Keep this book. You will need it and use it throughout your career.

About the American Hotel & Lodging Association (AH&LA)

Founded in 1910, AH&LA is the trade association representing the lodging industry in the United States. AH&LA is a federation of state lodging associations throughout the United States with 11,000 lodging properties worldwide as members. The association offers its members assistance with governmental affairs representation, communications, marketing, hospitality operations, training and education, technology issues, and more. For information, call 202-289-3100.

LODGING, the management magazine of AH&LA, is a "living textbook" for hospitality students that provides timely features, industry news, and vital lodging information. For information on subscriptions and student rates, call 202-289-3113.

About the Educational Institute of AH&LA (EI)

An affiliate of AH&LA, the Educational Institute is the world's largest source of quality training and educational materials for the lodging industry. EI develops textbooks and courses that are used in more than 1,200 colleges and universities worldwide, and also offers courses to individuals through its Distance Learning program. Hotels worldwide rely on EI for training resources that focus on every aspect of lodging operations. Industry-tested videos, CD-ROMs, seminars, and skills guides prepare employees at every skill level. EI also offers professional certification for the industry's top performers. For information about EI's products and services, call 800-349-0299 or 407-999-8100.

About the American Hotel Foundation (AHF)

An affiliate of AH&LA, the American Hotel Foundation provides financial support that enhances the stability, prosperity, and growth of the lodging industry through educational and research programs. AHF has awarded hundreds of thousands of dollars in scholarship funds for students pursuing higher education in hospitality management. AHF has also funded research projects on topics important to the industry, including occupational safety and health, turnover and diversity, and best practices in the U.S. lodging industry. For information, call 202-289-3100.

UNDERSTANDING HOSPITALITY LAW

Educational Institute Books

UNDERSTANDING HOSPITALITY LAW

Fourth Edition

Jack P. Jefferies, J.D., LL.M., J.S.D.
Banks Brown, J.D.

EDUCATIONAL INSTITUTE
American Hotel & Lodging Association

Disclaimer

This publication is designed to provide accurate and authoritative information in regard to the subject matter covered. It is sold with the understanding that the publisher is not engaged in rendering legal, accounting, or other professional service. If legal advice or other expert assistance is required, the services of a competent professional person should be sought.

—From the Declaration of Principles jointly adopted by the American Bar Association and a Committee of Publishers and Associations

The authors, Jack P. Jefferies and Banks Brown, are solely responsible for the contents of this publication. All views expressed herein are solely those of the authors and do not necessarily reflect the views of the Educational Institute of the American Hotel & Lodging Association (the Institute) or the American Hotel & Lodging Association (AH&LA).

Nothing contained in this publication shall constitute a standard, an endorsement, or a recommendation of the Institute or AH&LA. The Institute and AH&LA disclaim any liability with respect to the use of any information, procedure, or product, or reliance thereon by any member of the hospitality industry.

Editor: Jennifer Smith

Contents

Part III: The Hotel's Duties to the Guest and Others 99

9 Americans with Disabilities Act—Public Accommodations 101

10 The Hotel's Duty to Protect Guests 111

11 The Hotel's Liability Regarding Guests' Property 161

Preface

Understanding Hospitality Law, Fourth Edition, is addressed to students and laypersons who are or may become involved in the lodging industry. This book alerts hotel and restaurant operators to a number of potential legal problems and pitfalls. My primary legal resources for this book come from many years of service to the American Hotel & Lodging Association and state hotel associations, and from working with individual hotel and motel properties to solve their legal problems or prevent potential legal problems insofar as possible.

As the Table of Contents indicates, this book is very concerned with the growth of federal government legislation and regulations that have a nationwide impact on the lodging industry. Such legislation and regulations include the Civil Rights Act of 1991 and other federal discrimination laws dealing with employment and sexual harassment, Occupational Safety and Health Administration (OSHA) regulations, the Family and Medical Leave Act of 1993, the Americans with Disabilities Act, the Hotel and Motel Fire Safety Act of 1990, antitrust regulations, the National Labor Relations Act, copyright music laws, tax laws and tip reporting regulations, telephone resale regulations, consumer protection laws, franchise regulations, product liability laws, and laws relating to the Internet.

Many years of reviewing state statutes and court decisions have made it clear that the New York State Legislature and court decisions have, in effect, often led the way in defining basic legal principles affecting hotels, and we have used many of these statutes and cases in this book as a means of illustrating basic legal issues. However, we have also included statutes and court decisions from many other states throughout the nation to demonstrate recent developments and trends in the laws affecting (1) the relationship of the hotel to its guests and others, and (2) the hotel's liability for guest protection and for losses of guest property. As indicated above, this book also discusses the major laws that impact the hotel's general operations and relations with its employees.

Understanding Hospitality Law, however, is not intended to be a how-to handbook whereby the hotel or restaurant operator, upon reading it, will become a legal expert on the subjects reviewed. This book is not presented as, or intended to be, a substitute for the services or legal opinion of your local attorney (though we hope it will be a valuable aid to your attorney). Hoteliers and restaurateurs should consult with their local attorneys on legal problems arising in the states concerned. However, readers of this book should be better able to recognize, early on, a legal problem or potential lawsuit, which will enable them to consult with a local attorney before the legal problem mushrooms and perhaps grows out of hand. Experience has shown that if a lawyer is contacted at the beginning of a legal problem, it will often prove far less costly to find a solution to the problem or resolve the dispute.

At the end of each chapter you will find "Important Points for Management," a section that summarizes the basic legal principles discussed in the chapter. This is followed by a series of review questions designed to stimulate discussion of the legal subjects covered in the chapter. These are valuable instructional aids for both teacher and student.

We dedicate this book to the late Herbert Brownell and the late Charles W. Merritt, who led the way.

Jack P. Jefferies, Esq.
Banks Brown, Esq.

About the Authors

Jack P. Jefferies

Banks Brown

Jack P. Jefferies and Banks Brown are recognized as perhaps the best known U.S. experts on laws and regulations affecting hotels.

Dr. Jefferies served as legal counsel for 21 years to the American Hotel & Lodging Association (AH&LA), New York State Hospitality & Tourism Association, Inc., and Hotel Association of New York City. His work consisted primarily of advising, upon request, individual hotels throughout the United States and the Caribbean on hotel management problems and the laws and regulations affecting hotels. He also represented the Hospitality, Lodging & Travel Research Foundation and the American Hotel Foundation, as well as *Lodging* magazine.

In 1993, Dr. Jefferies was appointed by the International Hotel Association as its representative to the United Nations and its Specialized Agencies. The International Hotel Association has offices in Paris, France, and represents over 400,000 hotels in some 146 countries.

Dr. Jefferies is also a recognized expert on convention and trade shows. For 21 years he served as general counsel for the International Hotel/Motel & Restaurant Show in New York City, one of the two largest trade shows in the hospitality industry. He has also lectured on convention and group sales contracts and legal issues.

Dr. Jefferies has been a guest lecturer at Cornell University and has lectured before such organizations as the International Council of Hotel/Motel Managers and the Hotel Sales Managers Association in New York.

Dr. Jefferies earned his J.D. Degree (Law Review) at the University of Virginia, and his LL.M. Degree (International Law) and J.S.D. Degree (International Law) at

Yale University. He is a member of the New York Bar, the Virginia Bar, and is admitted to practice before the U.S. Supreme Court. He was a partner for 28 years with the law firm of Lord Day & Lord, Barrett Smith, and now is a Special Consultant to the international law firm of McDermott, Will & Emery. He has been listed in *Who's Who in America* and *Who's Who Among American Lawyers*.

Banks Brown is a partner of the firm of McDermott, Will & Emery. He is now legal counsel to the American Hotel & Lodging Association, the Hotel Association of New York City, Inc., the Travel Business Roundtable, and the International Hotel, Motel & Restaurant Show. He advises a number of hotel compaines on various aspects of their businesses. He is the primary author of *Lodging Law*. He graduated fro Harvard University in 1974 with a B.A. Degree and from the University of Virginia School of Law in 1977 with a J.D. Degree. He then joined the firm of Lord, Day & Lord, where he was a partner until its dissolution 1994, whereupon he became a partner in McDermott, Will & Emery, and founded its Hospitality Group.

March 1, 2001

Part I

Some Basic Legal Principals Governing Hospitality Operations

Chapter 1 Outline

Common Law
State Court Decisions
Federal Court Decisions
Defining Hotels, Motels, and Inns
    Definition of a Hotel
    Definition of a Motel
Important Points for Management
References
Key Terms
Review Questions
Internet Sites

Competencies

1. Describe the development of rules regarding the rights and liabilities of innkeepers under the common law system. (pp. 3–4)

2. Provide examples of common law rules uniquely applicable to innkeepers. (p. 4)

3. Explain why the laws of two states may differ with regard to essentially the same general issue. (p. 5)

4. Explain why two federal circuit courts can reach different decisions while addressing the same type of legal problem. (p. 5)

5. Describe any legal distinctions that may be made in the terms "hotel," "inn," and "motel." (pp. 6–8)

1

The Common Law Basis for Laws Governing the Hotelkeeper

Common Law

The laws governing hotels and motels in the United States are myriad. They include many common law rules that have evolved from early English judicial decisions and social customs. The **common law** system was developed in England during the Middle Ages as **courts** sought to resolve disputes between individuals by applying generally accepted rules and principles of justice. As society evolved from the feudal into the industrial era, courts under the common law system continued to apply many of the rules and principles enunciated by courts in earlier, similar cases. Within this developing common law system, special common law rules regarding the rights and liabilities of innkeepers and their guests also evolved. This special body of rules applicable to innkeepers under the common law resulted from the public nature of the occupation. In *Crapo* v. *Rockwell*[1] the court noted the public nature of innkeeping in reviewing the history of innkeeping:

> The primary and fundamental function of an inn seems clearly to have been to furnish entertainment and lodging for the traveler on his journey. This at all times seems to have been its distinguishing feature. This idea has been expressed in the literature of ages, in history, sacred and profane, in fiction, and in poetry. So true is this that the term "inn" seems always to have been used in connection with the corresponding notion of travelers seeking the accommodation and protection of the inn. Thus the Christian era dawned on a Judean scene, where travelers away from home, who had gone up to be taxed pursuant to the decree of the Roman Emperor, sought refuge in a manger, "because there was no room for them in the inn." Sir Walter Scott characterized the inn of the old days of Merry England as "the free rendezvous of all travellers," of which the bonny Black Bear of Cumnor village, not conducted merely, but "ruled, by Giles Gosling, a man of goodly person," as landlord, was a typical instance. And so the most illustrious bard of England says, referring to the time of approaching twilight, with the west glimmering with streaks of day, "now spurs the lated traveller apace to gain the timely inn."

> Turning from the pages of literature to those of legal lore, we find that the same idea is carried out with remarkable constancy. An inn is defined by Bacon to be a

3

house for the entertainment of travelers and passengers, in which lodging and necessaries are provided for them and for their horses and attendants.

* * *

In *Cromwell* v. *Stephens*, 2 Daly, 22, it is said, referring to the case of *Thompson* v. *Lacy*, 3 B. & A. 283:

"Justice Bayley declares it to be 'a house where a traveler is furnished with everything which he has occasion for while upon his way,' and in the same case Best, J., says it is a 'house, the owner of which holds out that he will receive all travelers and sojourners who are willing to pay a price adequate to the sort of accommodation provided, and who come in a situation in which they are fit to be received.'"

* * *

In *Mowers* v. *Fethers*, 61 N.Y. 37, 19 Am. Rep. 244, it is said:

"An innkeeper, at common law, has been said to be the keeper of a common inn for the lodging and entertainment of travelers and passengers, their horses and attendants, for a reasonable compensation. 5 Bacon, Abr. 'Inns,' etc., 228; Story on Bailments, § 475. The person or persons undertaking this public employment were bound to take in and receive all travelers and wayfaring persons."

Examples of old common law rules uniquely applicable to innkeepers are: (i) innkeepers as operators of public places must as a general rule provide available accommodations to travelers who are willing and able to pay for such accommodations, and (ii) an innkeeper under common law would be **liable** as an **insurer** for the loss of guests' property brought to the inn, with certain exceptions.

Throughout the years, the common law rules governing innkeepers* have, however, been refined by court decisions, and modified by federal, state, and municipal legislation and administrative agency rules and regulations, which, in turn, have then been further defined by federal, state, and municipal court decisions and administrative agency rulings.

In addition, hotels and motels today are subject to numerous federal, state, and municipal **statutes** and administrative rules and regulations governing a multitude of subjects never covered by common law. These governing statutes, rules, and regulations have, in turn, been further defined by federal, state, and municipal court decisions and administrative agency rulings.

Over 135,000 new federal and state laws are issued annually, as well as hundreds of thousands of federal and state administrative rules.** A great number of these laws, rules, and regulations affect hotels and motels directly or indirectly.

---

* We have to make an exception, of course, as to Louisiana, where the Code Napoleon, as incorporated in the Louisiana Civil Code, governs.
** For example, there are over 1,200 interpretations by the Federal Reserve staff of the Truth-in-Lending Act.

State Court Decisions

It is important for the layperson to note in using this book that since the United States is a federation of states, each state through its state court system develops its own case law and judicial precedent on issues involving state laws. State courts generally decide issues involving local and state laws and disputes between citizens of the state. In this respect each state court system is independent of other state **jurisdictions.** Thus, for example, the decision of the highest state court in California may be **binding** on lower courts in California, but is not binding on the courts in another state, such as New York. This is true even though a New York court in interpreting a New York State statute could indeed look at a California State court decision interpreting a similar California statute, and find the California court decision reasoning to be "persuasive" or "interesting" or "of no effect whatsoever" in New York. It is thus that a New York court can reach a different result from California courts on the same general issue.

Federal Court Decisions

The layperson should also be aware that the federal court system includes 94 district courts* and a court of **appeals** for each of 13 judicial circuits, and the Supreme Court of the United States (see Exhibits 1.1 and 1.2).** Federal courts generally decide disputes involving federal laws and disputes between citizens from different states (subject to certain jurisdictional requirements). One federal circuit court of appeals may reach a decision different from that of another federal circuit court of appeals on the same type of legal problem. It is left to the U.S. Supreme Court to determine which of the circuit courts is correct (or to decide to leave the different decisions of both circuit courts standing).

This is an oversimplification in your introduction to the laws governing hotels, motels, and restaurants, but it is intended to help you understand why a decision in California may differ from a court decision in New York, Iowa, or Hawaii, and to understand why two federal circuit courts render what appear to be directly contrary decisions on apparently the same question when the courts are both part of the same federal court system.

It is important that the layperson also recognize that the law is a continually changing body of rules and cannot be viewed as frozen in time and space. For example, common law rules established a standard of absolute liability of the hotel operator for the loss of a guest's property. The state legislatures in most states then limited this common law liability, often to $500. In some states, the legislatures then increased the amount of this liability to more than $500. Moreover, some state courts today appear to exercise a quasi-legislative function in redefining and modifying the meaning of said statutes with the effect of increasing liability. Many other laws (common law, statutory, and regulatory) affecting hotel and motel operators are also undergoing constant evolution and change over the years.

---

 * Including Puerto Rico, Guam, Virgin Islands, and the Northern Mariana Islands.
** In addition, there are a number of special courts in the federal system, such as the U.S. Court of Claims and U.S. Tax Court.

Exhibit 1.1   The Thirteen Federal Judicial Circuits

Thus, from both a historic and national perspective, the laws affecting hotels and motels present a slowly changing kaleidoscope of legislation, regulations, rules, and court and administrative decisions affecting the legal rights, responsibilities, and liabilities of hotel and motel operators.

Defining Hotels, Motels, and Inns

The following basic definitions will help the reader understand this text, and the statutes and cases relating to hotels, motels, and inns.*

A "hotel" and an "inn" mean the same. Court decisions and statutes use the two terms interchangeably.

Whether or not a particular establishment is a "hotel" often depends upon the nature of the legal problem that gives rise to the question. This is because various statutes define a "hotel" in different terms to accomplish the specific objectives of the particular law. In the absence of a statutory definition, it may be necessary to determine whether a particular establishment is a "hotel" in the general sense of that term in order to determine the common law rights and obligations of the establishment and its guests or employees.

Definition of a Hotel

A broad definition of the term "hotel" preferred by the author is as follows:

Exhibit 1.2   The United States Court System

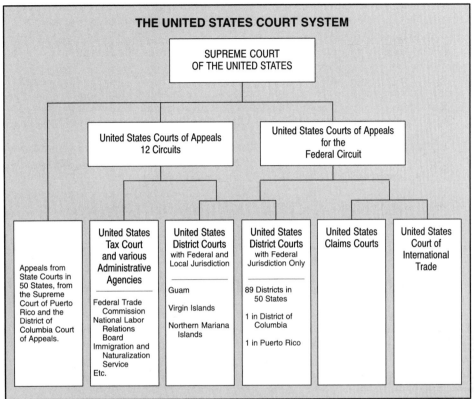

A "hotel" is a structure used primarily for the business of providing lodging facilities for the general public and which furnishes one or more customary hotel services such as a restaurant, room attendant service, bell service, telephone service, laundering of linen, and use of furniture and fixtures.

You must remember, however, that when a question concerning a "hotel" operation arises under a specific statute, you must always consider any different definition of a "hotel" given in such statute.

Definition of a Motel

A "motel" is a lodging facility deriving the greater part of its room business from members of the general public who are traveling by automobile and which ordinarily provides space for the parking of guests' automobiles on the premises.

Thus, the motel has been referred to on occasion as a "motorists' hotel." The motel may have fewer or more services (particularly recreational services) than an ordinary "hotel," depending on the particular property. Today some former motels have been renamed "hotels" in certain cities.

The common law rules* of the innkeepers' liability that apply to guests in hotels generally also apply to guests in motels. Court rulings with respect to hotels will often be used as precedents in determining the liability or rights of motels in subsequent cases.

In an action to recover **damages** for personal injuries, the Kentucky Court of Appeals in *Langford* v. *Vandaveer*[2] stated:

> It is clear the character of the place as respects the relationship of guest and the legal responsibility of the operator as an innkeeper is not lost because of the type of structure or facility being called by a different name.

Some statutes, such as zoning ordinances, building codes, fire laws, and rate posting laws, may, however, set forth different requirements for motels and hotels, usually because of the location, physical layout, and structure of the property.

Whenever we use the term "hotel" in the text which follows, the term generally applies also to "motels" and "inns," unless otherwise indicated.

Important Points for Management

The myriad laws governing hotels and motels in the United States include many common law rules that evolved from early English judicial decisions and social customs.

Through the years, the common law rules governing innkeepers have been refined by various court decisions, by federal, state, and municipal legislation, and by administrative agency rules and regulations. Furthermore, hotels today are subject to many governmental regulations covering subjects never addressed by common law. These, in turn, are defined by various court decisions and administrative agency rulings.

Each state through its court system develops its own case law and judicial precedent on issues involving state laws. State courts generally decide issues involving local and state laws and disputes between citizens of the state.

The federal court system includes 94 district courts, a court of appeals for each of 13 judicial circuits, and the U.S. Supreme Court. Federal courts generally decide disputes involving federal laws and disputes between citizens from different states, subject to certain jurisdictional requirements.

The law is a continually changing body of rules. It is not frozen in time and space.

Court decisions and statutes use the terms "hotel" and "inn" interchangeably. Whether a particular establishment is a "hotel" often depends upon the nature of the legal problem giving rise to the question. Various statutes define a "hotel" in different terms to accomplish the specific objectives of a particular law.

When a question concerning a "hotel" operation arises under a specific statute, management must always consider any different definition of a "hotel" given in such statute.

---

* Discussed earlier in this chapter.

The common law rules of the innkeepers' liability that apply to hotel guests generally also apply to motel guests. Court rulings with regard to hotels will often be used as precedents in determining the liability or rights of motels in subsequent cases.

However, some statutes may establish requirements for motels that are different from requirements for hotels, usually because of the location, physical layout, and structure of the property.

References

1. 48 Misc. 1, 94 N.Y.S. 1122 (Sup. Ct. Albany Co. 1905).
2. 254 S.W.2d 498, 500 (Ky. Ct. of App. 1953).

Key Terms

appeal—The removal of a cause from an inferior court to one of superior jurisdiction for the purpose of obtaining a review. The term "appeal" indicates a re-examination by a higher tribunal of issues determined in original trial. The term "appeal" has a double significance and may be used to designate the act of lodging the action in the appellate court and also the action itself, when in the appellate court.

binding—Legally enforceable.

common law—The general Anglo-American system of legal concepts and the traditional legal technique that forms the basis of the law of the states that have invoked it.

While there have been conflicting theories as to the origin of the common law in the North American Colonies, it is generally settled that the Law of England, as it existed at the time of the colonial settlements, is the basis of the common law in this country (with the exception of Louisiana).

The common law is a system of unwritten law not evidenced by statute, but by traditions and the opinions and judgments of courts of law.

court—A tribunal empowered to hear and determine questions of law and fact, either with or without a jury, upon pleadings either oral or written and upon evidence to be adduced under well-defined and established rules according to settled principles of law.

damages—Pecuniary compensation which may be recovered in court by a person who has suffered a loss or injury to his/her person or property through an unlawful act, omission, or negligence of another.

insurer—One who undertakes or is obligated to compensate the other for loss or damage to person or property.

jurisdiction—May be defined simply as the court's right or authority to adjudicate concerning subject matter of a particular controversy.

liable—Obligated in law or equity to make satisfaction, pay compensation, or make restitution.

statute—An act of the legislature; a particular law enacted by the legislative branch of the government.

Review Questions

1. What are two examples of old common law rules specifically applicable to innkeepers?

2. What issues do state courts generally decide? What disputes do federal courts generally decide?

3. How is it possible that the courts of two different states (for example, Wisconsin and Minnesota) can reach varying results on the same general issue?

4. How can two federal circuit courts render seemingly contrary decisions on the same question?

Internet Sites

For more information, visit the following Internet sites. Remember that Internet addresses can change without notice.

Common Law
http://www.encyclopedia.com/articles/02984.html

http://lawyers.com/lawyers-com/content/aboutlaw/judicial_1.html

Federal Judiciary
http://www.uscourts.gov

FindLaw
http://www.findlaw.com

Chapter 2 Outline

Competencies

1. Identify the necessary elements of a contract. (p. 13)

2. Define "offer," "acceptance," and "consideration." (pp. 13–14)

3. Explain the differences between express and implied contracts. (p. 15)

4. Distinguish between bilateral and unilateral contracts. (p. 15)

5. Define "void," "voidable," and "unenforceable" contracts. (pp. 15–16)

6. Explain why statutes of limitations have been enacted. (p. 16)

2

The Hotelkeeper and the Law of Contracts

Introduction

Before we proceed further with a discussion of the rights and duties of an innkeeper, it is important that we understand some basic principles of contract law.

When the hotel confirms and accepts a guest reservation, the innkeeper usually enters into a contract relationship with the guest. When the hotel purchases goods, hires employees, builds a swimming pool, or makes repairs, the innkeeper enters into various written or oral contracts. Therefore, it is important to understand what constitutes a contract, and why it is important to have a written contract whenever possible to set forth the terms agreed upon by the parties to the contract.

Definition of a Contract

A **contract** is a promise or a set of promises for the **breach** of which the law gives a remedy, or the performance of which the law in some way recognizes as a duty.[1] A contract is an agreement which creates legally enforceable obligations between two or more parties. There must be an *offer,* an *acceptance,* and *consideration* to support the formation of a legally enforceable agreement. Thus, the elements which are necessary to the formation of a contract are:

1. A manifestation of mutual assent, comprising:
   (a) an offer, and
   (b) its acceptance
2. A legally valid consideration
3. Parties who have legal capacity to enter into a contract
4. A subject which is not illegal

"Offer" Defined

An *offer* to contract is a proposal to exchange a promise or an act for a specified promise or act of another, and requires the latter's assent in order that the transaction shall be complete.[2]

That is, an offer is an expression by the offeror of his/her agreement that something shall be done or happen or shall not be done or happen if the conditions stated in the offer are complied with.[3]

Thus, an offer is an act on the part of one person whereby he/she gives to another person the legal power of creating an obligation called a *contract.*

An offer must be so definite in its essential terms, or require such definite terms in its acceptance, that promises and performances to be rendered by each **party** are reasonably certain.

In stating that the offer must be definite in its essential terms, we mean that it must at least identify the parties, the subject matter, the time of performance, and the compensation or price.

A person making an offer makes it to a specific person. In effect, he/she says, "I am willing to contract with you on these terms."

"Acceptance" Defined

An offer must be accepted in order to create a contract, since, as it has often been said, "it takes two to make a bargain."

Acceptance of an offer is a manifestation of assent to the terms thereof made by the *offeree* in a manner invited or required by the offer.[4]

The acceptance must manifest assent to the same bargain proposed by the offer, and must also comply with the terms of the offer as to the identity of the offeree and the mode of manifesting acceptance.[5]

Acceptance of an offer, to result in a contract, must be absolute and unconditional, identical with the terms of the offer, in the mode, at the place, and within the time expressly or impliedly required by the offer.[6]

Such acceptance is the final step in the making of a contract. Upon acceptance, the *offeror* is bound by the promise embodied in the offer.[7]

Note that the acceptance of an offer must always be identical with the terms of the offer or there is no meeting of minds and no contract.

Where a person offers to do a definite thing, and another accepts conditionally or introduces a new term into the acceptance, his/her answer is a mere expression of willingness to treat, or it is a counterproposal, and in neither case is there an agreement or contract.

"Consideration" Defined

Generally speaking, *consideration* can be money, property, or a promise. Consideration can be an act, forbearance, or promise bargained for and given in return for a promise. Readers should note that, generally speaking, the law is not concerned with whether the consideration and return promise were substantially equivalent. The adequacy of the consideration is usually a matter for the parties to determine. It is not for the court to determine.

For example, the delivery of a letter by A to B, erroneously believed by B to be necessary to win a lawsuit against a hotel for breach of its contract for a convention reservation, was held by a court to be valid consideration to enforce B's promise to pay A $1,000 for such letter.

Express and Implied Contracts

An *express contract* is one that is definitely set forth in words, either oral or written. Thus, a contract can be written or oral.[8]

An *implied contract* is one that is inferred from the acts and conduct of the parties.

For example, following negotiations, D drew up an agreement to deliver 1,000 doorknobs to P hotel in New York "at eighteen dollars each, cash upon such delivery." P hotel accepted this written memorandum signed by D. D then refused to deliver the doorknobs, alleging that there was no contract, since D received no consideration for his promise, inasmuch as P never agreed to accept the doorknobs or pay for them. The court held for P hotel. The assent and agreement to receive and pay for these doorknobs is clearly to be inferred from P hotel's acceptance of the memorandum prepared and tendered by D. In this case, both sides clearly intended to be bound by the terms of the memorandum.

Bilateral and Unilateral Contracts

A *bilateral (two-sided) contract* is a contract in which promises are made on both sides. Each party is both a promisor and a promisee.

For example, A says to B, "I'll give you $200 if you will agree to snowplow the hotel driveway. B replies, "I agree." Thus, there is a bilateral contract between A and B.

A *unilateral (one-sided) contract* is a contract in which only one party makes a promise. The other party acts or refrains from acting.

For instance, A says to B, "I'll give you $200 to snowplow the hotel driveway." B says nothing, but does snowplow the driveway. There is now a unilateral contract between A and B, and A is liable on his promise to pay $200 for the work.

The essential distinction between bilateral and unilateral contracts is in the type of acceptance required. In bilateral contracts, acceptance is indicated by a promise; in unilateral contracts, acceptance is indicated by an act.

Void and Voidable Contracts

A *void contract* is one which cannot possibly have any legal effect. It is just as if the agreement had never been made. Although such an agreement has all the outward appearances of a contract, it is void and unenforceable. Hence, it is not a contract at all.

To illustrate, B, by a contract in writing, wagers $1,000 with A in State M that a certain horse named "Winning Colors" will win the Kentucky Derby. The horse performs badly and comes in tenth. A sues B in State M, a state which by statute forbids gambling and declares *all* gambling contracts illegal and void. B need not bother appearing in court, because A's case will be thrown out. The contract was void because it never legally existed.

A *voidable contract* is one which may be either affirmed or disaffirmed at the option of one or more of the contracting parties, but which is valid and binding until thus disaffirmed. Disaffirmance voids or destroys the legal relations and obligations created by the contract; affirmance ratifies the contract and makes it enforceable.

Thus in *Holt* v. *Clarencieux,* 1732, 2 Strange (Eng.) 937, Plaintiff, an infant, and Defendant, an adult, entered into a contract to marry in England. D married X instead, so P sued D. D defended by saying P could have voided her promise since she was an infant, although she had not done so in fact; hence, his return promise should not be held to be binding on him. It was held in this English case that even a voidable promise, as of an infant, is good consideration for a counter promise, since the adult assumes the chance that the infant may disaffirm. *Note:* In the United States, the result may be different and the contract declared void since the infant may be held to have no legal capacity to enter into such a contract.

Unenforceable Contracts

It is possible to have a legally valid contract which no longer can be enforced.

For instance, X contracts with the U.S. Government to supply beds for its army lodging facility. The Government refuses to pay. X cannot enforce his contract since a sovereign state cannot be sued except with its consent.

The U.S. Government later consents to be sued on such contracts. X can now proceed to bring his action.

Statutes of Limitation

In order to protect persons from suits brought after witnesses have died, evidence has been lost, and claims perhaps forgotten, various **statutes of limitations** have been enacted by the states. These state statutes fix the time within which particular lawsuits must be instituted, although the parties may always by contract agree upon a reasonably shorter period of time for bringing the lawsuit.

For example, in Virginia, the statute of limitations for bringing a lawsuit on a contract claim is *six* years.

We have now introduced the basic principles of the law of contracts. In subsequent chapters, we will present the requirements of the law of contracts with regard to hotel convention contracts (Chapter 6), guest relations (Chapters 7 and 8), restaurant operations and the sale of food and beverages (Chapters 16–18), warranties and product liability laws (Chapter 36), and antitrust laws prohibiting illegal contracts (Chapter 37).

Important Points for Management

- A *contract* is a legal agreement creating legally enforceable obligations between two or more parties. There must be an *offer,* an *acceptance,* and *consideration* to support the formation of a legally enforceable agreement.

- An *express contract* is definitely set forth in words, either oral or written. An *implied contract* is inferred from the acts and conduct of the parties.

- A *bilateral contract* is a contract between two parties with promises made on both sides. A *unilateral contract* is a contract in which only one party makes a promise. The other party acts or refrains from acting.

- A *void contract* is one which cannot possibly have any legal effect, and is just as if the agreement was never made. In other words, it is not a contract at all. A *voidable contract* is one which may be either affirmed or disaffirmed at the option of one or more of the contracting parties, but which is treated as valid and binding until disaffirmed.

- Statutes of limitations establish the time within which particular lawsuits must be instituted, although the parties may always by contract agree upon a reasonably shorter period of time for bringing the lawsuit.

References

1. See *Restatement (Second) of Contracts*, § 1 (1981).
2. See S. Williston, *A Treatise on the Law of Contracts*, 3d ed. (1957), p. 211, § 64.
3. *Id.* at § 24A at p. 56 (3d ed. 1957).
4. See *Restatement (Second) of Contracts* § 50 (1981).
5. *Ibid.*
6. See *Baird Bros.* v. *Walter Pratt & Co.*, 89 S.W. 648, 653, 6 Ind.T. 38, quoting and adopting the definition in Clark, *Contracts*, § 36.
7. See E.A. Farnsworth, *Contracts*, at § 3.3 *et seq.* p. 109 (1982).
8. This general statement is qualified by the Statutes of Fraud; see Chapter 14.

Key Terms

breach of contract—A failure, without legal excuse, to perform any promise that forms the whole or part of a contract.

contract—A legal agreement creating legally enforceable obligations between two or more parties.

et seq.—(Latin) "And the following."

party—A person who is actively included in the prosecution or defense of a legal proceeding.

statute of limitations—Any law which fixes the time within which parties may take judicial action to enforce rights or else be thereafter barred from enforcing them.

Review Questions

1. What elements are necessary for the formation of a contract?

2. What is the difference between an *offer* and an *acceptance*?

3. Give examples of valid consideration for a contract.

4. What do we mean when we say that an offer must be definite in its essential terms?

5. How does an express contract differ from an implied contract?

6. What type of acceptance is required for a bilateral contract? for a unilateral contract?

7. What is a void contract? What is a voidable contract?

8. Give an example of a legally valid contract which may be unenforceable.

9. What is the purpose of statutes of limitations?

Internet Sites

For more information, visit the following Internet sites. Remember that Internet addresses can change without notice.

Contracts

http://www.catalaw.com/topics/Contract.shtml

http://www.lawyers.com/lawyers-com/content/aboutlaw/about_contr.html

Chapter 3 Outline

Competencies

1. Distinguish between a tort and a crime. (p. 21)

2. Define negligence. (p. 21)

3. Identify the four elements necessary to bring an action based in tort. (pp. 21–22)

4. Explain the doctrine of *res ipsa loquitur*. (p. 22)

5. Describe the concept of contributory negligence. (pp. 22–23)

6. Explain the rule of comparative negligence, and distinguish between the two types of comparative negligence. (pp. 23–24)

3

The Hotelkeeper and the Laws of Torts and Negligence

Definition of a Tort

A **tort** is an unlawful act done in violation of the legal rights of someone. When there has been an invasion of a legally recognized right of a person or of a property right of a person, the law will compel the wrongdoer to compensate the injured party. This right of compensation is not created by agreement between the parties; rather, it is imposed by the law regardless of their wishes. (Hence a right of action arising out of a tort is not a contract right. Contract law, as we have seen, covers an *agreement* between or among two or more persons.)

Although an act may constitute both a *crime* and a *tort*, a **crime** is an offense against the public pursued by the government, while a tort is a private injury which is redressed at the suit of the injured party.

A tort may involve physical (or mental) injury to a person, or it may involve damage to property. For example, a tort may involve an assault and battery on a person. An **assault** is an attempt by violence to hurt another; a **battery** occurs when the attempted violence is accomplished. A battery is an actual infliction of a blow without the consent of the person who receives it.

A tort may involve an accident or injury that is caused by an act of *negligence*.

Negligence Defined

Negligence is generally defined as the doing of that thing which a reasonably prudent person would not have done, or the failure to do that thing which a reasonably prudent person would have done, under like or similar facts and circumstances.

As hereinafter discussed, hotels (and restaurants) owe a duty of reasonable care to their guests.

When a hotel guest suffers an injury which was the result of the hotel's failure to act with reasonable care, the injury which is caused by such negligence on the part of the hotel may constitute a tort. This would give the injured guest a right to sue the hotel for damages based upon the law of torts.

Elements of a Tort Action Based on Negligence

To bring an action based in tort, four elements must be present:

1. The defendant must owe a duty of care to the guest. For example, a hotel has a duty to provide working door locks on guestroom doors.

21

2. There must be a breach of such duty. For example, a hotel's failure to fix a broken door lock on a guestroom door could constitute a breach of its duty of care to the guest.

3. This breach of duty must be the *proximate cause* of the injury to the guest. **Proximate cause** is often defined as that primary moving predominating cause from which an injury follows as a natural, direct, and immediate consequence, and without which it would not have occurred. For example, suppose an intruder gains entry to a guestroom and assaults the guest because the guestroom door lock was broken, even though it appeared to work. The test is whether the intruder's assault of the guest was reasonably foreseeable by the hotel when the hotel failed to fix the broken lock.

4. The guest must suffer injury and damages.

Res Ipsa Loquitur ("the thing speaks for itself")

The doctrine of *res ipsa loquitur* recognizes that common experience sometimes permits a **reasonable** inference of negligence from the occurrence itself.

In *Page* v. *Sloan*,[1] the rules governing the application of the doctrine of *res ipsa loquitur* in North Carolina were stated as follows:

> When a thing which causes injury is shown to be under the exclusive management of the defendant and the accident is one which in the ordinary course of events does not happen if those in control of it use proper care, the accident itself is sufficient to carry the case to the jury on the issue of defendant's negligence.

In this case, the **plaintiff** was the administratrix of the estate of Changing Nelson Page, who was killed on August 29, 1964, at a motel in North Carolina. The death allegedly resulted from the explosion of an 82-gallon electric hot water heater located in a utility room of the motel. The plaintiff alleged that Mr. Page was a paying guest in said motel which was owned and operated by the defendants as co-partners, and that Mr. Page was assigned a corner room adjoining the utility room containing the motel's hot water heater. This electric hot water heater was installed and operated by defendants for the purpose of furnishing hot water to the various guestrooms of the motel. The plaintiff alleged that the explosion of the electric hot water heater was the direct and proximate cause of Page's death and that at all times the said water heater was in the exclusive possession and control of the defendants. The plaintiff further alleged that the explosion of said electric hot water heater was caused by, or due to, the actionable negligence of the defendants. The court ruled that the doctrine of *res ipsa loquitur* was applicable in this case, and thus the case should be submitted to the jury to decide whether the hotel was negligent.

You have now been introduced to some of the basic principles of negligence and the law of torts. In subsequent chapters, we will discuss in greater detail the "duty of reasonable care" hospitality operations owe to their guests and other **business invitees**, and their liability for failure to exercise such reasonable care.

Contributory Negligence Rule

Until recently in a number of states, a guest who suffered injury due to a hotel or motel's negligence could not recover damages if the guest, himself or herself, through contributory negligence, was wholly or even partly responsible for the injury. An older case that illustrates the defense of contributory negligence is *Kurna* v. *Byron Reed Syndicate.*[2]

In this case a guest, on his third night in a Nebraska hotel, stopped by the front office. The desk was only a step away from two double glass doors, one of which was kept open, and the other locked shut. Upon leaving the desk, the guest ran into the shut glass door and broke it, causing permanent damage to his nose.

The court found that the hotel was negligent in placing a locked glass door near the check-out desk where a guest could turn and step into it. The court also found, however, that the guest was contributorily negligent because he had been in the hotel for three days and thus should have been aware of the location of the glass door. Consequently, under the rule of contributory negligence, the guest was not entitled to recover anything from the hotel. The old rule of contributory negligence often served as a complete bar to recovering damages in many states.

Another case involving the defense of contributory negligence centered on a guest's claim of inadequate lighting by a motel in New Mexico.[3] On December 21, 1976, the New Mexico Court of Appeals held that a jury should decide the question of whether a motel with an automatic timed outdoor light switch could be held to be negligent and liable for personal injuries a guest suffered when she fell while leaving her room before dawn. Upon checking in, the guest had stated that she would be leaving at 5:00 the following morning. The motel had a master timer switch that automatically shut off the outside lights at 4:30 A.M. At 5:00 A.M. the guest unsuccessfully tried to turn on the porch light in order to pack her car. She then left her room door open in order to allow the inside light to shine onto the motel porch. Upon entering the parking lot, she was unable to see where the side-walk ended and missed her footing.

The trial court granted **summary judgment** for the defendant-motel. The New Mexico Court of Appeals reversed the trial court. It held that there were issues of fact which must be decided by the trial court jury as to whether the defendant-motel was negligent. In addition, the court rejected the motel's argument that the plaintiff's stepping into the darkness made her contributorily negligent as a matter of law. The court noted that the guest had attempted to turn on the outside light, then tried to get light from her room, and proceeded cautiously. The court of appeals then **remanded** the case for trial, leaving to the jury the questions of the motel's negligence and the guest's contributory negligence. In effect, the court stated that the lack of lighting caused by the hotel's automatic timed light mechanism might be a known and discoverable dangerous condition causing the plaintiff's fall, depending on how the jury weighed all the facts.

More Than Half of States Have Changed from Rule of Contributory Negligence to Rule of Comparative Negligence

Heavily criticized by legal scholars, the rule of contributory negligence has been replaced by new rules of comparative negligence in at least 36 states.[4] California made this change by court decision. In most states, New York among them, the change was accomplished by statute. These laws vary from state to state.

Comparative negligence rules may act only to reduce the amount of damages that can be recovered. Consequently, it is possible that more suits may be brought against hotels and motels, and insurance rates will foreseeably rise to cover the increased number of suits and possible recoveries.

Under the new rules of comparative negligence, fault is attributed to each party—the hotel and the guest—according to their respective negligence. Basically, there are two kinds of comparative negligence: the so-called "pure" form and the "50%" form. California, New York, Florida, and a few other states have the pure form; most of the other states, the 50% form. Under the 50% form, the plaintiff may recover as long as the percentage of his/her fault does not exceed 50% of the total fault.

The difference between these types of negligence can best be explained by the following example. Suppose a hotel or motel operator negligently provides scalding hot bath water, and a guest, without testing the water, plunges into the bathtub and is seriously burned.

If this accident occurred in a state where contributory negligence is still the rule, it is quite possible that a jury would find that, in not testing the bath water before entering the tub, the guest was contributorily negligent and therefore could recover nothing from the hotel.

If, however, the accident occurred in a state with the pure form of comparative negligence, then a jury would decide to what extent the hotel operator was at fault and to what extent the guest was at fault, and apportion damages to the hotel accordingly. If the jury found the hotel 40% at fault and the guest 60% at fault, the hotel would have to pay 40% of the guest's damage.* (See the *Edgewater Motels, Inc.* v. *Gatzke* case at the end of this chapter for an opinion on a question of comparative negligence in a motel fire.)

In a case in Hawaii, the jury found the hotel, Island Holidays Ltd., was 64% liable in a negligence lawsuit.[5] The suit involved Lyle Nakaahiki, whose jaw was allegedly broken in November 1984 after he was punched in a parking lot at the Poipu Beach Hotel on Kauai. Nakaahiki's lawsuit contended that hotel employees failed to inform security or the police that trouble was developing between two men at the hotel. The trouble continued in the parking lot, where Nakaahiki allegedly suffered a broken jaw.

Fifth Circuit Court Judge Kei Hirano ordered Island Holidays to pay $243,200 of the $380,000 award to Nakaahiki, while Nakaahiki's assailant was ordered to pay the rest.

Readers should remember that the laws vary considerably from state to state, and may change rapidly. Therefore, hotels and restaurants should refer particular problems or claims to local counsel.

---

 * The hotel can also counterclaim for its own damages, if any. In the example cited, the hotel would have to bear 40% of its damages claimed.

Important Points for Management

- A *tort* is an unlawful act done in violation of the legal rights of someone. It may involve physical or mental injury to a person, or damage to property. For example, it may involve assault and battery on a person. It is a private injury which is redressed at the suit of the injured party.

- When a hotel guest suffers an injury which was the result of the hotel's failure to act with reasonable care, the injury which is caused by such negligence on the part of the hotel may constitute a tort. This would give the injured guest a right to sue the hotel for damages based upon the law of torts.

- Hotels and restaurants owe a duty of reasonable care to their guests.

- The doctrine of *res ipsa loquitur* may be stated as follows: "When a thing which causes injury is shown to be under the exclusive management of the defendant and the accident is one which in the ordinary course of events does not happen if those in control of it use proper care, the accident itself is sufficient to carry the case to the jury on the issue of defendant's negligence" (see discussion of *Page* v. *Sloan* in this chapter).

- Until recently in a number of states, a guest who suffered injury due to a hotel or motel's negligence could not recover damages if he/she was wholly or partly responsible for the injury through *contributory negligence.*

- The rule of contributory negligence has been replaced by new rules of *comparative negligence* in at least 36 states. The rules vary according to state. Under comparative negligence rules, fault is attributed to each party—the hotel and the guest—according to their respective negligence. Comparative negligence rules may act only to reduce the amount of damages that can be recovered. Thus, it is possible that more suits may be brought against hotels and motels, and insurance rates will probably rise to cover the increased number of suits and possible recoveries.

References

1. 12 N.C. App. 433, 183 S.E.2d 813 (1971).

2. 374 F. Supp. 687 (D. Neb. 1974).

3. *Withrow* v. *Woozencraft*, 90 N.M. 48, 559 P.2d 425 (N.M. App., 1976), *cert. denied,* 90 N.M. 255, 561 P.2d 1348 (1977).

4. Including Alaska, Arkansas, California, Colorado, Connecticut, Florida, Georgia, Hawaii, Idaho, Maine, Massachusetts, Minnesota, Mississippi, Nebraska, Nevada, New Hampshire, New Jersey, New York, North Dakota, Oklahoma, Oregon, Rhode Island, South Dakota, Texas, Utah, Vermont, Washington, Wisconsin, Wyoming. See also 49 L.W. 2707 (1981).

5. Reported in *Pacific Business News,* Nov. 23, 1987.

🔑 Key Terms _____

assault—An attempt to commit violent injury upon the person of another. Physical contact is not necessary. An assault is an act done toward the commission of a battery, and immediately precedes the battery.

battery—An actual infliction of a blow without the consent of the person who receives it. While an "assault" is an attempt by violence to hurt another, a "battery" occurs when the violence is accomplished.

business invitee—A person who is invited or permitted to enter or to use such part of the premises as the visitor reasonably believes are held open to him/her as a means of access to or egress from the place where that person's business is to be transacted.

crime—An act or omission that is prohibited by law as injurious to the public and punished by the state in a proceeding in its own name or in the name of the people.

negligence—In absence of statute, negligence is generally defined as the doing of that thing which a reasonably prudent person would not have done, or the failure to do that thing which a reasonably prudent person would have done, under like or similar facts and circumstances.

plaintiff—A person who brings a lawsuit against another person.

proximate cause of injury—That primary moving predominating cause from which an injury follows as a natural, direct, and immediate consequence, and without which it would not have occurred.

reasonable—Just and proper; ordinary or usual; not excessive.

remand—To send a case brought into the appellate court back to the lower court it came from so that further proceedings in the case, if any, may be taken there.

summary judgment—Loosely defined, a judgment decreed by a court in a case pending before it when, as a matter of law, proceedings show that there is no issue of fact between the parties.

tort—A civil wrong resulting in damage. The essence of a tort is that it is an unlawful act, done in violation of the legal rights of someone.

Although the same act may constitute both a "crime" and a "tort," the crime is an offense against the public pursued by the government, while the tort is a private injury which is redressed at the suit of the injured party.

❓ Review Questions _____

1. How does a *crime* differ from a *tort*?

2. How is *negligence* defined?

3. What elements must be present to bring an action based in tort?

4. What is the doctrine of *res ipsa loquitur*?

5. What is meant when one says a person was contributorily negligent?

6. What is the concept of *comparative negligence*? Give an example in a state where the 60/40 rule applies.

Internet Sites

For more information, visit the following Internet sites. Remember that Internet addresses can change without notice.

Torts

http://www.lawyers.com/lawyers-com/content/aboutlaw/about_personal.html

http://www.findlaw.com/01topics/22tort/index.html

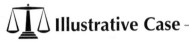

Illustrative Case

Edgewater Motels, Inc. v. Gatzke

277 N.W.2d 11 (Minn. Sup. Ct. 1979)

SCOTT, Justice.

This matter consists of two consolidated appeals from the post-trial orders of the St. Louis County District Court. Plaintiff Edgewater Motels, Inc., and defendant A. J. Gatzke contend that the trial judge erred by ordering judgment for defendant Walgreen Company notwithstanding a jury verdict which found that Gatzke, a Walgreen employee, negligently caused a fire in plaintiff's motel while he was in the scope of his employment. Plaintiff also claims that the trial judge erred in refusing to set aside a jury finding that plaintiff's negligence caused 40 percent of the damages sustained by Edgewater. We reverse in part and affirm in part.

The fire in question broke out on August 24, 1973, in a room at the Edgewater Motel in Duluth, Minnesota, occupied by Arlen Gatzke. In July 1973, Gatzke, a 31-year Walgreen employee and then district manager, spent approximately three weeks in Duluth supervising the opening of a new Walgreen's restaurant. During that time, he stayed at the Edgewater Motel at Walgreen's expense. On about August 17, 1973, Gatzke returned to Duluth to supervise the opening of another Walgreen-owned restaurant. Again, he lived at the Edgewater at the company's expense. While in Duluth, Gatzke normally would arise at 6:00 A.M. and work at the restaurant from about 7:00 A.M. to 12:00 or 1:00 A.M. In addition to working at the restaurant, Gatzke remained on call 24 hours per day to handle problems arising in other Walgreen restaurants located in his district. Gatzke thought of himself as a "24 hour a day man." He received calls from other Walgreen restaurants in his district when problems arose. He was allowed to call home at company expense. His laundry, living expenses, and entertainment were items of reimbursement. There were no constraints as to where he would perform his duties or at what time of day they would be performed.

On August 23, 1977, Gatzke worked on the restaurant premises for about seventeen hours. This was the seventh consecutive day that he put in such long hours. One of his responsibilities that day was to work with Curtis Hubbard, a Walgreen district manager from another territory who was in Duluth to observe a restaurant opening and learn the techniques employed. Gatzke's supervisor, B. J. Treet, a Walgreen's regional director, was also present.

Between 12:00 and 12:30 A.M., Gatzke, Hubbard, Treet, and a chef left the restaurant in a company-provided car. The chef was dropped off at his hotel, the Duluth Radisson, and the other three proceeded to the Edgewater, where they each had a room. Upon arrival at the Edgewater, Treet went to his room. Gatzke and Hubbard decided to walk across the street to the Bellows restaurant to have a drink.

In about an hour's time Gatzke consumed a total of four brandy Manhattans, three of which were "doubles." While at the Bellows, Gatzke and Hubbard spent part of the time discussing the operation of the newly-opened Walgreen restaurant. Additionally, Gatzke and the Bellows' bartender talked a little about the mixing and pricing of drinks. The testimony showed that Gatzke was interested in learning the bar business because the new Walgreen restaurant served liquor.

Between 1:15 and 1:30 A.M. Gatzke and Hubbard left the Bellows and walked back to the Edgewater. Witnesses testified that Gatzke acted normal and appeared sober. Gatzke went directly to his motel room, and then "probably" sat down at a desk to fill out his expense account because "that was (his) habit from travelling so much." The completion of the expense account had to be done in accordance with detailed instructions, and if the form was not filled out properly it would be returned to the employee unpaid. It took Gatzke no more than five minutes to fill out the expense form.

While Gatzke completed the expense account he "probably" smoked a cigarette. The record indicates that Gatzke smoked about two packages of cigarettes per day. A maid testified that the ash trays in Gatzke's room would generally be full of cigarette butts and ashes when she cleaned the room. She also noticed at times that the plastic waste basket next to the desk contained cigarette butts.

After filling out the expense account Gatzke went to bed, and soon thereafter a fire broke out. Gatzke escaped from the burning room, but the fire spread rapidly and caused extensive damage to the motel. The amount of damages was stipulated by the parties at $330,360.

One of plaintiff's expert witnesses, Dr. Ordean Anderson, a fire reconstruction specialist, testified that the fire started in, or next to, the plastic wastebasket located to the side of the desk in Gatzke's room. He also stated that the fire was caused by a burning cigarette or match. After the fire, the plastic wastebasket was a melted "blob." Dr. Anderson stated that X-ray examination of the remains of the basket disclosed the presence of cigarette filters and paper matches.

The jury found that Gatzke's negligence was a direct cause of 60 percent of the damages sustained by Edgewater. The jury also determined that Gatzke's negligent act occurred within the scope of his employment with Walgreen's. Plaintiff was found to be negligent (apparently for providing a plastic wastebasket) and such negligence was determined to be responsible for 40 percent of the fire damage sustained by Edgewater. The jury also decided that "The Bellows" was not liable.

Thereafter, Walgreen's moved for judgment notwithstanding the jury findings and, in the alternative, a new trial. Plaintiff moved to set aside the jury's findings that Edgewater was negligent and that such negligence was a direct cause of the fire. The district court granted Walgreen's motion for judgment notwithstanding the verdict, ruling that Gatzke's negligence did not occur within the scope of his employment, and denied all other motions.

The following issues are presented in this case:

(1)   Did the trial court err in setting aside the jury finding that Gatzke's negligent conduct occurred in the scope of his employment?

(2)   Did the trial court err in refusing to set aside the jury's findings that Edgewater was contributorily negligent and that such negligence was a direct cause of the damages sustained by Edgewater?

* * *

It is reasonably inferable from the evidence, and not challenged by Walgreen's or Gatzke on appeal, that Gatzke's negligent smoking of a cigarette was a direct cause of the damages sustained by Edgewater. The question raised here is whether the facts of this case reasonably support the imposition of vicarious liability on Walgreen's for the conceded negligent act of its employee.

It is well settled that for an employer to be held vicariously liable for an employee's negligent conduct the employee's wrongful act must be committed within the scope of his employment. *Seidl* v. *Trollhaugen, Inc.,* 305 Minn. 506, 232 N.W.2d 236 (1975); *Nelson* v. *Nelson,* 282 Minn. 487, 166 N.W.2d 70 (1969). As this court stated in *Laurie* v. *Mueller,* 248 Minn. 1, 4, 78 N.W.2d 434, 437 (1956):

> "* * * This doctrine of vicarious liability of the master rests upon the sound principle that, if an employer expects to derive certain advantages from the acts performed by others for him, he, as well as the careless employee, should bear the financial responsibility for injuries occurring to innocent third persons as a result of the negligent performance of such acts. But this responsibility is not carried to the point where an employer is absolutely liable for every tortious act of his employees, and there is incorporated within the doctrine a requirement that the servant's acts must be within the scope of his employment in order that the employer may be held liable.* * *"

* * *

To support a finding that an employee's negligent act occurred within his scope of employment, it must be shown that his conduct was, to some degree, in furtherance of the interests of his employer. *Lange* v. *National Biscuit Co.,* 297 Minn. 399, 211 N.W.2d 783 (1973); *Laurie* v. *Mueller, supra.* This principle is recognized by Restatement, Agency 2d, § 235,[1] which states:

> "An act of a servant is not within the scope of employment if it is done with no intention to perform it as a part of or incident to a service on account of which he is employed."

Other factors to be considered in the scope of employment determination are whether the conduct is of the kind that the employee is authorized to perform and whether the act occurs substantially within authorized time and space

---

[1]   Restatement, Agency 2d, § 235, is cited with approval in *Gackstetter* v. *Dart Transit Co.,* 269 Minn. 146, 150, n. 4, 130 N.W.2d 326, 329, n. 4 (1964), and *Laurie* v. *Mueller,* 248 Minn. 1, 5, n. 5, 78 N.W.2d 434, 437, n. 5 (1956).

restrictions. *Boland* v. *Morrill,* 270 Minn. 86, 132 N.W.2d 711 (1965); Restatement, Agency 2d, § 228. No hard and fast rule can be applied to resolve the "scope of employment" inquiry. Rather, each case must be decided on its own individual facts. *Seidl* v. *Trollhaugen, Inc., supra; Laurie* v. *Mueller, supra.*

The initial question raised by the instant factual situation is whether an employee's smoking of a cigarette can constitute conduct within his scope of employment.[2] This issue has not been dealt with by this court. The courts which have considered the question have not agreed on its resolution. See, Annot., 20 A.L.R.3d 893 (1968). A number of courts which have dealt with the instant issue have ruled that the act of smoking, even when done simultaneously with work-related activity, is not within the employee's scope of employment because it is a matter personal to the employee which is not done in furtherance of the employer's interests.[3] [citations omitted]

Other courts which have considered the question have reasoned that the smoking of a cigarette, if done while engaged in the business of the employer, is within an employee's scope of employment because it is a minor deviation from the employee's work-related activities, and thus merely an act done incidental to general employment. See, e.g., *Wood* v. *Saunders,* 228 App. Div. 69, 238 N.Y.S. 571 (1930); *Vincennes Steel Corp.* v. *Gibson,* 194 Ark. 58, 106 S.W.2d 173 (1937); cf., *De Mirjian* v. *Ideal Heating Corp.,* 129 Cal. App.2d 758, 278 P.2d 114 (1955) (employee's negligent filling of cigarette lighter with fluid found to be within the scope of his employment).

* * *

The question of whether smoking can be within an employee's scope of employment is a close one, but after careful consideration of the issue we are persuaded by the reasoning of the courts which hold that smoking can be an act within an employee's scope of employment. It seems only logical to conclude that an employee does not abandon his employment as a matter of law while temporarily acting for his personal comfort when such activities involve only slight deviations from work that are reasonable under the circumstances, such as eating, drinking, or smoking. As was stated by the court in *De Mirjian* v. *Ideal Heating Corp., supra:*

> "A mere deviation by an employee from the strict course of his duty does not release his employer from liability. An employee does not cease to be acting within the course of his employment because of an incidental personal act, or by slight deflections for a personal or private purpose, if his main purpose is still to carry on the business of his employer. Such deviations which do not amount to a turning aside completely from the employer's business, so as to be inconsistent

---

[2] The district court did not address this issue, and thus apparently assumed that an employer could be held vicariously liable for an employee's negligent smoking, if done concurrently with an activity which is otherwise within the employees' scope of employment.

[3] We also note that Restatement, Agency (2d), supports the position that, in a situation similar to the instant case, the negligent smoking of a cigarette is outside an employee's scope of employment. Compare Restatement, Agency (2d), § 235, comment d, illustration 5 and illustration 6; see, also, *Minamayor Corp.* v. *Paper Mill Suppliers, Inc.,* 297 F. Supp. 524, 526 (E.D. Pa. 1969).

with its pursuit, are often reasonably expected and the employer's assent may be fairly assumed. In many instances they are the mingling of a personal purpose with the pursuit of the employer's business. In order to release an employer from liability, the deviation must be so material or substantial as to amount to an entire departure. * * *" 129 Cal. App.2d 765, 278 P.2d 118 (citation omitted).

We agreed with this analysis and hereby hold that an employer can be held vicariously liable for his employee's negligent smoking of a cigarette [if] he was otherwise acting in the scope of his employment at the time of the negligent act.

Thus, we must next determine whether Gatzke was otherwise in the scope of his employment at the time of his negligent act. In setting aside the jury's scope of employment determination, the trial court stated that:

> "* * * it is difficult to discount the effect of four drinks—three of which were 'double'—taken within the period of about 30 minutes. Had Gatzke gone imme-diately to his room, as did his supervisor, and then filled out his expense account, there might be some validity to his claim that he was within the scope of his employment."

It appears that the district court felt that Gatzke was outside the scope of his employment while he was at the Bellows, and thus was similarly outside his scope of employment when he returned to his room to fill out his expense account. The record, however, contains a reasonable basis from which a jury could find that Gatzke was involved in serving his employer's interests at the time he was at the bar. Gatzke testified that, while at the Bellows, he discussed the operation of the newly-opened Walgreen's restaurant with Hubbard. Also, the bartender stated that on that night "[a] few times we [Gatzke and the bartender] would talk about his business and my business, how to make drinks, prices."

But more importantly, even assuming that Gatzke was outside the scope of his employment while he was at the bar, there is evidence from which a jury could reasonably find that Gatzke resumed his employment activities after he returned to his motel room and filled out his expense account.[4] The expense account was, of course, completed so that Gatzke could be reimbursed by Walgreen's for his work-related expenses. In this sense, Gatzke is performing an act for his own personal benefit. However, the completion of the expense account also furthers the employer's business in that it provides detailed documentation of business expenses so that they are properly deductible for tax purposes.[5] See, 26 U.S.C.A. § 274 (1978). In this light, the filling out of the expense form can be viewed as serving a dual purpose; that of furthering Gatzke's personal interests and promoting his employer's business purposes.[6] Accordingly, it is reasonable for the jury to find that the completion of the expense account is an act done in furtherance of the employer's business purposes.

---

[4] It is well settled that a temporary departure from an employee's scope of employ-ment will suspend an employer's vicarious liability only until the deviation has ended. *Nelson* v. *Nelson*, 282 Minn. 487, 166 N.W.2d 70 (1969).

[5] Although this fact was not brought out at trial, it is a matter within the jury's com-mon knowledge.

[6] To be within the scope of employment the act need only be motivated in part to fur-ther the interests of the employer. *Laurie* v. *Mueller,* supra, Restatement, Agency (2d), § § 228, 236.

Additionally, the record indicates that Gatzke was an executive type of employee who had no set working hours. He considered himself a 24-hour-a-day man; his room at the Edgewater Motel was his "office away from home." It was therefore also reasonable for the jury to determine that the filling out of his expense account was done within authorized time and space limits of his employment.

In light of the above, we hold that it was reasonable for the jury to find that Gatzke was acting within the scope of his employment when he completed his expense account. Accordingly, we set aside the trial court's grant of judgment for Walgreen's and reinstate the jury's determination that Gatzke was working within the scope of his employment at the time of his negligent act.

Edgewater contends that the jury's findings relating to Edgewater's contributory negligence are not reasonably supported by the record. It first claims that it owed no duty to protect against its guests' negligence. This court, in *Jacobs v. Draper*, 274 Minn. 110, 142 N.W.2d 628 (1966), stated that: "* * * there are many situations in which a reasonable man is expected to anticipate and guard against the conduct of others." 274 Minn. 116, 142 N.W.2d 633. In that case we quoted from Prosser, Torts (3 ed.), § 33 at 173, as follows, in part:

> "* * * In general, where the risk is relatively slight, he is free to proceed upon the assumption that other people will exercise proper care. * * * But when the risk becomes a serious one, either because the threatened harm is great, or because there is an especial likelihood that it will occur, reasonable care may demand precautions against 'that occasional negligence which is one of the ordinary incidents of human life and therefore to be anticipated.' 'It is not due care to depend upon the exercise of care by another when such reliance is accompanied by obvious danger.'* * *" 274 Minn. 116, 142 N.W.2d 633.

The record indicates that Edgewater had notice of its guests' practice of placing cigarette materials in their motel rooms' plastic wastebaskets. The Edgewater maid who regularly cleaned the room in which Gatzke was staying testified that she had seen cigarette butts in the wastebasket in Gatzke's room. She also stated that, in her experience, she had observed that many other motel residents would often "dump" ash trays and cigarettes in the motel rooms' plastic wastebaskets. She further testified that the head housekeeper had knowledge of the motel guests' habit of leaving cigarette butts in these plastic baskets. In light of these facts, and consistent with the principle articulated in *Jacobs* v. *Draper, supra,* it was reasonable for the jury to find that Edgewater had a duty to protect against the dangers which might flow from its guests' disposal of smoking materials in the motel rooms' wastebaskets.

Edgewater further contends that defendants failed to prove that the use of a plastic wastebasket in and of itself can amount to a breach of a duty of due care. Again, however, the record does not support this contention. Edgewater's own expert witness, Dr. Anderson, testified that the plastic material out of which the wastebasket was made "burns readily." In fact, he had no difficulty igniting the remains of the wastebasket with a common household match. Based on this alone, the jury could quite reasonably conclude that a motel owner, aware that smoking materials were often dumped into wastebaskets, breached a duty of due care by providing a highly combustible plastic wastebasket.

It is also argued by Edgewater that its use of plastic wastebaskets was not negligent because "the use of such wastebaskets is commonplace." Of course, there is no merit to this contention as it is basic hornbook law that "[e]ven an entire industry, by adopting such careless methods to save time, effort or money, cannot be permitted to set its own uncontrolled standard." Prosser, Torts (4 ed.), § 33 at 167. Edgewater's conduct must be compared to that of the reasonably prudent motel owner, not that of a similarly negligent one.

Edgewater finally claims that, even if its use of a plastic wastebasket was negligent, such negligence was not a proximate cause of the fire damage. This contention is premised on the theory that the evidence does not show that the fire originated in the wastebasket. Plaintiff's expert, Dr. Anderson, in reference to the origin of the fire, testified on direct examination as follows:

* * *

"Q   Where, in your opinion, with reference to the wastebasket, did the fire originate, Doctor?

"A   Basically in the wastebasket."

* * * * * *

"Q   All right, Sir. Now, is that—Can you tell us whether that opinion that the fire originated in the wastebasket, is that consistent with all of the pointers and all of the char and all of the burn that you saw in that area, or is it not?

"A   Yes, it is consistent.* * *

[Following the noon recess the questioning continued as follows:]

"Q   Doctor Anderson, at the noon break I was talking to you about the place of origin of the fire and I think—tell us, again, where did you say you felt that it originated?

"A   I felt—it's my opinion that it originated right in the wastebasket or right next to it where I put the 'X' on the figure.

"A   Well, that's what I wanted to ask you about. The 'X' that appears on Plaintiff's Exhibit Z does not appear to be directly in the wastebasket and I wonder if that's an accident or whether you intended that?

"A   No, that's where I think it started.

"Q   Well, that's what I want to understand. You mean in the wastebasket or outside of the wastebasket?

"A   Right next to it.

"Q   So it could have been either one place or the other?

"A   Yes."

The above testimony, coupled with the reasonable inferences which may be drawn from the facts of this case (i.e., a person would presumably dispose of a cigarette in a wastebasket, rather than next to it), provides a reasonable basis from which the jury finding of proximate cause is supported.

The trial court's granting of judgement to Walgreen is hereby set aside, and the jury's verdict is hereby reinstated in its entirety.

Reversed in part; affirmed in part.

OTIS, J., took no part in the consideration or decision of this case.

Part II

The Hotel-Guest Relationship

Chapter 4 Outline

Competencies

1. Describe a hotel's duty under the common law to receive guests. (p. 37)

2. Explain how hotels come under the coverage of the Civil Rights Act of 1964. (pp. 37–38)

3. Explain the remedies allowed an aggrieved person under the Civil Rights Act of 1964. (p. 38–39)

4. Describe a hotel's further obligations under state civil rights law. (p. 39)

5. Explain a hotel's duty to receive married women and minor children. (pp. 39–40)

6. List the circumstances under which a hotel may refuse a guest. (p. 40)

7. Indicate possible liabilities for a hotel's wrongful refusal to receive a guest. (pp. 40–41)

8. Describe anti-discrimination restrictions on hotel advertising. (p. 41)

The Hotel's Duty to Receive Guests and Its Right to Refuse Guests

Duty to Receive Guests

Obligation Under the Common Law

It is a fundamental principle of hotelkeeping, derived from the common law, that the hotelkeeper is engaged in a "public employment"* and must take into the hotel travelers who apply to be received as guests. Under certain circumstances, however, the hotelkeeper may refuse to receive persons applying. These circumstances are discussed in this chapter. Unless such circumstances exist, the hotel must take the person in. This obligation is derived from the public nature of the hotel operation.**

This obligation has been supplemented and strengthened by specific statutory requirements prohibiting discrimination both in the penal and **civil rights** laws of the various states and in the federal Civil Rights Act of 1964.

Federal Civil Rights Law

The Civil Rights Act of 1964 contains certain laws prohibiting places of "public accommodation" from discriminating against any person on the grounds of race, color, religion, or national origin. As stated in 42 U.S.C. § 2000a *et seq.*:

§ 2000a   Prohibition against discrimination or
segregation in places of public assembly

(a) All persons shall be entitled to the full and equal enjoyment of the goods, services, facilities, privileges, advantages, and accommodations of any place of public accommodation, as defined in this section, without discrimination or segregation on the ground of race, color, religion, or national origin.

---

* See Chapter 1 and *Mowers* v. *Fethers* case for discussion of "public employment" under common law.

** Note that in California the Penal Code § 365 provides that it is a *crime* for an innkeeper to refuse accommodations to any person without "just cause or excuse."

This section specifically defines a "place of public accommodation" as including hotels, motels, inns, taverns, roadhouses, barrooms, barbershops, and beauty parlors, as well as many other places.[1]

The federal law applies to any establishment affecting interstate "commerce."* In the case of hotels, motels, or other establishments that provide lodging to transient guests, such are *deemed* to affect interstate commerce under § 2000a(c)(1). Therefore, hotels are covered by the federal civil rights laws.[2]

Remedies Under Federal Law

A person who alleges discriminatory acts by a hotel or other "place of public accommodation" in violation of the provisions of Title II of the Civil Rights Act of 1964 may bring a **civil action** in federal district court to seek "preventive relief," such as an **injunction** or other order directing relief to the aggrieved person.[3] The court may, at its discretion, award the prevailing party reasonable attorney's fees. However, **compensatory damages** are not provided for in the statutory provisions of Title II.

In addition to civil actions brought by individuals, the Attorney General of the United States is authorized to bring a civil action if there is "reasonable cause to believe that any person or group of persons is engaged in a pattern or practice of resistance to the full enjoyment" of any of the rights provided by Title II.[4] Also, when an individual brings an action for injunctive relief, the Attorney General may seek the court's permission to intervene if the case is of "general public importance."[5]

On December 16, 1999, the U.S. Justice Department charged that the Adam's Mark hotel chain discriminates against blacks by charging them more than whites, offering them less desirable rooms and requiring more security. The St. Louis-based chain, which owns 21 full-service hotels around the country, was sued earlier by blacks who alleged that Adam's Mark hotel in Daytona Beach, Florida, singled them out as security risks.

The hotels were charged with engaging in a pattern of racial discrimination against blacks in its hotels, clubs, restaurants, and lounges. The complaint alleged that the company violated Title II of the Civil Rights Act, which requires equal access to public accommodations. Hotel management, the lawsuit said, applied "more onerous terms and conditions to non-white persons at its hotels with regard to such things as prices for goods and services."

This case was settled in 2000 when Adam's Mark Hotels reportedly agreed to pay $4.4 million to individuals who were either guests of, or visitors to, its Daytona Beach resort during the 1999 Black College Reunion. In addition, the luxury hotel chain will reportedly pay $1.5 million to four historically black Florida colleges

---

* For purposes of this Act, "commerce" means travel, trade, traffic, commerce, transportation, or communication among the several states, or between the District of Columbia and any state, or between any foreign country or any territory or possession and any state or the District of Columbia, or between points in the same state but through any other state or the District of Columbia or a foreign country (see also *Heart of Atlanta Motel, Inc.* v. *United States,* 379 U.S. 241 (1964), at the end of this chapter for a discussion of "commerce").

and $112,000 to help them coordinate the annual college reunion over the next three years. As part of the agreement, Adam's Mark will provide training to its officers, hotel managers, and other personnel on their responsibilities under state and federal accommodation laws.[6]

State Civil Rights Laws

In addition to the above federal civil rights laws directly applicable to hotels, some states also make it unlawful for any person to deny to another the full enjoyment of any of the accommodations of a hotel, tavern, or restaurant because of race, religion, color, or national origin. Some states, such as New York, also forbid discrimination on the basis of sex, marital status, blindness, or physical or mental handicaps.[7] In addition to providing a person bringing a civil action the remedy of civil damages (often limited by statute), state laws may also provide criminal penalties.

In New York State, § 40 of the New York Civil Rights Law provides that all persons "shall be entitled to the full and equal accommodations, advantages, facilities and privileges of any places of public accommodations, resort or amusement, *subject only to the conditions and limitations established by law and applicable alike to all persons*" (emphasis added). As the language of the statute indicates, the general rule requiring a hotel to provide equal and full access to hotel accommodations is limited by certain common law reasons for refusing a guest, so long as such refusal or limitation is applied "alike to all persons."

Hotel's Duty to Receive Married Women or Minors

The hotelkeeper's duty to receive guests is not confined or limited to the reception of guests who have the ability to contract. Under the common law a hotelkeeper is required to receive a married woman or a minor on the theory that they are as much in need of the protection of the hotel while upon a journey as any other person.[8]

A married woman today may bind herself by agreement to pay for accommodations that are furnished to her, but her husband may also be liable for the charges incurred either (1) where he has expressly agreed to pay these charges, (2) where apparent authority of the wife to invoke her husband's credit is shown by a prior course of dealings, or (3) in the absence of such authority, where the husband is liable for his wife's support pursuant to an agreement or duly constituted judicial directive.[9] Hotels cannot assume in all cases, however, that a husband is liable for his wife's support, because there may be marital litigation pending or a settlement agreement that has determined otherwise.

Minor Child. What has been said above regarding the charges incurred by a married woman for lodging and meals may also apply in the case of a minor child (in New York, one under 18). In most cases a father is liable under common law for meals and lodging furnished to a minor child whom he is obligated to support. In the absence of special agreement, this liability applies only to meals and lodging, which at law are called "necessaries." In general it does not apply to other items, such as bar charges and theater, airplane, or railroad tickets.

Except for the obligation of husband or father, the hotel can collect directly from the married woman for any charges she incurs; in the case of minors it can enforce collection directly from the minor only for "necessaries."

Right to Refuse Persons

There are circumstances under which a hotel may refuse a guest, notwithstanding the general common law and statutory obligation to receive a person. In some jurisdictions, courts have indicated that a hotel can refuse to receive a guest if:

- The person is drunk or disorderly so as to create a public nuisance

- The person is suffering from a contagious disease

- The person is bringing property into the hotel which it does not customarily receive, such as an animal; or if the person is bringing in property which may be dangerous to others, such as firearms or explosives

- The person is unwilling or unable to pay for hotel services

- The hotel has no accommodations to offer a person (However, if the person has a valid reservation, the hotel may be contractually liable for not providing accommodations.)

A hotel *cannot* refuse a person accommodations merely because the person arrives at an unusual hour, such as the middle of the night. The hotel is presumed to be open for the reception of travelers at all times.

In some states, the hotel's common law right to refuse a person has been further modified by Statute.[10] For example, Minnesota laws provide:

"(a) An innkeeper may refuse to admit or refuse service or accommodations to a person

(1) while on the premises of the hotel acts in an obviously intoxicated or disorderly manner, destroys or threatens to destroy hotel property, or causes or threatens to cause a public disturbance;

(2) the innkeeper reasonably believes is seeking accommodations for the unlawful possession or uses of controlled substances in violation of chapter 152 or the use of the premises for the consumption of intoxicating liquor by a person under the age of 21 years in violation of [Minnesota law]; or

(3) the innkeeper reasonably believes is bringing property into the hotel that may be dangerous to other persons; such as firearms or explosives."

Possible Liabilities for Wrongful Refusal to Receive a Guest

If a hotel *wrongfully* refuses to receive a guest who has reservations, the guest may institute a civil lawsuit against the hotel for damages based on the common law theory of **breach of contract.** Damages may include his/her expenses in going and staying elsewhere and damages sustained by reason of having been turned away.

If the refusal to receive the guest was because of race, creed, color, or national origin, the person may also sue under an applicable state civil rights statute. For example, § 41 of the New York Civil Rights Law allows an aggrieved party to bring a civil action and receive an award of not less than $100 nor more than $500.

In addition, the violation of § 40 may result in criminal charges against the hotel, since under § 41 of the New York Civil Rights Law such violation is a **misdemeanor** punishable upon **conviction** by a fine of not less than $100 nor more than $500 and/or imprisonment of not less than 30 days nor more than 90 days. (See Chapter 9 for information about the accessibility rights of persons with disabilities.)

Restrictions on Advertising

State laws may also prohibit the use of any circulars, advertising, or letters that contain *any implication* or statement that any of the accommodations, facilities, etc., will be refused on account of race, creed, color, or national origin or that any person is unwelcome, objectionable, not acceptable, not desired, or not solicited because of race, creed, color, or national origin. (For example, see § 40 of the New York Civil Rights Law.) It is, therefore, important that hotel advertising, whether by circular or in newspapers or magazines, contain no phrases or words indicating that the hotel is discriminating in the selection of its guests because of race, creed, color, or national origin.

This also applies to letters written by hotels to prospective guests with regard to accommodations or facilities.

Other laws relating to discrimination against employees are addressed in Chapter 21.

Important Points for Management

The common law is the basis for our laws. Our federal and state laws (with the exception of Louisiana) have evolved from court decisions and social customs rooted in our English heritage. The common law as modified by federal, state, and local legislation and court decisions still governs hotel and guest relationships and business transactions in the United States.

Each state is independent and can pass legislation meeting its needs. It is important to remember that state courts can reach decisions separate from court rulings of other states in similar cases.

Under common law, hotelkeepers were obligated to take all travelers who applied to be received as guests. This requirement derived from the common law of England during a time when it was not safe to stay on the open road because there were highway robbers. The common law rule still applies unless it has been changed by legislative statute.

The federal Civil Rights Act of 1964 supplemented the old common law rule by providing that hotels could not discriminate in providing accommodations against any person on the grounds of race, color, religion, or national origin. As noted earlier, some states also enacted state civil rights laws.

References

1. 42 U.S.C. § 2000a(b).

2. See *Heart of Atlanta Motel, Inc.* v. *United States* (following this chapter), 379 U.S. 241 (1964), for the United States Supreme Court's review of the constitutionality of these provisions of the Civil Rights Act of 1964 as applied to hotels.

3. 42 U.S.C. § 2000a-3(a).

4. 42 U.S.C. § 2000a-5.

5. 42 U.S.C. § 2000a-3.

6. *N.Y. Times*, December 17, 1999 at pg. A-23, col. 5 and May 21, 1999 at pg. A-21; USA Today, December 17, 1999 at pg. 3A, col 6. Reprinted with permission from Hospitality Law copyright 2000 by LRP Publications, 747 Dresher Road, Horsham, PA 19044-0980. All rights reserved. For more information on Hospitality Law or for a free 30-day trial subscription, please call 1-800-341-7874, ext. 310.

7. A New York State statute in this connection states, in part, that:

   > It shall be an unlawful discriminatory practice for any person, being the owner, lessee, proprietor, manager, superintendent, agent or employee of any place of public accommodation, resort or amusement, because of the race, creed, color, national origin, *sex, or disability or marital status* of any person, directly or indirectly, to refuse, withhold from, or deny to such person any of the accommodations, advantages, facilities, or privileges thereof.... (emphasis added). N.Y. Exec. Law § 296(2).

   See also § 296(14) of the New York Executive Laws and Article 4-B of the New York Civil Rights Laws on the rights of blind persons.

8. *Watson* v. *Cross*, 63 Ky. 147 (1865). See also Brownell and Merritt, *Manual of Laws Affecting Hotels and Restaurants in New York State* (1947), pp. 22–23.

9. *C. Ludwig Baumann & Co.* v. *Burman*, 155 Misc. 314, 278 N.Y.S. 80 (App. term, 2d Dept. 1935); *Birney* v. *Wheaton*, 2 How. Prac. (NS) 519 (1855). See also *Gabel* v. *Blackburn Operating Corp.*, 442 S.W. 2d 818 (Ct. Civ. App. Tex. 1969); *Jersey Shore Medical Center-Fitkin Hospital* v. *Estate of Baum*, 84 N.J. 137, 417 A.2d 1003 (Sup. Ct. N.J. 1980); But see, *Condore* v. *Prince George's County*, 289 Md. 516, 425 A.2d 1011 (Ct. App. Md. 1981) (court held husband not liable for wife's medical expenses in hospital case and that common law doctrine of necessaries was rendered invalid by Maryland's state equal rights law).

10. See Minn. Stat. § 327.73, subdiv. 2, as amended October 1, 1993.

Key Terms

breach of contract—A failure, without legal excuse, to perform any promise that forms the whole or part of a contract.

civil action or civil suit—A proceeding in a court by one party against another for the enforcement or protection of a private right or the redress of a private wrong.

civil rights—Those personal and natural rights of each human being protected by the U.S. Constitution, in particular the Thirteenth and Fourteenth Amendments, and other federal and state laws. Examples of such civil rights include the freedom of speech, press, and religion, the right to be free of discrimination based on race, color, creed, religion, etc.

compensatory damages—Awarded to make good or to replace loss caused by a wrong or injury; are confined to compensating for injuries sustained. They do not include *punitive damages* (See Chapter 6 and Glossary).

conviction—The final consummation of prosecution against the accused, including judgment or sentence rendered pursuant to a verdict, confession, or plea of guilty to criminal offense.

injunction—A judicial process whereby a party is required by the court to do or refrain from doing a particular thing.

misdemeanors—Generally, less serious crimes that are punishable by fines or jail terms not to exceed one year.

 ## Review Questions

1. Under what circumstances may a hotelkeeper refuse to accept a prospective guest?

2. What are the possible consequences if a hotel wrongfully refuses to receive a guest?

3. How does the Civil Rights Act of 1964 affect hotels?

4. What recourse does a person have who feels he/she was discriminated against by a hotel?

5. In addition to prohibiting discrimination on the basis of race, religion, color, or national origin, under federal law, some states prohibit other forms of discrimination. Name two other forms of discrimination prohibited under state statutes.

6. Why is a hotel obligated under common law to receive married women and minors?

7. How do state discrimination laws place restrictions on hotel advertising?

 ## Internet Sites

For more information, visit the following Internet sites. Remember that Internet addresses can change without notice.

Civil Rights

http://www.ojp.usdoj.gov/ocr/

http://www.law.cornell.edu/topics/civil_rights.html

Federal Court System

http://www.uscourts.gov

Illustrative Case ———————————————————

Heart of Atlanta Motel, Inc. v. United States et al.

379 U.S. 241 (1964)

1. *The Factual Background and Contentions of the Parties.*

The case comes here on admissions and stipulated facts. Appellant owns and operates the Heart of Atlanta Motel which has 216 rooms available to transient guests. The motel is located on Courtland Street, two blocks from downtown Peachtree Street. It is readily accessible to interstate highways 75 and 85 and state highways 23 and 41. Appellant solicits patronage from outside the State of Georgia through various national advertising media, including magazines of national circulation; it maintains over 50 billboards and highway signs within the State, soliciting patronage for the motel; it accepts convention trade from outside Georgia and approximately 75% of its registered guests are from out of State. Prior to passage of the Act the motel had followed a practice of refusing to rent rooms to Negroes, and it alleged that it intended to continue to do so. In an effort to perpetuate that policy this suit was filed.

The appellant contends that Congress in passing this Act exceeded its power to regulate commerce under Art. I, § 8, cl. 3, of the Constitution of the United States; that the Act violates the Fifth Amendment because appellant is deprived of the right to choose its customers and operate its business as it wishes, resulting in a taking of its liberty and property without due process of law and a taking of its property without just compensation; and, finally, that by requiring appellant to rent available rooms to Negroes against its will, Congress is subjecting it to involuntary servitude in contravention of the Thirteenth Amendment.

The appellees counter that the unavailability to Negroes of adequate accommodations interferes significantly with interstate travel, and that Congress, under the Commerce Clause, has power to remove such obstructions and restraints; that the Fifth Amendment does not forbid reasonable regulation and that consequential damage does not constitute a "taking" within the meaning of that amendment; that the Thirteenth Amendment claim fails because it is entirely frivolous to say that an amendment directed to the abolition of human bondage and the removal of widespread disabilities associated with slavery places discrimination in public accommodations beyond the reach of both federal and state law.

At the trial the appellant offered no evidence, submitting the case on the pleadings, admissions and stipulation of facts; however, appellees proved the refusal of the motel to accept Negro transients after the passage of the Act. The District Court sustained the constitutionality of the sections of the Act under attack (§§ 201 (a), (b) (1) and (c) (1)) and issued a permanent injunction on the counterclaim of the appellees. It restrained the appellant from "[r]efusing to accept Negroes as guests in the motel by reason of their race or color" and from "[m]aking any distinction whatever upon the basis of race or color in the availability of the goods, services, facilities, privileges, advantages or accommodations offered or made available to the guests of the motel, or to the general public, within or upon any of the premises of the Heart of Atlanta Motel, Inc."

2. *The History of the Act.*

Congress first evidenced its interest in civil rights legislation in the Civil Rights or Enforcement Act of April 9, 1866.[1] There followed four Acts,[2] with a fifth, the Civil Rights Act of March 1, 1875,[3] culminating the series. In 1883 this Court struck down the public accommodations sections of the 1875 Act in the *Civil Rights Cases,* 109 U. S. 3. No major legislation in this field had been enacted by Congress for 82 years when the Civil Rights Act of 1957[4] became law. It was followed by the Civil Rights Act of 1960.[5] Three years later, on June 19, 1963, the late President Kennedy called for civil rights legislation in a message to Congress to which he attached a proposed bill. Its stated purpose was

> "to promote the general welfare by eliminating discrimination based on race, color, religion, or national origin in...public accommodations through the exercise by Congress of the powers conferred upon it...to enforce the provisions of the fourteenth and fifteenth amendments, to regulate commerce among the several States, and to make laws necessary and proper to execute the powers conferred upon it by the Constitution." H. R. Doc. No. 124, 88th Cong., 1st Sess., at 14.

Bills were introduced in each House of the Congress, embodying the President's suggestion, one in the Senate being S. 1732[6] and one in the House, H. R. 7152. However, it was not until July 2, 1964, upon the recommendation of President Johnson, that the Civil Rights Act of 1964, here under attack, was finally passed.

After extended hearings each of these bills was favorably reported to its respective house, H. R. 7152 on November 20, 1963, H. R. Rep. No. 914, 88th Cong., 1st Sess., and S. 1732 on February 10, 1964, S. Rep. No. 872, 88th Cong., 2d Sess. Although each bill originally incorporated extensive findings of fact these were eliminated from the bills as they were reported. The House passed its bill in January 1964 and sent it to the Senate. Through a bipartisan coalition of Senators Humphrey and Dirksen, together with other Senators, a substitute was worked out in informal conferences. This substitute was adopted by the Senate and sent to the House where it was adopted without change. This expedited procedure prevented the usual report on the substitute bill in the Senate as well as a Conference Committee report ordinarily filed in such matters. Our only frame of reference as to the legislative history of the Act is, therefore, the hearings, reports and debates on the respective bills in each house.

The Act as finally adopted was most comprehensive, undertaking to prevent through peaceful and voluntary settlement discrimination in voting, as well as in places of accommodation and public facilities, federally secured programs and in employment. Since Title II is the only portion under attack here, we con-

---

[1] 14 Stat. 27.

[2] Slave Kidnaping Act. 14 Stat. 50; Peonage Abolition Act of March 2, 1867, 14 Stat. 546; Act of May 31, 1870, 16 Stat. 140; Anti-Lynching Act of April 20, 1871, 17 Stat. 13.

[3] 18 Stat. 335.

[4] 71 Stat. 634.

[5] 74 Stat. 86.

[6] S. 1732 dealt solely with public accommodations. A second Senate bill, S. 1731, contained the entire administration proposal. The Senate Judiciary Committee conducted the hearings on S. 1731 while the Committee on Commerce considered S. 1732.

fine our consideration to those public accommodation provisions.

3. *Title II of the Act.*

This Title is divided into seven sections beginning with § 201 (a) which provides that:

> "All persons shall be entitled to the full and equal enjoyment of the goods, services, facilities, privileges, advantages, and accommodations of any place of public accommodation, as defined in this section, without discrimination or segregation on the ground of race, color, religion, or national origin."

There are listed in § 201 (b) four classes of business establishments, each of which "serves the public" and "is a place of public accommodation" within the meaning of § 201 (a) "if its operations affect commerce, or if discrimination or segregation by it is supported by State action." The covered establishments are:

> "(1) any inn, hotel, motel, or other establishment which provides lodging to transient guests, other than an establishment located within a building which contains not more than five rooms for rent or hire and which is actually occupied by the proprietor of such establishment as his residence;
> "(2) any restaurant, cafeteria…[not here involved];
> "(3) any motion picture house…[not here involved];
> "(4) any establishment…which is physically located within the premises of any establishment otherwise covered by this subsection, or…within the premises of which is physically located any such covered establishment…[not here involved]."

Section 201 (c) defines the phrase "affect commerce" as applied to the above establishments. It first declares that "any inn, hotel, motel, or other establishment which provides lodging to transient guests" affects commerce *per se*. Restaurants, cafeterias, etc., in class two affect commerce only if they serve or offer to serve interstate travelers or if a substantial portion of the food which they serve or products which they sell have "moved in commerce." Motion picture houses and other places listed in class three affect commerce if they customarily present films, performances, etc., "which move in commerce." And the establishments listed in class four affect commerce if they are within, or include within their own premises, an establishment "the operations of which affect commerce." Private clubs are excepted under certain conditions. See § 201 (e).

Section 201 (d) declares that "discrimination or segregation" is supported by state action when carried on under color of any law, statute, ordinance, regulation or any custom or usage required or enforced by officials of the State or any of its subdivisions.

In addition, § 202 affirmatively declares that all persons "shall be entitled to be free, at any establishment or place, from discrimination or segregation of any kind on the ground of race, color, religion, or national origin, if such discrimination or segregation is or purports to be required by any law, statute, ordinance, regulation, rule, or order of a State or any agency or political subdivision thereof."

Finally, § 203 prohibits the withholding or denial, etc., of any right or privilege secured by § 201 and § 202 or the intimidation, threatening or coercion of any person with the purpose of interfering with any such right or the punishing, etc., of any person for exercising or attempting to exercise any such right.

The remaining sections of the Title are remedial ones for violations of any of the previous sections. Remedies are limited to civil actions for preventive relief. The Attorney General may bring suit where he has "reasonable cause to believe that any person or group of persons is engaged in a pattern or practice of resistance to the full enjoyment of any of the rights secured by this title, and that the pattern or practice is of such a nature and is intended to deny the full exercise of the rights herein described...." § 206 (a).

A person aggrieved may bring suit, in which the Attorney General may be permitted to intervene. Thirty days' written notice before filing any such action must be given to the appropriate authorities of a State or subdivision the law of which prohibits the act complained of and which has established an authority which may grant relief therefrom. § 204 (c). In states where such condition does not exist the court after a case is filed may refer it to the Community Relations Service which is established under Title X of the Act. § 204 (d). This Title establishes such service in the Department of Commerce, provides for a Director to be appointed by the President with the advice and consent of the Senate and grants it certain powers, including the power to hold hearings, with reference to matters coming to its attention by reference from the court or between communities and persons involved in disputes arising under the Act.

4.   *Application of Title II to Heart of Atlanta Motel.*

It is admitted that the operation of the motel brings it within the provisions of § 201 (a) of the Act and that appellant refused to provide lodging for transient Negroes because of their race or color and that it intends to continue that policy unless restrained.

The sole question posed is, therefore, the constitutionality of the Civil Rights Act of 1964 as applied to these facts. The legislative history of the Act indicates that Congress based the Act on § 5 and the Equal Protection Clause of the Fourteenth Amendment as well as its power to regulate interstate commerce under Art. I, § 8, cl. 3, of the Constitution.

The Senate Commerce Committee made it quite clear that the fundamental object of Title II was to vindicate "the deprivation of personal dignity that surely accompanies denials of equal access to public establishments." At the same time, however, it noted that such an objective has been and could be readily achieved "by congressional action based on the commerce power of the Constitution." S. Rep. No. 872, *supra,* at 16–17. Our study of the legislative record, made in the light of prior cases, has brought us to the conclusion that Congress possessed ample power in this regard, and we have therefore not considered the other grounds relied upon. This is not to say that the remaining authority upon which it acted was not adequate, a question upon which we do not pass, but merely that since the commerce power is sufficient for our decision here we have considered it alone. Nor is § 201 (d) or § 202, having to do with state action, involved here and we do not pass upon either of those sections.

5.   *The Civil Rights Cases, 109 U.S. 3 (1883), and their Application.*

In light of our ground for decision, it might be well at the outset to discuss the *Civil Rights Cases, supra,* which declared provisions of the Civil Rights Act of 1875 unconstitutional. 18 Stat. 335, 336. We think that decision inapposite, and without precedential value in determining the constitutionality of the present Act. Under Title II of the present legislation, the 1875 Act broadly proscribed discrimination in "inns, public conveyances on land or water, theaters, and other places of public amusement," without limiting the categories of affected businesses to those impinging upon interstate commerce. In contrast, the applicability of Title II is carefully limited to enterprises having a direct and substantial relation to the interstate flow of goods and people, except where state action is involved. Further, the fact that certain kinds of businesses may not in 1875 have been sufficiently involved in interstate commerce to warrant bringing them within the ambit of the commerce power is not necessarily dispositive of the same question today. Our populace had not reached its present mobility, nor were facilities, goods and services circulating as readily in interstate commerce as they are today. Although the principles which we apply today are those first formulated by Chief Justice Marshall in *Gibbons* v. *Ogden,* 9 Wheat. 1 (1824), the conditions of transportation and commerce have changed dramatically, and we must apply those principles to the present state of commerce. The sheer increase in volume of interstate traffic alone would give discriminatory practices which inhibit travel a far larger impact upon the Nation's commerce than such practices had on the economy of another day. Finally, there is language in the *Civil Rights Cases* which indicates that the Court did not fully consider whether the 1875 Act could be sustained as an exercise of the commerce power. Though the Court observed that "no one will contend that the power to pass it was contained in the Constitution before the adoption of the last three amendments [Thirteenth, Fourteenth, and Fifteenth]," the Court went on specifically to note that the Act was not "conceived" in terms of the commerce power and expressly pointed out:

> "Of course, these remarks [as to lack of congressional power] do not apply to those cases in which Congress is clothed with direct and plenary powers of legislation over the whole subject, accompanied with an express or implied denial of such power to the States, as in the regulation of commerce with foreign nations, among the several States, and with the Indian tribes.... In these cases Congress has power to pass laws for regulating the subjects specified in every detail, and the conduct and transactions of individuals in respect thereof." At 18.

Since the commerce power was not relied on by the Government and was without support in the record it is understandable that the Court narrowed its inquiry and excluded the Commerce Clause as a possible source of power. In any event, it is clear that such a limitation renders the opinion devoid of authority for the proposition that the Commerce Clause gives no power to Congress to regulate discriminatory practices now found substantially to affect interstate commerce. We, therefore, conclude that the *Civil Rights Cases* have no relevance to the basis of decision here where the Act explicitly relies upon the commerce power, and where the record is filled with testimony of obstructions and restraints resulting from the discriminations found to be existing. We now pass to that phase of the case.

6. *The Basis of Congressional Action.*

While the Act as adopted carried no congressional findings the record of its passage through each house is replete with evidence of the burdens that discrimination by race or color places upon interstate commerce.... This testimony included the fact that our people have become increasingly mobile with millions of people of all races traveling from State to State; that Negroes in particular have been the subject of discrimination in transient accommodations, having to travel great distances to secure the same; that often they have been unable to obtain accommodations and have had to call upon friends to put them up overnight. S. Rep. No. 872, *supra,* at 14–22; and that these conditions had become so acute as to require the listing of available lodging for Negroes in a special guidebook which was itself "dramatic testimony to the difficulties" Negroes encounter in travel. Senate Commerce Committee Hearings, *supra,* at 692–694. These exclusionary practices were found to be nationwide, the Under Secretary of Commerce testifying that there is "no question that this discrimination in the North still exists to a large degree" and in the West and Midwest as well. *Id.,* at 735, 744. This testimony indicated a qualitative as well as quantitative effect on interstate travel by Negroes. The former was the obvious impairment of the Negro traveler's pleasure and convenience that resulted when he continually was uncertain of finding lodging. As for the latter, there was evidence that this uncertainty stemming from racial discrimination had the effect of discouraging travel on the part of a substantial portion of the Negro community. *Id.,* at 744. This was the conclusion not only of the Under Secretary of Commerce but also of the Administrator of the Federal Aviation Agency who wrote the Chairman of the Senate Commerce Committee that it was his "belief that air commerce is adversely affected by the denial to a substantial segment of the traveling public of adequate and desegregated public accommodations." *Id.,* at 12–13. We shall not burden this opinion with further details since the voluminous testimony presents overwhelming evidence that discrimination by hotels and motels impedes interstate travel.

7. *The Power of Congress Over Interstate Travel.*

The power of Congress to deal with these obstructions depends on the meaning of the Commerce Clause. Its meaning was first enunciated 140 years ago by the great Chief Justice John Marshall in *Gibbons* v. *Ogden,* 9 Wheat. 1 (1824), in these words:

> "The subject to be regulated is commerce; and...to ascertain the extent of the power, it becomes necessary to settle the meaning of the word. The counsel for the appellee would limit it to traffic, to buying and selling, or the interchange of commodities... but it is something more: it is intercourse...between nations, and parts of nations, in all its branches, and is regulated by prescribing rules for carrying on that intercourse. [At 189–190.]

* * *

> "To what commerce does this power extend? The constitution informs us, to commerce 'with foreign nations, and among the several States, and with the Indian tribes.'
> "It has, we believe, been universally admitted, that these words comprehend every species of commercial intercourse.... No sort of trade can be carried on...to which this power does not extend. [At 193–194.]

* * *

> "The subject to which the power is next applied, is to commerce 'among the several States.' The word 'among' means intermingled....

* * *

"...[I]t may very properly be restricted to that commerce which concerns more States than one.... The genius and character of the whole government seem to be, that its action is to be applied to all the...internal concerns [of the Nation] which affect the States generally; but not to those which are completely within a particular State, which do not affect other States, and with which it is not necessary to interfere, for the purpose of executing some of the general powers of the government. [At 194-195.]

* * *

"We are now arrived at the inquiry—What is this power?"

"It is the power to regulate; that is, to prescribe the rule by which commerce is to be governed. This power, like all others vested in Congress, is complete in itself, may be exercised to its utmost extent, and acknowledges no limitations, other than are prescribed in the constitution.... If, as has always been understood, the sovereignty of Congress...is plenary as to those objects [specified in the Constitution], the power over commerce...is vested in Congress as absolutely as it would be in a single government, having in its constitution the same restrictions on the exercise of the power as are found in the constitution of the United States. The wisdom and the discretion of Congress, their identity with the people, and the influence which their constituents possess at elections, are, in this, as in many other instances, as that, for example, of declaring war, the sole restraints on which they have relied, to secure them from its abuse. They are the restraints on which the people must often rely solely, in all representative governments. [At 196-197.]"

In short, the determinative test of the exercise of power by the Congress under the Commerce Clause is simply whether the activity sought to be regulated is "commerce which concerns more States than one" and has a real and substantial relation to the national interest. Let us now turn to this facet of the problem.

That the "intercourse" of which the Chief Justice spoke included the movement of persons through more States than one was settled as early as 1849, in the *Passenger Cases*, 7 How. 283, where Mr. Justice McLean stated: "That the transportation of passengers is a part of commerce is not now an open question." At 401. Again in 1913 Mr. Justice McKenna, speaking for the Court, said: "Commerce among the States, we have said, consists of intercourse and traffic between their citizens, and includes the transportation of persons and property." *Hoke* v. *United States*, 227 U.S. 308, 320. And only four years later in 1917 in *Caminetti* v. *United States*, 242 U.S. 470, Mr. Justice Day held for the Court:

"The transportation of passengers in interstate commerce, it has long been settled, is within the regulatory power of Congress, under the commerce clause of the Constitution, and the authority of Congress to keep the channels of interstate commerce free from immoral and injurious uses has been frequently sustained, and is no longer open to question." At 491.

* * *

In framing Title II of this Act Congress was also dealing with what it considered a moral problem. But that fact does not detract from the overwhelming evidence of the disruptive effect that racial discrimination has had on commercial intercourse. It was this burden which empowered Congress to enact appropriate legislation, and, given this basis for the exercise of its power, Congress was not restricted by the fact that the particular obstruction to interstate commerce with which it was dealing was also deemed a moral and social wrong.

It is said that the operation of the motel here is of a purely local character. But, assuming this to be true, "[i]f it is interstate commerce that feels the pinch, it does not matter how local the operation which applies the squeeze." As Chief Justice Stone put it in *United States* v. *Darby, supra*:

> "The power of Congress over interstate commerce is not confined to the regulation of commerce among the states. It extends to those activities intrastate which so affect interstate commerce or the exercise of the power of Congress over it as to make regulation of them appropriate means to the attainment of a legitimate end, the exercise of the granted power of Congress to regulate interstate commerce. See *McCulloch* v. *Maryland,* 4 Wheat. 316, 421." At 118.

Thus the power of Congress to promote interstate commerce also includes the power to regulate the local incidents thereof, including local activities in both the States of origin and destination, which might have a substantial and harmful effect upon that commerce. One need only examine the evidence which we have discussed above to see that Congress may—as it has—prohibit racial discrimination by motels serving travelers, however "local" their operations may appear.

Nor does the Act deprive appellant of liberty or property under the Fifth Amendment. The commerce power invoked here by the Congress is a specific and plenary one authorized by the Constitution itself. The only questions are: (1) whether Congress had a rational basis for finding that racial discrimination by motels affected commerce, and (2) if it had such a basis, whether the means it selected to eliminate that evil are reasonable and appropriate. If they are, appellant has no "right" to select its guests as it sees fit, free from governmental regulation.

There is nothing novel about such legislation. Thirty-two States now have it on their books either by statute or executive order and many cities provide such regulation. Some of these Acts go back fourscore years.[7] It has been repeatedly held by this Court that such laws do not violate the Due Process Clause of the Fourteenth Amendment. Perhaps the first such holding was in the *Civil Rights Cases* themselves, where Mr. Justice Bradley for the Court inferentially found that innkeepers, "by the laws of all the States, so far as we are aware, are bound, to the extent of their facilities, to furnish proper accommodations to all unobjectionable persons who in good faith apply for them." At 25.

As we have pointed out, 32 States now have such provisions and no case has been cited to us where the attack on a state statute has been successful, either in federal or state courts. Indeed, in some cases the Due Process and Equal Protection Clause objections have been specifically discarded in this Court. *Bob-Lo Excursion Co.* v. *Michigan,* 333 U. S. 28, 34, n. 12 (1948). As a result the constitutionality of such state statutes stands unquestioned. "The authority of the Federal Government over interstate commerce does not differ," it was held in *United States* v. *Rock Royal Co-op., Inc.,* 307 U. S. 533 (1939), "in extent or character from that retained by the states over intrastate commerce." ...

It is doubtful if in the long run appellant will suffer economic loss as a result of the Act. Experience is to the contrary where discrimination is completely obliterated as to all public accommodations. But whether this be true or not is of

---

[7] State statutes omitted.

consequence since this Court has specifically held that the fact that a "member of the class which is regulated may suffer economic losses not shared by others...has never been a barrier" to such legislation. *Bowles* v. *Willingham, supra,* at 518. Likewise in a long line of cases this Court has rejected the claim that the prohibition of racial discrimination in public accommodations interferes with personal liberty.... [cases omitted] See District of *Columbia* v. *John R. Thompson Co.,* 346 U.S. 100 (1953), and cases there cited, where we concluded that Congress had delegated lawmaking power to the District of Columbia "as broad as the police power of a state" which included the power to adopt "a law prohibiting discriminations against Negroes by the owners and managers of restaurants in the District of Columbia." At 110. Neither do we find any merit in the claim that the Act is a taking of property without just compensation. The cases are to the contrary....

We find no merit in the remainder of appellant's contentions, including that of "involuntary servitude." As we have seen, 32 States prohibit racial discrimination in public accommodations. These laws but codify the common-law innkeeper rule which long predated the Thirteenth Amendment. It is difficult to believe that the Amendment was intended to abrogate this principle. Indeed, the opinion of the Court in the *Civil Rights Cases* is to the contrary as we have seen, it having noted with approval the laws of "all the States" prohibiting discrimination. We could not say that the requirements of the Act in this regard are in any way "akin to African slavery."...

We, therefore, conclude that the action of the Congress in the adoption of the Act as applied here to a motel which concededly serves interstate travelers is within the power granted it by the Commerce Clause of the Constitution, as interpreted by this Court for 140 years. It may be argued that Congress could have pursued other methods to eliminate the obstructions it found in interstate commerce caused by racial discrimination. But this is a matter of policy that rests entirely with the Congress not with the courts. How obstructions in commerce may be removed—what means are to be employed—is within the sound and exclusive discretion of the Congress. It is subject only to one caveat—that the means chosen by it must be reasonably adapted to the end permitted by the Constitution. We cannot say that its choice here was not so adapted. The Constitution requires no more.

Affirmed.

Chapter 5 Outline

Form and Effect of Agreement
Guest Lawsuits for Damages
    Potential Liability for Fraud in
      Overbooking
Laws on Overbooking
Important Points for Management
References
Key Terms
Review Questions
Illustrative Cases

Competencies

1. List the material points that must be present to constitute a binding agreement between a hotel and a prospective guest. (p. 55)

2. Explain the basis for a hotel's liability for not honoring a reservation. (p. 55)

3. Indicate the damages a guest may sue for if a hotel fails to furnish reserved accommodations. (pp. 55–56)

4. Describe laws on overbooking. (pp. 56–57)

Guest Reservations

Form and Effect of Agreement

When a hotel and a person seeking to become a guest enter into an agreement wherein the hotel is to reserve a room for a definite period of time at a specified price, if either the hotel or prospective guest breaches this agreement, that party may become liable to the other party for damages. This is general contract law. The agreement may be oral or may be embodied in telegrams or correspondence between the parties. To be binding, the agreement must be in definite terms indicating the intent of the parties and reciting the material points of the agreement, such as the dates of the reservation, the rate, the number of rooms, the nature of the accommodations, and the number of persons. Confirming a reservation to a prospective guest in language that states definitely that he/she will be accommodated for a particular date or dates can constitute a contract binding on the hotel to provide accommodations on the date(s) mentioned. If the hotel's confirmation is in response to a request from the prospective guest for this reservation, it is also binding on the prospective guest to take up the reservation. This is particularly important when the guest contemplates an extended stay, as in a resort hotel.

The case of *Freeman* v. *Kiamesha Concord, Inc.*[1] involved a guest who solicited a reservation at a resort hotel through a travel agent and was offered a room for a minimum stay of three nights. The guest forwarded and the hotel accepted a $20 deposit. The guest departed after two nights, alleging dissatisfaction with the advertised entertainment. The hotel demanded payment for the third night's stay. The New York court held that the resort hotel in such a situation may recover payment from the guest for the entire contractual period of the minimum three nights. In this case the minimum reservation occurred during a peak demand period at the resort hotel and under circumstances in which no other guest was available to occupy the room left vacant. (See the full text of the opinion in this case at the end of this chapter.)

In another case where, as the judge said, "there was room at the inn," the court found that Qwip Systems, Inc., had breached its contract to occupy up to 250 rooms of a luxury hotel for a four-day period. (This case is discussed in Chapter 6, and the full opinion appears at the end of that chapter.)

Guest Lawsuits for Damages

If the hotel fails to furnish the accommodations pursuant to its agreement, the guest may sue for damages, which could be the difference between the contract price and the cost to the guest of obtaining accommodations elsewhere. The damages sought may also include travel or other expenses the guest necessarily incurred. Some courts have recently extended traditional concepts of compensatory damages in contract to include monetary recovery for emotional distress and discomfort.

In the case of *Scher* v. *Liberty Travel Service, et al.*,[2] a New York doctor and his wife, who was convalescing from surgery performed three months before the trip, made prepaid reservations with a travel agent for a three-week stay at a Caribbean hotel. A snowstorm closed the New York airports, making it impossible for the couple to arrive at the hotel on their scheduled first night. They notified the travel agent, who informed the hotel chain's reservation service of the delay in their planned arrival. When they arrived at the Caribbean destination, they were initially refused accommodations despite their confirmed reservations. However, the hotel finally agreed to allow them to stay for two nights on condition that they would then leave.

Despite considerable effort, the plaintiffs were unable to find suitable alternative accommodations for their vacation or to get a flight back to New York. Eventually, they flew to another Caribbean island and booked passage on an ocean liner returning to New York.

Subsequently, they brought suit against the travel agent and the hotel for failure to honor their confirmed reservations. A jury awarded them $15,000 as compensatory damages, including damages for their emotional distress and disappointment. The claim against the travel agent was dismissed.

On appeal, the decision was reversed because the damages were held to be somewhat excessive as a matter of law. Thereafter, the plaintiffs agreed to accept $6,000 (a figure suggested by the **appellate court**) in settlement of their claim.

In a Hawaiian case, a jury awarded a travel agency $151,467 in damages in a suit brought against a hotel that failed to honor confirmed reservations for a group of tourists during Christmas 1977. The travel agency had featured the hotel in its travel literature and television advertisements. Because the hotel refused to honor reservations booked through the agency, the court found that the agency's reputation was damaged.[3]

Potential Liability for Fraud in Overbooking

In a precedent-setting case, *Rainbow Travel Service* v. *Hilton Hotel Corp.*,[4] the U.S. Court of Appeals for the Tenth Circuit in 1990 upheld a jury decision that had found Hilton Hotels Corporation guilty of fraud and awarded $37,500 to the plaintiff, Rainbow Travel Service, for damages to goodwill.

Rainbow Travel had reserved a block of 45 rooms at the Fontainebleau Hilton in Miami Beach, Florida. After the Fontainebleau walked a number of Rainbow Travel's clients, Rainbow Travel sued on the basis that its business reputation had been damaged. (The opinion in this case appears at the end of this chapter.)

Laws on Overbooking ─────────────────────────────

In addition to the potential common law liability that a hotel may face if it overbooks, there has been a good deal of consumer agitation on both the federal and state levels for legislation prohibiting overbooking. The Federal Trade Commission and the U.S. Congress spent a number of years investigating reservation practices of the hotel industry.

States have produced various overbooking bills and enacted regulations. At least one state, Florida, has already enacted regulations prohibiting overbooking. Under these regulations, the hotel must guarantee space when the guest has made a reservation accompanied by a deposit. If the space is later unavailable, the hotel must make "every effort" to find alternate accommodations, must refund the deposit, and is liable for a fine of up to $500 for each guest turned away because of the overbooking.[5]

In addition to possible liability to the guest for damages, if the hotel actually has accommodations but fails to supply them as agreed, the hotel may also become liable for breach of its duties as a hotelkeeper to receive guests (see Chapter 4).

On the other hand, if the hotel were to sue the guest for failure to use the reservation, damages due the hotel are the difference between the agreed contract price and the cost of supplying the accommodations. In addition, if the hotelkeeper rents the rooms to other guests, the original guest is entitled to a credit therefor.

Important Points for Management

- A confirmed reservation can constitute a binding agreement between a prospective guest and the hotel.

- If a hotel breaches a reservation contract, the guest could sue the hotel for damages.

- If a hotel overbooks, the guest may file a lawsuit, especially if he/she had a confirmed reservation.

References

1. 76 Misc.2d 915, 351 N.Y.S.2d 541 (1974). See court's opinion in this case immediately following this chapter.

2. 38 A.D.2d 581, 328 N.Y.S.2d 386 (2d Dept., 1971).

3. *Pleasant Hawaiian Tours* v. *Makani Kai* (unreported).

4. 896 F.2d 1233 (10th Cir. 1990).

5. Rules and Regulations under Chap. 509 of Florida statutes.

Key Terms

appellate court—A court of review to determine whether the rulings and judgment of the court below on the case were correct. It is not a forum in which to make a new case.

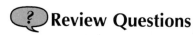

Review Questions

1. Is a confirmed reservation an enforceable contract?

    (a) Does a reservation have to be confirmed in writing to constitute an enforceable contract?

    (b) Does an oral request for a reservation constitute a contract? If so, when? If not, why not?

2. Is a deposit necessary to make a reservation a binding contract? If not, why not?

3. What does the case of *Freeman* v. *Kiamesha Concord, Inc.* teach us with respect to contractual agreements between a hotel and a guest?

4. What may happen if a hotel fails to live up to its obligations under a contractual agreement:

    (a) with a guest?

    (b) with a convention?

5. What steps have been taken on a state level to regulate overbookers?

6. What have AH&MA members done in order to improve reservation practices?

Illustrative Cases

Freeman **v.** *Kiamesha Concord, Inc.*

76 Misc.2d 915, 351 N.Y.S.2d 541
(Small Claims Pt. N.Y. Co. 1974)

SHANLEY N. EGETH, Judge.

Determination of the issues in this Small Claims Part case requires a present construction of the meaning of language contained in Section 206 of the General Business Law as it applies to current widespread and commonplace practices and usages in the hotel and resort industry. Although the pertinent statutory provision has essentially been in effect since its original enactment ninety years ago (L.1883, ch. 227, § 3), there appears to be no reported decision which directly construes or interprets its meaning and applicability.

* * *

The relevant portion of Sec. 206 reads as follows:

"...No charge or sum shall be collected or received by any...hotel keeper or inn keeper for any service not actually rendered or for a longer time than the person so charged actually remained at such hotel or inn...provided such guest shall have given such hotel keeper or inn keeper notice at the office of his departure. For any violation of this section the offender shall forfeit to the injured party three times the amount so charged, and shall not be entitled to receive any money for meals, services, or time charged."

* * *

Is a resort hotel which contracts with a guest for a minimum weekend or other fixed minimum period stay in violation of Sec. 206 General Business Law, and subject to the liability provided therein, if it insists upon full payment from a guest who checks out prior to the expiration of the contract period?

* * *

Plaintiff, a lawyer, has commenced this action against the defendant, the operator of the Concord Hotel (Concord), one of the more opulent of the resort hotels in the Catskill Mountain resort area, to recover the sum of $424.00. Plaintiff seeks the return of charges paid at the rate of $84.80 per day for two days spent at the hotel ($169.60), plus three times said daily rate ($254.40) for a day charged, and not refunded after he and his wife checked out before the commencement of the third day of a reserved three day Memorial Day weekend. Plaintiff asserts that he is entitled to this sum pursuant to the provisions of Sec. 206, General Business Law.

The testimony adduced at trial reveals that, in early May, 1973, after seeing an advertisement in the *New York Times* indicating that Joel Gray would perform at the (Concord) during the forthcoming Memorial Day weekend, plaintiff contacted a travel agent and solicited a reservation for his wife and himself at the hotel. In response he received an offer of a reservation for a "three night minimum stay" which contained a request for a $20.00 deposit. He forwarded the money confirming the reservation, which was deposited by the defendant.

While driving to the hotel the plaintiff observed a billboard, located about 20 miles from his destination which indicated that Joel Gray would perform at the Concord only on the Sunday of the holiday weekend. The plaintiff was disturbed because he had understood the advertisement to mean that the entertainer would be performing on each day of the weekend. He checked into the hotel notwithstanding this disconcerting information, claiming that he did not wish to turn back and ruin a long anticipated weekend vacation. The plaintiff later discovered that two subsequent *New York Times* advertisements, not seen by him before checking in, specified that Gray would perform on the Sunday of that weekend.

After staying at the hotel for two days, the plaintiff advised the management that he wished to check out because of his dissatisfaction with the entertainment. He claims to have told them that he had made his reservation in reliance upon what he understood to be a representation in the advertisement to the effect that Joel Gray would perform throughout the holiday weekend. The management suggested that, since Gray was to perform that evening, he should remain. The plaintiff refused and again asserted his claim that the advertisement constituted a misrepresentation. The defendant insisted upon full payment for the entire three day guaranteed weekend in accordance with the reservation. Plaintiff then told the defendant's employees that he was an attorney and that they had no right to charge him for the third day of the reserved period if he checked out. He referred them to the text of Sec. 206, General Business Law, which he had obviously read in his room where it was posted on the door, along with certain other statutory provisions and the schedule of rates and charges. The plaintiff was finally offered a one day credit for a future stay, if he made full payment. He refused, paid the full charges under protest and advised the defendant of his intention to sue them for treble damages. This is that action.

* * *

I find that the advertisement relied upon by the plaintiff did not contain a false representation. It announced that Joel Gray would perform at the hotel during the Memorial Day weekend. Gray did actually appear during that weekend. The dubious nature of the plaintiff's claim is demonstrated by the fact that when he checked in at the hotel he had been made aware of the date of Gray's performance and remained at the hotel for two days and then checked out prior to the performance that he had allegedly travelled to see.

The advertisement contained no false statement. It neither represented nor suggested that Gray would perform throughout the holiday weekend. The defendant cannot be found liable because the plaintiff misunderstood its advertisement. [citations omitted]

* * *

We now reach plaintiff's primary contention. Simply put, plaintiff asserts that by requiring him to pay the daily rate for the third day of the holiday weekend (even though he had given notice of his intention to leave and did not remain for that day), the defendant violated the provisions of Sec. 206, General Business Law and thereby became liable for the moneys recoverable thereunder. Plaintiff contends that the language of the statute is clear, and that under its terms he is entitled to the relief sought irrespective of whether he had a fixed weekend, week, or monthly reservation, or even if the hotel services were available to him.

It must be noted at the outset that the plaintiff checked into the defendant's hotel pursuant to a valid, enforceable contract for a three day stay. The solicitation of a reservation, the making of a reservation by the transmittal of a deposit and the acceptance of the deposit constituted a binding contract in accordance with traditional contract principles of offer and acceptance. Unquestionably the defendant would have been liable to the plaintiff had it not had an accommodation for plaintiff upon his arrival. The plaintiff is equally bound under the contract for the agreed minimum period.

The testimony reveals that the defendant was ready, willing, and able to provide all the services contracted for, but that plaintiff refused to accept them for the third day of the three day contract period. These services included lodging, meals, and the use of the defendant's recreational and entertainment facilities. In essence, plaintiff maintains that under the terms of the statute, his refusal, for any reason, to accept or utilize these facilities for part of the contract period precludes the defendant from charging him the contract price.

Section 206 is silent as to its applicability to circumstances which constitute a breach of contract or a conscious refusal to accept offered services. This is one of those instances in which, upon analysis, a statute which appears to be clear and unambiguous is sought to be applied to a situation not envisioned by its framers. Nothing contained in the statute provides assistance in answering the question presented in the case, i.e., may a resort hotel hold a guest to his contract for a stay of fixed duration when that guest has, without cause, breached his contract.

There is no legislative history available to assist in determining the intention of the legislature, nor are there any reported decisions construing the statute which can be of assistance in this regard. Recourse must therefore be had to general principles of statutory construction.

Plaintiff argues that Section 206 must be strictly construed against the hotel. In support of this position he cites a number of decisions construing Sections 201 and 202 of the General Business Law. These cases all deal with construction of the statutory right of hotels to limit their monetary liability for the loss of a guest's property. They are inapplicable to the instant situation. The statutory right of a hotel to limit its liability to its guests is in derogation of its unlimited pre-statutory common law liability.

The decisions thereunder universally and appropriately mandate a strict construction of the statutes. However, this case presents the converse situation. Section 206 limits the prior common law unlimited right of a hotel to contract to charge its guests for services and facilities. The statutory restriction upon the hotel is in derogation of the common law. Such a statute must be strictly construed in favor of the hotel and against any expansion of the restriction of its common law right.

The requirement of strict construction in favor of the hotel is buttressed by the penal-like treble damage penalty contained in the statute. A statute which is quasi-penal in nature should be strictly construed against the extension of its application to areas not expressly mandated or contemplated by the legislature. [citations omitted]

It is not sufficient to merely conclude that the statute must be strictly construed in favor of the hotel. The construction to be accorded the statute must also harmonize with the other general principles which have evolved to assist courts in arriving at a determination of legislative intent. Consideration must be given to the "mischief sought to be remedied by the new legislation." [citations omitted]

* * *

In most instances the industry is seasonal in nature. Its facilities are most sought during vacation and holiday periods. Hotels such as the one operated by the defendant have developed techniques to provide full utilization of their facilities during periods of peak demand. One such method is the guaranteed minimum one week or weekend stay, which has gained widespread public acceptance. Almost all of these enterprises have offered their facilities for minimum guaranteed periods during certain times of the year by contracting with willing guests who also seek to fully utilize their available vacation time. These minimum period agreements have become essential to the economic survival and well being of the recreational hotel industry. The public is generally aware of the necessity for them to do so, and accepts the practice.

Adoption of plaintiff's statutory construction in this case would have far-reaching consequences with impact well beyond this case or this defendant. Changes during the past 90 years have transformed the conditions which required urgent redress by statutory enactment in 1883, into a rarity in the year 1973. Absurd results would follow were the statute to be literally and strictly construed in the manner urged by plaintiff. The statute could then become an instrumentality for the infliction of grave harm and injustice, rather than a buffer or shield against the activities of rapacious hotelmen. Plaintiff's construction would create the anomaly of rendering a proper contract illusory while unjustly continuing to obligate only one of the parties to the performance of the contract. The defendant, and most similarly situated hotel keepers have utilized their minimum reservation contracts as a means of achieving economic survival. Chaos and financial disaster would result from the invalidation of such agreements.

A hotel such as the defendant's, services thousands of guests at a single time. The maintenance of its facilities entails a continuing large overhead expenditure. It must have some means to legitimately ensure itself the income which its guests have contracted to pay for the use of its facilities. The minimum period reservation contract is such a device. The rooms are contracted for in advance and are held available while other potential guests are turned away. A guest who terminates his contractual obligations prior to the expiration of the contract period will usually deprive the hotel of anticipated income, if that guest cannot be held financially accountable upon his contract. At that point, replacement income is virtually impossible. Indeed, on occasion, some hotels contract out their entire facilities to members of a single group for a stipulated period many months in advance. No great imagination is required to comprehend the economic catastrophe which would ensue if all such guests were to cancel at the last minute or to check out prior to the end of their contract period without continuing contractual liability. I cannot believe that the public policy of the state sanctions such contractual obliteration.

The construction sought by the plaintiff could result in other consequences which are equally bizarre. The defendant has contracted to supply the plaintiff with a room, three meals a day, and access to the use of its varied sports, recreational or entertainment facilities. As long as these are available to the plaintiff the defendant has fulfilled its contractual commitment. If the plaintiff's construction of the statute is tenable, he might also argue with equal force that unless a guest receives an appropriate rebate or adjustment of bill, the defendant would incur statutory liability, if such guest visited a friend in the vicinity, slept over and failed to use his room for one or more nights of his contracted stay; became enmeshed in an all-night game of cards and failed to use his room; was dieting and failed to avail himself of all the offered meals; did not play tennis, golf, or swim, or became sick and made no use of the available recreational or entertainment facilities.

I conclude that plaintiff may not recover because he has not proved a cause of action based upon a violation of Section 206 of the General Business Law. The evidence does not prove the existence of the type of wrong for which redress was provided in the 1883 enactment. The statute was not intended to prevent a hotel from insisting that its guest comply with the terms of a contract for a fixed minimum stay. There can be no statutory violation by a hotel which fulfills its part of the contract by making its services and facilities available to a guest who refuses to accept them. Such act of refusal by the guest does not justify imposition of the penalties set forth in the statute.

Judgment is accordingly awarded to the defendant with costs.

Rainbow Travel Service v. *Hilton Hotel Corp.*

896 F.2d 1233 (10th Cir. 1990)

The Fontainebleau Hilton is a deluxe resort hotel in Miami Beach, Florida. The hotel is operated by the defendant Hilton Hotels, Inc. ("Hilton"), a Delaware corporation, on behalf of the hotel's owner, defendant Hotelerama Associates, Ltd., a Florida limited partnership. Plaintiff Rainbow is a travel agency with its principal place of business in Oklahoma City, Oklahoma.

* * *

In the spring of 1986, Rainbow began organizing several tour packages for Oklahoma football fans who wanted to attend a University of Oklahoma versus University of Miami football game. The game was scheduled for September 26, 1986, in Miami, Florida. Rainbow initially contacted the Fontainebleau concerning the possibility of reserving hotel rooms for Rainbow's groups. After telephone calls and correspondence between the parties, the Fontainebleau sent Rainbow two contracts which called for the hotel to reserve one hundred and five rooms for Rainbow on the weekend of September 27, 1986. The second of these contracts, which is at issue in this case, provided that forty-five rooms were to be reserved for Rainbow on September 26, 1986. Rainbow executed the agreements and returned them to the Fontainebleau. In June of 1986, the Fontainebleau confirmed Rainbow's reservation by mail and requested prepayment for one night for Rainbow's groups. In response, Rainbow sent a partial payment of over $6,000.00. The Fontainebleau sent another confirmation in August and requested the remainder of the first night's payment. Rainbow then sent a final customer list and the remainder of the requested payment. The payments were made by checks drawn on Rainbow's account in Oklahoma.

Rainbow's president, A.J. Musgrove, went to Miami on September 24, 1986, to make sure that all arrangements had been made for his groups' stay at the Fontainebleau. One group from Rainbow arrived on September 25 and was accommodated as planned. Musgrove met with the hotel's tour representative, Livia Cohen, on September 24, twice on September 25, and again on the morning of September 26. Ms. Cohen assured Mr. Musgrove that everything was fine and that all of the reserved rooms would be available. When the Rainbow group arrived at the hotel on the afternoon of September 26, however, they were told by Hilton representatives that no rooms were available at the Fontainebleau. Hilton made arrangements for the group to stay at the Seacoast Towers, a hotel/apartment complex located about ten blocks away from the Fontainebleau. Rainbow subsequently filed this action in the U.S. District Court for the Western District of Oklahoma, alleging breach of contract and fraud.

* * *

Appellants next argue that the evidence was not sufficient to support an award of damages for injury to goodwill or to support a finding of fraud. Our review of these issues is limited to inquiring whether the record contains substantial evidence to support the jury's verdict, viewing the evidence in the light most favorable to the prevailing party....

Damage—Good Will

The jury found that Rainbow had sustained $37,500.00 in damages to its good will. Rainbow's primary witness on this issue was its president, A.J. Musgrove, who testified that he was familiar with the value of Rainbow's good will from his history with the company and from reviewing Rainbow's financial statements. Mr. Musgrove estimated that the incident at the Fontainebleau damaged Rainbow's good will in the amount of $250,000.00. His opinion was based in part on his observation that when customers are dissatisfied they tell others about it, meaning that a bad incident such as this one has a "rippling effect" on a business' reputation. He indicated that this is particularly true for a travel agency because it relies heavily on its reputation in the community. Addition-ally, Rainbow presented the testimony of witnesses who had traveled to Miami on the Rainbow tour. These witnesses stated that they were dissatisfied with Rainbow because of the hotel incident and stated that they probably would not choose Rainbow again as a travel agent.

Viewing this evidence in the light most favorable to the plaintiff, we find that there was substantial evidence reasonably tending to support the jury's verdict.

* * *

Fraud

Appellants next argue that the evidence was insufficient to support the jury's verdict on fraud. Under Oklahoma law, fraud consists of a false material representation made as a positive assertion which is known either to be false, or is made recklessly without knowledge of the truth, with the intention that it be acted upon by a party to his or her detriment.... [citation omitted] As the jury was instructed, fraud must be shown by clear and convincing evidence.... [citation omitted] Rainbow argued in the district court that a Hilton agent's assurances that rooms would be available amounted to fraud because the representations were made recklessly without knowledge of the truth. Most of the evidence at trial centered on whether Hilton knew or should have known there would be a shortage of rooms at the Fontainebleau on September 26, 1986. Interpreting the evidence in the light most favorable to the plaintiff, we find there was sufficient evidence to raise a question of fact for the jury on the issue of fraud.

Rainbow presented evidence that Hilton accepted reservations for more rooms than were available on September 26, 1986. Hilton admitted that its policy was to book the Fontainebleau up to one hundred and fifteen percent of its capacity, but argued that it did so based on a historic fifteen per cent "no-show" rate for guests with reservations. Hilton insisted that this policy allowed the hotel to honor almost all of its reservations. Although Hilton showed that an exceedingly high percentage of reservations were in fact honored over the course of a year, Rainbow presented evidence showing that on fifty per cent of those occasions when the hotel was operating at capacity the hotel had to dishonor reservations. Additionally, Rainbow presented evidence tending to show that Hilton was aware of a substantial likelihood that Rainbow's reservation might be dishonored. Rainbow showed that Hilton knew at least one month in advance that a large number of rooms would be closed for maintenance during September of 1986. Rainbow also argued that departure figures from the Fontainebleau showed that the hotel knew that a substantial number of people would stay over past their announced departure date. Additionally, Rainbow showed that on the date in question Hilton gave a block of rooms to a group from the University of Oklahoma even though the group had not reserved the rooms. Despite these factors, and pursuant to Hilton policy, Rainbow was not informed of the practice of overbooking and was not told there was a possibility that "guaranteed" reservations might be dishonored. Instead, Hilton assured Rainbow that the rooms would be available.

Hilton argued strenuously in the district court that the overbooking situation was due to factors beyond its control, such as guests extending their stay at the Fontainebleau and rooms being out of order for repairs. These explanations may have sounded rather hollow to the jury, however, in light of a portion of the Fontainebleau's policy manual which read:

Overboard

We never tell a guest we "overbooked."

If an overboard situation arises, it is due to the fact that something occurred that the hotel could not prevent.

Examples:

1.   Scheduled departures do not vacate their rooms.

2.   Engineering problems with a room (pipe bursted, thus water leaks, air conditioning, heating out of commission, broken glass, etc.)

Always remain calm and as pleasant as possible.

(Plaintiff's Exhibit 25-2)

Hilton also argued that its agent could not have known about the lack of rooms without performing a series of complicated calculations. If this proposition is true, however, it serves as some support for the allegation that Hilton made positive assertions about the availability of rooms without knowledge of the truth.

In addition to the foregoing, the record contains much circumstantial evidence showing that Hilton had knowledge of a likelihood of dishonoring reservations at the time in question. The Fontainebleau was extremely busy during the week of Rainbow's visit. On September 22 and 23 for instance, the hotel was completely sold out and the Fontainebleau had to dishonor reservations. Although there were some vacant rooms on September 24 and 25, the number of vacancies was very few. (Pl.Ex. 65). Also, the "no-show" rate for reservations was much less during this period than the fifteen per cent annual average used by Hilton. Although Hilton's agent indicated to Mr. Musgrove on the morning of September 26 that his rooms would be available, the Night Clerk Summary for September 25 indicated that the hotel would be short of rooms even if fifteen per cent of the reservations for the 26th failed to show.

Some of the testimony at trial raised questions about the candor of Hilton's explanation concerning its treatment of Rainbow's reservations. Hilton said that it only became aware of a shortage of rooms after Mr. Musgrove had gone to the airport to pick up his group, yet when the group arrived back at the hotel they had already been assigned specific rooms at the Seacoast Towers.

* * *

Hilton explained that the shortage of rooms was caused by guests not checking out on the 26th, but the decision to move Rainbow was made well before checkout time on that date. Moreover, Hilton's representative testified at trial that all requests for extended stays on the 26th were refused by the hotel. Finally, members of Rainbow's group testified that several groups that arrived at the Fontainebleau after Rainbow had been bumped were given rooms at the Fontainebleau.

Clearly, the evidence in the record before us may be interpreted in more than one way. Yet, as we noted at the outset, our inquiry is limited to whether the record contains substantial evidence to support the jury's verdict.

* * *

We find substantial evidence in the record that Hilton was aware of having overbooked the hotel to such an extent as to create a substantial likelihood that Rainbow's reservation would be dishonored.... [citation omitted] Despite this, Hilton repeatedly told Rainbow that its rooms would be available and did not tell Rainbow that the group might be "bumped." Based on this and all of the evidence in the record before us, we find that a reasonable juror could find by clear and convincing evidence that Hilton recklessly made statements without knowledge of their truth, that Hilton did so with the intention that plaintiff rely on them, and that plaintiff relied on the statements to its detriment.... [citations omitted]

Damages for Breach of Contract

Appellants contend that the jury's award of $5,493.10 for breach of contract was not supported by the evidence. We have examined the record in detail and we agree with appellant that this figure is not supported by the record. There was little evidence presented as to damages from the breach of the contract. Rainbow did not seek damages for lost profits from the Miami trip. Indeed, the evidence was that the travel agency realized its expected profit from the trip. Rainbow only suffered out of pocket expenses of $796.00 from the breach.... Aside from these expenses, however, Rainbow sought to recover $8,740.00, which was the amount paid by Rainbow's clients to Rainbow for the Miami trip (excluding airfare). A.J. Musgrove testified that he would like to repay his customers since they did not get the rooms that Rainbow promised they would get. Hilton argued that this was an improper attempt to recover on behalf of Rainbow's clients. Rainbow's response was to argue that this was a necessary expense to help repair Rainbow's good will.

We agree that under the evidence in this case it was improper to allow Rainbow to recover an amount to pay back to its customers. Clearly, Rainbow had no right to re-cover on behalf of its clients. Thus, the amounts paid by Rainbow's customers were only relevant insofar as Rainbow's good will was concerned. Awarding Rainbow both the full extent of injury to its good will, however, *and* the means to repair that damage amounts to a double recovery. Mr. Musgrove's opinion that Rainbow had suffered damage to its good will did not take into account the effect of giving refunds to its customers for the Miami trip. In fact, Rainbow's argument that its good will had been injured relied heavily on the fact that its customers had not been paid back. Yet, under the instructions on the fraud count, the jury was told that if it found fraud it should fully compensate Rainbow for any loss of good will arising from Hilton's conduct. The jury did so, awarding $37,500.00 in damages attributable to loss of good will. Rainbow cannot have it both ways. It cannot recover the full extent of damage to its good will while seeking additional money that it claims is necessary to repair the injury to good will. In view of this fact, there is simply no evidence to support the jury's award of $5,493.10 for breach of contract.

Under the instructions given to the jury in this case, the defendants were entitled to a setoff of $5,892.90 on any damages arising from a breach of the parties' agreement. This setoff was due to the fact that Hilton refunded a portion of Rainbow's initial payment for the hotel rooms. Accordingly, we must offset the amount of $5,892.90 against the $796.00 loss claimed by Rainbow. When this is done, it is apparent that Rainbow is not entitled to recover any damages from Hilton for the breach of contract.

* * *

Conclusion

The judgment is AFFIRMED in all respects except as to the damages for breach of contract; on that issue we REVERSE the judgment as unsupported by the evidence.

IT IS SO ORDERED.

Chapter 6 Outline

Convention Contract Format
A Word About Insurance
    Contract Review
    Recent Case Law
Important Points for Management
References
Key Terms
Review Questions
Internet Sites
Illustrative Case

Competencies

1. List some major items that should be included in a written contract between a hotel and its convention or group travel clients. (pp. 69–73)

2. Identify the types of insurance that a hotel might advise a convention or group travel client to carry. (pp. 73–74)

3. Indicate how often a hotel should review its convention or group contracts, and cite cases illustrating the importance of proper contracts with conventions or groups. (pp. 74–76)

6

Convention and Group Contracts with the Hotel

CONVENTION AND GROUP travel business has grown tremendously and plays an ever larger role in a hotel's economic life. For many years convention agreements were made primarily by a handshake between the convention manager and the hotel manager. Because convention planning has become more difficult and complex over the years, the parties have grown more accustomed to setting forth their understandings and agreements in written contract form.

Convention Contract Format

The contract format presented in this chapter (Exhibit 6.1) offers some idea of the subjects covered by a convention contract. Each hotel usually develops its own contract form for reserving guestrooms, meeting rooms, banquet facilities, exhibit space, and services at the property. Whenever the hotel enters into a written contract with a convention manager or group travel representative, there are a myriad of items that must be discussed and specified in the contract in order to avoid misunderstandings between the parties. A hotel's printed contract form may have to be modified by riders and additional clauses to tailor the agreement to the parties' requirements. The advice of a hotel's attorney is important before the hotel commits to any contractual agreement since such agreements could result in liability for the hotel.

The simplified convention contract format presented here is derived largely from a document distributed by the American Society of Association Executives, and, foreseeably, it may be used by associations in framing their requests for provisions to include in the hotel convention contract.

The convention contract would probably also include so-called "protection clauses" covering the following:

- Impossibility of performance by reason of labor strikes, civil disorders, etc.
- Cancellation clauses

Other matters that might be included in a hotel convention contract are:

- Pre-registration procedures
- Luggage handling
- Transportation arrangements and charges, if any, and gratuities, if any

Exhibit 6.1   Sample Convention Contract

Sample Convention Contract

This will confirm the arrangements made by _____ (name of Association) and _____ (name of hotel) concerning the _____ forthcoming meeting/convention.

The _____ (hereafter referred to as the "Association") and _____ Hotel (hereafter referred to as the "Facility") agree that:

1. The Association hereby engages the Facility and its staff for a meeting/convention and the Facility agrees to furnish same on the following terms: (By mutual agreement in writing, these rates, as well as the rates set forth in paragraph 1 (f) hereof may be revised or otherwise changed.)
(a) Scheduled dates and days of meeting/convention from _____ to _____
(b) Start exhibit setup _____ A.M./P.M.
(c) The rates to be charged by the Facility for sleeping rooms are as follows:

Single Room from	$	to	$	or Flat Rate
Double Room from	$	to	$	or Flat Rate
Twin Rooms from	$	to	$	or Flat Rate
Suites from	$	to	$	or Flat Rate
Other from	$	to	$	or Flat Rate

(d) The Association presently estimates the number of rooms required to be as follows:

No. of Single

minimum and maximum

No. of Double

minimum and maximum

No. of Twin

minimum and maximum

No. of Suites

minimum and maximum

No. of Other (Specified)

minimum and maximum

(NOTE: If room is from X to Y dollars [paragraph c] then specify at each rate.)
It is anticipated that _____ of those attending may wish to have an earlier check-in. The dates for early check-in are _____, in which case the Facility will provide rooms therefor at convention rates specified. The same rates will apply for _____ days following the convention/meeting.
The Facility guarantees it will provide at least the maximum number of rooms set forth in paragraph (d) and the Association agrees to provide occupancy for the minimum number of rooms specified.

Exhibit 6.1 *(continued)*

The Association agrees to keep the Facility informed periodically of registrations received in advance so that more exact estimates can be made as to room requirements. It is agreed that periodic changes in the above estimates (d) may be made from time to time up to _____ days prior to the meeting/convention, but in no case shall the minimum or maximum number set forth in this agreement be changed except by written agreement. The Association and Facility should agree in advance on a mutually satisfactory review schedule of convention developments and specify when and how rooms may be released by either party. (Review dates and times should be specified in this letter of agreement.) After the agreed upon cutoff date(s) the Association and Facility will be held responsible to meet the final agreement.

Facility agrees to refer all requests for suites (if any are held) and/or public rooms to Association for approval before assignment if the applicant is identified with the Association or industry it serves.

The Association shall/shall not request room deposits of convention delegates.

The Facility agrees to provide the Association with a final occupancy report showing number of rooms occupied each day of the convention period.

(e) Specify here any agreement by the Facility to improve, remodel, or create certain rooms or areas or add services prior to the event covered by this contract. The specifics of the changes in the Facility should be spelled out in this contract and it should be stated if failure to meet the requirements by a specified date would be cause for cancellation of the agreement by the Association. Reasonable and adequate notification of the association should be required of any remodeling which would result in a change in the number of suites or public space available.

(f) Anticipated meeting room requirements:

Room Reserved   From Date and Hour to Date and Hour

_____   _____

_____   _____

_____   _____

Type of Function Anticipated   Rental Charge (if any)

_____   _____

_____   _____

_____   _____

A tentative schedule of meeting rooms required will be submitted to the Facility at least _____ months in advance of the meeting/convention. A firm and detailed schedule of meeting rooms required will be furnished the Facility not

(continued)

Exhibit 6.1   *(continued)*

later than _____ months before the meeting/convention. Unless otherwise specified in this agreement, public space as outlined above shall be reserved for the Association unless released in writing. (If total facility is being booked the later language should state "All public space shall be reserved for the Association without charge" (or with charges as specified) for use at the discretion of the Association. If the Association is utilizing only a part of the facility, the above room schedule should be completed.)

(g)   Anticipated exhibit space required. The Facility agrees to reserve _____ rooms for use as exhibit space. Cost for space shall be _____ (if any). Services to be provided in exhibit hall by Facility include (here specify such items as cleaning, extra lighting, carpeting, advance storage, security, number of microphones available, audio-visual equipment available, operator rates, power supply, or other times agreed upon):

The Facility warrants that the following union regulations prevail in the exhibit hall and will promptly notify the Association of any change. Current conditions are (outline union requirements in exposition hall):

Special equipment needs of the Association (description and rates):

(h)   Banquet facilities required.

(i)   A guarantee of the number of persons attending each food or beverage function will be given to the Facility at least _____ hours in advance of the function. The Facility agrees to set for _____ % over the guarantee. The above food functions (package) shall be provided at a per person cost of $_____. Beverage/liquor by drink and/or bottle shall be provided at a cost of $ _____. Such prices are subject to review up to six months prior to the event.

If a meal function is to be added to the package, the price applied shall be the same as that included in the above package for a like meal.

(j)   Complimentary accommodations, if any, to be furnished by the Facility to the Association (description of rooms and suites, dates of availability and number):

(k)   The Facility will give the Association notice of any construction or remodeling to be performed in the Facility which might interfere with the event. In such event, Facility must provide equal alternate space within the facility under contract.

2.   The Facility and Association agree that the following procedure shall be followed with regard to gratuities.

(NOTE: Specific individuals, amount or percent and procedure may be spelled out.)

3.   It is agreed by the parties that the foregoing sets forth the essential features of the agreement between the parties, and that specific details as to registration, assigning rooms for persons attending, handling of materials, special services, collection of tickets, accounting, master account billing procedures, promotion, publicity and other matters will be worked out and confirmed in writing to the satisfaction of both parties prior to the meeting/convention.

4.   This agreement will bind both the Association and the Facility and except as above provided in paragraph 1 (e), may be canceled by either party only upon the giving of written notice at least _____ (years) _____ (months) _____ (days) prior to the dates of the meeting/convention; that is no later than _____ (specific date).

Exhibit 6.1   *(continued)*

---

5.   The Facility and the Association each agree to carry adequate liability and other insurance protecting itself against any claims arising from any activities conducted in the Facility during the meeting/convention, namely (specify):

_____

(Hotel)

By _____ General Manager

_____ Sales Manager

The Undersigned Accepts and Agrees to all terms, conditions and the rates above set forth in this Agreement.

_____ Association

By _____ Chief Elected Office (title)

_____ Chief Paid Executive (title)

- Applicable federal, state, and local taxes, and percentages of same
- Procedures with respect to speedy check-outs
- Distribution of any gift merchandise to the guestrooms

A Word About Insurance

In preparing a contract with the convention manager or group travel representative, hotel representatives should review the insurance carried by the convention or group. The convention or group should be advised of general liability insurance for protection against claims involving bodily injury and/or property damage.

Groups should also consider fire legal liability insurance and broad form property damage protection. Medical payment insurance is also available to reimburse medical expenses because of injuries occurring at the hotel. If the convention or group sets up a first aid station, or hires a doctor or nurse, it should consider malpractice insurance coverage.

If the convention or group operates a food stand or serves food or drink at a reception or dinner, it may wish to take host liability and/or liquor liability insurance.

If **independent contractors** are used, they should provide the hotel with workers' compensation and general liability insurance with adequate liability limits. Independent contractors liability insurance, in addition to a hotel's general liability, can insure against any suit brought as a result of negligence on the part of the independent contractor.

If the convention or group uses charter buses, automobiles, watercraft, or aircraft, it should consider proper liability insurance to cover injury to persons or damage to property.

The hotel can also consider "no-show" insurance to protect it against losses if the convention or group does not attend the meeting because of fires, blizzards, strikes, bombings, or other hazards. (Also, the insurance could cover extra expenses incurred in seeing that the event does go on. For example, if there is a taxicab strike, the hotel may have to hire buses to pick up people at the airport.)*

Contract Review

As the convention and group travel business grows, requirements for meeting rooms, facilities and equipment, and amenities increase proportionately. A hotel should review its contracts every two or three years to see that they cover all matters involved in modern day convention and group planning.**

Pertinent Case Law

The importance of hotels having a written contract with the convention or tour group was demonstrated in the case of *Hotel Del Coronado* (San Diego, California) v. *Qwip Systems*.[1] In this case, the court decided that the plaintiff-hotel could recover damages of $15,300 from the defendant-corporation, a division of Exxon. The breach arose when Qwip attempted to cancel an agreement to use the hotel facilities for a four-day bonus trip for outstanding sales personnel. (The full opinion in this case appears at the end of this chapter.)

The hotel sales manager sent a letter to Qwip on December 17, 1977, stating that the accommodations would be held. The group representative responded to the hotel by letter dated December 22, 1977, "confirming" the reservation "for 250 accommodations" for the four-day period and the determination of the specific number of occupancies 21 days before the date of arrival, as required by the hotel.

In December, 1978, Qwip wrote to the hotel that the corporation would be sending its employees to Spain instead of to Hotel Del Coronado in February, 1979. The hotel sued Qwip for damages for breach of contract.

The judge calculated damages totaling $15,300 by multiplying the actual number of vacancies for the four-day period, which he determined to be 306, by $50, the average price per room. The plaintiff's claim that the hotel lost an additional $46 per room due to lost revenue on "meals, gifts shops, beverages, and miscellaneous items" was rejected. *The court pointed out that the agreement made no reference to any other activity in the hotel except occupancy.*

Usually, if a group cancels its reservations after a specified date, the group is responsible for the cost of any reserved guestroom that cannot be resold. In 1999, the Court of Appeals of Tennessee found that when a convention was canceled, the Opryland Hotel must calculate liability by treating each guestroom sold after the cancellation as one of the rooms reserved by Millbrook Distribution Services, Inc.,

---

* See *Convention Liaison Council Manual*, published by the Convention Liaison Council (Washington, D.C., 1985).

** In this regard, several AH&MA *Lodging* magazine articles contain useful information, namely: "How to Service Conventions," March 1982, pp. 25 *et seq.*, and "Master Account Billing," June 1980, pp. 49 *et seq.*

which booked the rooms for the group. To this extent, the court agreed with Millbrook that the reserved rooms moved to the top of the hotel's inventory. However, the ascension did not take place until Millbrook released the rooms by canceling its reservation. In this manner, the court found the hotel was obligated to sell the Millbrook guestrooms from the top of its inventory. Based on this approach by the Court, Millbrook's liability was calculated to be $170,690 for cancelling the group's room reservations.[2]

When the hotel has an agreement with a convention or a group, the hotel must make every effort to honor the agreement. In the case of *Sweet Adelines, Inc.* v. *Hyatt Hotels Corporation* (filed in the U.S. District Court for the District of Arizona; an unreported case), the plaintiff organization sought damages in excess of $30,000, plus **punitive damages** for the defendant hotel operator's alleged breach of contract. The **complaint** alleged that during a meeting with the hotel sales manager in July 1976, a commitment was made to provide 600 rooms for a convention to be held in November 1981. In November 1976, the sales manager in a letter allegedly indicated that 600 rooms would be held on a "definite basis" for certain days during the convention and that the room rates would be confirmed in November 1980 for 1981. As requested, the plaintiff organization signed and returned this letter.

The complaint stated that in January 1981, the general manager of the hotel informed a representative of the plaintiff organization that only 175 of the hotel rooms could be provided during the convention period. The plaintiff then obtained rooms at other hotels farther away from the convention site. The plaintiff-organization sued for the additional administrative expenses and travel expenses in arranging for alternate accommodations, and alleged losses in connection with the management of its convention. Punitive damages for a "willful" breach of contract and attorney's fees were also sought. The suit was settled for an undisclosed amount.

In another case, the National Council of Savings Institutions (NCSI) agreed to pay up to $800,000 to the Westin Kauai in Hawaii after the NCSI canceled a convention two months before it was scheduled to take place.[3] The cancellation meant an estimated loss to the Westin Kauai of $900,000 to $1 million in room rental fees and food and beverage expenditures.

The NCSI had reserved rooms for its members four years earlier. Then, in light of the nation's savings and loan crisis in the 1980s, the association decided that a convention in Hawaii was inappropriate and instead chose to hold a half-day meeting in Washington, D.C., for its 90 board members.

The contract between the NCSI and Westin Kauai provided for graduated damages in the event of cancellation within 12 months prior to the event: the closer the notice of cancellation occurred to the convention date, the larger the damages. The exact amount of the penalty was negotiated out of court.

Liquidated damage clauses in contracts, like the one in the Westin Kauai contract, serve to protect the hotel.

Important Points for Management

Because convention and group planning has become increasingly complex in recent years, a hotel should set forth its agreement with the client in written contract form. Each hotel usually develops its own contract form for reserving guestrooms, meeting rooms, banquet facilities, exhibit space, and services at the property.

In order to avoid misunderstandings, many details must be specified in any contract entered into by a hotel and a convention or group. A hotel's printed contract may be amended by additional clauses or by riders to meet the needs of a particular convention or group. It is important that a hotel seek its attorney's advice before entering into such a contract, because such agreements could result in liability for the hotel. When a hotel has an agreement with a convention or group, the hotel must make every effort to honor the agreement.

A hotel must review its convention contract forms every five or six years to make certain that they address all matters pertinent to modern convention and group planning.

Items to cover in contracts with conventions or groups include:

- What the hotel is required to provide—guestrooms, meeting rooms, banquet food, exhibition space, audiovisual aids, etc.

- Cost to the group or convention

- What the group or convention will do—buy and furnish evidence of insurance, purchase a set number of rooms, and so forth

- Payment dates

- "Protection clauses," including:

    a. Impossibility of performance by reason of labor strike, civil disorders, etc.

    b. Cancellation clauses

These are only a few of the items covered by a convention or group contract. Review the types of insurance that the hotel, convention, or group should purchase in order to help protect the hotel against potential liability claims. They may include fire legal liability insurance, broad form property damage protection, medical payment insurance, malpractice coverage, host and/or liquor liability insurance, workers' compensation, general liability insurance, independent contractors liability insurance, no-show insurance, and proper liability insurance to cover injury to persons or damage to property.

 ## References

1. 186 N.Y.L.J. at 13, col. 4 (N.Y. Sup. Ct. Nassau Co., July 16, 1981).

2. *Opryland Hotel, L.P.,* v. *Millbroook Distribution Services, Inc.,* 1999 Tenn. App. LEXIS 647, 80 F. Supp. 2d 88, No. 01-A-01-9810-CH- 00551 (Tenn. App. 09/29/99). Reprinted with permission from Hospitality Law copyright 2000 by LRP Publications, 747 Dresher Road, Horsham, PA 19044-0980. All rights reserved. For more information on Hospitality Law or for a free 30-day trial subscription, please call 1-800-341-7874, ext. 310. And see *Hyatt* v. *WIBC* (97 Civ. 767A(f) W.D.N.Y., August 25, 1999).

3. Unreported case. See *N.Y. Times,* Mar. 16, 1989, p. 23D, col. 3.

Key Terms

complaint—Gives the adverse party notice of the claims asserted against it. It does not narrow the issues, or give notice of precise factual basis of plaintiff's claim, or provide a means for an early adjudication of a claim.

independent contractor—One who, in exercise of an independent employment, contracts to do a piece of work according to his/her own methods and is subject to his/her employer's control only as to end product or final result of the work.

punitive damages—Damages, other than compensatory or nominal damages, awarded against a person to punish him/her for outrageous conduct. The chief purpose of punitive damages is to inflict punishment as an example and a deterrent to similar conduct.

Review Questions

1. Why is it important for hotels to have written convention and group contracts?

2. What are some of the matters which should be covered by a convention contract?

3. When, if ever, should the hotel update its forms for convention contracts? Why?

4. Why is it important to seek the advice of an attorney before entering into a convention or group contract?

5. Why is it important for the hotel to make certain that the convention or group has adequate insurance coverage?

6. What are some of the insurance policies that a convention or group should have?

Internet Sites

For more information, visit the following Internet sites. Remember that Internet addresses can change without notice.

American Society of Association
Executives
http://www.asaenet.org

Illustrative Case ────────────────────────────

Hotel Del Coronado v. Qwip Systems

186 N.Y.L.J., July 16, 1981 at 13,
Col. 4 (N.Y. Sup. Ct., Nassau Co. 1981)

This breach of contract action which was tried before me without a jury involves a situation where there was room at the inn.

Hotel Del Coronado, the plaintiff, operates a 585-room luxury hotel situated on an island in San Diego Harbor. It seeks damages from defendant, Qwip Systems, Inc., a division of Exxon Enterprises, Inc., for their failure to occupy 250 rooms for the 4-day period commencing Feb. 28, 1979.

The parties' agreement is set forth in a series of letters exchanged during Dec. of 1977 and Jan. of 1978. Some background is essential to their proper interpretation.

In 1977 Qwip employed between 350 and 400 sales personnel. It also maintained a "Sales Compensation and Recognition Program" headed by Mr. William J. Bradley whose purpose it was to "motivate" Qwip sales and customer support people. In the latter part of 1977 the motivators determined that a 4-day expense paid trip would represent an excellent carrot to dangle in front of its motivatees. Qualification for the trip was to be based on exceeding an established sales criteria for the sales year beginning Jan. of 1978. Bradley and his staff were neophytes in such matters. Having no past experiences upon which to draw, they were unsure how many of Qwip's employees might ultimately qualify. Realizing that counter-productive results might occur if adequate arrangements were not made, they were concerned with insuring sufficient space for those who might possibly qualify.

In Dec. of 1977, Qwip contacted Mr. Warford Drown, the Hotel Coronado's sales manager, for the purpose of reserving rooms at the "Coronado" during Feb. of 1979. The problems with respect to numbers were explained to Drown.

On Dec. 12, 1977 (Ex. 2) Drown wrote the following letter to Bradley:

"Thank you for your call recently, it was a pleasure to discuss with you arrangements to accommodate the meeting of Kwip [*sic*] Systems—Division of Exxon.

"This will confirm that we have reserved on a tentative basis one hundred and eighty five accommodations for arrival on Feb. 11, 1979 and departure Feb. 15, 1979.

"We cannot confirm room rates at this time, but we are able to confirm the rates one year in advance of your arrival date.

"We do not have any information on your meetings or planned food functions and will need this as soon as possible so that we may set aside the proper and adequate space.

"We will hold a total of one hundred and eighty five accommodations up to TWENTY ONE DAYS PRIOR to the arrival date specified above. If such accommodations have not been reserved for specifically named occupants from your group by that time, it will be assumed that the number of accommodations required for your meeting at the hotel will not equal the number now confirmed. The accommodations not reserved for specifically named occupants by TWENTY ONE DAYS prior to the arrival date specified will revert to the hotel for sale. If members of your group wish to make reservations during the

TWENTY ONE DAYS prior to the arrival date specified above, or should you have a larger attendance than expected we will provide accommodations on a space available basis.

"If you will be utilizing a rooming list for your accommodations it is necessary that it be accompanied by individual names and addresses. If the attendees will be making their individual reservations directly with the hotel or to your office we will be happy to provide the individual reservation forms without charge. Each individual reservation, whether made by the person himself or pursuant to a rooming list, must be accompanied by one night's deposit, or the first night must be guaranteed by the group in writing.

"Now that your plans are firm and the foregoing meets with your approval, kindly sign the enclosed carbon copy of this letter in the space provided and return it to the undersigned. This will serve as notice to the Hotel del Coronado of your approval of the arrangements, terms and provisions set forth herein and your agreement to have your meeting here. Upon receipt of the signed copy of this letter, we will change our records from "tentative" to "firm" for your meeting. Until such time, these arrangements are tentative only."

After receipt of this letter Bradley telephoned Drown. On Dec. 22nd Bradley sent the following (Ex. 3):

"This will confirm our telephone conversation of Monday, Dec. 19 accepting confirmed reservations for 250 accommodations for arrival Feb. 28, 1979 and departure March 4, 1979.

"In addition to our confirmed accommodations, we have several second options with you in the month of Feb. 1979. We have requested and given you permission to interchange our confirmed accommodations by the second options listed below: ... .

"We understand that you can hold accommodations up to 21 days prior to arrival without a specified list of occupants. After that point in time, our reservations would be equal to the list of occupants supplied by QWIP SYSTEMS to that date, and any additions after that would be made by QWIP on a space available basis.

"We appreciate your assistance in this matter, and in the near future we will be discussing activities, meeting plans, menus, etc.

"I look forward to meeting with you personally."

In December of 1978 Qwip changed its mind (Ex. A):

"The Hotel Del Coronado is magnificant [sic] and has nothing to do with the decision to cancel. We look forward to hopefully visiting with you soon and to continue our professional relationship. Perhaps, we will be able to use the Del Coronado one day in the future.

"I want to thank you personally for all the assistance given to me during the formulation of our Business Conference scheduling and plans. I appreciate all that you have done very much."

During February of 1979, 160 of Qwip's employees and their families were sent to the south of Spain. This action followed.

It is Qwip's contention that the quoted agreements in no way obligated it to occupy any rooms at the Coronado.

Qwip contends it cannot be held liable. Categorizing the 21-day specific registrant notification as a "drop dead date," counsel argues that no obligation existed on defendant's part unless, and until, it notified the hotel which of its employees would occupy the rooms. In other words, defendant would have me hold that the Coronado, without receiving any consideration, provided Qwip with an option to occupy 250 rooms exercisable 21 days before arrival.

Not only does such an argument run contrary to the sense of the situation, it is at variance with the parties' intent both expressed or to be implied.

The exchange of correspondence and the testimony at the trial clearly establish an intent on the parties to be obligated to the other—the Hotel to furnish up to 250 rooms, Qwip to send its contest winners to the "Coronado." Viewed in context, the 21-day notification provision does nothing more than evidence the fact that both sides were aware that the actual rooms required would not be fixed until January of 1979.

There can be no doubt that defendant desired to insure availability of rooms. It was they who changed what had been designated "tentative" reservations to "confirmed" in their letter of December 22nd. The argument that defendant was unaware of the trade usage of such terms is unconvincing. Qwip is a division of Exxon Enterprises, Inc., not the Little Sisters of the Poor. They must be assumed to have sufficient commercial sophistication to appreciate that a confirmed reservation obligated plaintiff to keep the rooms available for Qwip's usage during the period in question.

The finding of an expressed intent is not essential to this determination, however, since such an intent on defendants must be implied. Although it is somewhat incongruous to equate people and bread crumbs, it can be said that the situation here is analogous to that in Feld v. Levy & Sons (37 N.Y. 2d 466) where the Court of Appeals implied a good faith obligation on the part of a manufacturer under an exclusive supply agreement (see also Wood v. Duff-Gordon, 222 N.Y. 88; Schlegel Mfg. Co. v. Cooper's Glue Factory, 231 N.Y. 459; Tauchner v. Burnett, 32 Misc. 2d 839).

Qwip has offered no valid explanation as to why it elected to send its employees to Spain rather than the Coronado. Under the circumstances, I find that Qwip Systems, Inc., has breached its contract with the Hotel Del Coronado and is liable to them for the damages arising out of its failure to send the 160 contest winners to plaintiff Hotel.

Having found that Qwip breached its agreement, the issue becomes the extent of their liability to plaintiff. Before a dollar amount can be fixed a general proposition must be considered—the extent of Qwip's obligation.

Although the testimony is sketchy it has been established that some 160 persons qualified for a free trip. Such a finding fixes the maximum number of rooms Qwip was obligated to take. It is, of course, only a reference figure being subject to reduction by the number of rooms actually vacant on the four days in question (2/28/79–3/3/79) and any allowances to be made for double occupancy.

With respect to the former, plaintiff, during the trial, attempted to establish a total vacancy for the four-day period of 598 rooms. Such testimony was objected to on the grounds that only a 483 total vacancy had been claimed in plaintiff's bill of particulars. In light of counsel's failure to offer a valid reason why amendment had not been sought prior to the time of trial, I sustained defendant's objection and limited the proof to a combined vacancy of 483 rooms broken down as follows:

Date 2/28/79, Rooms 47
Date 3/1/79, Rooms 242
Date 3/2/79, Rooms 176
Date 3/3/79, Rooms 18

Total Rooms 483

From the total of 483 some allowance must be made with respect to double occupancy. In that regard the only testimony is that of the 160 people on the trip approximately 40 were spouses of contest winners. Assuming that all 40 couples were on speaking terms and would share accommodations, we have a situation where a total 120 rooms would be required for each of the 4 nights.

Plaintiff must be deemed to have lost 305 occupancies over the 4-day period. Said number to be computed as follows:

2/28/79—47 (actual vacancies)
3/1/79—120 (maximum liability)
3/2/79—120 (maximum liability)
3/3/79—18 (actual vacancies)

Plaintiff's claim for damages is based on a rate of $146.00 per room. This amount is calculated by taking an average price per room of $50.00 plus an additional $96.00 per room in additional revenue losses. Included in this $96.00 figure are loss of revenue on meals, gift shops, beverages, and miscellaneous items. The figure was arrived at by computing the hotel's average income per room over the past two years.

While it is clear that the parties had an agreement with respect to the taking of rooms, no such agreement can be said to exist with respect to any other activities at the hotel. Plaintiff's witnesses, in response to a question put by me, admitted that Qwip was under no obligation to conduct any functions at the hotel. The parties' agreement makes no reference to such an obligation. Accordingly, plaintiff is not entitled to recover for its "additional revenue" for 305 lost vacancies.

Plaintiff is entitled to recover for the revenue lost as a result of its rooms being vacant at the rate of $50.00 per room. The use of an average figure for the computation of such loss is appropriate under the circumstances since the accommodations reserved were not fixed as to the nature of rooms, and were dependent upon the number and nature of the qualifiers. Defendant's objection with respect to plaintiff's failure to put in evidence the records is without merit. The copies of said records were available to counsel during the trial and were used by him during cross-examination of plaintiff's witness. Therefore, it cannot be said defendant was in any way prejudiced.

In accordance with the foregoing I concluded that defendant has breached the agreement entered into with plaintiff in December of 1977 and that it has been damaged in the amount of $15,300.00 representing "loss to it for 306 rooms at the rate of $50.00 per room."

Submit judgment on notice.

Chapter 7 Outline

Competencies

1. Explain a hotel's affirmative duty not to allow unregistered and unauthorized third parties access to guestrooms. (p. 83)

2. Describe the guest's constitutional protection against unreasonable search and seizure and warrantless searches. (pp. 83–84)

3. Explain the concept of a guest's right to privacy as it relates to the hotel. (pp. 84–85)

7

The Guest's Right to Privacy

GENERALLY SPEAKING, a hotel has an **affirmative duty,** stemming from a guest's rights of privacy and peaceful possession, not to allow unregistered and unauthorized third parties to gain access to its guests' rooms. However, it is understood that the hotel will have access for routine housekeeping and in the case of an emergency such as fire.

In *Campbell* v. *Womack,* the court affirmed the right of hotels to exclude unregistered persons—even a guest's spouse. The Court of Appeals of Louisiana, First Circuit, held that a motel was not liable for damages for refusing to admit a wife to her husband's room when she was not a registered guest.[1] In this case, the husband had obtained a double room in the motel on a month-to-month basis. On occasion his wife joined him for weekends and holidays, but she was never given a key to the room. On one such weekend, the wife arrived while her husband was out and asked the desk clerk for the key. The desk clerk denied the request, since the wife was not a registered guest and her husband had not authorized the motel to release his key to his wife. The wife then went to another motel and her husband joined her there. Thereafter they sued the motel and the desk clerk, alleging that the wife was entitled to the key on the grounds that she had obtained the status of a guest as a result of her previous stays with her husband in the motel room. They demanded damages for embarrassment, humiliation, and mental anguish as a result of the hotel's alleged breach of contract. The trial court granted the defendant's motion for summary judgment, and the plaintiffs appealed.

The Louisiana Court of Appeals affirmed. The court held that the motel clerk was under no duty to give the wife the key to one of the motel's guestrooms, and stated "in fact, the motel had an affirmative duty, stemming from a guest's rights of privacy and peaceful possession, not to allow unregistered and unauthorized third parties to gain access to the rooms of its guests."[2] The court recognized that marriage alone did not imply the husband's authorization for access to his room, noting that a motel would never be able to know that a marital situation was amicable.

In *People* v. *Lerhinan*[3] the New York State Supreme Court rendered an opinion on the guest's right to privacy in a case regarding the validity of a search of the defendant's hotel room and the admission of evidence of goods stolen from the hotel. In this case, the hotel manager entered the defendant's room for the purpose of removing his belongings since he was two weeks in arrears of hotel charges that were payable on a weekly basis. The manager entered the room to put the defendant's belongings in storage, change the lock, and re-rent the room. Upon recognizing cases of liquor and a tool and die set as items stolen from his own hotel earlier, the manager called the police. The police entered the room without a **search**

warrant. The New York State Supreme Court allowed the confiscated items to be introduced as evidence in the defendant's criminal trial.

The question of the validity of the **warrantless search** hinged on the guest's right to privacy and the Fourth Amendment to the U.S. Constitution (protecting citizens from warrantless searches). The court held that *during* the guest's rental period when the guest has paid for the room, a hotel manager or other employee may *not* validly consent to a warrantless search. The court stated, however,

> Under New York law, there is an express or implied understanding between guest and hotel owner that the former shall be the sole occupant during the time that is set apart for his use. The owner retains a right of access only for such reasonable purposes as may be necessary in the conduct of the hotel, not only to take action in the event of a fire or gas leakage, but obviously to take routine care of necessary housekeeping as well. But since no conventional landlord-tenant relationship is involved in the ordinary rental of hotel rooms, a hotel owner [in New York] may dispossess an occupant without resort to the use of **summary proceedings**. Under § 181 of the [New York] Lien Law, the owner also has the right to seize the defaulting guest's property and sell it at public auction.* This contrasts with the rental of an apartment, the possession of which may not be disturbed until a warrant of eviction has been executed.

* * *

> As a consequence of the hotel keeper's lien and the transitory nature of hotel tenancies, mere non-payment of the rent terminates any reasonable expectation of privacy in the hotel room and the property contained in it. The cases have uniformly held that the operator of a motel, essentially similar to a hotel, may consent to a warrantless search as soon as the rental period has expired. [citations and footnotes omitted]

The U.S. Supreme Court has made it clear that when the hotel guest has paid for the room, the guest is entitled to constitutional protection against unreasonable search and seizure, and the hotel would generally have no authority to permit the search of the guest's room without a search warrant. This would violate the hotel guest's right to privacy.[4]

In a recent Minnesota case, *United States* v. *Rambo*,[5] the police were summoned to the Curtis Hotel in Minneapolis by the hotel security officers and an assistant manager after guests reported a naked man running and screaming down the seventh-floor halls. When approached by the security officer and assistant

---

* In a footnote to the court's discussion of the hotelkeeper's remedy of seizing the defaulting guest's property (quoted above), the court stated,

> Although the *ex parte* sale of the property was declared unconstitutional in *Blye* v. *Globe–Wernecke Realty Co.* (33 NY 2nd 15, 20), the innkeeper's right to seize and sell the property was not questioned, so long as the guest was afforded notice and the opportunity to be heard prior to permanent deprivation of the property (see also *Sharrock* v. *Del. Buick–Cadillac*, 45 NY 2nd 152).

manager, the naked man, Mr. Rambo, stated that there was no problem and returned to his room.

When the police arrived at Mr. Rambo's room he opened the door, still naked. The police informed him that the management wanted him removed from the hotel, but Mr. Rambo refused to leave. The police then arrested him in his room where they conducted a search and allegedly found cocaine. He was charged with disorderly conduct and possession of illegal drugs. Mr. Rambo made a motion in court to suppress the evidence of the narcotics on the ground that his arrest on a misdemeanor was illegal since the police had not actually observed his disorderly conduct.

However, the court ruled that the evidence of narcotics was obtained pursuant to a lawful arrest because a Minnesota disorderly guest statute specifically provides:

> An innkeeper may remove or cause to be removed from a hotel a guest...who acts in a disorderly manner...or causes a public disturbance. A guest who has engaged in such conduct and refuses to leave is guilty of a misdemeanor.

Because Mr. Rambo refused to comply when the police told him that the hotel management wanted him to leave because of his disorderly conduct, he was found guilty of the misdemeanor described in the above Minnesota statute on disorderly guests. The subsequent police search of his room was therefore upheld by the court as a search incident to a lawful arrest.

Important Points for Management

A hotel owes a guest the rights of privacy and peaceful possession while the guest is in the guestroom. However, the hotel does have access to occupied guestrooms for routine housekeeping and during emergencies.

Police officers must usually have a search warrant in order to enter guestrooms. The U.S. Supreme Court has made it clear that when the hotel guest has paid for the room, the guest is entitled to constitutional protection against unreasonable search and seizure, and the hotel would generally have no authority to permit the search of the guest's room without a search warrant. This would violate the hotel guest's right to privacy.

Desk clerks and bell personnel should *never* announce a guest's room number aloud so that bystanders can overhear.

Hotel employees should be instructed *not* to give out guests' room numbers to callers.

Hotel employees should *not* give out a guestroom key to anyone but the guest who has rented that particular room.

References

1. *Campbell* v. *Womack*, 345 So.2d 96 (La. App. 1977).

2. 345 So.2d 98.

3. 189 N.Y.L.J., Jan. 4, 1983 at 1, col. 6 (2d Dept., Nov. 22, 1982).

4. See *Stoner* v. *California,* 376 U.S. 483 (1964). See also *People* v. *Blair,* 25 Cal.3d 640, 602 P.2d 738 (1979); the opinion in this case appears at the end of this chapter.

5. *United States* v. *Rambo,* 789 F.2d 1289 (8th Cir. 1986).

Key Terms

affirmative duty—The duty or obligation of making proof, in the first instance, of matters alleged or in the pleadings of the court; in other words, the duty to sustain the burden of proof.

ex parte—Refers to a judicial proceeding taken or granted at the insistence of and for the benefit of one party only, and without the necessity of the other party's presence.

search warrant—An order in writing in the name of the state, signed by a magistrate and directed to a peace officer commanding him/her to search for personal property and bring it before the magistrate.

summary proceedings—Any proceedings by which a controversy is settled, case disposed of, or trial conducted in a prompt and simple manner, without the aid of a jury.

warrantless search—A search of property without a search warrant.

Review Questions

1. What are the guest's rights to privacy within the guestroom? When do these rights cease?

2. What relevance did *Campbell* v. *Womack* have in a hotel guest's right of privacy?

3. When is it necessary to have a search warrant to enter a guestroom?

4. For what purposes does a hotel retain the right of access to a guest's room?

Internet Sites

For more information, visit the following Internet sites. Remember that Internet addresses can change without notice.

FindLaw
http://www.findlaw.com

Illustrative Case

People **v.** *Blair*

25 Cal.3d 690, 602 P.2d 738 (Cal. Sup. Ct. 1979)

MOSK, Justice.

We held in *Burrows* v. *Superior Court* (1974) 13 Cal.3d 238, 118 Cal. Rptr. 166, 529 P.2d 590, that a depositor's bank statements provided to the police by the bank without the benefit of legal process were obtained as the result of an illegal search and seizure, in violation of article 1, section 13 of the California Constitution.* In this case we are called upon to decide, inter alia, whether the rationale of *Burrows* applies to copies of bills charged to a credit card used by defendant, to the record of a telephone call made by him from a hotel room in California,... obtained by federal authorities in that city and provided by them to the police in California.

Defendant was convicted of the murders of Alan and Renate Wellman, which occurred at their home in Los Angeles on the night of December 14, 1975. He appeals from the judgment of conviction.

* * *

We next consider whether the police acted improperly in obtaining from an employee of the Hyatt House, without legal process, a list of telephone calls made from defendant's room while a guest at the hotel. Among those calls was one to Wellman on the day of the murders.

In *People* v. *McKunes* (1975) 51 Cal. App.3d 487, 124 Cal. Rptr. 126, it was held, under the authority of *Burrows*, that the police may not, without legal process, obtain from the telephone company records revealing the calls dialed by a defendant from his home or office. The court reasoned that, as with bank records, a telephone subscriber has a reasonable expectation that the calls he makes will be utilized only for the accounting functions of the telephone company and that he cannot anticipate that his personal life, as disclosed by the calls he makes and receives, will be disclosed to outsiders without legal process. As with bank records, concluded the court, it is virtually impossible for an individual or business entity to function in the modern economy without a telephone, and a record of telephone calls also provides "a virtual current biography."

The fact that the telephone calls in the present case were made by defendant from a hotel room rather than his home does not render the *McKunes* rationale inapplicable. As in the case of a telephone call from a private residence, a hotel guest may reasonably expect that the calls which he makes from his room are recorded by the hotel for billing purposes only, and that the record of his calls will not be transmitted to others without legal process. The People argue that because there is no "ongoing relationship" between a hotel and a guest who rents a room for a limited period, the situation is distinguishable from *McKunes* and *Burrows*. But the hotel room is in reality a residence, however temporary. Thus the critical issue is whether there is an expectation of privacy in the information sought; such an expectation may exist even in the briefest encounter between the persons who impart and receive the information. We conclude, therefore, that the motion to suppress should have been granted as to the telephone call which defendant made from the Hyatt House to Wellman on December 14.

---

* Article 1, section 13 provides in part, "The right of the people to be secure in their persons, houses, papers, and effects against unreasonable seizures and searches may not be violated;..."

* * *

We have concluded above that the trial court erred in failing to suppress the evidence regarding the charges made by defendant on his Diner's Club card and the telephone call made by defendant to Wellman from the Hyatt House.

Chapter 8 Outline

Competencies

1. Distinguish between a guest and a tenant. (p. 91)

2. Explain the legal implication of the difference between a guest and a tenant. (pp. 91–92)

3. List some conditions under which a hotel can rightfully evict guests or restaurant and bar patrons. (pp. 92–93)

4. Describe the actions that the hotel should follow when evicting a guest. (pp. 92–93)

5. Indicate the circumstances under which a hotel may evict persons who are not guests or patrons. (pp. 93–95)

8

The Hotel's Right to Evict a Guest, Tenant, Restaurant Patron, or Others

Distinction Between Guest and Tenant

In deciding whether a person can be evicted from the hotel premises without court proceedings, the hotelkeeper must first make certain that a person occupying a room has the legal status of a "guest" and is not a "tenant." In general, a traveler who is staying at a hotel for a limited period of time is commonly described as a "guest." However, many hotels permit guests to stay for such an extended length of time that the question arises as to whether the so-called "guest" is in fact a "tenant," making the relationship between the hotelkeeper and the guest that of landlord and tenant. If the person has the legal status of a tenant, he/she can be compelled to leave the premises only if the hotel brings a dispossession proceeding in the proper local court. In this case, the hotel is in the same position as any other landlord, and, insofar as evictions are concerned, has no special rights.

How to Distinguish Guests from Tenants

There is no specific rule of law that applies in all cases to distinguish a guest from a tenant. Each case must be decided on its particular facts. Residential hotels in cities frequently use written leases that describe the hotel as a landlord and the person occupying the room or apartment as a tenant. In these cases, there is no doubt that the status of the person occupying the room or apartment is that of a tenant. In other hotels, the so-called guests sometimes stay for a long period of time and pay room charges by the week or month. The fact that the room charges are paid on a weekly or monthly basis is not conclusive, but it is one point that must be taken into account in showing that the person is a tenant.

Since no specific rule can be made to apply to all cases, the hotel with a doubtful case should never assume that the person it wishes to evict from the premises for any reason is a guest. The only safe course is to consult an attorney concerning whether to commence a dispossession proceeding. With a dispossession proceeding, the hotel will gain the protection of a court order for the actual eviction. If the person to be dispossessed denies that he/she is a tenant and claims that he/she is a hotel guest, the hotel gains the same end because it always has the right, *for proper reason,* to evict a guest without a court proceeding.

Patrons in Hotel Restaurants and Bars

The hotel has the same rights under the proper circumstances to evict restaurant and bar patrons as it has with guests occupying rooms. The following discussion applies to these patrons as well as to room guests.

When and How a Hotel Can Evict a Guest

Violation of Hotel Regulations

The hotel may make reasonable regulations governing the conduct of its guests, provided that such regulations are applied to all persons without discrimination. These regulations can be designed to prevent immorality, drunkenness, or any form of willful misconduct that may offend other guests, or that may bring the hotel into disrepute, or that may be inconsistent with the generally recognized proprieties of life. The hotel has the right to evict any guest who willfully violates these rules. (As discussed above, be sure the person is a guest and not a tenant.) Obviously, the eviction must be done in a reasonable manner. If a guest refuses to leave the hotel after his/her attention has been called to the violation and he/she has been requested to leave and given a reasonable opportunity to do so, the hotel may forcibly evict him/her. In doing so, the hotel may use only such force as is reasonably necessary to accomplish this end. Management personnel and security officers should be carefully instructed on this point, and the assistance of the local police should be obtained.

Eviction for Non-Payment

The hotel has the right to evict a guest who has failed to pay the hotel bill when due. (Again, the procedure suggested applies only to a guest and not to a tenant.) Ordinarily, the hotel makes a demand upon the guest for the amount of the bill and requests him/her to leave by a certain hour if the bill is not paid. If the guest fails to pay after this demand, the hotel can evict him/her unless local laws forbid this. In New York, if the guest refuses to leave the room, the hotel has the right to evict him/her physically, but, as pointed out above, should never use more force than necessary under the circumstances. It is recommended that you consult your local attorney before making an eviction, and that assistance from the local police be obtained for any eviction.

Refusal of Service Because of Unpaid Bill

The hotel is not required to provide food or service to a guest who refuses to pay a proper charge. The hotel can exercise this right to refuse food or service without exercising its right to evict the guest from the premises. In some cases, the refusal of service may cause a recalcitrant guest to leave the premises and thus eliminate the need for an eviction.

Eviction of a Guest Because of Illness

When a hotel guest is taken ill with a contagious disease, the proprietor, after notifying the guest to leave, has the right to remove such guest *in a careful manner* and at an appropriate hour to some hospital or other place of safety, *provided* this does not imperil the guest's life. As a practical matter, however, it is preferable to consult your local attorney and report these matters to the proper local authorities. Usually, the local authorities will take charge and remove the sick guest. The illness of an indigent guest should be reported to the local department of welfare; communicable diseases should be reported to the local health authorities; and mental cases should be reported to the police.

The Guest Who Overstays

In the case of a guest (not a tenant) who has overstayed the agreed number of days at a hotel, the hotel has the right to require such guest to leave unless applicable state laws forbid this. Many hotels specifically provide that the guest may stay only a limited period of time (for example, three days). Such a limitation should be clearly expressed to the guest when he/she registers. Some hotels have adopted the practice of stating this limitation on the registration card.

When the guest has overstayed the agreed number of days or when an indefinite stay has been extended for an unreasonable length of time, the hotel has the right to ask the guest to leave. The guest should receive reasonable notice, especially in those cases in which no advance agreement has been made regarding the duration of the stay. After the period of notice has expired, the hotel has the right to evict the guest, unless applicable state laws forbid this. This right must, of course, be exercised in a reasonable manner without inflicting unnecessary physical force or undue humiliation upon the guest. Again, it is recommended that you consult with local counsel before evicting, and that the assistance of local police be obtained in the eviction. In most cases in which the guest refuses to leave, the hotel can accomplish its purpose by taking possession of the room during the guest's absence, and, if necessary, changing the lock on the door.

Eviction of Persons Other Than Guests

As a general rule, a person who is not a guest or a patron may not enter or remain upon the hotel premises against the proprietor's will. A person who is an invitee of a guest may call upon a guest at a hotel, subject to such reasonable rules and regulations as the hotel may **promulgate** on a non-discriminatory basis. This right of the visitor, like that of the guest, may be forfeited by his/her misconduct.

Persons who are not hotel guests or patrons do not have the same privileges as guests, so that hotels may in certain cases exclude such persons. In *People* v. *Thorpe*,[1] the City Magistrate's Court of New York convicted two Jehovah's Witnesses ministers of disorderly conduct. The two ministers entered a hotel in New York City and went from door to door to talk to the guests about their religion. The hotel's management asked the ministers to leave. When the ministers refused, the management called the police who advised the ministers that they had no right to return to the hotel. Following this discussion with the police officers, however, the ministers re-entered the hotel and were arrested. The court stated that a person who is not a guest of the hotel has no legal right to enter or remain in the hotel. Because the ministers returned defying the orders of the police, they were found guilty of disorderly conduct.

A more recent case in Washington, D.C., *Kelly* v. *United States*,[2] concerned prostitution. Staff at the hotel noticed a woman frequenting the hotel lobby and bar and occasionally going into guestrooms with different men. A member of the police vice squad told the hotel's security officer that the woman was a prostitute and showed him a copy of her criminal record. When the woman was subsequently noticed leaving a guest's room, the hotel security officers told her that the hotel did not permit non-guests above the lobby and that if she returned to the hotel she would be arrested and charged with unlawful entry. Five months later, the hotel's security officers arrested the woman when she left a fifth floor guestroom with two men. The woman was convicted of unlawful entry in violation of D.C. laws.[3]

The court of appeals affirmed the conviction. It rejected the woman's argument that she was visiting a legally registered guest. The court held that in the case of persons who are not guests and did not have the intention of becoming guests, the hotel had the right to exclude them. In addition, it held that in such instances the hotel had the right to use reasonably necessary force to do so. The court then argued that since the hotel had the right to exclude the woman and she had received appropriate notice of her exclusion, she was without lawful authority to remain in the hotel and was subject to arrest for unlawful entry.

Hotels contemplating the forcible eviction of guests or non-guests for any reason should proceed carefully so that they do not subject themselves to a potential claim of assault and battery. In particular, hotels should contact their legal counsel and the police in such circumstances.

Important: See also Chapter 14, "Frauds Committed Against Hotels and Crimes of Trespass," regarding possible lawsuits by evicted persons for wrongful detention, false imprisonment, slander, etc.

New State Laws on Eviction

In 1993, Idaho enacted a law[4] stating:

    (2)   A hotelkeeper also shall have the right to evict a person, whether or not such person is a guest of the hotel, who:

        (a)   Is under the influence of alcohol, drugs or any other intoxicating substances;

        (b)   Is disorderly so as to disturb the peace of other guests;

        (c)   Seeks to use the hotel for any unlawful purpose;

        (d)   Seeks to bring property into the hotel which may be dangerous to other persons (such as firearms, explosives or hazardous or toxic substances) or the possession of which by such person is unlawful;

(e) Destroys, damages or defaces property of the hotel or its guests or threatens to do so;

(f) Would cause or permit any hotel room to exceed its maximum allowable occupancy as established by the hotelkeeper; or

(g) Refuses to abide by reasonable standards or policies established by the hotelkeeper for operation and management of the hotel.

Important Points for Management

Before evicting a person from a hotel room, the hotelkeeper should first review the facts with an attorney to determine if that person is a "guest" or a "tenant." If the person has a lease, he/she is occupying the room as a tenant. If the person is paying room charges by the month and has been in the room for 30 days or more, check the local laws, because he/she may be considered a tenant. The eviction of a tenant would require dispossession court proceedings.

When a guest—not a tenant—has overstayed an agreed number of days, the hotel has the right to require him/her to leave unless state laws forbid it. Many hotels specifically state that a guest may stay for a limited time only (for example, three days). Such a limitation should be clearly conveyed to the guest when he/she registers.

Hotels considering the forcible eviction of guests or non-guests for any reason should act carefully to protect themselves from a potential claim of assault and battery. It is important to contact legal counsel and the police in such circumstances.

References

1. 198 Misc. 101 N.Y.S. 2d 986 462 (Mag. Ct. 1950). See also *People* v. *Vaughan*, 65 Cal. App. 2d Supp. 844, 150 P. 2d 964 (Cal. App. Dept. Super. Ct. 1944), and see *SOC Inc.* v. *County of Clark*, 152 F. 3d 1136 (1998 U.S. App. LEXIS 18791, Eighth Cir., Aug. 14, 1998) on right in Las Vegas to distribute leaflets on exotic dancers for hire.

2. 348 A. 2d 884 (D.C. Cir., 1975).

3. D.C. Code Ann. § 22-3102.

4. Idaho Code, Title 39, Chap. 18, § 1805 (1993). See also Minn. Stat., Chap. 327, § 327.73 (1993) for somewhat similar provisions.

 ## Key Terms

promulgate—To publish; to announce officially.

 ## Review Questions

1. Why is it difficult to distinguish between a guest and a tenant?

2. How do the hotel's rights differ when evicting a guest? a tenant?

3. Under what circumstances might a hotel decide to evict a guest?

4. When can a hotel expel a sick guest?

5. What rights does the hotel have to evict a non-guest or visitors of a guest?

6. What caution should hotels use in forcible eviction of either guests or non-guests?

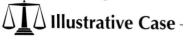 **Illustrative Case** ————————————————————————

Kelly v. United States

348 A.2d 884 (D.C. Cir. 1975)

YEAGLEY, Associate Judge:

Appellant was convicted in a nonjury trial of unlawful entry a violation of D.C.Code 1973, § 22-3102. This appeal followed.

Between the months of January and March, 1974, appellant was seen by the chief of security at the Statler Hilton Hotel on approximately five occasions. He first noticed her in the hotel bar speaking with a guest with whom she later went upstairs. On one occasion when she was in the lobby all night, a police officer assigned to the vice squad told the hotel's security officer that appellant was a prostitute and showed him a copy of her criminal record and her mug shot.

On March 18, hotel security officers again noticed appellant in the hotel. At that time she was once more observed going upstairs with a guest. After about an hour in the guest's room, she came out of the room alone. She was stopped by the hotel security officers and informed of the hotel policy of not allowing any unregistered guests above the lobby. She was also told of the conversation with the police vice squad officer and was read a "barring notice."[1] Furthermore, she was told that if she returned to the hotel, she would be arrested and charged with unlawful entry.

On August 19, security officers were called to the fifth floor of the hotel. They waited outside one of the rooms until appellant emerged with two male companions. She was then placed under arrest.

Appellant was tried without a jury and on her motion for judgment of acquittal counsel argued that the statute was not applicable to a hotel and accordingly a hotel could not issue a valid barring notice. The court denied the motion.... We discern no error in that ruling.

* * *

The proffered evidence that appellant was visiting a legally registered guest at the hotel was properly excluded as inadmissible hearsay. Even if we were to assume *arguendo,* however, that the person she was visiting was legally registered at the hotel, we could still not agree with appellant's contention. It is a general rule that

---

[1] The notice said:

> You are hereby notified that you are not permitted entry in the Statler Hilton Hotel, 1001 Sixteenth Street, Northwest. In the future, if you return to the Statler Hilton Hotel and gain entry you may be subject to criminal prosecution for unauthorized entry.

..."an innkeeper gives a general license to all persons to enter his house. Consequently, it is not a trespass to enter an inn without a previous actual invitation," but, "Where persons enter a hotel or inn, not as guests, but intent on pleasure or profit to be derived from intercourse with its inmates, they are there, not of right, but under an implied license that the landlord may revoke at any time." The respondent did not enter the hotel as a guest nor with the intention of becoming one and it was his duty to leave peaceably when ordered by the landlord to do so, and in case of his refusal to leave on request appellant was entitled to use such force as was reasonably necessary to remove him. [*Hopp* v. *Thompson,* 72 S.D. 574, 38 N.W.2d 133, 135 (1949)] (citations omitted).

* * *

[I]f a hotel has the right to exclude someone, and he, or she, receives appropriate notice of his exclusion, that person's subsequent presence in the hotel is without lawful authority. Thus he or she is subject to arrest for the crime of unlawful entry.[2]

In the instant case appellant concedes that she was warned not to return to the hotel. She also admits that she was in the hotel on the evening of August 19, 1974. Consequently, under the authorities cited above, with which we agree, her entrance into the hotel was unlawful being in violation of D.C.Code 1973, § 22-3102.

* * *

Appellant seems to imply that she was barred from the hotel solely on the basis of the conversation between the hotel security officer and the police officer. This fails to take into account that the security officer also observed appellant sitting in the lobby all night and that he had observed her previously on several other occasions meeting guests in the bar or lobby with whom she later went upstairs. There was thus an independent basis for the barring of appellant and the barring notice was issued by the hotel. The policy is solely within the hotel's discretion and to be invoked by it when the hotel manager or security officer concludes the person is undesirable. The police lack authority to bar persons from the hotel and evidence is absent that the police officer requested or even suggested that the hotel advise appellant she was prohibited from further entry.

Appellant's other grounds for reversal, namely that the hotel policy was unreasonably and discriminatorily applied and that the government's evidence was insufficient, are without substance.

Accordingly, the judgment appealed from below is

Affirmed.

---

[2] The unlawful entry statute, D.C.Code 1973, § 22-3102, provides:

Any person who...being [in or on any public or private buildings] without lawful authority to remain therein or thereon shall refuse to quit the same on the demand of...the person lawfully in charge thereof, shall be deemed guilty of a misdemeanor....

Part III

The Hotel's Duties to the Guest and Others

Chapter 9 Outline

Competencies

1. State the purpose of the Americans with Disabilities Act (ADA) and briefly describe how Title III of the Act affects lodging and food service establishments. (p. 101)

2. Describe the "full enjoyment" requirement of the ADA, describe how the Act defines an individual with a disability, and describe the "auxiliary aids or services" requirement of the Act. (pp. 101–102)

3. Summarize what the ADA considers "readily achievable" removal of barriers, and state the suggested priorities for removing barriers in public accommodations. (pp. 102–103)

4. Explain what the ADA requires of new or renovated hotels, with special attention to "path of travel" requirements and guestroom requirements. (pp. 103–105)

5. Describe how Title III of the ADA may be enforced. (pp. 106–107)

9

Americans with Disabilities Act—Public Accommodations

O<small>N</small> J<small>ULY</small> 26, 1990, President Bush signed into law the Americans with Disabilities Act[1] (the ADA) which prohibits discrimination against "qualified individuals with disabilities." The ADA covers five areas: employment, public services, public transportation, public accommodations, and telecommunication services. The sections of the ADA that are of primary concern to hotel and restaurant operators are Title III, which covers public accommodations, and Title I, which covers employment. This chapter discusses the public accommodation requirements of Title III.[2] Chapter 21, which covers laws against discrimination in employment, discusses Title I.

Title III—Public Accommodations

Title III of the ADA became effective on January 26, 1992. It prohibits discrimination against individuals with disabilities in the full and equal enjoyment of the goods, services, facilities, privileges, advantages, or accommodations of any place of public accommodation, requiring that these be offered in the setting appropriate to the needs of the individual, except where it poses a direct threat to the health or safety of others.

Title III covers inns, hotels, motels, and other places of lodging, except those in which the proprietor resides and rents out five or fewer rooms. Title III also applies to gathering places (such as auditoriums and convention centers), places of entertainment, and establishments serving food or drink.

Full Enjoyment Requirement

Operators of public accommodations may not generally impose or apply eligibility criteria that screen out individuals with disabilities from fully enjoying goods, services, facilities, advantages, privileges, or accommodations. Failing to make reasonable modifications in policies, practices, and procedures to afford people with disabilities access to and use of public accommodations is also discriminatory.

An "individual with a disability" is broadly defined as anyone who has a physical or mental impairment that substantially limits one or more life activities, has a record of such an impairment, or is regarded as having such an impairment. Examples of disabilities include visual/speech/hearing impairments, orthopedic impairments, cerebral palsy, epilepsy, muscular dystrophy, multiple sclerosis,

101

AIDS, HIV, cancer, heart disease, diabetes, mental retardation, emotional illness, learning disabilities, tuberculosis, drug addiction, and alcoholism, and may include obvious as well as hidden disabilities.

Auxiliary Aids or Services Requirement

Goods and services cannot be denied to guests because of the absence of "auxiliary aids or services," unless providing such aids would fundamentally alter the nature of the good or service or result in an undue burden on the owner or operator of the public accommodation. Auxiliary aids or services include interpreters, readers, audio taped texts, or other effective methods of making aurally or visually delivered materials available to impaired individuals; the acquisition or modification of equipment or devices; and other similar services or actions. Overall, the ADA requires that individuals with disabilities be given opportunities to enjoy the same goods or services as non-disabled persons, but does not mandate the type of auxiliary aids or services that must be provided. A restaurant, for example, would not be required to provide braille menus for blind patrons if it instead provides an employee to read the menu aloud for such patrons.

The Removal of Barriers in Existing Facilities

Under the ADA, it is discriminatory to fail to remove architectural and communication barriers at existing facilities where such removal is "readily achievable." **Readily achievable** removal means removal that is easily accomplished and can be carried out without much difficulty or expense. In determining whether removing a structural barrier is readily achievable, such considerations as the nature and cost of the structural modification and the size, financial resources, and type of business of the company and parent corporation, if any, are also pertinent.

Any determination of what is readily achievable must be made on a case-by-case basis. Some measures that might be considered readily achievable include:

- Making curb cuts in sidewalks
- Widening doorways and changing door hardware
- Installing offset hinges to widen doorways
- Installing ramps
- Adding raised and braille symbols at elevators
- Rearranging furniture, vending machines, and displays
- Removing high-pile, low-density carpeting
- Repositioning shelves and telephones
- Installing grab bars in toilet stalls
- Installing raised toilet seats
- Installing insulation on lavatory pipes under sinks
- Installing flashing alarm lights.[3]

Priorities for Barrier Removal. The regulations implementing Title III set forth the following suggested priorities for public accommodations where it is not readily achievable to remove all architectural and communication barriers:

- Provide access that provides entry to the facility itself. This includes providing accessible routes from public sidewalks, parking, or public transportation. This may require providing accessible parking spaces and ramped or widened entrances.

- Provide access to the primary goods and services provided by the public accommodation. This includes providing accessible routes and signage. The hotel or motel must determine what it believes its primary goods and services to be. For most properties, the primary goods and services are the guestrooms, meeting rooms, and/or restaurants.

- Provide access to public restroom facilities that are used by the customers or guests.

- Provide access to other services or features.[4]

If the removal of a barrier is not readily achievable, the goods or services are to be made available through alternative methods, whereby doing so is readily achievable.

In 1993, the U.S. Department of Justice required the Hotel Intercontinental (built in 1926) in New York City to carry out a major renovation program to comply with the ADA, costing the hotel some $1.7 million.

The cost of the renovation included aesthetically designed permanent access ramps to the main entrance, restaurant, and bar; modifications to public restrooms; and modifications to 21 guestrooms of different price ranges. A lift to the ballroom and the modification of elevators for people with sight, hearing, and mobility impairments were included in any subsequent renovations. Other changes include modifying public telephones, installing Telecommunications Devices for the Deaf (TDDs) at the front desk and in rooms, and providing outlets for portable TDDs (also called a TTY, an abbreviation for "teletypewriter").[5]

Accessibility of New or Renovated Hotels

New or renovated hotels must be readily accessible and usable by individuals with disabilities.* This includes parking, public toilets, and water fountains, as well as access to the goods, services, programs, facilities, and work areas in the hotel. When the hotel has no control over accessible elements at streets, curbs, parking, or sidewalks, it should request such modifications from the responsible entity.

Alterations begun after January 26, 1992, must, to the maximum extent feasible, be readily accessible to and usable by individuals with disabilities, including individuals who use wheelchairs.

---

* Except where it is structurally impractical under regulations that have been issued by the U.S. Attorney General.[6] Such regulations are consistent with the guidelines and requirements of the Architectural and Transportation Barriers Compliance Board.

Exhibit 9.1   ADA Rooms Accessibility Requirements

Number of Guest Rooms	Wheelchair Accessible Guest Rooms	Additional Wheelchair Guest Rooms With Roll-in Showers
1 to 25	1	
26 to 50	2	
51 to 75	3	1
76 to 100	4	1
101 to 150	5	2
151 to 200	6	2
201 to 300	7	3
301 to 400	8	4
401 to 500	9	4 plus one for each additional 100 over 400
501 to 1,000	2% of total	
1,001 & over	20 plus 1 for each 100 over 1,000	

Source: ADA Accessibility Guidelines, and John P.S. Salmen, AIA, *Accommodating All Guests* (Washington, D.C.: The American Hotel & Motel Association and Universal Designers & Consultants, Inc., 1992), p. 54.

New construction designed and constructed for first occupancy after January 26, 1993, must be readily accessible to and usable by individuals with disabilities.

Path of Travel Requirements. When an alteration to an existing facility affects an area with a primary function (a major activity for which the facility is intended; for example, altering conference rooms in a hotel), an additional obligation is placed upon the business. In this case, the "path of travel" to the altered area must also be made readily accessible and usable.

A **path of travel** is a continuous, unobstructed way of pedestrian passage by which the altered area may be approached, entered, and exited, and which connects the altered area with an exterior approach (including sidewalks, streets, and parking areas), an entrance to the facility, and other parts of the facility.

The path of travel includes restrooms, telephones, and drinking fountains serving the altered area. However, the cost of these "path of travel" alterations is limited to 20% of the cost of the primary alteration.

Room Requirements. New hotels must provide wheelchair accessible sleeping rooms or suites that comply with ADA Accessibility Guidelines (ADAAG) for accessible units, sleeping rooms, and suites. The number of wheelchair accessible rooms required per property is based on the overall size of the property. Additional wheelchair accessible sleeping rooms or suites that include a roll-in shower must be provided in hotels having 51 or more sleeping rooms or suites (see Exhibit 9.1).

Exhibit 9.2   ADA Rooms Requirements for Hearing-Impaired Guests

All Wheelchair Accessible Guest Rooms *and* the Following Rooms must Provide Equipment for Hearing Impaired Guests	
Number of Rooms	Rooms for Hearing-Impaired
1 to 25	1
26 to 50	2
51 to 75	3
76 to 100	4
101 to 150	5
151 to 200	6
201 to 300	7
301 to 400	8
401 to 500	9
501 to 1,000	2% of total
1,001 & over	20 plus 1 for each 100 over 1,000

Source: ADA Accessibility Guidelines, and John P.S. Salmen, AIA, *Accommodating All Guests* (Washington, D.C.: The American Hotel & Motel Association and Universal Designers & Consultants, Inc., 1992), p. 54.

Fully accessible sleeping rooms and suites—plus a specific number of other sleeping rooms and suites—must be equipped for hearing-impaired guests (see Exhibit 9.2). The special equipment required in these rooms includes visual alarms, notification devices, and telephones.

A hotel or motel that provides in-room telephone service to its guests must make a text telephone (TDD) available in the room on request. A hotel or motel with guestroom telephones is also required to have a text telephone at the front desk so that guests with hearing or speech impairments can contact the front desk from their rooms and enjoy the same in-house services as other guests. Similarly, if telephones are provided to the public for receiving and/or making telephone calls, as with public telephones provided at a conference facility, text telephones would also have to be made available. In addition, a hotel or motel with five or more guestrooms must provide, upon request, a device for decoding captions.

Furthermore, a reasonable number, but at least one, of the following must be available for use in a hotel's guestrooms: closed caption TV decoders, visual alarm smoke detectors, visual door knock alerting devices, and visual devices available or in place so that guests with hearing disabilities are afforded the effective communication services and benefits equal to those provided to other guests.

Accessibility of Transportation Services

Transportation services are also governed by Title III and must be made readily accessible to disabled individuals (at the same costs as other guests). The U.S.

Secretary of Transportation has promulgated regulations governing these requirements.[7]

Enforcement and Penalties

Title III may be enforced by the U.S. Attorney General or by private lawsuit. The Attorney General investigates and undertakes compliance reviews. The procedures and remedies are the same as those under Title II of the Civil Rights Act of 1964 and can include such actions as ordering that facilities be altered to make them accessible or ordering that the public accommodation provide auxiliary aids to enable individuals with disabilities to use the facilities or services. Also, courts may award monetary damages to aggrieved persons and may assess civil penalties in the amount of $55,000 for a first violation and $110,000 for any subsequent violation.

The U.S. Department of Justice is not coy in its enforcement strategy. "Ensuring compliance by the hotel and motel industry is one of our chief priorities," says John Wodatch, chief of the disability rights section in DOJ's Civil Rights division. "We continue to receive a number of complaints that facilities are inaccessible, that reservations are not held, and that people are being excluded because they use service animals (guide dogs)."

Hoping to get the industry's attention with maximum impact, the Department identifies high-profile properties and publicizes the cases in the media and on their ADA web site. For example, targets included leading properties in major markets:

- The Inter-Continental Hotel in New York City spent $800,000 to achieve compliance.

- Three Hawaiian resorts agreed to make numerous improvements, from the parking lots to the luau center, and to pay two guests who use wheelchairs $25,000 in damages and another $25,000 in penalties.

- Courtyard by Marriott agreed to design its chainwide reservation system and procedures so that persons with disabilities are assured of getting the accessible rooms they reserved. The federal case arose when a guest was mistakenly checked into a room next door to one of eight accessible ones at the Memphis property. Damages and fines were $17,500.

- The Justice Department sued not only the Days Inn proprieties owners (franchisees) of Days Inn, but also the architect and Days Inns of America, Inc., a unit of Cendant Corporation's hotel division (the franchisor). It sued in five separate cases in five different U.S. District Courts.

  In 2000, these cases against Days Inn were settled. Days Inn of America, Inc. and its parent company, Cendant Corp., in effect promised the Justice Department it would make all of its properties built since 1993 fully accessible to persons with disabilities. The hotel chain agreed to establish a $4.75 million fund to provide interest-free loans to franchise owners to finance repairs and renovations. Days Inn also undertook to ensure that before a new hotel is opened for business using the Days Inn name, the architect, the contractor, and the hotel owner will all certify that the hotel meets all ADA requirements.

The Justice Department has an ADA web site (www.usdoj.gov/crt/ada/adahom1.htm) that contains a wealth of resources on the ADA. Included there are "Common ADA Problems at Newly Constructed Lodging Facilities" and "Five Steps to Make New Lodging Facilities Comply with the ADA." These guides are extensive. However, even if followed, they do not guarantee compliance. The DOJ has made it clear that compliance is the duty of the hotel owner and operator, the designer, and the architect.

- In 1998 the Holiday Inn and Crown Plaza hotel chains agreed to guarantee reservations for rooms accessible to disabled people and pay for mediation of their complaints under agreements with the U.S. Department of Justice that settled a Justice Department Inquiry. (Disabled people had complained that accessible rooms they had reserved were not available when they got to the hotel.)

   The Justice Department is investigating other hotel chains and 200 individual hotels because of complaints filed by disabled people under the ADA.

New ADA Guidelines. In 1999, the U.S. Access Board and the Department of Justice began the process (still continuing in 2001) of revising the federal rules (American Disabilities Act Access Guidelines) governing accessibility, including access to hotels and motels.

Important Points for Management

"Readily achievable" under the ADA means easily accomplishable and able to be carried out without much difficulty or expense.

Building alterations begun after January 26, 1992, must, to the maximum extent feasible, be readily accessible to and usable by individuals with disabilities, including those who use wheelchairs.

New construction designed and constructed for first occupancy after January 26, 1993, must be readily accessible to and usable by individuals with disabilities.

New facilities that must be accessible include parking, public toilets, water fountains, and access to the goods, services, programs, facilities, and work areas. When the public accommodation or commercial facility has no control over accessible elements at streets, curbs, parking, or sidewalks, it should request such modifications from the responsible public entity.

When an alteration to an existing facility affects an area with a primary function (a major activity for which the facility is intended; for example, altering guestrooms in a hotel), an additional obligation is placed upon the public accommodation. In this case, the "path of travel" to the altered area must also be made readily accessible and usable.

Hotels must provide accessible sleeping rooms and suites that comply with ADA Accessibility Guidelines (ADAAG). The number of accessible rooms required per property is based on the overall size of the property.

In addition to the wheelchair accessible sleeping rooms and suites required, the ADAAG requires new hotels to have a specific number of sleeping rooms and suites specially equipped for hearing-impaired guests. The special equipment includes visual alarms, notification devices, and telephones.

References

1. Pub. L. No. 101-336, 42 U.S.C. § 12101. See also 47 U.S.C. §§ 225 and 611.

2. For further information, see John P.S. Salmen, AIA, *Accommodating All Guests* (Washington, D.C.: The American Hotel & Motel Association and Universal Designers & Consultants, Inc., 1992) http://www.UniversalDesign.com. Also, the Educational Institute of AH&MA has produced two ADA videotapes: *ADA: The Hiring Process* and *ADA: Communication and Service Skills*. For ordering information, call toll-free 1-800-344-4381.

3. Salmen, pp. 24–25.

4. Salmen, pp. 25–26.

5. See *Hotel Business*, Aug. 7–20, 1993, pp. 1 and 29.

6. See 28 C.F.R. Part 36.

7. 549 C.F.R. Part 37 and § 37.101 and 36 C.F.R. Part 1191.

8. See also 1999 U.S. Supreme Court ruling on the availability of punitive damages for violation of the discrimination statutes, including the American Disabilities Act. *Kolstad* v. *American Dental Association* 525 U.S. 526 (1999).

 ## Key Terms

path of travel—A continuous, unobstructed three foot wide way of pedestrian passage by which an altered area may be approached, entered, and exited, and which connects the altered area with an exterior approach (including sidewalks, streets, and parking areas), an entrance to the facility, and other parts of the facility. It includes restrooms, telephones, and drinking fountains serving the altered area.

readily achievable—Easily accomplishable and able to be carried out without much difficulty or expense.

Review Questions

1. What are some examples of a "disability" under the ADA, as far as hotel guests are concerned?

2. What does "readily achievable" barrier removal mean?

3. What are some measures that might be considered readily achievable?

4. What priorities would you consider in removing barriers?

5. What does "path of travel" mean under the ADA?

6. What aids for individuals with hearing impairments must be provided at the front desk? in the guestroom?

Internet Sites

For more information, visit the following Internet sites. Remember that Internet addresses can change without notice.

ADA
http://www.usdoj.gov/crt/ada/adahom1.htm

ADAAG
http://www.access-board.gov/adaa/html/adaag.htm

U.S. Department of Justice
http://www.usdoj.gov

Chapter 10 Outline

Reasonable Care Rule
    Recreational Facilities, Exercise Rooms,
      and Health Clubs: Liability for
      Guests' Injuries
    Agreements Seeking to Relieve Hotels
      from Liability
Acts of Hotel Employees
Acts of Other Guests and Patrons
Assault by Third Parties in Restrooms
Assault by Third Parties in Hotel Parking
    Lots
Acts by Third Parties at Hotel Entrances
Educating the Public in Travelers' Safety
Important Points for Management
References
Key Terms
Review Questions
Internet Sites
Illustrative Cases

Competencies

1. Describe the hotel's obligation to
   protect its guests. (p. 111)

2. Describe how a hotel's duty to exercise
   reasonable care may not be delegated,
   and cite cases illustrating the
   reasonable care rule. (pp. 111–114)

3. Describe the hotel's liability when a
   guest is injured in the hotel's
   recreational facilities. (pp. 114–117)

4. Explain how the doctrine of *respondeat
   superior* affects the hotel as an
   employer. (pp. 117–119)

5. Explain how the hotel might be held
   liable for injuries a guest receives at
   the hands of other guests, patrons, or
   third parties. (pp. 119–122)

10

The Hotel's Duty to Protect Guests

Reasonable Care Rule

What is the hotelkeeper's duty to protect the guest? The general rule in many states is that hotels are not insurers of the personal safety of guests. However, the hotelkeeper must exercise reasonable care to prevent injury to a guest.* Otherwise, the establishment may be held liable for damages caused by its negligence. Whether reasonable care is exercised depends upon the facts and circumstances in each case. The hotel is generally not held liable for acts that it could not reasonably foresee.

The hotel may not delegate its duty to exercise reasonable care in order to relieve it from liability. Thus, in an early New York case, a hotel was held liable for injuries a woman received when an elevator fell due to the breaking of a corroded piston rod, even though the hotel had employed experts to examine and repair the elevator before the accident.[1]

In *Kiefel* v. *Las Vegas Hacienda, Inc.,*[2] the hotel was found liable for failure to provide a reasonably safe sleeping room accommodation to plaintiff, who was attacked in the early morning by an unknown person who entered her room. (The full opinion in the case appears at the end of this chapter.)

In *Splawn* v. *Lextaj Corporation, d/b/a Lexington Hotel,*[3] a TWA stewardess was raped by an intruder in her room at the Lexington Hotel in New York City on November 26, 1985. A jury awarded the woman $1,800,000 for past pain and suffering and $200,000 for future pain and suffering over a five-year period. An appeal was denied.

In another case, the entertainer Connie Francis was awarded $2.5 million (and her husband $150,000) against Howard Johnson's Motor Lodges, Inc., by a jury in a federal district court. The award stemmed from an alleged criminal assault that occurred while Ms. Francis was a guest at a Howard Johnson hotel in Westbury, Long Island, New York. In this case the rapist entered her room through a sliding glass door. The door gave the appearance of being locked but was capable of being unsecured from the outside without much difficulty.

---

* But note State of Illinois standard of care imposed in *Yamada* v. *Hilton Hotels Corp.,* 60 Ill. App.3d 10, 376 N.E.2d 227 (1977), *cert. denied* by Sup. Ct. of Ill. This case was settled.

Howard Johnson filed a motion in federal court asking that the damage award be set aside as "excessive." On September 20, 1976, the court upheld Ms. Francis's $2.5 million damage award, but reduced her husband's award to $25,000.[4]

In a case involving a Motel 6 in Fort Worth, Texas, a woman guest who was a professional photographer was leaving for the hotel to go to dinner one September night in 1988. Two ex-convicts allegedly bullied their way into her room, raped her repeatedly, stole her photographic equipment, and drove off in her car. Motel 6 has settled her negligence lawsuit for $10 million.[5]

In *Orlando Executive Park, Inc. (OEP)* v. *P.D.R.,*[6] a Florida appellate court upheld an award of $750,000 as compensatory damages against the hotel operators and franchisor. In this case, a guest was allegedly beaten, robbed, and sexually attacked by an unidentified man. The guest was accosted as she was returning to her room and was dragged to a secluded stairwell in the building. The guest claimed that the hotel's duty to exercise reasonable care for her safety was breached by allowing the building to remain open to anyone who cared to enter, by failing to have adequate security on the premises to deter criminal activity against guests, by failing to install TV monitoring equipment in the public areas, by failing to establish and enforce standards of operation that would protect guests from attack, and by failing to warn of previous criminal activity. The appellate court upheld the jury's conclusion that the hotel operators (OEP) did not provide adequate security, noting that there were reasonable measures in this case that could have been taken to deter the incident.

On appeal, the Supreme Court of Florida affirmed the decision of the lower court,[7] and in doing so stated:

> We agree…with the district court's assessment of OEP's liability. In commenting on OEP's attack on the lack of standards the district court stated that the "absence of industry standards does not insulate the defendants from liability when there is credible evidence presented to the jury pointing to measures reasonably available to deter incidents of this kind, against which the jury can judge the reasonableness of the measures taken *in this case*" 402 So.2d at 447 (emphasis in original). In this case Robbins presented credible evidence, namely, that numerous episodes of criminal activity, of which the management had knowledge, had occurred during the immediately preceding six-month period and that the situation required the presence of security guards.

> The district court properly characterized the question as one of foreseeability. [citations omitted] An innkeeper owes the duty of reasonable care for the safety of his guests, *Rosier* [v. *Gainsville Inns Associates, Ltd.,* 347 So.2d 1100 (Fla. Dist. Ct. App. 1977)], *Phillips Petroleum Co.* v. *Dorn,* 292 So.2d 429 (Fla. 4th DCA 1974), rev'd on other grounds, 347 So.2d 1057 (Fla. 4th DCA 1977), and it is "peculiarly a jury function to determine what precautions are reasonably required in the exercise of a particular duty of due care." *Holley,* 382 So.2d at 100-01. On the facts of this case the district court correctly stated that "the jury may consider competent evidence on the need or effect of any of these security measures or combination thereof in the context of the circumstances and evidence before it, in determining whether the innkeeper has met his duty of providing his guest with

reasonable protection for his safety." 402 So.2d at 448. Credible evidence supported the jury's verdict, and we approve the portion of the district court opinion dealing with OEP's liability.

(The opinion of the Supreme Court of Florida and the lower court's opinion appear at the end of this chapter.)

In another case,[8] a guest stopped at an Econolodge motel in Louisiana at 4 A.M. After registering, the guest drove to the back of the motel and parked under a light. As he began unloading his car, a gunman approached and demanded money. The guest gave the robber all of his cash, and the robber then shot him.

The guest sued the motel, claiming that the motel had breached a duty to take reasonable precautions to protect its guests. The jury decided in favor of the motel.

On appeal, the court acknowledged that:

> innkeepers owe their guests a high degree of care and protection, and that reasonable precautions must be taken to protect patrons from the acts of criminals.

The Econolodge had only one entrance to the property, and an eight-foot-high fence topped with barbed wire surrounded the premises. Additionally, evidence revealed that the robber had followed the guest by car onto the motel premises.

The appellate court held that there was enough evidence to support the jury's conclusion that Econolodge had met its duty of care—in other words, Econolodge had taken reasonable precautions to protect its guests.

In 1994 a registered guest at a Days Inn in Rome, Georgia, walked next door to the Shoneys Restaurant with two co-workers. On the way back to the hotel, they were jumped by four men, beaten, and robbed. The guest's left eye socket, cheekbone, and nose were broken, and the injuries were permanent. He sued the Days Inn.

The evidence at trial showed that there had been prior incidents of vandalism and trespassing, as well as an assault on a security guard. The evidence also showed that the Days Inn had hired a security guard, but that his shift did not begin until 11:00 P.M., and, therefore, he wasn't on the premises when the attack occurred. Further inquiry revealed that the security guard had very little training, had a criminal record, and had assaulted one of the other security guards in the past. There was no video camera or other monitoring system for the parking lot.

Nevertheless, the trial judge threw the case out. He held that a motel owed its guests a duty of reasonable care, and that part of that duty had to do with whether a particular injury was foreseeable. The judge reasoned that since there was no prior history of violent attacks on guests at the motel, the motel had no reasonable basis to anticipate that one of its guests might be jumped in the parking lot.

The appeals court reversed the decision. It reasoned that, in order for a particular incident to be foreseeable, there need be no history of precisely the same type of incident on the premise. Rather, it is enough that there is evidence of similar types of problems. Such evidence, the appeals court said, is enough to take *McNeal* v. *Days Inn of America* to the jury.[9]

In *Stahlin* v. *Hilton Hotels Corporation*,[10] a guest, while hurriedly dressing in the room of the defendant-hotel in Illinois, got his foot tangled in his shorts and fell backward, banging his head against the wall. The injury caused some pain and a large bump. His roommate called the hotel later that evening to report that the guest had a large bump on the back of his head and was vomiting. The hotel responded by sending up a woman to offer assistance and medical help who claimed to be a licensed practical nurse but who was, in fact, unlicensed. She did not diagnose serious injury, whereas the guest was suffering a subdural hematoma.

As a result, when the guest finally did seek the services of a doctor, it was too late to prevent major surgery and permanent brain damage. This allegedly could have been prevented if immediate diagnosis had been made. The hotel was found liable to the guest and his wife for $210,000. The court stated that the hotel had no duty, under Illinois law, to provide medical aid or assistance in this case, but that if the hotel did come forward to offer to assist with medical help, it must exercise reasonable care in providing such medical assistance. The hotel, in the opinion of the court, had volunteered to come forward and supply medical aid, but had failed to supply a competent person to administer the medical aid.

In *Sneider* v. *Hyatt Corporation,*[11] a U.S. District Court in Georgia ruled, on a motion for summary judgment, that there could be instances under Georgia law in which a hotel could be held liable in connection with the suicide of a guest, depending on the circumstances. In this case, the plaintiff's wife registered at an Atlanta hotel late in the evening. She had no luggage. The plaintiff alleged that he telephoned the hotel on more than one occasion to inquire about the whereabouts of his wife and to inform the defendant-hotel that she had suicidal tendencies.

Furthermore, during previous years, several people had committed suicide by leaping from the upper stories of the defendant-hotel. This allegedly put the hotel on notice that its upper floors had attracted potential suicides. Also, the defendant's employees saw the woman in question acting in a dazed manner the day before she jumped to her death.

In these circumstances, the Georgia court stated that a jury could find the hotel negligent in not preventing the wife from committing suicide, and could thereby be liable to the plaintiff. The court refused to grant the hotel's request for a summary judgment.

On the other hand, in *Reichenbach* v. *Days Inn of America, Inc.,*[12] the court held that the motel was not liable for an assault on one of its guests in the motel parking lot. One of the judges in a concurring opinion discussed the concept of **foreseeability** and precautionary measures on the part of the hotel. (The full opinions appear at the end of this chapter.)

Recreational Facilities, Exercise Rooms, and Health Clubs: Liability for Guests' Injuries

Today many hotels and motels provide recreational sports facilities, exercise rooms, and health clubs for guests' use. As guests utilize such facilities, injuries may occur. What is the hotel's liability, if any, for such injuries? The duty a hotel owes to the guest is the duty of reasonable care under the facts and circumstances of the case.[13]

Should a guest become injured while using the exercise room or recreational facilities, the guest's own negligence may in some cases be a valid defense for the hotel.* The guest's contributory negligence is a question of whether the guest exercised reasonable care in the circumstances. In *Luftig* v. *Steinhorn* (see Reference 13), the plaintiff was injured when he tripped on a plainly visible hole in a baseball field owned by the hotel. At trial, plaintiff admitted that he saw the holes in the outfield, and he failed to prove that the hotel was negligent. Therefore, the plaintiff could not recover any damages from the defendant hotel owner.

Another possible defense is that the injured guest assumed the risk of his/her activities. For instance, in *Luftig*, the court stated that one reason the plaintiff could not recover was that he was playing the outfield with knowledge of hazards, and therefore, he assumed the risk of the accident.**[14]

Posting notices warning the user of the recreational facilities or exercise room that there are dangers (i.e., heart attacks, pulled muscles, etc.) involved in the use of the equipment may not exonerate the hotel. However, such notices may put the guest on notice of the risks involved, and thereby facilitate the hotel's invoking the defense of assumption of risk by the guests.[15]

In *Hooks* v. *Washington Sheraton Corp.*[16] a federal court in 1977 upheld an award of $4.6 million to a hotel guest injured in a diving accident at the hotel swimming pool. The guest dived off the pool's diving board and landed in such a manner as to break his neck and injure his spine so severely that he became a quadriplegic. Evidence introduced at trial indicated that the Sheraton Park Hotel's diving board was not of the standard fiberglass design generally used for hotel swimming pools. Employees of the Sheraton had arranged to replace an aging board with a "duraflex" diving board, made of extruded aluminum, that was used generally in competitive swimming events. Testimony showed that the duraflex board was designed to throw a diver higher and farther than a fiberglass board. The Sheraton's employees allegedly were aware of these properties when they purchased the duraflex board.

A federal jury in the Virgin Islands awarded $6.8 million to a guest injured in an American Motor Inns (AMI) swimming pool at the chain's Frenchman's Reef Holiday Inn. The guest charged AMI with negligence in construction and maintenance of the pool where he broke his neck in a dive in 1977 and subsequently became a quadriplegic. A settlement for $4.4 million was reached while the case was being appealed.

Several recent tragic incidents involved pool drains. In one incident, a swimmer's hair became caught in a malfunctioning drain and, despite valiant rescue

---

  * The injured party's own negligence, or contributory negligence, is no longer a complete defense in most jurisdictions. In New York State, for example, § 1411 of the Civil Practice Laws and Rules adopts the *comparative* negligence rule. This section provides that the claimant's contributory negligence *or assumption of risk* shall not bar recovery, "but the amount of damages otherwise recoverable shall be diminished in the proportion" which the claimant's fault bears to the the defendant's negligence. In other words, if a jury decided that the injured guest was 60% negligent and the defendant-hotel was 40% negligent, then the claimant's award would be reduced by 60%.
 ** This defense of assumption of risk may bar recovery in contributory negligence jurisdictions and reduce recovery in comparative negligence jurisdictions. The *Luftig* case was decided before the enactment of New York's comparative negligence statutes.

efforts, the individual drowned. In 1996, a 16-year-old New Jersey girl was held underwater by drain suction in a hot tub and drowned. In 1993, at the Medfield Area Recreation Club in Cary, North Carolina, five-year-old Valerie Lakey was in a wading pool whose drain cover had been pried off earlier in the day by other children. When she sat down, the resulting suction held her to the bottom of the pool and literally disemboweled her. Although the child survived, she must now take nourishment intravenously and may require several organ transplants in the future. The Lakelys subsequently sued the pool's manufacturer, the pump's manufacturer, the county (which certified the pool), and recreation club. After three years of lawsuits, the family finally received payments of $25 million from the pool's manufacturer (a record in North Carolina), $2.5 million from the county, $2.9 million from the pump manufacturer, and $500,00 from the club itself. This and similar judgments have led to the recommendation that an emergency switch be visible and readily accessible in the pool area to turn off the pump. Furthermore, dual drains, which reduce the suction at any given drain, are becoming more common.

Vermont[17] and New Hampshire[18] have enacted laws that serve to limit the liability of ski area operators for injuries to skiers using the area. As a safeguard against possible negligence suits against the ski area operators, the laws establish that persons participating in the sport of skiing assume the risk and accept, as a matter of law, the dangers inherent in the sport, and therefore may not maintain an action against a resort based on injuries suffered as a result of these inherent dangers.

The laws followed judgment by a Vermont court in the case of *Sunday* v. *Stratton Corporation.*[19] The plaintiff, a novice skier, was awarded $1.5 million for injuries sustained as a result of what the court found to be negligent trail maintenance, resulting in his skis becoming entangled with underbrush on the edge of the trail.

These laws were designed to prevent further awards along the lines of the *Sunday* case in Vermont. In both Vermont and New Hampshire, however, ski area operators will continue to be responsible for guarding against risks to skiers in their ascent of the ski trail and to be held to official standards in the operation of mechanisms such as uphill passenger tramways.

In New York State, the Industrial Commissioner promulgated a new Downhill Skiing Safety Code in 1979.[20] In addition to setting forth responsibilities for skiers, the code provides rules to be observed by ski area operators, including, among others, rules regarding snowmaking equipment, marking trails, equipping trail maintenance vehicles with flashing or rotating lights, and inspecting trail conditions. Violation of the code is punishable by fines and imprisonment.

The Michigan Ski Area Safety Act protects ski resorts from liability for skiing accidents. Skiers assume the risk that they could be injured by variations in terrain, surface or subsurface snow, or ice conditions. The Act was passed to reduce litigation and provide economic stabilization to the ski industry. In *Shukoski* v. *Indianhead Mountain Resort, Inc.*, the court rejected the argument that the Act did not pertain to a snowboarder, noting that snowboarders are exposed to identical risks as traditional alpine skiers.[21]

In 1977, the New York Appellate Division reversed a judgment that Kiamesha-Concord, Inc., was guilty of negligence in connection with an accident occurring on its ice skating rink.[22] On June 4, 1972, the defendant's employee had checked the rink every 10 or 15 minutes to make sure it was suitable for skating. At trial, the Supreme Court, Kings County, charged the jury that if the rut or hole in the ice alleged to have caused the personal injuries existed for more than fifteen minutes, then the defendant should have corrected the condition. The Appellate Division held that this charge was erroneous and stated that: "Under the circumstances defendant's failure to discover the hole within fifteen minutes does not necessarily establish negligence."[23] The Appellate Division then reversed the judgment based on the jury **verdict** and granted a new trial, holding that the verdict was contrary to the weight of the evidence and was based upon an erroneous charge that was highly misleading in its suggestion of an arbitrary time as a criterion of constructive negligence.

Agreements Seeking to Relieve Hotels from Liability

Some states' statutes address the validity of "exculpatory" clauses in contracts of membership or admission to gymnasiums or recreational facilities. An exculpatory clause is an agreement whereby one party seeks to absolve itself from liability even if negligent. In New York State, however, § 5-326 of the General Obligations Law states:

> Every covenant, agreement or understanding in or in connection with, or collateral to, any contract, membership application, ticket of admission or similar writing, entered into between the owner or operator of any pool, gymnasium, place of amusement or recreation, or similar establishment and the user of such facilities, which exempts the said owner or operator from liability for damages caused by or resulting from the negligence of the owner, operator or person in charge of such establishment, or their agents, servants or employees, shall be deemed to be void as against public policy and wholly unenforceable.

This statute overrules the earlier Court ruling in *Ciofalo* v. *Vic Tanny Gymnasium*,[24] which upheld the validity of an exculpatory agreement between the owner of the gymnasium and a user of the facilities.

Therefore, a hospitality operation should consult local counsel to see if similar state statutes exist which void any exculpatory agreements.

Acts of Hotel Employees

A hotel employer may be held liable for the acts of his/her employee acting within the course of employment under the doctrine of *respondeat superior*. Under this doctrine, the act of the employee becomes the act of the employer by operation of law. Once the employer hires the employee and has the power to control his/her acts, the employer becomes liable for any wrongful acts of the employee.[25] Therefore, if an employee commits a wrongful act while working within the scope of employment, the employer will be deemed liable whether or not he/she exercised reasonable care in hiring that employee.

A lawsuit was brought against a Louisville, Kentucky, hotel by a plaintiff-guest stemming from an incident in which the hotel clerk allegedly gave the plaintiff-guest the key to a room which was already occupied. According to the plaintiff, when he attempted to open the door to the room with the key, he was shot in the chest when the person occupying the room fired a gun through the door. Criminal charges were not prosecuted against the occupant who fired the gun, and the hotel was sued for damages resulting from the plaintiff's injuries.

It should be noted that in some jurisdictions there is some recent authority for holding the hotel as employer liable to guests for the **tortious** acts of its employees *committed outside the scope of employment.*[26] For example, in *Crawford v. Hotel Essex Boston Corp.,*[27] the guest recovered damages on the theory that the hotel breached a plaintiff-guest's contractual rights of "immunity from rudeness, personal abuse and unjustifiable interference." In a recent San Francisco case, a hotel was held liable for $250,000 in an assault case. The assailant admitted that he heard the newly trained desk clerk call out to bell personnel the room number of the female guest; he then followed her to the eighth floor where he committed the assault on her person. In *McKee v. Sheraton-Russell, Inc.,*[28] the Second Circuit Court of Appeals, applying New York law, held that a hotel may be liable for a bellboy's improper advances to a female guest in her room. The court noted that this would be so even if the bellboy by making such advances was acting outside the scope of employment. The action was based upon the breach of the hotel's contractual requirement of decent and respectful treatment implied from the relationship of hotelkeeper and guest.[29]

The foregoing concept of liability is generally understood within the industry. But certain cases have shown some of the outer reaches of alleged liabilities. Consider the following: In *Tobin v. Slutsky,*[30] the United States Court of Appeals for the Second Circuit discussed the liability of a New York hotel for failure to protect the guest from assaults by the hotel's employees.

An employee at a family resort in upstate New York molested a 15-year-old guest at knife point. The court decided that the hotel was not an "insurer" of the guest's safety but must exercise "reasonable care" to prevent such harm. This federal court declared:

> We construe the law of New York to oblige an innkeeper to use reasonable care, commensurate with the quality of the accommodations offered, to see that his guest is not abused, injured or insulted by his employees. In the case of a first class family resort, reasonable care would mean a high degree of care. Indeed, examination of the New York cases leads us to believe that the duty of reasonable care has generally been interpreted to be a severe one.

The federal court held that the hotel, being a first class family resort, had a high degree of care, and that whether the resort had met this degree of care was a jury question. Accordingly, the court of appeals remanded to the trial court for a decision on this issue. The court of appeals held that $30,000 would not be excessive under the facts, but that punitive damages could not be awarded in this case.

In another case, a lounge paid a male patron $115,000 because he was assaulted by the employee door attendant. It appears in this case that the door attendant made advances to the patron's girlfriend. The patron objected, and an argument ensued. The door attendant struck the patron and fractured his jaw. The medical bills were $23,000. The pre-trial discovery proceedings allegedly revealed that the door attendant had never been specifically trained with regard to security and safety of the guest, and that there was negligence in the supervision and in the delegation of authority by the employer to the door attendant (this is an unreported case).

In 1998 a Tennessee woman sued the posh Essex House hotel in New York City for $16 million, allegedly charging a security guard with groping her and "sucking and biting her breast" while she lay ill waiting for an ambulance.[31]

In *Sistler* v. *Liberty Mutual Insurance Company*,[32] the Supreme Court of Louisiana upheld a verdict for Lola Sistler for $175,000, which she was awarded for severe knee injuries that resulted from a fall in a restaurant because of a change of elevation in the floor. The state Supreme Court noted:

> Mrs. Sistler was a restaurant invitee, using the premises as they were intended to be used.... While entering its foyer, she was looking ahead instead of down. No signs, warnings or indicators drew her attention to or notified her to look down or to beware of [a one-inch] change in elevation.... The steakhouse had a duty to attract Mrs. Sistler's attention to the change in elevation. Placement of warning signs in the entryway or placement of yellow highlighting on the face of the elevated surface would not have encumbered the utility of the elevation. The failure to take such precautions caused the face of the elevation, where Mrs. Sistler caught the toe of her shoe, to become unreasonably dangerous.

Acts of Other Guests and Patrons

In New York, a hotel may be held liable for injuries received by a guest that were reasonably foreseeable and that might have been prevented through the exercise of reasonable care. Thus, when a football team made a hotel its headquarters and the lobbies were crowded with celebrating people, the hotel was held liable for injuries an elderly woman received when two of the crowd ran through a revolving door at great speed. This was because the hotel had not provided a door attendant to supervise the door. In its opinion, the court said that if the hotel had exercised reasonable care and diligence for the safety of its patrons, it could have readily foreseen that without precautions to control the use of the door, some patron might be injured by the unrestrained cavorting of some celebrant.[33]

In 1993, Linda and Robert Millan stayed with their four children at a Georgia Residence Inn. During their stay, another guest, Roy Dowty, allegedly sexually assaulted the Millans' 14-year-old daughter, Audrey, who is developmentally disabled. The alleged assault took place in the swimming pool.

The Millans sued Dowty, Residence Inn by Marriott Inc., and Marriott International Inc. The Millans' theory of liablitiy for the hotel defendants was the inn had knowledge of previous criminal acts by Dowty.

The Georgia Court of Appeals looked at evidence on the earlier sexual touching of both a hotel employee and children. This should have given the employees

---

Selected Security and Law Enforcement Publications

Hospitality Law
747 Dresher Road
P.O. Box 980
Horsham, PA 19044-0980
(215) 784-0860

*Hotel/Motel Security and Safety
Management*
Rusting Publications
402 Main Street
Port Washington, NY 11050
(516) 883-1440

The Police Chief
International Association of Chiefs
of Police
515 N. Washington Street
Alexandria, VA 22314-2357
(703) 836-6767

Research in Brief
National Institute of Justice
Office of Justice Programs
810 7th Street, NW
Washington, DC 20531
(202) 307-2942

Security Letter
166 East 96th Street
New York, NY 10128
(212) 348-1553

Security Management
American Society for Industrial Security
1655 North Fort Meyer Drive
Arlington, VA 22209
(703) 522-5800

Security Technology & Design
Locksmith Publishing Corp.
850 Busse Highway
Park Ridge, IL 60068
(847) 692-5940

Security World
Cahners Publishing Company
Cahners Plaza
1350 East Touhy Avenue
Des Plaines, IL 60018
(847) 635-8800

Source: Raymond C. Ellis, Jr., and David M. Stipanuk, *Security and Loss Prevention Management,* Second Edition (East Lansing, Mich.: Educational Institute of the American Hotel & Motel Association, 1999), p. 17.

sufficient warning of Dowty's character, said the court. Notice to an employee was considered notice to the inn.*

The matter of a restaurant's liability for injuries to patrons by other patrons is addressed in *Kimple* v. *Foster.*[34] A jury awarded three plaintiffs $6,500 each in damages for personal injuries sustained during a violent episode in a tavern. (The opinions in this case appear at the end of this chapter.)

In October 1994 a jury ordered the Las Vegas Hilton Hotel and its parent company, Hilton Hotel Corporation, to pay former Navy Lt. Paula A. Coughlin $1.7 million in compensatory damages[35] for emotional distress plus $5 million punitive damages for failure to provide adequate security at the hotel, where she was allegedly groped by drunken male aviators in a crowded third floor gauntlet

---

* Reprinted with permission from Hospitality Law copyright 2000 by LRP Publications, 747 Dresher Road, Horsham, PA 19044-0980. All rights reserved. For more information on Hospitality Law or for a free 30-day trial subscription, please call 1-800-341-7874, ext. 310.

during the infamous Tailhook Association convention at the hotel in September 1991. This was the notorious gathering at which some 83 women were allegedly assaulted or harmed by Navy aviators at the Las Vegas Hilton Hotel.

In *Maher* v. *Best Western Inn*, the Florida Court ruled that a hotel that permitted dogs to stay on its premises created a forseeable risk which required the hotel to take certain precautions to protect its other guests from the dogs.[36]

Assault by Third Parties in Restrooms

The Missouri State Supreme Court found a St. Louis hotel liable when a woman was raped in one of the hotel restrooms.[37] The court upheld the jury award of $100,000 to the plaintiff, even though there had been no such previous incidents at the hotel. In this case the plaintiff was a patron of one of the restaurants in the hotel. An apparently neat, well-dressed man followed her down into a restroom in the hotel's lower lobby (where convention meeting rooms and offices were located), and there assaulted her.

In a 1990 New York case,[38] a man was attacked by an unidentified assailant in the restroom of a restaurant. The restaurant patron was stabbed in the neck and suffered other injuries. He sued the restaurant, alleging negligence in maintaining adequate security.

The appellate court held that the plaintiff failed to demonstrate that the restaurant owed a duty to protect the patron from a sudden, unforeseeable, and unexpected attack, despite a similar attack five months earlier. The court stated:

> The mere fact that a single similar incident, involving different patrons, may have occurred in the defendant's restaurant approximately five months prior to the instant incident does not, without more, render the present incident any less unexpected and sudden. The plaintiff has failed to establish that the defendant owed a duty to protect the plaintiff against such an unexpected and sudden assault.

Because the court held that the restaurant in this case had no duty to protect patrons from unforeseeable, unexpected, and sudden attacks on its premises, the plaintiff could not recover damages for any of the injuries sustained in the restroom assault. The result of this case would have been quite different if the plaintiff had been able to demonstrate that the restaurant knew or should have known of the potential for danger in the unattended restroom and subsequently failed to take preventive measures.

Assault by Third Parties in Hotel Parking Lots

In *McCoy* v. *Gay,*[39] the Georgia Court of Appeals affirmed the trial court's directed verdict in favor of the defendant-hotel sued by a plaintiff-patron for alleged negligence in protecting patrons from assaults by third parties. In this case, the plaintiff-patron alleged that an assault occurred in the hotel's parking lot. Plaintiff claimed that poor lighting and inadequate security in the parking lot was the proximate cause of the plaintiff's injuries, and alleged that previous criminal assaults on the hotel premises constituted notice to the defendant-hotel of the allegedly dangerous condition. The trial court and the appellate court disagreed.

The Court of Appeals held that evidence of two assaults within the hotel building a couple of years before the incident, and one criminal assault of a guest in the parking lot 10 years before the incident, would not constitute a "reasonable apprehension" of danger by the hotel alerting it to act to prevent the injury to plaintiff.

See also *Reichenbach* v. *Days Inn of America, Inc.,* at the end of this chapter.

Acts by Third Parties at Hotel Entrances

In *Banks* v. *Hyatt Hotel Corp.,*[40] the plaintiffs sued the hotel operators as well as the operators of a shopping mall which was part of the building complex in which the hotel was located. The action was a derivative claim brought by the family of a guest who was murdered in a robbery attempt as he was returning to the hotel after walking through sections of New Orleans. The assault occurred on a public sidewalk only four feet from entrance doors which led to the shopping mall and the hotel. On appeal, the Fifth Circuit Court of Appeals affirmed the lower court's decision in holding the defendant hotel operators liable for damages of $975,000, while absolving the shopping mall operator from any liability.

In discussing the geographic area for which the hotel could be found liable for inadequate security, the court indicated that such area would extend only to the hotel's own premises and the area immediately surrounding its entrance. The court indicated that it was not prepared to say that a hotel had a duty to provide security beyond this limited area or to warn guests of crime hazards in other parts of the city.

In *Zerangue* v. *Delta Towers, Ltd.,*[41] the United States Court of Appeals for the Fifth Circuit on June 25, 1987, upheld the jury verdict of the lower court holding the Ramada Hotel in New Orleans liable for damages resulting from personal injuries sustained by an invitee of a hotel guest when she was sexually assaulted on a public sidewalk outside the hotel. (This case is discussed at the end of this chapter.)

Educating the Public in Travelers' Safety

On November 27, 1992, Ken Hine, then president of the American Hotel & Motel Association (AH&MA), appeared on the television show *Larry King Live* to discuss the status of security safeguards in hotels. He also explained the need for educating the public on taking proper precautions whenever they travel and introduced the AH&MA's "Traveler Safety Tips," a list of do's and don'ts for the traveling public (see Exhibit 10.1).

Important Points for Management

Hospitality operations have a duty of "reasonable care" to protect guests. Reasonable care depends on the facts and circumstances. Hotels cannot guarantee (be the insurer) that nothing will happen to the guest. The hotel is generally not liable for acts that it could not reasonably foresee.

Exhibit 10.1   Traveler Safety Tips Card

TRAVELER SAFETY TIPS

American Hotel & Motel Association

1. Don't answer the door in a hotel or motel room without verifying who it is. If a person claims to be an employee, call the front desk and ask if someone from their staff is supposed to have access to your room and for what purpose.

2. When returning to your hotel or motel late in the evening, use the main entrance of the hotel. Be observant and look around before entering parking lots.

3. Close the door securely whenever you are in your room and use all of the locking devices provided.

4. Don't needlessly display guest room keys in public or carelessly leave them on restaurant tables, at the swimming pool, or other places where they can be easily stolen.

5. Do not draw attention to yourself by displaying large amounts of cash or expensive jewelry.

6. Don't invite strangers to your room.

7. Place all valuables in the hotel or motel's safe deposit box.

8. Do not leave valuables in your vehicle.

9. Check to see that any sliding glass doors or windows and any connecting room doors are locked.

10. If you see any suspicious activity, please report your observations to the management.

We Support the National Citizens' Crime Prevention Campaign. **TAKE A BITE OUT OF CRIME**®

Printed on recycled paper

Copyright 1993 by The American Hotel & Motel Association 1201 New York Avenue, N.W. Washington, D.C. 20005-3931

Source: American Hotel & Motel Association, Washington, D.C.

If the hotel is sued in a civil suit, the hotel should determine whether there was:

- Contributory negligence by the plaintiff
- Assumption of a known risk by the plaintiff

Under the doctrine of *respondeat superior,* the hotel is liable for torts committed by hotel employees in the course and scope of employment. Courts can be very liberal in deciding what is in the course and scope of employment.

Desk clerks and bell personnel should *never* announce a guest's room number so that bystanders can overhear.

References

1. *Stott* v. *Churchill,* 15 Misc. 80, 36 N.Y.S. 476 (1895), *aff'd,* 157 N.Y. 692, 51 N.E. 1094 (1898). See also *Blansit* v. *Hyatt Corp. of Delaware,* 874 F.2d 1015 (5th Cir. 1989), involving a fall on a hotel escalator; the opinion of the court appears at the end of this chapter. See also *Kauffmann* v. *Royal Orleans, Inc.,* 216 So.2d 394 (La. 1968), involving a hotel restaurant's duty of reasonable care; the opinion of the court appears at the end of this chapter.

2. 404 F.2d 1163 (7th Cir. 1968), *cert. denied,* 395 U.S. 908, (1969) *reh'g. denied* 395 U.S. 987 (1969).

3. 197 A.D.2d 479 (1st Dept. 1993), 83 N.Y.2d 753 (1994).

4. *Garzilli* v. *Howard Johnson's Motor Lodges, Inc.,* 419 F.Supp.1210 (E.D.N.Y., 1976). On appeal, the case was settled for $1,475,000.

5. Unreported case. *Wall Street Journal,* July 18, 1991, p. 1A.

6. 402 So.2d 442 (Dist. Ct. of App., 5th Dist. 1981). See also *Wassell* v. *Adams,* 865 F.2d 849 (7th Cir. 1989); the opinion of the court appears at the end of this chapter.

7. Supreme Court of Florida, Case No. 61,165 and 61,166, March 3, 1983.

8. *Franklin* v. *Paul Dupuis & Associates, d/b/a Econolodge, and United States Fidelity & Guaranty Company,* 543 So.2d 971 (La. Ct. of App., 3d Cir., April 19, 1989).

9. 230 Ga. App. 786, Ga. App. LEXIS 281 (Feb. 26, 1998).

10. 484 F.2d 580 (7th Cir. 1973). See also *Gingeleski* v. *Westin Hotel Company* (1998 U.S. App. LEXIS 10535, 9th Cir., May 22, 1998) on the duty of care that a hotel owes its guests once it is known or there is reason to know of a patron's illness.

11. 390 F.Supp. 976 (N. D. Ga., 1975).

12. 401 So.2d 1366 (Fla. Dist. Ct. App., 5th Dist. 1981), *petition denied,* 412 So.2d 469 (Fla. 1982).

13. *Luftig* v. *Steinhorn,* 21 A.D.2d 760, 250 N.Y.S.2d 354 (1st Dept. 1964), *aff'd mem.,* 16 N.Y.2d 568, 260 N.Y.S.2d 840 (1965). See also *Jungjohann* v. *Hotel Buffalo,* 5 A.D.2d 496, 173 N.Y.S.2d 340 (4th Dept. 1958); *Kane* v. *Ten Eyck Co.,* 10 Misc.2d 398, 175 N.Y.S.2d 88 (1943).

14. See also *Kulaga* v. *State of New York,* 37 A.D.2d 58, 322 N.Y.S.2d 542 (4th Dept. 1972), *aff'd,* 31 N.Y.2d 756, 338 N.Y.S.2d 436 (1972).

15. *Olsen* v. *State of New York,* 30 A.D.2d 759, 291 N.Y.S.2d 833 (4th Dept. 1968), *aff'd* 25 N.Y.2d 665 (1969), 306 N.Y.S.2d 474 (1969).

16. No. 76-1958 (D.C. Cir. 1977). See also *Wiegman* v. *Hitch-Inn Post of Libertyville Inc.*, 308 Ill. App. 3d 789, No. 2-98-1494 (Ill. Ct. App. 1999) where the jury awarded a guest $52,500 when she slipped on a wet floor at the swimming pool.

17. 12 V.S.A. § 1037.

18. R.S.A. 225-A:24(I).

19. 136 Vt. 293, 390 A.2d 398 (1978).

20. 12 NYCRR Part 54.

21. 166 F. 3d 848, No. 97-2241 (6th Cir. 1999).

22. *Bushman* v. *Kiamesha-Concord, Inc.*, 58 A.D.2d 638, 396 N.Y.S.2d 44 (2d Dept. 1977).

23. *Id.* at 44.

24. 10 N.Y.2d 294, 220 N.Y.S.2d 962 (1961). See also *Wurzer* v. *Seneca Sport Parachute Club*, 66 A.D.2d 1002, 1003 (4th Dept. 1978).

25. 53 Am. Jur. 2d. § 417.

26. *Clancy* v. *Barker* 71 Neb. 83, 98 N.W. 440 (1904), *aff'd* 71 Neb. 91, 103 N.W. 446 (1905).

27. 143 F.Supp. 172 (D.C. Mass. 1956).

28. 268 F.2d 669 (2d Cir. 1959).

29. *Id.* at 672.

30. 506 F.2d 1097 (2d Cir. 1974). See also *Crawford* v. *Hotel Essex Boston Corp.*, 143 F.Supp. 172 (D. Mass. 1956). See also *Moore* v. *Florida Innkeepers, Inc., et al.*, 20 ATLA Newsletter 152-54 (1977), where hotel was charged with falsely advertising hotel as a safe place. This case was settled.

31. *New York Post,* March 18, 1998, p. 22, Col. 5.

32. 558 So.2d 1106 (La. 1990).

33. *Schubart* v. *Hotel Astor, Inc.,* 168 Misc. 431, 5 N.Y.S.2d 203 (1938), *aff'd* 255 A.D. 1012, 8 N.Y.S. 2d 567 (1938).

34. 205 Kan. 415, 469 P.2d 281 (1970).

35. See *New York Times,* Oct. 29, 1994, p. 1, col. 4; and Nov. 1, 1994, p. A-24; and Nov. 6, 1994, p. 46, col. 1.

36. No. 97-2450 (Fla. Dist. Ct. App. 1998).

37. *Virginia* v. *Madesco Investment Corp., d/b/a Bel Air Hilton Hotel,* 648 S.W.2d 881 (Sup. Ct. Mo. 1983).

38. *Lindskog* v. *Southland Restaurant, Inc.,* 554 N.Y.S.2d 276 (Sup. Ct. App. Div., 2nd Dept. 1990).

39. No. 65117, slip opin. (Ga. Ct. App., March 2, 1983).

40. Docket No. 81-3377 (5th Cir., January 9, 1984). See also *Holland* v. *Days Inn Motel* 705 So. 2d 1126, KA 5474 (La. Ct. Apps 1997) aff'd in material part, rev'd on another point, 747 So. 2d 1133 (Sup. CT. LA. 1999) 262 A.D. 2d 193, where court denied hotel liability when attack was 150 yards from hotel or public property not adjacent to the hotel. See also *Joseph McAndrew* v. *Pierre Hotel* (199 N.Y. App. Div. Lexis 7426, June 22, 1999) where the court said that the "hotel's duty to keep its business secure" extended to guests, not to the non-guest plaintiff, who "was assaulted on a public sidewalk." Moreover, said the court, the "duty" to keep a sidewalk safe "applied only in trip and fall cases and we decline to extend it." See also "Selected Security and Law Enforcement Publications" feature earlier in the chapter. But see Alamo Rent-A-Car case where the jury found the company acted negligently in not warning the customer of dangerous areas in Miami. (Cited in Hospitality Law copyright 2000 by LRP Publications, 747 Dresher Road,

Horsham, PA 19044-0980. All rights reserved. For more information on Hospitality Law or for a free 30-day trial subscription, please call 1-800-341-7874, ext. 310.

41. U.S. Court of Appeals (Fifth Circuit No. 86-3357, June 25, 1987).

Key Terms

foreseeability—In a suit alleging negligence, the plaintiff generally must show in part that the defendant innkeeper had a duty to use reasonable care to protect the plaintiff or victim from foreseeable acts. An injury is foreseeable if a person of ordinary prudence would have foreseen that such an injury might and probably would result from the act of negligence. It does not mean that the negligent party ought reasonably to have foreseen a particular consequence or precise form of injury, or a particular manner of occurrence, or that it would occur to a particular person.

tortious—Wrongful.

verdict—A decision made by the jury and reported to the court on matters lawfully submitted to the jury in the course of the trial of a case.

Review Questions

1. What is the hotel's duty to protect guests?

2. Is the hotel an "insurer" of the guest's safety? If so, why? If not, why not?

3. What does "reasonable care" mean?

4. How has the increase of recreational facilities, exercise rooms, and health clubs affected the hotel's liabilities?

5. What are exculpatory agreements? How do they pertain to hotels?

6. What is the doctrine of *respondeat superior*?

7. What is the hotel's responsibility in the case of assault on a guest by other guests and patrons?

8. Should a hotel be responsible for its guests' safety outside the hotel premises? If not, why not?

9. What is the rule of "contributory negligence"?

10. What is the difference between the rules of "contributory negligence" and "comparative negligence"?

Internet Sites

For more information, visit the following Internet sites. Remember that Internet addresses can change without notice.

American Hotel & Lodging Association (AH&LA)
http://www.ahla.com

Educational Institute of the AH&LA
http://www.ei-ahla.org

FindLaw
http://www.findlaw.com

International Association of
Chiefs of Police
http://www.theiacp.org

International Association of
Professional Security Consultants
http://www.iapsc.org

International Foundation for
Protection Officers
http://www.ifpo.com

Loss Prevention Management Institute
http://www.hrm.uh.edu

National Crime Prevention Council
http://www.ncpc.org

National Fire Protection Association
(NFPA)
http://www.nfpa.org/

National Institute of Justice
http://www.ojp.usdoj.gov/nij/

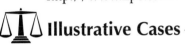 **Illustrative Cases** ────────────────────────────────────

Blansit v. Hyatt Corp. of Delaware

874 F.2d 1015 (5th Cir. 1989)

DUHE, Circuit Judge:

A "runaway" escalator is the culprit in this personal injury action. Hyatt Corporation, the lessor of the escalator, appeals the trial court's determination that it was strictly liable under La.Civ.Code Art. 2317 for injuries sustained by Mr. and Mrs. Leslie Blansit when the escalator's brakes failed. Alternatively, Hyatt seeks to decrease the amount of damages awarded to the Blansits. We affirm.

FACTS

The escalator is located in a building owned by Refco Poydras Hotel Joint Venture (Refco) and leased by Hyatt Corporation. It connects the third floor of the New Orleans Hyatt Regency Hotel to the first floor lobby. At the time of the accident, the escalator was turned off and was being used as a stationary stairway. Nevertheless, it began moving rapidly downward, hurling the Blansits onto the lobby floor. Mr. Blansit sustained three fractured ribs, a fractured vertebra, a contusion of the lower back which lasted two to three months, swelling of the left knee, and a hematoma on the left leg. Mrs. Blansit sustained a contusion of her right ribs.

TRIAL COURT OPINION

The trial court found that due to the problem with its brakes, the escalator created an unreasonable risk of injury to others. The court also found that under the lease between Refco and Hyatt, Hyatt had assumed custody (garde)[1] of the escalator. The trial court further found that Hyatt paid Westinghouse Electric Corporation to maintain the escalator and it considered this evidence of Hyatt's control over the maintenance of the escalator. Accordingly, the district court held

---

[1] For a discussion of the civilian concept of "garde" in relation to La.Civ.Code Art. 2317 see *Ross* v. *Las Coste de Monterville*, 502 So.2d 1026 (La.1987); *Loescher* v. *Parr*, 324 So.2d 441 (La.1975).

Hyatt liable for the Blansits' injuries under La.Civ.Code Art. 2317 which provides for the liability of the guardian of a thing for damages caused by its defect without proof of negligence.

The trial court awarded Mr. Blansit $67,500 for disability, pain and suffering, and mental anguish; $10,000 for loss of enjoyment of life; and $3,898.52 for past medical expenses. Mrs. Blansit received $1,500 for pain and suffering and mental anguish; and $5,000 for loss of consortium.

ANALYSIS

1. *Custody*

Hyatt contends the trial court erred in finding it had "custody" (garde) of the escalator. It asserts several theories in support of this claim. First, Hyatt contends it did not have custody of the escalator because it did not supervise or control the *maintenance* of the escalator. This argument is without merit. It is well settled that things are in one's custody for purposes of Art. 2317 liability if one bears such a relationship to them as to have the right direction and control over them and to draw benefit from them. Although this relationship is ordinarily associated with ownership, the owner may transfer the guardianship by transferring the thing to another, such as a bailee, lessee or usufructuary, who will bear such a relationship to the thing as to himself have the custody (guardianship) of it. *Loescher* v. *Parr*, 324 So.2d 441 (La.1975). Paragraph 18 of the lease between Refco and Hyatt provides that Hyatt "shall solely and exclusively be responsible for operation of the leased property and shall enjoy the exclusive possession thereof and revenues therefrom, all costs and liabilities arising from such operation being costs and liabilities of Hyatt." This paragraph of the lease transferred to Hyatt the care (garde) of the escalator. Hiring Westinghouse to maintain the escalator did not strip Hyatt of its right of direction and control of the escalator. On the contrary, as the trial court found, it is proof of Hyatt's dominion over the escalator.

Next, Hyatt contends that it did not have custody (garde) of the escalator because, under the lease with Refco, it merely agreed to be responsible for operation of the hotel and did not assume responsibility for any liabilities arising out of the condition of the escalator. This argument is frivolous. Hyatt agreed to be responsible for operations of the leased property. The escalator was part of the leased property.

Next, Hyatt contends it did not have custody of the escalator because an owner [Refco] who leases a defective thing retains custody (garde) of the thing for Article 2317 purposes. This argument is without merit. None of the cases relied on by Hyatt[2] is applicable to the instant case. In *Detillier* and *Ross* there was evidence that the structural defect causing the loss existed at the time the offending device was transferred by the owner. There is no proof that the escalator was defective when Refco leased it to Hyatt. In *Willis* the language relied upon is dicta only. There was no transfer of the offending device by the owner. The district

---

2 *Detillier* v. *Scafco, Ltd.*, 507 So.2d 829 (La.App. 5th Cir.), *cert. denied*, 508 So.2d 820 (1987); *Ross* v. *La Coste de Monterville*, 502 So.2d 1026 (La.1987); and *Willis* v. *Cajun Electric Power Co-op, Inc.*, 484 So.2d 726 (La.App. 1st Cir.), *cert. denied*, 488 So.2d 200 (1986).

court correctly concluded that Hyatt had "custody" (garde) of the escalator.

2. *Third Party Fault*

Hyatt asserts Westinghouse's negligent failure to maintain and/or repair the brakes on the escalator as a defense to its liability under Article 2317. However, it is well settled that the defense of third-party fault does not apply where the third party is acting with the consent of the custodian of the defective thing. *Olsen* v. *Shell Oil Co.*, 365 So.2d 1285 (La.1979). Westinghouse was acting with the consent of Hyatt. Therefore, Westinghouse's negligence, if any, did not relieve Hyatt of its liability.

3. *Damages*

Hyatt contends Mr. Blansit's awards for disability, pain, suffering, mental anguish, and loss of enjoyment of life are excessive because Mr. Blansit was 50-60% disabled by an arthritic condition before the accident and his impairment was only marginally increased by the accident.

Much discretion is left to the trial judge in assessment of damages in cases of offenses. La.Civ.Code 2324.1. Before the court of appeal can disturb an award by a trial court, the record must clearly reveal that the trier of fact abused his discretion in making the award. *Perniciaro* v. *Brinch*, 384 So.2d 392, 395 (La.1980). The trial court found Mr. Blansit's back injuries were extremely painful, required the use of a back brace occasionally for one year and continued to cause Mr. Blansit lower back pain at the time of the trial—more than two years after the accident. Additionally, Mr. Blansit fractured three ribs, had swelling and tenderness in his left knee, and a slight loss of motion and ecchymosis about his lower leg. The awards made by the trial court were supported by the record and were not an abuse of discretion.

Hyatt contends that the trial court erred in awarding $5,000 to Mrs. Blansit for loss of consortium. Hyatt argues that no proof of such a loss was established at trial, that Mr. Blansit's participation in household activities before the accident was minimal due to his arthritic condition and therefore, the award to Mrs. Blansit was excessive. Under Louisiana law loss of right of performance and material services is one of the elements of consortium for which a plaintiff may recover. *Finley* v. *Bass*, 478 So.2d 608 (La.App. 2d Cir. 1985). The trial court specifically found, as a result of the accident, Mr. Blansit could no longer perform household chores, rake leaves or shop for groceries. This constitutes a loss of right to material service for which Mrs. Blansit was entitled to recover and for which the trial court's award was not excessive.

AFFIRMED.

Kauffmann v. *Royal Orleans, Inc.*

216 So.2d 394 (La.1968)

JOHNSON, Judge.

This plaintiff fell to the floor of the restaurant called the Rib Room operated by defendant, The Royal Orleans, Inc. She filed this suit against the hotel and its public liability insurer for alleged personal injury damages. After trial the Civil

District Court for the Parish of Orleans rendered judgment for the defendants and the plaintiff has appealed.

On December 30, 1964, the plaintiff took her cousin, Mrs. Pearla Schwartz, and Mrs. Schwartz's two young grandsons to The Royal Orleans Hotel to have lunch in the Rib Room. All tables were occupied when they arrived. After they had waited some thirty minutes, the headwaiter, Hans Mueller, went to the cocktail lounge to tell Mrs. Kauffmann that a table was available, and he led Mrs. Kauffmann to the table. With Mr. Mueller in the lead, followed closely by Mrs. Kauffmann, they were walking between the other tables occupied by other patrons toward the table where Mrs. Kauffmann and her guests were to sit. When Mr. Mueller reached the table, he turned to pull out a chair to seat Mrs. Kauffmann. Right at that instant, Mrs. Kauffmann fell to the floor alongside her table. Mrs. Kauffmann described her fall by saying that the waiter was leading her to the table and she stepped on a piece of orange or lemon peel and "my legs just slipped from under me and I fell, and I was in a sitting position when I realized that I was down." She did not see the peel until after she fell. She said it was on the floor close to her right side. She was given assistance to get up, after which she sat at the table and had lunch with her guests. After lunch, she took her guests to the Steamer President on the Mississippi River for a boat ride in the afternoon. Mrs. Kauffmann said she and Mr. Mueller were walking between other tables and she thinks she could have touched the other tables as she walked along. She would not exactly describe the space where they walked as an aisle. At first she testified that she slipped on the peel, but when asked how she could be certain about it she answered: "Because I slid on it and it was there and it was the only thing." When she saw the peel, it was by her side and not at her feet.

Mr. Mueller testified that the lunch hour started at 11:30 A.M., when the floors were cleaned and then inspected by him and the housekeeper, at which time the peel was not on the floor. He said the peel could not have been on the floor for any period of time because he walked back and forth over that area many times and if it had been there he would have picked it up; that all the waiters are instructed to watch out for foreign material on the floor; that if anything is found they must pick it up; that a busboy is always assigned to constantly check for such objects and, if any appear, to clean them up during the meal period; that when he was assisting Mrs. Kauffmann to get up, he saw a very small piece of orange or lemon peel close beside her and that it was fresh in appearance. Other employees of the hotel described the system followed to clean and keep the floors clean of foreign objects, and the instructions given the waiters and busboys, who keep close watch on the floor for any object that should not be there; but, on this occasion, none had been found and none reported to them. Some of these witnesses had started employment there after this occasion, but their explanations were the same as those who were working there on that day.

Mrs. Schwartz testified by deposition that she did not see Mrs. Kauffmann fall because she and her grandsons were not following Mr. Mueller and Mrs. Kauffmann to the table, though Mr. Mueller said Mrs. Kauffmann and her whole party were following him to the table.

Counsel for plaintiff wrote in his brief that the captain, meaning the headwaiter, Hans Mueller, testified that Mrs. Kauffmann "slipped and fell on an orange or lemon peel." Mr. Mueller did not say that, but only said that after the fall, he saw the piece of peel in the vicinity of where she fell.

We quite agree with the argument of counsel for plaintiff that Mrs. Kauffmann had every reason to believe that the headwaiter would not conduct her through an aisle that was dangerous or on which there was some foreign object on which she might slip and fall. We will add that this would be true if Mr. Mueller knew of the presence of such an object or had any reason to suspect that the object was on the floor. That argument does not relieve plaintiff of the burden of proving there was negligence on the part of any hotel employee in carelessly dropping the foreign object on the floor, or that the employee had actual knowledge that such an object was on the floor at the time, or, if the employees had no actual knowledge of the object being on the floor, that the object had gotten on the floor by some other means and had been there long enough to constitute constructive notice or knowledge of its presence. We also agree that Mrs. Kauffmann was not required under these circumstances to keep her eyes constantly on the floor when she was following the headwaiter on that occasion.

In many decisions by appellate courts in many slip and fall cases in this state, it has been held that each case must be judged on the facts of that particular case. The issue before this court now is: Do these facts prove that the hotel employees failed to exercise reasonable care in the hotel's floor cleaning and inspection system, and did Mrs. Kauffmann slip on a foreign object, the presence of which on the floor the employees had actual or constructive knowledge?

We find that the testimony in our case is convincing that the hotel employees were instructed to keep the floors free of any foreign objects, and that the system followed in the Rib Room was sufficient to enable the court to find and hold that the premises were kept in a reasonably safe condition. There is no evidence that the waiters, busboys, and porters did not perform the duties assigned them. The time lapse between observations and inspections of the floor make it reasonable to assume that the small piece of peel found on the floor could have been there only a very short time, probably only a very few minutes or few seconds. No one had seen it, and we believe that there was no knowledge or notice of it and there was no negligence proven on the part of these employees. We are not even sure that Mrs. Kauffmann's foot slipped on the peel. It was not near her feet and it still had a fresh appearance. If her foot had slipped on it, it is most likely that it would have been crushed....

Counsel for the defendant has correctly and concisely stated the principles of law that support our findings against the plaintiff in this case, as follows:

"Plaintiff has failed to carry burden of proof; plaintiff has failed to show that the alleged extraneous substance on the floor of the Rib Room of The Royal Orleans was placed there by the owner or one of his employees, or if placed by someone else, that the owner or his employees had actual knowledge of the presence of the substance or that it had remained in such a position of danger for such a length of time that the owner or his employees should have had knowledge of the presence of the substance."

Counsel has cited a number of decisions that adhere to these principles. Some of the cases he cites contain facts that do not bring those cases in line with the present case.

Of course we have here again, as in many, many cases of all types, that there has been no showing that the trial court committed manifest error in its factual and legal determination. The only decision we can make is to affirm the trial court.

Ruling of the Court: For these reasons, the judgment appealed from is affirmed with costs to be paid by plaintiff.

Kiefel v. Las Vegas Hacienda, Inc.

404 F.2d 1163 (7th Cir. 1968)
cert. denied 395 U.S. 908 (1969).

Before HASTINGS, FAIRCHILD and KERNER, Circuit Judges.
KERNER, Circuit Judge.

* * *

Plaintiff-appellee Kiefel and her husband purchased a package air travel and hotel plan to Las Vegas in February, 1962. They were lodged in Room 315 of the Las Vegas Hacienda. On the evening and morning of February 28-March 1, 1962, plaintiff and her husband visited three night club shows and consumed several drinks. Returning to their hotel, another drink was had at the bar and plaintiff went off to their room to bed, while her husband remained in the casino stating he remained there until 6:30 A.M. Sometime before 5:20 A.M. someone entered Room 315 and attacked plaintiff, striking her on the head with a bottle of champagne, fracturing her skull and causing severe facial lacerations.

The complaint and amended complaint are founded in contract and tort for failure of defendant, Las Vegas Hacienda, to provide a reasonably safe sleeping room accommodation resulting in the personal injuries to plaintiff.

* * *

The primary issue raised by this appeal is whether the facts were sufficient in law to support the jury's verdict. The three particular questions asked by Hacienda are:

1. Was the lock actually forced open on the night of the occurrence?

2. Was the assailant an unknown intruder or might it have been Carl Kiefel, plaintiff's husband?

3. Did Donna Kiefel lock the door before going to bed, or did she leave it open for her husband?

The testimony in the record indicates the lock used on the door to room 315 was a Schlage lock, model A 51-PD. The projection of the bolt in the lock taken from the door is 3/8 of an inch. Witness James Busch, a master locksmith, testified the lock was defective, since there was 1/8 of an inch of play or 33 1/3% of the total length of the bolt. Additionally, there was testimony that the door was loose fitting and the cutting of the door for the installation of the lock was larger than necessary, allowing additional play of another 1/8 of an inch, leaving only 1/8 of an inch security in the lock. Daniel G. Olson, Schlage Lock Company representative, testified there was evidence of a "gouge" on the lock resulting in damage. The local police department was on the scene and in the course of the investigation noted there were fresh paint chips from the door and molding at the base of the lock and chips on the floor at the door entry to the room "that appeared to be of the same type of paint that was present on the door and door jamb and appeared to be relatively fresh." The police report recorded that "upon closer examination noted the door had recently been shimmed."

Additionally, on the night of the incident, travelers checks were reported stolen from Donna Kiefel's purse which was in the room when the assault occurred. These checks were located by the police the following day and were determined to have been forged and cashed at a hotel several blocks from the Hacienda by an unknown person.

All of this information was before the jury through exhibits, depositions, and examination and cross-examination of the witnesses. There was adequate latitude allowed by the trial court for the defense to raise the questions of fact now placed before this court as well as the tactical interplay by defense counsel. The jury found the factual questions in favor of the plaintiff and there are adequate grounds for its so finding.

* * *

We perceive no error in the other objections raised by Hacienda.

The judgment on the verdict and the order taxing costs are hereby affirmed. Affirmed.

Wassell v. Adams

865 F.2d 849 (7th Cir.1989)

POSNER, Circuit Judge.

The plaintiff, born Susan Marisconish, grew up on Macaroni Street in a small town in a poor coal-mining region of Pennsylvania—a town so small and obscure that it has no name. She was the ninth of ten children, and as a child was sexually abused by her stepfather. After graduating from high school she worked briefly as a nurse's aide, then became engaged to Michael Wassell, also from Pennsylvania. Michael joined the Navy in 1985 and was sent to Great Lakes Naval Training Station, just north of Chicago, for basic training. He and Susan had decided to get married as soon as he completed basic training. The graduation was scheduled for a Friday. Susan, who by now was 21 years old, traveled to Chicago with Michael's parents for the graduation. The three checked into a double room at the Ron-Ric motel, near the base, on the Thursday (September 22, 1985) before graduation. The Ron-Ric is a small and inexpensive motel that caters to the families of sailors at the Great Lakes Naval Training Station a few blocks to the east. The motel has 14 rooms and charges a maximum of $36 a night for a double room. The motel was owned by Wilbur and Florena Adams, the defendants in the case.

Four blocks to the west of the Ron-Ric motel is a high-crime area: murder, prostitution, robbery, drugs—the works. The Adamses occasionally warned women guests not to walk alone in the neighborhood at night. They did not warn the Wassells or Susan.

Susan spent Friday night with Michael at another motel. On Saturday the Wassells checked out and left for Pennsylvania, and at the Wassells' suggestion Susan moved from the double room that she had shared with them to a single room in the Ron-Ric. Michael spent Saturday night with her but had to return to the base on Sunday for several days. She remained to look for an apartment where they could live after they were married (for he was scheduled to remain at the base after completing basic training). She spent most of Sunday in her room reading the newspaper and watching television. In the evening she went to look at an apartment.

Upon returning to her room at the motel, she locked the door, fastened the chain, and went to bed. She fell into a deep sleep, from which she was awakened by a knock on the door. She turned on a light and saw by the clock built into the television set that it was 1:00 A.M. She went to the door and looked through the peephole but saw no one. Next to the door was a pane of clear glass. She did not look through it. The door had two locks plus a chain. She unlocked the door and opened it all the way, thinking that Michael had come from the base and, not wanting to wake her, was en route to the Adamses' apartment to fetch a key to the room. It was not Michael at the door. It was a respectably dressed black man whom Susan had never seen before. He asked for "Cindy" (maybe "Sidney," she thought later). She told him there was no Cindy there. Then he asked for a glass of water. She went to the bathroom, which was at the other end of the room, about 25 feet from the door (seems far—but that was the testimony), to fetch the glass of water. When she came out of the bathroom, the man was sitting at the table in the room. (The room had a screen door as well as a solid door, but the screen door had not been latched.) He took the water but said it wasn't cold enough. He also said he had no money, and Susan remarked that she had $20 in her car. The man went into the bathroom to get a colder glass of water. Susan began to get nervous. She was standing between the bathroom and the door of her room. She hid her purse, which contained her car keys and $800 in cash that Michael had given her. There was no telephone in the room. There was an alarm attached to the television set, which would be activated if someone tried to remove the set, but she had not been told and did not know about the alarm, although a notice of the alarm was posted by the set. The parking lot on which the motel rooms opened was brightly lit by floodlights.

A few tense minutes passed after the man entered the bathroom. He poked his head out of the doorway and asked Susan to join him in the bathroom, he wanted to show her something. She refused. After a while he emerged from the bathroom—naked from the waist down. Susan fled from the room, and beat on the door of the adjacent room. There was no response. The man ran after her and grabbed her. She screamed, but no one appeared. The motel had no security guard; the Adamses lived in a basement apartment at the other end of the motel and did not hear her screams.

The man covered Susan's mouth and dragged her back to her room. There he gagged her with a wash cloth. He raped her at least twice (once anally). These outrages occupied more than an hour. Eventually Susan persuaded the rapist to take a shower with her. After the shower, she managed to get out of the bathroom before he did, dress, and flee in her car. To save herself after the rapes, she had tried to convince him that she liked him, and had succeeded at least to the extent that his guard was down. The Adamses' lawyer tried halfheartedly to show that she had consented to the rapes, but backed off from this position in closing argument.

The rapist was never prosecuted; a suspect was caught but Susan was too upset to identify him. There had been a rape at the motel several years previously (a sailor had opened the door of his room to two men who said they were "the management," and the men raped his wife). There had also been a robbery, and an incident in which an intruder kicked in the door to one of the rooms. These were the only serious crimes committed during the seven years that the Adamses owned the motel.

Susan married Michael, but the rape had induced posttrauma stress that has, according to her testimony and that of a psychologist testifying as her expert witness, blighted her life. She brought this suit against the Adamses on January 21, 1986. It is a diversity suit that charges the Adamses with negligence in failing to warn Susan or take other precautions to protect her against the assault. The substantive issues are governed by the law of Illinois. A jury composed of four women and three men found that the Adamses had indeed been negligent and that their negligence had been a proximate cause of the assault, and the jury assessed Susan's damages at $850,000, which was the figure her lawyer had requested in closing argument. But in addition the jury found that Susan had been negligent too—and indeed that her negligence had been 97 percent to blame for the attack and the Adamses' only 3 percent. So, following the approach to comparative negligence laid down in *Alvis* v. *Ribar,* 85 Ill.2d 1, 52 Ill.Dec. 23, 421 N.E.2d 886 (1981)—the decision in which the Supreme Court of Illinois abolished the common law rule that contributory negligence is a complete bar to a negligence suit—the jury awarded Susan only $25,500 in damages. This happens to be approximately the midpoint of the psychologist's estimate—$20,000 to $30,000—of the expense of the therapy that the psychologist believes Susan may need for her post-traumatic stress.

Susan's lawyer asked the district judge to grant judgment in her favor notwithstanding the verdict, on the ground either that she had been nonnegligent as a matter of law or that her negligence was immaterial because the Adamses had been not merely negligent but willful and wanton in their disregard for her safety. In the alternative, counsel asked the judge to grant a new trial on the ground that the jury's apportionment of negligence was contrary to the manifest weight of the evidence. There were other grounds for the motion, but they have been abandoned. The judge denied the motion, and Susan appeals.

Had she filed her suit after November 25, 1986, she could not have recovered any damages, assuming the jury would have made the same apportionment of responsibility between her and the Adamses. Illinois' new comparative negligence statute (Ill.Rev.Stat. ch. 110, ¶ 2-1116; see also ¶ 2-1107.1) bars recovery in negligence (or strict liability product) cases in which the plaintiff's "fault... is more than 50% of the proximate cause of the injury or damage for which recovery is sought." But as her suit was filed before that date, the new statute is inapplicable. See Ill.Rev.Stat. ch. 34, ¶ 429.7 Historical Note.

Susan Wassell's counsel argues that the jury's verdict "reflected a chastened, hardened, urban mentality—that lurking behind every door is evil and danger, even if the guest is from a small town unfamiliar with the area." He takes umbrage at the defendant's argument that Susan's "antennae" should have been alerted when she didn't see anyone through the peephole. He rejects the metaphor, remarking unexceptionably that human beings do not have antennae and that this case is not a Kafka story about a person who turned into an insect (i.e., is not *The Metamorphosis*). He points out that a person awakened from a deep sleep is not apt to be thinking clearly and that once Susan opened the door the fat was in the fire—if she had slammed the door in the rapist's face he might have kicked the door in, as had happened once before at this motel, although she didn't know that at the time. The Adamses' counsel argued to the jury (perhaps with the wisdom of hindsight) that Susan's "tragic mistake" was failing to flee when the man entered the bathroom. Susan's counsel insists that Susan was not negligent at all but that, if she was, she was at most 5 percent responsible for the catastrophe, which, he argues, could have been averted costlessly by a simple warning from the Adamses. To this the Adamses' counsel replies absurdly that a warning *would* have been costly—it might have scared guests away! The loss of business from telling the truth is not a social loss; it is a social gain.

The common law refused to compare the plaintiff's and the defendant's negligence. See 4 Harper, James & Gray, The Law of Torts § 22.1 (1986). The negligent plaintiff could recover nothing, unless the defendant's culpability was of a higher degree than simple negligence. See *id.*, §§ 22.5, 22.6, and the discussion of "degrees" of negligence in *Alvis* v. *Ribar, supra,* 85 Ill.2d at 9-10, 52 Ill.Dec. at 26-27, 421 N.E.2d at 889-90. Susan argues that the defendants were willful and wanton, which, she says, would make her negligence as irrelevant under a regime of comparative negligence as it would be in a jurisdiction in which contributory negligence was still a complete defense. See *id.,* 85 Ill.2d at 10, 52 Ill.Dec. at 27, 421 N.E.2d at 890; 4 Harper, James & Gray, *supra*, § 22.6.

Both the premise (that the Adamses were willful and wanton) and the conclusion (that if so, her own negligence was irrelevant) are wrong. As we guessed in *Davis* v. *United States,* 716 F.2d 418, 429 (7th Cir.1983), that it would, Illinois appears to be lining up with the states that allow the plaintiff's simple negligence to be compared with the defendant's "willful and wanton conduct," see *State Farm Mutual Automobile Ins. Co.* v. *Mendenhall,* 164 Ill.App.3d 58, 115 Ill.Dec. 139, 517 N.E.2d 341 (1987); see also *Bofman* v. *Material Service Corp.,* 125 Ill.App.3d 1053, 81 Ill.Dec. 262, 466 N.E.2d 1064 (1984); *Soucie* v. *Drago Amusements Co.,* 145 Ill.App.3d 348, 99 Ill.Dec. 262, 495 N.E.2d 997 (1986). We say "appears to be" because only *Mendenhall* discusses the issue and it is not a decision of the Illinois Supreme Court, and because a critical premise of the decision may be shaky. That is the proposition that "willful and wanton" under Illinois law denotes merely a heightened form of negligence, so that there is only a small difference between simple negligence and willful and wanton misconduct despite the ominous sound of the words "willful" and "wanton." See 164 Ill.App.3d at 61, 115 Ill.Dec. at 141-42, 517 N.E.2d at 343-44; *Davis* v. *United States, supra,* 716 F.2d at 425-27. As we noted in *Davis,* there are two lines of "willful and wanton" decisions in Illinois. One, which seemed to be in the ascendancy when we wrote *Davis,* and is the position taken in section 342 of the Second Restatement of Torts (1965), indeed regards "willful and wanton" as merely a heightened form of "negligent." Section 342 requires only that the defendant "knows *or has to reason to know* of the [dangerous condition of his premises] and *should* realize that it involves an unreasonable risk of harm" (emphasis added). But the cases since *Davis* appear to have swung round to the narrower concept, under which willful and wanton conduct denotes "conscious disregard for . . . the safety of others," *Rabel* v. *Illinois Wesleyan University,* 161 Ill.App.3d 348, 356, 112 Ill.Dec. 889, 895, 514 N.E.2d 552, 558 (1987), or "knowledge that [the defendant's] conduct posed a high probability of serious physical harm to others." *Albers* v. *Community Consolidated #204 School,* 155 Ill.App.3d 1083, 1085, 108 Ill.Dec. 675, 677, 508 N.E.2d 1252, 1254 (1987). See also *Soucie* v. *Drago Amusements Co., supra,* 145 Ill.App.3d at 352, 99 Ill.Dec. at 264, 495 N.E.2d at 999. These formulations come close to—perhaps duplicate—the standard of recklessness that we limned in *Duckworth* v. *Franzen,* 780 F.2d 645, 652 (7th Cir.1985), a prisoners' suit involving a claim that reckless disregard for prisoners' safety violates the Eighth Amendment's prohibition against cruel and unusual punishments. *Bresland* v. *Ideal Roller & Graphics Co.,* 150 Ill.App.3d 445, 457, 103 Ill.Dec. 513, 522, 501 N.E.2d 830, 839 (1986), describes willful and wanton misconduct as "so close to . . . intentional misconduct that a party found liable on that basis should not be able to obtain contribution [from his joint tortfeasors]."

If the more recent formulations are authoritative, this would undermine the argument in *Davis* and *Mendenhall* for allowing a plaintiff's simple negligence to be compared with a defendant's willful and wanton misconduct. But it would not help Susan Wassell win her case. No rational jury could find that the Adamses *consciously* disregarded a *high* probability of serious physical harm. Cf. *Doe* v. *United States*, 718 F.2d 1039 (11th Cir.1983). If the laxer version of "willful and wanton" is used, Susan's argument against permitting the jury to compare her culpability with that of the Adamses falls, yet she might seem in that event to have a powerful fallback position. The laxer the standard for "willful and wanton," the stronger the inference that the Adamses *were* willful and wanton—and if so, surely Susan's own negligence was not so great as to outweigh theirs by a factor of more than 30. But as we shall see in a moment, the defendants' negligence in this case was at most simple, not aggravated, negligence. Indeed, the jury may not have thought the defendants negligent at all.

The district judge was right to deny Susan's request for judgment notwithstanding the verdict. But was he right to deny her request for a new trial? This court treats the question as one of federal law, even in a diversity case. *Davlan* v. *Otis Elevator Co.*, 816 F.2d 287, 289 (7th Cir.1987); see also *Abernathy* v. *Superior Hardwoods, Inc.*, 704 F.2d 963, 971 (7th Cir.1983). And the federal standard is that "a new trial can be granted only when the jury's verdict is against the clear weight of the evidence," *Davlan* v. *Otis Elevator Co., supra,* 816 F.2d at 289, and we can reverse only when persuaded that in applying this standard the district judge abused his discretion, *id.*; see also *Foster* v. *Continental Can Corp.*, 783 F.2d 731, 735 (7th Cir.1986); *Babb* v. *Minder*, 806 F.2d 749, 752 (7th Cir.1986). The Illinois approach to these questions is similar. See, e.g., *Lowe* v. *Kang*, 167 Ill.App.3d 772, 782, 118 Ill.Dec. 552, 558, 521 N.E.2d 1245, 1251 (1988); *Mazikoske* v. *Fire-stone Tire & Rubber Co.*, 149 Ill.App.3d 166, 181-82, 102 Ill.Dec. 729, 739, 500 N.E.2d 622, 632 (1986); *Junker* v. *Ziegler*, 113 Ill.2d 332, 339-40, 101 Ill.Dec. 627, 630, 498 N.E.2d 1135, 1138 (1986); *Ford* v. *City of Chicago*, 132 Ill.App.3d 408, 412-13, 87 Ill.Dec. 240, 244, 476 N.E.2d 1232, 1236 (1985). So Susan has a tough row to hoe to get the district court's refusal to grant her a new trial reversed.

The old common law rule barring the contributorily negligent plaintiff from recovering *any* damages came eventually to seem too harsh. That is why it has been changed in most jurisdictions, including Illinois. It was harsh, all right, at least if one focuses narrowly on the plight of individual plaintiffs, but it was also simple and therefore cheap to administer. The same cannot be said for comparative negligence, which far from being simple requires a formless, unguided inquiry, because there is no methodology for comparing the causal contributions of the plaintiff's and of the defendant's negligence to the plaintiff's injury. In this case, either the plaintiff or the defendants could have avoided that injury. It is hard to say more, but the statute requires more—yet without giving the finder of facts any guidance as to how to make the apportionment.

We have suggested in previous cases, such as *Davis* v. *United States, supra,* 716 F.2d at 429, that one way to make sense of comparative negligence is to assume that the required comparison is between the respective costs to the plaintiff and to the defendant of avoiding the injury. If each could have avoided it at the same cost, they are each 50 percent responsible for it. According to this method of comparing negligence, the jury found that Susan could have avoided the attack at a cost of less than one thirty-second the cost to the Adamses. Is this possible?

It is careless to open a motel or hotel door in the middle of the night without trying to find out who is knocking. Still, people aren't at their most alert when they are awakened in the middle of the night, and it wasn't crazy for Susan to assume that Michael had returned without telling her, even though he had said he would be spending the night at the base. So it cannot be assumed that the cost—not to her (although her testimony suggests that she is not so naive or provincial as her lawyer tried to convince the jury she was), but to the reasonable person who found himself or herself in her position, for that is the benchmark in determining plaintiff's as well as defendant's negligence, see, e.g., *Blacconeri* v. *Aguayo*, 132 Ill.App.3d 984, 988, 88 Ill.Dec. 231, 234-35, 478 N.E.2d 546, 549-50 (1985); 4 Harper, James & Gray, *supra*, § 22.10, at pp. 334-38—was zero, or even that it was slight. As innkeepers (in the increasingly quaint legal term), the Adamses had a duty to exercise a high degree of care to protect their guests from assaults on the motel premises. See, e.g., *McCarty* v. *Pheasant Run, Inc.*, 826 F.2d 1554, 1558 (7th Cir.1987) (Illinois law); *Yamada* v. *Hilton Hotel Corp.*, 60 Ill.App.3d 101, 112, 17 Ill.Dec. 228, 237, 376 N.E.2d 227, 236 (1977); *Mrzlak* v. *Ettinger*, 25 Ill.App.3d 706, 712, 323 N.E.2d 796, 800 (1975); *Fortney* v. *Hotel Rancroft, Inc.*, 5 Ill.App.2d 327, 125 N.E.2d 544, 546, 548 (1955); *Peters* v. *Holiday Inns, Inc.*, 89 Wis.2d 115, 278 N.W.2d 208 (1979). And the cost to the Adamses of warning all their female guests of the dangers of the neighborhood would have been negligible. Surely a warning to Susan would not have cost the Adamses 32 times the cost to her of schooling herself to greater vigilance.

But this analysis is incomplete. It is unlikely that a warning would have averted the attack. Susan testified that she thought the man who had knocked on the door was her fiance. Thinking this, she would have opened the door no matter how dangerous she believed the neighborhood to be. The warning that was not given might have deterred her from walking alone in the neighborhood. But that was not the pertinent danger. Of course, if the Adamses had told her not to open her door in the middle of the night under any circumstances without carefully ascertaining who was trying to enter the room, this would have been a pertinent warning and might have had an effect. But it is absurd to think that hoteliers are required to give so *obvious* a warning, any more than they must warn guests not to stick their fingers into the electrical outlets. Everyone, or at least the average person, knows better than to open his or her door to a stranger in the middle of the night. The problem was not that Susan thought that she *should* open her bedroom door in the middle of the night to anyone who knocked, but that she wasn't thinking clearly. A warning would not have availed against a temporary, sleep-induced lapse.

Giving the jury every benefit of the doubt, as we are required to do especially in a case such as this where the jury was not asked to render either a special verdict or a general verdict with answers to written interrogatories (Fed.R.Civ.P. 49), we must assume that the jury was not so muddle-headed as to believe that the Adamses' negligence consisted in failing to give a futile warning. Rather, we must assume that the jury thought the Adamses' negligence consisted in failing to have a security guard, or telephones in each room, or alarms designed to protect the motel's patrons rather than just the owners' television sets. (The Adamses did, however, have an informal agreement with the local police that the police would cruise through the parking lot of the Ron-Ric whenever they drove down the street at night—and this was maybe three or four times a night.) The only one of these omitted precautions for which there is a cost figure in the record was the security guard. A guard would have cost $50 a night. That is almost $20,000 a year. This is not an enormous number. The plaintiff suggests that it would have been even lower because the guard would have been needed only on busy nights.

But the evidence was in conflict on whether the Sunday night after a Friday graduation, which is the night that Susan was attacked, was a busy night. And the need for a security guard would seem to be greater, the less busy rather than the busier the motel; if there had been someone in the room adjacent to Susan's, she might have been saved from her ordeal. In any event the cost of the security guard, whether on all nights or just on busy nights—or just on unbusy nights— might be much greater than the monetary equivalent of the greater vigilance on the part of Susan that would have averted the attack.

The assumption that the jury was clear-thinking and instruction-abiding is artificial, of course. During its deliberations, the jury sent the judge a question about the duty to warn (the judge did not answer it). This is some indication that the jury thought that the Adamses' negligence consisted in failing to warn Susan. But it is equally plausible that the jury didn't think the Adamses were negligent at all toward Susan, but, persuaded that she had suffered terribly, wanted to give her a token recovery. Concern with sympathy verdicts appears to lie behind Illinois' new statute barring the plaintiff from recovering any damages if he is more than 50 percent negligent. "The adoption of the pure comparative negligence doctrine [the doctrine, adopted in *Alvis* v. *Ribar*, that allows the plaintiff to recover something however great his negligence was relative to the defendant's] was thought to have increased a plaintiff's chances for winning at trial from about 50% to 60%, even though at the same time it tended to reduce the amount of the damage awards made at trial." Smith-Hurd Ill.Ann.Stat. ch. 110, ¶ 2-1116 Historical Note. It may be more than coincidence that the jury awarded Susan just enough money to allow her to undertake the recommended course of psychological therapy. We are not supposed to speculate about the jury's reasoning process, see, e.g., Fed.R.Evid. 606(b), and we have just seen that it would not necessarily strengthen Susan's case if we did. The issue for us is not whether this jury was rational and law-abiding but whether a rational jury could, consistently with the evidence, have returned the verdict that this jury did.

If we were the trier of fact, persuaded that both parties were negligent and forced to guess about the relative costs to the plaintiff and to the defendants of averting the assault, we would assess the defendants' share at more than 3 percent. But we are not the trier of fact, and are authorized to upset the jury's apportionment only if persuaded that the trial judge abused his discretion in determining that the jury's verdict was not against the clear weight of the evidence. We are not so persuaded. It seems probably wrong to us, but we have suggested an interpretation of the evidence under which the verdict was consistent with the evidence and the law. And that is enough to require us to uphold the district judge's refusal to set aside the verdict.

AFFIRMED.

Orlando Executive Park, Inc.* v. *P.D.R.

402 So.2d 442 (Fla. Dist. Ct. App. 1981)

ORFINGER, Judge.

In an action for damages brought by appellee against the appellants, Orlando Executive Park, Inc. (OEP), and Howard Johnson Company (HJ), the jury returned a verdict for the appellee in the amount of $750,000 as compensatory damages against both defendants jointly, and awarded punitive damages in the amount of $500,000 against each defendant separately. Upon defendants' post-trial motions for directed verdict, the trial judge directed verdicts in favor of the defendants on the punitive damage claims, but denied a motion for new trial, remittitur or directed verdict on the claim for compensatory damages. The defendants have appealed the final judgment for compensatory damages, and the plaintiff has cross-appealed the order directing verdict on the punitive damage claim.

The factual circumstances giving rise to this litigation, viewed in the light most favorable to the plaintiff, follow: Plaintiff, a 33-year-old married woman, and the mother of a small child, was employed as a supervisor for a restaurant chain. Her duties required that she travel occasionally to Orlando and because of the distance from her home, she stayed overnight in the Orlando area on those occasions.

On October 22, 1975, she was in Orlando performing the duties of her employment. She telephoned the Howard Johnson's Motor Lodge involved in this action at approximately 9:30 P.M. and made a room reservation.[1] Approximately ten minutes later she left the restaurant and drove directly to the motor lodge. When she arrived, she signed the registration form which had already been filled out by the desk clerk and was directed to her room which was located on the ground level in building "A," the first building behind the registration office. Plaintiff parked her car, went to her room and left her suitcase there. She then went back to her car to get some papers and when starting back to her room, she noticed a man standing in a walkway behind the registration office. Having reentered the building and while proceeding back along the interior hallway to her room, she was accosted by the man she had seen behind the registration office, who struck her very hard in the throat and on the back of her neck and then choked her until she became unconscious. When consciousness returned, plaintiff found herself lying on the floor of the hallway with her assailant sitting on top of her, grabbing her throat. Plaintiff was physically unable to speak and lapsed into an unconscious or semi-conscious state. Her assailant stripped her jewelry from her and then dragged her down the hallway to a place beneath a secluded stairwell, where he kicked her and brutally forced her to perform an unnatural sex act. He then disappeared in the night and has never been identified.

Plaintiff's action for damages was based on her claim that defendants owed her the legal duty to exercise reasonable care for her safety while she was a guest on the premises. And she alleged that this duty had been breached by, *inter alia,* allowing the building to remain open and available to anyone who cared to enter, by failing to have adequate security on the premises either on the night in question or prior thereto so as to deter criminal activity against guests which had occurred before and which could foreseeably occur again, failing to install TV monitoring equipment in the public areas of the motel to deter criminal activity, failing to establish and enforce standards of operation at the lodge which would protect guests from physical attack and theft of property, and failure to warn

---

[1] She had stayed at this same motor lodge approximately one week earlier. Arrangements had been made for the billing of her room charges directly to her employer.

plaintiff that there had been prior criminal activity on the premises and that such activity would or might constitute a threat to her safety on the premises.

There was evidence submitted tending to show serious physical and psychological injury as a result of this assault which was susceptible of the conclusion that within a year following the assault, plaintiff lost her job because of memory lapses, mental confusion and inability to tolerate and communicate with people. There was evidence from which the jury could conclude that this injury was permanent and that she would require expensive, long-term medical and psychiatric treatment, and that she had suffered a great loss in her earning capacity.

The motor lodge is a part of a large complex known as "Howard Johnson's Plaza" located just off Interstate 4. The complex includes a Howard Johnson's Restaurant, the Howard Johnson's Motor Lodge, a pub, an adult theater, and five office buildings. The motor lodge contains approximately three hundred guest rooms in six separate buildings, plus a registration office, and it was owned and operated by defendant Orlando Executive Park, Inc., under a license agreement with the parent company, Howard Johnson Company. The restaurant, the pub and the adult theater on the property were operated by the defendant, Howard Johnson Company. Approximately 75% of the Howard Johnson motor lodges throughout the country are owned and operated by licensees. The Howard Johnson Company never established any standards or procedures to be followed by licensees relating to the matter of guest security, although it has established such procedures for the lodges which it owns and operates. Each licensee handled that problem as it deemed best.

There was no regular security force at the motor lodge, nor were there other security devices such as TV monitors in hallways or other common areas. One security guard was employed from time to time, on a sporadic basis. For the six-month period prior to the incident in question, management of the motor lodge was aware of approximately thirty criminal incidents occurring on the premises. While most of these involved burglary, some of them involved direct attacks upon the guests. Following one of the attacks, approximately ten weeks prior to the incident in question, the motor lodge owners had hired a full-time security guard, but he was terminated a short time later. Anticipating high occupancy, one security guard had been employed for the evening in question commencing at 10:00 P.M. While it is not clear whether the attack occurred during the period this guard was on duty, the jury could have concluded that he was not on duty at the time, although he was on the premises becoming familiar with the layout because he had never been on the property before. Additionally, the evidence indicated that the guard had been employed to patrol the parking areas, and not the motor lodge buildings. The security service which provided the guards from time to time, had recommended the employment of two to three guards on a full-time basis. Plaintiff's security expert testified that three guards on staggered shifts would be necessary to deter criminal activity, although he agreed that there were no industry standards for security guards and that it was impossible to say that the assault would not have occurred if three guards had been on the premises. He did, however, testify that in his opinion, a proper security force would serve as a deterrent to this type of activity and the chance of this happening would be slight.

I. LIABILITY OF ORLANDO EXECUTIVE PARK, INC.

It seems clear in Florida registered guests in a hotel or motel are business invitees to whom the hotel or motel owes a duty of reasonable care for their safety. *Phillips Petroleum Company of Bartlesville, Oklahoma v. Dorn,* 292 So.2d 429 (Fla. 4th DCA 1974). While recognizing this principle and conceding this duty, appellants say, nevertheless, that there is no evidence of a breach of their duty, since the injury to appellee was caused by the criminal act of a stranger, thus acting as an intervening efficient cause for which they are not responsible.

The evidence clearly shows numerous criminal activities on the premises in the six-month period immediately prior to this occurrence.[2] The testimony of a security expert produced by plaintiff indicated adequate security at this motor lodge required the presence of at least three full-time security guards. Thus the question becomes one of foreseeability. Could a jury, under the facts of this case reasonably conclude that the absence of adequate security would lead to the robbery and attack here?[3] Such is ordinarily a question for the jury. *Rosier v. Gainesville Inns Associates, Ltd.,* 347 So.2d 1100 (Fla. 1st DCA 1977).

* * *

We first reject, as entirely fallacious, the defendant's claim that the brutal and deliberate act of the rapist-murderer constituted an "independent intervening cause" which served to insulate it from liability. It is well-established that if the reasonable possibility of the intervention, criminal or otherwise, of a third party is the avoidable risk of harm which itself causes one to be deemed negligent, the occurrence of that very conduct cannot be a superseding cause of a subsequent misadventure. As said in *Restatement (Second) of Torts,* § 449 (1965):

> If the likelihood that a third person may act in a particular manner is the hazard or one of the hazards which makes the actor negligent, such an act whether innocent, negligent, intentionally tortious, or *criminal* does not prevent the actor from being liable for harm caused thereby (emphasis supplied).

* * *

See also, W. Prosser, Torts, supra, Section 44, at 275, nn. 20-21. The application of this principle to the case at bar is obvious. *Since Mt. Zion is liable, if at all, for only*

---

[2] Although aware of a formal request by plaintiff's attorneys to produce records of criminal incidents predating this six-month period, after the trial court ordered production of these records, defendant's agent admitted that she had ordered them to be destroyed. The court instructed the jury that they could infer from this action that the evidence suppressed would have been unfavorable to the party who destroyed it. While appellants appeal the giving of this instruction, we do not consider this point because it was not property preserved for review.

[3] This question, one of causation, should be distinguished from a plaintiff's initial burden of demonstrating a duty to take reasonable measures against foreseeable criminal activity. If the criminal activity is not foreseeable, no duty arises. See *Relyea v. State,* 385 Se.2d 1378 (Fla. 45th DCA 1980). Defendants in this case stipulated that they were on notice of criminal activity, admitting the duty to take reasonable measures against this type of attack.

failing to protect its tenant from a criminal attack, it cannot escape responsibility because the attack has actually taken place (emphasis supplied).

Id. at 101. In a suit for damages arising out of a robbery and rape in a hotel room, the court, in *Nordmann* v. *National Hotel Company*, 425 F.2d 1103 (5th Cir. 1970), summarized its holding thusly:

> The evidence was ample to support the jury's verdict. For its twelve hundred rooms, and with a large ball in progress, the hotel had on duty at the time of the robbery and assault only one security officer, one room clerk and one bell boy. The jury could, with reason, determine that the defendants had failed to perform their general duty to protect their guests.

Id. at 1107.

Appellant continues, however, with its argument that there was no evidence that security was inadequate or more to the point, that any specific quantity of security guards or other measures would have prevented this robbery and attack. They say that since there are no standards for security in the motel industry, there is no way for a jury to determine the reasonableness (or unreasonableness) of any particular security measure. The absence of industry standards does not insulate the defendants from liability when there is credible evidence presented to the jury pointing to measures reasonably available to deter incidents of this kind, against which the jury can judge the reasonableness of the measures taken in this case.

Obviously, a six-unit, one building "Mom and Pop" motel will not have the same security problems as a large highrise thousand room hotel, or of a three hundred room motor lodge spread out over six buildings. Each presents a peculiar security problem of its own. How the means necessary to fulfill the duty of care varies with the peculiar circumstances of each case is explained by the Wisconsin Supreme Court in *Peters* v. *Holiday Inns, Inc.*, 89 Wis.2d 115, 278 N.W.2d 208 (1979) in the following language which we approve:

> Thus, in meeting its standard of ordinary care a hotel must provide security commensurate with the facts and circumstances that are or should be apparent to the ordinarily prudent person. In other words, an innkeeper's standard of care in providing security will vary according to the particular circumstances and location of the hotel. Accordingly, as the degree of care that an innkeeper must exercise will vary in relation to the attendant circumstances, relevant factors in deciding whether a hotel has exercised ordinary care in providing adequate security are: industry standards, the community's crime rate, the extent of assaultive or criminal activity in the area or in similar business enterprises, the presence of suspicious persons, and the peculiar security problems posed by the hotel's design. A hotel's liability depends upon the danger to be apprehended and the presence or absence of security measures designed to meet the danger. The particular circumstances may require one or more of the following safety measures: a security force, closed circuit television surveillance, dead bolt and chain locks on the individual rooms as well as security doors on hotel entranceways removed from the lobby area.

Id. at 212. See also *Yamada* v. *Hilton Hotel Corporation*, 60 Ill. App.3d 101, 17 Ill. Dec. 228, 376 N.E.2d 227 (1977).

The reference to these standards is not to be interpreted as an opinion of this court that the absence of any of the mentioned security measures will result in a finding of liability of the innkeeper, because this is not the test. We only intend to say that the jury may consider competent evidence on the need or effect of any of these security mea-sures or combination thereof in the context of the circumstances and evidence before it, in determining whether the innkeeper has met his duty of providing his guest with reasonable protection for his safety.

Here, the jury had the right to consider the size and layout of the complex, its various accessory uses and the apparent ease of entrance into the motel buildings, and could have concluded that these factors required some security measures. They could also conclude from the evidence that the type of activity within the complex increased the security risk and that no security was provided at the time of this attack.

And while appellant suggests plaintiff was required to show the attack would have been prevented had reasonable measures been taken, this is not the test. Causation, like any other element of plaintiff's case, need not be demonstrated by conclusive proof:

> and it is enough that [plaintiff] introduces evidence from which reasonable men may conclude that it is more probable that the event was caused by the defendants, than that it was not. The fact of causation is incapable of mathematical proof, since no man can say with absolute certainty what would have occurred if the defendant had acted otherwise.

W. Prosser, *Law of Torts*, Section 41 at 242 (4th Ed. 1977).

Plaintiff adduced evidence that reasonable measures were not taken. Expert testimony, as well as reasonable inferences from the suggested measures, allowed a conclusion that the chance of this attack was "slight" had reasonable measures been taken. Thus the question of whether defendant's negligence was the proximate cause of plaintiff's injury was properly a jury question. [citations omitted]

Plaintiff also proved that the area under the stairwell where she was dragged was dark and secluded and was in itself a security hazard which should have been boarded up as had other similar stairwells in the motel. OEP management actively discouraged criminal investigations by sheriff's deputies, minimizing any deterrent effect they may have had. Thus, the totality of the circumstances presented a jury question regarding causation. See *Rosier* v. *Gainesville Inns. Assoc. Ltd.*[4] It cannot be said that there was a complete absence of probative facts to support the jury's conclusion. See *Yamada* v. *Hilton Hotel Corp.*, 17 Ill. Dec. at 233, 376 N.E.2d at 232.

* * *

II.   LIABILITY OF HOWARD JOHNSON COMPANY

Appellant Howard Johnson Company contends that the trial court erred in not granting its motion for directed verdict. Appellee proceeded against this appellant on the theory of apparent agency. Appellant argues strongly that the evidence fails to show any control or right of control by HJ over the operation of

---

[4] In agreeing that a jury question was presented on the security issue, the court re-stated the traditional rule on intervening cause:

> While the question of proximate cause in a negligence action is one for the court where there is an active and efficient intervening cause, *Nance* v. *James Archer Smith Hospital, Inc.*, 329 So.2d 377 (Fla.3d DCA 1976), still if such intervening cause is either foreseeable or might reasonably have been foreseen by the defendant, his negligence may be considered the proximate cause of the injury notwithstanding the intervening cause. 347 So.2d at 1102.

the motel, but while this argument may be relevant to a claim of *actual* agency, it has no relevance to the theory of *apparent* agency. Appellee sought damages against HJ solely on the *apparent* agency doctrine, and the jury was so instructed.

The doctrine of apparent agency, sometimes referred to as agency by estoppel, consists of three primary elements: (1) a representation by the principal; (2) reliance on that representation by a third person; and (3) a change of position by the third person in reliance upon such representation to his detriment. The principal is estopped to deny the authority of the agent, because he has permitted the appearance of authority in the agency and thereby justified the third party in relying on that appearance of authority as though it were actually conferred upon the agent. 2 Fla.Jur.2d, *Agency and Employment*, sec. 36 (1977).[5] Put another way,

> Where a principal has, by his voluntary act, placed an agent in such a situation that a person of ordinary prudence, conversant with business usages and the nature of the particular business, is justified in presuming that such agent has authority to perform a particular act, and therefore deals with the agent, the principal is estopped, as against such third person, from denying the agent's authority. [citations omitted]

* * *

HJ attacks the verdict of the jury by arguing that (1) there was insufficient evidence of representations by it, and (2) there was insufficient evidence of reliance by plaintiff. We will address both issues.

Appellant asserts that the only representations of HJ to be considered are the sign announcing the lodge as a "Howard Johnson's," and the distinctive color scheme. Appellant correctly points out that gas station signs alone do not make a gas station operator a general agent of the oil company. *Cawthon* v. *Phillips Petroleum Co.*, 124 So.2d 517 (Fla.2d DCA 1960). The reason for this is that it is common knowledge that gas station operators are independent contractors, and "these signs and emblems represent no more than notice to a motorist that a given company's products are being marketed at the station." *Coe* v. *Esau*, 377 P.2d 815 (Okl. 1963); *accord, Cawthon* v. *Phillips Petroleum Co.* Thus, the "representation" made by service station signs is only that a certain kind of gasoline is sold, not that the operator is an agent for the oil company with respect to any standard of service,[6] car repair,[7] or maintenance of premises.[8] In *Cawthon,* Phillips' advertisements (for products sold at "Phillips" gasoline stations) did not subject Phillips to liability for a station operator's negligent brake repair, because

> There appeared in the advertisement no statement that mechanical or repair services were solicited or offered by the oil company or its employees or agents; neither did the advertisement indicate agency.

---

[5] It is important to note that the doctrine rests on appearances created by the principal rather than on appearances created by the agent.

[6] *B.P. Oil Corp.* v. *Mabe*, 279 Md. 632, 370 A.2d 554 (1977) (operator negligently fills radiator).

[7] *Crittendon* v. *State Oil Co.*, 78 Ill. App.2d 112, 222 N.E.2d 561 (1966) (signs might allow belief that "State Oil" products are sold, but do not warrant assumption that station operator was agent in repairing and driving plaintiff's car).

[8] *Apple* v. *Standard Oil, Div. of American Oil Co.*, 307 F. Supp. 107 (N.D. Cal. 1969) (American Oil not liable when station operator's dog bites plaintiff).

124 So.2d at 521.

While OEP might not be HJ's agent for all purposes, the signs, national advertising, uniformity of building design and color schemes allow the public to assume that this and other similar motor lodges are under the same ownership.[9] A HJ official testified that it was the HJ marketing strategy to appear as a "chain that sells a product across the nation." Additionally, the license agreement between HJ and OEP clearly gives HJ the right to control the architectural design and the "standards of operation and service . . . and the licensee agrees at all times to conform to such standards."[10]

Florida had adopted section 267 of the *Restatement (Second) of Agency* (1958), which says:

> One who represents that another is his servant or other agent and thereby causes a third person justifiably to rely upon the skill of such apparent agent is subject to liability to the third person for harm caused by the lack of care or skill of one appearing to be a servant or other agent as if he were such...

See *Mercury Cab Owners Association* v. *Jones*, 79 So.2d 782 (Fla. 1955).

There was sufficient evidence for the jury to reasonably conclude that HJ represented to the traveling public that it could expect a particular level of service at a Howard Johnson Motor Lodge. The uniformity of signs, design and color scheme easily leads the public to believe that each motor lodge is under common ownership or conforms to common standards, and the jury could find they are intended to do so.[11] [citations omitted]

On the question of reliance, the jury had a right to conclude that appellee believed exactly what appellant wanted her to believe, i.e., that she was dealing with Howard Johnson's, "a chain that sells a product across the nation." Appellee testified that when she realized her need for a room, she called the Howard Johnson Motor Lodge. She had stayed there once before. Thus, she was calling a specifically identified establishment, not just any motel. She also testified that she was not aware that any of the HJ motels were individually owned, but assumed "they were Howard Johnson's." While more could have been presented, we believe that this, coupled with the evidence of the extensive efforts of HJ to market a uniform product, presented an issue to the jury on the question of reliance which they obviously resolved in appellee's favor. In *Economy Cabs* v. *Kirkland*,

---

[9] Even in service station cases some courts have found the existence of apparent agency where the representations involved more than advertising the product being sold, as e.g., *Gizzi* v. *Texaco, Inc.*, 437 F.2d 308 (3d Cir. 1971), dealing with Texaco's "you can trust your car to the man who wears the star" slogan.

[10] The agreement also provides that in the event of termination, licensee will discontinue use of signs and other indicia of operation as a Howard Johnson Motor Lodge and will discontinue use of the color scheme and remove the cupola and all orange tile from the holdings or structures "effectively to distinguish the same from its former appearance as a designation of a 'Howard Johnson's Motor Lodge'... "

[11] A vice president of HJ testified:

> Q. Well do you consider the Howard Johnson name to be a valuable name?
> A. Yes, we do.
> Q. *Do you consider the name to imply cleanliness and safety* and all of those good things?
> A. Yes, we do. (R-893). (emphasis supplied).

127 Fla. 867, 174 So. 222 (1937), a passenger in a taxicab was injured and sued the company whose name was carried on the cab. The passenger had telephoned this company, and a cab bearing the colors and insignia of the company responded. The suit was defended on the ground that this taxicab, like some others, was in reality owned and operated by a third party, hence the company was not liable. Justice Terrell, in speaking for the court, said:

> Under such state of facts the law will presume as to the public generally and the plaintiff that defendant cab and driver were a common carrier for hire *and in the service of the company whose name it bore.* One of the first principles of hornbook law we were taught in the law school was that for every wrong the law provides a remedy. If the law is to be circumvented by litigants as proposed here, then we were taught a futile lesson. They should not be permitted to parade under a flag of truce to garner a profit and then raise the black flag when called on to make restitution for damage perpetrated (emphasis added).

* * *

> Third parties who happen to own a cab and use it in the name of the company at the call of the company will be treated as the company.

* * *

174 So. at 224. See also, *Sapp* v. *City of Tallahassee, supra.*

Appellant's remaining points on appeal have been considered and are without merit.

Appellee cross appeals the action of the trial court in granting appellant's motion to set aside the punitive damage award. The trial court found that the evidence and reasonable inferences thereon, viewed in this light most favorable to appellee, were insufficient to support the award of punitive damages against either defendant. We do not find the conduct of defendants to be of such egregious nature as to support a punitive damage award.

The judgment appealed from is AFFIRMED. Frank D. Upchurch, Jr., J., concurs. Cowart, J., dissents with opinion. [dissenting opinion omitted]

Orlando Executive Park, Inc. v. *Robbins*

Case Nos. 61,165 and 61,166 (Fla. Sup. Ct. March 31, 1983)
affirming on application for review, 402 So.2d 442
(Fla. Dist. Ct. App. 5th Dist. 1981).

McDONALD, J.

Both Orlando Executive Park, Inc., and the Howard Johnson Co. have petitioned for review of *Orlando Executive Park, Inc.* v. *P.D.R.*, 402 So.2d 442 (Fla.5th DCA 1981). We have jurisdiction, article V, section 3(b)(3), Florida Constitution, and approve the district court decision.

An unidentified man attacked Robbins while she was a registered guest at a Howard Johnson (HJ) Motor Lodge owned and operated by Orlando Executive Park, Inc. (OEP). Robbins sued for damages, claiming that HJ and OEP violated their legal duty to exercise reasonable care for her safety while she was a guest on the premises. The jury agreed and awarded her $750,000 compensatory damages against the defendants jointly and $500,000 punitive damages against each defendant separately. The trial court vacated verdicts for OEP and HJ on the punitive damages, but refused to grant their other post-trial motions. The district court of appeal affirmed the judgment, holding that the jury could properly find that OEP breached its duty of care and that liability could be extended to HJ under the doctrine of apparent agency.

OEP petitioned for review, which we granted on the basis of conflict with *Winer v. Walo, Inc.,* 105 So.2d 376 (Fla.3d DCA 1958). In *Winer* a motel guest slipped and fell on a wet terrazzo walkway. His expert witness, a local builder, testified as to the unsuitability of terrazzo for outdoor walkways because it becomes slippery when wet. The trial court directed a verdict for the defendant, finding that Winer had not proved prima facie negligence. In affirming the directed verdict the district court commented that Winer had made "no showing that such terrazzo was not safe when measured by the general standard of building construction practice in the area." *Id.* at 378.

As its points on review, OEP claims that the district court erred as to the basis for expert testimony and as to imposing upon an innkeeper the duty to prevent a criminal assault. Upon further reflection we find no conflict with *Winer* regarding the first point, on which we based the exercise of our jurisdiction in granting OEP's petition. Because we have jurisdiction regarding HJ's petition for review, however, we will review the portion of the district court opinion discussing OEP's liability as well as that part concerning HJ. [footnote omitted]

In the instant case Robbins' security expert testified that three guards should have been on round-the-clock duty at this 300-room motel. OEP's former security service had also suggested the necessity for three guards. Robbins' witness also testified, however, that no industry standards covering the instant situation existed. In *Winer* industry standards existed, but Winer failed to present them at trial. Here, industry standards did not exist, and we find no conflict with *Winer.*

We agree, however, with the district court's assessment of OEP's liability. In commenting on OEP's attack on the lack of standards the district court stated that the

> absence of industry standards does not insulate the defendants from liability when there is credible evidence presented to the jury pointing to measures reasonably available to deter incidents of this kind, against which the jury can judge the reasonableness of the measures taken *in this case.*

402 So.2d at 447 (emphasis in original). In this case Robbins presented credible evidence, namely, that numerous episodes of criminal activity, of which the management had knowledge, had occurred during the immediately preceding six-month period and that the situation required the presence of security guards.

The district court properly characterized the question as one of foreseeability. [citations omitted] An innkeeper owes the duty of reasonable care for the safety of his guests, *Rosier, Phillips Petroleum Co.* v. *Dorn,* 292 So.2d 429 (Fla.4th DCA 1974), rev'd on other grounds, 347 So.2d 1057 (Fla.4th DCA 1977), and it is "peculiarly a jury function to determine what precautions are reasonably required in the exercise of a particular duty of due care." [citations omitted] On the facts of this case the district court correctly stated that

> the jury may consider competent evidence on the need or effect of any of these security measures or combination thereof in the context of the circumstances

and evidence before it, in determining whether the innkeeper has met his duty of providing his guest with reasonable protection for his safety.

402 So. 2d at 488. Credible evidence supported the jury's verdict, and we approve the portion of the district court opinion dealing with OEP's liability.

Turning to HJ, we granted its petition for review because of conflict between the instant district court opinion and *Sydenham* v. *Santiago*, 392 So.2d 357 (Fla.4th DCA 1981), on the issue of apparent authority. In *Sydenham* a tire repaired at Santiago's Gulf Service Station exploded and injured the plaintiff. Sydenham sued both Santiago, who owned the station, and Gulf Oil Co., whose products Santiago sold. Relying on *Cawthon* v. *Phillips Petroleum Co.,* 124 So.2d 517 (Fla.2d DCA 1960), the fourth district found Gulf not liable under an apparent agency theory because

> [a]n oil company does not confer apparent authority, subjecting itself to vicarious liability for negligence, upon a retail service station by allowing the use of its trade name and selling its products to the station.

392 So.2d at 357-58.

> The instant district court, on the other hand, stated:

> While OEP might not be HJ's agent for all purposes, the signs, national advertising, uniformity of building design and color schemes allows the public to assume that this and other similar motor lodges are under the same ownership.

402 So.2d at 450 [footnote omitted]. On the facts of this case the district court has set out the proper standard, limiting *Sydenham* and other oil company cases to their facts, and we disapprove extending the language of *Sydenham* into cases such as the instant one to the extent of conflict with this opinion.

As HJ concedes, the district court correctly set out the three elements needed to establish apparent agency: "(1) a representation by the principal; (2) reliance on that representation by a third person; and (3) a change of position by the third person in reliance upon such representation to his detriment." 402 So.2d at 449. The existence of an agency relationship is ordinarily a question to be determined by a jury in accordance with the evidence adduced at trial [citations omitted] and can be proved by facts and circumstances on a case-by-case basis. *Sapp* v. *City of Tallahassee,* 348 So.2d 363 (Fla.1st DCA), cert. denied, 354 So.2d 985 (Fla. 1977).

As it did before the district court, HJ now claims that Robbins failed to present enough legally sufficient evidence tending to show the applicability of the doctrine of apparent agency to enable the case to go to the jury. We agree with the district court to the contrary. Robbins presented sufficient evidence to allow the jury to conclude that HJ represented to the public that it could find a certain level of service at this motel. Besides the evidence pointed out by the district court, we note that HJ, rather than OEP, operated the restaurant, lounge, and adult theater at the motel. The complex was an integrated commercial enterprise, and HJ's direct participation was significant. The district court also correctly pointed out the sufficiency of Robbin's evidence regarding her reliance on HJ.

We therefore approve the instant district court opinion.

It is so ordered. (Alderman, C.J., Adkins, Overton and Ehrlich, J.J., concur. Boyd, J., dissents with an opinion.) [dissenting opinion omitted]

AUTHOR'S NOTE: See also, *Billop's* v. *Magness Construction Co., Hilton Hotels Corporation, et al.* 391 A.2d 196 (Del. Sup. Ct. 1978).

Reichenbach v. Days Inn of America, Inc.

401 So. 2d 1366 (Fla. Dist. Ct. App., 5th Dist. 1981),
petition denied, 412 So.2d 469 (Fla. 1982)

FRANK D. UPCHURCH, Jr., Judge.

This is an appeal from a summary final judgment holding a motel not liable for an assault on one of its guests. We affirm.

Appellant, Alfred E. Reichenbach, was a guest at appellee's motel. At approximately 10:00 P.M., he parked his car in the parking lot and proceeded to step out of the car. At this point, an assailant came up and stated: "Don't do anything foolish." Reichenbach responded, "what" and was immediately shot twice. The assailant fled. The incident occurred so quickly that appellant could not identify or describe the assailant. A bus driver, the only eyewitness, was present with a charter group as a guest of the motel. Just before the shooting he had noticed a security guard making his rounds in the area where the event took place. Another employee was also patrolling. A few minutes after seeing the guard he saw a young, white male on the walkway. They greeted each other and he noticed "nothing unusual whatever" about the man and nothing to indicate he was armed. The bus driver walked upstairs onto the breezeway overlooking the parking lot. He then noticed appellant drive into the parking lot. As appellant got out of the car, the young man ran up to him, shot twice, ran to another car in the parking lot and left.

An innkeeper may be liable if he fails to take reasonable precautions to deter the type of criminal activity which resulted in a guest's injury. See *Orlando Executive Park* v. *P.D.R.,* 402 So.2d 442 (Fla.5th DCA 1981). In the case before us, there was no evidence that the innkeeper could have deterred or prevented appellant's injury by reasonable precautions which were not taken. There was no evidence that this incident was foreseeable or that the motel had any practical or reasonable method to protect its guest from or prevent this unprovoked hit and run attack.

AFFIRMED.

COBB, J., concurs.

* * *

COWART, Judge, concurring specially:

I specially concur with the majority opinion but write to point up what I perceive as an aberration of existing tort principles.

A registered guest of a motel is entitled to receive from the innkeeper the degree of care owed a business invitee.[1] Generally, an innkeeper stands in such a special relation to guests that the innkeeper has a duty to take reasonable action to protect them against unreasonable risks of physical harm and this duty can include the obligation to exercise control over the conduct of third persons[2] and to prevent a third person from criminally assaulting a guest.[3]

---

[1] See *Steinberg* v. *Irwin Operating Co.,* 90 So.2d 460 (Fla. 1956).
[2] W. Prosser, *The Law of Torts,* 349 n. 39 (4th Ed. 1971).
[3] *Restatement (Second) of Torts* § 314A(2)(1965).

The duty of an innkeeper to protect guests from the danger of a criminal assault by a third person presents an interesting problem relating to the concept of foreseeability. Appellants maintain that the location or particular character of a specific motel business, or past experience, should cause the innkeeper to reasonably anticipate that criminal assaults are likely to endanger the safety of guests.[4] It is contended that ability to generally foresee such danger creates a duty on the innkeeper to take affirmative action to deter persons intent on such wrongful conduct and to warn guests of prior criminal activity.[5] From these broad premises it is argued that a specific criminal assault on a guest by a third person was the proximate cause of, or resulted from, the failure of the innkeeper to meet this duty.

That motel guests will be criminally assaulted in the future is not only foreseeable—it is a certainty. This will occur not because innkeepers do not protect guests but because crime will continue and citizens generally will continue to be criminally assaulted and motel guests will be no exception. However, the general foreseeability of the risk of a criminal assault upon a guest by a third person only permits such precautionary measures as will deter crime generally. Employing security guards, and installing closed circuit video cameras and lights may *deter* crime generally, but can not reasonably be expected to *prevent* all crime or any one specific criminal act.[6] This is evident from the fact that, although society takes

---

4 The motel in the instant case was undisputedly the location of prior criminal acts. Prior to this assault there had been one rape complaint, two armed robberies of motel guests in their rooms, two robberies of the gas station on the premises, and numerous instances of police response to complaints of unidentified activity in and around the motel. However, the innkeeper had no prior warning or notice that Dr. Reichenbach might be harmed or that the assailant might harm any guest.

5 It is hard to envision just what type of warning would be appropriate. Must the prudent innkeeper maintain highway signs and placards at the registration desk warning potential customers that if they become guests of his motel they may be criminally assaulted by unknown third persons?

6 To deter is to inhibit, to turn aside or to discourage and the success of efforts to deter depends on the person sought to be deterred. To prevent is to stop, to obstruct or to deprive another of the power to act regardless of his will or desire to act. The success of an effort to prevent depends largely on the opportunity, means and ability of the one who seeks to prevent an act of result. The difference in these terms illustrates the innkeeper's plight and the fallacy in the argument that a failure to deter criminal acts generally is evidence of the breach of a duty to prevent a threatened assault. Only law-abiding citizens and timid would-be offenders are deterred. Bold determined robbers, rapists, murderers, and other criminal assailants are not deterred and are rarely thwarted. As a practical matter their failures result from the inadequacy of their own abilities and efforts and not from the intervention of others. This unhappy truth should be obvious to all who are experienced in the criminal justice system, or who have contemplated the history of assassinations, or who observed Jack Ruby shoot Lee Harvey Oswald. Indeed, since the oral argument in this case, two staggering events have occurred. First, on March 30, 1981, a man attempted to assassinate President Ronald Reagan, possibly the most intensely protected individual in the United States. Barely a month and a half later, a similar assassination attempt was made on the life of Pope John Paul II. Although no one would contend these events resulted from the negligence of the property owner, it is interesting to note that President Reagan's assassination attempt occurred as he was exiting from a hotel, the entity involved in both this case and *Orlando Executive Park* v. *P.D.R.*, 402 So.2d 442 (Fla.5th DCA 1981).

action to deter crime generally, law enforcement[7] rarely prevents a crime and then only when, by chance or by specific information relating to a threatened or planned crime, there is opportunity to take specific action to prevent a particular crime. Innkeepers should not be legally required to do that which organized society cannot do.[8] No reasonable standard of care should require one to be ever on guard, ever present, ready and able, to prevent an unforeseeable personal criminal attack upon another.[9] Although crime is foreseeable, generally an innkeeper, as well as others, may, under ordinary circumstances, reasonably assume that third persons will not violate the criminal law and will not intentionally cause harm to guests. Since the innkeeper is not an insurer of the guest's safety and is not liable, strictly or otherwise, for the acts of third persons,[10] he is under no duty to exercise any care to warn or to take preventive action[11] until he knows, or has reason to believe, that a third person is acting, or is about to act, in a manner as will, or is likely to, cause harm to a guest.[12] By their very nature assaults usually occur suddenly and without warning and without giving an opportunity to defend. Therefore, to prevent an assault by one person upon another requires an opportunity arising from some specific knowledge, notice or warning.[13]

Additionally, even where an innkeeper has reason to believe a third person is likely to assault a guest, an innkeeper's duty should be coextensive with his ability to meet that duty. This means the innkeeper should not be held responsi-

---

[7] It should also be noted that, in the performance of its duties, law enforcement has certain immunities and rights to use force that citizens do not have.

[8] The Florida Crime Index released by the Florida Department of Law Enforcement on November 13, 1980, shows that violent assaultive crimes (murder, rape, robbery and aggravated assault) comprised 11.7 percent of all reported index offenses for the first nine months of 1980 and reflected a 28.9 percent increase over the same period in 1979. Certainly bank robbery is the one assaultive crime most easy to anticipate and to prevent, yet in the 10 years following the Bank Protection Act of 1968, bank robberies increased fourfold and last year reached 7,037 nationwide. Employees of motels, along with those of convenience stores and service stations, are themselves prime victims of robberies and other assaults.

[9] W. Prosser, *The Law of Torts*, 282 n. 97 (4th Ed. 1971).

[10] Perspective requires one to bear constantly in mind that the assaultive act of the criminal assailant is the legal efficient, or proximate cause of a victim's injuries. This is not a case where the assailant's acts and the innkeeper's acts join together to contribute to the guest's injuries. We are here only concerned with an innkeeper's duty to take steps to prevent an injury which he in no way affirmatively causes or to which he contributes.

[11] The argument will be made that the failure to impose liability on the innkeeper under the facts of this case will result in motels foregoing all precaution to protect their guests. I do not believe this will result. There is an economic incentive to provide general deterrent measures. With a growing concern for crime, a traveler will choose the safest accommodations available. In an industry peculiarly dependent upon goodwill, it is in an innkeeper's own interest to employ general deterrent measures to enhance its good name and reputation. Secondly, the innkeeper must be reasonably prepared to meet his duty to prevent assaults on guests when he has an adequate opportunity and it is reasonably possible for him to do so.

[12] See *Restatement (Second) of Torts* § 344, Comment f (1965).

[13] Generally, criminal acts have been found foreseeable, creating a duty to prevent them, only when a defendant with a duty knew or should have known that a specific person was likely to assault someone. [citations omitted] (No liability was found

ble for an assault by a third party on a guest unless the innkeeper, acting reasonably, could have feasibly prevented it. There are severe limitations on the capability of anyone to prevent an assault on another person by a third party. First, it is in the nature of things that mobile or free moving objects are difficult to protect and secure. It is for this reason that more vehicles are stolen than other less mobile chattels and that valuable objects are kept in vaults, safety boxes and other various stationary places. Motel guests, like other free citizens, go and come at their pleasure. Also, persons intent on making a criminal assault, especially those not acting on impulse or merely upon an opportunity or perceived necessity, have the advantage of surprise and select the time, place, method and circumstances, rarely giving the victim, the police or an innkeeper an opportunity to prevent the particular assault.[14] Additionally, in earlier times innkeepers were required to accept the public generally but could with some impunity reject or eject persons considered disorderly, intoxicated, dangerous or undesirable. However, now in Florida, motels are not entirely free to exclude guests[15] or persons[16] who visit guests or other members of the public who come to use facilities and services which are customarily available to the public.[17] Thus, the character of a motel is essentially that of a public place and innkeepers lack the usual possessor's peculiar ability to exercise control over third persons using his property. This "open door policy" extends to all public areas and, while it impairs security, it is a necessary consequence of a free society and of motels and other public and semi-public places. Considering these circumstances, even when there is reason to be apprehensive of potential risk of harm to guests from an assault by a particular individual, the innkeeper must act reasonably and lawfully toward everyone, including third persons who may appear to be suspicious. Unless the circumstances not only give reasonable opportunity but also demand immediate action, when criminal acts are threatened the reasonable prudent present-day innkeeper can normally only call the police.[18]

Lastly, even if the innkeeper realizes, or should realize, that an assault is probable and circumstances do not permit police to be summoned, yet give the innkeeper a reasonable opportunity to act, the innkeeper should have a reasonable ability and method to prevent the assault before he is held liable for not doing so. An innkeeper who personally resorts to physical force risks harm to himself and legal consequences in the form of compensation and punitive damages. Even where physical force is justified, the innkeeper and his employees

---

when the wrongdoers were complete strangers to the landowner and to the victims, and where the incident occurred precipitously.) In the absence of actual or constructive knowledge of the particular risk and a reasonable opportunity to protect from that harm by preventing the act, duties have not been imposed. [citations omitted]

[14] Man's best efforts to control a potential assailant are impotent. On July 16, 1980, Richard Sherman "Bush Ax" Williams, a Florida State Prison inmate, fatally stabbed a fellow inmate through the bars of his cell. Since then, Thomas Knight, a death row inmate, fatally stabbed his prison guard, Richard Burke.

[15] See § 509.092, Fla. Stat. (1979). See also Annot., 7 A.L.R. Fed. 450 (1971).

[16] "[B]y the very nature of the business, the operator of the hotel is bound to anticipate that a registered guest is apt to have business and social calls." *Steinberg* v. *Irwin Operating Co.*, 90 So.2d 460, 461 (Fla. 1956).

[17] *Restatement (Second) of Torts* §§ 318, 866 (1965).

[18] This reasonable and proper action creates police reports suggesting criminal activity in the area which, as here, is used as evidence against the innkeeper.

may not be able to physically restrain a strong, violent or dangerous third person. What if, as here, the assailant is armed? An unarmed innkeeper is no match for an armed assailant. If the innkeeper had been standing at alert beside Dr. Reichenbach when this assault with a firearm occurred, as a practical matter exactly what could the innkeeper have done to have protected his guest? There are no limitations on the assailant, but the innkeeper's right to arm himself is severely limited,[19] and there is great penalty if the legal restrictions are disregarded.[20]

This is not a case where an innkeeper[21] or an employee or other person within the control of the innkeeper commits an assault on a guest. Nor does this case involve an innkeeper who neglected to take action after learning of the potential need of a particular guest for protection from some threatened harm. Nor does this case involve a cause of action based on express or implied contract. Nor does this case involve locking devices or other security measures relating to a private room which not only deter crime but, under some circumstances, might be capable of physically preventing access by members of the public generally, thereby preventing an assault. This case involves an alleged neglect of a duty of the innkeeper to prevent a third person from doing intentional harm to a guest in a public area where there was only general knowledge of the possibility of criminal assault but nothing is claimed to have given the innkeeper foresight that a particular person might assault some guest or that a particular guest might be assaulted by someone.

In order for an innkeeper to be liable for breach of his duty to take affirmative action to protect guests from the unlawful assaults of third parties, I would require that specific facts be alleged and proved that would put a reasonable innkeeper on notice that a particular person was likely to assault some guest or that a particular guest was likely to be assaulted by some assailant and, also, specific facts would be required to detail circumstances that afforded the innkeeper a reasonable and feasible opportunity and ability to prevent the particular attack. I would hold here that an innkeeper is not responsible to a guest for a sudden violent criminal assault by a third person which occurred in a public area without warning and under circumstances giving the innkeeper no reason to anticipate the particular assault, no opportunity to act and no reasonable way to prevent it.

Kimple v. *Foster*
205 Kan. 415, 469 P.2d 281 (1970)

FONTRON, Justice

This action was commenced by the three plaintiffs, John Stanley Kimple, Ernest I. Stahly and Larry A. Morris, to recover for personal injuries sustained while guests at The Roaring Sixties, a Wichita nightspot. The case was tried to a jury which awarded damages to each plaintiff in the sum of $6,500. The defendant, Bill G. Foster, owner of the offending tavern, has appealed.

---

[19] See § 790.25(3)(n), Fla. Stat. (1979); *Brevard County* v. *Bagwell,* 388 So.2d 645 (Fla.5th DCA 1980).

[20] *Herring* v. *State,* 393 So.2d 67 (Fla.5th DCA 1981).

[21] Of course in such event the innkeeper would be liable not for negligence but for the intentional tort.

For the three victims, the evening of July 7, 1966, began innocently enough. The men met in the afternoon for a business conference, following which they had dinner together. About 9:00 P.M. they dropped into The Roaring Sixties, where they ordered a pitcher of beer. Soon thereafter the tavern exploded with a frenetic violence which more than matched the picturesque character of its name.

The record reflects that when the plaintiffs entered the tavern, a group of males was gathered around a table some distance away. These characters had been patronizing the tavern since afternoon, drinking beer, pyramiding empty beer cans on their table, harassing patrons, brawling and behaving generally in a fashion that may be termed, at best, obnoxious.

Shortly after they had taken their seats the plaintiffs, none of whom were in anywise boisterous or unruly, were approached by one of the aforesaid male characters who bummed a light for his cigarette. After being accommodated he returned to his peer group across the room. In a matter of minutes several members of the graceless group surrounded the table at which the plaintiffs were seated, all seemingly itching for trouble. One of their number accused the plaintiffs of making uncomplimentary remarks about his girl friend (one of the go-go dancers who also served as waitresses) and invited them outside for a fight. When this gracious invitation was firmly declined, the gang began its vicious attack by kicking the chair out from under Mr. Kimple. The ultimate result of the ensuing affray was that all three plaintiffs were injured amidst an unrelenting rain of blows, kicks and missiles. Further details of the gory assault will be related when and as required.

The basis of the plaintiffs' claims against Mr. Foster, the proprietor of The Roaring Sixties, was his failure to provide them with the protection to which they were entitled as his guests. There is actually little dispute between plaintiffs and defendant with respect to the general proposition that a tavern operator owes his patrons the duty to exercise reasonable care for their personal safety. In this jurisdiction the general rule has been phrased in *Huddleston* v. *Clark*, 186 Kan. 209, 349 P.2d 888, in these words:

> "While the owner and operator of a public tavern and grill is held to a stricter accountability for injuries to patrons than is the owner of private premises generally, the rule is that he is not an insurer of the patrons, but owes them only what, under the particular circumstances, is ordinary and reasonable care." (Syl. 2.)

We find this rule to be in substantial accord with the prevailing doctrine which is expressed in 40 Am.Jur.2d, Hotels, Motels, Etc., § 112, p. 987:

> "A proprietor of an inn, hotel, restaurant, or similar establishment is liable for an assault upon a guest or patron by another guest, patron, or third person where he has reason to anticipate such assault, and fails to exercise reasonable care under the circumstances to prevent the assault or interfere with its execution. * * * "

To similar effect is *Reilly* v. *180 Club, Inc.*, 14 N.J.Super. 420, 82 A.2d 210, wherein the court said:

> "It is in the law the duty of a tavern-keeper to exercise reasonable care, vigilance, and prudence to protect his guests from injury from the disorderly acts of other guests. * * * " (p. 424, 82 A.2d at 212.)

* * *

Although, as we have said, the defendant does not seriously question this legal maxim, he calls our attention to its qualification in the following particular: That the proprietor's duty to protect his patrons does not arise under the rule until the impending danger becomes apparent to the tavern keeper, or the circumstances are such that an alert and prudent person would be placed on notice of the probability of danger. [citations omitted]

Pursuing this theme, the defendant asserts that the record is entirely bereft of evidence which would tend to place him on notice of impending danger. In making this assertion, we believe the defendant is mistaken. As we view this record, there is ample evidence to have alerted both the defendant himself and his go-go girl manager to the probability of violence erupting from the rowdy and unruly gang which had infested the tavern since afternoon.

We shall make no attempt to set out the evidence in detail. It is sufficient to say that "the guys" around the beer can pyramid, who ranged in number as high as eight or ten, were high and belligerent at 4:30 that afternoon and "maybe wanted to start a fight"; that about 5:15 or so the male manager (Mr. Foster) was in the tavern and set the boys up for a free beer; about 5:30 or 6:00 a fight broke out in which one of the fellows from the "pyramid" table hit and ran another guy out of the tavern; that the group was loud and boisterous and "would have gotten thrown out [of any other bar], because of the noise they were creating and the belligerence or sarcasm toward other people."

There is further evidence from a member of the gang that Foster's employees knew of this prior fight because they turned on the lights to stop it; and that there was another incident at the tavern over a hat involving some farm boys and one of the gang took the hat and everyone got to joking about it.

Mr. Foster himself testified that he was in the tavern from 5:00 to 6:00 that afternoon; that the boys were then building the pyramid of beer cans; and that he bought the boys a round of free beer.

We think the foregoing evidence was clearly sufficient, if believed by the jury, to warrant the jury in concluding that the defendant Foster, himself, had knowledge of facts which should reasonably have placed him on notice that trouble might well be expected from the unruly, belligerent group, and that an explosion might erupt which would endanger the safety of his patrons. True, Mr. Foster denied that any disturbance took place in the tavern while he was there, but there is evidence from which a contrary inference could well be drawn. Moreover, the defendant was aware of the gang's presence when he left his place of business and had helped to assuage its members' thirst by providing free beers all around.

Not only may notice be imparted to the defendant himself, but his go-go manager, whose duty it was to maintain order in the absence of her employer, was on the scene as the storm clouds gathered, and she took no steps to forestall the approaching tempest. The evidence is to the effect that before the physical attack commenced, the plaintiffs and other patrons repeatedly told the girls to summon the police, but to no effect. In fact, it may fairly be concluded from the evidence that the police were not called until the battle had raged for some ten minutes or so, during which time at least two of the go-go girls joined in the fray and belted the plaintiffs.

A case with similar overtones arose in our sister state of Minnesota (*Priewe* v. *Bartz*, 249 Minn. 488, 83 N.W.2d 116, 70 A.L.R.2d 621). There, a barmaid was in charge of her employer's place of business when an inebriated customer challenged another intoxicated customer to a fight. The barmaid did no more than to tell both inebriates to step outside if they wanted to fight. The police were not called although there was ample time for doing so. In upholding a verdict against the tavern owner in favor of an innocent third party who sustained injuries as a result of the fight, the Minnesota court said:

> " * * * [T]here can be no doubt that Mogen, the operator of a 3.2 beer establishment, owed a duty to those coming upon his premises to exercise reasonable care to protect them from injury at the hands of other patrons. * * * " (p. 491, 83 N.W.2d at 119.)

> " * * * The duty of the proprietor was not met by the admonition of the barmaid that the parties should go outside if they wanted to fight. * * * There must be some affirmative action to maintain order on the premises by demanding that such a person leave or by calling the authorities to enforce such demand. * * *" (pp. 492, 493, 83 N.W.2d at 120.)

In *Peck* v. *Gerber*, 154 Or. 126, 59 P.2d 675, 106 A.L.R. 996, the plaintiff was a guest in a restaurant at which alcoholic drinks were served. He was injured when two young men had an altercation, one of whom was knocked over and against him. The Oregon court upheld a verdict in the plaintiff's favor and in the course of its opinion stated:

> "A guest or patron of such an establishment has a right to rely on the belief that he is in an orderly house and that the operator, personally or by his delegated representative, is exercising reasonable care to the end that the doings in the house shall be orderly. * * *" (p. 136, 59 P.2d at 679.)

In our opinion there is ample evidence to establish that both the defendant and his designated manager had notice of sufficient facts to have alerted them to the potentiality of danger to the guests of The Roaring Sixties. A case in point is *Coca* v. *Areceo*, 71 N.M. 186, 376 P.2d 970, wherein the court said:

> " * * * The rule [of notice] does not require a long and continued course of conduct to find that the proprietor had knowledge of the violent disposition of the other patron—all that is necessary is that there be a sequence of conduct sufficiently long to enable the proprietor to act for the patron's safety. It is not necessary that the proprietor know of a history of a series of offenses against the peace. * * * " (p. 190, 376 P.2d at 973.)

The defendant complains of instructions given the jury to the effect that none of the plaintiffs were guilty of contributory negligence. Under the circumstances shown by the record we find no error in this respect. There is no evidence to indicate that plaintiffs were misbehaving or rowdy in any particular; the evidence, indeed, is quite to the contrary. They consistently sought to evade trouble until it was forced upon them.

Although the chief instigator of the attack accused one of the men of making a derogatory remark about his girl, this was rank hearsay on his part. Patrons sitting near the plaintiffs' table heard no remarks of an objectionable nature. The plaintiffs denied any disparaging utterances on their part, and the go-go girl herself, who may or may not have inflamed her boy friend's ire to fighting pitch, did not appear at the trial to favor the court with her version of the affair.

* * *

Prejudicial error has not been made to appear, and the judgments are affirmed as to each plaintiff.

Zerangue v. Delta Towers, Ltd.

U.S. Ct. App., 5th Cir., 86-3357 (1987)

The United States Court of Appeals for the Fifth Circuit on June 25, 1987, upheld the jury verdict of the lower court holding the Ramada Hotel in New Orleans liable for damages resulting from personal injuries sustained by an invitee of a hotel guest when she was sexually assaulted on a public sidewalk outside the hotel. AH&MA filed a brief *amicus* in this case.

In this case, the plaintiff, Susan Zerangue, left the hotel at 3:00 A.M. by an emergency side-lobby door, fronting Claiborne Avenue, after spending part of the night in the room of a hotel guest. The six side doors to this lobby were locked *for security reasons during the Mardi Gras.* However, the plaintiff used an emergency, push-bar door, which could be opened from the inside but not the outside, to enter the street where she met a stranger who forced her to a parking lot located across the street from the hotel and assaulted her there. The plaintiff testified at trial that she attempted to reenter the hotel when she saw the stranger but the push-bar door she used to exit the hotel was locked. She also testified that she saw no security guard posted in the side lobby of the hotel, which she used to leave the hotel's premises. Although a hotel security guard testified that signs were posted on the side doors advising persons to use the main lobby entrance of the hotel, plaintiff claimed she did not see them. The Court of Appeals construed the facts disclosed at trial as establishing that *no signs were posted* on the side doors.

While the Court of Appeals ruled that the duty owed by a hotel to a guest's visitor was one *of "ordinary and reasonable care,"* it held that the hotel breached this duty by failing to have a *security guard* posted in the side lobby and by failing to *properly warn* the plaintiff, an invitee of a guest, that she could not reenter the hotel through the side-lobby door once she left through that door. The Court of Appeals ruled that there was *sufficient evidence* before the jury for the jury to conclude that the public street in question was a *dangerous place* to be at 3:00 A.M. and that adequate security measures required that at least one side-lobby door afford both egress and ingress, with a *guard permanently* stationed at the side door.

The Court of Appeals stated:

> "Plaintiff's expert on hotel security and crime prevention testified that the police department *statistics showed an increase in criminal offenses in this vicinity the year prior to the incident* and that under the circumstances the Ramada security program was inadequate. He concluded that at least one Claiborne Street door should have afforded both ingress and egress, with a guard permanently stationed at that door. No guard was actually present even though under the hotel's plan one was supposed to be there. Most importantly, there was *no warning* to Susan Zerangue against exiting to Claiborne Street and that once outside, she would be unable to return.

> The defendants argue that it was the rapist that hurt the plaintiff and did so away from the hotel premises. The answer is that, *but for* her having been locked out at the mercy of the rapist, no harm would have occurred. This was a

danger that the security guard on duty foresaw; the jury was justified in finding that the hotel operator should have *foreseen the risk* to its invitees." (Emphasis added)

The Court of Appeals further held that the jury properly found the hotel liable under a Louisiana strict liability statute for defects on the premises, by reasoning that the jury was entitled to find that the "unguarded" and "warningless" exit, denying the visitor the option of reentering, created an unreasonable risk of harm.

The Court of appeals did, however, reduce plaintiff's damages from $200,000 to $150,000.

Both the plaintiff and the defendant filed applications for an *en banc* hearing before the Fifth Circuit Court of Appeals, requesting a new hearing of the case. This application was denied on July 22, 1987.

Chapter 11 Outline

Competencies

1. State the common law rule regarding a hotel's liability for loss of the guest's property. (p. 161)

2. Identify the steps a hotel must take to limit its liability for loss of guest valuables, and cite cases illustrating a hotel's liability for guests' property. (pp. 161–165)

3. Explain how a hotel can limit its liability for loss of the guest's personal property other than valuables. (p. 165)

4. Describe a hotel's liability if guest property disappears from a guest's room, the hotel lobby, hallways of the hotel, checkrooms, baggage rooms, and storerooms, or is lost by fire. (pp. 165–167)

5. Describe a hotel's liability with regard to unclaimed property. (p. 168)

6. Summarize a hotel's liability for handling guests' mail. (pp. 168–169)

7. Describe a hotel's liability for automobiles belonging to guests. (pp. 169–170)

8. Explain the theory of bailment. (p. 170)

9. Describe the common law doctrine of *infra hospitium.* (pp. 170–171)

The Hotel's Liability Regarding Guests' Property

State Statutes Limiting Liability

Many states have statutes that may limit the amount a guest may recover from a hotel for loss of personal property. In states where hotels are not so protected, the common law rule applies. In many of these common law states, the hotel is considered practically an insurer and held strictly liable for loss of a guest's property—unless the loss is caused by a guest's negligence, an **act of God**, or an act of a common enemy. Unless there is a modification or limitation of common law liability in the state statutes, the common law liability for the full value exists.

In states that have enacted protective legislation, the statutes are considered to be in **derogation** of the common law and will be strictly construed. Thus, hotels in states having such protective statutes must be careful to comply fully with the terms of the statutes, particularly with requirements concerning the posting of "Notices to the Guest on the Limitations of Liability." The limitations set forth in the state statutes are usually conditioned upon the posting of such notice.

Space prohibits reviewing the legislation of all the states. Therefore, this discussion deals primarily with New York State statutes, since many states have adopted similar statutes. Local counsel can advise whether a hotel's procedures strictly comply with applicable state statutes.

Liability for Valuables

In order to limit its liability for loss of a guest's "valuables," a hotel in New York must provide a safe or safe deposit boxes in the hotel office or other convenient place for the deposit of valuables, and must post notices to the guests regarding the existence of the safe or safe deposit boxes. This notice must be posted "in a public and conspicuous place and manner in the office and public rooms, and in the public parlors of such hotel, motel or inn" (§ 200, N.Y. General Business Law; see also Exhibit 11.1).

If a New York hotel satisfies the statutory prerequisites, it will normally be free of all liability in the event that the guest neglects to deposit valuables in the safe or safe deposit boxes during his/her stay.

Similar statutes exist in other states. In *Walls* v. *Cosmopolitan Hotels, Inc.*,[1] arising in the state of Washington, a watch valued at $3,685 was allegedly taken from

Exhibit 11.1   New York General Business Law

NOTICE TO GUESTS

A Safe is Provided in the Office for the Safekeeping of Money, Jewels, Ornaments, Bank Notes, Bonds, Negotiable Securities and Precious Stones Belonging to Guests.

DAILY RATES FOR ROOMS

Single from $ . . . . to $ . . . .
Double from $ . . . . to $ . . . .
Extra Persons
  (each) from $ . . . . to $ . . . .
Suites from $ . . . . to $ . . . .

*SUBJECT TO
APPLICABLE
TAXES

MEALS*

Table d'hote Breakfast from $ . . . . to $ . . . .
    "   "   Luncheon   " $ . . . . to $ . . . .
    "   "   Dinner   " $ . . . . to $ . . . .
    A la Carte as per menu

GENERAL BUSINESS LAW—SECTIONS 200, 201, 203-a, 203-b, 206, 206-d

SECTION 200. SAFES; LIMITED LIABILITY. Whenever the proprietor or manager of any hotel, motel, inn or steamboat shall provide a safe or safe deposit boxes in the office of such hotel, motel or steamboat, or other convenient place for the safe keeping of any money, jewels, ornaments, bank notes, bonds, negotiable securities or precious stones, belonging to the guests of or travelers in such hotel, motel, inn or steamboat, and shall notify the guests or travelers thereof by posting a notice stating the fact that such safe or safe deposit boxes are provided, in which such property may be deposited, in a public and conspicuous place and manner in the office and public rooms, and in the public parlors of such hotel, motel or inn, or saloon of such steamboat; and if such guest or trav-eler shall neglect to deliver such property, to the person in charge of such office for deposit in such safe or safe deposit boxes, the proprietor or manager of such hotel, motel, or steamboat shall not be liable for any loss of such property, sustained by such guest or traveler by theft or otherwise; but no hotel, motel or steamboat proprietor, manager or lessee shall be obliged to receive property on deposit for safe keeping, exceeding one thousand five hundred dollars in value; and if such guest or traveler shall deliver such property, to the person in charge of such office for deposit in such safe or safe deposit boxes, said proprietor, manager or lessee shall not be liable for any loss thereof, sustained by such guest or traveler by theft or otherwise, in any sum exceeding the sum of one thousand five hundred dollars unless by special agreement in writing with such proprietor, manager or lessee.

SECTION 201. LIABILITY FOR LOSS OF CLOTHING AND OTHER PERSONAL PROPERTY LIMITED. 1. No hotel or motel keeper except as provided in the foregoing section shall be liable for damage to or loss of wearing apparel or other personal property in the lobby, hallways or in the room or rooms assigned to a guest for any sum exceeding the sum of five hundred dollars, unless it shall appear that such loss occurred through the fault or negligence of such keeper, nor shall he be liable in any sum exceeding the sum of one hundred dollars for the loss of or damage to any such property when delivered to such keeper for storage or safe keeping in the store room, baggage room or other place elsewhere than in the room or rooms assigned to such guest, unless at the time of delivering the same for storage or safe keeping such value in excess of one hundred dollars shall be stated and a written receipt, stating such value, shall be issued by such keeper, but in no event shall such keeper be liable beyond five hundred dollars, unless it shall appear that such loss occurred through his fault or negligence, and such keeper may make a reasonable charge for storing or keeping such property, nor shall he be liable for the loss of or damage to any merchandise samples or merchandise for sale, unless the guest shall have given such keeper prior written notice of having the same in his possession, together with the value thereof, the receipt of which notice the hotel or motel keeper shall acknowledge in writing over the signature of himself or his agent, but in no event shall such keeper be liable beyond five hundred dollars, unless it shall appear that such loss or damage occurred through his fault or negligence; as to property deposited by guests or patrons in the parcel or checkroom of any hotel, motel or restaurant, the delivery of which is evidenced by a check or receipt therefor and for which no fee or charge is exacted, the proprietor shall not be liable beyond two hundred dollars, unless such

value in excess of two hundred dollars shall be stated upon delivery and a written receipt, stating such value, shall be issued, but he shall in no event be liable beyond three hundred dollars, unless such loss occurs through his fault or negligence. Notwithstanding anything hereinabove contained, no hotel or motel keeper shall be liable for damage to or loss of such property by fire, when it shall appear that such fire was occasioned without his fault or negligence.

2. A printed copy of this section shall be posted in a conspicuous place and manner in the office or public room and in the public parlors of such hotel or motel. No hotel, motel or restaurant proprietor shall post a notice disclaiming or misrepresenting his liability under this section.

SECTION 203-A. HOTEL AND MOTEL KEEPER'S LIABILITY FOR PROPERTY IN TRANSPORT. No hotel or motel keeper shall be liable in any sum exceeding the sum of two hundred and fifty dollars for the loss of or damage to property of a guest delivered to such keeper, his agent or employee, for transport to or from the hotel or motel, unless at the time of delivering the same such value in excess of two hundred and fifty dollars shall be stated by such guest and a written receipt stating such value shall be issued by such keeper; provided, however, that where such written receipt is issued the keeper shall not be liable beyond five hundred dollars unless it shall appear that such loss or damage occurred through his fault or negligence.

SECTION 203-B. POSTING OF STATUTE. Every keeper of a hotel or motel or inn shall post in a public and conspicuous place and manner in the registration office and in the public rooms of such hotel or motel or inn a printed copy of this section and section two hundred three-a.

SECTION 206. RATES TO BE POSTED; PENALTY FOR VIOLATION. Every keeper of a hotel or inn shall post in a public and conspicuous place and manner in the office or public room, and in the public parlors of such hotel or inn, a printed copy of this section and sections two hundred and two hundred and one, and a statement of the charges or rate of charges by the day and for meals furnished and for lodging. No charge or sum shall be collected or received by any such hotel keeper or inn keeper for any service not actually rendered or for a longer time than the person so charged actually remained at such hotel or inn, nor for a higher rate of charge for the use of such room or board, lodging or meals than is specified in the rate of charges required to be posted by the last preceding sentence; provided such guest shall have given such hotel keeper or inn keeper notice at the office of his departure. For any violation of this section the offender shall forfeit to the injured party three times the amount so charged, and shall not be entitled to receive any money for meals, services or time charged.

SECTION 206-D. POSTING OF RATES OF VARIOUS TYPE ACCOMMODATIONS. In addition to other provisions in this article relating to posting of rates, every keeper of a hotel, motel, or inn shall post publicly and conspicuously at the place maintained for the registration of guests so that it can be easily and readily seen and read by guests registering, a statement of the charges or rate of charges by the day indicating the standard rates for rooms or suites of different accommodations, and for meals furnished. The standard rates shall be that schedule of rates available to guests who do not qualify for special discounts or rate deductions.

NEW YORK STATE HOTEL & MOTEL ASSOCIATION, INC.
(HOTELS)

Check Out Time . . . .

the guest's hotel room. After the guest discovered this loss, he noticed that the door to his room had been severely damaged previously and one could "easily" obtain entry by pushing on the door, even if it appeared to be locked. The court, however, refused to impose any liability on the hotel because the guest had not deposited the watch in the hotel safe, as required by the Washington statute.

A guest of a hotel in New Orleans sued for a diamond ring which the guest reported missing from the guest's room. The guest sued for the alleged loss of the $10,000 value of the ring.[2]

The Louisiana Innkeepers' Statute specifies that the hotel's liability for the loss of a guest's property from a guestroom is limited to $100 absent some proof that the hotel was negligent. Plaintiff claimed that the ring was stolen due to the hotel's negligence.

However, various pieces of valuable jewelry, some traveler's checks, and cash were all left intact in the guest's room. The ring was reportedly the only item missing. The court held there was no evidence to support a finding of negligence on the part of the hotel. Therefore, the court upheld the innkeepers' statutory liability limit of $100 (in New York, this would now be $1,500; note, however, that in New York, the hotel would arguably not be liable; see Chapter 12 regarding valuables).

This case again points out the importance of posting the notice of the statutes limiting the hotel's liability.

In New York, a well-known actress was robbed in a hotel elevator of a reported $253,000 worth of jewelry.[3] Although the hotel had complied with the statutory requirements to provide a safe and post notices, the guest sued on the ground that the loss of valuables was caused by the hotel's negligence. The jury, however, found in favor of the hotel, reportedly deciding that the guest had had a reasonable amount of time in which to deposit the jewelry in the hotel safe, but had failed to do so.

In *Hisako Nagashima* v. *Hyatt Wilshire Corporation*, a bag of jewelry was stolen from a guest while she was standing at the check-out desk in the lobby of a California hotel. The guest had just taken possession of the small bag of jewelry *after* checking it out from the hotel safe. She had not informed hotel personnel about the value of the jewelry or the fact that the bag held jewelry. While the guest was in possession of the bag, and still at the check-out counter, an unidentified person stole the bag of jewelry from her.[4]

The guest sued the hotel. The parties stipulated that the reasonable value of the jewelry was $72,000. However, the hotel had not agreed with the guest to assume any liability greater than the $500 limit specified by California statute. The hotel had complied with the California statutory requirement to post printed notices in each hotel room informing the hotel's guests that a safe was available and that the hotel would not be liable for property of unusual value unless it was placed in the hotel safe.

The appellate court found that the trial judge committed error in holding the California innkeeper statute not applicable to the case. The California innkeeper statute provides that if an innkeeper "keeps a fireproof safe and gives notice" about the safe to hotel guests, the innkeeper "is not liable, except so far as his own acts shall contribute," for loss or damage to a guest's property unless deposited with the innkeeper, but in no case is an innkeeper liable for more than $500 for each guest's property, "unless he shall have given a receipt in writing...to such guest."

The California appellate court ruled that if a guest wants property protection greater than the $500 limit, then the guest should declare the value of the property in order to give the innkeeper the chance to confirm the estimated value. The innkeeper can then refuse to assume the higher liability or, if he decides to do so, he can take added precautions to protect such property. Thus, liability over the $500 limit is based on the hotel's agreement to assume the higher limit.

In this case, the hotel was protected by the California innkeeper statute because it maintained a fireproof safe and gave notice to guests about the availability of the safe as required by the California statute. Also, the hotel did not agree to assume any liability over the $500 limitation. *The California court then noted that the statute does not restrict the $500 liability limitation to the period of time in which a guest's property is actually located inside the safe. The limitation of liability therefore applied in this situation, where the valuables had been withdrawn from the safe and were stolen from the guest while she was checking out of the hotel.*

Accordingly, the appellate court reversed the trial judge's decision and remanded the case to him with direction to enter judgment in favor of the guest, *but limiting the amount to $500.*

Lawsuit on In-Room Safes. A Massachusetts couple filed a civil lawsuit against the Boca Raton Resort and Club on August 2, 1991, for the theft of jewelry worth $250,000 from an in-room safe.

In February 1991, the Caryes moved into the Boca Raton Resort and Club, in Flor-ida. They were concerned about safeguarding their jewelry, *and* hotel officials allegedly recommended that the couple store their jewelry in the in-room safe located in the Caryes' guestroom.

The stolen items allegedly included a nine-karat diamond anniversary ring valued at $95,000; five watches made of platinum, gold, and diamonds; and a pair of earrings worth $15,000.

Recently a Days Inn hotel was held liable for the entire contents of a room safe stolen from one of its guestrooms. The front desk clerk was told that the guest was a jewelry salesman and that this bag contained sample jewelry. The clerk recommended that he use the safe in his room to store the bag. The Court stated "Where an innkeeper misleads its guest into believing that the latter's property may be safely placed at a particular location in the inn, this [statement] leads a guest to disregard whatever posted statutory procedures there might be for safeguarding a guest's property generally." The judgment was in the amount of $142,834 plus $46,606 in interest.[5]

If a hotel offers in-room safes, the safes should contain a conspicuous notice that the hotel also provides a safe in the front office for the safekeeping of valuable jewelry and other valuables.

In a New York case, *Spiller* v. *Barclay Hotel,*[6] the hotel was held liable for the full value of valuables lost while the guest was checking out. In this case, the guest gave the bellboy her bags to take to the hotel cab area and watch over while she checked out of the hotel. When she went to the cab area, she noticed that one bag containing jewelry and other articles was missing. The court awarded the plaintiff over $1,700 for the lost articles, holding that the New York statutory limitations did not apply in these circumstances, and that the hotel's bellboy was negligent in failing to watch the guest's bag after leaving it in the cab area.

A Word about Guest Valuables. A hotel may not be obligated to receive all valuables proffered by the guest for safekeeping. For example, in New York, a hotel need not accept valuables that exceed $1,500 in value. The hotel's rights to refuse to accept such guest valuables are discussed in detail in Chapter 12.

Personal Property Other Than Valuables

In New York, the General Business Law, § 201, permits the hotel to limit its liability vis-à-vis the guest's personal property other than valuables, provided that the hotel posts "in a public and conspicuous place and manner in the office or public room, and in the public parlors of such hotel or inn a printed copy" of the applicable statutes. The limits of liability vary, however, depending upon the nature of the property lost and the general location where the property was lost.

Guest's Room, Hallways, and Lobby

If the property is lost from the guest's room, lobby, or hallways of the hotel, the New York statute provides that the hotel is not liable for the loss of wearing apparel or other personal property in excess of $500. However, if the guest is able to prove that the hotel's negligence resulted in the loss of such personal property, the $500 limitation may not be binding. In that event, the guest could recover the full value of the property—unless the guest was also negligent.

In *Cohen* v. *Janlee Hotel Corp.*,[7] a guest in a large metropolitan hotel went to bed leaving the door unlocked so that her girlfriend, who was sharing the room, could get in without awakening her. The next morning a valuable coat was missing from the room. The New York court refused to find the hotel liable on the ground that the guest's negligence was a contributing factor in the loss.

A question has been raised concerning the applicability of the comparative negligence statute in New York when property is lost or stolen due in part to the "contributory negligence" of the guest. The statute awaits interpretation by the courts.

A Nevada statute provides that the keeper or owner of a hotel or motel shall not be liable "for the loss of any property left in the room of any guest of any such establishment by reason of theft, burglary, fire or otherwise, in the absence of *gross neglect* upon the part of such keeper or owner" (emphasis added).

In the case of *Levitt* v. *Desert Palace, Inc.*,[8] a couple staying at a Las Vegas hotel left valuable jewelry on the dresser without availing themselves of the safe deposit box they had used earlier that very day. The jewelry disappeared by the next morning. At the trial, the plaintiffs' own expert witness testified about the superiority of the hotel's security program. The plaintiffs admitted that they had not used all the security precautions the hotel furnished them. They also had disregarded notices on the hotel's registration cards and on the doors of its guestrooms that safe deposit boxes were available for valuables.

In the face of the evidence and despite the judge's instructions that "gross neglect" is equivalent to the failure to exercise even a slight degree of care, the jury found the hotel liable and awarded the plaintiff-guests $500,000 for the loss of their jewelry. The hotel filed an appeal in the U.S. Court of Appeals (Second Circuit), which reversed the decision of the lower court, and held that the hotel was not liable under the Nevada statute since the hotel had exercised *more* than slight care, and **gross negligence** had not been proven.

Checkrooms

Hotels usually provide a place to keep the belongings of guests and of patrons who are not guests but are using the hotel facilities, such as a restaurant or banquet room. Although under common law the hotel will only be liable as a **bailee** to patrons, and, therefore, must be proven to be negligent if it fails to redeliver their belongings, a bailee nevertheless generally bears a heavy **burden of proof** to avoid liability. Many states have thus passed legislation limiting the hotel's liability under such circumstances.

The New York Court of Appeals in *Weinberg* v. *D-M Restaurant Corp.*[9] summarized the rules of liability relating to a restaurant's checkroom in New York. The court stated that § 201 of the New York General Business Law limits recovery by a patron who sues for negligence:

1. to $75 if the restaurant does not charge a fee for the checkroom service, and if the person checking the garment does not declare a value that exceeds $75 and obtain a written receipt when delivering the coat to the checkroom;

2. to $100 if a value in excess of $75 is declared, no charge or fee is exacted for checking the coat, and if negligence cannot be proved to be the cause of the loss;

3. to the full value of the garment if a value in excess of $75 is declared and a written receipt stating such value is issued when the coat is delivered to the checkroom attendant and either (i) negligence is shown or (ii) a fee or charge is exacted for checking the coat.*

In *Aldrich* v. *Waldorf-Astoria Hotel, Inc.,*[10] a hotel permitted an independent contractor to operate a checkroom on its premises. The independent contractor charged a $.35 **gratuity** for checking services. The plaintiff was attending a ball at the hotel. She checked her mink jacket at the checkroom. When she returned, the mink jacket was gone. (The opinion in this case appears at the end of this chapter.)

The court held the independent contractor liable on the grounds that he was not a hotel, motel, or restaurant, and therefore not entitled to the limitations of liability set forth in the New York statute, § 201 of the General Business Law. The court stated the statute was in derogation of common law liability and therefore

---

* In 1983, § 201 of the New York General Business Law was amended to increase the statutory limits on liability for checkrooms to $200 and $300, respectively, under items 1 and 2 above.

must be strictly construed. The court then held the hotel liable under principles of **agency** and pointed out that the hotel had failed to disclose to the plaintiff that the checkroom was not operated by the hotel. So far as the plaintiff was concerned, she was entrusting her coat to the safekeeping of the hotel. When the hotel attempted to assert the statutory limits on liability in this case, the court rejected such limitations, asserting that the $75 limitation applied only where no fee or charge was exacted and that in this case the $.35 "gratuity" was actually a "fee" for checking the coat. The court thus held that the New York statute was inapplicable in this case and awarded the plaintiff judgment against the defendant independent contractor and hotel for $1,400.

Therefore, if a hotel's checkroom is operated by an independent contractor, the hotel would be wise to indicate in a posted notice and on claim tickets that the checkroom is operated by an independent contractor that is not an agent of the hotel. Moreover, the hotel's agreement with the independent contractor should include a clause to the effect that the independent contractor will **indemnify** and hold the hotel harmless against any claims by a guest or patron for loss of property from the checkroom, and that proper insurance will be provided that also covers the hotel's liability.

Baggage Rooms and Storerooms

The New York statute (§ 201) also limits the hotel's liability for losses from baggage rooms and storerooms to a maximum of $100, unless the guest, at the time of delivery, obtains a written receipt from the hotel agreeing that the value of the guest's property is in excess of $100. Even if the guest obtains a receipt stating a higher value, the hotel's liability is still limited to a maximum of $500 unless the loss occurs as a result of the hotel's negligence.

Merchandise Samples

The New York statute (§ 201) also limits the hotelkeeper's liability for loss of or damage to merchandise samples or merchandise for sale (whether the property remains in the guest's possession or has been given to the hotel for storage). In connection with these items, the hotelkeeper is under *no liability whatsoever* unless the guest has given written notice stating the value to the effect that he/she has the samples or merchandise, which written notice the hotelkeeper *must* acknowledge in writing. Even in that event, the hotelkeeper's liability is limited to $500 unless the guest can show that the loss or damage occurred through the hotel's fault or negligence.

Loss by Fire

The New York statute (§ 201) also deals with the loss of a guest's personal property by reason of fire. This statute will only free the hotel from liability if the hotel can prove that the fire occurred without any fault or negligence of the hotel. This means that there is an initial presumption that the hotel is negligent, and the hotel must disprove this presumption of negligence in order to limit liability.

Unclaimed Property

Some states have statutes which provide that any hotel that has any unclaimed baggage or other property in custody for six months may sell the same at public auction. The statutory requirements may differ in each state (see, for example, New York's Abandoned Property Laws).

This procedure applies only to *unclaimed* property. Before selling the property, the hotel must be certain that no agreement was made to hold it for a period of time, or that at least six months have elapsed since the expiration of an agreed time. The statutory procedure for a sale must be strictly followed.

If the hotel has no record whatsoever of the address of the owner of the unclaimed property and does not know the name of the property's owner, it should not make the sale under such statute. This is because the hotel cannot mail the notice required by the law. This failure to comply strictly with the statutory procedure may make a hotel liable if the owner subsequently appears and asks for the property.

Note that in some states, such as New York, the hotel's right to sell unclaimed property has been questioned. In New York, the *ex parte* sale of guest property was declared unconstitutional in *Blye* v. *Globe-Wernecke Realty Co.*,[11] and the guest must be afforded notice and the opportunity to be heard prior to permanent deprivation of the property.[12]

In light of the foregoing, the simpler course is to turn over all such lost or mislaid property to the police.

Liability for Handling Mail for Hotel Guests

If a hotel accepts delivery of guests' mail from the post office, it may be liable for negligence for any failure to deliver such mail to the guest. In addition, the hotel may have to assume specific contractual liability for registered mail under its agreement with the post office or the guest to handle such mail.

Section 153.6 of the U.S. Postal Service's *Domestic Mail Manual* states:

153.6 Delivery to Persons at Hotels, Institutions, Schools, Etc.

* * *

.62 Mail Addressed to Persons at Hotels, Schools, Etc. Mail addressed to persons at hotels, schools, and similar places is delivered to the hotel or school. If the addressee is no longer at the address, the mail will be redirected to his current address. If the forwarding address is unknown, the mail will be returned to the post office.

.63 Registered Mail Addressed to Persons at Hotels and Apartment Houses. Registered mail addressed to persons at hotels and apartment houses will be delivered to the persons designated by the management of the hotel or apartment house in a written agreement with the Postal Service. Form 3801-A, *Agreement by the Hotel, Apartment House or the Like,* MUST be executed for this purpose. If delivery of the registered mail has been restricted by the sender, it may not be delivered to the representative of the hotel or apartment house unless the addressee has specifically authorized this person in writing to receive his restricted delivery mail. The authorization may be made on Form 3849-A, *Delivery Notice or Receipt;* Form 3849-B, *Delivery Reminder or Receipt;* Form 3801, *Standing Delivery Order;* or by a letter to the postmaster.

The hotel may make a special agreement to hold mail for guests. Section 153.211 of the *Domestic Mail Manual* states, "A person or a number of persons may designate an-other to receive their mail. Designation of another person to receive mail should be in writing, but no special form is furnished or required."

The hotel should consider whether it is prepared to assume responsibility for such mail during that period. The same precaution should be taken in agreeing to forward mail to a guest. Such an agreement should always have some time limitation, such as 10 days, 20 days, or other fixed period. Otherwise, the guest might expect mail to be forwarded indefinitely.

Liability for Automobiles of Guests and Others

Many hotels provide space for parking guests' automobiles. The hotel may operate its own garage or parking space or have a working agreement with an independently owned garage. In either case, where the hotel has been entrusted with the automobile, it may be liable for its loss or damage. The scope of the hotel's duty and the legal standard of care to which a hotel may be held with respect to guests' automobiles and contents vary from state to state. For example, in some states a hotel may be held liable under the common law rule as an insurer against loss or damage, while in other states the hotel is required to exercise ordinary and reasonable care under the circumstances.

In a few states, the hotelkeeper's liability for loss of a guest's car and property and requisite standard of care may be determined by statute. For example, in *Kushner* v. *President of Atlantic City, Inc.,*[13] the court held that under the state's hotelkeeper statute an automobile was considered "personal property" for which a hotel would not be liable unless the loss was caused by fault or negligence of the hotel proprietor. The hotelkeeper was thus absolved from any common law liability as insurer.[14]

Under the common law rule, hotels are liable as insurers for guests' property that is on the hotel premises, or *infra hospitium.*[15] This common law concept defining the scope of the innkeeper's liability itself may depend on various factors. For example, in *Merchants Fire Assurance Corp.* v. *Zion's Security Corp.,*[16] the hotel was held liable because its bellboy kept the key to the car. In cases in which the automobile was held not to be *infra hospitium,* factors such as the guest's keeping the keys, the lack of a fee charged by the hotel, and the lack of control exercised by the hotelkeeper over the guest's car were all considered relevant.[17]

The courts have held that even when the car was placed in a public garage, the garage company was the agent of the hotel in performing its contract for the safekeeping of the car. Therefore, the guest was entitled to sue the hotel for damages to the automobile, the hotel being liable for the acts of its agents.[18]

In a case in Virginia,[19] the trial judge refused to render summary judgment in favor of the defendant-hotel when a guest's automobile and its contents were stolen from the hotel's own outdoor parking lot. The judge's order apparently was based on the principle that the hotel did have some duty to protect guests' property on the hotel premises. Therefore, a jury should decide at trial whether the hotel took necessary and reasonable precautions in this case. The judge also refused to limit the hotel's liability for the loss of the guest's personal property contained in the vehicle under the Virginia hotelkeeper's statute since "the alleged loss did not take place from a room or rooms or the office of" the hotel, as required by that statute.

Theory of Bailment

Hotels have also been held liable for loss or damage to a guest's automobile and/ or its contents on the theory of **bailment.** Again, the question of whether a hotel is liable may depend on the amount of control the hotel exercises over the automobile and parking facilities. Some jurisdictions may distinguish between gratuitous bailments and bailments for hire. If a fee is charged for parking, if a fee is included in the guest's bill for the hotel's parking service, or if the hotel benefits from "free" parking, the bailment may fall within the category of bailment for hire, for which the standard of care in most states is generally that of ordinary and reasonable care. On the other hand, if the arrangement is classified as a gratuitous bailment, the hotel may have a lesser duty of care, namely, to be free of gross negligence in some jurisdictions. (**Caution:** In a number of jurisdictions, the distinction is not clear, and the **gratuitous bailee-**hotel may today be held to the standard of ordinary and reasonable care.)[20]

The Horseshoe Casino in Tunica, Mississippi, required its employees to park their cars in a particular lot. An employee had her car stolen from the employee's lot. Because the casino required that the cars of its employees be parked in a particular designated lot for the employer casino's own convenience and interests, a special relationship—a bailment—arose. Thus the court held Horseshoe Casino liable.[21]

The Hotel's Claim When the Hotel Does Not Own or Manage the Garage

In certain circumstances, a hotel may be able to bring a separate legal action against the garage operators for indemnification or a cross claim against the garage for contribution, alleging that the garage's negligence caused the loss or damage to the guest's car. For example, in *Governor House* v. *Schmidt,*[22] the hotel was held directly liable to a guest for property stolen from the guest's automobile in a connected and adjacent garage facility on the common law doctrine of *infra hospitium.* However, the appellate court held that the hotel could maintain an action against the garage operators for contribution or indemnification in which the garage's negligence, if proven at trial, would be the basis of liability.

The hotel might also obtain an indemnity agreement from the outside garage. In this case, even if a claim were made against the hotel, it could seek recovery from the garage for losses or damages. One sample form appears in Exhibit 11.2.

Exhibit 11.2   Form of Garage Indemnity Agreement

Garage Indemnity Agreement

Date _____

In consideration of the storage in the garage owned and/or operated by the undersigned at _____ of automobiles belonging to guests at
　　　　　　(address of garage)

the HOTEL _____ which automobiles may have been
　　　　　(name of hotel)
delivered to the garage either by Hotel employees or by the guests themselves upon recommendation from the Hotel and in consideration of payment of the agreed charges for such storage, either by the guests or by the Hotel, the undersigned agrees

(1) To pay to the Hotel the following commissions or other compensation [insert details of arrangement for payment to Hotel, if any. If no compensation is paid, this paragraph may be omitted].

(2) To indemnify and hold the hotel harmless from any and all claims, suits, judgments or demands from the owners of said automobiles based upon or arising from loss of or damage to the said automobiles, the accessories thereto or property in said automobiles occurring while the said automobile, accessories and contents are in the possession of the undersigned, his agents, servants or employees or under their operation or control, or otherwise, during the period subsequent to the delivery of said automobile to the undersigned, its agents, servants or employees and prior to its redelivery to the Hotel or to the owner of said automobile.

(3) Concurrently herewith the garage has furnished a surety bond in the sum of $_____ to cover the faithful performance by the garage of this agreement of indemnity.

In Witness Whereof, the undersigned has affixed his hand and seal the day and year first above written.

In the presence of:

_____(LS.)

_____

The hotel should consider obtaining insurance against liability for loss or damage. In all cases, insurance should be obtained to cover the hotel's liability if its door attendant drives the car to and from the garage.

As a matter of public policy, courts in a number of states may not give any effect to the fact that the hotel has posted a notice to guests attempting to absolve it from liability for loss or damage to guests' automobiles or personal property therein, unless it is a statutory notice pursuant to state statutes limiting such liability.[23]

Important Points for Management

- Hotels must post copies of required state statutes in accordance with the statutes' provisions in order to limit the hotel's liability for lost or stolen guest property.

- The hotel should exercise care with the guest's property from the time of the guest's arrival through the time of the guest's departure.

- The hotel may be sued for property lost from the hotel checkroom.

- It is recommended that unclaimed property be turned over to the police.

- If a garage on hotel premises is not operated by the hotel, the hotel should take steps to prevent its liability for property losses from guest cars parked in the garage. Tickets should be issued in the name of the garage, not in the name of the hotel. The garage should contractually agree to indemnify the hotel if the hotel suffers any loss due to the garage's operations. The hotel should also consider insurance to protect against loss.

References

1. 13 Wash. App. 427, 534 P. 2d 1373 (Wash. Ct. App. 1975).

2. *Phillip* v. *Fairmont-Roosevelt Hotel, Inc.,* 469 So. 2d 1140 (La. 1985).

3. *Gabor* v. *Hotel Waldorf-Astoria Corp.,* 70 Civ. 4310 (S.D.N.Y. 1973). See also *H.K. Mallak, Inc.* v. *Fairfiled FMC Corp.,* 33 F. Supp. 2d 748, No. 96-C-1207 (E.D. Wis. 1999).

4. 279 Cal. Rptr. 265 (Ct. App. 1991).

5. *Charles Bernard, Ltd. d/b/a Days Inn Art Deco/Convention Center* v. *Tobias Jewelry Ltd.,* 751 So. 2d 711, No. 3D98–3150 (Fla. Dist. Ct. App. 2/16/00).

6. 68 Misc. 2d 400, 327 N.Y.S. 2d 426 (Civ. Ct. N.Y. Co. 1972).

7. 276 App. Div. 67, 92 N.Y.S. 2d 852 (1949), reversed on other grounds, 301 N.Y. 736, 95 N.E. 2d 410, confirmed to 277 App. Div. 1097, 101 N.Y.S. 2d 622 (1st Dept. 1950).

8. *Levitt* v. *Desert Palace Hotel, Inc.,* 601 F. 2d 684 (2nd Cir. 1979).

9. 53 N.Y. 2d 499, 426 N.E. 2d 459 (1981).

10. 74 Misc. 2d 413, 343 N.Y.S. 2d 830 (Civ. Ct. N.Y. Co. 1973).

11. 33 N.Y. 2d 15, 20, 300 N.E. 710 (1973).

12. See also *Sharrock* v. *Del Buick-Cadillac,* 45 N.Y. 2d 152, 379 N.E. 1169 (1978); *People* v. *Lerhinan,* 90 A.D. 2d 74 (2d Dept. 1982); *U.S.* v. *Rahme,* 813 F. 2d 31 (2nd Cir. 1987).

13. 251 A. 2d 480, 105 N.J. Super. 203 (1969).

14. See also *Park-O-Tel Co.* v. *Roskamp,* 203 Okla. 493, 223 P. 2d 375 (Supreme Ct. Okla. 1950); *Savoy Hotel Corp.* v. *Sparks,* 57 Tenn. App. 537, 421 S.W. 2d 98 (1967).

15. See *Dispeker* v. *New Southern Hotel Co.,* 52 Tenn. App. 379, 373 S.W. 2d 897 (1963), *cert. denied,* 213 Tenn. 378, 373 S.W. 2d 904 (1963).

16. 109 Utah 13, 163 P. 2d 319 (1945).

17. See, for example, *Cloward* v. *Pappas,* 79 Nev. 482, 387 P. 2d 97 (1979); *Sewell* v. *Mountainview Hotel, Inc.,* 45 Tenn. App. 604, 325 S.W. 2d 626 (1959).

18. See *Kallish* v. *Meyer Hotel Co.,* 182 Tenn. 29, 184 S.W. 2d 45 (1944); *Savoy Hotel Corp.* v. *Sparks,* 57 Tenn. App. 537, 421 S.W. 2d 98 (1967). See also cases in Annot., 156 A.L.R. 233 (1945).

19. *Coates* v. *Second Richmond Motel Enterprises, Inc.* (Docket No. LC-1138).

20. See *Edwards Hotel Co.* v. *Terry,* 185 Miss. 824, 187 So. 518 (1939).

21. *Robinson Property Group Limited Partnership* v. *Debra Rodman.* (1998 Miss. LEXIS 359, Sup. Ct. Miss., July 23, 1998).

22. 284 A. 2d 660 (D.C. Ct. App. 1971).

23. See *Savoy Hotel Corp.* v. *Sparks,* 57 Tenn. App. 537, 421 S.W. 2d 98 (1967). See also 1999 Iowa Code Ann. §§ 671.7 and 671.8.

🔑 Key Terms

act of god—A casualty, loss, or event caused by direct, immediate, and exclusive operation of the forces of nature, uncontrolled or uninfluenced by the power of human beings.

agency—Presupposes a directing principal and a directed agent under delegation of authority to the agent, either by contract, express or implied, or by operation of law, estoppel, or ratification.

bailee—A person with whom personalty (personal property) is entrusted; generally bears a heavy burden of proof to avoid liability.

bailment—The delivery of personalty (personal property) for some particular purpose, or on mere deposit, upon a contract, express or implied, that after purpose has been fulfilled it shall be redelivered to the person who delivered it, or otherwise dealt with according to his/her directions, or kept until he/she reclaims it, as the case may be.

burden of proof—The burden or duty of satisfying the minds of the jury of the truth of all the material facts alleged by the plaintiff and denied by the defendant.

derogation—The partial repeal or abolishing of a law.

gratuitous bailee—A person who comes into possession of the personal property of another, receives nothing from the owner of the property, and has no right to recover from the owner for what he/she does in caring for the property. A gratuitous bailee is liable only to the bailor for bad faith or gross negligence.

gratuity—Something given voluntarily or beyond obligation.

gross negligence—Negligence that is substantially and appreciably higher in magnitude and more culpable than ordinary negligence. Gross negligence is equivalent to the failure to exercise even a slight degree of care. It is very great negligence, or the absence of slight diligence, or the want of even scant care; and a disregard of consequences that may ensue from the act; and indifference to rights of others.

indemnify—To secure against loss or damages.

infra hospitium—Means "within the inn." Under the doctrine of *infra hospitium,* the innkeeper's liability for loss of a guest's property attaches only where property was within the walls of the inn itself, or, if outside, was in the care and under the charge of the innkeeper.

❓ Review Questions

1. Under common law, what is the innkeeper's liability for losses of a guest's property?

2. In what ways do states limit the hotel's liability with respect to the loss of the guest's property?

3. Why is it important to post notices to the guest concerning the statutory limitations of liability?

4. What are the limitations on the hotel's liability with regard to checkrooms, baggage rooms, and storerooms?

5. How should the hotel handle unclaimed property?

6. What are some of the ways in which a hotel may be liable for loss or damage to guests' automobiles?

7. What is a bailment, and how does it apply to hotel and guest property?

8. If a hotel restaurant patron is not a guest staying in the hotel, what liability does the hotel have if the patron leaves his/her coat on a chair?

9. What steps should the hotel take with respect to abandoned property?

Internet Sites

For more information, visit the following Internet sites. Remember that Internet addresses can change without notice.

Hotel and Restaurant Law
http://www.law.cornell.edu/topics/hotel_restaurants.html

Illustrative Cases

Aldrich v. Waldorf-Astoria Hotel, Inc.

74. Misc. 2d 413,
343 N.Y.S. 2d 830 (Civ. Ct. N.Y. Co. 1973)

RICHARD S. LANE, Judge.

When Mr. and Mrs. Aldrich presented themselves at the Waldorf's check room at the conclusion of the Viennese Opera Ball, Mrs. Aldrich's mink jacket was missing. The check room was operated for the Waldorf by Harry Cantor but this fact was not revealed in any way to the guests.

The Waldorf and Mr. Cantor seek to avoid the ordinary consequences of the law of bailments by relying on the limitation of liability contained in Section 201 of the General Business Law. Such limitation is not available to Mr. Cantor because he is not a hotel, motel or restaurant. The statute is in derogation of common law liability and must be strictly construed. [citations omitted] Nor can the Waldorf hide behind the statute because it is applicable only where no fee or charge is exacted for checking. Here the 35 [cents] per garment familiar to those who participate in New York's social whirl was paid. Whether called a gratuity or otherwise, one need only try to check a coat without paying it to realize it is indeed a fee.

The above determinations render it unnecessary for the court to reach the issue of whether there has been sufficient posting to comply with the statute. The Waldorf uses the standard card approved by the New York State Hotel Association which bears a legend at the top "Notice to guests" in large black type. The legend is followed in equally large black type by a message concerning the availability of a safe in the office, and then in slightly smaller, lighter but still eminently readable type comes information concerning rates. Finally and occupying two-thirds of the card in legible but very tiny type are printed the provisions of several sections of the General Business Law including Section 201. Such a card in a frame was hung on the wall between the elevators on the ballroom floor where departing guests would have ample opportunity to see it but arriving guests would have their backs to it. There was also evidence that such cards were at either end of the forty- to forty-five foot checking counter at the Waldorf which is divided by pillars into four or five checking stations. The court is highly dubious as to whether this constitutes the posting "in a conspicuous place and manner" as required by the statute. It is clear that without a showing of such posting no limitation is available. [citations omitted] But what constitutes "conspicuous" posting has not been delineated in any recorded decision to the court's knowledge.

The Waldorf and Mr. Cantor also defend by alleging contributory negligence on the part of Mr. and Mrs. Aldrich in accepting only one check for two garments. This is not an uncommon practice in check rooms across the City. It was initiated here and generally by and for the convenience of the check room, and plaintiffs will not be held contributorily negligent for merely failing to protest it.

Finally the Waldorf defends on the grounds that it was not responsible for the check room, having franchised it to Mr. Cantor. Under the circumstances, this position flies in the face of the ordinary principles of agency. So far as Mr. and Mrs. Aldrich and the other guests were concerned, they were entrusting their coats to the safe keeping of the Waldorf. To the extent that *Jacobson* v. *Richards & Hassen Enterprises, supra,* is to the contrary, it will not be followed.

Plaintiff may have judgment against defendants for $1,400 together with the cost and disbursements of this action. The Waldorf has cross-claimed against Mr. Cantor based upon an indemnity agreement. No evidence thereon was adduced, however. Accordingly, the cross-claim will not be adjudged and this determination is specifically without prejudice to its renewal.

Salisbury v. St. Regis-Sheraton Hotel Corp.

490 F. Supp. 449 (S.D.N.Y. 1980)

On the morning of November 22, 1978, Mr. and Mrs. Roger Salisbury concluded a three day stay at the St. Regis-Sheraton Hotel in New York. While Mr. Salisbury paid the bill and surrendered their room key, Mrs. Salisbury checked their luggage with a bellhop in the lobby. The couple was to spend the day in town and return for the luggage that afternoon. Mrs. Salisbury did not inform the hotel, when she checked the luggage, that one of their pieces, a cosmetics case, contained jewelry and cosmetics worth over $60,000, and did not ask that the case be kept in the hotel's safe. Nor did she inform the hotel that the value of the case and its contents exceeded $100.

When the Salisburys returned to the hotel to retrieve their luggage at about 4:30 that afternoon, the cosmetics case containing the jewelry was missing. Mrs. Salisbury sues to recover the value of the case and its contents.

It is undisputed that posted conspicuously in the public areas of the hotel was a notice informing guests that the hotel provided a safe for the safekeeping of their valuables, and notifying them of the provisions of sections 200 and 201 of the New York General Business Law, which provide:

> "Whenever the proprietor or manager of any hotel, motel, inn or steamboat shall provide a safe in the office of such hotel, motel or steamboat, or other convenient place for the safe keeping of any money, jewels, ornaments, bank notes, bonds, negotiable securities or precious stones, belonging to the guests of or travelers in such hotel, motel, inn or steamboat, and shall notify the guests or travelers thereof by posting a notice stating the fact that such safe is provided, in which such property may be deposited, in a public and conspicuous place and manner in the office and public rooms, and in the public parlors of such hotel, motel, or inn, or saloon of such steamboat; and if such guest or traveler shall neglect to deliver such property, to the person in charge of such office for deposit in such safe, the proprietor or manager of such hotel, motel, or steamboat shall not be liable for any loss of such property, sustained by such guest or traveler by theft or otherwise;...." (§ 200)
>
> "No hotel or motel keeper except as provided in the foregoing section shall be liable for damage to or loss of wearing apparel or other personal property in the lobby, hallways or in the room or rooms assigned to a guest for any sum exceeding the sum of five hundred dollars, unless it shall appear that such loss occurred through the fault or negligence of such keeper, *nor shall he be liable in any sum exceeding the sum of one hundred dollars* for the loss of or damage to any such property when delivered to such keeper for storage or safe keeping in the store room, baggage room or other place elsewhere than in the room or rooms assigned to such guest, unless at the time of delivering the same for storage or safe keeping such value in excess of one hundred dollars shall be stated* and a written receipt, stating such value, shall be issued by such keeper, but in no event shall such keeper be liable beyond five hundred dollars, unless it shall appear that such loss occurred through his fault or negligence,...." (§ 201) (emphasis supplied)

* * *

It is not uncommon for a hotel to hold luggage for a few hours after guests check out as an accommodation to them. This would appear to be one of the services which a hotel performs for its guests in the normal course of its business, and there is no reason why it should be deemed to alter the otherwise existing legal relationship between them. Accordingly, we conclude that sections 200 and 201 are fully applicable in the circumstances of this case, and precludes [sic] any recovery against the hotel for the loss of Mrs. Salisbury's jewelry, and limits any recovery for the loss of the case and its other contents to $100....

While we thus conclude that the hotel has an absolute defense to Mrs. Salisbury's suit for the value of her jewelry, we note that even if the relationship involved here were deemed a gratuitous bailment, as Mrs. Salisbury contends it should be, the hotel's liability would be limited to the value of articles ordinarily

---

* Authors' note: In 1983, Section 201 was amended to increase this statutory liability to $200.

found in a cosmetics case, even if Mrs. Salisbury could establish that the hotel was grossly negligent in caring for her case…. Even under her own view of the law, Mrs. Salisbury could not recover the value of her lost jewelry.

Fennema v. Howard Johnson Co.

559 So. 2d 1231 (Fla. 1990)

HUBBART, Judge.

This is an appeal by the plaintiffs Robert and Kimberly Fennema from an adverse final summary judgment entered below in an innkeeper's negligence action. The central question presented for review is whether an innkeeper may rely on Section 509.111, Florida Statutes (1985), which limits an innkeeper's liability for loss of a guest's personal property, when, as here, (a) the innkeeper affirmatively advises his guest to park the guest's motor vehicle in a particular location in the inn's parking lot for safekeeping, after being told by the guest concerning the valuable nature of the vehicle's contents, and (b) the vehicle and its contents are thereafter stolen. We hold that the innkeeper's conduct estops him from setting up as a defense the aforesaid limitation of liability statute, and, accordingly, reverse the final summary judgment under review.

The material facts of this case are undisputed. In August, 1985, the plaintiffs Robert J. Fennema and his wife Kimberly A. Fennema came to Dade County, Florida, from the state of Washington so that Robert Fennema could become a university professor at Florida International University. They travelled to Dade County in a Chevrolet Camaro and a rented twenty-four-foot U-Haul truck which, in turn, towed their 1970 Toyota Land Cruiser; they placed nearly all their possessions in the U-Haul truck. Mr. Fennema drove the U-Haul truck, and Mrs. Fennema drove the Camaro. Upon their arrival in Dade County, they stopped at a Howard Johnson Motor Lodge located at 1430 South Dixie Highway, Coral Gables, Florida, at approximately 6:00 P.M. on August 10, 1985. This lodge was owned and operated by the defendants H. William Prahl, Jr. and Robert A. Prahl, under a franchise from the defendants Howard Johnson Company and Palmetto Management Company.

Mrs. Fennema went into the motel office and registered for her and her husband. She specifically advised the registration clerk that they had a Toyota Land Cruiser towed by a large U-Haul truck with nearly all their personal belongings in it; she asked where would be a safe place to park this vehicle. The clerk directed her to park the vehicle in a particular area of the motel parking lot behind a building where presumably it would be safe from vandalism or theft. Mrs. Fennema conveyed this information to Mr. Fennema who, in turn, parked the vehicle in the place designated by the clerk. Although there had been numerous incidents of criminal activity including motor vehicle thefts on or about the grounds and parking lot of this motel, the plaintiffs were not provided with this information nor warned of the risks of leaving their vehicle in the lot. The Fennemas thereafter spent the night in the motel without incident, and, the following day, went for a drive in the Camaro. When they returned to the motel at 3:00 P.M. that afternoon, they discovered that the U-Haul truck with all of its contents and the attached Toyota Land Cruiser had been stolen by unknown third parties from the place in the parking lot where the clerk had told them to park it for safekeeping.

The plaintiffs brought a negligence action below against the defendant inn-keepers for the property loss sustained as a result of the above theft in the amount of $177,000. They alleged that the defendants were negligent in failing to warn the plaintiffs that there had been criminal activity in the motel parking lot, and that the defendants failed to take other steps to warn their guests and/or to pre-vent criminal activity from occurring in the parking lot. The plaintiffs also claimed that the defendant Howard Johnson, as owner, departed from a standard of care nationally advertised by it, that all the defendants knew the parking lot was dangerous, and that as owners, lessees and operators of the motel, they had an obligation, at a minimum, to warn their guests. The defendant filed an answer denying any liability for the theft loss and setting up various affirmative defenses, including that the plaintiff's recovery was limited by Section 509.111, Florida Statutes (1985).

The defendants moved for a summary judgment which the trial court granted on the basis of the statute. Specifically, the trial court ruled that the defen-dants had posted Section 509.111, Florida Statutes (1985) in a "prominent place," [as required by Section 509.101, Florida Statutes (1985)]—namely, the inside of an open closet in the plaintiffs' motel room—and, consequently, were absolved of all liability for the theft loss sued upon when the plaintiffs failed to comply with the provisions of Section 509.111. This appeal follows.

The plaintiffs contend that the trial court erred in applying the aforesaid limitation of liability statute to the instant case inasmuch as the statute had no application to their vehicle and its contents under the circumstances of this case, and that otherwise genuine issues of material fact exist as to the defendants' alleged negligence. We entirely agree.

It is settled in Florida that "[a]n innkeeper owes the duty of reasonable care for the safety of his guests['] [person and property]," that generally speaking, "it is 'peculiarly a jury function to determine what precautions are reasonably required in the exercise of a particular duty of due care,'" and that an innkeeper's knowledge, as here, of prior criminal activity on or around the grounds of his inn imposes a duty to take adequate security precautions for the safety of his guests and their property.... With respect to any damage to or loss of a guest's property, however, an innkeeper's negligence liability is specifically limited by Section 509.111, Florida Statutes (1985)—provided a copy of that statute is posted "in the office, hall, or lobby or another prominent place of such public lodging... establishment."...

Under the...statute:

> "a hotel's liability for a guest's loss of property is limited to $500 unless the hotel accepts property for safekeeping pursuant to subsection (1) or the guest, in accordance with subsection (2) provides an inventory of effects not tendered and accepted pursuant to subsection (1). In either event, if the proper procedures are followed, the hotel's liability is limited to $1,000."...

It does not follow, however, that an innkeeper may, under all circumstances, rely on the above statute to limit his liability even if the statute is properly posted at the inn.... [A]n innkeeper is estopped to rely on the innkeeper's limitation of liability statute if he personally misleads his guest into believing that the latter's property may be safely placed at a particular location in the inn, as this causes a guest to disregard whatever posted statutory procedures there might be for safe-guarding a guest's property generally.

* * *

[I]n our view, the defendant innkeepers are estopped to invoke whatever protection Section 509.111, Florida Statutes (1985), may afford. This is so because the defendant's motel clerk affirmatively misled the plaintiffs into believing that their motor vehicle and its valuable contents were safe if parked at a particular location in the motel parking lot. Mrs. Fennema specifically informed the motel registration clerk concerning the valuable contents of the plaintiffs' motor vehicle and asked where would be a safe place to park the vehicle; the clerk, in turn, directed the Fennemas to park their vehicle at a particular spot in the motel guest parking lot behind a building where presumably the vehicle would be safe. The plaintiffs had every right to believe and did believe that their vehicle would be safe at that location; they parked their vehicle in the exact spot as directed and later the vehicle was stolen from that spot.

Having affirmatively misled the plaintiffs that it was, in effect, safe to leave their vehicle and its contents at this location in the motel parking lot, the defendant innkeepers are in no position to claim the limited liability protection of Section 509.111, Florida Statutes (1985). The plaintiffs had every right to rely on the defendant's affirmative assurance of safety for their property and to believe that these personal assurances of safety overrode whatever statutory procedures might exist for safeguarding guests' property generally—if, indeed, they had later read the statute as posted in their motel room.… [T]he defendants, by their conduct, are estopped to rely on the protection of the subject statute because they, in effect, misled the plaintiffs into disregarding the procedure stated in the posted statute as being unnecessary, given the motel's personal directive which they followed for safeguarding their property. Beyond that, there are otherwise genuine issues of material fact on this record as to whether the defendants were negligent in failing to take adequate security precautions to protect the plaintiffs' property or, at the very least, to warn the plaintiffs of the potential dangers to their property based on the past criminal activity and car thefts on and about the defendant's parking lot.…

Chapter 12 Outline

Competencies

1. Describe a hotel's liability for loss of a non-guest's property under the theory of bailment. (pp. 181–182)

2. Distinguish between actual custody and constructive custody of property, and describe a hotel's liability for a restaurant patron's property. (p. 182)

3. Explain a hotel's defenses to liability claims. (p. 183)

12

The Hotel's Liability for Loss of Property of Non-Guests

General Nature of Liability

As discussed in Chapter 11, most states have statutes limiting the common law liability of hotels as insurers of guests' property. Many of the state statutes relate to a hotel's or restaurant's liability for the property of persons who are not technically "guests" of the hotel (i.e., persons who are attending social functions at the hotel, bar and restaurant patrons, visitors of registered guests, etc.). Hotels and restaurants often provide checking facilities for such persons to deposit their coats, briefcases, and other personal belongings. In New York State, the General Business Law provides a statutory schedule of liability for the loss of personal property of guests or patrons from checkrooms of any hotel, motel, and restaurant. (See the discussion on checkroom liability in Chapter 11.)

Bailments for Non-Guests

In the absence of any state statute limiting liability, hotels may be liable for loss of property under a theory of bailment. When the hotel agrees to accept the non-guest's property for safekeeping, the hotel is legally a "bailee" and is generally bound by the applicable legal standard of care. For example, in *Crosby* v. *20 Fifth Avenue Hotel Co., Inc.*,[1] a court held that upon checking out of the hotel and leaving property checked in storage, a person no longer is a guest. However, the relationship between that person and the hotel with respect to the stored property is that of **bailor** and bailee, respectively. In this case, the guest checked out of the hotel leaving two trunks in storage. He returned to claim the trunks after two years and four months. During this time, the hotel had sold the trunks pursuant to a state law then in effect that allowed hotels to sell "unclaimed chattels" at auction after following certain notice procedures. The court held that as a gratuitous bailee, the hotel would be held to the duty to be free of gross negligence. However, the court went on to say that under the common law, a bailee had no right to sell goods without the bailor's consent. Therefore, because of the "unauthorized" sale, the court rendered a judgment in favor of the plaintiff-bailor for the value of the trunks and their contents. On appeal, the appellate court modified this judgment by reducing the award by the value of an antique item left in the trunk because the hotel should not be expected to know that such an extraordinary item was left in the trunk.

In another case, a departing guest stored a trunk at a hotel while she was temporarily absent. It was held that the hotel was not liable for the loss of a diamond pendant from the trunk on the ground that the hotel never agreed to assume liability for a diamond pendant, but only for such articles as are *"ordinarily* contained (emphasis added)" in a trunk.[2]

Rosin v. *Central Plaza Hotel, Inc.,*[3] a case in Chicago, involved the loss of luggage delivered to the hotel *before* the plaintiff's arrival. The Illinois court held that the hotel was merely a gratuitous bailee, and, under Illinois common law, liable only for any loss of bailed property caused by the hotel's gross negligence or **fraud.**

The hotel's custody of the property may be actual or constructive. It is actual custody if a hotel employee takes possession of the property. It may be constructive custody if the property is brought upon the premises with the hotel's consent. In either case, the hotel as bailee may be liable for loss caused by its negligence.[4]

The Supreme Court of Minnesota, in *National Fire Insurance Company* v. *Commodore Hotel, Inc.,*[5] held that the hotel will not be considered a bailee if it or its agent has no knowledge of the presence of the property on the premises or the acceptance of such property for safekeeping. The court held that the defendant-hotel was not a bailee of a mink jacket placed in an *unattended* cloakroom by a person attending a luncheon party at the hotel. The court held that on the facts of this case the hotel was not informed that the coat would be left in the unattended room. Therefore, the plaintiff maintained custody and control over the fur coat. Likewise, there was no evidence showing constructive (or implied) delivery of the coat for the hotel's safekeeping.

Hotel Liability for Restaurant Patrons' Property

In Washington, D.C., a case was brought by two patrons of a major hotel restaurant, claiming $35,680 in damages for jewelry that disappeared from their hand luggage while they ate lunch.

When the couple entered the hotel, a bellman offered to check their bags. The couple turned the bags over to the bellman, making no mention of the bag's contents. Allegedly the hotel failed to post any notice setting forth the statutory limits on the hotel's liability in such a case. The courts held that, under Washington, D.C. law, the relationship between restaurant and patron could not be considered the relationship of innkeeper and guest, and therefore the patrons could not premise their actions on strict liability imposed on innkeepers.

The court of appeals held that under the "bailee-for-hire" theory there was a question of fact to be determined by the jury as to whether the hotel had constructive knowledge that the patrons' hand luggage might contain valuable jewelry (or less valuable items). The court of appeals, therefore, remanded the case to the trial court for the jury's determination as to the contents of the bag. The jury rendered a verdict for the hotel.[6] (The opinion in this case appears at the end of this chapter.)

Hotel Defenses to Liability Claims

In the event of a suit against a hotel as bailee, the hotel has the burden of proof to show that it complied with the required standard of care with respect to the property. The degree of care required may vary, depending upon the state law governing the hotel. Even if the hotel has received no payment for holding or storing the property, it may still be liable depending upon the particular state law.

In *Coykendall* v. *Eaton*,[7] the trial court held the innkeeper not liable for property of a non-guest because the court ruled that the non-guest turned the property over to an unauthorized clerk, and the hotel never agreed to become a bailee. On appeal, the court reversed and remanded the case to the trial court, holding that the question of the clerk's authority should have been presented to the jury. It was held that the hotel clerk had no authority to receive property of persons who were not guests. In *Booth* v. *Litchfield*,[8] it was held that since there was no evidence of authority for a clerk to receive property after the guest had surrendered his room, the hotel was not liable for such property. However, a hotel may be estopped (prevented) from asserting in court that the clerk did not have authority to receive the property if the hotel in fact "holds out" the clerk as apparently having such authority.[9]

However, the negligence of the property owner, if such can be shown to be the cause or a contributing cause to the loss, may be asserted by the hotel to reduce (or, in some states, to eliminate) its liability.

Important Points for Management

- A hotel's liability for the property loss of a non-guest is covered by the law of ordinary bailments.

- The owner of property is legally liable for any loss of the property unless there is a bailment. To become a bailee, the hotel must assume possession and control over the property. The hotel's custody of the property may be actual or constructive. In either case, the hotel as bailee may be liable for loss caused by its negligence.

References

1. 173 Misc. 595, 20 N.Y.S. 2d 227 (1939), *modified on other grounds*, 173 Misc. 604, 17 N.Y.S. 2d 498 (1940).

2. *Waters* v. *Beau Site Company*, 114 Misc. 65, 186 N.Y.S. 731 (1920). See also *Crosby* v. *20 Fifth Avenue Hotel Company, Inc.*, 173 Misc. 595, 20 N.Y.S. 2d 227 (1939), *modified on other grounds*, 173 Misc. 604, 17 N.Y.S. 2d 498 (1940); *Ticehurst* v. *Beinbrink*, 72 Misc. 365, 129 N.Y.S. 838 (1911).

3. 345 Ill. App. 411, 103 N.E. 2d 381 (App. Ct. Ill. 1952).

4. *Adelphia Hotel Co.* v. *Providence Stock Co.*, 277 F. 905, 76 A.L.R. 213 (3rd Cir. 1922) (applying Pennsylvania law); *Bean* v. *Ford*, 119 N.Y.S. 1074, 65 Misc. 481 (1909).

5. 259 Minn. 349, 107 N.W. 2d 708 (1961).

6. *Blakemore* v. *Coleman*, 701 F.2d 967 (D.C. Cir. 1983).

7. 55 Barb. 188, 37 How. Pr. 438 (1869).

8. 201 N.Y. 466, 94 N.E. 1078 (1911). See also *Arcade Hotel Co.* v. *Waitt*, 44 Ohio St. 32, 4 N.E. 398 (1886).

9. *Adelphia Hotel Co.* v. *Providence Stock Co.*, 277 F. 905, 76 A.L.R. 213 (3rd Cir. 1922).

Key Terms

bailor—A person who entrusts his/her property to another.

fraud—An action calculated to deceive (including acts, omissions, and concealments) involving a breach of a legal or equitable duty, trust, or confidence which results in damage to another.

Review Questions

1. How does *Crosby v. 20 Fifth Avenue Hotel Co., Inc.* pertain to the theory of bailment?

2. Under what circumstances does a hotel become a bailee?

3. What is a bailee-hotel's relationship to a bailor?

4. What is a gratuitous bailee?

5. What is the difference between actual custody and constructive custody?

6. What does *National Fire Insurance Company v. Commodore Hotel, Inc.* teach us regarding a hotel's lack of knowledge about the presence of property on its premises?

7. What is a bailee-hotel's burden of proof in the event of a lawsuit brought against it?

8. What can hotels do to reduce or eliminate liability for losses of guest property?

Internet Sites

For more information, visit the following Internet sites. Remember that Internet addresses can change without notice.

FindLaw
http://www.findlaw.com

Illustrative Case

Blakemore **v.** *Coleman*

701 F.2d 967 (D.C. Cir. 1983)

MIKVA, C.J.

I. Background

The decision in this case turns uniquely on the facts. The Blakemores were in Washington, D.C. to celebrate President Reagan's inauguration, staying as overnight guests at a hotel in Georgetown. Before returning home, they decided to have lunch at The Jockey Club, a restaurant with a reputation for elegance. Upon arriving at the restaurant, which was then part of The Fairfax hotel, the Blakemores checked their car and three large suitcases with the hotel doorman. At the same time, they carried two pieces of hand luggage—a briefcase and a small, carry-on bag—into the hotel themselves. It was the carry-on bag that contained the jewelry that eventually disappeared; specifically, the missing jewelry was in one of the two small jewelry pouches that the Blakemores had stored in the bag. The bag itself was made of leather, was two feet long by nine-and-one-half inches wide, and was closed only by means of a zipper. No other locks or safety devices secured the main compartment of the bag.

When the Blakemores entered the hotel, they checked their two bags with the hotel bellman, who proceeded to place the bags in a small holding room or checkroom adjacent to the lobby. That room had neither a door separating it from the lobby nor any posted sign that would limit the defendant's liability under D.C. Code Ann. § 34-101 (1981) (allowing hotels to limit liability if, *inter alia*, they conspicuously post such notice). The Blakemores did not inform the bellman of the valuable jewelry contained in their bags or ask about locked storage areas; neither did the bellman inquire whether such valuables existed or inform the Blakemores that safety deposit boxes or other locked storage compartments were available for their use.

Following their lunch in the restaurant, the Blakemores returned to the hotel lobby to retrieve their belongings. Having done so, Mrs. Blakemore immediately opened the carry-on bag only to discover that one of the jewelry pouches was missing. It was at this point that the defendants actually were notified of the jewelry's existence and apparent disappearance. A search of the hotel by employees of The Fairfax and the police was unsuccessful in locating the missing pouch or any of the jewelry that it contained....

II. Innkeeper's Liability

Before discussing the issue of constructive knowledge that is central to this appeal, we must consider an alternative basis urged by the Blakemores for upholding the judgment of the district court. Specifically, the Blakemores argue that the trial judge should have found the defendants subject to innkeeper's liability, making them responsible for the contents of luggage belonging to their guests regardless of their knowledge about those contents. [Footnote omitted.] *See, e.g., Governor House* v. *Schmidt*, 284 A.2d 660 (D.C. 1971). It is true that application of the strict liability imposed on innkeepers would require affirmance of the district's court's judgment; but the Blakemores misconstrue the basis on which D.C. law premises an innkeeper-guest relationship. Indeed, in the latest case to define the scope of that relationship, *Wallace* v. *Shoreham Hotel Corp.*, 49 A.2d 81 (D.C. Mun. App. 1946), the D.C. Municipal Court of Appeals explicitly held that '[o]ne who is merely a customer at a bar, a restaurant, a barber shop or [a] newsstand operated by a hotel does not thereby establish the relationship of innkeeper and guest.' *Id.* at 82; *cf. Governor House*, 284 A.2d at 661-62 (applying innkeeper's liability in action brought by overnight guest of hotel); *Hotel Corp. of America* v. *Travelers Indemnity Co.*, 229 A.2d 158 (D.C. App. 1967) (same). Absent any indication that the D.C. courts have subsequently modified that definition, the federal courts are bound to follow that holding when applying D.C. law.

Nor is there any sound justification for distinguishing between the Blakemores and other restaurant patrons simply because the restaurant they happened to visit is located within a hotel. *Cake v. District of Columbia*, 33 App. D.C. 272 (D.C. Cir. 1909), heavily relied on by the Blakemores, is not to the contrary. In that case, the court defined 'bona fide registered guests' to include customers partaking of a hotel's food or lodging. *Id.* at 277. That court, however, was interpreting language included in a criminal statute, and was not delineating the scope of the innkeeper-guest relationship created by the common law. Thus, the district court was correct to conclude that the Blakemores could not premise their action on the strict liability imposed on innkeepers.

III. Constructive Knowledge

The Blakemores can sustain their damages award, therefore, only under a bailee-for-hire theory. The law of bailment for the District of Columbia, which the defendants admit is applicable to this case, requires that the subject matter of the bailment be delivered to, and accepted by, the bailee. It is not required, however, that the bailee have actual knowledge of the property in its custody in order to be liable for the property's eventual loss. Rather, when the property that is subject to the bailment is enclosed within a container, responsibility for its disappearance may rest with the bailee even though the bailee has only constructive or imputed knowledge of its existence. *See Dumlao v. Atlantic Garage, Inc.*, 259 A.2d 360 (D.C. App. 1969) (contents of an automobile); *Hallman v. Federal Parking Services*, 134 A.2d 382 (D.C. Mun. App. 1957) (same). Such constructive knowledge about the contents of a container has been defined to include those items that are in plain view, *see Dumlao*, 259 A.2d at 362, or that could be expected, given 'common knowledge and experience,' to be in a container under the specific facts and circumstances of a particular case, *see Hallman*, 134 A.2d at 385.

The mere articulation of this legal standard inescapably leads to the conclusion that a finding of constructive knowledge is a mixed question of law and fact. As with a finding of negligence, the specific facts underlying a given situation must be determined by the trier of fact before the legal standard can be properly applied. In the usual trial setting, the trial judge will explain the legal standard in his or her instructions, but the jury, uniquely qualified to make factual determinations, will apply that standard to the particular facts at issue. *See generally W. Prosser, Handbook of the Law of Torts* § 37 (4th ed. 1971) (discussing respective functions of court and jury in finding of negligence). In the present case, therefore, whether the defendants had constructive knowledge that the Blakemores' carry-on bag might contain valuable jewelry should have been left to the jury.

The district court ruled first that '[t]he evidence mandated a finding of constructive notice, leaving no question of fact for the jury in this regard,' RE 8, and then that '[a]rticles of jewelry are, as a matter of law, commonly and appropriately carried in hand luggage,' *id.* Both rulings, which had the effect of conclusively removing this issue from the jury's deliberations, were erroneous. [Footnote omitted.]

The first ruling quoted above—that the evidence 'mandated a finding' of constructive knowledge—effectively concluded that every reasonable juror necessarily would have found that the defendants had implied notice of the valuable jewelry contained in the Blakemores' carry-on bag. Although such a finding would not be clearly erroneous if the trial judge were serving as the trier of fact, the trial court committed reversible error when it removed the issue from the jury. The only fact that was conclusively established at trial was that the bag had some tangible contents. Whether those contents were valuable jewelry or just dirty laundry, however, could not be considered a foreclosed issue. Indeed, facts clearly existed from which conflicting inferences could be drawn. For example, it is conceded that the Blakemores arrived at the hotel only to have lunch, that they neither mentioned the valuables stored inside the bag or complained when the bag was placed in an unlocked holding room, and that the bag itself was unlocked. By themselves, these facts would seem to require submission of the case to the jury. *Cf. Dumlao*, A.2d at 362 (upholding a directed verdict in a bailment case when there was 'no evidence to show knowledge') (emphasis added). *Compare Wilkerson* v. *McCarthy*, 366 U.S. 53, 57, 69 S.Ct. 413, 415, 93 L.Ed. 497 (1949) ('It is the established rule that in passing upon whether there is sufficient evidence to submit an issue to the jury we need look only to the evidence and reasonable inferences which tend to support the case of a litigant against whom a peremptory instruction has been given.') with *Drapaniotis* v. *Franklin*, 504 F.2d 236, 237 (D.C. Cir. 1974) (per curiam) ('[i]n resolving [whether the trial court erred in directing a verdict for appellee] we must, of course, view the evidence, and the permissible inference therefrom, in the light most favorable to appellant') (citing *Brady* v. *Southern Railway*, 320 U.S. 476, 479, 64 S.Ct. 232, 234, 88 L.Ed. 239 (1943) and *Muldrow* v. *Daly*, 329 F.2d 886, 888 (D.C. Cir. 1964). *See generally Vander Zee* v. *Karabatsos*, 589 F.2d 723, 726-28 (D.C. Cir. 1978) (discussing standard for entering a directed verdict of j.n.o.v.), *cert. denied*, 441 U.S. 962, 99 S.Ct. 2407, 60 L.Ed.2d 1066 (1979). This is especially true when, as in this case, the trial judge takes an issue from the jury by ruling in favor of the party that bears the burden of persuasion. *Cf. Lucas* v. *Auto City Parking*, 62 A.2d 557, 559 (D.C. Mun. App. 1941) (burden on plaintiff to prove bailment).

Nor can we approve of the district court's ruling that valuable jewelry is, 'as a matter of law, commonly and appropriately carried in hand luggage.' To support that ruling, the trial judge relied on *Hasbrouck* v. *New York Cent. & H.R.R.*, 202 N.Y. 363, 95 N.E. 808 (N.Y. 1911), and the Blakemores cite *Sherman* v. *Pullman Co.*, 79 Misc. 52, 139 N.Y.S. 51 (App. Div. 1913). Even if these New York cases are somehow controlling in a diversity case applying D.C. law, they do not stand for the proposition stated. In *Hasbrouck*, for example, the specific paragraph relied on, 95 N.E. at 813, was an appellate court conclusion that there was sufficient evidence to support the trial judge's findings of fact; no conclusion of law about jewelry was made at the trial level. Similarly, in *Sherman*, the appellate court simply held that the lower court's conclusion that the term 'baggage' included jewelry found inside was not 'against the weight of the evidence.' 139 N.Y.S. at 52. Thus, in both cases the courts were affirming findings of fact made by trial judges serving as triers of fact; neither opinion is appropriate precedent for the lower court's action in the present case.

In sum, a straightforward application of the law of bailment for the District of Columbia requires that the jury determine whether the defendants in this case had constructive knowledge of the existence of valuable jewelry in the Blakemores' carry-on bag. To this extent, the district court's judgment must be reversed, and the case remanded for a new trial.

IV. Proceedings on Remand

Our holding requires that a retrial on all issues be held. Any decision concerning the defendant's constructive knowledge of valuable jewelry is too enmeshed with the other issues presented to allow for separate consideration.

Even assuming the jury concludes that the defendants had constructive knowledge that valuable jewelry was contained in the Blakemores' carry-on bag, it does not follow that the defendants would be liable for an unlimited amount or value of jewelry. The defendants had a right to assume that patrons of the restaurant would not check articles having an unreasonably high value without informing the bellman. Thus, the trial judge should further instruct the jury to limit its potential damage award to the maximum value of goods which the defendants reasonably could expect to be left in baggage checked under the particular circumstances of the present case. Only in this way can the necessary and appropriate limits be set on the liability that might be imposed on the defendants.

It is so ordered.

Chapter 13 Outline

Competencies

1. Explain what a hotel must do to limit liability for loss of guest valuables according to state statutes. (p. 191)

2. Explain the importance of strict compliance with statutory regulations limiting liability for loss of guest valuables. (pp. 191–192)

3. Describe statutory limits on a hotel's liability when the hotel's negligence is alleged as the cause of a loss of guest valuables. (pp. 193–194)

13

Safekeeping Facilities

Guests' Valuables

As pointed out in Chapter 11, hotels wishing to meet a state's statutory requirements for limiting liability for any loss of money, jewelry, or other valuables
belonging to a guest must provide a safe or safe deposit boxes for safekeeping of
such valuables. Most small hotels maintain a safe or safe deposit boxes to which
only the hotel manager and front desk agent have access. The guest delivers the
money or articles to the manager or front desk agent, who then places the guest's
property in the safe or safe deposit boxes. Some form of receipt may be used. Any
receipt should contain a statement to the effect that the hotel is in no case liable
beyond the sum of the statutory limitation (which is $1,500 in New York) because
of loss or damage occurring by theft or otherwise. In some cases, the guest places
the money or articles in an envelope and then seals it. Since some insurance companies require it, it is a good idea to take an inventory of the guest's valuables in
front of the guest before the envelope is sealed.

In 1979, the New York Court of Appeals ruled that the New York General
Business Law § 200, which limits a hotelkeeper's liability to $1,500 for the loss of
guests' jewelry or other valuables if the hotelkeeper provides guests with a safe in
his/her office, does *not* apply if the safe is not available to guests *at all times*.[1]

Posting Notices

In order to limit liability for the loss of guests' valuables, the hotel is usually
required to post notices in accordance with the state statute to inform guests of the
existence of the safe or safe deposit boxes (whichever is required by state statute)
and the limits placed on the hotel's liability.

In *DePaemelaere* v. *Davis*,[2] the New York County Civil Court held that a hotel
owner had *not* given proper notice to the guest as required by the New York statutes. In this case, the hotel was held liable for $10,000 in cash allegedly missing
from the hotel's safe deposit box. The Appellate Term of the New York Supreme
Court (First Department) upheld the lower court's decision.

The importance of strictly complying with the statutory regulations is demonstrated by *Carlton* v. *Beacon Hotel Corp.*[3] In this case, a guest delivered money and
jewels to a hotel desk clerk for deposit in the hotel's safe. The desk clerk testified at
trial that it was his usual practice to place guests' valuables left with him in the
safe, but that he had no specific recollection of having done so in the plaintiff's

case. Justice Breitel, writing for a unanimous court, held that the then $500 limitation of liability contained in New York's General Business Law § 200 would apply even when the hotel, after receiving valuables from a guest for deposit in the hotel's safe, failed to put the valuables in the safe:

> Even apart from the absence of any evidence in the record to indicate that in fact defendant did not deposit plaintiff's valuables in its safe, the verdict and judgment must be reduced [to the $500 limitation]. Section 200 of the General Business Law, in language that is quite clear, states that a hotelkeeper who provides a safe and posts requisite notices is not liable at all for the loss of guests' valuables unless the guest delivers the valuables for deposit in the safe. Where the valuables have been delivered to the person in charge of the safe "for deposit in such safe", the hotel's liability is limited to $500, unless it otherwise agrees in writing.[4]

Justice Breitel noted that the purpose of § 200 was not solely relief of hotels from their common law burden as insurers. In addition, "the purpose of the section is to protect the hotel from an undisclosed excessive liability."[5]

In *DeLema v. Waldorf-Astoria Hotel, Inc.*,[6] the guest sued the hotel for theft of an attaché case containing jewelry allegedly worth $300,000 which was allegedly stolen from the guest while he was registering at the hotel. The U.S. District Court (S.D.N.Y.) found that the guest had failed to disclose to the hotel's representatives that he had valuable jewelry in his attaché case at the time that he was registering and to state that he wished to place the jewelry in a safe. Therefore the court held that the hotel's liability was limited to the New York statutory amount (then $500). The court pointed out that if the hotel had been advised of the value of the jewelry, it could then have decided whether or not it wished to take responsibility for jewels valued in excess of $500. The court stated:

> The hotel owner is entitled to that opportunity to consider the matter because the statute provides that "no hotel...shall be obliged to receive property on deposit for safekeeping, exceeding five hundred dollars in value." Absent such declaration by the guest, the hotel keeper's liability is limited to $500.

The Supreme Court of Maine, in *Levesque v. Columbia Hotel*,[7] stated the public policy considerations in limiting a hotel's liability for guests' valuables by statute. The court stated:

> The hotelkeeper is not a banker, and he is not in the business of operating a safe deposit vault except as an incident to operating a hotel. It is not, therefore, unreasonable to restrict his liability for such incidental services rendered to his guests within such limits as will meet their ordinary needs. Those who carry with them large amounts of money or jewelry must take other measures for their protection. The added cost to the hotelkeeper of providing for such protection even as against the willful act or negligence of an employee, is in the last analysis one of his costs of operation reflected in the rates charged to all. *Why should those guests who do not need such protection pay for the cost of those who do?*[8] [emphasis added]

This policy discussion was quoted with approval by a federal district court in a case involving Missouri law in *Link-Simon, Inc. v. Muehlebach Hotel, Inc.*[9]

Statutory Limits on Hotel's Liability When Hotel's Negligence Is Alleged as Cause of Loss —————————

Often statutes enacted by various state legislatures do not expressly indicate whether the statutory limit of liability applies when the hotel's negligence is alleged as the cause of the loss. Should this issue arise, hotels should ask local counsel to review the language of the statute as well as court decisions and legislative history regarding state laws.

Various state courts have come to different conclusions in interpreting similar provisions.[10] For example, in *Hoffman* v. *Louis D. Miller & Co.,*[11] the Supreme Court of Rhode Island, after reviewing the history of the applicable Rhode Island statute, concluded that the legislature intended "to limit the innkeeper's liability only as an insurer and not generally as to the care and diligence it ordinarily owed the guest for the protection of his property while it was within the innkeeper's house." Thus, in such a state, a guest suing a hotel for lost valuables alleged to be worth more than the statutory limit of liability merely alleges that the hotel was negligent with respect to the deposit of these items. Then, the hotel must prove in court that it was not negligent. Only if the hotel meets its burden of proof does the statutory limit of liability apply in that state.

However, many jurisdictions[12] have adopted a contrary and more reasonable rule that limits the hotel's common law burden as insurer of guests' property to the stated statutory amounts (provided the hotel strictly complies with the requirements of the statutes), whether or not negligence is alleged as the cause of a particular loss. As the U.S. Court of Appeals for the Tenth Circuit in *Kalpakian* v. *Oklahoma Sheraton Corporation*[13] pointed out:

> The trend of the decisions considering state statutes relating to a hotel's liability for lost property deposited with it, is to strictly construe the obligation of a hotel guest to disclose the value of deposited property and to refuse to impose on hotels without notice a greater liability than the statutory amount, regardless of negligence. [citations omitted] Kalpakian [the plaintiff-guest] argues that the statutory provisions do not relieve the hotel from liability for loss of deposited articles if caused by negligence whatever their value. To accept this construction would permit a guest to accomplish by nondisclosure what he could not accomplish by giving notice of value.[14]

In *Ricketts* v. *Morehead Co.,*[15] the California District Court of Appeals, in a case charging a hotel with negligent loss of a guest's property delivered for deposit in the hotel's safe, held that negligence would not defeat application of the California statutes limiting the hotel's liability to $250. The court said that the statutes "are as applicable to losses resulting from theft by employees as to losses from negligence."[16]

In *Latini* v. *Lowes Corp. and LRI, Inc.,*[17] the plaintiffs sought compensation for alleged loss of their jewelry, valued at $24,345, from their guestroom at a major New York City hotel. The hotel argued that there were safe deposit boxes for such jewelry and that proper notice regarding the availability of such safe deposit boxes was given to the guests, and, therefore, the hotel's liability was limited by the New York statutory amount (then $500). On a motion for summary judgment, the court pointed out that the General Business Law of New York State requires that the notice to limit liability be posted "in a public and conspicuous place and manner in the office and public rooms, and in the public parlors of such hotel." The plaintiff-guests claimed, however, that one notice posted at the cashier's desk was obscured by a vase of flowers on one side, and that a second notice was obscured by mail. The court held that there were material issues of fact as to whether notice of availability of the safe was conspicuously posted on each side of the registration desk, thus precluding summary judgment for the hotel.

In a recent case in Las Vegas, the plaintiffs alleged that money and jewels disappeared from their VIP suite while they were guests at the MGM Grand Hotel. They sued the hotel, alleging that it had assigned several hospitality suites on the same floor to a trade show. As a result, many people were roaming the floor from suite to suite, and the plaintiffs claimed that the hotel failed to provide enough security guards for the floor. The guests sought to recover the value of their property losses, blaming the losses on the hotel's breach of contract in failing to provide appropriate security for their suite, and the hotel's alleged gross negligence in failing to provide appropriate security. The jury in this case found damages in the guests' favor in the amount of $100,000.[18]

Constitutionality of Statutory Limits

Pacific Diamond Company, Inc. v. *Superior Court of San Francisco and The Hilton Hotel Corp.*[19] arose out of a theft of approximately $150,000 in diamonds at the Denver Hilton. Suit was brought in California (which is permissible). Among other things, the plaintiff claimed that the California and Colorado innkeepers statutes—regardless of which state's laws applied—were unconstitutional since they violated the equal protection and **due process** clauses.

On November 7, 1978, the California District Court of Appeals upheld the constitutionality of the Colorado innkeepers law, which limits a hotel's liability for stolen guest valuables to $250 if a safe is present on the premises, notice thereof is posted properly, and the guest does not place his/her valuables in the safe.

The plaintiff then sought a hearing in the California Supreme Court to press his arguments that he had been denied due process and equal protection of the laws. On December 20, 1978, that court denied his petition.

Important Points for Management

Hotels wishing to meet a state's statutory requirements for limiting liability for any loss of money, jewelry, and other valuables belonging to a guest must provide a safe or safe deposit boxes for safekeeping of such valuables.

In order to limit liability for the loss of guests' valuables, the hotel is usually required to post notices in strict compliance with the state statute to inform the guest of the existence of the safe or safe deposit boxes (whichever is required by state statute) and the limits placed on the hotel's liability.

References

1. *Zaldin* v. *Concord Hotel*, 48 N.Y. 2d 107, 421 N.Y.S. 2d 858, 397 N.E. 2d 370 (1979).

2. 77 Misc. 2d, 1, 351 N.Y.S. 2d 808 (Civ. Ct., N.Y. Co. 1973), aff'd, 79 Misc. 2d 800, 363 N.Y.S. 2d 323 (App. Term, 1974).

3. 3 A.D. 2d 28, 157 N.Y.S. 2d 744 (1st Dept. 1956), *aff'd,* 4 N.Y. 2d 789, 173 N.Y.S. 2d 26, 149 N.E. 2d 527 (1958).

4. 3 A.D. 2d at 30, 157 N.Y.S. 2d at 745-46.

5. 3 A.D. 2d at 30-31, 157 N.Y.S. 2d at 746. *Accord, Millhiser* v. *Beau Site Co.,* 251 N.Y. 290, 294, 167 N.E. 447, 448 (1929); *Federal Insurance Co.* v. *Waldorf-Astoria Hotel,* 60 Misc. 2d 996, 997, 303 N.Y.S. 2d 297, 299 (Cir. Ct., N.Y. Co. 1969).

6. *DeLema* v. *Waldorf-Astoria Hotel, Inc.,* 588 F. Supp. (S.D.N.Y. 1984). But see *H.K. Mallak, Inc.,* v. *Fairfield FMC Corp.,* 209 F. 3d. 960, No. 99 1766 (7th Cir. 4/11/00), where the court held a Wisconsin hotel liable for jewelry theft before the guest had read the notice limiting liability—and the robbery appeared to be an inside job.

7. 141 Me. 393, 44 A. 2d 728 (1945).

8. 141 Me. at 398, 44 A. 2d at 730.

9. 374 F. Supp. 789, 795 (W.D. Mo. 1974).

10. See "Innkeepers—Loss of Guests' Property," 37 A.L.R. 3rd 1276 (1971).

11. 83 R.I. 284, 115 A. 2d 689 (1955).

12. Such jurisdictions include Arkansas, California, Florida, Georgia, Hawaii, Illinois, Maine, Missouri, New York, Oklahoma, Tennessee.

13. 398 F. 2d 243 (10th Cir., 1968).

14. 398 F. 2d at 247.

15. 122 Cal. App. 2d 948, 265 P. 2d 963 (3d Dist. 1954).

16. 122 Cal. App. 2d at 953, 265 P. 2d at 965-66, quoting *Gardner* v. *Jonathan Club,* 35 Cal. 2d 343, 349, 217 P. 2d 961, 964 (1950). *Accord, Link-Simon, Inc.* v. *Muehlebach Hotel, Inc.,* 374 F. Supp. 789 (W.D. Mo. 1974) (Missouri Law); *Levesque* v. *Columbia Hotel,* 141 Me. 393, 44 A. 2d 728 (1945).

17. No. 85 Civ. 3275 (PNL), in the United States District Court for the Southern District of New York, decided April 8, 1987, 657 F. Supp. 475.

18. *MGM Grand Hotel, Inc.* v. *Siegel,* 506 So. 2d 451 (D.C. App. Fla. (3d Dist., 1987)), reh'g denied, in part, *MGM Grand Hotel, Inc.* v. *Siegel,* 12 Fla. Weekly 1340 (Fla. Dist. Ct. App. 3d Dist. 1987).

19. *Pacific Diamond Co., Inc.* v. *Superior Court of San Francisco and the Hilton Hotel Corp.,* 149 Cal. Rptr. 813, 85 Cal. App. 3d 871 (1st Dist., 1978).

☞ Key Terms

due process of law—When applied to judicial proceedings, a course of legal proceedings according to those rules and principles which have been established in our systems of jurisprudence for the enforcement and protection of private rights.

? Review Questions

1. Why should a hotel provide a safe or safe deposit boxes?

2. What must a hotel do to limit its liability for loss of a guest's valuables?

3. Why is it important that hotels post notices regarding the hotel's liability for guest property which is lost or stolen?

4. What information should hotels include in the posted notices referred to in question 2?

5. Why do hotels often take inventory of the guest's valuables in the guest's presence before placing the valuables in the safe or safe deposit boxes?

6. If receipts are given to guests who place valuables in the hotel safe or safe deposit boxes, what information should the receipts include?

7. What is the hotel's liability in your state for loss of a guest's property if the guest does not request that the property be placed in a hotel safe or safe deposit box?

8. When can hotels in your state refuse to accept valuables for placement in hotel safes or safe deposit boxes?

Chapter 14 Outline

Competencies

1. Identify types of crimes that are often committed against hotels. (pp. 199–201)

2. Describe how some state statutes may ease the burden of the prosecution in a case involving the defrauding of a hotel. (pp. 199–200)

3. Describe how hotelkeepers can maximize the protection of criminal statutes. (p. 201)

4. Explain why hotelkeepers should be wary of detaining guests they suspect of theft or fraud. (pp. 201–202)

5. Describe what a hotel should do when detaining guests suspected of wrongdoing. (pp. 201–202)

Frauds Committed Against Hotels and Crimes of Trespass

Crimes Against Hotels

Hotels are often victims of crime—"skips," credit card frauds, bad checks, and theft by guests. This chapter will examine some of the hotelkeeper's legal protections against these crimes and suggest some ways to become less susceptible to them. Since most criminal laws relating to hotels stem from individual state legislation, however, this discussion will be general. Hotels should check with local counsel concerning their state laws.

Defrauding a Hotel

Hotels are often victimized by skips—persons who obtain food or lodging but abscond without paying for them. To protect the innkeeper, many states have enacted penal statutes making it a crime for a person to obtain credit, food, or lodging fraudulently with no intention to pay for them.[1] As the Wisconsin Supreme Court has noted, these penal statutes are especially important today when innkeepers, especially motel owners, no longer supervise the handling of a guest's baggage on arrival and departure. Consequently, they are no longer as readily able to recover payment for lodging by enforcing a **lien** on detained baggage.[2]

The penal statutes relating to skips generally prohibit a person's leaving a hotel with the *intent* of avoiding payment for food, lodging, or other services.[3] Many states ease the prosecutor's burden by creating a presumption of an intent not to pay,[4] or stating that the prosecutor may establish a *prima facie* case of intent, upon a showing of certain facts.[5] To establish a *prima facie* case, the jury must consider and weigh the evidence concerning a defendant's leaving the hotel, "and, after such reflection may determine whether the evidence is sufficient to establish the fact of guilt beyond a reasonable doubt."[6] In either case, these state statutes enable the prosecutor to establish the defendant's intent to defraud merely by establishing the defendant's action, subject to the defendant's showing that his/her actions were justified or that there was actually no intent to defraud. For instance, in *People* v. *Astor*,[7] a guest was charged with defrauding a hotel of a small amount of charges. She overcame the presumption of intent by showing that she had paid all charges for a period of six months and that the hotelkeeper had requested her to leave. Consequently, she established that she did not intend to defraud the proprietor when she originally registered as a guest.

Generally, the previously described statutes require that the guest leave the hotel or motel premises without paying for accommodations in order to establish a *prima facie* case of intent. The presumption of intent would not arise when a "guest" continues to reside at the property but refuses payment. In 1981, California adopted a law that allows hotels to involve the police in dealing with "deadbeats." The law provides that a person is guilty of **trespass** if he/she refuses to leave a hotel or motel after obtaining accommodations and failing to pay for such accommodations following a request to leave the premises by the hotel proprietor or manager.[8]

In 1982, California also passed a law that makes it a **felony** to obtain credit, lodging, or food without paying the hotel for the same where the amount owed is in excess of $400.[9]

Credit Card Fraud

A second crime of concern to many hotels is credit card fraud—using stolen, forged, or altered cards to obtain the hotel's services. The federal government has made the fraudulent use of credit cards a criminal offense. The federal government has enacted legislation providing, among other things, for fines of up to $10,000 and imprisonment for up to ten years for fraudulent use of credit cards in a transaction affecting interstate or foreign commerce to obtain goods or services worth $1,000 or more within any one-year period.[10] The legislation imposes the same penalty on persons who furnish money, services, or anything else worth $1,000 or more in any one-year period to a person whom they know to be fraudulently using a card. Consequently, the federal statute could be invoked against outsiders seeking to defraud a hotel and unscrupulous employees furnishing services to persons they know are engaged in credit card fraud. In addition to the federal legislation, many states have enacted penal statutes relating to credit card fraud.[11]

Bad Checks

Practically all states make it a crime to pass a bad check, that is, a check written with the intent to deceive the payee.[12] Because intent is difficult to prove, some state statutes establish a **rebuttable presumption** that the check writer intended to issue a worthless check if there were in fact insufficient funds to cover the check when issued.[13] Other state statutes provide that, if a check is dishonored for insufficient funds, the payee must be paid within a certain time period or the issuer's criminal intent is established.[14] This latter type of statute is more defendant-oriented since it allows the issuer an opportunity to make good on the check after an error is discovered.

Another problem arises with post-dated checks. Although some states treat a post-dated check just as any other bad check,[15] other states view a post-dated check as a promise to pay money in the future and attach only civil, not criminal, liability when the promise is broken.[16] Clearly, hotels in those states attaching no criminal liability to issuing bad post-dated checks should be wary in accepting them. Hotels should check with their local counsel to determine whether criminal liability attaches to post-dated bad checks.

How Hotels Can Take Advantage of Criminal Statutes ———

The criminal statutes provide strong weapons in hotels' fights against persons seeking to defraud them. First, they enable hotelkeepers to go to state and federal law enforcement authorities for apprehension of those who engaged in crimes against hotels. In addition, the criminal statutes provide stiff penalties of prison terms and large fines. Enforcement of these penalties acts as a deterrent against such criminal activity.

What can hotelkeepers do to maximize the protection of these criminal statutes? First, they should establish procedures that provide evidence facilitating the conviction of those perpetrating crimes.[17] A State of Washington Supreme Court case illustrates how a hotel can establish such evidence.[18] At the trial, the defendant was convicted of defrauding a hotelkeeper. The Washington Supreme Court affirmed, noting that the hotel had a standard procedure for creating extensive records. The hotel room attendant turned in a daily written report to the cashier showing which rooms had been vacated. The cashier, in turn, entered the guest's room charges, compared that with the amounts paid by each guest, and indicated those persons who had failed to check out. Subsequently, statements were sent to persons still owing money. Thus, through its standard procedures, the hotel had established a written record showing the amount of the defendant's hotel account and that the hotel had mailed a statement to the defendant at the address he gave at registration, which was returned unclaimed. Since the hotel had established regular recordkeeping procedures, the records were admitted into evidence and the conviction resulted.

Hotels, therefore, should establish regular procedures for showing the circumstances under which guests check out of the hotel and in which payment is or is not made.

Caveats on Detention of Guests ————————————

Hotels should be wary of detaining guests they suspect of theft or fraudulently avoiding payment of their bills. Such detention, especially if unjustified or improperly instituted, might open the hotel to suits for **false imprisonment** and **slander,** depending on the circumstances of the case and state laws. Consequently, hotels should check with counsel before establishing any procedures for detaining guests suspected of wrongdoing.

Some jurisdictions permit hotels to detain temporarily for investigation persons whom they reasonably believe are guilty of theft and failure to pay for property or ser-vices received.[19] In these jurisdictions, the hotel may only detain the guest "for the time necessary for a reasonable investigation of facts."[20] Before detaining a guest in states so permitting, the hotel must have reasonable grounds for believing the guest is committing the theft or absconding without paying.[21] Normally a guest would be detained only long enough to make such inquiry as may be reasonable, considering the nature of the suspected misconduct, the amount involved, the explanation offered by the guest, and the time required to consult readily available sources of information. If the guest is detained too long, the hotel may be liable for false imprisonment.[22]

Many states do not permit even brief periods of detention, however. The Court of Appeals of Maryland, for instance, has stated that a person detaining another for theft is liable for false imprisonment if the person detained does not have any of the detainer's property unlawfully in his/her possession.[23] Hotels in states such as Virginia and Maryland are liable for false imprisonment if a detained guest is later found to be innocent. Hotels in such states should be extremely careful before detaining a guest to investigate possible theft. In any event, hotels in all states should check with local counsel before instituting any procedures for detaining guests.

Hotels should also be careful in dealing with detained guests in order to avoid possible charges of slander. If a guest is wrongfully accused of criminal activity in the presence of others, the hotel might be sued for slander. In *Zayre of Virginia, Inc.* v. *Gowdy*,[24] the Virginia Supreme Court held that a store's security officer's words to two patrons suspected of theft constituted an actionable claim. The security officer said, "Hey, young ladies, let me see what you have in that suitcase."[25] The court upheld a verdict that the security officer's statement had falsely and insultingly accused the customers of **larceny.** The customers were each awarded $750 in damages. Consequently, hotels should be certain that their security personnel are properly trained to avoid incidents enabling guests to sue the hotel for slander. Local counsel can advise hotels about the best procedures to use to guard against potentially slanderous statements that perhaps overzealous security employees may make.

In addition to slander, if a guest or patron is arrested without justification at the instigation of the hotel, the hotel might face a suit for **malicious prosecution.** For instance, in *Lind* v. *Schmid*[26] the New Jersey Supreme Court held that the restaurant could be sued for potential malicious prosecution where patrons had been arrested without **probable cause** for allegedly obtaining food with intent to defraud. Again, hotels seeking to prosecute persons suspected of fraud should consult with local counsel before proceeding in order to protect themselves against malicious prosecution actions.

Important Points for Management

Crime against hotels may involve:

- Skips—guests who leave without paying for room or food
- Fake or invalid credit cards
- Bad checks
- Theft of linens or towels

Knowingly using a stolen, forged, or altered credit card to get food or lodging at a hotel is a federal crime and often a state crime.

Knowingly using a check to pay for goods or services when there are insufficient funds is usually a state crime. Check your state law.

When detaining persons suspected of committing a crime, *be careful.* The detention of a person who has not committed a crime can lead to civil suits against the hotel for the torts of false imprisonment or slander.

References

1. See, for example, Cal. Penal Code § 537; Conn. Gen. Stat. Ann. § 53a-119(7) (1); Del. Code Ann. Supp. Tit. 11, § 845; Fla. Stat. Ann. Supp. 509.151; N.Y. Penal Law § 165.15. (McKinney Supp., 1994).

2. *State* v. *Croy,* 32 Wis. 2d 118 145 N.W. 2d 118 (1966).

3. See, for example, statutes listed in note 1, *supra.* See also, *e.g.,* Del. Code Ann. Supp. Tit. 11, § 845 (1982), *People* v. *Ausely,* 523 P. 2d 460 (Colo., 1974). See also *Agnew* v. *State,* 474 S.W. 2d 218 (Texas Crim. App., 1971).

4. See, for example, N.Y. Penal Law § 165.15 (McKinney Supp., 1994).

5. See, for example, Cal. Penal Code § 537.

6. *State* v. *Cummings,* 267 N.E. 2d 812, 814 (Ohio, 1971); 25 Ohio St. 2d 219, 54 Ohio Ops. 2d 325.

7. 55 N.Y.S. 2d 283, 269 A.D. 250 (1945). See also *State* v. *Gledhill,* 67 N.J. 565, 342 A. 2d 161 (1975).

8. Chapter 349, Statutes of 1981, amending § 602 of the California Penal Code.

9. Bill AB 3074-1982.

10. 15 U.S.C. § 1644.

11. See, for example, Cal. Penal Code § 484g (West Supp. 1983); Conn. Gen. Stat. Ann. § 53a-128a *et seq.* Fla. Stat. Ann. Supp. § 817.60.

12. See, for example, N.Y. Penal Law § 190.5 *et seq.* (McKinney Supp. 1988); and Conn. Gen. Stat. Ann. § 53a-128.

13. See, for example, Conn. Gen. Stat. Ann. § 53a-128(b).

14. New York, for example, permits a defendant to pay the amount in full within ten days of dishonor by the drawer. N.Y. Penal Law § 190.15 (McKinney 1988). See also *State* v. *Blasi* 64 N.J. 51, 312 A. 2d 135 (1973). See, for example, Fla. Stat. Ann. Supp. § 832.05(2).

15. *Mercer* v. *Commonwealth,* 332 S.W. 2d 655 (Ky. Ct. App. 1960).

16. See, for example, *State* v. *Downing,* 83 N.M. 62, 488 P. 2d 112 (N.M. Ct. App., 1971). See also "Application of 'Bad Check' Statute with Respect to Postdated Checks," 52 A.L.R. 3d 464 (1973).

17. *People* v. *Miller,* 188 Colo. 400, 534 P. 2d 1218 (Colo., 1975).

18. *State* v. *Higgins,* 67 Wash. 2d 147, 406 P. 2d 784 (1965), *cert. denied* 385 U.S. 827 (1966).

19. Restatement (Second) of Torts § 120A.

20. *Id.*

21. *Prieto* v. *May Department Stores Company,* 216 A. 2d 577 (D.C., 1966).

22. Restatement (Second) of Torts § 120A, Comment F.

23. *Great Atlantic & Pacific Tea Co., Inc. v. Paul*, 256 Md. 643, 261 A. 2d 731 (1970). See Art. 57 Md. Code § 551(A) (creating an exception for shoplifting). See also *Zayre of Virginia, Inc. v. Gowdy*, 207 Va. 47, 147 S.E. 2d 710 (1966).

24. *Zayre of Virginia, Inc. v. Gowdy, supra.*

25. 147 S.E. 2d at p. 712.

26. 67 N.J. 255, 337 A. 2d 365 (1975). See also Del. Code Ann. Supp. Tit. 11, § 846 (4).

🔑 Key Terms

false imprisonment—The detention of a person without his/her consent and without lawful authority.

felony—A criminal offense usually punishable by a jail term of over one year (and generally by confinement in the state penitentiary).

larceny—An unlawful taking and carrying away of personal property without the consent of and against the will of the owner, and with a felonious intent to deprive the owner of the property permanently.

lien—A charge upon real or personal property for the payment of a debt or obligation owed. A hold or claim which one person has upon the real or personal property of another as security for some debt or charge.

malicious prosecution—A criminal prosecution instituted upon no, or such slight, grounds of suspicion as to indicate general disregard of the rights of others.

prima facie **evidence**—That degree of proof which unexplained or uncontradicted by other evidence is sufficient, if credited by a jury, to establish an unlawful intent.

probable cause—Exists when facts and circumstances within one's knowledge, and of which one has reasonably trustworthy information, are sufficient in themselves to warrant a person of reasonable caution to act in the belief that a crime has been or is being committed.

rebuttable presumption—Gives particular effect to a certain group of facts in the absence of further evidence, and presumption provides *prima facie* case which shifts to defendant the burden to go forward with evidence to contradict or rebut fact presumed.

slander—Words falsely spoken which are injurious to the reputation of another. False defamatory words, when written, constitute a *libel*.

trespass, common law act of—Every unauthorized entry is a trespass, regardless of the degree of force used.

❓ Review Questions

1. How are hotels protected from "skips" under state penal statutes?

2. How are hotels protected from credit card fraud under federal legislation?

3. How do state laws protect the hotel with respect to bad checks?

4. What measures can hotels take to ensure protection against bad checks under state criminal statutes?

5. How do various state laws treat post-dated checks? How does your state treat them?

6. What precautions should a hotel take when detaining a guest suspected of theft or fraudulent acts?

7. In what cases might a hotel be liable for false imprisonment?

8. What consequences might a hotel suffer if a guest is unjustly arrested at the hotel's instigation?

9. What are some examples of "crime of defrauding a hotel"?

Chapter 15 Outline

Competencies

1. Describe the procedures a hotel must follow if a guest dies while at the hotel. (p. 207)

2. Explain how a hotel should dispose of a deceased guest's or patron's property. (pp. 207–208)

3. Describe the roles the public administrator, medical examiner, and police department may play when a guest dies on hotel premises. (pp. 208–209)

15

Deceased Guests

WHEN A GUEST DIES in the hotel, state laws may impose obligations upon hotelkeepers in certain circumstances with respect to the body and personal property of the deceased guest. New York and California law are cited as examples of statutory duties imposed upon hotelkeepers. However, hotels in all jurisdictions should consult with their legal counsel or local health authorities to establish procedures to follow if a person dies while on the hotel premises.

If a physician is in attendance when the death occurs, it is the physician's duty to make the necessary reports to the local health authorities. In this case, the body should be removed by an undertaker authorized by the decedent's relatives. If there is no attending physician and if no undertaker is called, local health authorities or the police department should be asked to arrange for removal of the body to a morgue. In New York State, if the death occurs without a physician in attendance, the New York Public Health Law states that it is the duty of the undertaker *"or other person to whose knowledge the death may come"* (emphasis added) to notify the coroner or the medical examiner of the death. The hotel should be sure that such notice is given and that the undertaker has notified the proper authorities. If there is any doubt, the hotel should give the notice itself.

If the guest appears to have died from anything but natural causes, the hotel should contact local police authorities. In California, a duty is imposed on the coroner "to inquire into and determine the circumstances, manner, and cause of all violent, sudden or unusual deaths; unattended deaths;" and deaths suspected to be caused by accident or injury, drug addiction, asphyxiation, or criminal act.[1]

Disposition of Property of Deceased Guest or Patron ———

Delivery to Executor or Administrator

The personal property of the deceased should not be moved, at least until the appropriate authorities arrive to investigate the cause of death. In California, a state law authorizes the coroner, in any death subject to inquiry, to "take charge of any and all personal effects, valuables, and property of the deceased at the scene of death and hold or safeguard them until lawful disposition thereof can be made."[2] In addition, another provision of this law makes it unlawful for *"any person to* search for or remove any papers, moneys, valuable property or weapons constituting the estate of the deceased from the person of the deceased *or from the premises,* prior to arrival of the coroner or without his consent" (emphasis added).[3] Therefore, upon discovery of a guest's death in California, or any other state with a similar statutory provision, the hotel should immediately seal the room, contact the coroner's office and/or local police authorities, and await their direction.

The deceased guest's property in the guestroom must be delivered to the proper person; otherwise, the hotel may face a claim for its value. Ordinarily, the hotel is fully protected if it delivers the property to the duly appointed **executor** or administrator of the deceased or to the Public Administrator, if appointed. Before delivering the decedent's property to any person, including the decedent's relatives, the hotel should ask for a certificate from the Surrogate's Court certifying that an executor, administrator, or Public Administrator has been appointed. The hotel should retain this certificate. The hotel should also get a detailed receipt when delivering the property.

In some cases, it may be several days or longer before an executor or administrator is appointed. In such cases, the hotel (after obtaining any necessary consent from an investigating official) may remove the property from the room to another place for safekeeping. As a precaution, a careful inventory of the property should be taken in front of a witness before it is removed from the room, and the witness should sign the inventory.

Tax Waiver

Before delivering the property of a deceased guest to an executor, administrator, or any other person, the hotel should ask to be furnished with a tax waiver, normally issued by the state taxation authorities.* This waiver is related to the state estate tax and is, in effect, the taxation authority's consent to the delivery of the property. In the absence of such a waiver, the hotel is at risk of paying such estate tax itself if the assets are delivered to an unauthorized person who later disposes of them without paying the estate tax. This is important even if the deceased person is a non-resident of the state.

Property of Little Value

In some cases, a deceased guest leaves property of little value in the hotel room. The same principles of law apply and the same requirements exist regardless of the property's value. If the property is obviously of very little value and no executor or administrator is appointed, the hotel may decide to turn over the property to a near relative of the deceased. In doing so, however, from a legal standpoint, the hotel is assuming a risk both to the extent of the value of the property and to the extent of the estate tax on it.

Role of Public Administrator and Police Department ———

State laws may specifically require hotelkeepers to report all deaths to public officials. For example, in New York, Articles 11 and 12 of the Surrogate's Court

---

* For example, in California, this waiver or consent should be obtained from the Inheritance Tax Department of the State of California; in New York, hotelkeepers should contact the State Department of Taxation and Finance.

Procedure Act (SCPA) require hotelkeepers in certain counties of the state to report the death of any hotel guest to the Public Administrator of that county within 12 hours after the death. This is to notify the Public Administrator of the property over which he/she might have jurisdiction and has nothing to do with removal of the body.

Under certain circumstances, the local police department may claim property left by the deceased guest, according to local ordinances of the town or city where the hotel is located. In New York City, for example, the police department has no jurisdiction when the guest dies of natural causes while being attended by a physician. However, if the guest dies from "criminal violence, by a casualty, by suicide, suddenly when in apparent health, when unattended by a physician . . . or in any suspicious or unusual manner,"[4] both the medical examiner and the police department must be notified. In general, the medical examiner has authority to take any property that may help establish the cause of death; the police department has the power, in the absence of next of kin, to take possession of the property found on the deceased's person.[5] In all such cases, the hotel should demand a receipt for the property taken.

Important Points for Management

When a guest dies on the hotel premises:

- Notify local authorities for removal of the decedent's body. Know whom to call in advance.

- Do not remove decedent's personal property until authorities approve. Take precautions against theft. Seal the room if necessary.

- Take the decedent's property into safekeeping. Sometimes the hotel must do this because no one else is going to do it. A written inventory should be made describing each item of property. The task should be assigned to two or three persons to ascertain that nothing is taken. Secure valuable personal property in a safe.

References

1. Cal. Gov't. Code § 27491.0.
2. Cal. Gov't. Code § 27491.3(a).
3. Cal. Gov't. Code § 27491.3(c).
4. New York, N.Y., City Charter § 557(b).
5. New York, N.Y.C., Admin. Code § 17–202.

Key Terms

executor—A person appointed by the testator to carry out the directions and requests in the testator's will, and to dispose of the testator's property according to the will.

Review Questions

1. If a guest dies in the hotel, what should hotel management do with the body?

2. What public authorities should be notified if a person dies in the hotel?

3. Whom should the hotel notify when a guest dies in a "suspicious or unusual manner"?

4. What should hotel authorities do with a deceased guest's personal property?

5. Under what circumstances might the local police department claim property found on the decedent's person?

6. Under what circumstances may a medical examiner take a deceased guest's property?

7. What should a hotel do to protect itself when delivering a deceased guest's property to a duly appointed executor, administrator, or any other person?

8. When there is a delay in the legal appointment of a deceased guest's executor or administrator, what should the hotel do with the deceased guest's property?

9. What is a tax waiver? Why is it important that a hotel obtain one before delivering a deceased guest's property to another person?

Part IV

Restaurants, Food Service, and Bars

Chapter 16 Outline

Federal Laws Regarding Food
State and Local Laws Regarding Food
General Liability for Unwholesome Food
Warranties
Privity of Contract
Uniform Commercial Code
Strict Liability
Important Points for Management
References
Review Questions
Internet Sites
Illustrative Case

Competencies

1. Describe the purpose of the federal Food, Drug, and Cosmetic Act. (p. 213)

2. Describe subjects typically covered by state and local health regulations. (pp. 213–214)

3. Explain the hotel or restaurant operator's general liability for serving unwholesome food. (pp. 214–215)

4. Describe the two theories under which a hotel may be sued for serving contaminated food. (pp. 214–215)

5. Explain the type of warranty that may be imposed on the sale of food. (pp. 215–216)

6. Describe privity of contract. (pp. 216–217)

7. Identify the purpose of the Uniform Commercial Code. (p. 217)

8. Explain what is meant by the foreign-natural test. (pp. 218–219)

9. Summarize the doctrine of strict liability in food cases. (p. 220)

16

General Laws Regarding Food

Federal Laws Regarding Food

Federal laws relating to food service are contained in the federal Food, Drug, and Cosmetic Act.[1] Section 331 (k) prohibits

> [t]he alteration, mutilation, destruction, obliteration, or removal of the whole or any part of the labeling of, or the doing of any other act with respect to food…if such act is done while such article is held for sale (whether or not the first sale) after shipment in interstate commerce and results in such article being adulterated or misbranded.

Courts have held that the purpose of this section is to safeguard the consumer from the time the food enters the channels of interstate commerce until the time it is delivered to the ultimate consumer.[2] Consequently, it may be argued that hotels come within the statute's purpose since the guest or restaurant patron is arguably the ultimate consumer. The Act defines adulterated food in § 342 (a), which states, in part, that "food shall be deemed adulterated if it has been prepared, packed, or *held* under insanitary conditions whereby it *may* have become contaminated with filth" (emphasis added).

State and Local Laws Regarding Food

Hotels and restaurants in all areas are also subject to state laws and regulations relating to health and sanitary conditions in handling food and drink. In addition, most hotels and restaurants are subject to supplemental regulations promulgated and enforced by local county, city, town, or village health departments.

The state and local health laws and agriculture laws (as well as the federal Occupational Safety and Health Administration and state OSHAs) cover subjects such as cleanliness in preparing and serving food; regulations on the sale and service of milk, meats, and desserts; regulations regarding adulterated or misbranded food; restrictions on the sale of margarine; the care and cleaning of silverware; etc.

In addition, state and/or local health regulations usually contain specific provisions relating to restaurants or other "food service establishments."[3] Such regulations may cover in detail the general topics of:

- Food supplies—contamination, potentially hazardous food, dairy products, and food processing

- Food protection—temperature and refrigeration requirements, prohibitions on re-serving unused portions of unprotected foods, storage of food, and refrigerated and hot storage

- Toxic materials—storage and labeling

- Personnel—employees' health, cleanliness, consumption of food, use of tobacco, and training

- Food preparation and service—provisions regarding washing, cooking, reheating, display, and service of food

- Equipment and utensils—materials prohibited and equipment lubrication, construction, and cleanability

- Equipment and utensil cleaning—frequency of cleaning, general sanitization requirements, manual and mechanical cleaning and sanitizing, and drying

- Water supply, sewage, plumbing, garbage and refuse, insect and rodent control, construction and maintenance of physical facilities, and other miscellaneous provisions

Because state and local regulations differ, each hotel and restaurant should be familiar with those in effect in its particular community. Hospitality operations can obtain such regulations from state and local health authorities.

General Liability for Unwholesome Food

Hotel and restaurant operators must exercise reasonable care and prudence in purchasing, preparing, and serving food to guests and patrons. Otherwise, they may be held liable if, due to negligence, unwholesome or improperly prepared food is served and a person becomes ill or is otherwise injured. The potential liability may arise from two theories: common law negligence, which is a *tort theory*, and/or a breach of an implied warranty that the food is fit for human consumption, which is a *contract theory*.

For example, in *McAvin* v. *Morrison Cafeteria Co.*,[4] the plaintiff-patron brought a lawsuit based on negligence for injuries caused by unwholesome shrimp salad. The appellate court upheld the verdict and judgment for the plaintiff, noting that the plaintiff at trial carried her burden of proving that "the food served to her was deleterious and caused her illness."[5] The court further explained that the defendant-restaurant failed to show that it was not negligent with respect to the preparation of the shrimp salad served to the plaintiff.

Food poisoning was to blame for the mass sickness that felled 50 guests at the famed Plaza Hotel on February 22, 1993, the New York City Health Department determined.[6] In this incident, lab tests revealed that the poisoning was caused by a bacterial contamination of seafood; the seafood was an ingredient of a seafood pasta served at the hotel during a fashion industry luncheon for fashion buyers. Over the 24 hours following the luncheon, the guests reported suffering from fever, chills, stomach cramps, and vomiting, and one Long Island woman was hospitalized. Plaza owner Donald Trump blamed the problem on the vendor who supplied the seafood. The incident reinforces the idea that hotel operators should check their vendor contracts to make sure the hotel is protected by appropriate warranties and insurance coverage.

In 1986, Mr. and Mrs. Jasiczek sued the Elbow Beach Hotel in Bermuda (as well as the travel agent, Liberty Travel, Inc., the Bermuda Hotel Association, and the American Hotel & Motel Association). Mrs. Jasiczek claimed that she found glass in a croissant sandwich served at the hotel. She alleged that the sandwich contained slivers of glass which caused bleeding when she swallowed the sandwich. She requested $50,000 in damages. This case was settled.[7]

In *Gardyjan* v. *Tatone*,[8] the Supreme Court of Oregon held that the plaintiff restaurant patron had presented sufficient evidence to allow the jury to decide the issue of whether the defendant restaurant operators were negligent in serving unwholesome food. The plaintiff suffered from a form of food poisoning. The appellate court rejected the restaurant owner's contention that the plaintiff's illness may have been caused by food eaten elsewhere. The court pointed out that in Oregon the plaintiff must merely prove that the defendant's food was the most likely cause and not necessarily the only cause of the plaintiff's illness.[9]

In 1995 a Hindu couple failed to convince a judge that Taco Bell should help pay their way to India because they were inadvertently served meat. Siva Rama Krishna Valluru and wife, Sailaja—lifelong vegetarians—reportedly said that they found meat in rice they had eaten at a Taco Bell restaurant. Eating meat is a sin for some Hindus, and the Vallurus wanted the fast-food chain to help pay for a trip to India so they could be cleansed in a purification ceremony in the Ganges River. Taco Bell refused, and the couple filed a claim in Lancaster County Small Claims Court, seeking $2,100 each. County Judge Jean Lovell dismissed the claim because it did not show the rice was tainted or unfit for human consumption. The Judge also said that damages claimed by the couple were not foreseeable, even if the restaurant broke its contract to serve them meatless rice.[10]

Warranties

Under common law, a number of questions arose regarding whether the sale of food should be treated as a service or a sale. If a court treated a transaction as a sale, an implied warranty could be imposed that the product was fit for consumption. If a court treated a transaction as a service, no warranty could be implied.

There are two basic kinds of warranties: express warranties and implied warranties. *Express warranties* are oral or written representations which the seller makes to the buyer relating to the goods which become part of the basis of the sale. *Implied warranties* are imposed by law on the sale unless the seller negates or limits them to the extent permitted by the law. Generally speaking, if the seller is a merchant with respect to the kind of goods being sold, a warranty that the goods shall be merchantable is implied in a contract for sale.*

In *Levy* v. *Paul*,[11] a three-year-old child consumed food at a restaurant in Virginia and became ill with food poisoning. Damages were sought against the restaurant in the amount of $25,000. The Virginia Court of Appeals stated:

---

* See Chapter 36 for a discussion of warranties in the sale of goods to hotels.

The question for decision here, of first impression in Virginia, is: Does a restaurant-keeper impliedly warrant the wholesomeness of the food he serves to his patrons?

The holding that the transaction between a restaurant-keeper and his patron is a sale, carrying an implied warranty of wholesomeness of the food served, is required to maintain consistency with our other decisions relating to foodstuffs…[W]e have consistently held that there is an implied warranty of wholesomeness imposed upon those who manufacture or sell foodstuffs.

The purpose of such a warranty…is "to require a person who sells or purveys articles of food to insure their being wholesome and fit for human consumption."

* * *

To hold that no implied warranty is applicable here would create a strange inconsistency in the law. In such a situation, a customer who is made ill from eating an unwholesome ham could recover from the corner supermarket where he purchased the ham. But if, instead, that same person becomes ill from eating a sandwich prepared with the same ham at the next-door restaurant, he would be denied recovery against the restaurateur.

The reasoning that would arrive at such a conclusion smacks of a lack of a sense of reality. Such reasoning stems from the old-fashioned notion that the patron acquired no title to or property in the food placed before him in an eating place. When a patron orders and pays for a meal in a restaurant, whose food is it if not his? Does it still belong to the restaurateur, who is free to retrieve it at will if not yet eaten?

These questions answer themselves. As was said in *Betehia* v. *Cape Cod Corporation*, 10 Wis. 2d 323, 103 N.W. 2d 64, 66, "Today if one takes home from a restaurant part of his steak for his dog, he could hardly be accused of larceny."

Sound considerations of public policy demand that we avoid the inconsistencies that would naturally arise from a holding that the restaurateur-patron relationship does not involve a sale carrying an implied warranty. We answer that demand by holding that the furnishing of food by a restaurant-keeper to a patron is a sale and does carry an implied warranty that the food is wholesome and fit for human consumption, for the breach of which the restaurant-keeper is liable for consequential damages.

Privity of Contract

Under common law, *privity of contract* is generally necessary to bring an action against a party for breach of an implied warranty. Privity of contract means that a contractual relationship exists between the person suing and the party sued. Note the following case:

In *Conklin* v. *Hotel Waldorf-Astoria*,[12] the plaintiff was invited by one of the guests of the hotel to have lunch at one of the hotel's restaurants. During the luncheon, the plaintiff bit into a roll and was injured by a piece of glass which was imbedded in it. When the injured woman sued, the hotel claimed that there was no privity of contract between her and the hotel because the luncheon bill was paid by her hostess, who was the hotel guest. The court, however, held that the hotel had agreed to serve the plaintiff and that there was an implied warranty that the hotel would serve both the plaintiff and her hostess food which was fit for human consumption. In this case, the court refused to adhere to the privity principle. The New York court ruled:

> An implied contract was formed when [injured] plaintiff and her friend became patrons of the restaurant, placed their orders for food and their orders were accepted. At that moment, an implied obligation on the part of both the plaintiff and her friend was individually created to pay for whatever was individually ordered. Simultaneously, the defendant impliedly agreed to serve each of them food fit for human consumption. The warranty arose then and ran to both of them. The warranty does not run only to the one who eventually pays the check. The actual payment of the check does not determine the time when the contract comes into being.
>
> Even if the plaintiff's friend placed the order, the hotel knew it was serving an order for two persons. When one person undertakes to give the order for several people, that person is acting as the agent for the others. Which person pays the check and whether they reimburse each other or not is only a matter of private arrangement between the customers themselves. This is of no concern to the restaurateur as long as he is paid. The plaintiff and her friend relied on defendant's implied promise to serve each of them with fit and wholesome food. Consequently, it makes no difference whether the plaintiff or her friend paid the check.

In other states, the courts might well have ruled otherwise, based on a stricter theory of privity of contract.

Such problems under the common law have largely been eliminated by the Uniform Commercial Code.

Uniform Commercial Code

The Uniform Commercial Code (UCC), which has been enacted into law in all states except Louisiana, seeks to set forth a uniform law to govern buyer-seller transactions, including food service liability.

Section 2-314 of the UCC states:

§ 2-314. Implied Warranty: Merchantability; Usage of Trade.

(1)   Unless excluded or modified (Section 2-316), a warranty that the goods shall be merchantable is implied in a contract for their sale if the seller is a merchant with respect to goods of that kind. Under this section the serving for value of food or drink to be consumed either on the premises or elsewhere is a *sale.*

(2)   Goods to be merchantable must be at least such as…

(c)   are fit for the ordinary purposes for which such goods are used.…

Thus, under the UCC, the service of food or drink is considered a sale and creates a warranty that the food or drink is fit for the purposes for which the items are sold. That is, the UCC automatically imposes, by operation of law, an implied warranty on the sale.

In the case of *Webster* v. *Blue Ship Tea Room, Inc.*,[13] the court discusses the question of breach of an implied warranty under the UCC (and apart from the UCC):

> On Saturday, April 25, 1959, about 1 P.M., the plaintiff, accompanied by her sister and her aunt, entered the Blue Ship Tea Room operated by the defendant.

* * *

> The plaintiff, who had been born and brought up in New England (a fact of some consequence), ordered clam chowder and crabmeat salad. Within a few minutes she received tidings to the effect that "there was no more clam chowder," whereupon she ordered a cup of fish chowder. Presently, there was set before her "a small bowl of fish chowder.... The fish chowder contained haddock, potatoes, milk, water and seasoning. The chowder was milky in color and not clear. The haddock and potatoes were in chunks" (also a fact of consequence). She agitated it a little with the spoon and observed that it was a fairly full bowl.... It was hot when she got it, but she did not tip it with her spoon because it was hot...but stirred it in an up and under motion. She denied that she did this because she was looking for something, but it was rather because she wanted an even distribution of fish and potatoes. She started to eat it, alternating between the chowder and crackers which were on the table with...[some] rolls. She ate about 3 or 4 spoonfuls then stopped. She looked at the spoonfuls as she was eating. She saw equal parts of liquid, potato and fish as she spooned it into her mouth. She did not see anything unusual about it. After 3 or 4 spoonfuls she was aware that something had lodged in her throat because she couldn't swallow and couldn't clear her throat by gulping and she could feel it." This misadventure led to two esophagoscopies at the Massachusetts General Hospital, in the second of which, on April 27, 1959, a fish bone was found and removed. The sequence of events produced injury to the plaintiff which was not insubstantial.
>
> We must decide whether a fish bone lurking in a fish chowder, about the ingredients of which there is no other complaint, constitutes a breach of implied warranty under applicable provisions of the Uniform Commercial Code [§§ 2-314, 2-316].... As the judge put it in his charge, "Was the fish chowder fit to be eaten and wholesome? [N]o-body is claiming that the fish itself wasn't wholesome.... But the bone of contention here—I don't mean that for a pun—but was this fish bone a foreign substance that made the fish chowder unwholesome or not fit to be eaten?"

The court, in this case, ruled in favor of the restaurant in applying the UCC. The court pointed to the *foreign-natural test* to determine whether the restaurant was liable to the customer for the injury. This test is used to determine whether an object found in food is *foreign* to the food, or whether it might naturally be in the food. In the *Blue Ship Tea Room* case, the court stated, a customer who sat down to eat a bowl of fish chowder in a New England restaurant might well expect to find a fish bone.

As indicated in the *Blue Ship Tea Room* case, other courts have applied the foreign-natural test with respect to unexpected objects found in food. This test, as its name implies, involves a factual determination concerning the nature of any object found in food. If an object that causes an injury is "natural" to the food served, the injured plaintiff cannot recover damages. For example, in *Mix* v. *Ingersoll Candy Company*,[14] the court denied recovery to a plaintiff alleging injuries caused by a chicken bone in a chicken pot pie which, according to the court, could be reasonably anticipated in such a dish.

In *Stark* v. *Chock Full O'Nuts*,[15] the court also adopted the *reasonable expectation* doctrine whereby a plaintiff can recover for breach of implied warranty if it is found that a foreign object or other harmful substance is not "reasonably anticipated to be in the food, as served." The courts have applied this rule when foreign or unexpected objects have been found in foods, such as whole walnuts in walnut ice cream, or struvite in shrimp and canned tuna fish.

In *Musso* v. *Picadilly Cafeterias, Inc.*,[16] the court held that the restaurant-keeper was not liable to a customer whose denture was broken by a cherry pit while the customer ate cherry pie. The court ruled that the restaurant-keeper did not breach the implied warranty of wholesomeness because the cherry pit might naturally be present in a cherry pie. The court stated:

> If the server permits alien, extraneous matter not constituting a natural part of the ingredients or finished product (such as glass or other noxious substances), to enter his product during preparation or processing, he is liable for breach of his implied duty to serve a product free of foreign, deleterious substances. However, should the restaurant-keeper inadvertently leave in the food substances natural to the ingredients or finished product[,] he is not liable to the customer, as the food is not thereby rendered unwholesome and unfit for human consumption. As a result there is no breach of the implied warranty of wholesomeness.

In *Allen* v. *Grafton*,[17] a restaurant patron was injured by a piece of oyster shell which was in an order of fried oysters. The court stated that "the possible presence of a piece of oyster shell in or attached to an oyster is so well known to anyone who eats oysters that we can say as a matter of law that one who eats oysters can reasonably anticipate and guard against eating such a piece of shell."

On the other hand, a famous actress was dining at a New York City hotel when she bit into a shrimp and chipped a tooth on an unknown substance. She sued the hotel-owner of the restaurant for $10 million in damages. The suit was settled for $50,000. (The actress had allegedly lost a contract for a fashion appearance in Italy because of the tooth injury.)

The Washington State Supreme Court held a restaurant liable for injuries a patron sustained when a wine glass broke as he drank from it. The court held that under the UCC, the restaurant warranted both that the wine was fit for drinking and that the container in which it was sold, the glass, was adequate for its purpose. In addition, the restaurant was found to be strictly liable for selling a defective product, which consisted of the wine and the glass as a unit.

Thus, liability claims may be based on a claim of breach of an implied warranty that the food served is fit for human consumption. The restaurant operator warrants that food is wholesome, fit for human consumption, and contains no foreign or harmful material. *Bronson* v. *Club Comanche, Inc.,*[18] and *Battiste* v. *St. Thomas Diving Club, Inc.,*[19] both involved restaurant patrons being stricken with ciguatera fish poisoning. Courts have held in numerous cases that serving unwholesome or improperly prepared food violates the implied warranty under the UCC.

Strict Liability

As noted earlier, the UCC requires that patrons prove a breach of warranty in claiming that the food product made them sick. In a number of recent cases, the patrons have asked the courts to go even further and hold the restaurant or hotel liable under the doctrine of *strict liability* in food cases. That is, the restaurant or hotel is treated as an insurer of the food product and held absolutely liable to the injured patron.

Under this legal doctrine, which has been adopted by some courts, the law holds the restaurant or hotel to be a guarantor of the food product as being fit for consumption without the requirement that there be an express or implied warranty between the seller of the food and the patron.

This doctrine of strict liability is discussed in the case of *Shoshone Coca-Cola Bottling Company* v. *Dolinski,*[20] in which the manufacturer of a food product was held liable. In this case, Mr. Dolinski suffered physical and mental distress when he consumed some of the contents of a bottle of Squirt containing a decomposed mouse. Consequently he filed an action for damages against Shoshone Coca-Cola Bottling Company, which manufactures and distributes Squirt. His complaint alleged two theories of liability: breach of the implied warranties of quality (which the court rejected, in the absence of privity of contract) and strict tort liability. The breach of warranty and negligence claims were later abandoned, and the case went to the jury solely upon the doctrine of strict tort liability. The jury favored Mr. Dolinski with its verdict and awarded him damages of $2,500. On appeal, the Supreme Court of Nevada affirmed the verdict and judgment (see the opinion in this case at the end of this chapter).

If a hotel restaurant had served the Squirt drink to the patron in the above case, the restaurant might be sued under the doctrine of strict liability. However, the hotel restaurant would then sue the manufacturer for indemnification in such a case.

Important Points for Management

Federal laws relating to food are contained in the Food, Drug, and Cosmetic Act which seeks to prevent adulteration of food shipped and sold in interstate commerce. Altering or removing the label on food held for sale is prohibited.

State laws relating to food cover the topics of sanitation, food storage, cleaning, water supply, sewage, and vermin control.

There are two theories under which a hotel may be sued for serving contaminated food to a guest:

- Negligence (tort theory) is the failure to exercise due care.

- Breach of the implied warranties of merchantability or fitness for a particular purpose (contract theory). This is the warranty that goes from the seller to the buyer that the food is fit for human consumption.

The Uniform Commercial Code provides for an implied warranty that food or drink sold is fit for the purposes for which it is sold.

Food and beverages must be served and prepared under sanitary conditions.

Many courts apply the foreign-natural test to determine whether the restaurant should be held liable for guest injuries suffered from objects found in the food. For example, is a fish bone found in a serving of fish a natural or foreign substance?

References

1. 21 U.S.C. § 331 *et. seq.*

2. *United States* v. *H.B. Gregory Co.,* 502 F. 2d 700 (7th Cir. 1974), *cert. denied,* 422 U.S. 1007 (1975); *United States* v. *J. Treffiletti & Sons,* 496 F. Supp. 53 (N.D.N.Y. 1980).

3. See, for example, N.Y. State Sanitary Code Tit. 10, Subpart 14-1.

4. 85 So. 2d 63 (La. Ct. App. 1956).

5. *Id.* at 65.

6. Reported in the *New York Post,* February 24 and 25, 1993.

7. *Jasiczek* v. *Elbow Beach Hotel-Bermuda,* Doc. No. L-093544-85, Sup. Ct. N.J. Law Div.: Essex Cty. (Oct. 9, 1986).

8. 270 Or. 678, 528 P. 2d 1332 (Sup. Ct. Or. 1974). But see *Renna* v. *Bishop's Cafeteria Co. of Omaha,* 218 N.W.2d 246 (Neb. 1974).

9. *Id.* at 1334. The Oregon Supreme Court reversed the judgment for plaintiff on the grounds of erroneous instructions to the jury on breach of implied warranty, a theory which the plaintiff failed to plead in the complaint.

10. *Newport Daily News,* Aug. 25, 1995 at pg. A-4, col.1.

11. 147 S.E. 2d 722 (Va. 1965).

12. 161 N.Y.S. 2d 205 (1957).

13. 198 N.E. 2d 309 (Mass. 1964).

14. 6 Cal. 2d 674, 59 P. 2d 144 (Cal. 1936).

15. 77 Misc. 2d 553, 356 N.Y.S. 2d 403 (1st Dept. 1974). See also *Coulter* v. *American Bakeries' Co.,* 530 So.2d 1009 (Fla. 1988).

16. 178 So. 2d 421 (La. App. 1965).

17. 170 Ohio St. 249, 164 N.E. 2d 167 (1960).

18. 286 F. Supp. 21 (D.C.V.I. 1968).

19. 26 U.C.C. Rep. Serv. (Callaghan) 324 (D.C.V.I. 1979).

20. 420 P. 2d 855 (Nev. Sup. Ct. 1966, rehearing denied 1967).

 # Review Questions

1. How does the Food, Drug, and Cosmetic Act define "adulterated food"?

2. What subjects do state and local health laws cover with regard to food preparation and service?

3. Name two legal bases for a guest lawsuit against a restaurant for food containing kitchen floor polish.

4. How do express warranties differ from implied warranties?

5. How did the court view the privity principle in *Conklin* v. *Hotel Waldorf-Astoria?*

6. How does the Uniform Commercial Code help the guest who sues the restaurant for food poisoning?

7. What is the "foreign-natural test"? How do courts apply it?

8. What is the "reasonable expectation" doctrine with regard to objects found in food?

9. What does the court say in *Allen* v. *Grafton* with respect to the reasonable expectation doctrine?

Internet Sites

For more information, visit the following Internet sites. Remember that Internet addresses can change without notice.

Federal Food, Drug, and Cosmetic Act
http://www.fda.gov/opacom/laws/fdcact/fdctoc.htm

Uniform Commercial Code
http://www.law.cornell.edu/ucc/ucc.table.html

Illustrative Case

Shoshone Coca-Cola Bottling Company v. *Dolinski*

420 P. 2d 855 (Nev. Sup. Ct. 1966, rehearing denied 1967)

The important question presented by this appeal is whether Nevada should judicially adopt the doctrine of strict tort liability against a manufacturer and distributor of a bottled beverage. Subordinate questions are also involved and will be discussed.

1. Leo Dolinski suffered physical and mental distress when he partially consumed the contents of a bottle of "Squirt" containing a decomposed mouse. As a consequence he filed this action for damages against Shoshone Coca-Cola Bottling Company, the manufacturer and distributor of "Squirt." His complaint alleged alternative theories of liability; breach of the implied warranties of quality (which theory this court has rejected, in the absence of privity of contract...); and strict tort liability. The breach of warranty and negligence claims were subsequently abandoned, and the case was pre-sented to the jury solely upon the doctrine of strict tort liability. The jury favored Dolinski with its verdict and fixed his damages at $2,500. This appeal by Shoshone ensued.

We affirm the verdict and judgment since, in our view, public policy demands that one who places upon the market a bottled beverage in a condition dangerous for use must be held strictly liable to the ultimate user for injuries resulting from such use, although the seller has exercised all reasonable care, and the user has not entered into a contractual relation with him. Perhaps the supporting policy reasons are best expressed by William L. Prosser in his article, "The Fall of the Citadel," 50 Minn. L. Rev. 791, 799 (1966): "The public interest in human safety requires the maximum possible protection for the user of the product, and those best able to afford it are the suppliers of the chattel. By placing their goods upon the market, the suppliers represent to the public that they are suitable and safe for use; and by packaging, advertising, and otherwise, they do everything they can to induce that belief. The middleman is no more than a conduit, a mere mechanical device, through which the thing is to reach the ultimate user. The supplier has invited and solicited the use; and when it leads to disaster, he should not be permitted to avoid the responsibility by saying that he made no contract with the consumer, or that he used all reasonable care."

In *Escola* v. *Coca-Cola Bottling Co.*, 24 Cal. 2d 453, 150 P. 2d 436, 440 (1944), Justice Traynor, in a concurring opinion, wrote: "Even if there is no negligence, however, public policy demands that responsibility be fixed wherever it will most effectively reduce the hazards to life and health inherent in defective products that reach the market." That point of view ultimately became the philosophy of the full court in *Greenman* v. *Yuba Power Products, Inc.*, 59 Cal. 2d 57, 27 Cal. Rptr. 697, 377 P. 2d 897 (1962). There Justice Traynor wrote: "The purpose of such liability is to insure that the cost of injuries resulting from defective products are borne by the manufacturer that put such products on the market rather than by the injured persons who are powerless to protect themselves."

We believe that the quoted expressions of policy are sound as applied to the manufacturer and distributor of a bottled beverage. Indeed, eighteen states have judicially accepted strict liability, without negligence and without privity, as to manufacturers of all types of products; and six more have done so by statute. See Prosser, "The Fall of the Citadel," 50 Minn. L. Rev. 791, 794, 795, 796 (1966). Though the appellant suggests that only the legislature may declare the policy of Nevada on this subject, the weight of case authority is contra. As indicated, most states approving the doctrine of strict liability have done so by court declaration.

2.   Our acceptance of strict tort liability against the manufacturer and distributor of a bottled beverage does not mean that the plaintiff is relieved of the burden of proving a case. He must still establish that his injury was caused by a defect in the product, and that such defect existed when the product left the hands of the defendant. The concept of strict liability does not prove causation, nor does it trace cause to the defendant.

In the case at hand Shoshone contends that insufficient proof was offered to establish that the mouse was in the bottle of "Squirt" when it left Shoshone's possession. On this point the evidence was in conflict and the jury was free to choose. The Vice-President and General Manager of Shoshone testified, in substance, that had the mouse been in the bottle while at his plant, it would have been denuded because of the caustic solution used and extreme heat employed in the bottle washing and brushing process. As the mouse had hair when examined following the plaintiff's encounter, the Manager surmises that the rodent must have gotten into the bottle after leaving the defendant's possession. On the other hand, the plaintiff offered the expert testimony of a toxicologist who examined the bottle and contents on the day the plaintiff drank from it. It was his opinion that the mouse "had been dead for a long time" and that the dark stains (mouse feces) which he found on the bottom of the bottle must have been there before the liquid was added. The jury apparently preferred the latter evidence which traced cause to the defendant.

We turn to the question of tampering. Shoshone insists that a burden is cast upon the plaintiff to prove that there was no reasonable opportunity for someone to tamper with the bottle after it left Shoshone's control. *Underhill* v. *Anciaux, supra*, where the claim was based upon negligence, may be read to suggest that such a burden is cast upon the plaintiff. We cannot agree with that suggestion.

The matter of tampering is inextricably tied to the problem of tracing cause to the defendant. This is so whether the claim for relief is based on negligence or strict liability. Whenever evidence is offered by the plaintiff tending to establish the presence of the mouse in the bottle when it left Shoshone's possession, the defense is encouraged to introduce evidence that the mouse must have gotten there after the bottle left Shoshone's control, thus interjecting the possibility that the bottle and its contents were tampered with by someone, perhaps as a practical joke or for some other reason. In this case, as in most cases, positive proof either way is not available. Inferences must be drawn from the best available evidence produced by each side. We have already alluded to that evidence.

It is apparent that the moment plaintiff produces evidence tending to show that the mouse was in the bottle while in the defendant's control, he has, to some degree, negated tampering by others. The converse is likewise true. A fortiori, once it is decided that enough evidence is present to trace cause to the defendant, that same evidence is sufficient to allow the jury to find an absence of tampering. For this reason, any notion that there is a burden of proof as to tampering, simply does not make sense. The sole burden is upon the plaintiff to prove that his injury was caused by a defect in the product and that such defect existed when the product left the hands of the defendant. The defendant, of course, may offer evidence suggesting tampering under a general denial of liability....

The Supreme Court of Oregon is in accord. In *Keller* v. *Coca-Cola Bottling Co.,* 214 Or. 654, 330 P. 2d 346 (1958), the court wrote: "We hold, therefore, that there was reasonable inference for the jury's consideration that the cigar stub entered or remained in the bottle while in the exclusive control of the defendant. It was not incumbent upon the plaintiff to prove that tampering did not exist. Having established the delivery to be in the normal course of processing and dispensing, plaintiff was not required to negative the doubtful possibility of unwarranted or unlawful acts by other persons."

3.   Shoshone next complains that there was not enough evidence to identify it as the manufacturer and distributor of the bottle in question. The record shows that Shoshone manufactured, bottled, and sold "Squirt"; that it furnished one of its vending machines to the Sea and Ski plant where the plaintiff was employed; and that it delivered beverages, including "Squirt," to the Sea and Ski plant to be placed in the machine. Almost immediately after the plaintiff drank from the bottle and became ill, an employee of Sea and Ski telephoned Shoshone and reported the incident, whereupon a Shoshone salesman came to the Sea and Ski plant to investigate. On this evidence it was permissible for the jury to conclude that Shoshone was the manufacturer and distributor of the bottle in question.

* * *

5.   The jury awarded Dolinski $2,500 as compensatory damages. Shoshone urges that the award is excessive. Upon drinking the "Squirt," Dolinski immediately became ill, visited a doctor, and was given pills to counteract nausea. At the time of trial more than two years later, he still possessed an aversion to soft drinks, described by a psychiatrist to be a "conditioned reflex" that could continue indefinitely. He lost 20 pounds. In these circumstances we cannot say that the damages must have been given under the influence of passion or prejudice or that our judicial conscience is shocked.

* * *

Judgment Affirmed.

Chapter 17 Outline

Truth-in-Menu Laws and Labeling Laws
    Kosher Food
    Prohibition Against the Use of
      Sulfiting Agents
    New York State Sought Pesticide
      Notice to Guests
Important Points for Management
References
Key Terms
Review Questions
Internet Sites

Competencies

1. Describe truth-in-menu laws and labeling laws. (pp. 227–229)

2. List some examples of inaccurate food descriptions that would violate typical truth-in-menu regulations. (pp. 228–229)

17

Other Laws Relating
to Food Service

Truth-in-Menu Laws and Labeling Laws

A number of states have enacted *truth-in-menu laws* or regulations. California, New Jersey, and Maryland, among others, have adopted regulations prohibiting misrepresentations in menu descriptions of food served and subjecting violators to fines.

In New Jersey, for example, statutes under the general heading of frauds in sales or advertising prohibit "misrepresentations of identity of food" in menus. The texts of the New Jersey truth-in-menu laws read:

56:8-2.9 Misrepresentations of identity of food in menus or advertisements of eating establishments

It shall be an unlawful practice for any person to misrepresent on any menu or other posted information, including advertisements, the identity of any food or food products to any of the patrons or customers of eating establishments including but not limited to restaurants, hotels, cafes, lunch counters or other places where food is regularly prepared and sold for consumption on or off the premises. This section shall not apply to any section or sections of a retail food or grocery store which do not provide facilities for on the premises consumption of food or food products.

56:8-2.10 Acts constituting misrepresentation of identity of food

The identity of said food or food products shall be deemed misrepresented if:

a. Its description is false or misleading in any particular;

b. Its description omits information which by its omission renders the description false or misleading in any particular;

c. It is served, sold, or distributed under the name of another food or food product;

d. It purports to be or is represented as a food or food product for which a definition of identity and standard of quality has been established by custom and usage unless it conforms to such definition and standard.[1]

Furthermore, any person who violates these statutes "shall be liable for the refund of all moneys acquired" from the deceptive menu description or advertisement. These refunds may be obtained pursuant to a "private action" or by any established county or municipal consumer affairs office.[2]

A bill was introduced before the City Council of New York City dealing with alleged misrepresentations by restaurants of items listed on their menus. Although the bill was never officially enacted, it shows some of the concerns for consumer protection with respect to menu representations. Menu descriptions mentioned in the bill included:

- Labels designating an item as "fresh"

- Indications of the place of origin of an item

- Listings of "whole" foods that are, in fact, prepared from chopped or reconstituted elements

- The designation of "homemade"

The National Restaurant Association (NRA) has published a booklet to assist food service operators in properly representing the items they sell. The booklet, entitled "Accuracy in Menus," discusses such topics as quantity, quality, price, brand names, product identification, points of origin, merchandising terms, means of preservation, food preparation, verbal and visual presentation, and dietary and nutritional claims. This booklet can be ordered from the NRA's Washington, D.C., office.*

In a case illustrating the potential liability under state or local truth-in-menu laws, on July 19, 1978, the California Superior Court fined the McDonald's hamburger chain $10,000 for violations cited by the Los Angeles County Health Department of local truth-in-menu regulations. The City Attorney charged in his suit that breakfast place mats used on trays at McDonald's contained two descriptions of food purportedly served by the establishment that were not accurate. The place mats advertised, first, that "maple" syrup was served on the premises, and, second, that "fresh" orange juice was served. The City Attorney claimed that the syrup in fact available was not pure maple and that the orange juice was frozen rather than fresh. McDonald's chose not to contest the charges brought by the Los Angeles City Attorney on the basis of the Health Department's investigation, but instead paid the fines levied for two **allegations** of false advertising, in addition to court costs.

A bill was introduced in the New York City Council that would require that:

- Customers be informed of substitutions on the menu

- The size of a beverage appear in ounces rather than only the words "small" or "large"

---

* National Restaurant Association, 311 First St., N.W., Washington, DC 20001.

- The term "homestyle" or "homemade" be used for dishes prepared "from scratch"
- If monosodium glutamate is used in the preparation of an item, it should be so indicated in the description of the item
- A copy of the menu with prices be posted so that it will be visible from outside the restaurant, and individual menus be provided or a large menu be posted visible to all diners
- Cover, mandatory, or minimum charges be written on the menu in type size no smaller than that used for the headings of food categories
- Restaurant owners retain records and invoices indicating authenticity of brand names
- A sign be posted next to the Health Department permit informing customers that they may request to examine the latest Health Department report

Kosher Food

State and local laws may also govern the sale of kosher food and its labeling. For example, in New York it is a misdemeanor to make certain representations of the kosher status of food products sold or consumed on or off the premises. Requirements relate not only to false representations made orally, but also to mislabeling, misbranding, advertising, and menus. In New York, the law also requires certain signs to be posted where both kosher and non-kosher meat or meat preparations or other food products are sold on the premises.*

Prohibition Against the Use of Sulfiting Agents

In 1985, New York State passed a law prohibiting state wholesale food distributors, retailers, and restaurants from adding sulfiting agents to any foods sold after August 5, 1985. Simply stated, this meant that food service operators had to find a substitute product to use as a freshener for salad bar items and peeled potatoes, if they had not already done so.**

New York State Sought Pesticide Notice to Guests

In 1988, the New York State Department of Environmental Conservation sought to establish regulations requiring that at least two hours prior to the application of a pesticide, a hotel or restaurant must post an appropriate notice to guests.

That is, all hotels and restaurants would have to post an 8 1/2" × 11" notice stating that such premises were to be treated with a pesticide. Moreover, such notice was to remain posted for 24 hours after the pesticide treatment.

However, the Supreme Court of New York State ruled that the Department of Environmental Conservation had exceeded its authority, and, therefore, ruled that the regulations were invalid.

---

* N.Y. Agriculture & Markets Law § 201-a.
** N.Y. Agriculture & Markets Law § 199-d.

Important Points for Management

A number of states have truth-in-menu laws. You should have on file a copy of any such laws in your state.

Be certain to label kosher foods properly, especially when required by your state and local laws.

Various states prohibit the use of sulfites. Check your state and local laws if you are using sulfite preservative agents.

References

1. N.J. Stat. Ann. § 56:8-2.9-56:8-2.10 (West 1989).
2. N.J. Stat. Ann. § 56:8-2.11-56:8-2.12 (West 1989).

Key Terms

allegation—The assertion or statement of a party to a lawsuit made in a pleading, setting out what the party expects to prove in court.

Review Questions

1. How do truth-in-menu laws protect consumers?

2. Under New Jersey truth-in-menu laws, what acts on the part of food service establishments constitute "misrepresentation of identity of food"?

3. As implied in the McDonald's case, what does the term "fresh" (as in "fresh orange juice") suggest? If syrup is labeled "maple" syrup, what must that legally signify?

4. According to a bill before the New York City Council, what do the terms "homestyle" and "homemade" mean?

5. How do New York laws protect purchasers of kosher food? What are the food labeling laws for kosher foods in your state?

6. What does your state or city require with respect to the posting of notices when restaurants or hotels use pesticides?

Internet Sites

For more information, visit the following Internet sites. Remember that Internet addresses can change without notice.

National Restaurant Association
http://www.restaurant.org

Chapter 18 Outline

General Nature of Control by State
Application for and Issuance of Licenses
General Restrictions on Licenses
    Removal
    Corporate Changes
    The Employment of Minors
    Illegal Sales
Liability Under State Dram Shop Acts
Common Law Liability for Serving
    Alcoholic Beverages to Intoxicated
    Persons
Hours and Premises of Sale
Books and Records
Important Warning
Important Points for Management
References
Review Questions
Internet Sites
Illustrative Case

Competencies

1. Explain how a hotel applies for licenses to sell alcoholic beverages. (p. 233)

2. List the types of alcoholic beverage licenses that the State Liquor Authority often issues. (p. 233)

3. Identify the general state restrictions typically placed on operations licensed to sell alcohol for on-premises consumption. (pp. 234–235)

4. Explain the purpose of Dram Shop Acts, cite a typical Dram Shop law, and identify four elements a plaintiff must prove for a statutory cause of action under that law. (pp. 235–236)

5. Describe a hotel's liability under state Dram Shop Acts. (pp. 235–236)

6. Describe the common law liability a hotel may face for serving alcoholic beverages to intoxicated persons. (pp. 236–337)

7. Describe restrictions imposed by state laws with regard to the sale of alcoholic beverages. (p. 237)

18

State Laws Relating to
Alcoholic Beverages

General Nature of Control by State

Under the Twenty-first Amendment of the U.S. Constitution, each state has the right to control the sale of alcoholic beverages within that state. In states that permit the sale of alcoholic beverages, sales are governed by alcoholic beverage control laws and rules and regulations of the State Liquor Authority.*

While Alcoholic Beverage Control Boards in each county generally have specific powers and responsibilities, the final control usually rests in the State Liquor Authority. Every hotel should have a copy of the rules and regulations of its State Liquor Authority, since these have the force of law. The State Liquor Authority office will probably have copies available.

The purpose of this chapter is to discuss the various subjects often covered by state laws. It is not intended to describe any particular state's regulations regarding the sale and service of alcoholic beverages.

Application for and Issuance of Licenses

Applications for a license must usually be made to the local county Alcoholic Beverage Control Board or directly to the State Liquor Authority. Licensees must usually file a bond in an amount fixed by the State Liquor Authority.

Often the State Liquor Authority issues three types of licenses for on-premises consumption:

- Beer license

- Liquor license, which includes the sale of wine and beer

- Wine license, which may or may not include the sale of beer

When a license is issued and when it is renewed each year, the hotel must usually publish a notice in a newspaper or newspapers in the form provided by law.

---

* Federal and state liquor taxes are covered in Chapter 35.

General Restrictions on Licensees

Before an on-premises license is first issued, the Alcoholic Beverage Control Board usually must inspect and approve the premises. Thereafter, no alterations, increase, or decrease in the size of the premises or change in equipment in the licensed premises are permitted without prior permission from the State Liquor Authority.

Removal

In most states, no license may be transferred from licensed premises to other premises without permission from the State Liquor Authority.

Corporate Changes

Generally, a corporate licensee must notify the State Liquor Authority of any change in its officers, directors, or stock ownership. This information must be submitted on forms furnished by the Authority. No change is effective until approved by the Authority. Failure to notify the State Liquor Authority of such changes is usually a violation of law and may subject the licensee to Authority action.

The Employment of Minors

Usually, a licensee is prohibited from employing or suffering to work on the licensed premises any person under the statutory age (which is normally 21 years of age)* as a hostess, waitress, waiter, or in any other capacity where duties require them to sell, dispense, or handle alcoholic beverages.

Illegal Sales

Further, in many states, a person who sells or gives away any alcoholic beverages to any child, actually or apparently under the statutory age, is guilty of a misdemeanor. It is essential that the utmost care be taken not to violate this law. A violation may well result in the suspension or revocation of a liquor license.

The alcoholic beverage control law may also prohibit sales to the following:

- Any visibly intoxicated person

- Any habitual drunkard known to be such to the person authorized to dispense any alcoholic beverages

- Other designated persons

New York State recently enacted a law[1] that requires the State Liquor Authority to print and distribute to liquor licensees for both on-premises and off-premises consumption a poster containing certain provisions of the Alcoholic Beverage Control Law. This poster states, among other things, "No person shall sell, deliver, or give away or cause or permit or procure to be sold, delivered, or given away any

---

*   In New York State, an 18-year-old may be employed in licensed premises even though the statutory drinking age has been raised to 21.

alcoholic beverages to… (a)ny visibly intoxicated person." The poster will be captioned with the word "warning" in at least two-inch lettering. The licensee must conspicuously display the poster once it is received from the State Liquor Authority. Failure to do so may result in a civil penalty not to exceed $100 for each day of the violation of the posting requirements.

Liability Under State Dram Shop Acts

State Dram Shop Acts* generally create a *statutory*, as distinguished from common law, cause of action in favor of "[a]ny person who shall be injured in person, property, means of support or otherwise by any intoxicated person, or by reason of the intoxication of any person" against "any person who shall, by *unlawful* selling to or unlawfully assisting in procuring liquor for such intoxicated person, have caused or contributed to such intoxication" (emphasis added).[2]

However, in 1978, California enacted a law that, unlike many other state laws, expressly provides that the server of alcoholic beverages to an "obviously intoxicated person" shall *not* be liable in a civil action to another person subsequently injured as a result of such intoxication. The full text of the California law follows.

> Section 25602. Sales to drunkard or intoxicated person; offense; civil liability
>
> (a) Every person who sells, furnishes, gives or causes to be sold, furnished, or given away, any alcoholic beverage to any habitual or common drunkard or to any obviously intoxicated person is *guilty of a misdemeanor.*
>
> (b) *No person who sells,* furnishes, gives, or causes to be sold, furnished, or given away, any alcoholic beverage pursuant to subdivision (a) of this section *shall be civilly liable to any injured person or the estate of such person for injuries inflicted on that person as a result of intoxication by the consumer of such alcoholic beverage.*
>
> (c) The Legislature hereby declares that this section shall be interpreted so that the holdings in cases such as *Vesely* v. *Sager* (5 Cal.3d 153), *Bernhard* v. *Harrah's Club* (16 Cal.3d 313) and *Coulter* v. *Superior Court* (21 Cal.3d 144) be abrogated in favor of prior judicial interpretation finding the consumption of alcoholic beverages rather than the serving of alcoholic beverages as the proximate cause of injuries inflicted upon another by an intoxicated person.[3] [emphases added]

Under many Dram Shop Acts, a plaintiff must prove the following elements of the statutory cause of action: (1) an unlawful sale (2) of liquor or other alcoholic beverages (that is, beer or wine) (3) to an intoxicated person (4) which causes injury to another party.[4] Under New York law, "unlawful sale" refers to the law

---

* At least 20 states today have some type of Dram Shop Act. The New York State Dram Shop Act language is cited here as an example of a state statutory cause of action. Hotels should consult their own counsel for questions that may arise under other states' statutes. For further information regarding states' Dram Shop Acts, contact the National Restaurant Association, 1200 17th St., N.W., Washington, DC 20036. See also *Summary of State Laws & Regulations Relating to Distilled Spirits*, Distilled Spirits Council of the United States, Inc., 31st Ed., 2000.

prohibiting the sale to minors, known habitual drunkards, or to visibly intoxicated persons (see previous discussion as well as Reference 1). Under a state's Dram Shop Act, the potential liability of taverns, restaurants, hotels, and motels that serve alcoholic beverages is usually tremendous. The owners may be directly liable to the injured or deceased party or parties for various damages including medical expenses, property damages, damages for pain and suffering, support for spouse and dependents, lost wages, funeral expenses, and perhaps punitive damages. Therefore, all establishments serving liquor should obtain insurance to cover these potentially devastating amounts of recoverable damages. Food and beverage service staff should regularly be reminded of their responsibilities under the state's Alcohol Beverage Control Laws and related Dram Shop Act. Establishments should develop service policies regarding when or when not to serve patrons or guests in order to comply with such Dram Shop laws.

Common Law Liability for Serving Alcoholic Beverages to Intoxicated Persons

A person who is injured by the acts of an intoxicated individual may also have the common law right to bring a lawsuit against the owners of a restaurant or bar where the person causing the injuries was served intoxicating beverages. Such suits may be based on a common law theory of negligence independent of any claim under a state's Dram Shop Act. For example, in *Grasser* v. *Fleming*,[5] the plaintiff sought to recover damages for the death of her father, a habitual alcoholic. After becoming intoxicated in the defendant's bar, he was fatally injured when he fell off a 20-inch unguarded projection of a bridge. The plaintiff brought an action under the Michigan Wrongful Death Act alleging gross negligence, as well as willful and wanton misconduct by serving the decedent, allegedly known to be an alcoholic, after agreeing not to serve him. The trial and the appeals courts held that the existence of a Michigan Dram Shop Act does not preclude a common law action for "wrongful service of intoxicants."[6] The appeals court upheld a common law cause of action against the defendants for serving a known drunk and explained that the Dram Shop Act in Michigan was a statutory remedy that did not bar an action under common law in that state. In *Rappaport* v. *Nichols*,[7] the New Jersey Supreme Court recognized a common law cause of action against a tavern for serving an intoxicated patron who subsequently injured another party. (See the opinion in this case following this chapter.)

Similarly, in New York State, a lower court in *Berkley* v. *Park*[8] concluded that the New York Dram Shop Act did not preclude a common law cause of action for negligence. The court decision included a historical analysis of the state law:

> At the time of the original enactment of the Dram Shop Act of 1873, the automobile had not been invented and modern highway traffic was a figment of the imagination. The rural Inn and small town Tavern were patronized by the local citizenry or by travelers in horse-drawn vehicles. Today, the hazards of travel by automobiles on modern highways has become a national problem. The drunken driver is a threat to the safety of many. The responsibility of a tavern keeper for contributing to the intoxication of a patron has long been regulated by statute

(Alcoholic Beverage Control Law). It is understandable that early cases did not recognize any duty of an innkeeper to the traveling public because a serious hazard did not exist. Through lack of necessity, this phase of negligence liability did not develop. However, there did exist General Common Law Rules of negligence liability based on foreseeability and proximate cause. It is a well established, sound principle of legal philosophy that the common law is not static. Under the skillful interpretation of our Courts, it has been adapted to changing times and conditions of our civilization.

Hours and Premises of Sale

During certain hours set by local Alcoholic Beverage Control Boards, no alcoholic beverages may be sold, offered for sale, or given away upon any premises licensed to sell alcoholic beverages at retail for on-premises consumption. For example, in New York State the prohibited hours are Sunday from 4 A.M. to 12 P.M. or any other day between 4 A.M. and 8 A.M. Also in New York State, local Alcoholic Beverage Control Boards may adopt rules further restricting the hours of sale of alcoholic beverages.[9] In many states, no retail licensee for on-premises consumption may deliver or give away any liquors or wines for consumption off the premises where sold.

Books and Records

State laws usually require every retail licensee for on-premises consumption to keep and maintain upon the licensed premises books and records of all transactions. These records must show the amount of alcoholic beverages purchased daily by the licensee together with the sellers' names, license numbers, and place of business. The licensee's daily sales of alcoholic beverages must also be recorded.

Important Warning

The laws in every state (and often every county) are different with regard to the on-premises and off-premises sales *or non-sale* of alcoholic beverages. As hotel operators are fully aware, these laws must be strictly followed to avoid the loss of their liquor licenses and severe civil and/or criminal penalties.

Important Points for Management

Dram Shop Acts make the seller of alcoholic beverages liable to a third person injured by the buyer of alcoholic beverages. These are the usual elements that make the seller liable:

1. Sale of alcoholic beverages;

2. To an intoxicated person;

3. Who causes injury to a third party.

While Dram Shop Acts modify the common law rule, an injured party could also bring suit against the seller of alcoholic beverages under common law if that person were negligent in serving the intoxicated person.

The Educational Institute offers video-driven alcohol awareness training programs. For more information, contact the Educational Institute, 1407 S. Harrison Road, P.O. Box 1240, East Lansing, Michigan 48826, or call 1-800-752-4567.

References

1. N.Y. Alco. Bev. Cont. Law § 65-d (McKinney and Supp. 1994).
2. New York Gen. Oblig. Law § 11-101 (McKinney 1989).
3. Cal. Bus. & Prof. Code § 25602 (West's 1985). But see § 25602.1 for exception regarding intoxicated minors.
4. See *McNally* v. *Addis*, 65 Misc. 2d 204, 317 N.Y.S. 2d 157 (Sup. Ct. Westch. Co. 1970).
5. 74 Mich. App. 338, 253 N.W. 2d 757 (1977).
6. *Id.* at 760.
7. 31 N.J. 188, 156 A. 2d 1 (1959).
8. 47 Misc. 2d 381, 262 N.Y.S. 2d 290 (Sup. Ct. Otsego Co. 1965).
9. N. Y. Alco. Bev. Cont. Law § 106(5) (McKinney 1987).

 # Review Questions

1. What are at least three types of alcoholic beverage sales that are considered illegal?

2. What is the minimum age at which a person may legally purchase alcohol in your state?

3. Are there days or time periods when it is illegal to sell alcohol in your state? If so, what are they?

4. What is a Dram Shop Act?

5. Under many Dram Shop Acts, a plaintiff must prove certain elements of a statutory cause of action. What are they?

6. In some places without a specific Dram Shop Act, operations and servers have been held liable for damages. The factor behind this liability is server negligence. What is server negligence, and how can hospitality operations avoid it?

7. Under a state's Dram Shop Act, hospitality operation owners may be directly liable to an injured or deceased party for various damages. What might the list of possible damages include?

8. What can hospitality operations do to help protect themselves from liability under state Alcoholic Beverage Control Laws and Dram Shop Acts?

9. What is the extent of a hospitality operation owner's potential liability under state Alcoholic Beverage Control Laws and Dram Shop Acts in your state?

10. If a guest got intoxicated in your establishment, what would you do?

Internet Sites

For more information, visit the following Internet sites. Remember that Internet addresses can change without notice.

FindLaw
http://www.findlaw.com

Illustrative Case

Rappaport v. Nichols

31 N.J. 188, 156 A.2d 1 (N.J. Sup. Ct., 1959)

JACOBS, J.

The plaintiff-appellant appealed to the Appellate Division from a judgment entered in the Law Division in favor of the defendants-respondents. We certified the matter on our own motion.

The plaintiff's complaint alleges that during the night of November 14 or the early morning of November 15, 1957 Robert Nichols, who was then about 18 years of age, was "wrongfully and negligently sold and served alcoholic beverages" at the tavern premises of the defendants Hub Bar, Inc., 146 Mulberry Street, Newark, Murphy's Tavern, Inc., 135 Mulberry Street, Newark, Nathan Sweet and Solomon Lustig, trading as Nate's Tavern, 116 Mulberry Street, Newark and El Morocco Cocktail Bar, Inc., 1011 Broad Street, Newark; that the alcoholic beverages were sold and served under circumstances which constituted "notice or knowledge" by the tavern operators that Nichols was a minor who could not lawfully be served by them; that during his visits to Murphy's Tavern and the El Morocco Cocktail Bar, Nichols was accompanied by the defendant Leonard Britton, an adult, who paid for the alcoholic beverages under circumstances which constituted notice or knowledge that Nichols should not be served because of "his age and apparent condition"; that by reason of the "negligence and wrongful conduct" of the defendants, Nichols was rendered "under the influence of alcoholic beverages and unfit and incompetent to safely and reasonably operate" the motor vehicle entrusted to him by his mother, the defendant Mary Nichols; that he nevertheless drove it along the public highway at Washington and Academy Streets in Newark in a careless manner, resulting in a collision with a car operated by Arthur Rappaport and owned by the plaintiff; that Arthur Rappaport died as the result of injuries received in the collision and the plaintiff was appointed as general administratrix and administratrix *ad prosequendum* and seeks damages as the representative of his estate and in her individual capacity as owner of the car. Upon the basis of the limited record before us we may, for present purposes, infer that Nichols had just attained his eighteenth birthday, that he was served with intoxicating beverages at each of the four named taverns, that he left the last of the taverns at about 2 A.M., that he was intoxicated and negligently drove the motor vehicle and collided with the plaintiff's car between 2:15 and 2:20 A.M., and that his negligent operation of the motor vehicle was the result of his intoxication.

The tavern operators moved for summary judgment on the ground that the complaint "fails to state a cause of action and that as a matter of law" they are entitled to judgment. On March 20, 1959 the Law Division judge granted the motion in a letter opinion which stated that "while in some other jurisdictions outside New Jersey one may be held responsible for the actions of another to whom he has served intoxicating liquors, such is not the present law in New Jersey and to apply the doctrine of foreseeability to the facts in the case would stretch the intent of the doctrine too far." On April 20, 1959 a formal order for summary judgment was entered; it contained a provision staying proceedings against the remaining defendants until the plaintiff's rights are finally determined on appeal as against the tavern keepers.

* * *

During prohibition days, New Jersey had a Civil Damage Law which imposed strict liability for compensatory and punitive damages upon unlawful sellers of alcoholic beverages. [citations omitted] The law was repealed in 1934 (L. 1934, c. 32, p. 104) along with other miscellaneous liquor enactments in the light of the abandonment of prohibition and its replacement by the Alcoholic Beverage Control Act. [citations omitted] The repealer left unimpaired the fundamental negligence principles which admittedly prevail in New Jersey and upon which the plaintiff grounds his common law claim. [citations omitted] Negligence is tested by whether the reasonably prudent person at the time and place should recognize and foresee an unreasonable risk or likelihood of harm or danger to others. [citations omitted] And, correspondingly, the standard of care is the conduct of the reasonable person of ordinary prudence under the circumstances [citations omitted]

The negligence may consist in the creation of a situation which involves unreasonable risk because of the expectable action of another. See *Brody* v. *Albert Lifson & Sons,* 17 N.J. 383, 389 (1955). Where a tavern keeper sells alcoholic beverages to a person who is visibly intoxicated or to a person he knows or should know from the circumstances to be a minor, he ought to recognize and foresee the unreasonable risk of harm to others through action of the intoxicated person or the minor. The Legislature has in explicit terms prohibited sales to minors as a class because it recognizes their very special susceptibilities and the intensification of the otherwise inherent dangers when persons lacking in maturity and responsibility partake of alcoholic beverages; insofar as minors are concerned the sale of the first drink which does "its share of the work" (*Taylor* v. *Wright,* 126 Pa. 17, 621, 17 A. 677, 678 (1889)) and which generally leads to the others is unequivocally forbidden. See R.S. 33:1-77. In furtherance of the legislative policy, the Division of Alcoholic Beverage Control has by its Regulation No. 20, Rule 1, provided that no licensee shall permit any minor to be served or consume any alcoholic beverages; and the same regulation contains a provision against service to or consumption by any person "actually or apparently intoxicated." It seems clear to us that these broadly expressed restrictions were not narrowly intended to benefit the minors and intoxicated persons alone but were wisely intended for the protection of members of the general public as well. See *State* v. *Dahnke,* 244 Iowa 599, 603, 57 N.W.2d 553, 556 (Sup.Ct.1953); *Waynick* v. *Chicago's Last Department Store, supra,* 269 F.2d at page 325; *cf. Essex Holding Corp.* v. *Hock,* 136 N.J.L. 28 (*Sup. Ct. 1947*); *Sportsman 300* v. *Board of Com'rs of Town of Nutley,* 42 N.J. Super. 488, (*App. Div. 1956*).

When alcoholic beverages are sold by a tavern keeper to a minor or to an intoxicated person, the unreasonable risk of harm not only to the minor or the intoxicated person but also to members of the traveling public may readily be recognized and foreseen; this is particularly evident in current times when traveling by car to and from the tavern is so commonplace and accidents resulting from drinking are so frequent. See *National Safety Council, Accident Facts*, p. 49 (1959 ed.); cf. *Resume of Annual Reports of the Chief Medical Examiner of the County of Middlesex, State of New Jersey* (1933-1958), p. 9 (1959); *Study No. 885.A13 Minnesota Department of Highways, The Relationship of Drinking & Speeding to Accident Severity*, p. 5 (1959). If the patron is a minor or is intoxicated when served, the tavern keeper's sale to him is unlawful; and if the circumstances are such that the tavern keeper knows or should know that the patron is a minor or is intoxicated, his service to him may also constitute common law negligence. In view of the standard of conduct prescribed by the statute and the regulations, a tavern keeper's sale of alcoholic beverages when he knows or should know that the patron is a minor or intoxicated may readily be found by the jury to be imprudent conduct. While the plaintiff here may introduce evidence that the defendants knew or should have known that Nichols was a minor, or intoxicated when served, and may avail herself of the violations of the statute and the regulations as evidence of the defendants' negligence, each of the defendants is at liberty to assert that it did not know or have reason to believe that its patron was a minor, or intoxicated when served, and that it acted as a reasonably prudent person would have acted at the time and under the circumstances. See *Evers* v. *Davis, supra; cf. Carlo* v. *Okonite-Callendar Cable Co.*, 3 N.J. 253, 264 (1949); *Moore's Trucking Co.* v. *Gulf Tire & Supply Co.*, 18 N.J. *Super.* 467, 472 (*App. Div.* 1952), certification denied 10 N.J. 22 (1952).

The defendants contend that, assuming their conduct was unlawful and negligent as charged in the complaint, it was nevertheless not the proximate cause of the injuries suffered. But a tortfeasor is generally held answerable for the injuries which result in the ordinary course of events from his negligence and it is generally sufficient if his negligent conduct was a substantial factor in bringing about the injuries. . . . The fact that there were also intervening causes which were foreseeable or were normal incidents of the risk created would not relieve the tortfeasor of liability. . . . Ordinarily these questions of proximate and intervening cause are left to the jury for its factual determination. . . . If, as we must assume at this stage of the proceeding, the defendant tavern keepers unlawfully and negligently sold alcoholic beverages to Nichols causing his intoxication, which in turn caused or contributed to his negligent operation of the motor vehicle at the time of the fatal accident, then a jury could reasonably find that the plaintiff's injuries resulted in the ordinary course of events from the defendants' negligence and that such negligence was, in fact, a substantial factor in bringing them about. And a jury could also reasonably find that Nichols' negligent operation of his motor vehicle after leaving the defendants' taverns was a normal incident of the risk they created, or an event which they could reasonably have foreseen, and that consequently there was no effective breach in the chain of causation. In the light of the foregoing, we are in no position to hold that as a matter of law there could have been no proximate causal relation between the defendants' unlawful and negligent conduct and the plaintiff's injuries. See *Menth* v. *Breeze Corporation, Inc., supra; Martin* v. *Bengue, Inc., supra; Andreoli* v. *Natural Gas Company, supra.*

In the *Menth* case, *supra*, the plaintiffs alleged that the defendant had negligently stored combustible materials in a shed and that the materials had become ignited and had burned the plaintiffs' household furnishings in a nearby apartment house; this court held that the questions of negligence and proximate cause were for the jury and in answer to the contention that there may have been an intervening cause which had ignited the materials, it had this to say:

> There may be any number of causes and effects intervening between the first wrongful act and the final injurious occurrence and if they are such as might, with reasonable diligence, have been foreseen, the last result as well as the first, and every intermediate result, is to be considered in law as the proximate result of the first wrongful cause. A tort-feasor is not relieved from liability for his negligence by the intervention of the acts of third persons, including the act of a child, if those acts were reasonably foreseeable. The theory being that the original negligence continues and operates contemporaneously with an intervening act which might reasonably have been anticipated so that the negligence can be regarded as a concurrent cause of the injury inflicted. One who negligently creates a dangerous condition cannot escape liability for the natural and probable consequences thereof although the act of a third person may have contributed to the final result. The law of negligence recognizes that there may be two or more concurrent and directly cooperative and efficient proximate causes of an injury.

* * *

Although it is evident that the strict civil liability prevailing by statute in many of the states is a much heavier responsibility, the defendants urge that the sustaining of the plaintiff's complaint will place an "inconceivable" burden on them. We are fully mindful that policy considerations and the balancing of the conflicting interests are the truly vital factors in the molding and application of the common law principles of negligence and proximate causation. But we are convinced that recognition of the plaintiff's claim will afford a fairer measure of justice to innocent third parties whose injuries are brought about by the unlawful and negligent sale of alcoholic beverages to minors and intoxicated persons, will strengthen and give greater force to the enlightened statutory and regulatory precautions against such sales and their frightening consequences, and will not place any unjustifiable burdens upon defendants who can always discharge their civil responsibilities by the exercise of due care. It must be borne in mind that the plaintiff's complaint has no relation to service by persons not engaged in the liquor business or to lawful sales and service by liquor licensees, or to sales by reasonably prudent licensees who do not know or have reason to believe that the patron is a minor or is intoxicated when served; the allegations of the complaint are expressly confined to tavern keepers' sales and service which are unlawful and negligent. Liquor licensees, who operate their businesses by way of privilege rather than as of right, have long been under strict obligation not to serve minors and intoxicated persons and if, as is likely, the result we have reached in the conscientious exercise of our traditional judicial function substantially increases their diligence in honoring that obligation then the public interest will indeed be very well served.

The judgment entered in the Law Division is reversed and the [case] is remanded for trial.

Part V

The Hotel and Its Employees

Chapter 19 Outline

Coverage of Federal and State Laws
Minimum Wage Rates Under Federal Law
Tip Credits
FICA and FUTA Taxes
Meals and Lodging
Uniform Maintenance
Student Employees
Important Points for Management
References
Review Questions
Internet Sites
Illustrative Case

Competencies

1. Cite those "enterprises" to which the federal wage and hour law applies. (p. 245)

2. Explain what is covered by the Fair Labor Standards Act (FLSA). (pp. 245–246)

3. Describe tip credits allowed by the FLSA. (p. 246)

4. Describe how tips are treated under FICA and FUTA taxes. (pp. 246–248)

5. Describe the U.S. Department of Labor's requirements with regard to meal credit. (pp. 248–249)

6. Describe federal regulations on the cost of maintenance of required uniforms. (p. 249)

7. Describe restrictions under federal law on the employment of students at subminimum wage rates. (pp. 249–250)

19

Wage and Hour Laws Applicable to Hotel Employees

Coverage of Federal and State Laws

The federal wage and hour law currently applies to "enterprises" consisting of one or more establishments under common control with an aggregate gross volume of sales made or business done totaling $500,000 a year. Thus, a single hotel or motel enterprise that is the employer's sole business is covered if it grosses $500,000 or more a year.* Moreover, a single hotel or motel establishment that is a component of a chain "enterprise" of hotel or motel establishments that grosses $500,000 or more a year is covered by the federal wage and hour law regardless of the component's own gross annual sales volume.

Hotels and motels which are subject to the federal wage and hour law may also be subject to state wage and hour laws. Section 18 of the federal wage and hour law provides that state laws may establish wage and hour standards that are more beneficial to the employee than the equivalent federal standards. *In this event, the employer must apply those standards, federal or state, that are the most beneficial to the employee.*

In addition, hotels or motels whose dollar amount of business is less than the amount required to bring them within the coverage of the federal wage and hour law may be subject to any state laws covering the hotel industry.

Minimum Wage Rates Under Federal Law

The Fair Labor Standards Act (FLSA) provides that, as of March 2001, a federal minimum wage rate covering most hotel and motel employees us $5.15 per hour. That rate changes whenever the U.S. Congress enacts a new federal minimum

---

* The Fair Labor Standards Act amendments also prohibit the reduction of the minimum wage applicable to employees of hotel or motel "enterprises" which become "uncovered" due to the higher dollar volume test in subsequent years. Consequently, a hotel or motel will be required to continue to pay to its employees the federal minimum wage rate *in effect on the date that such "enterprise" becomes "uncovered."*

wage. As stated above, hotels or motels *not* covered by the federal laws may nevertheless be subject to state minimum wage rates. In addition, hotels or motels which are covered by the federal law may nevertheless be subject to state rates that are more beneficial to the employee.

Federal law requires that all hotel and motel employees of covered enterprises be paid at the rate of one and one-half times their regular hourly rate for all hours worked in excess of 40 hours per week.

Hotels and motels should also be aware of any applicable state law standards with respect to overtime pay. (For an interesting case on who is an employee and thus entitled to minimum wage, see *Weisel* v. *Singapore Joint Venture, Inc.*, at the end of this chapter.)

Tip Credits

Tips are relevant to federal and state minimum wage laws. An employer may, under certain circumstances, use a *tip credit* applied to the cash wage which must be paid to a *tipped employee* to meet the minimum wage standards.

The FLSA allows an employer to take a tip credit of a percentage of the minimum wage. The FLSA allows a credit toward the hourly minimum wage rate resulting in a lower cash wage per hour for straight time hours. The credit is equal to the amount of tips actually received; however, the law provides that tips cannot be used to reduce the cash amount paid by the employer to less than $2.13 per hour. A tipped employee is defined by the FLSA as an employee who customarily and regularly receives more than $30 per month in tips.[*]

For purposes of the FLSA, the U.S. Department of Labor defined a tip in its regulations:

> A tip is a sum presented by a customer as a gift or gratuity in recognition of some service performed for him. It is to be distinguished from payment of a charge, if any, made for the service. Whether a tip is to be given, and its amount are matters determined solely by the customer, and generally he has the right to determine who shall be the recipient of the gratuity.[1]

Only gratuitous tips may be applied toward the tip credit. The Wage and Hour Division of the Department of Labor has ruled that "service charges" are not tips, and therefore cannot be considered for tip credit purposes.

FICA and FUTA Taxes

The Internal Revenue Service requires that an employee who receives $20 or more per month in tips must report the total amount of tips he/she receives to the employer (see Exhibit 19.1 for a copy of IRS Form 4070, Employee's Report of Tips to Employer). The amount of tips reported is considered wages for purposes of income tax withholding, FICA taxes, and Federal Unemployment Tax Act (FUTA) taxes.

---

[*] Note that federal tax laws require each service employee to report to his/her employer tips amounting to $20 a month or more. See Chapter 25.

Exhibit 19.1   IRS Form 4070

Form **4070** (Rev. June 1999) Department of the Treasury Internal Revenue Service	**Employee's Report** **of Tips to Employer** ▶ For Paperwork Reduction Act Notice, see back of form.	OMB No. 1545-0065
Employee's name and address		**Social security number**
Employer's name and address (include establishment name, if different)		**1** Cash tips received
		2 Credit card tips received
		3 Tips paid out
Month or shorter period in which tips were received from to		**4** Net tips (lines 1 + 2 - 3)
Signature		Date

Instructions

You must keep sufficient proof to show the amount of your tip income for the year. A daily record of your tip income is considered sufficient proof. Keep a daily record for each workday showing the amount of cash and credit card tips received directly from customers or other employees. Also keep a record of the amount of tips, if any, you paid to other employees through tip sharing, tip pooling or other arrangements, and the names of employees to whom you paid tips. Show the date that each entry is made. This date should be on or near the date you received the tip income. You may use **Form 4070A**, Employee's Daily Record of Tips, or any other daily record to record your tips.

Reporting Tips to Your Employer. If you receive tips that total $20 or more for any month while working for one employer, you must report the tips to your employer. Tips include cash left by customers, tips customers add to credit card charges, and tips you receive from other employees. You must report your tips for any one month by the 10th of the month after the month you receive the tips. If the 10th day falls on a Saturday, Sunday, or legal holiday, you may give the report to your employer on the next business day that is not a Saturday, Sunday, or legal holiday.

You must report tips that total $20 or more every month regardless of your total wages and tips for the year. You may use **Form 4070**, Employee's Report of Tips to Employer, to report your tips to your employer. See the instructions on the back of Form 4070.

You must include all tips, including tips not reported to your employer, as wages on your income tax return. You may use the last page of this publication to total your tips for the year.

Your employer must withhold income, social security, and Medicare (or railroad retirement) taxes on tips you report. Your employer usually deducts the withholding due on tips from your regular wages.

(continued on inside of back cover)

Purpose. Use this form to report tips you receive to your employer. This includes cash tips, tips you receive from other employees, and credit card tips. You must report tips every month regardless of your total wages and tips for the year. However, you do not have to report tips to your employer for any month you received less than $20 in tips while working for that employer.

Report tips by the 10th day of the month following the month that you receive them. If the 10th day is a Saturday, Sunday, or legal holiday, report tips by the next day that is not a Saturday, Sunday, or legal holiday.

See **Pub. 531,** Reporting Tip Income, for more details.

You can get additional copies of **Pub. 1244,** Employee's Daily Record of Tips and Report to Employer, which contains both Forms 4070A and 4070, by calling 1-800-TAX-FORM (1-800-829-3676).

Paperwork Reduction Act Notice. We ask for the information on these forms to carry out the Internal Revenue laws of the United States. You are required to give us the information. We need it to ensure that you are complying with these laws and to allow us to figure and collect the right amount of tax.

You are not required to provide the information requested on a form that is subject to the Paperwork Reduction Act unless the form displays a valid OMB control number. Books or records relating to a form or its instructions must be retained as long as their contents may become material in the administration of any Internal Revenue law. Generally, tax returns and return information are confidential, as required by Code section 6103.

The time needed to complete Forms 4070 and 4070A will vary depending on individual circumstances. The estimated average times are: **Recordkeeping**—Form 4070, 7 min.; Form 4070A, 3 hr. and 23 min.; **Learning about the law**—each form, 2 min.; **Preparing** Form 4070, 13 min.; Form 4070A, 55 min.; and **Copying and providing** Form 4070, 10 min.; Form 4070A, 28 min.

If you have comments concerning the accuracy of these time estimates or suggestions for making these forms simpler, we would be happy to hear from you. You can write to the Tax Forms Committee, Western Area Distribution Center, Rancho Cordova, CA 95743-0001.

Employers must pay the Social Security Tax (FICA) with respect to (1) all tip income which the employee declares to the employer for income tax purposes and (2) on actual wages paid to the employee.

Employers must also deduct and withhold from their employee's wages the FICA taxes payable by the *employee* on his/her wages *and* the total tips he/she reports to the employer for income tax purposes.

All tips reported to the employer are subject to both the employer *and* employee portions of FICA.

Employers, in addition to withholding income tax due and collecting FICA taxes, must pay FUTA taxes on any tips reported by an employee.

Tips to employees are wages that are taxable for FUTA purposes. All tips reported in writing to the employer are taken into account in determining the employee's compensation under the minimum wage laws.

Hotels and motels should also consult applicable state regulations with respect to credits toward state minimum wage compliance for tips that employees receive.

Meals and Lodging

Federal law provides, in general, that the employer may use the reasonable cost of furnishing an employee with meals and lodging as a credit when determining compliance with the requirements of the federal law only.

The U.S. Department of Labor has issued regulations[2] on meal credits listing requirements for employee meals for purposes of the meal credit which include the following:

1. The employee must voluntarily accept the meal in lieu of cash.

2. The employer must inform the employee of the amount of the meal credit to be taken, and the employee must accept the amount prior to accepting the meal in lieu of cash.

3. The acceptance of meals instead of cash cannot be a mandatory condition of employment. That is, the employer cannot require employees to "voluntarily" accept meals in lieu of cash as a condition of their initial or continued employment.

4. Where the employer meets the voluntary condition, he/she must still maintain records to show:

   a. actual meals consumed,

   b. who ate the meals, and

   c. the actual cost of the meals to the employer.

As these regulations show, the Department of Labor has been taking the position that no meal credit would be allowed unless employees "voluntarily accepted" the meals in lieu of cash, that is, they were given the option of choosing between receiving either money or meals. For practical purposes, the regulations eliminated the meal credit.

The U.S. Court of Appeals (11th Circuit) does not agree with the U.S. Department of Labor regulations on meal credits. In *Davis Brothers, Inc.* v. *Raymond J. Donovan, Secretary of Labor, et al.,*[3] the court held that there was not room in the statutory language for such a "voluntary acceptance" requirement. The court ruled that an employer can take a meal credit against the minimum wage as long as the meals are "customarily furnished" to the employees. "Customarily furnished," the decision says, means "regularly provided."

This case could have an impact in the 11th Circuit at least (Georgia, Florida, and Alabama) for those food service or lodging employers who customarily provide free meals to employees, and wish to take a "meal credit."

As above, hotels and motels should consult state regulations with respect to analogous credits toward compliance with state minimum wage rates.

Uniform Maintenance

Under federal law, an allowance for maintenance of required uniforms can *not* be used as a credit toward the federal minimum wage. According to federal law, when the employer requires but does not maintain the employee's uniform, the employer shall pay the employee an amount in addition to minimum wage equal to the actual cost of maintaining the uniform (if the employer arranges with a laundry or rental service that charges the employee) or an amount per week equal to one hour at the applicable minimum hourly wage rate. If the uniform is wash and wear, no uniform maintenance need be paid.

Under applicable state laws, an allowance for maintenance of required uniforms may or may not be used as a credit toward the state minimum wage. Since each state has different requirements, hotels and motels should check individual state law requirements with respect to allowances for uniform maintenance.

Student Employees

The FLSA provides that the Secretary of Labor shall certify for employment, at a wage rate of not less than 85% of the minimum wage rate, up to six full-time student employees whom a retail establishment (including hotels and motels) may employ, but only if such employment does not reduce employment opportunities for persons other than full-time students.

Some restrictions under federal law on the employment of students at subminimum wage rates are:

1. The employee must be a full-time student.

2. Such full-time students may be employed for not more than 8 hours a day and 20 hours a week when school is in session (including summer schools).

3. When school is out of session (that is, holidays and vacation days), the maximum number of hours that full-time students may work during the week is increased by 8 hours for each holiday, but shall not exceed a total of 40 hours during the work week.

4. Full-time students under 16 years of age may be employed only during hours outside of their scheduled hours of instruction.

5. No full-time students may be hired under any full-time student certificate while "abnormal labor conditions," such as a strike or lockout, exist at the hotel, motel, or restaurant.

6. Employers must comply with any more stringent applicable state or federal laws, including child labor laws, with respect to the employment of student or child labor.*

Any employer who wishes to pursue such authorization for student employees should obtain and complete Form WH-202, the "Application for Authority to Employ Not More Than Six Full-Time Students at Subminimum Wages on any Workday in a Retail or Service Establishment or in Agriculture." This form and its instructions (Form WH-200) may be obtained from the district office of the U.S. Department of Labor, Wage and Hour Division.

Important Points for Management

The Fair Labor Standards Act (FLSA) is a federal law passed in 1938 and subsequently amended many times, particularly with regard to the minimum wage.

If a hotel or business produces $500,000 or more in sales for the year, it is covered under the federal law. Some states have similar laws. The employer must follow those laws, federal or state, that are the most beneficial to the employee.

To meet the minimum wage, tips can be credited against the minimum wage as long as at least $2.13 per hour is paid as cash wages. A "tipped" employee is one who earns customarily and regularly more than $30 per month in tips. Service charges imposed by the operator are not considered tips.

An employer must pay "time and a half" for all time worked over 40 hours a week.

The employer can use the cost of a meal as a credit to minimum wage if the employee voluntarily accepts it.

References

1. 29 C.F.R. § 531.52.
2. 29 C.F.R. § 531.30.
3. 700 F. 2d 1368 (11th Cir. 1983), *reh'g denied*, 708 F. 2d 734 (1983).

---

* There are also special child labor provisions of the FLSA and state laws which should be carefully reviewed. Note that the child labor laws under the FLSA do not apply to children who work in businesses solely owned by their parents (except in manufacturing or occupations determined to be "hazardous" by the U.S. Secretary of Labor).

Review Questions

1. If the state minimum wage rate is more beneficial to the employee than the federal minimum wage rate, which wage rate must an employer apply?

2. What is the purpose of the Fair Labor Standards Act (FLSA)?

3. What is a tip credit? What tip credit does the FLSA allow an employer to take?

4. How does the U.S. Department of Labor define a tip?

5. How does the FLSA define a tipped employee? Are tips counted toward the employer's obligation to pay the minimum wage? If so, when?

6. What are FICA taxes? Who pays them?

7. What requirements are provided in the U.S. Department of Labor's regulations regarding meal credits for employees?

8. What are the maintenance requirements for uniforms under applicable federal laws? your state laws?

9. What restrictions on student employment at subminimum wage rates are included under federal law?

10. When employers are faced with applicable state and federal laws regarding child labor, which law should they comply with?

11. When is a retail establishment allowed to employ full-time students? How many such full-time students may a retail establishment employ?

Internet Sites

For more information, visit the following Internet sites. Remember that Internet addresses can change without notice.

Minimum Wage Laws in the States
http://www.dol.gov/dol/esa/public/minwage/america.html

U.S. DOL Employment Standards Administration
http://www.dol.gov/dol/esa

Illustrative Case

Weisel v. *Singapore Joint Venture, Inc.*

602 F. 2d 1185 *(5th Cir. 1979)

JOHN R. BROWN, Chief Judge:

While the case before us will have little or no effect on the course of Anglo-American jurisprudence, the outcome is of vital importance to Gary E. Weisel, the plaintiff-appellant. From April 1, 1974, to December 31, 1975, Weisel worked as a parking valet at the Singapore Hotel/Motel (the Singapore Hotel),[1] owned and operated by the defendant, Singapore Joint Venture, Inc. (Singapore J.V.). Throughout his period of employment at the hotel, Weisel's compensation consisted entirely of gratuities from hotel guests and others using the parking facilities. All was quiet on the Singapore Hotel front until one day—several months after quitting his job—Weisel learned about something called "minimum wage." Weisel decided to explore the possibility of filing a lawsuit and thereafter brought this suit. Sitting without a jury, the Trial Court ruled that minimum wage laws did not apply because Weisel was not an "employee" of the hotel for purposes of the Fair Labor Standards Act, 29 U.S.C.A. Section 201 *et seq.* (FLSA). The Trial Court reasoned that Weisel's service was a mere "luxury" and that his day-to-day orders came from individuals outside the hotel.

We hold that the Trial Court incorrectly concluded that Weisel was not an employee of the hotel for purposes of the FLSA. We therefore reverse and remand for a determination of the proper relief.

I

Most of the essential facts of this case are not in dispute. Defendant admits that the Singapore Hotel is subject to the minimum wage provisions of the FLSA[2] and must therefore pay the statutory minimum wage to all employees. It is also undisputed that if Weisel was indeed an employee of the Singapore Hotel, he is entitled to unpaid minimum wages totaling $4,657.60.

The following facts are also undisputed. Gary Weisel was hired by Ben Pascal and his partner Al Valone to serve as a parking valet. Pascal and the Singapore Hotel had an unwritten agreement whereby Pascal would park cars, keep the front of the hotel clean, rent cars to hotel guests, and assist guests in carrying their luggage into the hotel. In consideration for these services, Pascal was entitled to tips of up to fifty cents per car for valet parking and to 50% of the rental car fees. He was also given permission to rent several hotel parking spaces to hotel employees and others and to keep all of the money he collected.[3] The fifty cent maximum gratuity on tips for parking was fixed by Meyer Wassell, President and Chairman of the Board of Singapore J.V.[4]

In addition to parking cars, Weisel was required to help unload luggage from cars arriving at the hotel and to sweep the floor at the hotel's entrance.[5]

---

[1] The Singapore Hotel is a resort hotel located in Bal Harbour, Florida. It can accommodate up to 600 guests.

[2] During the time period involved here (April 1, 1974-December 31, 1975), the Singapore Hotel was an enterprise engaged in commerce with an annual gross business (exclusive of taxes) of not less than $250,000. See 29 U.S.C.A. §§ 203(s) and 206.

[3] The only limitation was that enough spaces be left for hotel guests.

[4] The parking valet was required to give a slip of paper to guests of the hotel informing them of the fifty cent limit on gratuities. Guests of the hotel could park their cars themselves if they desired. Others had to use the valet's services.

[5] Weisel testified that he also drove Mr. Wassell home on occasion and sometimes brought drinks to the hotel cardroom. Meyer Wassell testified that he had no knowledge of Weisel carrying drinks to the cardroom and that Weisel was not even allowed in the cardroom because he was under 18 years of age.

During working hours, Weisel was required by the defendant, Singapore J.V., to wear a uniform designating the name "Singapore Hotel." The uniform was supplied by the hotel at no expense to Weisel.

Concerning Weisel's supervision, Meyer Wassell admitted at trial that if he gave an instruction concerning the parking valet to either Al Ronin, the hotel's general supervising manager, or to Pascal, he expected these instructions to be carried out. Wassell also testified that he had the power to hire and fire Pascal and that he did in fact fire him.[6]

While working at the Singapore Hotel, Weisel was issued an identification card by the Bal Harbour Police Department. The $2.00 fee for obtaining the card was paid by the Singapore Hotel. Moreover, the card indicated that Weisel was employed by the Singapore Hotel.[7]

Weisel received a couple of small benefits from the hotel. First, he received two Christmas bonuses. Second, he got his meals at the hotel restaurant at an employees' discount.[8]

On one occasion, while parking a car, Weisel accidently struck and killed a guest of the hotel. Although the hotel's insurance policy explicitly excluded independent contractors from coverage, the insurance company nonetheless paid out over $100,000 for settlement of a claim filed as a result of the accident. In a deposition taken during the course of the law suit brought by the deceased's estate, Meyer Wassell stated that Weisel was an employee of the hotel. Mr. Wassell also admitted that he, Wassell, had the power to fire anyone hired by Pascal and could veto the hiring of any individual selected by Pascal. Moreover, Mr. Wassell claimed that he told Mr. Pascal "how to run the operation."

One of the few truly disputed facts concerned who gave Weisel his day-to-day orders. Weisel testified at trial that he received advice and commands from hotel manager Ronin. Meyer Wassell, during the course of his testimony, implied that Weisel's day-to-day orders came from Pascal, although Wassell provided no concrete evidence of this. Moreover, Wassell admitted that *he* gave Pascal the orders which Pascal apparently gave to Weisel.[9]

After hearing all of the testimony presented, the Trial Court entered its findings of fact and conclusions of law. The Court found that Gary Weisel was not an employee of the Singapore Hotel.

---

[6] Weisel testified that after Pascal was fired, he, Weisel, stayed on as a parking valet for a few days and left *voluntarily* when he found a new job.

[7] According to Weisel, Al Ronin instructed him to list the Singapore Hotel as his employer when applying for the card.

[8] Although the defendant refused to stipulate that Weisel got such a discount, no evidence was presented to the contrary.

[9] For example, Wassell testified as follows:

> Q: [Plaintiff's lawyer]: Do you have any personal knowledge as to whether Gary E. Weisel ever engaged or aided in helping the loading and unloading of luggage of certain cars that would pull up to the hotel?
> A: Yes, sir, I do.
> Q: And at whose instructions or requests were those?
> A: I don't know. But probably by his boss, the concessionaire, Mr. Pascal.
> Q: And who would have given these instructions to Pascal?
> A: I would have.

II

In 1938, Congress enacted the FLSA to eliminate the low wages and long working hours then plaguing the American labor market. An important part of the solution was the guarantee of a minimum wage to every "employee" engaged in interstate commerce or working for an enterprise engaged in interstate commerce. 29 U.S.C.A. Section 206. Since the FLSA is limited to employees, an employer can avoid the minimum wage requirement by establishing that a particular person is an independent contractor rather than an employee.

The FLSA explains what is meant by the term "employee," but the "definition" provides little help. An employee is one "employed by an employer." 29 U.S.C.A. Section 203(e)(1). "Employer" is not defined except for the cryptic remark that the term "includes any person acting directly or indirectly in the interest of an employer in relation to an employee." 29 U.S.C.A. Section 203(d). "Employ" is defined as including "to suffer or permit to work." 29 U.S.C.A. Section 203(g).

The Supreme Court has attempted to provide guidance to lower courts in distinguishing between employees and independent contractors (and given the definition discussed above, courts need all the guidance they can get). In its 1947 "trilogy," the Court explained that such terms as "independent contractor" and "employee" are to be given flexible definitions and should not be limited to their common law meanings. [citations omitted]

In *Silk,* the Supreme Court provided a number of guidelines to differentiate between an employee and an independent contractor, including the degree of control the business has over the worker and the worker's opportunities for profit or loss.[10] The Court emphasized, however, that "no one [factor] is controlling nor is the list complete." 331 U.S. at 716, 67 S. Ct. at 1469, 91 L. Ed. at 1769.

It is often possible for both sides to point to the presence or absence of particular *Silk* factors. Yet such an attempt to apply mechanically the components of *Silk* represents a distortion of that case. *Silk* clearly emphasized that the ultimate issue is whether as a matter of "economic reality" the particular worker is an employee.... [citations omitted]

In *Mednick* v. *Albert Enterprises, Inc.,* 5 Cir., 1975, 508 F. 2d 297, this Court attempted to apply the precise guidelines of *Silk* in determining whether one whose job was to oversee the operation of cardrooms at an apartment house-hotel was an employee or an independent contractor. The Court observed that these guidelines, when "considered in isolation...produce no clear cut conclusion." *Id.* at 300. Yet the Court noted that the mechanical approach taken by both sides gave "too little weight" to matters of economic reality. Based on economic realities, the Court found that the worker qualified as an employee.

As in *Mednick,* we think that a rigid application of the *Silk* guidelines would be a futile exercise. Instead of quibbling over the presence or absence of particular *Silk* factors, we proceed to an analysis of the economic realities. The touchstone of "economic reality" in analyzing a possible employee/employer relationship for

---

[10] Specifically, the Court observed:

> [The] degrees of control, opportunities for profit or loss, investment and facilities, permanency of the relation and skill required in the claimed independent operation are important for decision.

331 U.S. at 716, 67 S. Ct. at 1469, 91 L. Ed. at 1769.

purposes of the FLSA is dependency. As we stated in *Usery* v. *Pilgrim Equipment Company, Inc.*, 5 Cir., 1976, 527 F. 2d 1308, 1311, *cert. denied*, 1976, 429 U.S. 826, 97 S. Ct. 82, 50 L. Ed. 2d. 89, the "final and determinative question" is whether the "personnel are so dependent upon the business with which they are connected that they come within the protection of FLSA or are sufficiently independent to lie outside its ambit."

We think that the Trial Court ignored economic realities in holding that Weisel was not an employee.[11] The Trial Court gave two separate reasons for its holding. Neither one can withstand analysis.

First, the Trial Court concluded that Pascal, not the hotel, gave Weisel his day-to-day commands.[12] However, even assuming that Pascal did give some or all daily directives, ultimate control was clearly in the hands of the hotel. Wassell, the defendant's President, admitted in a deposition concerning Weisel's tragic accident that he, Wassell, had the power to fire anyone hired by Pascal and would veto Pascal's hiring decisions.[13] Moreover, Wassell testified at the trial in the instant case that when he gave an order concerning the parking valet, he expected that order to be carried out. Finally, Weisel's compensation was limited to the maximum gratuity of fifty cents for each car parked, and this limitation on gratuities was set not by Pascal but by the hotel. Thus even Weisel's salary was to a large extent controlled by the hotel.

Second, the Trial Court characterized Weisel's work as a "luxury" and of interest to few of the guests of the hotel.[14] This finding ignores the fact that Weisel not only parked cars, but also unloaded luggage for guests and kept the hotel entrance clean. At a minimum, all—including peripatetic judges—would hope that a clean hotel is not a mere "luxury." In any event, given that Weisel's valet

---

[11] In reviewing the Trial Court's ultimate finding that Weisel was not an employee, we are not constrained by the "clearly erroneous" test. Rather, that finding is treated as a legal determination. See *Shultz* v. *Hinojosa*, 5 Cir., 1970, 432 F. 2d 259, 264. However, the individual findings of fact leading to that conclusion are examined under the "clearly erroneous" test. See *Mitchell* v. *Strickland Transportation Co.*, 5 Cir., 1955, 228 F. 2d 124, 126.

[12] As the Trial Court stated:

> The plaintiff worked for and took orders from one Mr. Pascal and his partner, Al Valone, with the understanding that gratuities or tips would be the plaintiff's only source of compensation. The infrequent directives of Mr. Wassell and the defendant's agents were insufficient to alter to fact [sic] that Pascal and Valone exercised primary and continuous control over the plaintiff. It was to Pascal that Mr. Wassell complained when the latter was dissatisfied with the performance of the parking attendants under the control of the former.

[13] In addition, as indicated in note 6, *supra*, when Wassell fired Pascal, Weisel did not feel compelled to leave also. Weisel left voluntarily a few days after Pascal because he found a better job.

[14] As the Trial Court observed:

> The notice and extent of the plaintiff's work was not an independent step in the essential operation of the defendant's motel; rather, it amounted to a convenient service performed tangentially to the defendant's principal endeavor. Namely, valet parking was but a luxury requested by only a portion of defendant's guests and their visitors, and by persons who have had no interest in or connection with the defendant motel.

services were used by at least some guests, the fact that these services were a "luxury" is irrelevant.[15]

Thus, we are persuaded by neither of the Trial Court's reasons for denying Weisel employee status. We think the Trial Court ignored the many facts indicative of an employer/employee relationship between the hotel and Weisel. For example, Weisel wore a uniform with the hotel's name on it supplied by the hotel. He was covered by the hotel's employee insurance in a tragic accident. His identification card (issued by the police department), procured at the direction and expense of the hotel, prescribed that he was an employee of the hotel. He received Christmas bonuses from the hotel. Finally, he ate meals at the hotel at the employees' discount.

In sum, the "economic reality" of Weisel's relationship with the hotel could hardly be clearer. The evidence demonstrates overwhelmingly that Weisel was an employee of the hotel.[16] And the Trial Court's finding is clearly erroneous since it is contrary to the right and justice of the case.[17] We therefore remand the case to the Trial Court for a determination of the appropriate relief.[18]

REVERSED and REMANDED

---

[15] In *Mednick,* the Court recognized that the worker's function "was not an integral part of the business." 508 F. 2d at 300. Nonetheless, the Court found the worker to be an employee, pointing out that his function was "very useful or even necessary in the market in which [the apartment house-hotel] competed." *Id.** at 301. Weisel's valet services clearly fit within the standard set forth in *Mednick.*

[16] Our holding in no way depends on whether Pascal was an independent contractor or was himself an employer, since we believe that, on the facts of this case, Weisel was in reality an employee of the hotel.

[17] See, e.g., *Bishop* v. *United States,* 5 Cir., 1959, 266 F. 2d 657, 666, quoting *Sanders* v. *Leech,* 5 Cir., 1946 158 F. 2d 486, 487. ("It is our positive duty to reverse findings as clearly erroneous…when [the decision below] does not reflect or represent the truth and right of the case"). Cf. *United States* v. *Morrison,* 5 Cir., 1957, 247 F. 2d 285, 288 (equitable lien arises "because equity in good conscience requires it to accomplish right and justice").

[18] Weisel is, of course, entitled to the $4,657.60 of unpaid minimum wages. In addition, Weisel seeks liquidated damages (equal to the amount of the unpaid minimum wages) and attorneys' fees. While under 29 U.S.C.A. Section 216 (b), the awarding of liquidated damages and attorneys' fees appears mandatory, 29 U.S.C.A. Section 260 makes clear that with respect to liquidated damages, a defendant can escape paying such damages by demonstrating that the failure to pay minimum wage was in good faith, i.e., defendant did not believe it was violating the FLSA. See, e.g., *Hays* v. *Republic Steel Corp.,* 5 Cir., 1976, 531 F. 2d 1307 (29 U.S.C.A. Section 260, although part of the Portal-to-Portal Act, served to amend the FLSA); *Nitterright* v. *Claytor, Jr.,* D.D.C. 1978, 454 F. Supp. 130 (29 U.S.C.A. Section 260 limits 29 U.S.C.A. Section 216 (b)). Reasonable attorneys' fees are mandatory, however. 454 F. Supp. at 141.

On remand, therefore, the Trial Court should determine whether liquidated damages are appropriate, and if so, how much. It should also award attorneys' fees in an amount deemed reasonable, including those for this appeal.

Chapter 20 Outline

Competencies

1. Identify which employers are subject to the Family and Medical Leave Act (FMLA), and which employees are eligible for leave and related benefits under the Act. (pp. 259–260)

2. Describe important rules regarding employee leaves under the FMLA. (p. 260)

3. Explain prohibitions for employers, how "serious health condition" is defined, and what a husband and wife who both work for the same employer are entitled to request under the FMLA. (pp. 261–262)

4. Summarize employee responsibilities under the FMLA. (p. 262)

5. Identify two provisions regarding the transfer of employees receiving FMLA leave to alternative positions, and describe the FMLA's position on altering or terminating the employment of employees on FMLA leave. (pp. 262–263)

6. Explain the employer penalties for non-compliance with the FMLA. (p. 263)

7. Describe the FMLA's effect on state laws and union collective bargaining agreements. (p. 263)

8. Summarize FMLA and Department of Labor regulations regarding notification of employees about the FMLA. (p. 264)

20

The Family and Medical Leave Act

THE FAMILY AND MEDICAL LEAVE ACT OF 1993[1] (the FMLA) became effective on August 5, 1993. This Act provides for a period of mandated unpaid employee leave of up to 12 weeks per year for the birth, adoption, or serious illness of a child, or serious illness of a parent or a spouse, with a return to the same or equivalent job. The Act also provides an exception for highly paid, "key" employees.

This chapter summarizes the major provisions of this Act.

Under the FMLA, employers with 50 or more employees are required to allow eligible employees to take unpaid leaves of absence of up to 12 weeks every 12 months in order to care for a newborn or newly placed adopted or foster child or because of a serious health condition of the employee or an immediate **family member.**

During a leave, the employer must maintain an employee's group medical coverage. Following this leave, the employee is entitled to be returned to his or her old job or an equivalent one, without any loss of accrued benefits. Employers cannot retaliate against or interfere with employees who exercise their rights under the FMLA or who participate in FMLA enforcement proceedings. Employees who believe their rights under the FMLA are violated are entitled to sue in state or federal court or to make administrative complaints to the U.S. Department of Labor.

Covered Employers and Eligible Employees

Any employer who employs 50 or more employees for each working day during each of 20 or more calendar workweeks in the current or preceding calendar year is subject to FMLA.

With two important exceptions, an employee is eligible for leave and related benefits if he or she has been employed for at least 12 months by a covered employer and has at least 1,250 hours of service with that employer during the previous 12-month period. The first exception is that salaried employees among the highest-paid 10% of an employer's staff may not be entitled to the full benefit of the FMLA under some circumstances. The second exception is that employees are not eligible if the employer has fewer than 50 employees within 75 miles of the work site.

The authors wish to acknowledge the contribution of Terri L. Ross, Esq., in preparing this chapter.

Leaves of Absence for Eligible Employees

An eligible employee is entitled to a total of 12 workweeks of leave during any 12-month period under the following circumstances:

- **Family leave:** The birth, adoption, or foster-care placement of a child in order to care for that child

- **Medical leave:** To care for a spouse, child, or parent with a "serious health condition," or because of a "serious health condition" that makes an employee unable to perform the function of his or her position

Leaves are not granted under the FMLA to care for parents-in-law or siblings. Leave to care for adult children is allowed only if the child is incapable of self care because of a mental or physical disability.

Leave Schedules

Family leave may *not* be taken on an intermittent or reduced work schedule without employer consent. Medical leave may be taken on an intermittent or reduced work schedule if medically necessary. A reduced-leave work schedule can be either fewer hours per week or fewer hours per day than an employee's usual schedule.

The Relationship of FMLA Leaves to Other Forms of Paid or Unpaid Leave

FMLA leaves may be unpaid. In addition, an employer may require—or an employee may elect—to substitute any accrued vacation leave, personal leave, or family leave for the unpaid leave, except the FMLA does not authorize the use of paid family leave for medical leave taken because the employee has a serious health condition.

The employer may also require—or the employee may elect—to substitute accrued paid medical or sick leave for unpaid medical leave.

Health Benefits During the Leave

During any leave under FMLA, the employer must maintain an employee's coverage under the company's group health plan at the existing level and under existing conditions.

The FMLA provides that the employer may recover health insurance premiums paid for coverage during leave if the employee fails to return and the failure is due to reasons other than a serious health condition or circumstances beyond the employee's control.

The FMLA does not expressly mandate continuing group benefits other than medical insurance during FMLA leaves. (However, the practical difficulties of interrupting life insurance, disability, or other similar coverages induce many employers simply to continue them.)

Additional Protection for Employees

Any employee who takes an FMLA leave is entitled, upon return from such leave:

- To be restored to the position held when the leave commenced, or
- To be restored to an equivalent position with equivalent benefits, pay, and other terms and conditions of employment

In addition, the leave must not result in the loss of any employment benefits accrued prior to the start of the leave. However, the FMLA does not require employers to provide returning employees with the accrual of any seniority or employment benefits during their leave, or any right, benefit, or position of employment other than those to which employees would have been entitled had they not taken the leave. Thus, under the FMLA, no accrual of employee pension benefits is required during an employee's leave. However, the employer's pension plan or state law may have such a requirement.

Exception for Highly Compensated Employees

An employer may deny restoration of employment to any salaried eligible employee who is among the highest-paid 10% of the employees within 75 miles of the work site. Such denial is permissible only if it is necessary to prevent grievous economic injury to an employer's operations. However, the employer must notify the employee of his or her intention not to reinstate the employee, and the employee must elect not to return.

This exception applies to restoration rights only; these employees still have the right to take FMLA leaves of absence and receive medical benefits at the employer's normal expense during their leaves.

Prohibitions for Employers

No employer may interfere with, restrain, or deny the exercise of an employee's rights under the FMLA. Further, it is unlawful for an employer to discharge or discriminate against any individual for opposing any practice made unlawful by the FMLA.

"Serious Health Condition" Defined

A **serious health condition** means any illness, injury, impairment, or physical or mental condition that involves either (a) in-patient care in a hospital, hospice, or residential medical care facility; or (b) continuing treatment by a health-care provider.

Serious health conditions are discussed at some length in federal FMLA regulations. Generally, any illness that disables someone for at least three days is likely to qualify. Prenatal care is also covered by the FMLA and is considered a "serious health condition."

Spouses Employed by the Same Employer

When a husband and wife are entitled to leave under the FMLA and are employed by the same employer, the number of weeks of leave to which both may be entitled may be limited to an aggregate of 12 workweeks during any 12-month period unless the leave is due to the "serious health condition" of one of the spouses or a child.

Employee Responsibilities

Whenever possible, the employee must generally provide the employer with no less than 30 days' notice for a requested leave. If the leave is not foreseeable, the employee is required to give as much notice as is practicable (defined as a maximum of two days). Where medical leave is based on foreseeable, planned medical treatment, the employee is required to make a reasonable effort to schedule the treatment so as not to "unduly" disrupt the employer's operations.

An employer may require that a request for medical leave be supported by certification issued by the health-care provider of the eligible employee or of the person the employee intends to care for. An employer may require a second opinion if there is reason to doubt the validity of the employee's certification. In the case of a conflict, the employer may require a third opinion. The employer pays the cost of second and third opinions. The third opinion is final.

The FMLA also specifically authorizes employers to require employees on leave to report periodically to the employer on their status and their intention to return to work.

The FMLA does not specify the penalty for an employee's failure to meet these requirements. For example, it is not clear whether failure to provide notice, certification, or status reports could be a basis for denying, reducing, or delaying a leave request or leave. The federal FMLA regulations place some limits on the use of these requirements by employers in some circumstances.

Employee Transfers to Alternative Positions

The FMLA contains two provisions regarding the transfer of employees receiving FMLA leave to alternative positions.

1. An employee on intermittent or reduced-schedule medical leave may be transferred temporarily to another position if:

    - The leave is based on foreseeable, planned medical treatment

    - The employee is qualified for the alternative position

    - The alternative position has equivalent pay and benefits

    - The alternative position better accommodates recurring periods of leave

2. An employee may be transferred to an alternative position at the conclusion of leave if the position has equivalent "benefits, pay, and other terms and conditions of employment."

If an employee's situation satisfies both tests, the employee can be transferred temporarily during his or her leave, and the transfer can be made permanent when the leave is concluded.

Change or Termination of Employment

The FMLA contains no provision expressly authorizing employers to alter or terminate the employment of employees on leave under the FMLA due to unrelated circumstances, such as business difficulties, reductions in force, or closings.

However, the FMLA does provide that restored employees are only entitled to those rights, benefits, or positions to which the employees would have been entitled if they had not taken leave. Thus, an employee on FMLA leave may be terminated if such an event had occurred without the FMLA leave. The FMLA also has a similar provision that requires maintenance of group medical benefits only at the level and under the conditions that employees would have received if they had not taken leave.

Employer Penalties for Non-Compliance

Any employer who violates the FMLA will be liable to any affected eligible employee for damages equal to the amount of the employee's lost wages, salary, benefits, or compensation. Where an employee has no lost wages (such as in leave denial), the employee can recover monetary losses sustained as a result of the violation, up to 12 weeks of salary or wages. Employees can recover interest and automatically receive liquidated damages equal to the sum of the damages and accrued interest, unless the employer can prove it acted in good faith on reasonable grounds. Employees may receive equitable relief including employment, reinstatement, or promotion.

Prevailing employees will be awarded attorneys' fees, expert witness fees, and other costs of the action. The FMLA does not provide for awards of attorneys' fees to prevailing defendants.

The FMLA's Effect on State Laws

The FMLA does not supersede any provision of any state or local law that provides greater family or medical leave rights. The FMLA does not diminish the obligation of an employer to comply with any collective bargaining agreement or employee benefit program or plan that provides greater family or medical leave rights to employees. Employers are not discouraged from adopting or retaining leave policies that are more generous.

Special Considerations for Unionized Employees

The FMLA provides that it does not supersede union collective bargaining agreement provisions that are more generous than the FMLA; however, no agreement provision may diminish the rights provided by the FMLA.

Regulations

The Secretary of Labor last issued regulations under the Act on March 30, 1995.[2] The FMLA and the Department of Labor regulations require action by covered employers. If employers maintain written guidance (such as employee manuals or handbooks) on employee benefits and leave, employees' FMLA rights must be added. Otherwise, employees must be given written guidance about all their FMLA rights whenever they request FMLA leave. All employees who request FMLA leave must also be given specific, written notice of the employer's requirements for such leave and the consequences of failing to meet them.

In addition, FMLA notices must be posted. A model notice is included in the regulations and copies are available from your local Department of Labor office. (See Exhibit 20.1.) Employers must also "responsively" answer any employee questions about the FMLA.

Important Points for Management

The FMLA provides for a period of mandated unpaid employee leave of up to 12 weeks per year for the birth, adoption, or serious illness of a child, or the serious illness of a parent or a spouse, with a return to the same or equivalent job.

The FMLA also provides an exception for highly paid, "key" employees.

An employer may require—or an employee may elect—to substitute any accrued vacation leave, personal leave, or family leave for the unpaid leave; however, the FMLA does not authorize the use of paid family leave for medical leave taken because the employee has a serious health condition.

During any leave under the FMLA, the employer must maintain an employee's coverage under the company's group health plan at the existing level and under existing conditions.

Any employee who takes an FMLA leave is entitled, upon return from such leave:

- To be restored to the position held when the leave commenced, or

- To be restored to an equivalent position with equivalent benefits, pay, and other terms and conditions of employment.

An employer may require that the request for a leave of absence be supported by a certification issued by the health care provider of the eligible employee or of the person the employee intends to care for. In some cases, an employer, provided the employer funds the cost, may require a second opinion and in the case of a conflict, a third opinion. The third opinion will be binding. An employer should promptly advise employees as to whether their absences will be governed by the FMLA.[3]

The Family and Medical Leave Act does not supersede any provision of any state or local law that provides greater family or medical leave rights. The Family and Medical Leave Act does not diminish the obligation of an employer to comply with any collective bargaining agreement or employee benefit program or plan that provides greater family or medical leave rights to employees.

Exhibit 20.1   FMLA Notice

Your Rights
Under The
Family and Medical Leave Act of 1993

FMLA requires covered employers to provide up to 12 weeks of unpaid, job-protected leave to "eligible" employees for certain family and medical reasons. Employees are eligible if they have worked for a covered employer for at least one year, and for 1,250 hours over the previous 12 months, and if there are at least 50 employees within 75 miles.

Reasons For Taking Leave:

Unpaid leave must be granted for *any* of the following reasons:

• to care for the employee's child after birth, or placement for adoption or foster care;

• to care for the employee's spouse, son or daughter, or parent, who has a serious health condition; or

• for a serious health condition that makes the employee unable to perform the employee's job.

At the employee's or employer's option, certain kinds of *paid* leave may be substituted for unpaid leave.

Advance Notice and Medical Certification:

The employee may be required to provide advance leave notice and medical certification. Taking of leave may be denied if requirements are not met.

• The employee ordinarily must provide 30 days advance notice when the leave is "foreseeable."

• An employer may require medical certification to support a request for leave because of a serious health condition, and may require second or third opinions (at the employer's expense) and a fitness for duty report to return to work.

Job Benefits and Protection:

• For the duration of FMLA leave, the employer must maintain the employee's health coverage under any "group health plan."

• Upon return from FMLA leave, most employees must be restored to their original or equivalent positions with equivalent pay, benefits, and other employment terms.

• The use of FMLA leave cannot result in the loss of any employment benefit that accrued prior to the start of an employee's leave.

Unlawful Acts By Employers:

FMLA makes it unlawful for any employer to:

• interfere with, restrain, or deny the exercise of any right provided under FMLA:

• discharge or discriminate against any person for opposing any practice made unlawful by FMLA or for involvement in any proceeding under or relating to FMLA.

Enforcement:

• The U.S. Department of Labor is authorized to investigate and resolve complaints of violations.

• An eligible employee may bring a civil action against an employer for violations.

FMLA does not affect any Federal or State law prohibiting discrimination, or supersede any State or local law or collective bargaining agreement which provides greater family or medical leave rights.

For Additional Information:

Contact the nearest office of the Wage and Hour Division, listed in most telephone directories under U.S. Government, Department of Labor.

U.S. Department of Labor
Employment Standards Administration
Wage and Hour Division
Washington, D.C. 20210

WH Publication 1420
June 1993

★ U.S. G.P.O. : 353-606

American Hotel & Motel Association Governmental Affairs • 1201 New York Ave., NW, Washington, DC 20005 • (202) 289-3120 •

American
Hotel & Motel
Association

References

1. Pub. L. No. 103-3, U.S.C. § 2601
2. 29 C.F.R. Part 825.
3. See *Drew* v. *Waffle House, Inc.* No. 3190. (S.C. App. 6/12/00).

Key Terms

family leave—Type of leave that can be taken under the FMLA for the birth, adoption, or foster-care placement of a child in order to care for that child.

family member—One's spouse, child, or parent. The FMLA definition does not include siblings or parents-in-law.

medical leave—Type of leave that can be taken under the FMLA to care for a spouse, child, or parent with a "serious health condition," or because of a "serious health condition" that makes an employee unable to perform the function of his or her position.

serious health condition—Any illness, injury, impairment, or physical or mental condition that involves either (a) in-patient care in a hospital, hospice, or residential medical care facility; or (b) continuing treatment by a health-care provider.

Review Questions

1. Which employers are subject to the FMLA?

2. Which employees are eligible for a leave of absence under the FMLA?

3. How much leave is an employee entitled to under the FMLA?

4. Under what circumstances is an employee entitled to take a leave of absence under the FMLA?

5. What rules apply with respect to the continuation of employee health benefits during his or her leave?

6. What employment protection is provided under the FMLA for the employee who takes a leave?

7. What exception applies to highly compensated employees under the FMLA?

8. What prohibitions apply to an employer under the FMLA?

9. How is a "serious health condition" defined?

10. What kinds of leaves are available to spouses employed by the same employer?

11. How much notice does an employee have to give the employer in order to take leave under FMLA?

12. What penalties apply to employers for non-compliance with the FMLA?

13. What effect does the FMLA have on state laws that already regulate family leave?

14. What effect does the FMLA have on union collective bargaining provisions?

Internet Sites

For more information, visit the following Internet sites. Remember that Internet addresses can change without notice.

Family and Medical Leave Act
http://www.dol.gov/dol/esa/fmla.htm

Chapter 21 Outline

Competencies

1. Describe the anti-discrimination terms of Title VII of the Civil Rights Act of 1964. (p. 269)

2. Describe federal laws adopted to prevent sex discrimination in employment. (pp. 269–270)

3. State the essential elements of the Age Discrimination in Employment Act of 1967. (pp. 270–271)

4. Explain how race discrimination is prohibited by Title VII of the Civil Rights Act of 1964. (pp. 271–272)

5. Describe the requirements of Title VII of the Civil Rights Act of 1964 with regard to religious discrimination. (p. 272)

6. Describe the Equal Employment Opportunity Commission (EEOC) "Guidelines on Discrimination Because of National Origin" with regard to an employer's responsibility. (p. 272)

7. Describe affirmative action programs. (pp. 272–273)

8. Explain when marital status discrimination is in violation of Title VII of the Civil Rights Act of 1964. (p. 273)

9. Describe the Civil Rights Act of 1991's effect on employment. (pp. 273–274)

10. Explain sexual harassment issues as addressed by EEOC regulations and Title VII of the Civil Rights Act of 1964, and cite court cases dealing with sexual harassment of employees. (pp. 274–278)

11. Summarize the Pregnancy Discrimination Act. (p. 278)

12. Describe how the Americans with Disabilities Act's Title I provisions affect hotel employment. (pp. 279–283)

13. Describe the Civil Rights Act of 1964's impact on advertising for employment. (p. 283)

21

Laws Against Discrimination in Employment

Federal and State Laws

Title VII of the 1964 Civil Rights Act[1] makes it unlawful for employers of 15 or more persons in any industry affecting commerce to discriminate against any individual with respect to compensation, terms, conditions, or privileges of employment because of race, color, religion, sex, or national origin.* The Act also prohibits employment agencies and labor unions from discriminating on these grounds. The Act allows an exception only in some "instances where religion, sex or national origin is a bona fide occupational qualification reasonably necessary to the normal operation of the particular business or enterprise." This exception has been given a very limited construction by the courts and it should not be relied upon without advice of counsel.

The Civil Rights Act of 1991[2] overturned a series of 1989 U.S. Supreme Court decisions and amended Title VII of the 1964 Civil Rights Act to allow damages and jury trials in cases of alleged intentional job discrimination.

In addition to the federal laws cited in this chapter, several states have enacted similar laws prohibiting discrimination in employment on the basis of race, creed, sex, national origin, age, physical handicaps, sexual orientation, etc. These laws are generally enforced by the respective state agencies or designated commissions. Hotelkeepers should consult local counsel regarding the applicability of such laws and any reporting requirements thereunder.

Some states require employers to put up a poster that summarizes the chief provisions of the state laws on discrimination. In New York, for example, such posters may be obtained from the New York State Division of Human Rights.

Sex Discrimination

Discrimination on the basis of sex has been pervasive in America throughout its history. While the Equal Protection Clause of the Fourteenth Amendment

---

The authors express appreciation to Ms. Terri Ross, Esq., and Mr. Sean Molloy, Esq., for their advice and assistance in preparing this chapter.

* The prohibitions against discrimination by a hotel as applied to a guest are described in Chapter 4.

guarantees that no state shall "deny to any person within its jurisdiction the equal protection of the laws," the Equal Pay Act of 1963 and amendments to Title VII of the 1964 Civil Rights Act for the first time gave women significant legal tools with which to oppose sex discrimination in employment.

One case in the hospitality industry that demonstrates the reach of these statutes is *Evans* v. *Sheraton Park Hotel.*[3] Two local unions supplied banquet personnel to the hotel. One union was a waiter's union, all male, and the other a waitress's union, all female. The hotel's banquet captain, a member of the waiter's union, allegedly assigned waiters rather than waitresses to more lucrative banquets. The court found this to be discriminatory and damages of $1,100 plus attorneys' fees were assessed against all the defendants jointly, while the hotel was fined an additional $500 for alleged harassment.

Glorious Food caterers agreed in 1998 to pay $425,000 to settle a class-action sex discrimination lawsuit brought by waitresses who said they were denied the opportunity to work at lucrative private parties.[4] In another case, "Hooters" agreed in 1997 to pay $3.75 million to settle a lawsuit filed by men who were denied jobs by the restaurant chain, which is known for its voluptuous and scantily clad female bartenders and servers.[5]

The federal Equal Pay Act[6] prohibits an employer from discriminating among employees in the same establishment on the basis of sex by paying wages to employees at a rate less than the rate paid to employees of the opposite sex for work on jobs which require substantially equal skill, effort, and responsibility and which are performed under similar working conditions, except where such payment is made pursuant to a differential based on any factor other than sex.

In *Brennan* v. *First Motor Inn, Inc.,*[7] the Department of Labor alleged that a New Jersey hotel discriminated by paying different wages to maids and housemen who performed substantially similar services. The case was settled without trial on November 13, 1975. The hotel agreed to equalize the pay rates of the maids and housemen, effective December 1, 1975. In addition, the hotel agreed to pay back wages for the period of July 1, 1973, through November 30, 1975.

Remember, however, that in any hotel case under the Equal Pay Act, it is the facts, and not the job titles, that determine whether men and women are performing "substantially similar service." Many hotels now follow strict lines regarding what work is done by room attendants ("maids") as distinguished from housepersons ("housemen").

Age Discrimination

The federal statute governing age discrimination in employment is the Age Discrimination in Employment Act of 1967, as amended.[8] This Act covers all employers engaged in an industry affecting commerce which have 20 or more employees for each working day in each of 20 or more calendar weeks in a year.

The Act makes it unlawful for an employer to discharge, to refuse to hire, or to otherwise discriminate against any person with respect to the terms of his/her employment because of his/her age, if the person is 40 years old or older. There is a narrowly construed exception, provided that the employer can show that age is a "bona fide occu-pational qualification reasonably necessary to the normal operation of the particular business." The Act does not prohibit age discrimination in hiring below the age of 40.

A 64-year-old room service waiter was recently awarded $290,125 by the court for back pay and damages when the hotel replaced him with a younger man.[9]

Discrimination cases have shown that the bona fide occupational qualification test mentioned above is a severe test that may be difficult for an employer to meet. The burden of proof is on the employer, who must show that persons over the age limit in question are generally incapable of performing the tasks required.

Individual states may also have concurrent age discrimination statutes or regulations. For example, New York State prohibits discrimination based on age against anyone 18 years old or older.[10]

Race Discrimination

In addition to the Fourteenth Amendment to the Constitution of the United States, Title VII of the Civil Rights Act prohibits discrimination based on race. The Civil Rights Act of 1964 applies to race discrimination in private employment. Additionally, Section 1983, Title 28 of the United States Code prohibits race discrimination in employment.

Most hotel and motel owners are well aware that they cannot discriminate by hiring qualified applicants from one race in preference to another race. Recent court decisions have attacked much more subtle forms of racial discrimination. For example, the federal government now takes the position, which the courts have upheld, that an employer may not use seemingly neutral criteria for employment that will in fact result in racial discrimination, unless those criteria are relevant to the performance of the particular job. For example, one court has found that, in the South, a smaller percentage of blacks have high school diplomas than whites. Consequently, a requirement that all employees have high school diplomas has been held to discriminate against blacks. That is, job requirements must be tied to legitimate skills and experience necessary to perform the job.

In *Parliament House Motor Hotel* v. *Equal Employment Opportunity Commission (EEOC)*,[11] the court held that when the employee's claim is broad enough, the EEOC is entitled to investigate the entire hotel operation to determine whether discrimination exists in any form, going far beyond the question of whether the single employee involved was discriminated against in a particular way. Thus, once a discrimination complaint has been filed, the EEOC may examine the hotel's entire operation for discrimination in any area of hiring, firing, or promotion with respect to any employee, not merely the complaining individual. If this occurs, consult an attorney.

The costs of racial discrimination can be significant. Recently, Interstate Bakeries Corp. was reportedly ordered by the Court to pay $120 million in punitive damages in addition to $11 million in actual damages to 21 black workers who said they suffered racial discrimination at a Wonder Bread plant.[12]

Recently, eight bellhops who were fired from the trendy Mondrian hotel on the Sunset Strip in 1996 and replaced by whites were awarded $120,000 each under a settlement announced by the Equal Employment Opportunity Commission. The commission had filed suit under the Civil Rights Act of 1964, charging that the

Mondrian's owner, Ian Schrager Hotels Inc., engaged in disciminartory recruit-ment practices against Hispanic, black, and Asian job applicants.[13]

Religious Discrimination

There have been a number of recent cases that deal with religious discrimination and the requirements of Title VII. For the full text of the opinion in a case of a Black Muslim alleging religious discrimination, see *Ali* v. *Southeast Neighborhood House* at the end of this chapter.

Generally speaking, if it is absolutely necessary from a business point of view, an employer may require a person to work on his/her Sabbath, and, if the employee refuses, the employer may discharge him/her for failure to work. Nevertheless, before discharging an employee, the employer must be able to demonstrate that he/she is unable to reasonably accommodate an employee's religious observance or practice without undue hardship on the conduct of the employer's business.

National Origin Discrimination

Several EEOC decisions indicate that it might charge a hotel with discrimination on the basis of national origin if it refuses to hire people who do not speak English fluently when the position does not require the fluent speaking of English.

The EEOC "Guidelines on Discrimination Because of National Origin" state that "an employer has an affirmative duty to maintain a working environment free of harassment on the basis of national origin." Under the Guidelines, an employer is responsible for acts that result in "creating an intimidating, hostile or offensive working environment," or which "unreasonably interfer[e] with an individual's work performance" or otherwise adversely affect an individual's employment opportunities.

The Guidelines also relate to any companies that have "Speak-English-Only" rules for employees. The Guidelines state that a rule requiring employees to speak English at *all* times is presumed to be a violation of Title VII of the Civil Rights Act and will be closely scrutinized. The Guidelines also provide that a "Speak-English-Only" rule applied at certain times may be valid if justified by business necessity. In 1981, the Supreme Court denied review of a decision of the Court of Appeals for the Fifth Circuit in *Garcia* v. *Gloor,* [14] which held that a "Speak-English-Only" rule applied to an employee in a workplace was not discrimination on the basis of national origin when the employee was in fact able to speak English.

The EEOC has amended its guidelines to extend antidiscrimination rights to illegal immigrant workders. The EEOC website provides a question and answer guide on this subject.

Affirmative Action Programs

Many employers have adopted affirmative action plans (that is, result-oriented programs which actively promote the hiring and promotion of qualified women and minorities in the work force). Broadly speaking, under such a plan, the employer evaluates the present work force and future needs to determine whether the work force is deficient in the utilization of available qualified women and minorities. Then the employer sets goals for increased hiring of such women and minorities if necessary to correct any underutilization in the present work force. In addition, the employer will continually review the establishment's employment procedures to ensure that such qualified women and minorities have upward mobility in the organization.

Federal regulation requires affirmative action of all employers who hold federal contracts that exceed $10,000. If federal contracts exceed $50,000 and the employer has 50 or more employees, the employer must develop and implement a written affirmative action plan, acceptable to and monitored under the auspices of the Department of Labor, Office of Federal Contract Compliance Programs.*

Marital Status Discrimination

Discrimination based on marital status is not necessarily a violation of the federal discrimination laws. However, if marital status discrimination affects one sex disproportionately, it may be viewed as sex discrimination in violation of Title VII. For example, under EEOC policy, an "employer's rule which forbids or restricts the employment of married women and which is not applicable to married men is a discrimination based on sex."

In *Sprogis* v. *United Airlines, Inc.*[15] the employer had an employment policy that required stewardesses to be unmarried, although no such marital status restriction existed against any male employee, whatever his position with the company. Plaintiff, a stewardess discharged because of her marriage, brought suit against United Airlines. The court found that the employer had discriminated in violation of Title VII because the employer had failed to demonstrate a rational connection between marital status, job performance, and the unmarried rule for stewardesses. The court ordered the employer to restore the plaintiff to her employment (including restoration of her seniority and longevity rights) and awarded her damages for loss of earnings.

There may be concurrent state laws in this area. For example, New York enacted legislation prohibiting employment discrimination on account of marital status as an unlawful discriminatory practice.[16]

The Civil Rights Act of 1991

As mentioned earlier, the Civil Rights Act of 1991[17] overturned a series of 1989 U.S. Supreme Court decisions and expanded Title VII of the Civil Rights Act to allow compensatory and punitive damages and jury trials in cases of intentional job discrimination based on race, color, sex, religion, national origin, and disability. The Act sets monetary caps for damages in cases based on sex, religious, and disability

---

* See *Schurr* v. *Resorts International Hotel Inc.*, 196 F.3d 486 (3rd Cir. 1999) for the court's decision on the requirements of an affirmative action plan. See also ADA—Enforcement and Damages, p. 282.

discrimination only. The caps range from $50,000 to $300,000, depending on the size of the employer's work force. A jury trial may be requested by any party to a case in which compensatory or punitive damages are sought.

The Civil Rights Act of 1991 also provides: "An unlawful employment practice is established when the complaining party demonstrates that race, color, religion, sex, or national origin was a motivating factor for any employment practice, *even though other factors also motivated the practice.*" However, if the employer demonstrates that the same action would have been taken even absent the discriminatory motive, the court may not award compensatory or punitive damages or require reinstatement, hiring, or promotion.

Sexual Harassment of Employees

The EEOC published regulations on April 11, 1980, explicitly forbidding sexual harassment of employees by their supervisors. The rules state that employers have an "affirmative duty" to prevent and eliminate sexual harassment, which may be "either physical or verbal in nature."

Thus, harassment on the basis of sex is a violation of § 703 of Title VII of the Civil Rights Act of 1964, as amended. Unwelcome sexual advances, requests for sexual favors, and other verbal or physical conduct of a sexual nature constitute sexual harassment when:

1. Submission to such conduct is made, either explicitly or implicitly, a term or condition of a person's employment

2. Submission to or rejection of such conduct by a person is used as the basis for employment decisions affecting such person

3. Such conduct has the purpose or effect of unreasonably interfering with a person's work performance or creating an intimidating, hostile, or offensive working environment[18]

Two types of sexual harassment have been identified by the courts. Both are unlawful. The first is *quid pro quo*. In this type, a supervisor promises an employee something (such as a raise) for sexual favors (or conversely, threatens something— such as a job demotion). The second is hostile environment, where the work place is "hostile" as the result of sexual comments, touching, and the like. In this type, a supervisor need not be involved.

Applying general Title VII principles, an employer, employment agency, joint apprenticeship committee, or labor organization is responsible for its acts and those of its agents and supervisory employees with respect to sexual harassment. Generally, this is true regardless of whether the employer authorized or forbade the specific acts complained of and regardless of whether the employer knew or should have known of their occurrence.

Specific examples of sexual harrasment cases are discussed below.

In *EEOC* v. *Sage Realty Corp.*,[19] the plaintiff, a female lobby attendant in an office building, filed a sex discrimination complaint alleging she was required to wear "a revealing and provocative uniform which subjected her to repeated and abusive sexual harassment." The plaintiff asserted that she was fired when she refused to wear the uniform. The defendant's motion for summary judgment was refused. The full text of this opinion appears at the end of this chapter.

The text of another case addressing this topic, *Huebschen* v. *Department of Health and Social Services,*[20] appears at the end of this chapter.

On June 19, 1986, the U.S. Supreme Court ruled unanimously in *Meritor Savings Bank* v. *Vinson*[21] that sexual harassment of an employee by a supervisor in the workplace violates Title VII of the Civil Rights Act of 1964. The Court's ruling supports the decisions of the lower federal courts which have consistently held that sexual harassment is a form of sex discrimination. In addition, the Supreme Court held that workers may sue their employers for sex discrimination on the grounds that sexual harassment by a supervisor created a "hostile or abusive work environment," even if loss of job or lack of promotion were not involved. (Such a claim does *not* depend upon a supervisor being involved.

However, the U.S. Supreme Court rejected a lower court ruling that a company is always liable for sexual harassment of workers by supervisors, even if company management is not aware of the problem. The opinion of the Court stated that an employer's liability depends on the circumstances. The Court added that an employer's lack of knowledge of harassment by a supervisor would "not necessarily insulate that employer from liability."[22]

Following the above U.S. Supreme Court ruling, the Chicago Holiday Inn was reportedly charged by the EEOC with violating the 1964 Civil Rights Act by permitting sexual harassment. In this case, the hotel operator allegedly failed to stop the sexual harassment of 13 women, mainly servers and bus help, by a male food and beverage director over a two-and-a-half-year period, even though the victims repeatedly informed management about the harassment. The alleged sexual harassment ranged from verbal abuse and physical contact to the performance of one sexual act, the EEOC suit alleges, and was so "severe and pervasive" that a "hostile environment" existed, causing some of the women to quit their jobs.

In another case, a restaurant employee in Minnesota was fired on the grounds of sexual harassment. Reportedly, the employee had kissed a 16-year-old server on the back of her head, and the management heard of other such incidents involving the same employee. The employee sued the management, claiming that he was really fired because of his age (60 years old) and that the sexual harassment charge was a pretext. The court ruled that under the Age Discrimination in Employment Act (ADEA), an employer may refute a discrimination charge by showing that the firing was "for good cause," or that it was based on reasonable factors other than age. The court dismissed the plaintiff's complaint.[23]

In 1998 the Benihana resaurant chain reportedly paid over $130,000 to settle a lawsuit brought by waitresses who said they were groped, hit on, or pressured to have sex with the manager of a Long Island franchise. The Tokyo-based chain settled with the Equal Employment Opportunity Commission rather than go to trial.[24]

In 1992, a Miami jury awarded $1.08 million to Amy Lytton Virgo, the former general manager of Sheraton Ocean Inn in Riviera Beach, Florida.[25] The judgment included money for Virgo's past and future lost wages, future medical bills, and pain and suffering. The U.S. District Court later awarded an additional $421,000 in damages, noting that the hotel management company and the owners violated federal laws that prohibit sexual harassment.[26]

Virgo said the harassment began in the mid-1980s as she worked her way up the corporate ladder from sales manager to general manager at Sheraton Ocean Inn. Allegedly, Virgo testified that her supervisor forced her to have sex with him in order for her to keep her job. She gave in at first, she said, but later refused. Her supervisor made her working conditions intolerable, then forced her to resign, the court was told.

In a written answer to her allegations in court documents, her supervisor had alleged that Virgo "by her conduct, did not indicate that the alleged sexual advances…were unwelcome." In 1994, the U.S. Court of Appeals upheld the ruling and damages awarded by the lower court.[27]

In 1994, a jury awarded more than $7 million in damages to a former secretary of the world's largest law firm who said she had been sexually harassed by a partner.[28] Rena Weeks, the plaintiff, was reportedly awarded $6.9 million in punitive damages from Baker & McKenzie; $225,000 more from Martin Greenstein, the former partner; and $50,000 in compensatory damages for the emotional distress she suffered as a result of Greenstein's alleged actions and crude remarks. The judge reportedly reduced the punitive damages against Baker & McKenzie from $6.9 million to $3.5 million.[29]

The award implies that employers have a grave responsibility to respond promptly and vigorously to complaints of harassment by employees against their supervisors.

In two cases decided in 1998, the U.S. Supreme Court held that although an employer is liable for a sexually hostile work environment caused by a supervisor, an employer can prevail in a law suit by showing that it acted reasonably to prevent and correct the harassment, while the employee did not act reasonably to avoid the harm.

In *Burlington Industries* v. *Ellerth*,[30] Kimberly Ellerth claimed she was subjected to repeated sexual comments by her supervisor as well as physical touching. When interviewing Ellerth for a promotion, the supervisor told her he had reservations because she wasn't "loose enough." However, Ellerth received the promotion. Even though Burlington had a sexual harassment policy, Ellerth never reported the harassment, and she quit. At issue in *Ellerth* was whether an employee can recover for unwelcome sexual advances with no tangible job consequences without showing the employer was somehow at fault for the supervisor's conduct.

The second case, *Faragher* v. *City of Boca Raton*,[31] involved a lifeguard who claimed lewd remarks and uninvited and offensive touching by two supervisors at the beach. Faragher discussed her complaints with a low level supervisor who assigned her daily tasks, but even she did not regard this as a formal complaint, merely as a discussion with a person she "held in high esteem." While the city had a sexual harassment policy, it never disseminated the policy to the employees working at the beaches. In addition, the policy did not allow an employee to bypass a harassing supervisor in order to complain.

In both cases, the Court held that an employer is liable for a "hostile work environmnet" created by a supervisor who is somewhere in the immediate chain of command over the employee. But when no tangible employment action is taken against the employee, such as discharge or demotion, the employer may defend itself by showing, first, that it exercised reasonable care to prevent and promptly correct the sexual harassment. Second, the employer must show that the employee unreasonably failed to take advantage of any preventive or corrective opportunities provided by the employer to avoid the harm which occurred.

According to the Court's holdings, an employer will be held liable for a hostile work environment created by a supervisor unless it can show that it adequately communicated a viable harassment policy and promptly took corrective action and the employee failed to use the complaint procedure. This makes a properly drafted and publicized harassment policy essential for employers to defend themselves against claims of sexual harassment. A policy should specify that the company absolutley forbids harassment on the basis of any protected category, including sex, and threaten sanctions against any violators of the policy. The policy should instruct employees to promptly report complaints and include a complaint procedure that allows the employee to bypass the immediate supervisor, who often is the harasser. Finally, complaints must be promptly investigated, and employers must take prompt corrective action in order to avoid legal liability.*

The U.S. Supreme Court in *Harris* v. *Forklift Systems, Inc.,*[32] held that the law does not require "concrete psychological harm," adding: "So long as the environment would reasonably be perceived as hostile or abusive...there is no need for it also to be psychologically injurious."

In this case, Teresa Howard worked as a manager at a forklift manufacturer. According to a U.S. Magistrate, company President Charles Hardy called Howard "a dumb-ass woman," remarked on several occasions, "You're a woman, what do you know?" and suggested that the two of them "go to the Holiday Inn to negotiate [her] raise." He occasionally threw objects on the ground, asking her to pick them up.

In mid-August 1987, Howard complained to Hardy about his behavior. Hardy said he was surprised, that he had only been joking; he apologized and promised to stop.

In early September, Howard was arranging a deal with a customer. Hardy allegedly asked her, "What did you do, promise the guy some [sex] Saturday night?"

On October 1, 1987, Howard quit. Shortly thereafter, she sued the company and won.

The Harris case sends a warning to all industries. Except in the weakest of cases, a jury will be empowered to decide whether a given course of conduct "would reasonably be perceived" and was, in fact, perceived to be, "hostile and abusive." The jury will decide how much, if anything, an employer has to pay one of its employees because of comments made by another employee.

---

* Used with permission of McDermott, Will and Emery.

In September 2000, a former woman chef at the White House reportedly filed a sexual harassment suit against her boss, the executive pastry chief, and against President Clinton, as head of the federal agency involved. The woman chef seeks $1 million from her boss and $1 million from the President.[33]

The 1998 the U.S. Supreme Court ruled that Federal law protects employees from being sexually harassed in the workplace by people of the same sex. The unanimous decision carried the law of sexual harassment beyond the classic male-female context. In the opinion for the Court, it was the conduct itself, and not the sex or motivation of the people involved, that determined whether sexual harassment amounted to "discrimination because of sex" within the meaning of the Title VII of the Civil Rights Act of 1964.[34]

Pregnancy Discrimination Act

In 1978 Congress amended Title VII with the Pregnancy Discrimination Act, which prohibits discrimination on the basis of pregnancy, childbirth, or related medical conditions. Pregnancy discrimination claims are analyzed like all other Title VII actions.

The PDA does not require employers to make it easier for pregnant employers to return to work or treat them specially. But consider the following requirements under the PDA:

- Innkeepers must treat pregnant workers the same as other employees on the basis of their ability or inability to work.

- Innkeepers must ignore an employee's pregnancy as far as practically possible.

- Pregnancy under the PDA is treated just like any other temporary disability.

- Employees who are able to work must be permitted to work in the same conditions as other employees.

- Pregnant employees who are unable to work must be accorded the same leave and fringe benefits provided to other employees who are temporarily unable to work.

- Pregnancy alone may not be a motivating factor for an adverse employment action, such as hiring, firing, or promoting an employee.*

---

* Reprinted with permission from Hospitality Law copyright 2000 by LRP Publications, 747 Dresher Road, Horsham, PA 19044-0980. All rights reserved. For more information on Hospitality Law or for a free 30-day trial subscription, please call 1-800-341-7874, ext. 310.

Americans with Disabilities Act—Employment

In Chapter 9, we discussed the Americans with Disabilities Act (ADA) provisions relating to accessibility in places of public accommodation. In this chapter, we discuss the Act's Title I provisions which relate to hotel employment.[35]

Title I of the ADA prohibits covered hotel employers from discriminating against a **"qualified individual with a disability"** in regard to job applications, hiring, advancement, discharge, compensation, and training, or other terms, conditions, or privileges of employment.

Specifically, hotel employers may not adversely limit, segregate, or classify applicants or employees due to their disabilities. Employers may not participate in any contractual or other form of relationship that has the effect of subjecting applicants or employees to disability discrimination. Nor may employers use administrative standards, criteria, or methods that have a discriminatory effect or perpetuate existing discrimination against disabled individuals.

Title I became effective on July 26, 1992. It covers all employers engaged in an industry affecting commerce and having 15 or more employees for each working day in each of 20 or more calendar weeks in the then-current or preceding calendar year.

Definition of "Disability"

An **"individual with a disability"** is broadly defined as anyone who (1) has a physical or mental impairment that substantially limits one or more major life activities, (2) has a record of such an impairment, or (3) is regarded as having such an impairment.

Examples of physical or mental disabilities include visual/speech/hearing impairments, orthopedic impairments, cerebral palsy, epilepsy, muscular dystrophy, multiple sclerosis, AIDS, HIV, cancer, heart disease, diabetes, mental retardation, emotional illness, learning disabilities, tuberculosis, drug addiction, and alcoholism.[36]

The ADA specifically states that homosexuality and bisexuality are not impairments and as such are not disabilities under the ADA. The ADA also excludes from its definition of disabled individuals transvestites, transsexuals, pedophiles, exhibitionists, voyeurs, individuals with gender identity disorders not resulting from physical impairments, individuals with other sexual behavior disorders, compulsive gamblers, kleptomaniacs, pyromaniacs, and those who are currently engaged in the use of illegal drugs.

Under the ADA, employers may hold alcoholics to the same qualifications and job performance standards as other employees, even if unsatisfactory performance is related to alcoholism.

Qualified Individuals

The term *"qualified* individual with a disability" means an individual with a disability who satisfies the requisite skill, experience, education, and other job-related requirements of the employment position such individual holds or desires and who, with or without reasonable accommodation, can perform the position's essential functions. Thus, a disabled individual can be said to be "qualified" even though he/she is unable to perform the "marginal functions" of a particular job and even though he/she is able to perform the essential functions only with some degree of accommodation by the employer.

The term **"essential functions"** is defined in the EEOC regulations as the fundamental job duties of a particular employment position and as specifically excluding the "marginal functions" of the position. According to the regulations, evidence of whether a particular function is essential includes the following:

- The employer's judgment as to which functions are essential

- The written job descriptions that were prepared before advertising or interviewing applicants for the job

- The amount of time spent on the job performing the functions

- The consequences of not requiring the incumbent to perform the function

Drug Testing

Nothing in Title I shall be construed to encourage, prohibit, or authorize the use of drug testing for illegal drugs or the making of employment decisions based on the test results. However, if, under the ADA, employers tend to use drug testing more readily than before, it is possible that drug and alcohol testing claims against employers could increase, particularly from employees claiming that such tests are inaccurate.

Infectious and Communicable Diseases

The U.S. Secretary of Health and Human Services publishes annual lists of infectious and communicable diseases that are transmitted through food handling, including the methods by which such diseases are transmitted. Employers may decline to assign applicants or employees with listed diseases to jobs involving food handling, but only if reasonable accommodation cannot eliminate the risk of transmission.

Reasonable Accommodations Requirements

Under Title I, employers are required to make **"reasonable accommodations"** for the known physical or mental limitations of an otherwise qualified applicant or employee with a disability, unless doing so would impose an "undue hardship."

According to EEOC regulations, the term "reasonable accommodations" means (1) modifications or adjustments to a job application process that enable a qualified applicant with a disability to be considered for employment, and (2) modifications or adjustments to the work environment, or to the manner or circumstances under which a job position is customarily performed, that enable a qualified individual with a disability to perform the essential functions of that position.

The use of qualification standards, employment tests, or other selection criteria that tend to screen out individuals with disabilities is prohibited, unless the standards, tests, or criteria are job-related.

"Reasonable accommodations" for individuals with disabilities may include making existing facilities readily accessible; restructuring jobs; modifying work schedules; reassigning employees to vacant positions; acquiring or modifying equipment or devices; adjusting or modifying examinations, training materials, or policies; and providing the disabled with readers, interpreters, or similar accommodations.

Exceptions for Undue Hardship

Accommodations are not required under the ADA if they would impose an "undue hardship" on the employer's business, meaning that they would require a significant difficulty or expense. Whether an undue hardship exists is based on a number of factors. These include the nature and cost of the accommodation; the size, financial resources, and financial circumstances of the specific facility and the "employer" as defined by the Act; and the employer's type of operation, including the composition, structure, and functions of its work force as well as the geographic separateness and administrative or fiscal relationship between the specific facility and the employer.

Pre-Employment Interviews

The ADA makes it unlawful to inquire as to whether an applicant has a disability or to ask about the nature or severity of such a disability. Thus, even when a disability is visibly apparent, an employer should not raise the issue or discuss the extent or nature of any accommodation that might be required, unless and until the applicant advises the employer of the disability and the need, if any, for an accommodation.

Employers are permitted to make pre-employment inquiries into the ability of an applicant to perform job-related functions and may ask an applicant to describe or demonstrate how, with or without reasonable accommodation, the applicant will be able to perform these functions. If such questions are asked or demonstrations required, however, they should be posed to all applicants and not only to those who are or appear to be disabled.

According to the EEOC's *Technical Assistance Manual*, current applications being used by employers should be screened in order to remove any questions that might run afoul of the requirements of the ADA.

The manual gives the following examples of questions that are prohibited both on job applications and during interviews:

- Have you ever had or been treated for any of the following conditions or diseases (followed by a checklist of various conditions and diseases)?

- Are there any conditions or diseases for which you have been treated in the past three years?

- Have you ever been hospitalized? If so, for what condition?

- Have you ever been treated by a psychiatrist or psychologist? If so, for what condition?

- Have you ever been treated for any mental condition?

- Is there any health-related reason why you may not be able to perform the job for which you are applying?

- Have you had a major illness in the last five years?

- How many days were you absent from work because of illness last year?

- Do you have any physical defects that prevent you from performing certain kinds of work? If yes, describe these defects and specific work limitations.

- Are you taking any prescribed drugs?

- Have you ever been treated for drug addiction or alcoholism?

- Have you ever filed for workers' compensation insurance?

ADA Posting Requirements

Effective July 26, 1994, employers of 25 or more employees were required to hang a federal poster in a prominent place in their workplace in order to notify job applicants and employees of their rights under the employment rules of the ADA.

This poster may be obtained from the U.S. Equal Employment Opportunity Commission (EEOC).*

Enforcement and Damages

The EEOC is designated as the enforcement agency for Title I of the ADA and has issued regulations to implement Title I.[37] Complainants must file charges of an alleged discriminatory act with the EEOC within 180 days of its alleged occurrence (or within 300 days in states with approved enforcement agencies, such as New York). Generally, the EEOC has 180 days after a charge has been filed to investigate and either sue the employer or issue a right-to-sue letter to the complainant. The complainant then has 90 days to file a private lawsuit.

Title I adopts all of the powers, procedures, and remedies set forth in Title VII of the Civil Rights Act of 1964. Relief can include hiring or reinstatement with or without back pay as well as reimbursement for attorneys' fees and legal costs. Employers may not retaliate against complainants or those who assist in the investigation of a complaint under the ADA.

Additional remedies may be available under Title VII of the Civil Rights Act of 1964, as amended by the Civil Rights Act of 1991.**

---

 * To obtain a copy of the poster, contact the EEOC Publications Distribution Center, P.O. Box 12549, Cincinnati, OH 45212-0549 or visit http://www.eeoc.gov.
** Note that under the federal Rehabilitation Act of 1973 and its regulations all non-exempt employers with federal contracts or subcontracts in excess of $2,500 must take affirmative action to employ and advance in employment (job assignment, promotion, training, transfer, etc.) qualified handicapped individuals.

State and Local Disability Discrimination Laws

ADA Section 501(b) specifies that nothing in the ADA shall be construed to invalidate or limit any procedures, rights, or remedies provided by any other federal, state, or local law that affords greater or equal protection for the rights of individuals with disabilities than are afforded by the ADA.

Some states have also enacted statutes or regulations that expressly prohibit employment discrimination against individuals with disabilities. For example, New York prohibits discrimination against any person with "a physical, mental or medical impairment" unless the disability is related to and affects the person's ability to perform the activities of the particular job. Hotels should seek the advice of local counsel to determine the law applicable in their particular state.

Discrimination in Advertising for Employment

The Civil Rights Act of 1964 prohibits the use of any advertisement or publication that expresses any limitation, specification, or discrimination, or any intent to make such limitation, specification, or discrimination unless based upon a bona fide occupational qualification. This means that when advertising for help, the employer cannot specify that the applicants must be of a particular race, creed, sex, or national origin. Nor can such a qualification be implied unless it can be shown that it is a bona fide occupational qualification. There are probably comparatively few instances in ordinary hotel operations where a bona fide occupational qualification can be legally based upon race, creed, color, na-tional origin, or sex. If a hotel believes that it has such a position, it should secure a ruling from state and federal authorities on discrimination before publishing the advertisement.

Some employers deny jobs to persons who smoke. The EEOC has indicated that denying employment for this reason alone is not a violation of Title VII, unless it results in discrimination on the basis of national origin, race, religion, sex, or age.

Important Points for Management

- The federal Civil Rights Act prohibits sex discrimination in employment practices; that is, in hiring, promoting, etc.

- The federal Equal Pay Act generally requires that employers pay the same wages to employees (male or female) who perform jobs that require substantially equal skill, effort, and responsibility and that are performed under similar working conditions.

- The Age Discrimination in Employment Act of 1967 prohibits employers from discriminating against employees who are 40 years of age or older. Some states have age discrimination laws which also protect those under 40 years of age.

- Race discrimination is prohibited by the Civil Rights Act of 1964. Race discrimination *cannot* be justified as a bona fide occupational qualification.

- Affirmative action programs attempt to rectify possible past discrimination through implementation of a policy actively seeking and hiring minorities.

- Marital status discrimination is not prohibited per se by federal law, but it might be considered sex discrimination if a company rule affects married women but is not applied to married men or vice versa.

- Sexual harassment of employees is prohibited by the Equal Employment Opportunity Commission under Title VII of the Civil Rights Act of 1964. Hotels should form a policy against sexual harassment which must contain a complaint procedure.

- The ADA prohibits discrimination in employment against "a qualified individual with a disability"; i.e., a person with a disability who satisfies the requisite skill, experience, education, and other job-related requirements of the employment position that the person holds or desires to hold and who, with or without reasonable accommodation, can perform the position's essential functions.

- Many state laws ban discrimination based on stated physical or mental disabilities.

References

1. 42 U.S.C. § 2000a *et seq.*
2. Pub. L. 102-166, Nov. 21, 1991, 105 Stat. 1071.
3. 503 F.2d 177 (D.C. Cir., 1974).
4. *N.Y. Times,* Aug. 28, 1998, p. A-23, cols. 2-6.
5. *N.Y. Times,* Oct. 1, 1997, p. A-20, col. 1.
6. 29 U.S.C. § 206(d)(i).
7. *Brennan* v. *First Motor Inn, Inc.,* Civil Action No. 74-379 (F.B.L.) (D.C. N.J. 1974).
8. 29 U.S.C. § 621 *et seq.* In 2000, a Citigroup Bank executive sued the company for over $500,000, accusing it of age discrimination when it allegedly sought to dismiss older executives as a way to cut costs (*N.Y. Times,* Feb. 3, 2000, p. C-13, col. 1).
9. *Munoz* v. *Oceanside Resorts Inc.* 223 F.3d 1340 (11th Cir. 2000).
10. N.Y. Exec. Law § 296 (McKinney 1993).
11. 444 F.2d 1335 (5th Cir., 1971).
12. *N.Y. Times,* Aug. 3, 2000, p. A-20, col. 1.
13. *N.Y. Times,* Aug. 10, 2000, p. A-16, col. 1.
14. 618 F.2d 264, *reh'g denied,* 625 F.2d 1016, (5th Cir., 1980) *cert. denied* 449 U.S. 1113 (1981).
15. 308 F.Supp. 959 (1970), *aff'd* 444 F.2d 1194 (7th Cir., 1971) *cert. denied* 404 U.S. 991 (1971).
16. N.Y. Exec. Law § 296 (McKinney 1993).
17. Pub. L. 102-166, Nov. 21, 1991, 105 Stat. 1071.
18. 29 C.F.R. § 1604.11 (1987).
19. 87 F.R.D. 365 (S.D.N.Y. 1980), *later proceeding,* 507 F.Supp. 599 (S.D.N.Y. 1981), *later proceeding,* 521 F.Supp. 263 (S.D.N.Y. 1981).
20. 547 F.Supp. 1168 (W.D.Wis. 1982).

21. 477 U.S. 57 (1986).

22. See also *Romero* v. *Howard Johnson Plaza Hotel* (1999 U.S. Dist. LEXIS 15264, S.D.N.Y., Sep. 28, 1999), where the court said that where there is evidence that an employer knew or should have known of alleged sexual harassment, the employer cannot escape liability by arguing that no one from management was the actual harasser.

23. *Johnson* v. *Perkins Restaurants, Inc.,* 815 F.2d 1220 (8th Cir. Minn., 1987).

24. *N.Y. Post,* Nov. 10, 1998, p. 24, cols. 1–4.

25. See *Miami Herald,* Oct. 10, 1992, p. 1, col. 5.

26. See *Miami Herald,* Nov. 19, 1992, p. 1C, col. 2.

27. See *Miami Herald,* Sept. 10, 1994, p. 1C, col. 2.

28. See *International Herald Tribune,* Sept. 3-4, 1994, p. 3, col. 1.

29. 63 Cal. App. 4th 1128 (May 4, 1998). See also *N.Y. Times,* Nov. 29, 1994, p. 22A, col. 3.

30. 524 U.S. 742 (1998).

31. 542 U.S. 775 (1998).

32. 62 *Law Week* 4004 (1993).

33. *N.Y. Times,* Sep. 14, 2000, p. 25, col. 4.

34. *Oncale* v. *Sundowner Offshore Services Corp.,* 523 U.S. 75 (1998).

35. The Educational Institute of AH&MA has produced two ADA videotapes: *ADA: The Hiring Process* and *ADA: Communication and Service Skills.* For ordering information, call toll-free 1-800-344-4381.

36. John P.S. Salmen, AIA, *Accommodating All Guests* (Washington, D.C.: American Hotel & Motel Association and Universal Designers & Consultants, Inc., 1992) p. 9.

37. 29 C.F.R. Part 1630

🔑 Key Terms

essential functions—The fundamental job duties of a particular employment position.

individual with a disability—Broadly, anyone who has a physical or mental impairment that substantially limits one or more life activities, has a record of such an impairment, or is regarded as having such an impairment.

qualified individual with a disability—A person with a disability who satisfies the requisite skill, experience, education, and other job-related requirements of the employment position that the person holds or desires to hold and who, with or without reasonable accommodation, can perform the position's essential functions.

reasonable accomodations—(1) Modifications or adjustments that are made to a job application process to enable a qualified applicant with a disability to be considered for employment, and (2) modifications or adjustments made to the work environment, or to the manner or circumstances under which a job position is customarily performed, that enable a qualified individual with a disability to perform the essential functions of that position.

Review Questions

1. What is the purpose of Title VII of the 1964 Civil Rights Act?
2. What federal statute gave women firmer grounds on which to protest sex discrimination in employment? What does this statute protect?
3. What rights does the Age Discrimination in Employment Act of 1967 protect?
4. What is the "bona fide occupational qualification" test?
5. What was the court's finding in *Parliament House Motor Hotel* v. *Equal Employment Opportunity Commission (EEOC)*?
6. According to the EEOC "Guidelines on Discrimination Because of National Origin," what duty does an employer have to employees with regard to national origin?
7. What is an affirmative action program? Why are such programs adopted?
8. How does the ADA define a "qualified individual with a disability" with respect to an individual seeking employment?
9. What is an "essential function" of a job under the ADA?
10. To what extent must an employer make existing facilities readily accessible to and usable by employees with disabilities?
11. What does "reasonable accommodation" for an employee mean?
12. What constitutes an "undue hardship"?
13. Does the ADA require that someone with an infectious disease be prohibited from handling food?
14. What are the ADA requirements with respect to testing applicants before hiring?
15. What types of questions does the ADA prohibit in a job interview?
16. What steps must an employer take to try to prevent sexual harassment of employees by their supervisors?

Internet Sites

For more information, visit the following Internet sites. Remember that Internet addresses can change without notice.

Age Discrimination Act
http://www.eeoc.gov/laws/
adea.html

Americans with Disabilities Act (ADA)
http://www.usdoj.gov/crt/ada/
adahom1.htm

Civil Rights Act of 1964
http://www.eeoc.gov/laws/vii.html

Civil Rights Act of 1991
http://www.eeoc.gov/laws/
cra91.html

Equal Employment Opportunity
Commission (EEOC)
http://www.eeoc.gov

Pregnancy Discrimination Facts
http://www.eeoc.gov/facts/
fs-preg.html

Appendix A

Federal Guidelines on
Sex Discrimination—Sexual Harassment

(29 C.F.R. Chap. XIV, § 1604.11 (1980))

A. Harassment on the basis of sex is a violation of Sec. 703 of Title VII. Unwelcome sexual advances, requests for sexual favors, and other verbal or physical conduct of a sexual nature constitute sexual harassment when (1) submission to such conduct is made either explicitly or implicitly a term or condition of an individual's employment, (2) submission to or rejection of such conduct by an individual is used as a basis for employment decisions affecting such individual, or (3) such conduct has the purpose or effect of unreasonably interfering with an individual's work performance or creating an intimidating, hostile, or offensive working environment.

B. In determining whether alleged conduct constitutes sexual harassment, the commission will look at the records as a whole and at the totality of the circumstances, such as the nature of the sexual advances and the context in which the alleged incidents occurred. The determination of the legality of a particular action will be made from the facts, on a case by case basis.

C. Applying general Title VII principles, an employer, employment agency, joint apprenticeship committee, or labor organization (hereinafter collectively referred to as "employer") is responsible for its acts and those of its agents and supervisory employees with respect to sexual harassment regardless of whether the specific acts complained of were authorized or even forbidden by the employer and regardless of whether the employer knew or should have known of their occurrence. The commission will examine the circumstances of the particular employment relationship and the job functions performed by the individual in determining whether an individual acts in either a supervisory or agency capacity.

D. With respect to conduct between fellow employees, an employer is responsible for acts of sexual harassment in the workplace where the employer (or its agents or supervisory employees) knows or should have known of the conduct, unless it can show that it took immediate and appropriate corrective action.

E. An employer may also be responsible for the acts of non-employees, with respect to sexual harassment of employees in the workplace, where the employer (or its agents or supervisory employees) knows or should have known of the conduct and fails to take immediate and appropriate corrective action. In reviewing these cases the commission will consider the extent of the employer's control and any other legal responsibility which the employer may have with respect to the conduct of such non-employees.

F. Prevention is the best tool for the elimination of sexual harassment. An employer should take all steps necessary to prevent sexual harassment from occurring, such as affirmatively raising the subject, expressing strong disapproval, developing appropriate sanctions, informing employees of their right to raise and how to raise the issue of harassment under Title VII, and developing methods to sensitize all concerned.

G. Other related practices: Where employment opportunities or benefits are granted because of an individual's submission to the employer's sexual advances or requests for sexual favors, the employer may be held liable for unlawful sex discrimination against other persons who were qualified for but denied employment opportunity or benefit.

Appendix B

Model Harassment Policy

This company, [name], does not and will not tolerate harassment of our employees. The term "harassment" includes, but is not limited to, slurs, jokes, and other verbal, graphic, or physical conduct relating to an individual's race, color, sex, religion, national origin, citizenship, age, or handicap. "Harassment" also includes sexual advances, requests for sexual favors, unwelcome or offensive touching, and other verbal, graphic, or physical conduct of a sexual nature.

VIOLATION OF THIS POLICY WILL SUBJECT AN EMPLOYEE TO DISCIPLINARY ACTION, UP TO AND INCLUDING IMMEDIATE DISCHARGE.

If you feel that you are being harassed in any way by another staff member or any other person in the workplace, you should make your feelings known to your supervisor immediately. The matter will be thoroughly investigated and, where appropriate, disciplinary action will be taken. If you do not feel that you can discuss the matter with your supervisor or if you are not satisfied with the way your complaint has been handled, please contact the Office Manager. You will not be penalized in any way for reporting such conduct concerning yourself or another person. Do not assume that the company is aware of your problem. It is your responsibility to bring your complaints and concerns to our attention so that we can help resolve them.

Illustrative Cases ————————————————————————

Ali v. Southeast Neighborhood House

519 F.Supp. 489 (D.C. 1981)

Memorandum Opinion

JOYCE HENS GREEN, District Judge.

Plaintiff, Peb Ali ("Ali"), brings this action against the defendant, the Southeast Neighborhood House ("SENH"), alleging a violation of Title VII of the Civil Rights Act of 1964, as amended, 42 U.S.C. § 2000e *et seq.* on the ground that the defendant discriminated against him on the basis of his religion. At the outset, it should be noted that the sincerity with which the plaintiff, a Black Muslim, holds his religious beliefs is undisputed.

Sincere beliefs, meaningful to the believer, need not be confined in either source or content to traditional or parochial concepts of religion. *Welsh v. United States*, 398 U.S. 333, 90 S.Ct. 1792, 26 L.Ed.2d 308 (1970). *See also, United States v. Seeger*, 380 U.S. 163, 85 S.Ct. 850, 13 L.Ed.2d 733 (1965) for the definition of "religious training and belief" as applied to a conscientious objector claim, which definition is no less appropriate here. The Court noted the "vast panoply of beliefs" prevalent in our country and interpreted "the meaning of religious training and belief so as to embrace *all* religions." *Id.*, at 165, 85 S.Ct. at 853 (emphasis added). "Intensely personal" convictions which some may find "incomprehensible" or "incorrect" fit within the framework of "religious belief." As the Court has said,

> Most of the great religions of today and of the past have embodied the idea of a Supreme Being or a Supreme Reality—a God—who communicates to man in some way a consciousness of what is right and should be done, of what is wrong and therefore should be shunned.

Welsh, supra, 398 U.S. at 340, 90 S.Ct. at 1796.

Under *Welsh-Seeger* then, as in this case, when logically we apply its rationale to Title VII cases also, the belief is protected if the belief sought to be protected is "religious" in that person's own scheme of things and if it is sincerely held.

The following evidence, stated herein as findings of facts and conclusions of law, developed through trial.

Plaintiff began his employment at the SENH on April 9, 1979, after discussing that possibility with Calvin Lockridge, a member of its Board of Directors ("Board"). After an interview by a panel of the Board, Ali was recommended to the Executive Director of SENH, Laplois Ashford, for the position of Associate Director, Community and Human Resources Division ("CHRD"), which plaintiff accepted. This position required Ali to exercise skills in management and administration over a staff of approximately twenty to twenty-three employees, and to preside over the role of SENH in various areas of the city, including housing and community organization. When plaintiff assumed his position, the Executive Director was aware of his religious beliefs and in fact had met him when both men lived and worked in Chicago, Illinois in the early 1970's.

Soon after he began his employment, Ali experienced difficulties because he felt that certain duties he was required to undertake conflicted with his religious beliefs. Some examination of the circumstances surrounding those matters warrant mention, as they indicate the nature of plaintiff's beliefs as well as his perception of his position, and the interrelationship of his religion, as he saw it, and his employment requirements. The examples are merely illustrative and not intended to be inclusive of all the problems these parties encountered.

One incident concerned a time sheet submitted by a Meredith Gilbert, who commenced employment at SENH as a consultant in the housing area on March 12, 1979 and later, in early May, became Housing Coordinator. When Gilbert submitted his time sheet for hours worked, plaintiff refused to sign the document because he had not seen Gilbert on the premises and therefore thought that he would be acting dishonestly if he verified Gilbert's hours in the absence of this personal observation. Although Ali testified that his own investigation revealed that Gilbert's work was unrelated to SENH, that it involved a political campaign and not work in the CHRD, and that he reluctantly signed the time sheet only because of Ashford's direction, the credible evidence verified Gilbert's employment as a consultant. The Executive Director testified that he did not order Ali to sign the time sheet, that he could have signed the attendance record without Ali's approval, and that, pursuant to his ultimate authority to resolve all such disputes, Ashford decided that the time should be credited. As further evidence made clear, however, this aspect of plaintiff's complaint had little to do with the charge of religious discrimination.

Another series of events concerned the role of Ms. Peggy Jackson and harbored a complicated scenario that began when all employees were informed in early February, 1979, as a result of the Board of Directors' decision, that a major reorganization of SENH was to be undertaken to avert imminent financial crisis. To reformulate the House's mission and to give the Board complete flexibility in deciding upon personnel to fill the staff positions in a differently structured organization, the Board agreed to send each employee a notice of termination and ask that the employee submit a new application for work at SENH. A notice was thereupon given to all employees at a staff meeting in February, with an effective date of February 26, 1979 for termination of employment. The Executive Director testified that there were a number of unqualified people in positions of responsibility at SENH, and Jackson was one of those.

At the time of the notice of terminations, Jackson was a Junior Housing Advisor, having worked at SENH for thirteen years. Plaintiff contends that even before he acquired employment here, and after, he was told to discharge Jackson but was given no work-related reasons for such action. Once again he conducted his own investigation which, he testified, produced evidence that Jackson had only raised the ire of the Executive Director due to a vote she cast in what Ali felt was an unrelated matter involving another community organization. To fire an employee for what Ali thought was a personal reason was violative of his Muslim beliefs and he, therefore, rejected Ashford's decision (as well as the Board's) to terminate Jackson from SENH employment.

Yet plaintiff's testimony is outweighed by the testimony of Ms. Jackson herself. She indicated, and facts fortified this conclusion, that the Board meeting at which she cast the criticized vote was indeed related to her work at SENH. Although Ashford had vested Jackson with what she characterized as "independent discretion," the entire matter was not a personal or political dispute between the Executive Director and her. Plaintiff's individual investigation had again produced incorrect results, yet his refusal to discharge Jackson was premised on those results.

Additionally, the evidence reflected that although Jackson was discharged from her position as Junior Housing Advisor, along with each and every other employee at SENH, she did have substantial problems performing effectively in her position. As the controversy about Jackson increased, she submitted her resignation in late April, effective May 31, 1979. A pervasive problem persisted in plaintiff's Department because the Executive Director had hired Meredith Gilbert to replace Jackson, yet Ms. Jackson was determined to remain in her old office and continue with her duties to the point her resignation took effect. The conflict between Jackson and Gilbert produced considerable tension in the CHRD, and Ali's failure to manage the Department during this dispute, and resolve the difficulties, was one of the significant causes of his discharge. He adamantly refused to follow Ashford's direction that Jackson be fired, and as a compromise, made her a consultant. This solution satisfied neither Jackson nor Gilbert and the matter eventually subsumed most normal responsibilities in CHRD to the point where nothing was being accomplished.

Apart from plaintiff's difficulties over Gilbert's timecard and the continued employment of Jackson, he alleged that his discharge was motivated by the Executive Director's discriminatory attitude towards Ali's Muslim beliefs. A chronology of the final days of Ali's employment at SENH will clarify the evidence concerning this serious complaint.

A meeting was held May 23 at Lockridge's house between Ashford, Gilbert, Ali and Lockridge to attempt to resolve the differences between Ali and Gilbert. While Ashford concurred that Gilbert was a difficult person, he was not the only problem Ali encountered, without resolution, during his brief employment. This session was not effective. On May 25, Ashford initiated another meeting with Ali to discuss procedures in his Department which conference, lasting almost ninety minutes, produced a list of ten specific steps that Ashford directed Ali to undertake to improve the management of CHRD. This list was reduced to writing May 29 in a memorandum from Ashford to Ali, Defendant's Exhibit 6.

Ali was ill and did not appear at work from May 28-30. Because operations at CHRD had reached a standstill, the Executive Director met with that Department's staff on May 30, in Ali's absence. After this meeting, where Ashford was confronted with representations of Ali's managerial incompetence, he deliberated whether to discharge Ali from his position. He concluded then, and later reinforced that determination, that Ali had not implemented any of the procedures discussed and agreed upon at the May 25th meeting: Ali and Gilbert had not reported *together* to Ashford and it was Ali's responsibility to arrange this, Ali had not called a staff meeting to outline the duties of each coordinator, Ali had not assumed control of supportive service immediately, relieving Gilbert of these responsibilities, and he had not instituted other specified actions aimed at smoothing operations at CHRD. It should be noted that at the May 25 meeting, Ashford had indicated that he would monitor the progress of Ali's Department for ten days, but in the last week of May, Ashford determined that prompter action was necessary for the functioning of the Department.

On May 31, Ali wrote to the Executive Director and mailed to his home address a lengthy personal letter describing his Muslim practices and beliefs and demonstrating his problems at SENH. (Plaintiff's Exh. 7). The plaintiff declared,

> I did not come to Southeast Neighborhood House under any false pretence (sic), but as a Muslim dedicated to a cause. If you [Ashford] are as alert about the

situations of the world as you seem to be about procedures then you should recognize what I am speaking of, if not you're the one that is in trouble.

Additionally, Ali wrote, "If I do not work toward the goals as outlined by the Holy Qur-an based on the knowledge given to me then I will be destroyed. I have come too far to allow this to happen." In this letter the plaintiff complained that he had not been given all of the facts needed to lay out proper work responsibilities, and noted a number of special items, such as a debt owed to a local church, about which he demanded to be consulted. The letter begins and ends with quotations from the Holy Quran, and is replete with references to plaintiff's religious ideals.

Ashford received this letter on June 1 when he arrived at his home at about 6:30 P.M. He viewed the letter as an expression of "some deep internal turmoil" in Ali and found it difficult to comprehend. He was upset further by the fact that some of Ali's references to aspects of work at SENH, for example the debt owed to the church, were totally outside of his field of responsibility, and that Ali, as the manager, did not seem to be coping with the problems then existing in the CHRD and which were Ali's responsibility. He interpreted the letter as "an exercise in catharsis," whereby Ali vented his frustrations on Ashford.

On Monday June 4, 1979, Ashford sent Ali a memorandum (Plaintiff's Exh. 9) discharging him from employment with SENH. Ashford informed Ali that his

> administrative actions over the past two weeks and the problems which resulted therefrom have led me to conclude that you are either unwilling or incapable of separating personal relationships from professional procedures which are a must if subordinates are to have a clear understanding of what is expected of them in short term and long range programmatic operations.
>
> ...you have failed to provide decisive directions to your staff, despite agreeing to do so immediately following our conference on May 25...as spelled out in the memorandum of May 29... [which was a followup to the May 23 memorandum.]

Ashford "fully concur[red]" that Ali "should not be expected to undertake procedures which are foreign to [his] basic nature, beliefs, and commitments," and expressed his hope that Ali "can and will be able to find another organization through which [he] can practice...Muslim and humanist beliefs."

This memorandum, which Ali received on June 5, was followed on June 6 by another communication from Ashford to Ali outlining in detail his reasons for discharging the plaintiff. Ashford testified that this was a common practice because he thought it only fair to give specific and detailed reasons for dismissing an employee. The reasons included "refusal, unwillingness, and/or negligence" in following instructions discussed at the May 25 meeting, citing examples of noncompliance. The memo also indicated that Ali "interject[s his] religious beliefs in every issue or problem we discuss and the results have been a lack of clear and decisive attention to managerial details. Even more distressing," Ashford said, were Ali's "attempts to impose [his] beliefs and managerial operating style on me and others." Declaring that the "bottom line is whether or not a particular staff member is able to satisfactorily execute the duties and responsibilities of his position," Ashford described in specific detail his perception of plaintiff's inabilities. This description was buttressed at trial by the Executive Director's credible testimony.

On June 7, Ali wrote Ashford requesting reconsideration of the decision indicating that Ashford had violated the law by firing him on the basis of his religious beliefs. Ashford responded that same day that he would not reconsider and that he had not violated any law. Pursuant to appropriate SENH procedures, Ali appealed the Executive Director's decision and a hearing was held with three Board members: Lockridge, James Brown and JePhunneh Lawrence. Voting 2-1, Lawrence dissenting, the panel affirmed the Executive Director's decision to discharge Ali. While Ali testified that he had heard at this meeting that Ashford stated he had discharged Ali because of his religion, the record is devoid of evidence, despite opportunity to obtain it, that Ashford made any such statement. A recording of the meeting was stolen along with the tape recorder and numerous other items in a burglary at SENH in 1980. Nonetheless, Ashford denied making any such statement, and Lawrence was not even examined on the issue. When plaintiff's counsel attempted to cross-examine Lockridge about the statement, the Court was required to sustain defendant's technical objections because the question was clearly beyond scope of the direct examination, but the Court made a direct suggestion to the plaintiff that he use the opportunity to call Lockridge in rebuttal for exploration of this matter. Plaintiff did not do so.

Plaintiff filed a complaint with the District of Columbia Office of Human Rights, which after a conference with the parties, dismissed the matter finding "no probable cause...for crediting the complaint." Plaintiff then petitioned the Equal Employment Opportunity Commission ("EEOC") to investigate his complaint and on May 1, 1980, the EEOC determined that there was "no reasonable cause to believe the charge," but pursuant to regulations and statute, forwarded a "right to sue" letter to Ali on September 29, 1980. Plaintiff instituted this action on December 29, 1980.

Title VII prohibits discrimination on the basis of one's religion. 42 U.S.C. § 2000e-2(a) makes it unlawful for an employer "(1) to fail or refuse to hire or to discharge any individual, or otherwise to discriminate against any individual...because of such individual's religion." The 1972 amendments to Title VII provided a definition of religion:

> The term "religion" includes all aspects of religious observance and practice, as well as belief, unless an employer demonstrates that he is unable to reasonably accommodate to an employee's or prospective employee's religious observance or practice without undue hardship on the conduct of the employer's business.

42 U.S.C. 20003(j).

The Supreme Court has determined that:

> The intent and effect of this definition was to make it an unlawful employment practice under § 703(a)(1) for an employer not to make reasonable accommodations, short of undue hardship, for the religious practices of his employees and prospective employees. But...the statute provides no guidance for determining the degree of accommodation that is required of an employer.

Trans World Airlines v. *Hardison* 432 U.S. 63 at 74, 97 S.Ct. 2264 at 2271, 53 L.Ed.2d 113 (1977).

Despite this lack of direction, some guideposts have been constructed by courts addressing the duty to make a reasonable accommodation. For example, in *Haring* v. *Blumenthal*, 471 F.Supp. 1172 (D.D.C.1979), District Judge Harold H. Greene explored the "critical issue [of] whether the level of hardship must be measured by the accommodation of the one employee seeking relief or by the precedent-setting effect of the grant of such relief to him and the conceivable actions of others." *Id.* at 1181. He concluded that to satisfy the statutory requirement, the employer must show *present* undue hardship, as distinguished from anticipated or multiplied hardship.

> Unless the statutory mandate is to be rendered meaningless, it must be held to provide that until facts or circumstances arise from which it may be concluded that there can no longer be an accommodation without due hardship, the employee's religious practices are required to be tolerated.

Id. at 1182.

Additionally, some duty is placed on the employee to reach a reasonable accommodation with his employer once the employer has attempted to accommodate to the individual's beliefs. In *Yott* v. *North America Rockwell Corp.*, 602 F.2d 904 (9th Cir. 1979), *cert. denied*, 445 U.S. 928, 100 S.Ct. 1316, 63 L.Ed.2d 761, the Court noted that when an employer makes a reasonable accommodation, rejection by the employee might constitute grounds for the employer to demonstrate undue hardship by further accommodation. Quoting a decision by the 8th Circuit, *Chrysler Corp.* v. *Mann*, 561 F.2d 1282 at 1285 (8th Cir. 1977), the Court declared:

> An employee cannot shirk his duties to try to accommodate himself or to cooperate with his employer in reaching an accommodation by a mere recalcitrant citation of religious precepts. Nor can he thereby shift all responsibility for accommodation to his employer. Where an employee refuses to attempt to accommodate his own beliefs or to cooperate with his employer's attempt to reach a reasonable accommodation, he may render an accommodation impossible.

The questions [sic] concerning plaintiff's discharge is whether it was predicated on Ashford's discrimination against Ali's Muslim beliefs or on Ali's failure to execute his work responsibilities satisfactorily. The overwhelming weight of the evidence is that Ali was sorely ineffective as a manager and could not competently perform his duties as described in his position description and prescribed by the Executive Director. It was Ali himself who continuously injected his philosophic and moralistic principles into the day-to-day operation of his Department, invoking the name of religion when challenged on his management of that Department and his failure to obey his employer's clear and insistent directives. The defendant, through its Executive Director, attempted to ignore the allusions to the Quran, and sought to determine the dilemmas and disputes then present in plaintiff's Department on their factual bases, concluding, wholly apart from any perception of the plaintiff's values, that Ali was simply not qualified as a manager for this important Department in SENH.

Ali's testimony at trial provides the strongest evidence that he could not perform his tasks as required and could only do so in the future on *his* conditions. He stated,

> I intended to do the things that were in my job description, and the things outlined for me to do as it relates to the Holy Quran, helping remake the world, changing images, changing other things like people's minds and their relationship to each other.

The evidence further demonstrated that Ali did not or could not perform the tasks listed on his job description, Plaintiff's Exh. 1. It also showed that while plaintiff's position at SENH was, in part, to improve SENH's community image, it was not to "remake the world" or to "change people's minds." Important as these matters were to Ali personally, and appropriate as they might seem to be in certain settings to anyone, these ideals collided with his employment's functional necessity to react to SENH business and decisional crises then and there, by directive or compromise. Additionally, Ali's May 30 letter demonstrates a disregard for express, detailed procedures to aid in managerial operations, finding the "situation of the world" more important to SENH than office procedures. The plain fact is, as Ashford's most persuasive testimony reflected, that Ali was incapable of following directions aimed at streamlining his Departmental operations, that he was unable to resolve the dispute between Gilbert and Jackson that had paralyzed work in CHRD, and that he incorrectly interpreted and responded to his job responsibilities, believing he had been hired exclusively (or chiefly) to improve the image of SENH, rather than manage his Department. Lockridge and Ashford both stressed the importance of good management in overseeing CHRD, Lockridge stating it was the most important quality he looked for in an applicant. Ashford, recalling most of the procedures he directed be implemented on May 25, was clear that his directions had persistently been ignored and that he therefore was justified in discharge of Ali. While plaintiff alleged that Gilbert was the chief problem at SENH, and Ashford testified that Gilbert was a significant problem, the Executive Director was exercising his administrative judgment in concluding that "a good manager could have handled Mr. Gilbert." Taking into account the credibility of the witnesses and the demonstrated situation at SENH, it cannot be said that Ashford's attitude was anything but patient and reasonable.

Ashford's testimony and the documentary evidence submitted supports the conclusion that Ashford was confronted with insurmountable obstacles as he struggled to work with Ali's petulance and resistance. There could be no accommodation. This is not a case where an employee wishes to take a Friday or a Saturday off work to practice his Sabbath, and where the question is presented as to what steps the employer could take to accommodate that scheduling. Difficult as that might be, it is certainly possible, at least in many instances. Rather, our action is one where Ali would impose his personal perception, from conscience, religion, or philosophy, on each and every day-to-day aspect of his employment while ignoring the basic responsibilities of that position. Present at SENH for only eight weeks, through the crescendo of controversy, Ali sought resolution solely by means of *his* ideals: the issue of Gilbert's timecard, the role of Peggy Jackson, the establishment of proper reporting procedures, and the interpersonal incidents within his Department were never answered by effective management. While Ashford had considered other positions at SENH where Ali might be more satisfied, it was determined that none such existed. Ashford testified, and the Court must concur that the evidence so presented, that nothing short of turning over the operation of SENH could have accommodated Ali's beliefs.

Here, Ali was able to establish only that his religious belief was sincerely held, that he was employed with the employer's knowledge that he was a Muslim, that he was formally discharged after he wrote a critical letter to his employer which, in part, described his religion and its concepts, and that he thought (erroneously) that someone mentioned he was discharged because of his religion. As recently as March 4, 1981, the Supreme Court, in a termination of employment case predicated on gender discrimination in violation of Title VII, *Texas Department of Community Affairs* v. *Burdine*, 450 U.S. 248, at –, 101 S.Ct. 1089, 1093-1095, 67 L.Ed.2d 207 (1981), resolved the conflicts in the Circuits concerning the burden of proof borne by a defendant. The Court outlined the basic allocations of burdens and order of presentation of proof presented in Title VII cases alleging discrimination, *McDonnell Douglas Corp.* v. *Green*, 411 U.S. 792, 93 S.Ct. 1817, 36 L.Ed.2d 668 (1973): 1) the plaintiff bears the burden of proving by a preponderance of the evidence a prima facie case of discrimination; 2) if the plaintiff succeeds in proving the prima facie case, the burden shifts to the defendant "to articulate some legitimate, nondiscriminatory reason for the employee's rejection." *Id.*, at 802, 93 S.Ct. at 1824; 3) should the defendant carry this burden, the plaintiff is given the opportunity to prove by a preponderance of the evidence that the legitimate reasons offered by the defendant were not its true reasons but were a pretext for discrimination. *Id.*, at 804, 93 S.Ct. at 1825.

The burden of persuasion "never shifts" and the ultimate burden of persuading the court that the defendant intentionally discriminated against the plaintiff remains with the plaintiff at all times. *See Board of Trustees of Keene State College* v. *Sweeney*, 439 U.S. 24, 25, n. 2, 99 S.Ct. 295, 296, n. 2, 58, L.Ed.2d 216 (1979); *Burdine, supra*, 450 U.S. at 253, 101 S.Ct. at 1098.

We strain to consider in light of his evidence, that the plaintiff, Ali, was even able to establish a prima facie case of discrimination, but that conclusion requires the burden to shift to the defendant to rebut this presumption of discrimination by simply explaining what he has done, *Sweeney*, 439 U.S., at 25, n. 2, 99 S.Ct. at 296, n. 2 by producing clear, admissible evidence that Ali was terminated for a legitimate, nondiscriminatory reason sufficient to allow the trier of fact to rationally conclude that the employment action had not been motivated by discrimination, thereby "rais[ing] a genuine issue of fact as to whether it discriminated against the plaintiff." *Id.* 450 U.S. at 254, 101 S.Ct. at 1094. If the defendant succeeds in carrying this burden, the prima facie presumption raised by plaintiff's initial burden is rebutted. The plaintiff is then given the opportunity to show that the defendant's reasons were not the reasons for the employment decision—i.e., were pretextual. This might be done "either directly by persuading the court that a discriminatory reason more likely motivated the employer or indirectly by showing that the employer's proffered explanation is unworthy of credence." *Id.* 450 U.S. at 256, 101 S.Ct. at 1095.

In this litigation, the defendant demonstrated through clear, specific and admissible evidence the reasons for Ali's termination of employment, reasons which were unquestionably legitimate and nondiscriminatory. While Ali was intelligent, articulate and capable for some activity, he was unsuited for the position he served at SENH due to his inability to function as the essential manager and his warrantless refusal to follow through with acknowledged, direct orders of his superior. It was Ali, not his employer, who viewed the plaintiff's problems at SENH from a religious perspective only. It was Ali who articulated his religion when confronted with a task at his workplace, and then declined in the name of that religion to perform that task. It was Ali who conducted unnecessary independent investigations (often with incorrect conclusions due to a failure of facts), then criticizing and rejecting his employer's commands by invocation of conscience and religion. All the while Ali superimposed his judgment for the employer's, accepting that as the only correct basis upon which he could or would perform his employment.

The overriding concern of Congress in enacting Title VII was the elimination of discrimination in employment. Employees are sheltered from bigotry and discrimination emanating from the employer's actions towards that employee's most personal, most cherished religious beliefs and values. These considerations should be viewed by a Court with special sensitivity to their meaningful uniqueness.

Ali's religious beliefs enveloped every fact of his life, personal or business. It must be evident that in SENH's employment no "reasonable accommodation," indeed, no accommodation at all, could make way for those religious beliefs as Ali envisioned them: "helping remake the world, changing...people's minds and their relationship to each other." Only a complete reversal of the employer-employee roles, with Ali in the former, rather than the latter, might provide the plaintiff the absolute power he requires to satisfy those beliefs.

Accommodation is not abdication. Title VII cannot and will not be so construed.

Accordingly, judgment will be entered in favor of the defendant, Southeast Neighborhood House, and against the plaintiff, Peb Ali, with costs assessed against the plaintiff, each party to bear its own counsel fees.

EEOC v. Sage Realty Corp.

87 F.R.D. 365 (S.D.N.Y. 1980), *later proceeding*, 507 F.Supp.599 (S.D.N.Y. 1981), *later proceeding*, 521 F.Supp. 263 (S.D.N.Y. 1981)

Margaret Hasselman was employed as a lobby attendant in an office building located at 711 Third Avenue in Manhattan, from February, 1973 until June, 1976. The building was managed by defendant Sage. Ms. Hasselman was hired by Sage in January, 1973, and placed on the payroll of National Cleaning Contractors ("National") until November 1, 1975, when she was placed on the payroll of defendant Monahan Cleaners. Defendant Sage trained Ms. Hasselman, established her job duties, and supervised her day-to-day work. In addition, Sage selected the uniforms for the lobby attendants, issuing new uniforms every six months.

On June 28, 1976, Ms. Hasselman filed a charge with the EEOC's New York District Office, alleging that defendants Sage and Monahan Cleaners discriminated against her because of sex in violation of Title VII of the Civil Rights Act of 1964, as amended, 42 U.S.C. §§ 2000e *et seq.* ("Title VII"). The EEOC, after investigation, found reasonable cause to believe that defendants Sage and Monahan Cleaners had engaged in unlawful employment practices in violation of Title VII and, on September 29, 1978, commenced this action.

Plaintiff Hasselman moved to intervene as a party plaintiff on October 30, 1978. On November 27, 1978, the Court granted her motion and on January 10, 1979 she filed her complaint. The complaint alleges that defendants maintained a continuous policy of sex discrimination from Ms. Hasselman's hiring in January, 1973 until June, 1976, when the defendants allegedly required her to wear a revealing and provocative uniform which subjected her to repeated and abusive sexual harassment. The uniform was known as the Bicentennial uniform. The complaint further asserts that when Ms. Hasselman refused to wear it she was fired.

Defendants argue that there are no material facts in dispute and that they are entitled to summary judgment as a matter of law. They assert that requiring Ms. Hasselman to wear the Bicentennial uniform did not offend propriety or constitute discrimination based on sex within the meaning of Title VII....

Plaintiffs, in turn, assert that inasmuch as there are material facts in dispute with respect to whether the defendants required plaintiff to wear a provocative and revealing uniform which subjected her to sexual harassment in violation of Title VII, defendants' motion for summary judgment must be denied....

Summary judgment is to be granted only when "there is no genuine issue as to any material fact and...the moving party is entitled to judgment as a matter of law...." In evaluating such a motion the Court cannot try issues of fact, it can only determine whether there are issues to be tried after resolving all ambiguities and drawing all reasonable inferences in favor of the non-movant.... Moreover, the burden is on the moving party to establish that no relevant facts are in dispute. Applying this standard to the case at bar, the Court concludes that summary judgment is inappropriate. [citations omitted]

Section 703(a) of Title VII provides:

> It shall be an unlawful employment practice for an employer—
>
> (1) to fail or refuse to hire or to discharge any individual, or otherwise to discriminate against any individual with respect to his compensation, terms, conditions, or privileges of employment, because of such individual's race, color, religion, sex, or national origin; or
>
> (2) to limit, segregate, or classify his employees or applicants for employment in any way which would deprive or tend to deprive any individual of employment opportunities or otherwise adversely affect his status as an employee, because of such individual's race, color, religion, sex or national origin.
>
> 42 U.S.C. § 2000e-2(a).

This prohibition was "intended to strike at the entire spectrum of disparate treatment of men and women resulting from sex stereotypes." [citation omitted] Thus, no matter what form the sex-based or sex-stereotyped decision may take, when it operates as an impediment to employment opportunity for women, Title VII requires its elimination.

Plaintiffs contend, *inter alia*, that defendants discriminated against Margaret Hasselman on the basis of sex by requiring her to wear the Bicentennial uniform and by discharging her when she refused to wear it. They assert that this uniform was revealing and provocative and, on the two days on which she wore it, subjected her to repeated sexual harassment. Plaintiffs also argue that the uniform requirement was sex-based and that, but for the fact that Ms. Hasselman is a woman, she would not have been required to expose her body and endure the public's sexual harassment as a term and condition of her employment. Finally, they contend that the uniform requirement bore no relation to her job duties but was simply an onerous and irrational condition imposed upon her employment which constituted sex discrimination in violation of Title VII.

In order to state a claim under section 703, 42 U.S.C. § 2000e-2(a), a plaintiff must establish that a term or condition of employment had been imposed and that this term or condition was imposed by the employer on the basis of sex. [citations omitted] Plaintiffs here have either established the elements required to make a *prima facie* showing of a section 703 violation or, at a minimum, raised factual questions with respect to these elements which preclude summary judgment.

The complaint alleges that defendants' uniform requirement is sex-based; affidavits and depositions have been submitted by plaintiffs to support this claim. A disputed issue of fact, however, apparently exists as to whether the

Bicentennial uniform was short and revealing on Ms. Hasselman. Plaintiffs contend that photographic exhibits submitted in opposition to defendants' motion fairly and accurately depict the manner in which the uniform looked on Ms. Hasselman. Defendants apparently dispute the accuracy of the photographs. An additional question of fact exists as to whether a new and larger uniform was made for Ms. Hasselman; plaintiffs dispute defendants' assertion that such a uniform was made. There is apparently no dispute, however, that Ms. Hasselman was sexually harassed when she wore the Bicentennial uniform, that no male personnel were hired for lobby attendant positions after 1975 and that no male personnel were ever required to wear revealing or provocative uniforms at any time. Thus, there would, at the very least, appear to be disputed issues of fact with respect to the first element of plaintiffs' claim.

With respect to the second of the three required elements for stating a *prima facie* case of sex discrimination, that the condition be imposed by the employer, there apparently is no dispute that defendant Sage selected the Bicentennial uniform and that both Sage and Monahan Cleaners insisted that Ms. Hasselman wear the uniform. It is also undisputed that both defendants continued to insist that she wear the uniform, even after they were told about the harassment that she was subjected to when she wore it. The facts underlying the question of defendant Sage's precise degree of control over Ms. Hasselman's employment, however, are in dispute.

The facts relevant to the final element required to demonstrate a *prima facie* case of sex discrimination, that the conduct at issue affect the terms and conditions of the plaintiff's employment, are also at least partly disputed. Plaintiff Hasselman contends that she was discharged when she refused to wear the Bicentennial uniform; defendants assert that she quit. In any event, even if plaintiff Hasselman were not discharged, the uniform requirement, according to plaintiffs' allegations, had an adverse, discriminatory impact on the terms and conditions of Hasselman's employment in violation of Title VII.

In sum, inasmuch as there are factual issues in dispute with respect to the elements of plaintiffs' *prima facie* showing of sex discrimination and those facts not in dispute would tend to support plaintiffs' claim, defendants' motion for summary judgment must be denied.

The Court finds unavailing defendants' reliance on a number of "grooming" cases for the principle that a uniform requirement does not involve discrimination in employment on the basis of sex. These cases merely hold that nothing in Title VII prohibits an employer from making reasonable employment decisions based on factors such as grooming and dress. [citations omitted] None of these cases supports the proposition that an employer has the unfettered discretion under Title VII to require its employees to wear *any* type of uniform the employer chooses, including uniforms which may be characterized as revealing and sexually provocative....

Huebschen v. Department of Health and Social Services

547 F.Supp. 1168 (W.D. Wis. 1982)

SHABAZ, District Judge.

Plaintiff David Huebschen has brought this action under Title VII, Civil Rights Act of 1964, 42 U.S.C. § 2000e *et seq.* and under 42 U.S.C. § 1983, requesting damages and equitable relief for alleged sexual harassment. Jurisdiction is based on 42 U.S.C. § 2000e-5 and 28 U.S.C. § 1848.

In his complaint, plaintiff alleged that he was an employee of the State of Wisconsin; that while serving as a probationary supervisor in the Bureau of Social Security and Disability Insurance (BSSDI), his immediate supervisor was defendant Jacquelyn Rader (denominated in the caption as Jane Roe); that Ms. Rader terminated his probation, causing his demotion to a non-supervisory position, because he refused to continue a sexual relationship with her.

Plaintiff further alleged that defendant Bernard Stumbras, Ms. Rader's supervisor, knew about the harassment, but upheld the termination. Plaintiff claimed that these acts denied his right under Title VII to be free from discrimination and denied him due process of the law. The due process claim was dismissed prior to trial.

After a four-day trial on liability, the jury returned a verdict in favor of plaintiff and against defendants Rader and Stumbras by its answers to the following special verdict questions:

> In the event you determine that defendant Rader made demands of a sexual nature on plaintiff, was plaintiff's refusal to submit to these demands a motivating factor in the decision to terminate plaintiff's probation?
>
> Answer: Yes.
>
> Would plaintiff's probation have been terminated in the absence of the sexual harassment?
>
> Answer: No.

In addition, the jury found both Ms. Rader and Mr. Stumbras personally and directly responsible for the impermissible termination, and that these defendants were not acting in good faith performance of their duties.

After two more days of testimony in the damage phase of the trial, the jury returned a verdict assessing the following punitive and compensatory damages:

Bernard Stumbras:	$45,000 compensatory damages
	$36,900 punitive damages
Jacquelyn Rader:	$90,000 compensatory damages
	$24,600 punitive damages

The Court approved the form of the judgment on July 27, 1982.[4] *See* Rule 58(2), Federal Rules of Civil Procedure. Defendants accepted the jury verdict as to the Title VII claim as well, stipulating that plaintiff be reinstated at an equivalent position and be awarded back pay of $7,913.64. The Court also awarded plaintiff $21,726 in attorney's fees.

Defendants have now filed a number of post-verdict motions and plaintiff seeks increased attorney's fees and costs.

I.   MOTION FOR JUDGMENT NOTWITHSTANDING THE VERDICT

[Footnotes 1-3 omitted]

[4] The parties stipulated that the judgment against defendants Rader and Stumras be entered in their official capacities.

Defendants have filed a motion for judgment notwithstanding the verdict, alleging that: 1) compensatory and punitive damages are not available in this case; 2) the verdict against defendant Rader is not supported by the evidence; and 3) the verdict against defendant Stumbras is not supported by the evidence. For the reasons that follow, the motion is granted as to defendant Stumbras and, in all other respects, denied.

* * *

B. *Verdict as to Ms. Rader's Liability*

Defendants next argue that the verdict as to Ms. Rader's liability is unsupported by the evidence.

In deciding whether a verdict is supported by the evidence, the Court must apply the following standard:

> [T]he motion should be denied where the evidence, along with all inferences to be reasonably drawn therefrom, when viewed in the light most favorable to the party opposing such motion, is such that reasonable men in a fair and impartial exercise of their judgment may reach different conclusions. [citations omitted]

Judged by the [above] standard, the evidence supports the jury's verdict as to Ms. Rader's liability. The jurors were entitled to believe plaintiff's testimony: that he and Ms. Rader had a consensual sexual relationship during Fall, 1979; that plaintiff, on November 12, 1979, told Ms. Rader that the sexual relationship should end; that one week later, despite her previous favorable evaluations of plaintiff's work, Ms. Rader informed plaintiff that she was attempting to extend his probation and wished to delay a final determination of whether he should be granted permanent supervisory status; and, that when she failed to receive approval for such an extension, Ms. Rader terminated plaintiff's probation in mid-December.

Defendants insist, however, that plaintiff offered no testimony of any specific demands for sexual activity subsequent to November 12, 1979, the time at which, according to plaintiff, the relationship ceased to be consensual. This contention must fail for a basic reason. Plaintiff did not need to prove that any specific and overt demands were made. Instead, he had to demonstrate that his probation was terminated for a discriminatory, and therefore impermissible, reason.[10] [citations omitted]

In other words, he had to show that his refusal to continue a sexual relationship motivated the decision to demote him.

Plaintiff sufficiently carried his burden by the following testimony:

[Footnotes 5-9 omitted]

[10] Defendants do not challenge plaintiff's implicit assumption that sexual harassment is sex-based discrimination within the ambit of Title VII. The Court therefore will not face the issue, but notes that this assumption is a matter of some dispute. Recent cases, however, support the view that sexual harassment is sexual discrimination. *Bundy* v. *Jackson,* 641 F.2d 934 (D.C.Cir. 1981); *Tomkins* v. *Public Service Electric,* 568 F.2d 1044 (3rd Cir. 1977). *See also Munford* v. *James T. Barnes & Co.,* 441 F.Supp. 459 (E.D.Mich. 1977) for an overview of earlier cases facing this issue.

MR. FOX: What occurred then? [shortly after December 6, 1979 and subsequent to his termination notice]

MR. HUEBSCHEN: I was still in my office since I was still officially at least a supervisor and I received a phone call and was told to come to her [Ms. Rader's] office right away.

MR. FOX: And why were you called to her office?

MR. HUEBSCHEN: When I came there she said that she wanted to warn me that I had better never discuss the true circumstances of my demotion and that if I did she would make sure that I lost all of my friends and everybody knew that I was a chronic liar.

Tr. Huebschen testimony, July 14, page 67. This testimony reinforces other significant evidence from which the jury might infer that Ms. Rader's action was based on an impermissible reason. Since this case turned almost completely on the credibility of plaintiff and Ms. Rader,[11] the application of the test enunciated above compels the denial of this motion. A reasonable juror could, from all of the evidence, conclude that plaintiff was demoted because he refused to continue a sexual relationship with Ms. Rader.

Whether plaintiff's demotion was justified regardless of the influence of the impermissible reason (proof of which was defendants' burden under *Mt. Healthy*) was the subject of significant evidence from both sides. Plaintiff introduced a generally favorable performance evaluation from August, 1979; his own testimony of his overall work record and conscientious efforts to improve his performance; and, significantly, the uniformly unfavorable performance evaluation prepared subsequent to the decision to demote. Plaintiff contrasted this last item to the results of an investigation carried out under the direction of defendant Bernard Stumbras. The investigation revealed both positive and negative performance information. Therefore, aside from plaintiff's testimony about his generally good work record, the jury did have evidence from which it could infer that criticisms of plaintiff's performance were a pretext. The fact that under Wisconsin law a probationary employee *could be* terminated for any reason does not compel a different conclusion. The question is whether plaintiff's probation *would have been* terminated absent the sexual harassment. Reasonable jurors might differ on this question, but the *Kolb* standard does not allow this Court to overturn this portion of the verdict.

C. *Verdict as to Mr. Stumbras' Liability*

Defendants urge that the Court set aside the jury verdict against defendant Stumbras. Because he acted in good faith reliance on the advice of an attorney, defendants' motion as to Mr. Stumbras is granted.[12]

---

[11] Ms. Rader not only denied the exchange quoted above, but also the existence of any romantic or personal relationship with plaintiff.

[12] Defendants also strenuously argue that the evidence shows no personal involvement by Mr. Stumbras because he did not take part in the sexual harassment. The argument is totally without merit. Liability depends upon whether the demotion was motivated by an impermissible reason. Mr. Stumbras admitted on the stand that once the demotion was challenged, the ratification of the demotion was his decision to make. That is sufficient personal involvement.

A significant portion of the evidence concerning Mr. Stumbras' actions is undisputed. He is the Administrator of the Division of Economic Assistance of the Department of Health and Social Services. The Bureau of Social Security and Disability Insurance, where plaintiff and Ms. Rader worked, is an agency within the Division of Economic Assistance. In January, 1980, shortly after plaintiff's demotion, plaintiff wrote a letter to Mr. Stumbras and Mr. Stumbras' superior, complaining that his demotion resulted from sexual harassment. Mr. Stumbras consulted with a Department attorney. The attorney advised him that if the sexual harassment charge had any merit, Mr. Stumbras should forego an investigation of the charge in favor of the state's Personnel Commission, the agency equipped to handle such matters. In that event, the attorney continued, he should confine his investigation to whether or not the demotion was justified by work-related factors, that is, those matters within his expertise. Mr. Stumbras then interviewed plaintiff and Ms. Rader and found that their stories conflicted. Mr. Stumbras ordered an investigation into the justification for the demotion. Based on information from the investigation, and other factors, Mr. Stumbras concluded that the demotion was justified by evidence unrelated to any possible sexual relationship between plaintiff and Ms. Rader.

Plaintiff attacked that conclusion with obvious success before the jury. However, plaintiff provided no evidence that Mr. Stumbras exerted any pressure on the investigators or attempted to foreordain the conclusion. Whether or not Mr. Stumbras' conclusion was correct, the Court has no evidence to infer any wrongdoing because of it.

One other piece of evidence also may have had a significant impact on the jury. Plaintiff asserted strongly that Mr. Stumbras' failure to fully investigate the specifics of the sexual harassment charge was evidence of his liability. In fact, Mr. Stumbras did exactly what the Department's attorney recommended. If good faith immunity is available, then Mr. Stumbras' failure to investigate the harassment charge cannot be considered probative.[14]

The Supreme Court recently summarized the standard for the good faith defense:

> We therefore hold that government officials performing discretionary functions generally are shielded from liability for civil damages insofar as their conduct does not violate clearly established statutory or constitutional rights of which a reasonable person would have known.

Harlow v. *Fitzgerald*, — U.S. —, 102 S.Ct. 2727, 2738, 73 L.Ed. 2d 396 (1982).

Mr. Stumbras' reliance on the advice of counsel under these circumstances established a good faith defense which plaintiff did not significantly rebut. While an employer may have a duty to investigate charges such as the one brought by plaintiff, the employer here is the state. The attorney advised that Mr. Stumbras leave the investigation of sexual harassment to another state agency. Since such an investigation was undertaken, the duty to investigate was met. In short, Mr. Stumbras, in relying on the attorney's advice, did exactly what a "reasonable person" would have done.

[Footnote 13 omitted]

[14] Plaintiff suggested during argument that Mr. Stumbras had threatened plaintiff with retaliation if he took his charge to the Personnel Commission. The Court finds that the evidence of such alleged retaliatory threat is too weak to overcome Mr. Stumbras' good faith defense. Furthermore, no retaliatory acts were alleged.

In addition, *Mt. Healthy* instructs the employer to examine the complainant's performance to see whether the employment action taken was justified regardless of the charge of discrimination. On that fact, after all, the employer's liability rests. Mr. Stumbras' reliance on the attorney's advice was, therefore, not only reasonable, but probably correct.

The Court must conclude, then, that Mr. Stumbras established the defense of good faith, that the defense was not rebutted, and that Mr. Stumbras deserves judgment notwithstanding the verdict. Therefore, defendants' motion as to Mr. Stumbras will be granted.

* * *

D.   *Excessive Verdict*

Finally, defendants request a new trial on the ground that the verdict against Ms. Rader was excessive and was the result of passion or prejudice. While the Court believes that the jury was neither inflamed with passion nor overwhelmed with prejudice, the Court finds the verdict as to damages to be so excessive as to shock the judicial conscience.

The Court will examine compensatory and punitive damage awards separately.

1.   *Compensatory damages*

* * *

Compensatory damages are not intended to punish, but instead to make plaintiff whole for his injury. Plaintiff simply failed to demonstrate at trial that he suffered such emotional and mental damage, proximately caused by defendant Rader's conduct, to justify an award anywhere near $90,000.

The Court carefully instructed the jury that plaintiff's medical condition and surgery, with its attendant pain, suffering, humiliation or medical care could not be considered in determining compensatory damages. Instead, the only injury for which plaintiff may receive compensatory damages is any mental or emotional pain, suffering and distress proximately caused by Ms. Rader's actions.

Considering the evidence in the light most favorable to plaintiff, he showed the following items of mental or emotional damage:

a.   *Relationships with Co-workers*

Plaintiff testified that the termination adversely affected his dealings with peers and supervisors at work:

> MR. HUEBSCHEN: I think I was in the hospital until mid-March sometime or early March, and then I came back to work almost immediately after that.

> MR. FOX: Can you describe the atmosphere at work when you came back in early March?

> MR. HUEBSCHEN: Well, it was—I felt really isolated and pretty much out of it. I was not even beginning to recover from the surgery. I couldn't stand up

straight or anything but I could mainly just recall being in a fog and trying to come in and do my work and trying to stay together.

* * *

MR. FOX: Apart from that surgery and the feelings about that surgery that you just expressed, can you describe your interaction or what kind of interaction you had with other employees?

MR. HUEBSCHEN: Almost no interaction. I sat in my cubicle and tried to do my cases and sometimes I would go talk to Vila a little bit about that I was having a hard time, but I really can't recall—maybe people coming by—

MR. FOX: How did that differ in terms of your social interaction with other employees? How did that differ from the way you were prior to this time?

MR. HUEBSCHEN: I used to be—I knew a lot of the people. I knew everyone in the office or just about anyway and, you know, say hello to people, you know, passed the time of day in the course of the work day. I think there was almost some—I don't know if people thought I was a double outcast or what between the demotion and the illness, and I think people felt bad and maybe they didn't know quite what to say to me either.

* * *

MR. HUEBSCHEN: Number two, people were very uncomfortable. Some people didn't seem comfortable saying hello, or if I would walk into a room and there was a conversation, the conversation would stop as soon as I walked into the room. Not that it was about me or anything, but just because I would walk into the room. If I tried to talk to somebody, they would immediately look around and see who might see them talking to me, and I would sense a lot of discomfort from the other people as well as some on my own part and so I started to be more withdrawn.

* * *

MR. HUEBSCHEN: At about this time is when LeRoy Stuczynski told me that he did not want to associate—did not want to be seen with me in the office. He was the first person that came out and actually said that.

MR. FOX: Are there any other instances that you can recall happening about that time?

MR. HUEBSCHEN: About specific statements by individuals, no.

* * *

MR. HUEBSCHEN: When the Personnel Commission investigation began I—then I was totally, completely isolated. After that there was a great deal of fear I perceived.

MR. FOX: You are saying that but what types of things did you observe?

MR. HUEBSCHEN: At that point I observed that even close friends were just not comfortable around me and that they looked around whenever I was near them to see who might be observing us. That is all I can recall on specifics right now.

* * *

MR. HUEBSCHEN: We had a very close relationship as friends and we had been peers. We were equals during the time I was a supervisor and in addition to our business relationship Vila would occasionally come to our home and we would occasionally go to her home and just discuss life in general as friends.

MR. FOX: How did that differ from the period you are talking about where you said there was a strain?

MR. HUEBSCHEN: The relationship became strictly business, no extraneous discussion.

* * *

MR. FOX: How did that or did it affect you emotionally at all?

MR. HUEBSCHEN: It did. I felt very bad. I felt a sense of loss because she had been very close to me.

* * *

MR. HUEBSCHEN: I had some interactions with my very closest friends.

MR. FOX: Who were they?

MR. HUEBSCHEN: Greg Nametz, Patty Hake, Tim Greenya.

MR. FOX: In terms of your relationship with those people, did you note any changes in your relationship with those people from before the termination to after the termination?

MR. HUEBSCHEN: Yes. There was a change.

MR. FOX: What was that change?

MR. HUEBSCHEN: Even those relationships seemed to be—I had trouble express-ing myself and I was holding myself back from them and worrying that they might get in trouble for being my friends. That was a big worry that I had.

* * *

MR. FOX: Again, describing the summer of '81, what if anything did your social life consist of at work?

MR. HUEBSCHEN: By this time I had none. I didn't go to any office parties or I didn't go to going-away parties for people. On one or two occasions I tried, but it just didn't work. People were not comfortable with me there. I wasn't comfortable. I almost felt out of fairness for the people I shouldn't be going so I stopped.

Tr. Huebschen testimony, July 19, pages 12, 13, 24, 29, 30, 37, 40, 41.

    b.   *Home Life*

Plaintiff also alluded to the change in his relationship with his wife:

> MR. FOX: Again, this time focusing on your own home life, what was happening as far as your own home life was concerned?
>
> MR. HUEBSCHEN: Our home life was—it had changed. I think the main focus was relief that the first surgery had come out all right and wishing that I didn't have to go into work every day because I was having a hard time going in emotionally and wishing the whole problem would just go away.

* * *

> MR. FOX: At that point in time what was your situation as far as your family was concerned?
>
> MR. HUEBSCHEN: There is becoming more and more strain at home financially due to loss of income...

* * *

> MR. FOX: How did you perceive that situation at work in your home life? Did it have any effect on your home life at all?
>
> MR. HUEBSCHEN: Yes. It had very much effect because it took so much out of me just to get out of bed and go in there and try to do my job and try to do it so well so I couldn't be criticized for bad job performance. It took so much out of me that when I came home I had nothing left.
>
> MR. FOX: When was your baby born?
>
> MR. HUEBSCHEN: October 12, 1981.
>
> MR. FOX: What was your emotional state at that particular time?
>
> MR. HUEBSCHEN: Again, it was—I felt real happy. We felt so lucky that she was healthy and it was a real nice time, and yet I felt like I had cheated Arimanda because I knew in my head that I was happy and yet it didn't come out good enough. I didn't live the happiness I felt, and I cheated her very badly because I just—I would only be happy temporarily, last a few hours, and then I would be right back where I was being withdrawn. I felt I made her miss something.
>
> MR. FOX: What was it that you felt you made her miss?
>
> MR. HUEBSCHEN: My full participation in being a father and just the terrific thrill. It was really terrific and I admired her even despite the way I was she didn't let that drag her down at all.

Tr. Huebschen testimony, July 19, pages 25, 30, 41, 42.

c. *Work Routine*

Plaintiff further testified that his work routine became regimented and unpleasant:

> MR. HUEBSCHEN: What happened was I realized at this point that I was going to try to commit myself on going to the Personnel Commission and that I emotionally could not afford—I needed to try to cancel out my feelings on things and just plod along day to day, and I became much more withdrawn and

just tried to go into work every day and keep my nose clean, do a good job and go home and just try to gut it out pending a decision.

* * *

MR. HUEBSCHEN: My work day was much more restricted, number one. I felt much higher pressure to make very sure that I was meeting every standard, every statistic that I felt vulnerable to. I didn't want to slip or have any slips in my job performance.

* * *

MR. FOX: At that particular time can you describe again during that fall period your own emotional state that you were experiencing at work?

MR. HUEBSCHEN: I am getting mixed up again. We are in the fall of '81?

MR. FOX: Fall of '81.

MR. HUEBSCHEN: Oh, Vila was still my supervisor. My emotional state at work—by this time I had developed a check list of everything I had to do in order to do my job well, and I plodded every day from one point to the next. I kept stroke tallies of just minor little things that I had to do on the job, and they became my means of just getting through each day one at a time.

Tr. Huebschen testimony, July 19, pages 22, 24, 41.

d.   *General Emotional State*

Finally, plaintiff described his emotional state during the months following his termination:

MR. FOX: Mr. Huebschen, I'm going to focus your attention if I can for the purposes of questioning in the damage phase of the trial to the period around December or mid-December after your probation was terminated. I would like to have you if you can describe to the jury your feelings immediately after the termination of that probation or let's say after that meeting with Jackie Rader that you already testified to where she informed you not to—or not to contest your termination of probation.

MR. HUEBSCHEN: Well, that is one of the factors, that meeting, and it came across so clearly of, you know, I'm going to make sure you lose all of your friends and make sure that everybody knows you are a chronic liar and knows you never bring up the true circumstances and, well, that added to I guess the degree of threat that I had already felt and what was going on at home at that time was just a mixture of many, many emotions of grief, of guilt and embarrassment I guess.

* * *

MR. HUEBSCHEN: I felt really down. I felt that my earlier feeling of optimism that he would look into this had been dashed and, I don't know, I felt crushed when I came home.

* * *

MR. FOX: During that period of time you described, and we are focusing on July, August of 1980, can you describe your own emotional state when you were going through that period of time?

MR. HUEBSCHEN: By this time, and this is the problem that I have been having, I can remember—I put myself on automatic pilot and everything just happened and I don't remember my emotions.

MR. REPASKY: It sounds very powerful but I don't know what it means.

MR. HUEBSCHEN: I don't remember my emotions. I tried my best not to have any.

* * *

MR. FOX: Can you describe what you mean? What was your emotional state at that time?

MR. HUEBSCHEN: All right, my emotional state was that I tried not to feel fear or hurt if someone did not want to talk to me. I tried not to feel anger if I felt something had been unfair. I tried not to feel too optimistic if I thought anything good might be happening to me at the moment. I tried not to be affected by anything that was happening and just do everything step by step by step.

Tr. Huebschen testimony, July 19, pages 2, 11, 31, 32.

In its examination of the evidence, the Court did not attempt to separate the pain and suffering attributable to plaintiff's surgery and serious health problems, to his admittedly consensual affair with Ms. Rader, or to his dealings with other defendants or others. Instead, assuming all of the preceding paragraphs fairly describe the damage proximately caused by defendant Rader's actions, $90,000 in compensatory damages shocks the judicial conscience and will not be permitted to stand.

2. *Punitive Damages*

The jury also assessed $24,600 in punitive damages against defendant Rader. Defendants' motion for a new trial on damages because of the excessiveness of the verdict applies to this award as well. The Court applies the same standard in evaluating the excessiveness of punitive and compensatory damages. *See Perfect Fit Industries, Inc.* v. *Acme Quilting Co.*, 494 F.Supp. 505, 509 (S.D.N.Y.1980). The Court finds that the punitive damage award against Ms. Rader is so excessive on its face that it shocks the judicial conscience.

In making this determination, the Court considers the twin aims of punitive damages: punishment of the wrongdoer and deterrence of similar illegal conduct in the future. *City of Newport* v. *Fact Concerts, Inc.*, 453 U.S. 247, 101 S.Ct. 2748, 69 L.ED.2d 616 (1981). The amount should be reasonably proportional to the evidence of purposeful conduct. *Maxey* v. *Freightliner Corp.*, 450 F.Supp. 955 (N.D.Tex.1978) *aff'd*, 623 F.2d 395 (5th Cir. 1980). Punitive damages should be large enough to deter and punish, but not larger. *Collins* v. *Brown*, 268 F.Supp. 198 (D.C.D.C.1967).

In this case, the punitive damages awarded exceeded any amount required to punish defendant Rader or to deter future misconduct of this kind. Further, judged by the foregoing criteria, $24,600 is so excessive as to shock the judicial conscience and will not be permitted to stand.

3. *Remittitur*

The Court need not order a new trial, however. The Court may offer the plaintiff a remittitur, or reduction in the damages assessed by the jury. If plaintiff refuses the reduced award, the Court may grant a new trial.

* * *

Remittitur is also available when the Court is faced with excessive damages.

* * *

The Court will therefore determine as a matter of law that $10,000 in compensa-tory damages and $15,000 in punitive damages is reasonable and shall order a new trial on damages unless plaintiff elects to accept judgment in the changed amount within ten days of the date of this order.

In this determination, the Court does not minimize the problem of sexual harassment in employment. Isolated excessive jury verdicts such as this one will not solve the problem, however. This Court has a solemn obligation to do justice between the parties. Permitting this verdict to stand would violate that sworn duty.

* * *

ORDER

IT IS ORDERED that defendants' motion for judgment notwithstanding the verdict is GRANTED as to defendant Bernard Stumbras, and in all other respects DENIED.

IT IS FURTHER ORDERED that defendants' motion to alter or amend the judgment against the Department of Health and Social Services is DENIED.

IT IS FURTHER ORDERED that defendants' motion for a new trial is GRANTED in part, unless plaintiff agrees to accept $10,000 in compensatory damages and $15,000 in punitive damages. If plaintiff does not agree to accept judgment in the changed amount within ten days of the date of this order, the Court will schedule a new trial on the issue of damages. If plaintiff agrees to accept the reduced judgment, the motion will be DENIED. For all other purposes, the Court's decision on pre-trial motions shall be deemed rendered on August 27, 1982.

IT IS FURTHER ORDERED that plaintiff's motion for an additional award of attorney's fees is GRANTED in part. Plaintiff is awarded an additional $2,045 in attorney's fees.

IT IS FURTHER ORDERED that plaintiff's motion for an award of costs is GRANTED in part. Defendants shall be taxed $1,246.62, plus an additional sum to be determined after an examination of the affidavit requested in Part V of this decision.

Chapter 22 Outline

Competencies

1. Identify general prohibitions outlined in the Employee Polygraph Protection Act of 1988. (p. 313)

2. Describe the Employee Polygraph Protection Act's limited exemptions for "ongoing investigations." (pp. 313–314)

3. Describe additional requirements and protections provided for by the Employee Polygraph Protection Act. (p. 314)

4. Describe enforcement and penalties provided for by the Employee Polygraph Protection Act. (pp. 314–315)

5. Describe how lie detectors function. (p. 315)

22

Use of Lie Detector Tests by Hotel Management

Employee Polygraph Protection Act of 1988

The Employee Polygraph Protection Act of 1988, which became effective on December 27, 1988, prohibits covered employers from using polygraphs, lie detector tests, and similar devices on employees or prospective employees, except in limited circumstances.[1]

General Prohibitions

Subject to the limited exemptions set forth in the next section, the Employee Polygraph Protection Act now prohibits employers engaged in interstate commerce, or in the production of goods in interstate commerce, from doing any of the following:

- Requiring, requesting, suggesting, or causing any employee or prospective employee to take or submit to a lie detector test

- Using, accepting, referring to, or inquiring about the results of a lie detector test of an employee or prospective employee

- Making employment-related decisions against any employee or prospective employee for refusing to submit to a lie detector test or on the basis of the results of a lie detector test

- Discriminating against employees for exercising their rights under the Employee Polygraph Protection Act

Exemptions

The Employee Polygraph Protection Act provides a limited exemption for "ongoing investigations." This permits an employer to request an employee to submit to a polygraph test in connection with an ongoing investigation which involves economic loss or injury to the employer's business. The exemption applies only if the employer satisfies rigorous procedural requirements for administering the polygraph test, and makes the following additional showings:

- The employee had access to the property which is the subject of the investigation; and

- the employer has a reasonable suspicion that the employee was involved in the incident or activity under investigation; and

313

- the employer provides a signed statement to the employee *before* the test which (1) fully sets forth the incident or activity being investigated; (2) identifies the specific economic loss or injury to the employer; and (3) states that the employee had access to the property, which is the basis of the employer's reasonable suspicion that the employee was involved in the incident or activity under investigation.

Unless the employer has additional supporting evidence, which at a minimum includes the information required in the employer's statement set forth above, the employer loses the benefit of the exemption and cannot use the results of the test or the employee's failure to take the test as a basis for making adverse employment decisions. The statement which the employer provides to the employee must be signed by a person authorized to bind the employer, and the employer must retain it for at least three years.

The Employee Polygraph Protection Act protects the rights of the examinee of the polygraph test by specifying rigid procedural requirements which must be followed in various phases of the test, including qualifications of text examiners. Due to the complexity of these procedural requirements, which, if not precisely followed, may result in the loss of the exemption, we recommend that any employer planning to administer a polygraph test consult with counsel to obtain specific instructions on how to proceed.

Additional Requirements and Protections

Posting of Notices. Under regulations promulgated by the secretary of labor, appropriate notices are to be prepared and distributed to employers setting forth the pertinent provisions of the Employee Polygraph Protection Act. These notices must be posted and maintained by the employer where notices to employees and applicants are customarily posted.

Disclosure of Information. The polygraph examiner may disclose information acquired from a polygraph test only to the examinee, the employer that requested the test, or in accordance with a court order. The employer may not disclose the results of the polygraph test to anyone other than the examinee, except pursuant to a court order, or to a government agency, provided that the information submitted to such government agency is an *admission* of criminal conduct.

Effect of Other Laws and Agreements. The Employee Polygraph Protection Act does not preempt state laws or collective bargaining agreements that are more restrictive than the federal law or that totally prohibit the use of lie detector tests.

Enforcement and Penalties

Employers who violate any provision of the Employee Polygraph Protection Act may be assessed fines of up to $10,000. Additionally, the secretary of labor may commence an action against an employer for injunctive relief for violations of the Act.

The Act also creates a private cause of action by an employee or prospective employee in state or federal court to recover damages of not more than $10,000 for violations of the Act.

Subject to this new federal law, many states* will continue to permit hotels to use specified types of lie detector tests in conducting security investigations of current employees. In recent years, however, the use of lie detector tests has involved much controversy. Critics cite the invasion of a person's right to privacy and the disputed credibility of some tests as reasons for restricting or entirely banning the use of polygraphs. On the other hand, as many businesspersons can attest, losses resulting from employee theft are substantial. (See the opinion in a relevant case, *State of New Jersey* v. *Berkey Photo Inc.*, at the end of this chapter.)

Efforts to balance employer and employee interests have led some states to enact legislation greatly restricting employers' use of polygraph lie detector tests, even in cases permitted by the federal polygraph act. Today, many states require lie detector operators to be licensed by the state.**

How Lie Detectors Function

A lie detector test is, in essence, a method of recording the subject's physiological reactions when responding to specific questions presented by an examiner. Polygraph machines may measure and record changes in the subject's heartbeat, respiration rate, and perspiration. These factors are measured by mechanical devices and electrodes, and the polygraph machine records the data on graph paper. An expert polygraph examiner evaluates the graph to determine the truthfulness of the subject's response.

In another type of test called *voice stress analysis*, a polygraph machine measures and records changes in stress on the subject's vocal cords. However, in New York State, the use of this particular type of lie detector test is prohibited. The New York statutes prohibit any person from administering or participating in a "psychological stress evaluator examination." This test is defined in New York statutes as one using a device "which purports to determine the truth or falsity of statements made by an employee or prospective employee on the basis of vocal fluctuations or vocal stress."[2]

Caution in Using Tests

In conducting security investigations where permitted by federal and state laws, hotel operators should nevertheless consult with legal counsel before engaging in this practice.

---

* States with statutes restricting employers' use of polygraphs include Alaska, California, Connecticut, Delaware, Hawaii, Idaho, Maine, Maryland, Massachusetts, Minnesota, Montana, Nebraska, Nevada, New Jersey, Oregon, Pennsylvania, Rhode Island, Washington, and Wisconsin.

** Alabama, Arizona, Arkansas, Florida, Georgia, Illinois, Kentucky, Massachusetts, Michigan, Mississippi, Nevada, New Mexico, North Carolina, North Dakota, Oklahoma, Oregon, South Carolina, Texas, Utah, Vermont, and Virginia.

Important Points for Management

The Employee Polygraph Protection Act of 1988, which became effective on December 27, 1988, prohibits covered employers from using polygraphs, lie detector tests, and similar devices on employees or prospective employees, except in limited circumstances.

The Employee Polygraph Protection Act provides a limited exemption for "ongoing investigations." This permits an employer to request an employee to submit to a polygraph test in connection with an ongoing investigation which involves economic loss or injury to the employer's business. The exemption applies only if the employer satisfies rigorous procedural requirements for administering the polygraph test, and makes the following additional showings:

- The employee had access to the property which is the subject of the investigation; and

- The employer has a reasonable suspicion that the employee was involved in the incident or activity under investigation; and

- The employer provides a signed statement to the employee *before* the test which (1) fully sets forth the incident or activity being investigated; (2) identifies the specific economic loss or injury to the employer; and (3) states that the employee had access to the property, which is the basis of the employer's reasonable suspicion that the employee was involved in the incident or activity under investigation.

Employers who violate any provision of the Employee Polygraph Protection Act may be assessed fines of up to $10,000. Additionally, the secretary of labor may commence an action against an employer for injunctive relief for violations of the Act.

The Act also creates a private cause of action by an employee or prospective employee in state or federal court to recover damages of not more than $10,000 for violations of the Act.

References

1. 29 U.S.C.A. 2001, *et seq.* The Department of Labor has issued regulations to implement this law. 29 C.F.R. § 801.1 *et seq.*
2. N.Y. Lab Law § 733 (5)(c).

Review Questions

1. What prohibitions are contained in the Employee Polygraph Protection Act of 1988 for the protection of current and prospective employees?

2. According to the Employee Polygraph Protection Act of 1988, when may employers use polygraphs or similar devices?

3. What types of employers are affected by the prohibitions outlined in the polygraph act?

4. When may an employer legally request a current employee to submit to a polygraph test?

5. What procedures must an employer follow before requesting an employee to undergo a polygraph test?

6. What must an employer include in the signed statement he/she provides to an employee designated to undergo a polygraph test?

7. What penalties would an employer suffer if he/she failed to provide substantial supporting evidence to an employee requested to take a polygraph test?

8. To whom may an employer disclose information acquired in an employee's polygraph test? When?

9. How do polygraph machines work?

Internet Sites

For more information, visit the following Internet sites. Remember that Internet addresses can change without notice.

Employee Polygraph Protection Act of 1988
http://www.dol.gov/dol/esa/public/regs/compliance/whd/whfs36.html

Illustrative Case

State of New Jersey **v.** *Berkey Photo Inc.*

150 N.J. Super. 56, 374 A. 2d 1226
(Sup. Ct. N.J., App. Div. 1977)

Before Judges HALPERN, MICHELS and BOTTER.

PER CURIAM.

Defendant was convicted in the municipal court and in the County Court, on appeal *de novo* on the record below, of violating *N.J. S.A.* 2A:170-90.1. This statute makes it a disorderly persons offense for an employer to

> ...influence, request or require an employee to take or submit to a lie detector test as a condition of employment or continued employment...[1]

Defendant asked certain employees to take a lie detector test as an aid in investigating a theft from its plant in Clifton, New Jersey. On this appeal defendant contends that the statute was not violated primarily because the initial suggestion of using lie detector tests came from the police and, contrary to the trial judge's

---

[1] Defendant was charged with five separate violations, each involving a different employee, and was fined $100 for each violation, plus court costs.

conclusion, the employees took the tests voluntarily and not as a condition of continued employment within the meaning of the statute.

The underlying facts are not in dispute. On October 22, 1974 defendant reported the theft of a case of cameras to the Clifton Police Department. Two detectives went to the plant and met with defendant's director of security, Jim Ahern. It was established that during the preceding weekend the cameras had been stolen from a small area of the plant which had been accessible to only six employees and an alarm repairman employed by an independent contractor.

The detectives interviewed four of the employees and asked each if they would be willing to submit to a polygraph test. The four agreed to do so. Thereafter the detectives recommended to Ahern that polygraph tests be used in the investigation. The detectives also recommended that defendant arrange for the tests privately because the Clifton Police Department did not have a polygraph team and there would be a delay of a month or more if the State Police were asked to perform the test.

Ahern conferred with the personnel director, Thomas Glynn, and they decided to ask the employees to take the test. Ahern and Glynn, and in some cases Ahern alone, asked the six employees as well as the alarm repairman to take the test. All agreed to do so and signed "waiver" forms stating that they were taking the test voluntarily. For the purpose of this appeal we accept the finding that all were informed in advance that under the laws of New Jersey no employer may require a person to take a polygraph test as a condition of employment or continued employment.[2]

The six employees and the alarm repairman submitted to the tests. The questions were limited to establishing knowledge or involvement in the particular theft, except that preliminary questions were asked to relieve tension and nervousness. All persons tested were "cleared of involvement," except one employee. The test established his involvement and he confessed his guilt while the test was being administered.

N.J.S.A. 2A:170-90.1 precludes an employer from influencing, requesting or requiring an employee to take or submit to a lie detector test as a condition of employment or continued employment. There is no question that defendant here did request the employees to take or submit to the test. It makes no difference that the police initiated or recommended the procedure. The sole issue before us is whether, in the circumstances of this case, the request to take the test "was a condition of employment or continued employment" within the meaning of the statute. On this issue the opinion of our Supreme Court in *State v. Community Distributors, Inc.,* 64 N.J. 479, 317 A.2d 697 (1974), aff'g 123 *N.J. Super.* 589, 304 A.2d 213 (Cty.Ct.1973), is persuasive and, in our opinion, dispositive.

In *Community Distributors* defendant, the operator of a chain of drug stores, used polygraph tests as a screening device in its hiring procedures. Each of the

---

[2]   One employee testified on cross-examination by defendant that Ahern did not tell him that the test was voluntary and that he could refuse to take it. His testimony was that he was told that others were taking the test and that they had a good chance of establishing that another employee and possibly two others were involved in the theft. However, he did sign the form when asked to do so by the person who administered the lie detector test.

Another involved employee, the plant manager, testified that he felt that it was his "duty to take the test voluntarily..."

employees involved in the charges brought against defendant was told that he or she did not have to take the test and signed a consent or waiver form. Two of the employees were unaffected by the test results, but one was fired immediately after the test revealed that she had been previously involved in a larceny. In upholding defendant's conviction for three separate violations relating to these employees, the Supreme Court stated: (at 484, 317 A.2d at 699), "Nor is there any assurance of true voluntariness for the economic compulsions are generally such that the employee had no realistic choice." The court went on to say:

> We readily reject, as did the County Court…the defendant's contention that its request was not a condition of employment or continued employment within the statutory contemplation. Surely the employee would understand that it was despite any formal assertion by the employer to the contrary and his understanding would be wholly realistic in view of the employment relationship. The legislative goal would obviously be frustrated if Drug Fair's procedure were now judicially declared to be outside the prohibitory orbit. In the light of the "breadth of the objectives of the legislation and the common sense of the situation"… there can be little doubt that the conduct of the defendant here was violative of the statute. [at 485, 317 A.2d at 700]

That a crime was being investigated and the police were involved does not justify the employer's intrusion of a lie detector test into an employment relationship. Nor do these factors lessen the compulsion inherent in the situation. In fact, it may heighten that unspoken compulsion. Here, for example, one employee testified that he "volunteered" to take the test, after being told he did not have to do so and that his refusal would not affect his continued employment, because he was a security guard, he was in the building when the theft occurred and he wanted "to clear" himself of suspicion. Another employee, the plant manager, testified that he had a "duty" to take the test "voluntarily." Surely the employees understood what was expected of them when told that others were taking the test. How else can one explain that the guilty employee, the one who confessed, submitted to the test knowing the risk he was taking?

Appellant seeks to distinguish *Community Distributors* from the case at hand. However, the use of the words "as a condition of…continued employment" clearly shows that the statute was intended to apply to an established employment relationship as well as to the initial hiring process, as in *Community Distributors*.

Finding no legal justification in these circumstances for defendant's requests to its employees and its administration of the tests, we affirm defendant's conviction for each separate violation.

Chapter 23 Outline

Competencies

1. Identify the principal functions of the National Labor Relations Board. (pp. 321–322)

2. Describe the rights of employees as they relate to unions. (p. 322)

3. Distinguish between representation elections, decertification elections, and deauthorization elections. (pp. 322–323)

4. Provide examples of unfair labor practices forbidden by the National Labor Relations Act. (pp. 323–324)

5. Explain how unfair labor practice cases are processed by the NLRB. (pp. 324–325)

6. Define "right-to-work" laws. (p. 325)

23

National Labor Relations Act

THE NATIONAL LABOR RELATIONS ACT (NLRA) protects the right of workers to organize and to bargain collectively with their employers, or to refrain from all such activity.[1] The NLRA applies to most employers engaged in interstate commerce.* However, the National Labor Relations Board (NLRB), at its discretion, generally limits the exercise of its jurisdiction to enterprises with a substantial effect on commerce. The Board's "jurisdictional standards" are based on the yearly amount of business done by the enterprise, or on its yearly amount of sales or purchases. The NLRB jurisdictional standards cover hotels and motels that do at least $500,000 total annual volume of business.**

The NLRB administers the NLRA. The NLRB's two principal functions are:

1. To conduct secret ballot elections in which employees decide whether unions will represent them in collective bargaining

2. To remedy unfair labor practices whether by labor organizations or by employers

The NLRB can act only when it is formally requested to do so. Individuals, employers, or unions may initiate cases by (1) filing charges of unfair labor practices or (2) petitioning for employee representation elections with the NLRB

---

* The NLRA does not apply to railroads and airlines, agricultural laborers, domestic servants, independent contractors, and certain other persons. Supervisors are also excluded. Section 2 (11) of the NLRA states:

> The term 'supervisor' means any individual having authority, in the interest of the employer, to hire, transfer, suspend, lay off, recall, promote, discharge, assign, reward, or discipline other employees, or responsibility to direct them, or to adjust their grievances, or effectively to recommend such action, if in connection with the foregoing the exercise of such authority is not of a merely routine or clerical nature, but requires the use of independent judgment.

See Appendix C for selected provisions of the NLRA.

** **Advisory Opinions.** Sometimes it is difficult to say whether the NLRB will assert jurisdiction even with the help of the published jurisdictional standards. Because of this and because the 1959 amendments to the Act provided that the states may assert their jurisdiction over labor disputes over which NLRB does not take jurisdiction, the NLRB has established an advisory opinion procedure. Under it, parties to a proceeding pending before a state or territorial agency or court, or the court or agency itself, can directly petition the NLRB in Washington for an advisory opinion on whether the NLRB would assert jurisdiction on the basis of the jurisdictional facts submitted with the petition. For further information, write to the Division of Information, National Labor Relations Board, Washington, DC 20570.

regional office serving the area where the case arises. NLRB regional offices are located in various cities throughout the United States and Puerto Rico.

Rights of Employees

The rights guaranteed employees covered by the law are found in § 7 of the NLRA stating:

> Employees shall have the right to self-organization, to form, join, or assist labor organizations, to bargain collectively through representatives of their own choosing, and to engage in other concerted activities for the purpose of collective bargaining or other mutual aid or protection, and shall also have the right to refrain from any or all of such activities except to the extent that such right may be affected by an agreement requiring membership in a labor organization as a condition of employment as authorized in section 8(a)(3).

In order to protect employees in the exercise of these rights, the NLRA gives the NLRB authority to:

1. Remedy or prevent unfair labor practices of either employers or labor organizations (§ 10)
2. Conduct elections to determine whether employees wish to have a representative bargain for them as a group (§ 9)
3. Conduct polls to determine whether employees who have been under a union-shop agreement want to revoke the authority of their bargaining agent to make such agreements (§ 9)

The right of employees to strike, except as specifically modified by the NLRA, is preserved (§ 13). However, the NLRB and the courts have ruled that "sitdown" strikes are not activities protected by the law because they involve the unlawful seizure of property. The NLRB has also held that the law does not protect slowdowns by employees who remain on the job, partial strikes such as a refusal to work on a certain day each week, or walkouts when the applicable contract between the employer and the employees' bargaining representative contains a no-strike provision, unless such walkouts result from serious employer unfair labor practices or conditions abnormally dangerous to health, for example.

Unfair labor practice charges should be filed with the NLRB regional offices *within six months from the date or dates of the alleged unfair activity.*

Employee Elections

The NLRA provides for three general types of employee elections:

1. *Representation elections* determine the employees' choice of a collective bargaining agent. These are held upon petition of an employer, employees, or a labor organization.
2. *Decertification elections* determine whether the employees wish to withdraw the bargaining authority of a labor organization which they previously had

designated as their representative. These are held upon petition of employees or labor organizations.

3. *Deauthorization elections* determine whether the employees wish to revoke the authority of their bargaining representative to make a union shop contract. These elections are held upon a petition of employees.

Section 9(a) provides that the representative designated by a majority of employees in a unit appropriate for collective bargaining shall be the exclusive representative of the employees in bargaining about rates of pay, wages, hours, or other conditions of employment. When a majority representative has been chosen, it is illegal for an employer to bargain with individual employees or minority groups of employees.

Unfair Labor Practices

The NLRA forbids employers to engage in a number of specified unfair labor practices.

It is a violation of § 8(a)(1) for an employer to interfere with, restrain, or coerce employees in the exercise of rights guaranteed by § 7.

Examples of such illegal conduct are:

- Threatening employees with loss of jobs or benefits if they should join a union
- Threatening to close down a plant if a union should be organized in it
- Questioning employees about their union activities or membership in such circumstances as will tend to restrain or coerce the employees
- Spying on union gatherings
- Granting wage increases deliberately timed to discourage union organization among employees

Section 8(a)(3) forbids an employer to discriminate against employees "in regard to hire or tenure of employment or any term or condition of employment to encourage or discourage membership in any labor organization." Violation of this provision of the law—discharge or other employment discrimination for union activity or other protected group activity—is the most common unfair labor practice.

Examples of discrimination in employment forbidden by this section are:

- Discharging an employee because he/she urged fellow employees to join or organize a union
- Refusing to reinstate an employee (when a job for which he/she can qualify is open) because he/she took part in a union's lawful strike
- Refusing to hire a qualified applicant for a job because the person belongs to a union
- Refusing to hire a qualified applicant for a job because the person does not belong to a union or because the person belongs to one union rather than to another union

It is also an unfair labor practice, in violation of § 8(a)(4), for an employer to discharge or otherwise discriminate against an employee because he/she has filed charges or given testimony under the NLRA.

Section 8(b)(1) to (6) of the NLRA sets forth unfair labor practices of *labor organizations*. For example, a union may violate § 8(b)(1)(B) by restraining or coercing an employer in the selection of its representatives for collective bargaining or the adjustment of grievances. In such cases, unfair labor practices may be filed by the employer with the NLRB.

Procedures in Unfair Labor Practice Cases

If an employee believes that an employer or a union is engaged in one or more unfair labor practices, the employee may file charges with the appropriate NLRB regional office on forms supplied by that office. A union or an employer also may file charges.*

After the charges are filed, the case is processed as follows:

1. Field examiners from the NLRB regional offices investigate the charges. During this investigation, charges may be adjusted, withdrawn, dismissed, or otherwise closed without formal action.

2. The regional director issues a formal complaint if charges are found to be well grounded and the case is not settled by adjustment.

3. A public hearing on the complaint is held before an NLRB administrative law judge.

4. The NLRB administrative law judge's findings and recommendations are served on the parties and sent to the NLRB in Washington in the form of a trial judge's decision. At this point, the case is transferred to the NLRB in Washington. Unless either of the parties files a statement of exceptions to the administrative law judge's findings within 20 days, his/her recommended order takes the full effect of an order by the NLRB. Parties who except to the findings also may file a brief to support their exceptions and may request oral argument before the NLRB. Exceptions are in effect an appeal of the administrative law judge's decision.

---

* An unfair labor practice claim was filed by the Bakery Wagon Drivers and Salesmen, Local 484, International Brotherhood of Teamsters, Chauffeurs, Warehousemen and Helpers of America against the Fairmont Hotel before the NLRB Regional Office in San Francisco. At issue was the question of the union's right to send its representatives onto the hotel premises for the purpose of distributing handbills to the hotel's guests or patrons with respect to a dispute between the union and one of the hotel's suppliers. The union did not have any dispute with the hotel itself, and it did not represent any of the hotel's employees. The California Hotel & Motel Association filed an *amicus curiae* brief with the NLRB administrative Law Judge pointing out the importance of hotelkeepers maintaining control over their properties because of the nature and extent of the hotelkeeper's obligations and responsibilities to the guests and patrons on the premises. U.S. N.L.R.B., Region 20, Case No. 20-CA-17443 (1983). The NLRB ruled in favor of the hotel (282 NLRB No. 27, 1986).

5. The NLRB reviews the case and issues a decision and order.

6. In case a union or an employer fails to comply with an NLRB order, the NLRB may ask the appropriate U.S. court of appeals for a judgment enforcing its order. Also, any party to the case who is aggrieved by the NLRB's order may appeal to an appropriate U.S. court of appeals.

7. The NLRB or an aggrieved party may petition the U.S. Supreme Court to review the decision of the U.S. court of appeals. Failure to obey a final court judgment is punishable as civil or criminal **contempt** of court or both.

Remedies in Unfair Labor Practice Cases

When the NLRB finds that an employer or union or the agent of either has engaged in unfair labor practices, the NLRB is empowered by § 10(c) to issue an order requiring such person or organization to "cease and desist from such unfair labor practice, and to take such affirmative action, including reinstatement of employees with or without back pay, as will effectuate the policies of this Act."

There are no penalties or fines as such under the NLRA. Only after a court has upheld an NLRB order and an employer or union has refused to comply can either be held on contempt of court and subject to penalties.

The NLRA, under § 10(j) and § 10(1), enables the NLRB or the general counsel to petition the appropriate U.S. district court for an injunction to stop conduct alleged to constitute an unfair labor practice.

"Right-to-Work" Laws

Twenty-one states have "right-to-work" laws. In those states, an employee cannot be required to join a union as a condition of employment, even though his/her place of employment may be unionized. The "right-to-work" states are:

Alabama	Iowa	North Carolina	Utah
Arizona	Kansas	North Dakota	Virginia
Arkansas	Louisiana	South Carolina	Wyoming
Florida	Mississippi	South Dakota	
Georgia	Nebraska	Tennessee	
Idaho	Nevada	Texas	

Important Points for Management

The National Labor Relations Act (NLRA) protects the right of workers to organize and to bargain collectively with their employers, or to refrain from all such activity.

The NLRB administers the NLRA. The NLRB's two principal functions are:

1. To conduct secret ballot elections in which employees decide whether unions will represent them in collective bargaining

2. To remedy unfair labor practices whether by labor organizations or by employers

The NLRA forbids an employer to discriminate against employees "in regard to hire or tenure of employment or any term or condition of employment to encourage or discourage membership in any labor organization." Violation of this provision of the law—discharge or other employment discrimination for union activity or other protected group activity—is an unfair labor practice.

Twenty-one states have right-to-work laws. In those states, an employee cannot be required to join a union as a condition of employment, even though his/her place of employment may be unionized.

References

1. Labor-Management Reporting and Disclosure Act of 1959 (Taft-Hartley Act, as amended), Act of July 5, 1955, as amended, 29 U.S.C. §§ 141-169.

Key Terms

contempt—A willful disregard of the authority of the court or disobedience of its lawful orders.

Review Questions

1. What is the National Labor Relations Board (NLRB)?

2. What hotels and motels are covered by the NLRB jurisdictional standards?

3. What are the NLRB's principal functions?

4. What is an "unfair labor practice" on the part of the employer?

5. When can the NLRB act on behalf of: (1) an individual employee; (2) an employer; or (3) a union?

6. What types of employee elections does the NLRA provide for? Who may petition for these elections?

7. The NLRA forbids employers to engage in a number of unfair labor practices. What are examples of such practices?

8. What is one of the most common unfair labor practices?

9. What are some examples of discrimination in employment forbidden by § 8(a)(3) of the NLRA?

10. What is an example of a unfair labor practice on the part of a labor organization?

11. After someone files charges with the NLRB, how is the case processed?

12. What are right-to-work laws?

13. Do you as a hotel employee in your state have to join a union?

Internet Sites ——————————————————

For more information, visit the following Internet sites. Remember that Internet addresses can change without notice.

National Labor Relations Act (NLRA)
http://www.nlrb.gov/publications/basicguide.html

U.S. National Labor Relations Board
http://www.nlrb.gov

Chapter 24 Outline

Verification of Employee Eligibility
    Documentation
    Completion of Form I-9
Penalties
Anti-Discrimination Provisions
Conclusion
Important Points for Management
References
Review Questions
Internet Sites

Competencies

1. Describe the key provisions of the Immigration Reform and Control Act of 1986. (p. 329)

2. Describe the documents an employer may rely on to establish an employee's identity and authority to work. (pp. 330–332)

3. Describe the important points of INS Form I-9, the Employment Eligibility Verification Form. (pp. 332–335)

4. Describe what penalties may be assessed against employers who "knowingly" employ an illegal alien or fail to complete and retain the required documents. (pp. 335–336)

24

Immigration Reform and Control Act of 1986

THE LAWS GOVERNING hotels and motels in the United States are myriad. They include many common law rules that have evolved from early English judicial decisions and social customs.

The Immigration Reform and Control Act of 1986 made it unlawful after November 6, 1986, for any employer, regardless of the number of employees he/she has, to "knowingly" hire any alien not authorized to work in the United States *or* to continue the employment of an alien who is hired after November 6, 1986, once the employer knows the alien is, or has become, "unauthorized."[1] It is also unlawful for any employer to hire or recruit an employee without complying with the law's verification requirements, which are discussed below. The prohibition against hiring illegal aliens does not apply to employees hired *before* the Act's effective date (i.e., November 6, 1986).

The term "employer" is defined by the Immigration and Naturalization Service (INS) Regulations to mean any person or entity who engages the services or labor of an employee to be performed in the United States for wages or other remuneration. However, in the case of an independent contractor, the term "employer" means the independent contractor and not the person or entity using the independent contractor's labor, unless such person or entity knowingly uses a contract to obtain labor or services of an unauthorized alien.[2]

The Act also contains anti-discrimination provisions, which, if violated after November 6, 1987, will render employers liable to their employees or prospective employees.

Pursuant to the final INS Regulations, the INS has designated Form I-9, entitled the Employment Eligibility Verification Form, as the form to be used by employers for purposes of complying with the verification requirements of the law.*

The following discussion summarizes the key points of the Act.

This chapter is based on "Immigration Reform: An Update on Regulations," by Jack P. Jefferies, Esq., and John G. Fellinger, Esq., which appeared in *Lodging*, Sept. 1987, pp. 97-98, 100.

* Form I-9 may be obtained at INS District Offices or ordered from the Superintendent of Documents, Washington, D.C. 20402. Form I-9 may be photocopied or printed by employers.

Verification of Employee Eligibility

Documentation

As part of the verification requirements of the law, the Act requires employers to obtain from *all new* employees hired after November 6, 1986, documentation which establishes the employee's *identity* and *authority to work*. Thus, even employers with no reason to question the lawful status of new employees must comply with the verification procedures. However, under the grace period provisions of the law, verification of employment eligibility need only be undertaken with respect to individuals who are hired after November 6, 1986, and continue to be employed after May 31, 1987.

The new law requires an employer to verify the identity and status of new employees based on certain documents specified in the Act and on additional documents designated by the INS Regulations.

Under the Act and INS Regulations, the following documents may be relied on by an employer to establish both an employee's *identity and authority to work* if such documents reasonably appear to be genuine:[3]

- A U.S. passport

- A Certificate of Citizenship, issued by the INS, Form N-560 or N-561

- A Certificate of Naturalization issued by the INS, Form N-550 or N-570

- An unexpired foreign passport which:

    (1) contains therein an unexpired stamp which reads, "Processed for I-551. Temporary Evidence of Lawful Admission for permanent residence. Valid until _____. Employment authorized"; or

    (2) has attached thereto a Form I-94 bearing the same name as the passport and contains an employment authorization stamp, so long as the period of endorsement has not yet expired and the proposed employment is not in conflict with any restrictions or limitations identified on the Form I-94.

- An Alien Registration Receipt Card, INS Form I-151, or Resident Alien, INS Form I-551, provided that it contains a photograph of the bearer

- A Temporary Resident Card, INS Form I-688

- An Employment Authorization Card, INS Form I-688A

If the prospective employee does not have one of these documents, the employer must require two documents: one to establish authority to work and one to establish the prospective employee's identity.

In accordance with the Act and the Proposed Regulations, an employer may use certain documents to establish separately the employee's *authority to work* and his/her *identity*.[4]

Establishing Authority to Work. The following documents are acceptable only to establish authority to work:

- A social security card, other than one which has printed on its face "not valid for employment purposes"

- An unexpired re-entry permit, INS Form I-327

- An unexpired Refugee Travel document, INS Form I-571

- A Certification of Birth issued by the Department of State, Form FS-545

- A Certification of Birth Abroad, issued by the Department of State, Form DS-1350

- An original or certified copy of a birth certificate issued by a state or county or municipal authority bearing a seal

- An employment authorization document issued by the Immigration and Naturalization Service

- A native American tribal document

- A U.S. Citizen Identification Card, INS Form I-197

- An identification card for use by resident citizens in the United States, INS Form I-179

Establishing Identity. The following documents are acceptable only to establish the *identity* of the individual:
For individuals 16 years of age or older:

- A state-issued driver's license or state-issued identification card containing a photograph. If the driver's license or identification card does not contain a photograph, identifying information should be included, such as: name, date of birth, sex, height, color of eyes, and address

- A school identification card with a photograph

- A voter's registration card

- A U.S. military card or draft record

- An identification card issued by federal, state, or local government agencies or entities

- A military dependent's identification card

- Native American tribal documents

- A U.S. Coast Guard Merchant Mariner Card

- A driver's license issued by a Canadian government authority

For individuals under age 16 who are unable to produce a document listed above, the following documents are acceptable to establish identity only:

- A school record or report card

- A clinic, doctor, or hospital record

- A day-care or nursery school record

Minors under the age of 16 who are unable to produce one of the identity documents listed above are exempt from producing such documents if one of the following procedures is followed:

- The minor's parent or legal guardian completes Form I-9, Section 1—"Employee Information and Verification"—and, in the space for the minor's signature, the parent or legal guardian writes the words "minor under age 16"

- The minor's parent or legal guardian completes on Form I-9 the "Preparer/Translator certification"

- The employer or the recruiter or referrer for a fee writes in Section 2—"Employer Review and Verification"—under List B in the space after the words "Document identification" the words "minor under age 16"

Completion of Form I-9

The verification requirements also call for completion of the Employment Eligibility Verification Form, known as Form I-9, by both the employer and the employee. (See Exhibit 24.1 for a copy of Form I-9 with step-by-step instructions and a verification checklist.) A "Handbook for Employers," which contains instructions for completing Form I-9, is available and may be obtained from the INS.

Form I-9 must be completed for *all* individuals who are hired, recruited, or referred for a fee for employment after November 6, 1986, and who continue to be employed after May 31, 1987. With respect to employees hired on or after June 1, 1987, the employee must complete and sign under penalty of perjury Section 1 of Form I-9—"Employee Information and Verification"—*at the time he/she is hired.*[5]

The verification form also requires the employer to verify, under penalty of perjury, that he/she has examined the documentation presented by an individual which establishes a prospective employee's right to work in the United States and his/her identity. The regulations provide that verification by the employer must be performed within three business days of the hire, unless an employer hires an individual for less than three days, in which case verification must be completed before the end of the employee's first working day.[6] If an individual is unable to provide the required document(s) within this time period, the regulations provide that, within three days of the hire, the individual must present a receipt showing he/she has applied for the necessary document(s). The required document(s) must then be presented within 21 days of the hire.[7]

Form I-9 must be retained by an employer for three years after the date of hire, or one year after termination of employment, whichever is later. The Act permits, but does not require, the photocopying of any documents an individual presents as part of the verification process. This is true whether or not any other federal or state law prohibits such photocopying. Employers therefore may wish to keep photocopies of the documents which they inspected and relied on as evidence of their good faith compliance with the verification requirements of the Act. However, photocopying is permitted only for the purpose of complying with the Act, and any copies made must be retained with Form I-9. In fact, employers who photocopy documents should consider keeping the photocopies and Form I-9 in files separate from their conventional personnel files.

Exhibit 24.1   INS Form I-9

U.S. Department of Justice
Immigration and Naturalization Service

OMB No. 1115-0136
Employment Eligibility Verification

Please read instructions carefully before completing this form. The instructions must be available during completion of this form. **ANTI-DISCRIMINATION NOTICE.** It is illegal to discriminate against work eligible individuals. Employers CANNOT specify which document(s) they will accept from an employee. The refusal to hire an individual because of a future expiration date may also constitute illegal discrimination.

Section 1. Employee Information and Verification. To be completed and signed by employee at the time employment begins

Print Name: Last	First	Middle Initial	Maiden Name

Address *(Street Name and Number)*	Apt. #	Date of Birth *(month/day/year)*

City	State	Zip Code	Social Security #

I am aware that federal law provides for imprisonment and/or fines for false statements or use of false documents in connection with the completion of this form.

I attest, under penalty of perjury, that I am (check one of the following):
☐ A citizen or national of the United States
☐ A Lawful Permanent Resident (Alien # A _____)
☐ An alien authorized to work until ___/___/___
(Alien # or Admission # _____)

Employee's Signature	Date *(month/day/year)*

Preparer and/or Translator Certification. *(To be completed and signed if Section 1 is prepared by a person other than the employee.) I attest, under penalty of perjury, that I have assisted in the completion of this form and that to the best of my knowledge the information is true and correct.*

Preparer's/Translator's Signature	Print Name

Address (Street Name and Number, City, State, Zip Code)	Date *(month/day/year)*

Section 2. Employer Review and Verification. To be completed and signed by employer. **Examine one document from List A OR examine one document from List B and one from List C** as listed on the reverse of this form and record the title, number and expiration date, if any, of the document(s)

List A	OR	List B	AND	List C
Document title: _____		_____		_____
Issuing authority: _____		_____		_____
Document #: _____		_____		_____
Expiration Date *(if any):* ___/___/___		___/___/___		___/___/___
Document #: _____				
Expiration Date *(if any):* ___/___/___				

CERTIFICATION - I attest, under penalty of perjury, that I have examined the document(s) presented by the above-named employee, that the above-listed document(s) appear to be genuine and to relate to the employee named, that the employee began employment on *(month/day/year)* ___/___/___ and that to the best of my knowledge the employee is eligible to work in the United States. (State employment agencies may omit the date the employee began employment).

Signature of Employer or Authorized Representative	Print Name	Title

Business or Organization Name	Address (Street Name and Number, City, State, Zip Code)	Date *(month/day/year)*

Section 3. Updating and Reverification. To be completed and signed by employer

A. New Name *(if applicable)*	B. Date of rehire *(month/day/year) (if applicable)*

C. If employee's previous grant of work authorization has expired, provide the information below for the document that establishes current employment eligibility.

Document Title: _____ Document #: _____ Expiration Date (if any): ___/___/___

I attest, under penalty of perjury, that to the best of my knowledge, this employee is eligible to work in the United States, and if the employee presented document(s), the document(s) I have examined appear to be genuine and to relate to the individual.

Signature of Employer or Authorized Representative	Date *(month/day/year)*

Form I-9 (Rev. 11-21-91) N

(continued)

Exhibit 24.1   *(continued)*

LISTS OF ACCEPTABLE DOCUMENTS

LIST A		LIST B		LIST C
Documents that Establish Both Identity and Employment Eligibility	**OR**	**Documents that Establish Identity**	**AND**	**Documents that Establish Employment Eligibility**

LIST A — Documents that Establish Both Identity and Employment Eligibility

1. U.S. Passport (unexpired or expired)

2. Certificate of U.S. Citizenship *(INS Form N-560 or N-561)*

3. Certificate of Naturalization *(INS Form N-550 or N-570)*

4. Unexpired foreign passport, with *I-551 stamp* or attached *INS Form I-94* indicating unexpired employment authorization

5. Alien Registration Receipt Card with photograph *(INS Form I-151 or I-551)*

6. Unexpired Temporary Resident Card *(INS Form I-688)*

7. Unexpired Employment Authorization Card *(INS Form I-688A)*

8. Unexpired Reentry Permit *(INS Form I-327)*

9. Unexpired Refugee Travel Document *(INS Form I-571)*

10. Unexpired Employment Authorization Document issued by the INS which contains a photograph *(INS Form I-688B)*

OR

LIST B — Documents that Establish Identity

1. Driver's license or ID card issued by a state or outlying possession of the United States provided it contains a photograph or information such as name, date of birth, sex, height, eye color, and address

2. ID card issued by federal, state, or local government agencies or entities provided it contains a photograph or information such as name, date of birth, sex, height, eye color, and address

3. School ID card with a photograph

4. Voter's registration card

5. U.S. Military card or draft record

6. Military dependent's ID card

7. U.S. Coast Guard Merchant Mariner Card

8. Native American tribal document

9. Driver's license issued by a Canadian government authority

For persons under age 18 who are unable to present a document listed above:

10. School record or report card

11. Clinic, doctor, or hospital record

12. Day-care or nursery school record

AND

LIST C — Documents that Establish Employment Eligibility

1. U.S. social security card issued by the Social Security Administration *(other than a card stating it is not valid for employment)*

2. Certification of Birth Abroad issued by the Department of State *(Form FS-545 or Form DS-1350)*

3. Original or certified copy of a birth certificate issued by a state, county, municipal authority or outlying possession of the United States bearing an official seal

4. Native American tribal document

5. U.S. Citizen ID Card *(INS Form I-197)*

6. ID Card for use of Resident Citizen in the United States *(INS Form I-179)*

7. Unexpired employment authorization document issued by the INS *(other than those listed under List A)*

Illustrations of many of these documents appear in Part 8 of the Handbook for Employers (M-274)

Form I-9 (Rev. 11-21-91) N

   In the case of a former employee who is rehired by an employer who has previously completed Form I-9 and the verification procedures with respect to such employee, the regulations provide that, when any such individual is rehired within three years of the initial execution of Form I-9, the employer need only inspect Form I-9; if he/she determines that the employee is still authorized to work, no additional verification or new Form I-9 need be completed.[8]

If a state agency has conducted the verification process, the employer can comply with the Act by obtaining from the employee the *original* of the Form I-9 completed by the state agency, and keeping it on file for three years, or one year after termination of employment, whichever is later.[9]

The Act, however, does *not* permit an employer to rely on a verification conducted by a private employment agency. Thus, the employer should examine documentation and complete Form I-9 for all individuals referred by such a private agency.

Notwithstanding the foregoing, the regulations *do* permit an employer to designate an agent for purposes of verifying employment eligibility. Thus, an employer may designate a private employment agency *or* union hiring hall as its agent for verification purposes under the Act. But, unlike the case where verification is conducted by a state employment agency, if the verification conducted by a private employment agency *or* union hiring hall fails to satisfy the requirements of the law, it is the employer who will be liable.

An employer who establishes that he/she has complied in good faith with the verification requirements of the Act will have an affirmative, yet rebuttable, defense that such a person has not violated the Act by "knowingly" hiring an illegal alien.

However, if an employer hires an alien who is authorized to work at the time of hire and continues to employ the alien after learning that the alien has become unauthorized with respect to such employment, he/she is in violation of the Act.

Penalties

Civil and criminal penalties may be assessed against employers who "knowingly" employ an illegal alien or fail to complete and retain the required identity and work authorization documents.

An employer who knowingly hires or continues to employ an unauthorized alien is, for the first offense, subject to a civil fine of at least $250 and up to $2,000 for each unauthorized alien. For a second offense, the fine increases to a minimum of $2,000 and up to $5,000 for each unauthorized alien. For the third or subsequent offense, fines increase to a minimum of $3,000 and as much as $10,000 for each illegal alien.[10] An employer who is found guilty of engaging in a "pattern or practice" of hiring illegal aliens is subject to a criminal penalty of up to $3,000 for each unauthorized alien employed, and six months in prison.[11]

An employer who fails to comply with the verification requirements under the Act may be fined between $100 and $1,000 per employee. It is important to note that an employer may be fined for failure to inspect and verify a worker's documentation *even if* the individual in question is in fact a citizen or an alien authorized to work in the United States.[12]

It is also important to note that, under the provisions of the Act, if the INS asserts that an employer has hired an unauthorized alien, the employer may show as an "affirmative defense" that he/she has complied in "good faith" with the documentation and recordkeeping requirements of the Act. However, even if the employer completes and retains the verification forms which are required, this will not necessarily provide an absolute defense. For example, the INS might offer sufficient proof that the documents the employer relied upon did not reasonably appear on their face to be genuine, that the verification process was merely a pretext or a sham, or that the employer conspired with the unauthorized employees in falsifying documents. This does not mean, however, that an employer is required to conduct an in-depth investigation to authenticate the documents. Employers are expected to accept documents which reasonably appear on their face to be genuine.

The law also provides that civil penalties and compensatory damages may be awarded against an employer who violates the anti-discrimination provisions of the Act, which are discussed below.

Anti-Discrimination Provisions

In addition to the prohibition against national origin discrimination contained in Title VII of the Civil Rights Act of 1964, employment discrimination on the basis of national origin or citizenship status is prohibited by the Act.[13] This anti-discrimination provision was included to ensure that job applicants, whom employers perceive to be foreign born, are not discriminated against because of employers' fears regarding the Act's sanctions. Employers who have four or more employees and who discriminate against persons (other than unauthorized aliens) on the basis of national origin or alienage, will be subject to back pay awards, additional paperwork requirements, and fines up to $1,000 for a first act of discrimination, and up to $2,000 for subsequent acts of discrimination.

Conclusion

The foregoing is only a summary of the more significant provisions of this complex law. Employers are advised to consult with their own legal counsel with respect to a more detailed explanation of the employer's responsibilities under the Act.

Important Points for Management

- The Immigration Reform and Control Act of 1986 has made it unlawful after November 6, 1986, for any employer to "knowingly" hire any alien not authorized to work in the United States.

- The Act also contains anti-discrimination provisions, which, if violated after November 6, 1987, will render employers liable to their employees or prospective employees.

- The INS has designated Form I-9, entitled the "Employment Eligibility Verification Form," as the form employers must use to comply with the verification requirements of the law. Form I-9 may be obtained at INS District Offices or ordered from the Superintendent of Documents, Washington, D.C. 20402. Form I-9 may be photocopied or printed by employers.

- Form I-9 must be completed for *all* individuals who are hired.

- Civil and Criminal penalties may be assessed against employers who "knowingly" employ an illegal alien or fail to complete and retain the identity and work authorization documents which are required.

References

1. Immigration Reform and Control Act of 1986, Pub. L. No. 99603 (1986). See also regulations issued by the Immigration and Naturalization Service (INS). 52 Fed. Reg. 16189 (8 C.F.R. 100, 103, 109, 210, 211, 212, 234, 242, 245a, 264, 274a, 299). *Id.* at Sec. 101 (a)(1), § 274A(a)(1) & (2) (8 U.S.C.A. § 1324a(a)(1) & (2)) (Supp. 1994).

2. 52 Fed. Reg. 16221 (8 C.F.R. § 274a.1(g)).

3. *Id.* at 16622 (8 C.F.R. § 274a.2(b)(1)(V)(A)).

4. *Id.* (§ 274a.2(b)(1)(V)(B) & (C)).

5. *Id.* (8 C.F.R. § 274a.2(b)(1)(i)(A)).

6. *Id.* (8 C.F.R. § 274a.2(b)(1)(ii) & (iii)).

7. *Id.* at 16223 (8 C.F.R. § 274a.2(b)(1)(vi)).

8. *Id.* at 16223 (8 C.F.R. § 274a.6(c)).

9. *Id.* (8 C.F.R. § 274a.2(d)).

10. Immigration Reform and Control Act of 1986, Pub. L. No. 99603 (1986), Sec. 101(a)(1) § 274A(e)(4)(A) (8 U.S.C.A. § 1324a(e)(4)(A)).

11. *Id.* at Sec. 101(a)(1) § 274A(f)(1) (8 U.S.C.A. § 1324a(f)(1)).

12. *Id.* at Sec. 101(a)(1), § 274A(e)(5) (8 U.S.C.A. § 1324a(e)(5)).

13. *Id.* at Sec. 102(a), § 274B(a)(1) (8 U.S.C.A. § 1324B(a)(1)).

Review Questions

1. Why does the employer have to complete a Form I-9 for all individuals who are hired?

2. What penalties are imposed by the federal government if the employer hires an illegal alien?

3. Under what circumstances would an employer's hiring practices discriminate against an alien in violation of federal law?

4. What documents can be used to establish an employee's authority to work?

5. What documents can be used to establish the identity of a prospective employee?

6. How long must an employer retain Form I-9 for an employee?

7. What penalties may be assessed against an employer who knowingly hires or continues to employ an illegal alien?

8. What penalties may be assessed against an employer who fails to comply with verification requirements under the Immigration Reform and Control Act of 1986?

Internet Sites

For more information, visit the following Internet sites. Remember that Internet addresses can change without notice.

Immigration and Naturalization Service
http://www.ins.usdoj.gov

Chapter 25 Outline

Federal Insurance Contributions Act (FICA)
  Withholding of Employee's FICA
  Employee's Social Security Card
  Returns and Payment of Tax
  Employer Credit for FICA Paid on
    Tip Income
  Records
  Social Security on Orchestras
  Important Points for Each Hotel to
    Check
Federal Unemployment Tax Act (FUTA)
  Employers Subject to FUTA
  Returns and Payment of FUTA Tax
  Rate of Tax and Credits Against Tax
  Amount of Wages Subject to Tax
  Records
  Penalties
  Unemployment Insurance Payments
    on Hotel Orchestras
  FICA and FUTA Taxes on Tips
  Employees' Free Meals Furnished for
    the Convenience of the Employer—
    the FICA and FUTA Tax Question
State Unemployment Insurance Programs
State Laws on Workers' Compensation
Important Points for Management
References
Review Questions
Internet Sites

Competencies

1. Identify two major federal employment taxes. (p. 341)

2. Define "wages" in the context of the Federal Insurance Contributions Act. (pp. 341–342)

3. List the essential procedures related to Social Security that an operation must follow. (pp. 342–344)

4. Explain when orchestra members may be subject to FICA and FUTA, and summarize how FUTA is applied and administered. (pp. 343–345)

5. Describe how FICA and FUTA are applied to employee tips and free meals. Describe the relationship between federal and state governments with regard to unemployment insurance. (pp. 345–346)

6. Explain the purpose of workers' compensation laws, summarize how states comply with these laws, and name four classifications of disabilities. (pp. 347–349)

25

Federal Social Security, Unemployment Insurance, and Workers' Compensation

T HIS CHAPTER DISCUSSES federal Social Security and unemployment taxes, as well as state unemployment, disability, and workers' compensation programs from the standpoint of the employer's obligations.*

The employment taxes under the federal Social Security program relevant to hotels** are presently levied under the Federal Insurance Contributions Act. Commonly known as FICA, this Act provides retirement benefits for employees and their survivors. All hotels with employees must pay contributions under FICA.

A second employer tax is the Federal Unemployment Tax Act (FUTA). As the name implies, it provides taxes to cover unemployment insurance. In general, hotels that employ one or more persons at any time in each of any 20 calendar weeks during a calendar year must pay contributions under FUTA. The payments are made to the federal government, but the benefits are paid out to the unemployed by state governments. (See the discussion of "State Unemployment Insurance Programs" later in this chapter.)

The administration and enforcement of both FICA and FUTA are under the general jurisdiction of the Federal Social Security Administration, Baltimore, Maryland. However, the taxes levied by these Acts are paid to the District Director of Internal Revenue. The Bureau of Internal Revenue has issued information about both of these Acts in "Circular E, Employer's Tax Guide." Hotels may secure copies of this publication from the nearest District Director of Internal Revenue.

Federal Insurance Contributions Act (FICA)

In general, FICA provides for a tax upon the employer and a second tax upon the employee that the employer must deduct from the "wages" paid. The term "wages" is a very broad concept and includes all remuneration for employment unless specifically excepted by provisions of the federal law.[1] Remuneration may

---

  * This chapter does not deal with the various benefits from this program payable to the employees, such as the old-age survivor's and disability insurance benefits.
 ** Self-Employment Contributions Act is only relevant to self-employed.

341

include cash payments as well as goods, lodging, food or clothing, and vacation allowances. Tips constitute wages unless (1) they are not paid in cash, or (2) the tips do not exceed $20 in any calendar month.*

As of January 1, 2001, the FICA tax rate was still divided into two portions: the Social Security tax portion of 6.2% and the Medicare tax portion of 1.45%, for a combined FICA tax rate of 7.65%. Thus, as of 2000, a Social Security tax rate of 6.2% was paid by employers and employees *each* on earnings (tip income and wages) up to $80,400, and the Medicare tax rate of 1.45% was paid by employers and employees each on all earnings.

The maximum wage base may increase in future years since it is determined annually by a statutory escalator formula.[2] The amount of wages subject to FICA taxes under this escalator provision is published in the Federal Register on or before November 1 of the year before any year in which the wage base will increase.

Withholding of Employee's FICA

Employers should also remember that they must *deduct* and *withhold* from their employee's *wages* the Social Security and Medicare taxes payable by the *employee* on his/her wages and on total tips he/she reports to the employer (6.2% and 1.45% of wages and tips reported) for income tax purposes.

Employee's Social Security Card[3]

Every employee who is working in an employment covered by Social Security is supposed to have a Social Security card bearing his/her Social Security account number. This is important because each employee's account number must appear on all returns the employer files at the time of paying the taxes. If the hotel hires an employee who does not have a Social Security card and number, then, according to FICA:

(1)   the *employee* is required to make application for an account number within seven days after he starts work. This application is made by him to the nearest District Office of the Social Security Administration on Form SS-5, copies of which can be obtained from any District Office of the Social Security Administration, or from the nearest District Director of the Internal Revenue Service [emphasis added].

Returns and Payment of Tax[4]

Under FICA, employers make returns on Form 941, secured from the District Office of the Internal Revenue Service. Once an employer has registered, this form is mailed to the employer every three months. The returns must be filed four times a year and the taxes paid before the end of the month following each calendar quarter of the year. If the employer has made timely deposits in full payment of the tax due for the entire quarter, then the return may be filed by the 10th of the second month following the quarter.

---

* Cash tips include tips charged to a guest's credit card and which the employer turns over to the service employee. Treatment of tip income is discussed later in this chapter.

FICA taxes owed by the employer and withheld from employees' wages are paid or deposited in an authorized commercial bank or a Federal Reserve Bank in the same manner and at the same time as are the amounts withheld from wages for income tax purposes. See Chapter 26, under the heading "Deposit of Tax," for a discussion of such payment procedures.

Employer Credit for FICA Paid on Tip Income

For taxes paid after 1993, the Budget Reconciliation Act of 1993* provides a general business tax credit for food or beverage establishments equal to the employer's share of FICA tax (7.65%) on a portion of an employee's tip income. The credit is available for FICA paid on reported tips in excess of those treated as wages under the minimum wage provision of the Fair Labor Standards Act (FLSA). (The law prohibits an employer from taking a deduction for any amount for which the employer received the FICA credit.) Tipped employees not involved with food and beverage service cannot be included in the tax credit.

Records

The Social Security regulations provide that every employer must keep accurate records of all remuneration (whether in cash or otherwise) paid to employees.

Social Security on Orchestras

Social Security payments are required only with respect to employees. Ordinarily it is not difficult to ascertain whether or not a person is a hotel employee; in connection with orchestras, however, the problem is more difficult. It is not always easy to determine whether an individual member of the orchestra is an employee of the hotel or an employee of the orchestra leader. This is because orchestras are frequently engaged by making a contract with the orchestra leader, under which he/she agrees to furnish the orchestra for a specific amount per week or per day.

In recent years there has been much litigation on the question. In these cases the hotel or ballroom operator has taken the position either that the orchestra members are employed by the orchestra leader rather than by the hotel, or that each individual member of the orchestra is an "independent contractor" rather than an employee. The question of whether or not a particular person is an employee is always a question of fact under the terms of the contract and taking into account all of the surrounding circumstances. For that reason, the individual musician might be an employee in one hotel but not in another. The determination of the employer-employee relationship may also depend upon the degree of control that the hotel exercises over the individual musician.

If a hotel has reason to believe that the individual musicians are not employees of the hotel but employees of the orchestra leader, it can refuse to pay Social Security on these individual musicians. In this case, however, a hotel should set up a cash reserve to cover its contribution in the event that it is ultimately held to be the

---

* IRS Code § 45B

musicians' employer. In addition, it should try to arrange with individual members of the orchestra and the orchestra leader to deduct the employee's contribution and either to hold it in escrow until the matter is finally determined, or pay it to the government with a protest statement to the effect that in making such deduction and payment, the hotel is not admitting its liability as an employer. Then, the hotel should apply for a refund.

The principles set forth above also apply to FUTA, except that under FUTA there is no problem with a deduction from wages since the employer pays the entire amount.

Important Points for Each Hotel to Check

1. *Make sure that each employee has a Social Security card.*
2. *Secure employer's identification number.*
3. *Make proper deductions from employee's pay.*
4. *File quarterly returns and pay tax in April, July, October, and January.*

Federal Unemployment Tax Act (FUTA)

FUTA[5] is a tax upon employers to provide federal unemployment insurance for workers. Several features and requirements of FUTA as they relate to hotel employers are summarized here. As mentioned earlier, the employer pays the *entire* amount of the FUTA tax.

Employers Subject to FUTA[6]

In general, to be covered by FUTA, an employer must either have (1) paid wages of $1,500 or more in any calendar quarter, or (2) had one or more employees at any time in each of any 20 calendar weeks. The employees need not be the same persons during the entire 20 weeks.

Returns and Payment of FUTA Tax[7]

The returns for the FUTA tax are made on Form 940, secured from the local District Director of Internal Revenue. After employers have filed one return, forms should be mailed to them each year thereafter. The return must be filed with the local District Director of Internal Revenue on or before January 31 following the close of the calendar year covered by the return, unless the taxpayer has made certain quarterly deposits of the FUTA tax due (discussed below), in which case a 10-day extension of the due date is allowed.

Although the FUTA tax return must be filed annually, the regulations generally require (with certain exceptions) the employer to compute the FUTA tax quarterly and to deposit the total amount of FUTA tax due each quarter with an authorized bank or a Federal Reserve Bank. These quarterly deposits are required only when the amount of FUTA tax due for a particular quarter (or for a prior quarter in which no deposit was required) is $100 or more. The required deposit must be made with a Federal Tax Deposit Form (Form 508), which the IRS computer-codes, labels, and sends to each employer.

Rate of Tax and Credits Against Tax[8]

For the tax year 2001, the FUTA tax rate is 6.2% of the total taxable wages up to $80,400. However, there is a credit against the tax to the extent that the employer has contributed into a state unemployment insurance fund. These credits are limited to a 5.4% maximum credit.

Amount of Wages Subject to Tax

Under FUTA, all remuneration for employment is subject to the tax, with certain exceptions. Most important, as of January 1, 1983, the employer pays a tax only on the first $7,000 paid to an individual employee during the calendar year.

Records[9]

The records that are required to be kept are similar to records under the FICA tax discussed earlier. In addition, however, the records must show the amount of contributions paid into the state unemployment insurance fund and any credits received therefrom.

Penalties[10]

Willful failure to pay the FUTA tax, make returns, or keep proper records is a misdemeanor and punishable by a fine of up to $25,000 ($100,000 if a corporation), or imprisonment of not more than one year, or both. In addition, there are penalties for various types of violations, such as liability for double the amount of the tax, an additional tax for late filing of returns, and others.[11]

Unemployment Insurance Payments on Hotel Orchestras

The same principles set forth in our earlier discussion of FICA and orchestra members apply with equal force to payments under FUTA. If a musician is an employee under either FICA or FUTA, he/she is also considered an employee under the other Act.

FICA and FUTA Taxes on Tips

As mentioned earlier, an employee who receives $20 per month or more in tips must report the total amount of tips received during the month to the employer. The amount of tips reported is considered wages for purposes of income tax withholding, FICA taxes, and FUTA taxes.

Therefore, in addition to withholding income tax due, employers must withhold FICA taxes and pay FUTA taxes on any tips an employee reports.

Employers must also continue to withhold amounts from salary payments for payments of the employee's FICA tax on total tips reported to the employer for income tax purposes.

Tips to employees are taxable wages for FUTA purposes, but only to the extent that the employer takes the tips reported in writing into account in determining the employee's compensation under the applicable minimum wage law.

Employees' Free Meals Furnished for the Convenience of the Employer—the FICA and FUTA Tax Question

On June 8, 1981, the U.S. Supreme Court ruled in *Rowan Companies, Inc.* v. *United States*[12] that meals and lodging furnished to employees that are not subject to federal income tax and federal income tax withholding under § 119 of the Internal Revenue Code (IRC) are not considered "wages" subject to FICA and FUTA taxes.

Section 119 of the IRC excludes the value of meals and lodging provided "for the convenience of the employer" from federal income tax and income tax withholding. Under this "convenience of the employer rule," the Supreme Court explained, "an employee may exclude from gross income the value of meals and lodging furnished to him by his employer if the employer furnished both the meals and lodging for its own convenience, furnished the meals on its business premises and required the employee to accept the lodging on the business premises as a condition of employment."[13] The court held that for FICA and FUTA purposes the definition of wages was identical to that for income tax withholding. Thus, the court has, in effect, adopted the "convenience of the employer" test under § 119 of the IRC to determine whether meals and lodging furnished employees are subject to FICA and FUTA taxes.* See Chapter 26 for further discussion of the "convenience of the employer" rule.

State Unemployment Insurance Programs

As mentioned earlier, the unemployment insurance programs of the federal government (FUTA) and of state governments are related. While tax payments or employer (and employee) contributions are generally paid over to the federal jurisdiction, the state administers benefits under federal and state unemployment insurance programs. The states and the District of Columbia (and U.S. territories) have laws that generally require only employer contributions to the unemployment insurance fund, based on a percentage of employee salaries. The tax rates and wage bases subject to the taxes (as well as unemployment insurance benefits) vary among the states. Therefore, employers must consult their local counsel with respect to the specific nature and requirements of the unemployment insurance program enacted in their own state.

The state unemployment insurance tax rates may also vary among taxpayers in the same state, since in many states employers who qualify under provisions of state law may pay a reduced tax rate for a proven record of low unemployment among its employees.**

---

* In *Hotel Conquistador, Inc.* v. *United States*,[14] the U.S. Supreme Court also refused to review the Court of Claims ruling that the value of meals and lodging provided to hotel employees that is not subject to income tax withholding is also not subject to FICA and FUTA taxes. The IRS, however, announced that it would not follow the decision.[15] The Supreme Court in the *Rowan* case, *supra,* settled the question, ruling against the position of the IRS.

** New Jersey, Rhode Island, Hawaii, California, and Puerto Rico also have varying tax rates.

The wage base subject to the New York State Unemployment Insurance Tax, after January 1, 1999, is $8,500 of "remuneration" for each employee.[16] The term "remuneration" is defined to include:

> [E]very form of compensation for employment paid by an employer to his employee; whether paid directly or indirectly by the employer, including salaries, commissions, bonuses, and the reasonable money value of board, rent, housing, lodging, or similar advantage received. Where gratuities are received by the employee in the course of his employment from a person other than his employer, the value of such gratuities shall be determined by the [Industrial] [C]ommissioner.[17]*

While FUTA and state unemployment insurance programs are related, they are separate programs. That is, under FUTA the value of employees' meals and lodging is considered wages if not given for the "convenience of the employer" under the IRC, as decided in the *Rowan Companies* case (see discussion under the "Meals and Lodging" heading in Chapter 26). However, this test may not apply under the definition of "remuneration" or "wages" under a particular state's law, such as in New York State, or state unemployment insurance contributions by the employer.

State Laws on Workers' Compensation

All 50 states have enacted workers' compensation laws that provide a statutory framework in each state for employees to receive compensation for work-related injuries.

Workers' compensation insurance is insurance, paid for by the employer, that provides cash benefits *and* medical care for workers who become disabled because of an injury or sickness related to their job. If death results, benefits are generally payable to the surviving spouse and dependents as defined by law.

In most states, the workers' compensation acts generally provide that an employee's exclusive remedy is to obtain compensation for such work-related injury under the acts, with certain exceptions under the workers' compensation acts of the states. In other words, under the state workers' compensation acts, an employee would generally be precluded from bringing a lawsuit against his/her employer on common law negligence theories.**

---

* The Industrial Commissioner of New York State has issued regulations establishing rules for the valuation of board and lodging as well as for tips of restaurant and dining room employees, hotel service employees, and checkroom attendants, among others.[18] For example, the "reasonable money value" of board and lodging for all year-round hotels is:

> Each meal $1.45
> Lodging . . . . $ .20 per hour

** Note, however, that the courts of some states have created a judicial exception to the general exclusive remedy rule. For example, the Ohio Supreme Court in *Blankenship* v.

In order to provide such compensation, the laws of such states require employers to obtain insurance from private insurance companies or from state agencies to cover claims stemming from work-related injuries. Some states allow some employers to self-insure against the risks and liabilities of work-related injuries. However, substantial security deposits are generally required for self-insurers.

In New York State, an employer is prohibited from charging any part of the cost of workers' compensation insurance to the employee.

Employers who are insured must usually post in a conspicuous place on their premises a Notice of Compliance (Form C-105 in New York), which advises workers of their rights and how to file a claim.

The New York employer who does not carry required workers' compensation insurance is subject to an assessment of $100 for every 10 days of noncompliance and may be prosecuted in criminal court for a misdemeanor. In addition, the employer may be personally liable for any workers' compensation benefits due the injured worker in New York.

Benefits under the state workers' compensation laws generally depend on specified statutory amounts or formulas which depend on the type and extent of the work-related injury or disease. The state acts usually distinguish among four classifications of disabilities including: (1) temporary total disabilities, (2) permanent total disabilities, (3) temporary partial disabilities, and (4) permanent partial disabilities. In addition, the acts generally provide for specified compensation for certain "scheduled" injuries (such as amputation of limbs and loss of eyesight). The payments that the employee receives are intended to cover the employee's loss of income, medical expenses, rehabilitation, and survivor benefits in the case of employee work-related fatalities.

In New York State, when an employee's claim for workers' compensation benefits is challenged, the Workers' Compensation Board holds hearings before an administrative law judge. The judge takes testimony, reviews medical and other evidence, and decides whether the claimant is entitled to benefits. If the claim is found compensable, the judge determines the amount and duration of the compensation award. Either side may appeal the decision, as specified in the statute.

The workers' compensation laws of each state are quite technical and diverse, and specific questions should be referred to the hotel's local counsel.*

In addition to the state unemployment insurance taxes and workers' compensation laws, some states** have enacted laws and related taxes to provide state disability programs. These programs are designed to provide additional compensation for medical expenses and lost wages to disabled employees. Local

---

Cincinnati Milacron Chemicals, Inc.,[19] held that an employee could maintain a lawsuit for work-related injuries allegedly caused by the employer's *intentional* tort.

* For a summary of the various state acts (including summaries in chart form) of the topics of (1) coverage, (2) benefits provided and (3) administration of the acts, see the annual publication of the Chamber of Commerce of the United States entitled *Analysis of Workers' Compensation Laws* (1983).

** New York, New Jersey, Rhode Island, Hawaii, California, and Puerto Rico.

counsel, accountants, or state agencies can provide information concerning any disability program and related tax for each particular state.

Important Points for Management

In general, the Federal Insurance Contributions Act (FICA) provides for a tax upon the employer and a second tax upon the employee that the employer must deduct from the "wages" paid. The term "wages" is a very broad concept and includes all remuneration for employment unless specifically excepted by provisions of the federal law. Remuneration may include cash payments as well as goods, lodging, food or clothing, and vacation allowances. Tips constitute wages unless (1) they are not paid in cash, or (2) the tips do not exceed $20 in any calendar month.

On January 1, 1991, the FICA tax rate was divided into two portions: the Social Security tax portion of 6.2% and the Medicare tax portion of 1.45%, for a combined FICA tax rate of 7.65%. As of 2000, a Social Security tax rate of 6.2% was paid by employers and employees *each* on earnings (tip income and wages) up to $76,200, and the Medicare tax rate of 1.45% was paid by employers and employees *each* on all earnings.

If a hotel has reason to believe that musicians are not employees of the hotel but employees of the orchestra leader, it can refuse to pay Social Security taxes on these individual musicians. However, a hotel should set up a cash reserve to cover its contribution in the event that it is ultimately held to be the employer of the musicians. In addition, it should try to arrange with individual members of the orchestra and the orchestra leader to deduct each employee's contribution and either to hold it in escrow until the matter is finally determined, or pay it to the government with a protest statement to the effect that in making such deduction and payment, the hotel is not admitting its liability as an employer, and then apply for a refund.

The unemployment insurance programs of the federal government (FUTA) and of state governments are related. While tax payments or employer (and employee) contributions are generally paid over to the federal jurisdiction, the state administers benefits under federal and state unemployment insurance programs.

Employers who are insured must usually post in a conspicuous place on their premises a Notice of Compliance with Workers' Compensation Laws (Form C-105 in New York), which advises workers of their rights and how to file a claim.

References

1. I.R.C. § 3121(a).
2. 42 U.S.C. § 430.
3. 26 C.F.R. §§ 31.6011(b)(1)-31.6011(b)(2).
4. 26 C.F.R. § 31.6011(a)(1).
5. Internal Revenue Code of 1954, Chapter 23, as amended.
6. I.R.C. § 3306(a)(1).
7. 26 C.F.R. § 31.6011(a)(3).

8. I.R.C. §§ 3301, 3302.
9. 26 C.F.R. § 31.6001-4.
10. I.R.C. § 7203.
11. 26 U.S.C. § 6672.
12. 452 U.S. 247 (1981).
13. See 26 U.S.C. § 119.
14. 220 Ct. Cl. 20, 597 F.2d 348 (1979), *cert. denied,* 444 U.S. 1032 (1980).
15. 1980-7 I.R.B. 14 (1980).
16. N.Y. Lab. Law § 518(1)(a).
17. N.Y. Lab. Law § 517.
18. 12 N.Y. CRR Tit. § 138-2.7.
19. 69 Ohio St. 2d 608, 23 Ohio Op. 3d 504, 433 N.E. 2d 527, *cert. denied,* 103 S.Ct. 127 (1982).

Review Questions

1. Why does the employer have to pay FUTA taxes on an employee's wages?

2. Does the employee have to report *all* of his/her tips to the employer? Why or why not?

3. Does the employee pay FICA taxes on his/her tips?

4. When does the hotel have to pay FICA taxes on members of an orchestra that the hotel hires to play at the hotel?

Internet Sites

For more information, visit the following Internet sites. Remember that Internet addresses can change without notice.

Employment Taxes
http://www4.law.cornell.edu/
uscode/26/stC.html

Social Security Online
http://www.ssa.gov/

Chapter 26 Outline

General Nature of Law—Federal Income
    Tax
Determination of Wages
Withholding Priorities
Deposit of Tax
Returns and Payment of Tax
Withholding Statements to be Furnished to
    Employees
Annual Report of Withholding
Meals and Lodging
Tip Reporting Requirements
    TEFRA
    The Regulations
Important Points for Management
References
Review Questions
Internet Sites

Competencies

1. State the conditions under which tips
    are not considered wages. (p. 353)

2. List the order in which an employer
    should deduct taxes from a tipped
    employee's cash wages. (pp. 353–354)

3. State the alternatives an employer has
    when cash wages are not sufficient for
    collecting required taxes on reported
    tips. Describe regulations regarding
    depositing federal tax, tax returns and
    payment of tax, and withholding
    statements. (pp. 354–355)

4. Identify two conditions required to
    exclude meals and lodging from an
    employee's income for federal tax
    purposes. (pp. 355–356)

5. State tip reporting requirements of the
    Tax Equity and Fiscal Responsibility
    Act (TEFRA). (pp. 356–359)

6. List the items that are included in
    gross receipts in order to calculate the
    "threshold" for tip reporting purposes.
    (pp. 359–362)

26

Federal Income Tax: Withholding and Reporting Requirements

General Nature of Law—Federal Income Tax

The federal government requires the employer to withhold income taxes from the wages and salaries of employees and pay these taxes directly to the federal government.[1] This constitutes part of the system under which most persons pay their income tax during the year in which income is received or earned. For many employees whose entire income is wages, the amount withheld approximates the total tax due, so that the employee must pay little or no additional tax at the end of the year. The Internal Revenue Service (IRS) has prepared a bulletin for employers, "Circular E," outlining the requirements for withholding income tax and including tables showing the amounts to be withheld. Circular E is available from the local IRS office upon request or on the web.

Determination of Wages

For the purpose of the ordinary hotel payroll, the term "wages" means all remuneration, whether in cash or goods, an employer pays to an employee for services performed. Living quarters or meals furnished to an employee are included, *unless* such living quarters or meals are furnished for the "convenience of the employer." (This is discussed in Chapter 25 and later in this chapter.)

Tips the employee receives in the course of employment are considered wages for federal income tax purposes, unless the tips are paid in any medium other than cash or the cash tips received in any calendar month are less than $20. An employer is required to deduct and withhold the tax on those tips that the employee reports to the employer in a written statement furnished to the employer (Form 4070, shown in Chapter 19).

Withholding Priorities

In some instances when employers calculate the taxes to be withheld from a tipped employee's wages, including amounts to be withheld because of the employee's reported tips, the total to be withheld exceeds the cash wages due to the employee. The IRS has issued rules that state the order in which taxes should be deducted from cash wages.[2] The priority is:

1. The employee's share of Social Security tax the employer is required to withhold on cash wages (exclusive of tips)

2. The federal income tax the employer is required to withhold on cash wages (exclusive of tips)

3. The state and local withholding taxes the employer is required to withhold on cash wages (exclusive of tips)

4. The employee's share of Social Security tax required to be withheld as computed on the tips reported to the employer

5. The federal income tax required to be withheld as computed on the tips reported to the employer

6. Any other payroll deductions, such as union dues or wage garnishments, only after taking into consideration the preceding five priorities

If the cash wages are not sufficient for collecting the taxes on reported tips, employers have the following options available:

- Collect Social Security tax and/or federal income tax from a future payroll

- Collect monies from the employee on a voluntary basis to cover Social Security tax and/or federal income tax not withheld

- Report any Social Security tax not withheld on the W-2 (box 6) as "Uncollectible FICA on Tips"

In some instances the *employee* can be penalized for underwithholding should the withholding be less than 80% of his/her total tax liability for the year.

Deposit of Tax

If the total tax withheld by the employer from all employees amounts to more than $500 at the end of a quarter, the tax must be deposited in an "authorized financial institution" or a Federal Reserve bank. An "authorized financial institution" means a bank authorized by the Treasury Department to receive such deposits; most banks have such authorization. The amount of taxes determines the frequency of deposits, and the rules are summarized in Circular E. Employers who withhold less than $1,000 during the quarter have the option of following the deposit procedure. Otherwise, employers with less than $1,000 in withholding may pay the tax over to the IRS at the time each quarterly report is filed.

Moreover, larger employers with correspondingly larger withholding liabilities have different deposit requirements. If, during the immediately preceding period July 1 to June 30 (the "lookback" period), an employer reported $50,000 or less of withholding taxes, that employer must deposit on a monthly basis. If during the "lookback" period the employer reported more than $50,000 in withholding, then that employer must make two deposits per month. Moreover, if the employer incurs a tax liability of $100,000 or more in any given month, an immediate deposit must be made. Finally, if in 1998, the employer incurred tax liability of over $200,000, then all deposits must be made by electronic transfer.

Returns and Payment of Tax

The employer must file quarterly returns on Form 941, available from the local IRS office, with the local IRS Center. These returns cover three-month periods and generally must be filed on or before the last day of the month following the end of each calendar quarter (April, July, October, and January) for the preceding quarter. An employer who is required to make deposits of taxes, and has made timely deposits in full payment of the taxes due, may file the quarterly return on or before the 10th day of the second month following the applicable period (May 10, August 10, November 10, February 10).

The employer must keep for *at least* four years the employees' withholding exemption certificates (Form W-4) and also maintain records showing the number of persons employed, the periods of employment, and the amounts and dates of payments to these employees.

Withholding Statements to be Furnished to Employees

Employers must furnish each employee from whose wages tax has been withheld two copies (Copies B and C) of the "Wage and Tax Statement," Form W-2, obtained from the local Internal Revenue office. It is a comparatively simple form reporting the total wages paid and the amount of tax withheld. This statement must be furnished in duplicate to each employee on or before January 31 following the close of the calendar year the wages were paid (including value of meals and lodging unless furnished for the "convenience of the employer") and the tax withheld during the preceding year. If an employee leaves before the end of the year and requests the statement before the end of the calendar year, the employer must provide the statement not later than 30 days after the last payment of wages or after the date of the request, whichever is later.

Annual Report of Withholding

The employer must file the "Transmittal of Income and Tax Statement," Form W-3, for the calendar year with the Social Security Administration annually on or before the last day of February following the calendar year. A copy of Form W-2 (Copy A) for the calendar year must be filed with Form W-3. The Social Security Administration transmits the income tax information on the form to the IRS. Under another section of the Internal Revenue Code (IRC), employers must make "information returns" on Forms 1096 and 1099 with respect to fees paid to non-corporate independent contractors for services rendered and for non-salary distributions (such as dividends). Such forms do not include the wage payment reported on the withholding statements.

Meals and Lodging

As pointed out earlier, living quarters or meals furnished to an employee are income and subject to withholding taxes, unless such meals and lodging are furnished "for the convenience of the employer." This is sometimes a difficult determination. However, the question must be considered and answered separately in each case. A hotel may furnish meals and lodging to some of its employees for its convenience. It may also furnish meals and lodging to other employees not for its convenience, but merely as additional employee remuneration. The circumstances surrounding the employment must be carefully considered in each individual case. If the withholding is not proper, the employer may become liable for the amount of the income tax due that the employee fails to pay.[3]

Treasury regulations make it clear that at least two conditions must be met if meals and lodging are excluded by the employer in computing the employee's income for federal tax purposes:

1. The meals and lodging must be furnished on the business premises of the employer; and

2. In the case of lodging, the employee must be required to accept such lodging in order to enable him/her to properly perform the duties of his/her employment.

Tip Reporting Requirements

In 1982 Congress enacted the Tax Equity and Fiscal Responsibility Act (TEFRA) which included provisions requiring certain "food and beverage establishments," including most hotels, to report to the IRS the tip income that tipped employees reported to their employers. Furthermore, TEFRA provides that if total reported tip income is less than 8% of the establishment's gross receipts, such establishment would be required to make an allocation of tips among tipped employees pursuant to IRS regulations. Below is an outline of the Act and the IRS regulations. (See 26 C.F.R. § 31.6053-3.)

TEFRA

A. Information Requirements

A food and beverage establishment which may be part of a larger operation such as a hotel and which normally employed more than 10 employees on a typical business day during the preceding calendar year will be required to report annually to the IRS:

1. Gross receipts of the establishment from food and beverage sales (other than receipts from carry-out sales and mandatory 10% or more service charge sales),

2. The amount of aggregate charge receipts (other than receipts from carry-out sales and 10% service charge sales),

3. The aggregate amount of tips shown on such charge receipts, and

4. Reported tip income, and mandatory service charges of less than 10%.

B. Threshold

If the employees voluntarily report tips aggregating 8% or more of gross receipts (as defined in #1 above), *no tip allocation is required.* But the employee must file Form 8027 with the IRS (see next).

C. If 8% Threshold Is Not Met

The employer must allocate an amount equal to the difference between 8% of gross receipts and the amount reported by employees for the year to all tipped employees pursuant to either an agreement between the employer and employees or, in the absence of such an agreement, according to the IRS regulations.

The regulations provide procedures for an establishment to show its tipped employees' average tip rate is less than 8% (but not less than 2%). In addition, a single application to the IRS district director may be made with respect to all of an employer's establishments within the same IRS region that are similar in operation and have the same tip rate.

In 1994, the IRS began to claim that hotels had not paid sufficient FICA taxes, even though they had met the 8% threshold. The IRS commenced audits of numerous hotels and restaurants and assessed many of them for FICA taxes. In some cases, the assessments were in the hundreds of thousands of dollars. This led to a number of lawsuits. In the meantime, the hotel industry and the restaurant industry negotiated a solution with the IRS. Now if a hotel or restaurant signs an agreement with the IRS, it can obtain protection from such FICA assessments. This agreement is known as a Tip Rate Alternative Commitment (TRAC). The IRS also offers another agreement, known as the Tip Rate Determination Agreement (TRDA). Both agreements are intended to help ensure that employees report the proper level of tips. The forms for the agreements can be found on the web at http://www.irs.gov.

The Regulations

Food or beverage establishments will have to keep records of gross sales, charge sales, tips shown on the charge sales, and tips reported by employees to properly file a tip reporting form (Form 8027) with the IRS. The following is a further explanation of how and when to allocate tip income to employees.

Large Establishment. The first thing to consider is whether the property—or properties—are covered by this law. Although the law is complicated about who is covered, most hotels and motels are covered by this tip reporting law. Your property is covered if it is a "large food or beverage establishment."

The regulations contain a two-part definition of a "large food or beverage establishment": (1) a food or beverage operation whose employer normally employed more than ten employees on a typical business day during the preceding calendar year; and (2) where the tipping of the food or beverage employees of the operation by customers is customary.

Analyzing the first part of the definition, the rules state that a food or beverage operation is any business activity that provides food or beverages for consumption on the premises, other than "fast food" operations. For the purpose of determining whether an establishment meets the ten-employee criterion, the employer shall include all employees at all food or beverage operations of a single employer. Thus, a hotel with a dining room and a coffee shop, with eight employees in the dining room and three in the coffee shop, is covered by this law since the hotel has "more than ten employees."

In addition, if an employer at a food or beverage operation is a member of a controlled group of corporations, all employees of all corporations that are members of such controlled group of corporations shall be treated as employed by a single employer. Or if you are a partnership owning, for example, three motels with five employees at each motel's food or beverage operation, you have more than ten employees and are covered.

Separate Establishments. The test for reporting purposes, however, may be different from the ten-employee coverage test. Although the employees of all establishments are added together just to see whether you meet the ten-employee criterion, for reporting purposes they are treated separately.

Each food or beverage activity in a single building is considered a separate food or beverage establishment if the customers of the activity, while being provided with food or beverage, occupy an area separate from that occupied by customers of other activities, and the gross receipts of the activity are recorded separately from the gross receipts of the other activities.

Example

A restaurant, a coffee shop, and a cocktail lounge, all in the same hotel, are treated as separate food or beverage operations if gross receipts from each activity are recorded separately and the areas occupied by customers are separate. Therefore, you would report separately for each of these three establishments—filing a form for each one and treating tip income separately for each establishment.

Also, different activities conducted at different times in the identical place may be treated as separate food or beverage operations by an employer, if the gross receipts of the activities at each time are recorded separately.

Customary Tipping. For a food or beverage operation to be covered by this law, the tipping of employees must be customary. The regulations provide that tipping is generally not customary in food and beverage operations where 95% of the total sales include a service charge of 10% or more, or in "fast food" and "cafeteria style" operations. In this regard, properties with buffets and smorgasbords should consult the regulations to determine whether to report cafeteria and buffet activity.

Example

An employer that records the gross receipts from its cafeteria style lunch operation separately from the gross receipts of its full service dinner operation, though the same room is used for both, may treat the lunch and dinner operations as two separate food or beverage operations.

What to Do. Form 8027, a copy of which is presented in Exhibit 26.1, spells out how to report. Basically, large food or beverage establishments have to keep records of their gross receipts, including gross receipts or total hours attributable to each tipped employee, charge sales, tips shown on the charge sales, and tips recorded to the employer by food or beverage employees. It is necessary to keep detailed records for each employee, because, even though only total amounts of these items will be needed to complete the forms to be filed with the IRS, *if the total of tips reported is less than 8% of qualified gross receipts for the payroll period, the required allocation of tip income must be made on an employee-by-employee basis, by calendar year or by payroll period, and only to directly tipped employees.*

You must keep records of gross receipts for a "payroll period." You have considerable flexibility in choosing a payroll period and may select any length of time up to a calendar year or some reasonable division of it for the purpose of making tip allocations. Determine the amount of tips reported to you by food and beverage employees for the same payroll period. If tips equal at least 8%, there is no need to allocate. If there is a shortfall, you will need to make an allocation. If you make an allocation in accordance with IRS rules, you won't be liable to an employee for an improper allocation.

Here is what employers are going to have to report annually and keep records on.

A.   You Must Report "Gross Receipts"

The gross receipts to be reported are the gross receipts from food or beverage operations excluding:

1. Carry-out sales,

2. Sales on which a 10% or more service charge is added,

3. Tips reported on charge sales if the tips have been paid to the employees in cash and cash sales have not been reduced by the amount of tips paid to the employees (this means that if a meal cost $80 and the tip is $20 and the employee receives the $20, the "gross receipt" here to the food or beverage establishment is $80—not $100), and

4. State or local taxes.

Included in your calculations of gross receipts are:

1. Food or beverage charges to a hotel room, but tips charged to a hotel room can be excluded from gross receipts if the employer's accounting procedures allow these tips to be segregated out;

2. The retail value of complimentary food or beverages served to customers. In general, if a hotel or restaurant provides complimentary food and beverage to guests and patrons and it is not customary for such guests or patrons to tip the service employees in connection with such complimentary food and beverages, the value of the complimentary food and beverages may be excluded from gross receipts. As the regulations explain,

Exhibit 26.1   IRS Form 8027

Form **8027**	**Employer's Annual Information Return of Tip Income and Allocated Tips**	OMB No. 1545-0714
Department of the Treasury Internal Revenue Service	▶ See separate instructions.	**2000**

Use IRS label. Make any necessary changes. Otherwise, please type or print.

Name of establishment

Number and street (See instructions.)   Employer identification number

City or town, state, and ZIP code

Type of establishment (check only one box)

☐ 1   Evening meals only
☐ 2   Evening and other meals
☐ 3   Meals other than evening meals
☐ 4   Alcoholic beverages

Employer's name

Establishment number (See instructions.)

Number and street (P.O. box, if applicable.)   Apt. or suite no.

City, state, and ZIP code (If a foreign address, see instructions.)

Check the box **only** if applicable: Final Return ☐   Amended Return ☐

1	Total charged tips for calendar year 2000	**1**
2	Total charge receipts (other than nonallocable receipts) showing charged tips.	**2**
3	Total amount of service charges of less than 10% paid as wages to employees	**3**
4a	Total tips reported by indirectly tipped employees	**4a**
b	Total tips reported by directly tipped employees	**4b**
	Note: *Complete the Employer's Optional Worksheet for Tipped Employees on page 4 of the instructions to determine potential unreported tips of your employees.*	
c	Total tips reported (Add lines 4a and 4b.)	**4c**
5	Gross receipts from food or beverage operations (other than nonallocable receipts). . .	**5**
6	Multiply line 5 by 8% (.08) or the lower rate shown here ▶ _____ granted by the IRS. Attach a copy of the IRS determination letter to this return	**6**
	Note: *If you have allocated tips using other than the calendar year (semimonthly, biweekly, quarterly, etc.), put an "X" on line 6 and enter the amount of allocated tips from your records on line 7.*	
7	Allocation of tips. If line 6 is more than line 4c, enter the excess here	**7**

This amount must be allocated as tips to tipped employees working in this establishment. Check the box below that shows the method used for the allocation. (Show the portion, if any, attributable to each employee in box 8 of the employee's Form W-2.)

a Allocation based on hours-worked method (See instructions for restriction.) . . . ☐
Note: *If you checked line 7a, enter the average number of employee hours worked per business day during the payroll period. (See instructions.)* _____
b Allocation based on gross receipts method . . . . ☐

c Allocation based on good-faith agreement (Attach copy of agreement.) . . . . . ☐

8   Enter the total number of directly tipped employees at this establishment during 2000 ▶

Under penalties of perjury, I declare that I have examined this return, including accompanying schedules and statements, and to the best of my knowledge and belief, it is true, correct, and complete.

Signature ▶   Title ▶   Date ▶

For Privacy Act and Paperwork Reduction Act Notice, see page 4 of the separate instructions.   Cat. No. 49989U   Form **8027** (2000)

For example, the retail values of complimentary hors d'oeuvres served at a bar or a complimentary dessert served to a regular patron of a restaurant would not be included in gross receipts because the receipts of the bar or restaurant would be included in the definition of gross receipts. The retail value of a complimentary fruit basket placed in a hotel room generally would not be included because tipping for the provision of such items is not customary. The retail value of complimentary drinks served to customers in a gambling casino would be included in gross receipts because tipping for the provision of such items is customary, the gambling casino is an activity engaged in for profit, and the gambling receipts of the casino would not be included in the definition of gross receipts.

3. In situations where food or beverages are provided with other goods or services, for instance, "package deals," a good-faith estimate of the gross receipts apportioned to the food or beverages (cost of food and beverages plus a reasonable profit).

B. You Must Report Aggregate "Charge Receipts" and Aggregate "Charge Tips"

"Charge Receipts" are credit card charges and charges under any other credit arrangement (for example, house charges, city ledger, and charge arrangements to country club members).

When computing "aggregate charge receipts" under the regulations, the "charge receipts" are defined as only those receipts on which tips were charged. (Do not include charge receipts on which there are no charge tips.)

However, the regulations also state,

Charges to a hotel room may be excluded from charge receipts if such exclusion is consistent with the employer's normal accounting practices and the employer applies such exclusion consistently for a given large food or beverage establishment. *Otherwise, charges to a hotel room shall be included in charge receipts* (emphasis added). Paragraph (8)(4).

C. You Must Report Aggregate Amount of Tips

All tips received by food or beverage employees of the establishment and reported to the employer must be reported.

D. You Must Report Tip Allocations

If reported tip income **(C)** is less than 8% of your gross receipts **(A)** for the chosen payroll period, you must allocate tip income. As noted above, allocation of tips may be made on an annual basis when the food and beverage employees' reported tips do not meet the 8% threshold of the food and beverage establishment's reportable "gross receipts."

E. Informational Statement to Employees

You must also furnish to each employee to whom a tip allocation was made an information statement of the aggregate amount of tips allocated to the employee. This statement consists of supplying the necessary information on the employee's W-2 form. Although not required by law, the AH&MA has printed a poster to notify employees of the federal tip reporting requirements.

Important Points for Management

The federal government requires the employer to withhold income taxes from the wages and salaries of employees and pay these taxes directly to the federal government.

For the purpose of the ordinary hotel payroll, the term "wages" means all remuneration, whether in cash or goods, paid by an employer to an employee for services performed. Living quarters or meals furnished to an employee are included, unless such living quarters or meals are furnished for the "convenience of the employer."

Tips an employee receives in the course of employment are considered wages for federal income tax purposes, unless the tips are paid in any medium other than cash or the cash tips received in any calendar month are less than $20. An employer is required to deduct and withhold the tax on those tips that are reported by the employee to the employer in a written statement furnished to the employer (Form 4070).

If the total tax withheld by the employer from all employees amounts to more than $500 at the end of a quarter, the tax must be deposited in an "authorized financial institution" or a Federal Reserve bank.

Employers must furnish each employee from whose wages tax has been withheld two copies (Copies B and C) of the "Wage and Tax Statement," Form W-2, obtained from the local Internal Revenue office.

In 1982 Congress enacted the Tax Equity and Fiscal Responsibility Act (TEFRA) which included provisions requiring certain "food and beverage establishments," including most hotels, to report to the IRS the tip income that tipped employees reported to their employers.

References

1. I.R.C. §§ 3401-3404.
2. AH&MA *Washington Report,* December 14, 1982.
3. Treas. Regs § 31.3403-1.

Review Questions

1. How are employee "wages" for federal withholding purposes defined?

2. What does the employer do with the taxes which the employer withholds from an employee's wages?

3. What are the federal tip reporting requirements for hotel employees?

4. How do TEFRA regulations define a "large food or beverage establishment"?

Internet Sites

For more information, visit the following Internet sites. Remember that Internet addresses can change without notice.

Circular E
http://www.irs.gov/prod/forms_pubs/pubs/p15toc.htm

Internal Revenue Service
http://www.irs.gov

Tax Equity and Fiscal Responsibility Act (TEFRA)
http://www.irs.gov/plain/bus_info/tax_pro/irm-part/part04/30371.html

Part VI
Laws Relating to General Hotel Operation

Chapter 27 Outline

Competencies

1. Define the term "guest register."
   (p. 367)

2. Explain what a hotelkeeper should do
   if asked to show the hotel's guest
   register to attorneys and others.
   (pp. 367–368)

27

Maintenance of Guest Registers

STATE AND LOCAL LAWS often require hotels to maintain guest registers. In New York State, for example, § 204 of the General Business Law requires every hotelkeeper to keep for *three years* a record showing guests' names, residences, and dates of arrival and departure. This statute expressly allows such records to be maintained on any photographic or photostatic reproduction of the original record. (In California, many city and county governments have ordinances requiring hotels to maintain guest registers.) In many cases, the law requires that a guest sign a card or a register, which can preclude hotels from adopting "paperless check-in."

Examination of Guest Registers and Records by Attorneys and Others

Often an attorney requests permission to examine a hotel's **register** or other guest records on behalf of a client, who may or may not be the guest in question. In such instances, the hotel should require the attorney to obtain the guest's written consent to the examination. The hotel should not divulge any information with respect to the guest's registration without this written consent and the advice of hotel counsel. If the records are required in connection with a litigated matter between private parties, a **subpoena** or a court order should be issued requiring the hotel to produce its records, and hotel counsel should be consulted.

If a request for examination of hotel records is made by a police officer or a duly authorized official investigator, either city, county, state, or federal, the hotel should, especially if it has any reason to believe that it may be involved as a party in a civil or criminal suit, consult with its own attorney before permitting the examination. (See *People* v. *Blair* at the end of this chapter for a case in which the police acted improperly in obtaining hotel records.)[1]

Election Laws

Section 3-107 of the New York State Election Law authorizes the state Board of Elections to appoint a special investigator to take charge of any investigation under the Election Law. The special investigator, when directed by the state Board of Elections, may investigate the qualifications of persons to register or vote. Among other things, the investigator may visit and inspect a hotel and interrogate the hotel owner or proprietor as to any person currently residing in the hotel; "[i]nspect and copy any books, records, papers or documents relating to or affecting the election...require any lodging-house...landlord or proprietor to exhibit his register of the lodgers therein at any time to such special investigator." The statute states that any person who refuses to furnish any information required by the Election Law is guilty of a misdemeanor. Other states may have requirements for inspections and/or reports by hotels.

Important Points for Management

State or local laws often require hotels to maintain guest registers. A guest register is a written record of the guest's name, address, date of arrival, and date of departure. Do not allow anyone to examine the guest register, unless you are presented with a court order or subpoena, or unless you have the guest's written consent. Always seek the advice of hotel counsel in such matters.

References

1.   Cf. *People* v. *Blair,* 25 Cal.3d 640, 159 Cal.Rptr. 818, 602 P.2d 738 (1979).

 ## Key Terms

register—A written record of the guest's name, address, date of arrival, and date of departure.

subpoena—A writ of process in the name of the court authorized by law to issue same. A subpoena is a command to appear at a certain time and place, on a certain date, to give testimony upon a certain matter. Subpoena is the order of an arm of the state compelling the presence of a person under threat of contempt.

   A "subpoena duces tecum" is a court process compelling production of certain specified documents and other items, material and relevant to the facts in issue in a pending judicial proceeding, which documents and items are in custody and control of the person or body served with the process.

 ## Review Questions

1.   How long should a hotel retain its guest register?

2.   What information does a guest register usually contain?

3.   Why should you consult with the hotel's attorney before letting another attorney look at your guest register?

 ## Internet Sites

For more information, visit the following Internet sites. Remember that Internet addresses can change without notice.

FindLaw
http://www.findlaw.com

Illustrative Case ———————————————————————————

People v. *Blair*

25 Cal.3d 690, 602 P.2d 738 (Cal.Sup.Ct. 1979)

MOSK, Justice.

We held in *Burrows* v. *Superior Court* (1974) 13 Cal.3d 238, 118 Cal.Rptr. 166, 529 P.2d 590, that a depositor's bank statements provided to the police by the bank without the benefit of legal process were obtained as the result of an illegal search and seizure, in violation of article 1, section 13 of the California Constitution.[1] In this case we are called upon to decide, inter alia, whether the rationale of *Burrows* applies to copies of bills charged to a credit card used by defendant, to the record of a telephone call made by him from a hotel room in California,... obtained by federal authorities in that city and provided by them to the police in California.

Defendant was convicted of the murders of Alan and Renate Wellman, which occurred at their home in Los Angeles on the night of December 14, 1975. He appeals from the judgment of conviction.

* * *

We next consider whether the police acted improperly in obtaining from an employee of the Hyatt House, without legal process, a list of telephone calls made from defendant's room while a guest at the hotel. Among those calls was one to Wellman on the day of the murders.

In *People* v. *McKunes* (1975) 51 Cal. App.3d 487, 124 Cal.Rptr. 126, it was held, under the authority of *Burrows,* that the police may not, without legal process, obtain from the telephone company records revealing the calls dialed by a defendant from his home or office. The court reasoned that, as with bank records, a telephone subscriber has a reasonable expectation that the calls he makes will be utilized only for the accounting functions of the telephone company and that he cannot anticipate that his personal life, as disclosed by the calls he makes and receives, will be disclosed to outsiders without legal process. As with bank records, concluded the court, it is virtually impossible for an individual or business entity to function in the modern economy without a telephone, and a record of telephone calls also provides "a virtual current biography."

The fact that the telephone calls in the present case were made by defendant from a hotel room rather than his home does not render the *McKunes* rationale inapplicable. As in the case of a telephone call from a private residence, a hotel guest may reasonably expect that the calls which he makes from his room are recorded by the hotel for billing purposes only, and that the record of his calls will not be transmitted to others without legal process. The People argue that because there is no "ongoing relationship" between a hotel and a guest who rents a room for a limited period, the situation is distinguishable from *McKunes* and *Burrows.* But the hotel room is in reality a residence, however temporary. Thus the critical

---

[1] Article 1, section 13 provides in part, "The right of the people to be secure in their persons, houses, papers, and effects against unreasonable seizures and searches may not be violated;..."

issue is whether there is an expectation of privacy in the information sought; such an expectation may exist even in the briefest encounter between the persons who impart and receive the information. We conclude, therefore, that the motion to suppress should have been granted as to the telephone call which defendant made from the Hyatt House to Wellman on December 14.

* * *

We have concluded above that the trial court erred in failing to suppress the evidence regarding the charges made by defendant on his Diner's Club card and the telephone call made by defendant to Wellman from the Hyatt House.

Chapter 28 Outline

Competencies

1. Describe the notification required to hotel customers under the Consumer Credit Protection Act. (p. 373)

2. List and summarize some types of consumer protection laws that states may have. (pp. 373–377)

28

Consumer Protection Laws Affecting Hotels

The Federal Truth-in-Lending Act

Of the many consumer protection laws, only a few of those relevant to hotel operations are discussed here.* For example, the Consumer Credit Protection Act,[1] and the regulations promulgated thereunder by the Federal Reserve Board, establish procedures for handling complaints of credit card and credit account customers regarding billing errors. Under this statute and its regulations thereunder, the creditor *must* mail semi- annual notices to the debtor specifying the debtor's rights to dispute billing errors.

Consequently, when a customer has an outstanding debt to the hotel in his/ her credit account of more than $1 at the close of any of the hotel's full billing cycles and approximately every six months thereafter, the hotel must print on its customer billing statements:

> NOTICE: **See accompanying statement for important information regarding your rights to dispute billing errors.**

The hotel must also include a statement outlining the procedures for disputing billing errors.

Sample forms of the notice to the credit customer required by the Consumer Credit Protection Act are available upon request from the American Hotel & Lodging Association (AH&LA) offices. See also the AH&LA Operations Bulletin No. 197, "How to Comply with New Consumer Complaints Legislation." New York and other states have similar credit laws to protect the consumer.

State Laws on Credit Reporting

Various states also have state laws on credit reporting. New York passed the Fair Credit Reporting Act, General Business Law, Article 25. Under this law no hotel may request a consumer report from a credit reporting organization on the credit standing, character, reputation, personal characteristics, etc., of an applicant for consumer credit or for employment unless the applicant is first informed in writing:

---

* See also Chapter 17.

1. That a report from a credit reporting organization may be requested in connection with the application; and

2. Of the name and address of the credit reporting organization furnishing the report.

If the applicant is refused credit or employment opportunity either wholly or partly because of the information in the credit report, the hotel *must* advise the applicant of:

1. The adverse action

2. The reasons for such adverse action

3. The name and address of the credit reporting organization

4. His/her right to inspect and receive a copy of the credit report by contacting the credit reporting organization

The law also generally prohibits a user of a consumer credit report from disseminating it to others.

State Credit Card Laws

New York Credit Card Law

Credit card laws have been passed in New York that place an undue burden on hotels. Under the laws, enacted as Article 29-B of the New York General Business Law, hotels must inform the consumer of the amount of credit that the hotel will request the credit card company to set aside and obtain the consumer's consent thereto.

Moreover, it is unlawful for the hotel to communicate with a credit card issuer for the purpose of reserving or setting aside an amount of credit in a consumer's credit card account *in excess* of the actual, agreed-upon cost of the services contracted for by the consumer unless, prior to such communication, the hotel informs the consumer in writing of the amount of credit which will be requested to be reserved or set aside and obtains the consumer's *written* consent to the reservation or setting aside of such amount.

Furthermore, after the hotel has determined the guest's final charges, the hotel must promptly communicate with the credit card company to request the release of any amount of credit set aside that exceeds by more than $25 the charges actually billed by the guest. Under the law, the state Attorney General is authorized to bring an action to prevent any violations.

California Credit Card Law

California's Song-Beverly Credit Card Act of 1971 provides that:[2]

1. The credit card can only be issued pursuant to a request, application, or a renewal

2. The cardholder's maximum liability for unauthorized use of the credit card is $50 and only if the cardholder fails to notify the issuer

3. The right of a card issuer to recover from a cardholder is subject to the cardholder's defenses against the retailer, if the cardholder meets the conditions provided for in Civil Code § 1747.90

4. A card issuer must furnish to each cardholder, no later than February 15 of each year, a statement of the amount of interest or finance charges that the cardholder has paid during the preceding calendar year

Such statutes are particularly important whenever a hotel or hotel chain issues its own credit cards.

Consumer Contracts: Print Size and Plain Language Laws —

Some state laws, such as New York's, require that any contract involving a consumer transaction should be no less than "eight points" in type size. Thus, hotels should review state and city laws on this subject and make certain that personal banquets, weddings, residential leases, etc., comply with all such laws.[3]

Moreover, some state laws state that consumer contracts must be written in "plain English." In New York, for example, the law requires consumer contracts to be:

1. Written in a clear and coherent manner using words with common and everyday meanings; and

2. Appropriately divided and captioned by its various sections.[4]

Hotels, therefore, should consult with their attorneys as to whether their states have similar laws, and, if so, standard contracts relating to personal banquets and tour groups should be revised in order to comply with these "plain language" laws.

Catering Contracts

A regulation in New York City restricts the charges that a hotel or other caterer in New York City may make upon cancellation of a catering contract. In the event of cancellation by a patron, the regulation allows a caterer to retain only 5% of the total contract price, not to exceed $100, if the caterer re-books the contracted date. If the caterer is unable to re-book, he/she is allowed to recover for lost profits, that is, the difference between the contracted price and the cost of performance. Additionally, the caterer is allowed compensation for any actual damages incurred for any goods and services provided to the patron. Moreover, the regulation presumes that a caterer who receives notice of cancellation six months or more before the scheduled affair will be able to re-book. The caterer has the burden of showing diligent efforts to re-book and thereby lessen the damages. The caterer's contract must conspicuously disclose the caterer's cancellation fee in compliance with the regulation. Other states and cities may have similar laws.

Posting of Rates

Most state laws require hotels to post their rates, as well as the section of law requiring such posting, for guest and public information. For example, under § 206 of the New York General Business Law, the hotel is required to post in a public and conspicuous place and manner in its "office or public room" _and_ in the "public parlors" a statement of charges or rate of charges by the day for meals furnished, and for lodging.* This section also provides that no charge or sum shall be collected or received by any such hotel or hotelkeeper:

- For any service not actually rendered, or

- For a longer time than the person so charged actually remained at the hotel or inn, or

- For a higher rate for room or board, lodging, or meals than is specified in the posted rate of charges, provided the guest shall have given the hotel or hotelkeeper notice at the office of his/her departure.**

For any violation of this section, the offender must forfeit to the injured party _three times_ the amount charged, and is not entitled to receive any money for meals, services, or time charged.

Most other states have similar laws on the posting of rates that must be followed.

No-Smoking Laws

In recent years, most states have enacted laws that require hotels and restaurants to designate no-smoking areas in their restaurants and other areas where food is served. Further, numerous city ordinances control smoking.

In general, such laws:

- restrict or prohibit smoking in public areas

- restrict or prohibit smoking in restaurants

- require no-smoking signs be posted

- require the removal of ashtrays from non-smoking rooms

- require that health warnings (including second-hand smoke warnings in some cases) be posted in smoking areas

---

* Some jurisdictions have more stringent posting requirements. For example, in California § 1863 of the California Civil Code requires such posting in a conspicuous place in the office _and_ in every guestroom. In New York, a separate section of law, § 206-b of the General Business Law, requires _motels_ to post notices of rates in each rental unit.

** Under California law, a guest who is charged more than the maximum amount specified in the notice must give the innkeeper notice of any overcharge "within 30 days after payment of such charges and such keeper shall not fail or refuse to make proper adjustment of such overcharge."

- often require hotel management to adopt a smoking policy governing employees
- often require that hotel management "police" the hotels' guests to tell them to stop smoking in non-smoking areas.

The fines for violating these restrictions can be quite high. For example, in New York City, a violation of the non-smoking ordinance (NYCC § 17-501, *et. seq.*) can be as high as $1,000 per violation and, in addition, the hotel can be prosecuted under the criminal law for a misdemeanor that can carry a fine of $5,000 per violation.

It is therefore imperative that each hotel check the laws applicable in the city and state in which it is located. Note also that the trend is to amend these laws on a regular basis in order to make them even more strict—a trend likely to continue.

Important Points for Management

- Consumer protection laws are enacted to prevent unfair practices against the consumer. Most of the laws specify a procedure for a particular activity or provide that information or disclosure be given to the consumer.

- Plain language laws are state laws that specify that consumer contracts must be written in plain and understandable English. This could apply to convention or group contracts or catering contracts a hotel uses.

- It is a state law in most states that the hotel must post the hotel's room rates.

- Most states and many cities have laws restricting or prohibiting smoking in public areas and in restaurants in the hotel.

References

1. 15 U.S.C. § 1601 *et seq.*
2. Cal. Civ. Code § 1747, *et seq.*
3. See, for example, N.Y. Civ. Prac. Law § 4544.
4. N.Y. General Obligation Law § 5-702.

Review Questions

1. How does the Consumer Credit Protection Act affect hotels?

2. What is a Credit Reporting Act?

3. What are some rules and regulations with regard to consumer contracts?

4. What do your state laws provide with regard to cancelling a catering contract?

5. What do your state laws require with regard to posting hotel rates? What information must be included?

Internet Sites

For more information, visit the following Internet sites. Remember that Internet addresses can change without notice.

Fair Credit Reporting Act
http://www.ftc.gov/os/statutes/fcrajump.htm

Federal Reserve Board
http://www.federalreserve.gov

Tobacco Information and Prevention Source (TIPS)
http://www.cdc.gov/tobacco

Chapter 29 Outline

Building Codes
Hotel Linens, Towels, and Glasses
Water Supplies, Sewage Systems, and
    Drainage
Contagious Diseases
Swimming Pools
Laws Regarding Aid to Choking Victims
Important Points for Management
References
Review Questions

Competencies

1. Describe some of the ways in which
   building codes affect hotels.
   (pp. 381–383)

2. Give examples of items for which
   cleanliness standards are often
   established by public health laws.
   (p. 383)

3. Identify the types of public health
   regulations that often apply to hotels
   not served by public water supplies
   and sewage systems. Explain under
   what circumstances it becomes a
   hotelkeeper's responsibility to report
   contagious diseases. (pp. 383–384)

4. Identify types of regulations
   pertaining to hotel swimming pools.
   (p. 384)

5. Describe major provisions of laws
   addressing aid to choking victims.
   (pp. 384–385)

29

Public Health and Safety Requirements

A HOTEL HAS NUMEROUS OBLIGATIONS to the general public because of federal, state, and local statutes enacted to protect the public's safety and health. Examples of protective legislation include state building and fire codes, sanitary codes, and health laws. (See Chapter 31 regarding the authority of state and local governments to enact such legislation and regulations.) Hotels may also be subject to laws concerning the preparation and service of food; contagious diseases; and hotel water supplies, sewage systems, and swimming pool operations. State and local codes often require hotels to take affirmative steps that go beyond the common law duty of reasonable care (See Chapter 10).

Public health and safety laws, by the nature of their objectives and purposes, affect many areas of hotel operations. Many federal, state, and local laws that fall within the broad category of "public health" laws are discussed in other chapters. For example, Chapter 34 deals with laws regarding fire safety and Chapter 18 discusses laws controlling the sale of alcoholic beverages.

There may be other areas of hotel operations affected by a particular law or regulation in local jurisdictions that may be characterized as a public health law. Hotels should consult their attorneys to find out if their operations are affected by such laws.

Building Codes

In most states, hotels are subject to building codes enforced and administered by state and/or local government agencies. Because building codes differ in every state and locality, and each hotel building has unique design and construction requirements, it is impossible to discuss the multitude of different code provisions here. However, it is important that hotels contact local or state officials or attorneys for information about these codes. Many contain provisions regulating the ways in which buildings may be operated as hotels or motels, as well as the manner in which they may be built. State and local building codes often contain requirements as to capacity, exits, safety, etc., in private guestrooms, places of public assembly, and all other public areas in a hotel. In addition, state public health laws and labor laws often contain provisions that may be considered building requirements.

Statutes or regulations in many jurisdictions establish a required standard of conduct for the hotel (which may be greater than the common law standard of reasonable care). In such jurisdictions, a hotel violating a particular regulation or ordinance might be held liable if the purpose of the statute or regulation is found to be exclusively or in part

(a) to protect a class of persons which includes the one whose interest is invaded [i.e., the guest], and

(b) to protect the particular interest which is invaded [i.e., the guest's safety], and

(c) to protect that interest against the kind of harm which has resulted, and

(d) to protect that interest against the particular hazard from which the harm results.[1]

For example, in *Northern Lights Motel, Inc.* v. *Sweaney*,[2] the Supreme Court of Alaska affirmed a jury award of $313,650.82 to the surviving relative of a guest who died in a fire at the defendant-motel in Anchorage, Alaska. The guest was located in an area of the motel constructed with plasterboard of $3/8$ to $1/2$ inch in thickness. The applicable state building and fire codes at the time required the motel to "be of no less than one-hour fire resistive construction throughout." According to the appellate court's decision, the thickness of plasterboard required for one-hour fire resistant construction is $5/8$ of an inch. The trial judge's instructions to the jury read in part,

> If, in accordance with these instructions, you find that the defendant has violated the law and that any such violation legally caused the accident in question, and you further find that defendant has failed to so excuse or justify such violation of law, then you must find that the defendant was negligent.[3]

The Supreme Court of Alaska upheld this instruction, noting:

> Substitution of an administrative or legislative enactment as the applicable standard of care is appropriate where the rule of conduct contained therein is expressed in specific, concrete terms. Substitution is not appropriate where the statute merely sets out a general or abstract standard of care. [citations omitted][4]

The trial court's instructions to the jury allowed the jury to presume negligence if it found the applicable code provisions had been violated.[5] In its opinion the Supreme Court of Alaska went on to say that, in Alaska at least, violating the building code provision may be negligence per se. That is, a violation of the provision may itself conclusively show that the defendant breached the standard of care owed to the plaintiff, as opposed to requiring the plaintiff to prove that the inadequate construction violated the common law duty of reasonable care.[6]

In other jurisdictions, the violation of a statute may not constitute negligence per se, but may nevertheless be evidence of negligence. In Florida, for example, the case of *Schulte* v. *Gold*[7] reflected this principle. In this case the plaintiffs, husband and wife guests, sued the defendant-hotel for damages because the wife fell and broke her hip when she tripped on outside steps that were not properly illuminated. At trial the plaintiffs presented a Florida statute[8] which required that each "public lodging establishment," shall, among other things, be "properly...lighted...," and shall be conducted in every department with strict regard to the health, comfort, and safety of the guests or tenants; provided that such proper lighting shall be construed to apply to both daylight and artificial illumination...." Over the objection of the defendant hotel operators, the trial judge instructed the jury that if it found the defendants to have violated this statute, the defendants were negligent. The jury awarded the plaintiff-guests $100,000, and also found the wife 15 percent negligent. On appeal the court reversed the judgment, remanded the case for a new trial, and held the trial court's jury instructions erroneous. The appellate court held that the violation of the statute in question did not result in strict liability for two reasons. First, the statute was not of the type designed to protect a particular class of persons from their inability to protect themselves, but was designed to protect the public generally; and second, the purpose of the law was not to make the hotel an insurer.[9]

In addition to the statutory requirements for the protection of workers, a hotel may take many additional practical steps to help safeguard both employees and guests from accidents. The insurance company that writes the public liability insurance the hotel carries ordinarily furnishes information and advises the hotel regarding practical steps to take in accident prevention. Private consultants also perform the same services. (See also Chapter 30.)

Hotel Linens, Towels, and Glasses

State public health laws also contain provisions regarding cleanliness standards of bedding, sheets, and towels; the size of these items; and sometimes the amount to be furnished to each guest.

Some states may have laws similar to California and Nevada laws that prohibit any hotel from maintaining any towel for common use, defined as the use of the towel by different persons without laundering between consecutive uses.[10] A similar provision in California prohibits the common use of a cup or glass for drinking purposes that the hotel has not cleaned and sterilized between consecutive uses.[11]

Water Supplies, Sewage Systems, and Drainage

Public health laws may also contain specific provisions applicable to hotels and motels not served by public water supplies and sewage systems. These regulations may cover:

- Water supply
- Toilet and sewage disposal facilities
- Sewage treatment works
- Purchase of milk and cream from licensed dealers
- Protection of food supplies
- Dishwashing
- Communicable diseases

Similarly, public health laws generally contain provisions on sewers and drainage in order to provide safeguards for the health of employees and guests.

Contagious Diseases

State public health laws contain sections requiring physicians to report every case of infectious and contagious or communicable disease through the health officer of the county, city, town, or village where the disease occurs. If no physician is in attendance, state laws often provide that it is the duty of a hotelkeeper or other person to give notice.[12]

Swimming Pools

Most state public health laws require hotels to maintain lifeguards at any swimming facility, whether a beach or swimming pool. In New York, for instance, the state Sanitary Code (10 N.Y.C.R.R. § 6-1.23 (2)) requires that lifeguards or "other responsible persons" attend bathers at swimming pools and bathing beaches operated for purposes other than the owner's private use. Section 6-1.2(k) of the Code states,

> The term *responsible person* shall mean a competent individual, at least 18 years of age, acceptable to the permit issuing official, who shall be present at the bathing area at all times when the pool or bathing beach is officially open and capable of exercising control over the bathers, using safety equipment, summoning help, and following the safety plan.

The code establishes strict requirements (based on the square footage of the pool) for the number of lifeguards and supervisors required.

Hotels are cautioned to check their own state and local water safety and swimming pool regulations.

Laws Regarding Aid to Choking Victims

The laws of some states and localities require dining facility operators to post diagrams and instructions in a conspicuous place on how to aid a choking victim. Under New York State law,[13] all "public eating establishments" must display a poster adopted and distributed by the State Commissioner of Public Health.

Section 3 of the legislation provides:

> 3. Posting. The proprietor of every public eating establishment in this state shall, upon receipt thereof, post such instructions in a conspicuous place or places in order that the proprietor and employees may become familiar with them, and in order that the instructions may be consulted by any person attempting to provide relief to the victim of a choking emergency; provided, that the fact that such instruction shall not have been posted as required by this section at the time of a choking emergency shall not in and of itself subject such a proprietor, or his employees or agents, to liability in any civil action for damages for personal injuries or wrongful death arising from such choking emergency.

Note that this state public health law also makes it clear that "nothing contained in this section shall impose any duty or obligation on any proprietor, employee, or other person to remove, assist in removing, or attempt to remove food from the throat of the victim of a choking emergency."

Under this New York State law, a proprietor or employee of a public dining establishment or other person who "voluntarily and without expectation of monetary compensation" aids a choking victim *"in accordance with the instructions adopted by the commissioner"* shall not be liable for any damages resulting from injury or death of the victim *"unless* it is established that such injuries were, or such death was, *caused by the gross negligence on the part of such proprietor, employee or person"* (emphasis added).

The New York City Council enacted § 17-172 of the New York City Administrative Code, requiring every establishment where food is sold and space is designated specifically as eating areas to post, in a conspicuous place easily accessible to all employees and customers, a sign graphically depicting the "Heimlich Maneuver" or a comparable technique for dislodging food from a choking person. The Department of Health of New York City publishes the poster. *This section of the city code, however, also expressly provides that the law does not impose any duty or obligation on any proprietor, employee, or other person to remove or assist in removing food from the throat of a choking victim.* Additionally, some states or cities require that resuscitation equipment—oxygen masks—be available and that notice of availability be posted. For example, regulations in New York City (NYCC § 17-178) require bars, health clubs, and restaurants to have such equipment, and to post notice of it. Liability for use of such equipment is limited to gross negligence and the regulations also state that the law does not impose any duty to act.

Hotels should consult their attorneys before establishing or initiating *any* policy for choking emergencies. Those who then decide to instruct their employees to act should also consult their attorneys as to employee training in order to comply with the law and instructions on the poster competently, that is, without negligence.

Important Points for Management

- Many state and local building codes contain provisions regulating the ways in which buildings may be operated as hotels or motels, as well as the manner in which they may be built. State and local building codes often contain requirements as to capacity, exits, safety, etc., in private guestrooms, places of public assembly, and all other public areas in a hotel.

- State public health laws contain numerous provisions regarding cleanliness standards of bedding, sheets, and towels; the size of these items; and sometimes the amount of the item to be furnished to each guest.

- State public health laws usually require physicians to report every case of infectious and contagious or communicable disease to the health officer of the county, city, town, or village where the disease occurs. If no physician is in attendance, state laws often provide that it is the duty of a hotelkeeper or other person to give notice.

- Most state public health laws require hotels to maintain lifeguards at any swimming facility, whether a beach or swimming pool.

- The laws of some states and localities require dining facility operators to post, in a conspicuous place, diagrams and instructions on how to aid a choking victim. Under New York State law, all "public eating establishments" must display such a poster.

- Hotels should consult their attorneys before establishing or initiating *any* policy for choking emergencies.

References

1. Restatement (Second) of Torts § 286 (1965).
2. 561 P. 2d 1176 (Sup. Ct. Alaska 1977), *on reh'g,* 563 P. 2d 256 (1977).
3. *Id.* at 1180.
4. *Id.* at 1176.
5. *Id.* at 1183 n. 9.
6. *Id.* at 1183.
7. 360 So. 2d 428 (Fla. App. 1978), *cert. denied,* 368 So. 2d 1367 (1979).
8. Fla. Stat. § 509.221(2) (1975).
9. 360 So. 2d at 430.
10. California Health and Safety Code § 3800 and § 3801.
11. California Health and Safety Code § 3700.
12. 10 N.Y.C. R.R. § 2.12.
13. N.Y. State Public Health Law § 1352-b.

 ## Review Questions

1. Why is it important for a hotel owner to contact local or state officials or a local attorney for information concerning building codes?

2. If a hotel develops a plan to act in the case of a choking emergency, what steps should it take before implementing the plan?

Chapter 30 Outline

Reporting and Recordkeeping
  Requirements
Posting Requirements
Inspections: Employers' and Employees'
  Rights and Remedies
State Workplace Safety and Health
  Programs Under OSHA
OSHA Regulations on Bloodborne
  Pathogens
Medical Emergencies
Hazard Communication Standard
Important Points for Management
References
Review Questions
Internet Sites

Competencies

1. Describe the employer's duty
   regarding a place of employment as
   mandated by OSHA. (p. 389)

2. List OSHA's major functions, state
   OSHA's jurisdiction, and cite examples
   of safety and health standards set forth
   by OSHA. (pp. 389–390)

3. Explain OSHA reporting and
   recordkeeping requirements.
   (pp. 390–392)

4. Describe the OSHA posting
   requirements. (p. 392)

5. Explain employers' and employees'
   rights and remedies with regard to
   OSHA inspections. (pp. 392–395)

6. Describe state workplace safety and
   health programs under OSHA.
   Summarize OSHA regulations on
   bloodborne pathogens. Review
   medical emergency policies.
   (pp. 395–398)

7. List and describe the primary
   requirements of the OSHA Hazard
   Communication Standard.
   (pp. 398–400)

30

Occupational Safety and Health Act

 T HE OCCUPATIONAL SAFETY AND HEALTH ACT of 1970[1] created the Occupational Safety and Health Administration (OSHA) of the U.S. Department of Labor to administer and carry out the purpose of the legislation. The purpose of the Act and of OSHA is "to assure so far as possible every working man and woman in the Nation safe and healthful working conditions and to preserve our human resources...."[2] The Act further states the duty of each employer to furnish to each of his/her employees a "place of employment which is free from recognized hazards that are causing or are likely to cause death or serious physical harm to his[/her] employees."[3]

To fulfill this purpose, OSHA establishes standards to protect employees from safety and health hazards, conducts inspections of workplaces to check compliance with safety standards, requires that certain records of work-related injuries be kept, and enforces its regulations by citations and fines for violations.

OSHA has jurisdiction over any employer of one or more employees engaged in a business "affecting commerce." Hotels and motels are clearly within the broad coverage of the Act, and, therefore, must comply with all of the applicable standards and procedures established by regulations promulgated by OSHA. This chapter gives hotel and motel operators a general overview of how OSHA operates. For specific details of health and safety requirements, consult your attorney or contact the regional or area offices of OSHA. (See Chapter 34, "Fire Safety Laws," for a discussion of certain OSHA regulations relating to fire safety.)

A hotel has certain responsibilities under the Act and OSHA regulations. The hotel management must become familiar with and comply with all occupational safety and health standards promulgated by OSHA.

The safety and health standards set forth by OSHA are extensive, and include such subjects as safeguards for walking and working surfaces, stairs, doors, and exits, personal protective equipment and clothing, laundry equipment, maintenance shops and equipment, machine and fan guards, the use of appliances and electrical equipment, hazardous and flammable materials, environmental safeguards (ventilation, noise, etc.), storage conditions and materials-handling rules, parking garages, rodent and vermin controls, drinking water safety, restrooms,

The authors express their appreciation to Raymond Ellis for his valuable assistance on this chapter on OSHA.

Exhibit 30.1   OSHA Log No. 200 Form

Log and Summary of Occupational
Injuries and Illnesses

NOTE: This form is required by Public Law 91-596 and Act 154, P.A. 1974 and must be kept in the establishment for 5 years. Failure to maintain and post can result in the issuance of citations and assessment of penalties. (See posting requirements on the other side of form.)				**RECORDABLE CASES:** You are required to record information about every occupational death, every nonfatal occupational illness, and those nonfatal occupational injuries which involve one or more of the following: loss of consciousness, restriction of work or motion, transfer to another job, or medical treatment (other than first aid). (See definitions on the other side of form.)	
Case or File Number	**Date of Injury or Onset of Illness**	**Employee's Name**	**Occupation**	**Department**	**Description of Injury or Illness**
Enter a nondupli-cating number which will facilitate com-parisons with supple-mentary records	Enter Mo./day.	Enter first name or initial, Middle initial, last name.	Enter regular job title, not activity employee was per-forming when injured or at onset of illness. In the absence of a formal title, enter a brief description of the employee's duties.	Enter department in which the employee is regularly employed or a description of normal workplace to which employee is assigned, even though temporarily working in another depart-ment at the time of injury or illness.	Enter a brief description of the injury or illness and indicate the part or parts of body affected. Typical entries for this column might be: amputation of 1st joint right forefinger; Strain of lower back; Contact dermatitis on both hands; Electrocution — body.
(A)	(B)	(C)	(D)	(E)	(F)
					PREVIOUS PAGE TOTALS ➤
					TOTALS (Instructions on other side of form.) ➤

O.S.H.A. #200

bloodborne pathogens, medical and first aid requirements, etc.[4] Management must inspect the hotel premises to insure compliance with OSHA regulations and to alleviate any hazardous condition that may develop. If any potential hazards to employees exist, posters, labels, or signs must warn them of this potential danger. Employers must establish or update any procedure required by OSHA, and must also communicate this to employees.

Reporting and Recordkeeping Requirements

OSHA regulations require an employer of eleven or more employees to maintain an annual record of work-related employee injuries and illnesses.[5] This informa-tion must be maintained in the employer's establishment on an OSHA Log No. 200 form (Exhibit 30.1) or an equivalent form. The employer may maintain the log at a

For Calendar Year 19 _____   Page _____ of _____

| Company Name | Form Approved O.M.B. No. 44R 1453 |

Establishment Name

Establishment Address

Extent of and Outcome of INJURY						Type, Extent of, and Outcome of ILLNESS						
Fatalities	Nonfatal Injuries					Type of Illness	Fatalities	Nonfatal Illnesses				
Injury Related	Injuries With Lost Workdays				Injuries Without Lost Workdays	CHECK Only One Column for Each Illness (See other side of form for terminations or permanent transfers.)	Illness Related	Illnesses With Lost Workdays				Illnesses Without Lost Workdays
Enter DATE of death. Mo/day/yr. (1)	Enter a CHECK if injury involves days away from work, or days of restricted work activity, or both. (2)	Enter a CHECK if injury involves days away from work. (3)	Enter number of DAYS away from work. (4)	Enter number of DAYS of restricted work activity. (5)	Enter a CHECK if no entry was made in columns 1 or 2 but the injury is recordable as defined above. (6)	(a) Occupational skin diseases or disorders (b) Dust diseases of the lungs (c) Respiratory conditions due to toxic agents (d) Poisoning (systemic effects of toxic materials) (e) Disorders due to physical agents (f) Disorders associated with repeated trauma (g) All other occupational illness (7)	Enter DATE of death. Mo/day/yr. (8)	Enter a CHECK if illness involves days away from work, or days of restricted work activity, or both. (9)	Enter a CHECK if illness involves days away from work. (10)	Enter number of DAYS away from work. (11)	Enter number of DAYS of restricted work activity. (12)	Enter a CHECK if no entry was made in columns 8 or 9. (13)

INJURIES   ILLNESSES

Certification of Annual Summary Totals By _____ Title _____ Date _____

OSHA No. 200   **POST ONLY THIS PORTION OF THE LAST PAGE NOT LATER THAN FEBRUARY 1.**

place other than the business establishment or by means of data processing equipment (or both), if (1) at this "other" place there is sufficient information to complete the log to a date within six working days of a reportable accident or illness (as is required for logs maintained on the premises), and (2) at each of the employer's establishments there is a copy of the log kept current to date within 45 calendar days.[6]

Even if a hotel has no employee work-related injuries or illnesses during the year, it may be in the hotel's best interests to maintain an OSHA Log No. 200 for that year indicating "no recordable work-related injuries or illnesses." This may help matters in a non-incident year if the hotel is subject to an inspection by an OSHA compliance officer.

Furthermore, the regulations require that, by February 1 of the calendar year, the employer shall conspicuously post in places where employee notices are generally posted an annual summary of the prior year's totals from the OSHA Log No. 200. A separate OSHA Log No. 200 form must be used to present this summary information.

Employers must retain these records, the OSHA Log No. 200 and annual summary, for five years following the end of the year to which each relates.[7] Other regulations requiring the maintenance of medical records for 30 years for work-related employee injuries or illnesses stemming from the use of or exposure to certain hazardous chemicals[8] might apply to hotels. For example, certain hotel employees may work with or be exposed to pesticides, fungicides, cleansing or bleaching chemical agents, or water purification chemicals (i.e., chlorine used in swimming pools) in the course of their work. Should a work-related injury occur in connection with the use of or exposure to such chemicals, hotels should consult their attorney or safety consultant with respect to the hotel's obligation as to recordkeeping and reporting.

Separate reports of any accidents that result in a fatality or the hospitalization of three or more employees must be made to the nearest Office of the Area Director of OSHA *within 8 hours after the occurrence.*[9] This report "may be by telephone or telegraph" and "shall relate the circumstances of the accident, the number of fatalities, and the extent of any injuries."[10]

Posting Requirements

Hotels must post a notice furnished by OSHA that informs employees of their rights and obligations under the Act (Exhibit 30.2). The notice must be posted in a conspicuous place or in places where notices to employees are usually posted. Hotel management is responsible for maintaining this poster and ensuring that it is not altered, defaced, or covered in any way. OSHA notices should be permanently posted under glass. In addition, employers must post any citation for violation of an OSHA safety and health standard at or near the place of the alleged violation referred to in the citation. If this is impractical, the citation may be posted where employees report to work each day.

Inspections: Employers' and Employees' Rights and Remedies

OSHA inspectors may visit the hotel premises at any time without delay during regular working hours and walk around with a selected employee to check compliance with OSHA regulations. Advance notice of inspections may be provided only in the event of a reported dangerous condition requiring immediate attention. Pursuant to a U.S. Supreme Court decision, *Marshall v. Barlow's, Inc.,*[11] an employer may demand that the inspector have a search warrant before being required to allow the inspector access to non-public work premises. A search warrant authorizing an OSHA inspection may be issued by a court on the showing of probable cause, based on specific evidence of an existing violation or on showing that reasonable legislative or administrative standards for conducting an inspection are satisfied with respect to the hotel. Employers have the right to request

Exhibit 30.2   Occupational Safety and Health Act Notice

You Have a Right to a Safe and Healthful Workplace.

IT'S THE LAW!

- You have the right to notify your employer or OSHA about workplace hazards. You may ask OSHA to keep your name confidential.

- You have the right to request an OSHA inspection if you believe that there are unsafe and unhealthful conditions in your workplace. You or your representative may participate in the inspection.

- You can file a complaint with OSHA within 30 days of discrimination by your employer for making safety and health complaints or for exercising your rights under the *OSH Act*.

- You have a right to see OSHA citations issued to your employer. Your employer must post the citations at or near the place of the alleged violation.

- Your employer must correct workplace hazards by the date indicated on the citation and must certify that these hazards have been reduced or eliminated.

- You have the right to copies of your medical records or records of your exposure to toxic and harmful substances or conditions.

- Your employer must post this notice in your workplace.

The *Occupational Safety and Health Act of 1970 (OSH Act)*, P.L. 91-596, assures safe and healthful working conditions for working men and women throughout the Nation. The Occupational Safety and Health Administration, in the U.S. Department of Labor, has the primary responsibility for administering the *OSH Act*. The rights listed here may vary depending on the particular circumstances. To file a complaint, report an emergency, or seek OSHA advice, assistance, or products, call 1-800-321-OSHA or your nearest OSHA office: • Atlanta (404) 562-2300 • Boston (617) 565-9860 • Chicago (312) 353-2220 • Dallas (214) 767-4731 • Denver (303) 844-1600 • Kansas City (816) 426-5861 • New York (212) 337-2378 • Philadelphia (215) 861-4900 • San Francisco (415) 975-4310 • Seattle (206) 553-5930. Teletypewriter (TTY) number is 1-877-889-5627. To file a complaint online or obtain more information on OSHA federal and state programs, visit OSHA's website at **www.osha.gov**. If your workplace is in a state operating under an OSHA-approved plan, your employer must post the required state equivalent of this poster.

1-800-321-OSHA
www.osha.gov

U.S. Department of Labor   •   Occupational Safety and Health Administration   •   OSHA 3165 proper identification from any OSHA inspector prior to an inspection and to be advised of the reason for the inspection. It is recommended that employers avoid taking a confrontational attitude toward OSHA inspectors.

During an OSHA inspection of a hotel, the compliance officer is entitled to take environmental samples, take relevant photographs, question privately any employer, owner, operator, agent, or employee of the hotel, and use other reasonable and necessary investigative techniques. Hotel management has the right to accompany the inspector on the inspection of the workplace and is further entitled to confer with the inspecting compliance officer at the conclusion of the inspection. At this time, the compliance officer may informally advise management of any apparent safety or health violations, and management may respond with any pertinent information regarding conditions of workplaces in the hotel.

The hotel operator may file a notice of contest with the nearest OSHA Assistant Regional Director within 15 days of receipt of a citation for an alleged violation and notice of penalty. Also, within 15 days the hotel may file a written notice with the Area Director alleging that the period of time fixed in the citation for alleviating the violation is unreasonable. The Regional Administrator may also hold an informal conference at the request of the hotel operator to discuss any issues raised by the inspection. When a citation is issued, the hotel should contact its attorneys to protect its rights under the Act.

Employees can request that an OSHA Area Director conduct an inspection of the hotel. This employee request must be in writing and must specify the hazard believed to violate OSHA standards. The name of the employee making such a request is never given to hotel management.

The Act prohibits an employer from discriminating against any employee who exercises his/her rights under the Act. For example, in *Whirlpool Corporation* v. *Marshall*,[12] the U.S. Supreme Court held that an employee may refuse to perform a task that he/she reasonably believes may result in serious physical injury or death. The employer may not then discriminate against the employee who refuses such a dangerous task; that is, the employer may not treat this employee less favorably than he/she treats other employees similarly situated. (The OSHA regulations, however, do not require employers to pay workers who refuse to perform assigned tasks.)

United States v. *Cusack*[13] established for the first time that the government can in some cases prosecute a corporate officer, as an "employer," for OSHA violations. On February 22, 1993, the U.S. District Court (Dist. New Jersey) sentenced John Cusack, president of Qualified Steel, Inc., to three years' probation, six months of home confinement, 200 hours of community service, and a $2,500 fine. The court held that an officer or director who exercises pervasive and complete control over the corporation can be held liable as an employer under the criminal provisions of OSHA.[14] An employer who willfully violates an OSHA standard rule, resulting in the death of an employee, may be criminally prosecuted under 29 U.S.C. § 666(e).

The extensive OSHA regulations have been criticized in recent years because of the high cost of administering the standards and the burden upon employers to fulfill the recordkeeping requirements. If a hotel has any questions concerning

OSHA standards or procedures, it should consult legal counsel. An additional source of information is the OSHA Regional or Area Office.

State Workplace Safety and Health Programs Under OSHA

OSHA provides that state jurisdictions may enact and administer their own occupational safety and health programs provided that such programs are "at least as effective" as the federal OSHA program. Such state programs must be approved by OSHA, and, if approved, OSHA will provide funding for 50% of the costs of the state programs. States and territories with approved plans (so-called Little OSHAs) include Alaska, Arizona, California, Connecticut,* Hawaii, Indiana, Iowa, Kentucky, Maryland, Michigan, Minnesota, Nevada, New Mexico, New York,* North Carolina, Oregon, Puerto Rico, South Carolina, Tennessee, Utah, Vermont, Virgin Islands, Virginia, Washington (state), and Wyoming. Hotels in such states should be aware that the safety standards promulgated and enforced by state safety and health agencies may in fact be more stringent than the federal OSHA standards.

OSHA Regulations on Bloodborne Pathogens

On December 6, 1991, the U.S. Department of Labor issued OSHA regulations on bloodborne pathogens.[15]

Bloodborne pathogens are defined as "pathogenic microorganisms that are present in human blood and can cause disease in humans. These pathogens include, but are not limited to, hepatitis B virus (HBV) and human immunodeficiency virus (HIV)."

The OSHA regulations on bloodborne pathogens are oriented to the health-care industry. However, aspects of the regulations apply to all industries since OSHA mandates a trained first-aider on each work shift.

Under the regulations, management determines those employees at risk of exposure. Hepatitis B vaccinations must be *offered* by an employer to those employees who have occupational exposure to blood or other potentially infectious materials. In addition, employers must provide certain employees with protective gear, clothing, and equipment. Employers must also maintain all records of on-the-job exposure incidents on file for 30 years, even if the employee involved in any of the incidents leaves the business's employ.

OSHA requires employers to schedule at least one employee who is trained in first aid on each work shift. Because such employees may come into contact with blood or body fluids, they must be *offered* hepatitis B vaccinations. They must also be provided with protective gloves, eye and face protection, and a tube-mouth mask unit, when necessary, for performing cardiopulmonary resuscitation (CPR).

Similarly, all staff members who are skilled in CPR must be *offered* hepatitis B vaccinations. Employees trained in first aid, security officers, and lifeguards are in this classification of employees.

---

* Connecticut and New York cover only the state agencies and other government agencies.

A special response team of employees should be trained to clean up vomit from bar or dining areas, in the event that it becomes necessary, and should be offered the vaccination series and provided with the proper protective equipment.

If room attendants, housepersons, lifeguards, janitors, or other maintenance staff should be pricked by a discarded hypodermic needle when making up the guestroom, removing bagged trash, or patrolling lake or beach areas, those employees must be *offered* the vaccinations. They must also be provided with the proper protective equipment. This equipment includes protective gloves and face and eye protection.

The accidental pricking of a room attendant, houseperson, or any other employee by a discarded hypodermic needle requires that the employee be sent to a physician within 24 hours of the incident. The physician would make the decision as to the necessity for administering the hepatitis B vaccine. The employee may refuse the vaccine but must sign a waiver in the form required by OSHA (Exhibit 30.3).

If blood or body fluids are in bedding, sheets, pillowcases, or towels, not only must the room attendants be fully protected, but laundry workers *must* also be offered the vaccinations, special gloves, face and eye protection, and a dust respirator to eliminate the "dust" and particles from dried fluid or blood in the bed linens or towels.

Some hotels provide laundry services for facilities other than the immediate property. Whenever a hotel's laundry customers include clinics, hospitals, or nursing homes, the hotel's laundry staff must receive the full protection as explained earlier.

Several on-staff specialists must be designated and trained for the responsibility of "taking over" whenever a room attendant enters a guestroom and finds blood and body-fluid stains on bedding or towels, or discarded condoms. The specialist employees would be provided special training through a nearby hospital, clinic, or infirmary that serves the hotel. All employees with this special assignment would also be offered the hepatitis B vaccine and would be provided with full personal protection. This would include protective gloves, face and eye protection, a gown, shoe covers, and a dust mask that prevents the employee from ingesting particles when handling bedding or towels with caked blood or body fluids.

Whenever contaminated hypodermic needles are found, they are to be placed in appropriate containers, which are to be properly discarded when full. The local medical facility serving a property can often be a hotel's source or reference for purchasing such containers, as well as heavy-duty plastic bags bearing an OSHA-approved biohazard symbol or red bags bearing a similar symbol. A local medical facility might also provide contacts for or arrange for appropriate removal of medically contaminated waste from a property. Hotels should deal only with contractors licensed to remove medical waste to an approved medical waste disposal site.

It is recommended that consideration be given to establishing an emergency response team that would be called upon when a room obviously is contaminated. OSHA Health Compliance has agreed to this approach and it reduces the cost of personal protective equipment as well as the cost of the Hepatitis B vaccination. However, it must be remembered that the room attendant must be provided with

Exhibit 30.3 Hepatitis B Vaccination Waiver Form

In response to the letter sent to me on _____, **I wish to receive the hepatitis B vaccination,** and understand that there is no financial cost to me.

_____   _____
Employee Signature   Witness

_____   _____
Employee Name Printed   Date

OR

I decline the hepatitis B vaccination at this time. I understand that due to the possibility of my becoming exposed to blood or other potentially infectious materials while performing my job, I may be at risk of acquiring hepatitis B virus (HBV) infection. I have been given the opportunity to be vaccinated with the hepatitis B vaccine at no charge. I understand that by declining this vaccine, I continue to be at risk acquiring hepatitis B, a serious disease. If in the future, I continue to have occupational exposure to blood or other potentially infectious materials, and I wish to be vaccinated with hepatitis B vaccine, I can receive the vaccination series at no cost to me.

_____   _____
Employee Signature   Witness

_____   _____
Employee Name Printed   Date

OR

I decline the hepatitis B vaccination at this time because I have previously received the complete hepatitis B vaccination series; or antibody testing has revealed that I am immune; or the vaccine is contraindicated for medical reasons.

_____   _____
Employee Signature   Witness

_____   _____
Employee Name Printed   Date

gloves and eye and face protection for use while cleaning the bathroom area. A dust mask should be provided to supplement the eye and face protection when the room attendant is using any powdered cleaners or doing any overhead dusting or cleaning.

All occupational bloodborne pathogen exposure incidents (including needlestick injuries, lacerations, or splashes) must be recorded on OSHA Log No. 200 (exhibit 30.2) if the incident results in: (1) medical treatment (e.g. immune serum globulin, hepatitis B vaccine, or other prescribed medical treatment); or (2) diagnosis of possible seroconversion (possible exposure to contaminated blood). In the instance of seroconversion, only the injury, such as "needlestick," shall be recorded—*not* the serologic status of the employee.

In areas where there is continuing exposure, as in a laundry, there would be a need for an employer to offer vaccinations to all employees. In the laundry, a few key employees might be assigned to the sorting and laundering of all red bags or bags bearing the biohazard symbol, and such employees would be offered vaccinations and be provided with the protective clothing as noted earlier.

The hotel should prepare an exposure control plan, and all housekeeping, laundry, and security staff, lifeguards, and other employees who are trained in CPR and/or first aid should be advised of this plan.[16]

There are 22 states that administer OSHA-approved plans to implement the OSHA requirements. A property should verify whether its state has such an OSHA-approved plan that must be followed in that state.

Medical Emergencies

Hotels need to face the possibility of guests becoming seriously ill, accidentally injured, or even dying. Management should consider a policy for dealing with such problems. It should review with legal counsel and the insurance company an appropriate response to medical emergencies. It should also review with legal counsel the applicability of "good Samaritan" laws, which protect, within limits, passersby who try to help.

The Occupational Safety and Health Act requires that a trained first-aider be present on each workshift in all hotels and motels, unless those properties have ready access to medical services on the premises or in close proximity. This may prove helpful in incidents involving guests, as the staff member trained in first aid will have some knowledge of how best to assist the guest. An important point is that first-aiders will also have a better idea of what *not* to do in certain situations.

The property should review with legal counsel the local regulations regarding calling an emergency medical service (EMS). This is important, for a guest may decline assistance and then later sue a property for its failure to provide appropriate aid. If legal counsel advises calling an EMS, the trained first-aider on staff should make the guest comfortable and only provide first aid assistance if a life threatening condition or situation exists.

Hazard Communication Standard

OSHA's Hazard Communication Standard became effective on May 23, 1988. Hotel and motel employers are now responsible for compliance with its requirements—the violation of which could be a $5,000 fine per count!

The following is an outline of the steps an employer must follow to comply with the standard. There is no right way to comply spelled out by OSHA because this is a performance-oriented standard. OSHA thus requires that you develop your own program that complies with various elements it has outlined.

The primary elements of the OSHA Hazard Communication Standard include the following:

1. *Evaluate the hazards in your workplace.* Chemical manufacturers are required to report to companies that distribute or use their products concerning any

OSHA INFORMATION SOURCES

OSHA
http://www.osha.gov

U.S. Government Printing Office
http://www.gpo.gov/su_docs/

OSHA has published *Hazard Communication—A Compliance Kit* ($19). Properties interested in obtaining this publication should visit either the U.S. Government Online Bookstore at http://bookstore.gpo.gov/ or contact the U.S. Government Printing Office at:

SUPERINTENDENT OF DOCUMENTS
P.O. Box 371954
Pittsburgh, PA 15250-7954
(202) 512-1800 (7:30am–4:30pm Eastern)
FAX: (202) 512-2250

Questions on OSHA health standards may be referred to (202) 219-8036.
Questions on OSHA safety standards may be referred to (202) 219-8031.

For further information on OSHA Regulations for the Lodging Industry, see Raymond C. Ellis, Jr., *OSHA: A Guide to Occupational Safety and Health Standards Compliance for the Lodging Industry* (Washington, D.C.: American Hotel Foundation, 1997).

---

hazardous chemicals they contain. Innkeepers are what OSHA calls "downstream employers" and can rely on these evaluations that come from a manufacturer or supplier. If you choose to evaluate the hazards yourself you become responsible for the quality of the hazard determination.

2. *Prepare an inventory of all hazardous chemicals in the workplace.* You must do this in a centralized fashion for the entire property; then you can divide it by department for training purposes. Make sure that every product for which you have a material safety data sheet (MSDS) (see #3 below) is included in the inventory. Be sure to update the inventory if any new hazard is introduced into the workplace.

3. *Prepare a master MSDS file and keep a file by department in each department.* An MSDS is a material safety data sheet which the manufacturer or supplier is required to provide to you at the time of the initial shipment.

 The MSDS is supposed to provide the necessary information on the chemical-containing product, including: health effects, exposure limits, whether it's a carcinogen, precautionary measures, emergency and first-aid procedures, and the name of the organization which prepared the MSDS.

 Copies of the MSDS must be readily accessible to employees. A copy of the master MSDS file should also be kept at the front desk for reference by any fire, police, or utility response service unit. When you receive a new MSDS for your master file be sure a copy is placed in the file of the appropriate department(s).

You are responsible for having an MSDS on each hazardous chemical product.

4. *Labels or a form of warning belong on all containers of hazardous chemicals.* This, once again, is the responsibility of the manufacturer or supplier. Your responsibility as an employer is to ensure the maintenance of the label, tag, or marking. The label should identify the product in such a way that an employee could readily find the MSDS for the product. It must also contain the appropriate hazard warning. Labels must be in English. Another language may appear on the label as long as the information also appears in English.

5. *You must develop a comprehensive written hazard communication program.* The program should include provisions for container labeling, MSDS, an employee training program, and generally describe how your organization will comply with the hazard communication standard. It must also contain a list of the hazardous chemicals in each work area and the means you will use to inform employees of the hazards of non-routine tasks. The written program must be available to employees, employee representatives, and to representatives of OSHA and the National Institute for Occupational Safety & Health (NIOSH). Your written program need not be lengthy or complicated.

6. *You must establish a training and information program for employees exposed to hazardous chemicals in their work area.**

Important Points for Management

The Occupational Safety and Health Administration (OSHA) is a federal agency established to help ensure that employers provide a safe working environment for their employees. The agency sets standards, conducts inspections, requires that records be kept regarding work-related injuries and illnesses, and enforces the Occupational Safety and Health Act.

Hotels are responsible for satisfying OSHA requirements, even though they are relatively safe places to work. Usually, hotels and motels are not a priority target industry for OSHA inspections. However, if operators do not follow safety practices, they may be subject to increased inspections.

OSHA regulations require that by February 1 of the calendar year, the employer shall conspicuously post in places where employee notices are generally posted an annual summary of the prior year's totals of work-related injuries and illnesses

---

* In *Halterman* v. *Radisson Hotel Corp.* (2000 Va. Lexis 18, 259 Va. 171, Circuit Court of Alexandria, January 14, 2000) the court held that the hotel was not liable to a repairman who inhaled toxic fumes. The court held that under OSHA the hotel had a duty to do more than post a warning of hazardous materials—that the hotel had a responsibility to warn H&H (Halterman's employer). The court ruled that there was insufficient evidence in this case that the property had not properly warned H&H of the potential risk

from the OSHA Log No. 200. A separate OSHA Log No. 200 form must be used to present this summary information.

Hotels must also post a notice furnished by OSHA that informs employees of their rights and obligations under the Act. The OSHA poster must be conspicuously posted in an area accessible to all employees.

OSHA notices must be permanently posted under glass to ensure that such notices are not altered, defaced, or covered by other material.

OSHA compliance officers are authorized to enter a business's premises *without delay* during regular working hours to inspect and investigate in order to determine compliance with OSHA regulations.

An employer may deny entry to an OSHA inspector; however, OSHA can then obtain a search warrant authorizing an inspection. It is recommended that employers avoid using confrontation tactics when dealing with OSHA compliance officers.

Advance notice of inspections may be provided only in the event of a reported dangerous condition requiring immediate attention. This condition usually would be reported by an employee.

The OSHA compliance officer has the authority to take environmental samples, take relevant photographs, employ reasonable and necessary investigative techniques, and question privately any employer, owner, operator, agent, or employee.

Under OSHA regulations on bloodborne pathogens, employers must offer hepatitis B vaccinations to any employee who has been exposed to bloodborne pathogens. The employee may decline the vaccine, but must sign a declination form whose specific wording is included in the regulations. Following an exposure incident, all records concerning that exposure must be maintained on file for 30 years.

Prepare a master MSDS file and keep a file by department in each department. A copy of the master MSDS file should also be kept at the front desk for reference by any fire, police, or utility response service unit.

References

1. 29 U.S.C. § 651 *et seq.*
2. 29 U.S.C. § 651.
3. 29 U.S.C. § 654.
4. See 29 C.F.R., Part 1910 (1993) for a list of standards and information on guidelines.
5. Recording and Reporting Occupational Injuries and Illnesses, 29 C.F.R. Part 1904 (1993).
6. 29 C.F.R. § 1904.2.
7. 29 C.F.R. § 1904.6.
8. 29 C.F.R. § 1910.20.
9. 29 C.F.R. § 1904.8.
10. *Id.*

11.   436 U.S. 307 (1978). See also *Brock* v. *Emerson Electric Co.*, 834 F.2d 994 (11th Cir. 1987). But see *McLaughlin* v. *A. B. Chance Co.*, 56 U.S.L.W. 2547 (April 5, 1988).

12.   445 U.S. 1 (1980).

13.   See 806 F. Supp. 47 (D.N.J. 1992).

14.   *Ibid.*

15.   29 C.F.R. Part 1910.1030, *et seq.* (1993).

16.   See 29 C.F.R. § 1910.1030(c) for requirements.

Review Questions

1.   What is the purpose of OSHA?

2.   What are the requirements of OSHA as to posting notices to employees?

3.   What laws does your state have on occupational safety programs for employees?

4.   Define bloodborne pathogens, and name two.

5.   What forms of protection against bloodborne pathogens must be offered under OSHA regulations and to which employees?

6.   What additional equipment must employees who are trained in first aid be offered for performing CPR?

7.   What is the role of on-staff specialists, and what protective measures must they take?

8.   What are MSDS data files, and where should they be kept?

Internet Sites

For more information, visit the following Internet sites. Remember that Internet addresses can change without notice.

OSHA
http://www.osha.gov

Chapter 31 Outline

Types of Regulation
  Licenses to Operate, Certificates,
    Permits, and Inspections
  Other Local Regulations
  Taxes
Important Points for Management
References
Key Terms
Review Questions
Internet Sites

Competencies

1. Indicate some of the subjects covered
   by laws and regulations promulgated
   on the state and local levels.
   (pp. 405–407)

2. Identify the licenses, certificates,
   permits, or inspections that state and
   local building codes may require
   hotels to obtain. (p. 406)

3. Cite examples of state and local taxes
   that hotels may be subject to or may be
   responsible for collecting.
   (pp. 406–407)

31

Licensing and Regulation of Hotels by Cities, Towns, and Villages

Hotels are generally subject to regulation in federal, state, and local jurisdictions. The authority of the federal government to exercise its regulatory powers over hotels, as in the area of civil rights, derives from the authority granted by the "commerce clause" and the Fourteenth Amendment to the U.S. Constitution. State and local jurisdictions often justify regulation of hotels on the grounds of protecting the public interests, welfare, health, morals, and safety, and as a legitimate exercise of their police powers.[1]

Often state legislatures pass laws that expressly provide the authority for local jurisdictions—counties, cities, and towns—to enact additional or even more stringent regulations in areas that the state has already chosen to legislate or regulate. However, in order for such local laws and regulations to be valid, they must be reasonable and not arbitrary or discriminatory. For example, in *McCain* v. *Davis*[2] the court held unconstitutional, as a violation of due process and equal protection, a Louisiana statute that prohibited "white" hotels from providing accommodations for blacks.

In another case, *Gawzner Corporation* v. *Minier*,[3] a California appellate court affirmed a lower court's conclusion that a state statute relating to permissible outdoor advertising applying only to motels and not to hotels was discriminatory in its application and thus invalid.* The court concluded:

> With respect to the avowed purpose…[of the statute in question], hotels and motels are similarly situated. To discriminate between them as to outdoor or outside rate advertising is to deny motels the equal protection of the law.[4]

Types of Regulation

Beyond the limitations that regulations must not be arbitrary or discriminatory in their application, the authority of state and local governments to regulate hotel operations is extensive. A review of a few of the general types of statutes and regulations affecting hotel operations will demonstrate this.

---

* For a case reaching the same conclusion and involving a similar city ordinance, see *Eskind* v. *City of Vero Beach,* 159 So. 2d 209 (Sup. Ct. Fla. 1963).

Licenses to Operate, Certificates, Permits, and Inspections

Most states and cities require by law that a hotel owner obtain a license to operate the hotel. Failure to do so may result in civil and/or criminal penalties, depending on the applicable law of the jurisdiction. Along with the general license to operate a hotel, most states require hotels to obtain licenses to sell alcoholic beverages and to prepare and serve food.

In addition, state and local building codes may require hotels to obtain various "certificates" or "permits" relating to occupancy. For instance, under the New York City Building Code, a hotel must obtain a certificate of occupancy for the entire building, and must also obtain a "permit for a place of assembly" for certain meeting rooms. To obtain such certificates and permits, the hotel must comply with all of the Code's relevant structural and design requirements.

In order to maintain a building's exterior walls and **appurtenances** in a safe condition, § 27-127 of the New York City Building Code, effective February 21, 1980, requires the inspection of exterior walls and appurtenances of hotels and other buildings within the city that are more than six stories in height. The first "critical examination" took place by February 21, 1982. For buildings erected after the effective date, the initial examination must be conducted in the *fifth year* following the erection of the exterior walls. Thereafter, critical examinations must take place every five years, and the architect or engineer who performs the examination must submit a written report of the examination to the New York City Commissioner of Buildings.

The examination requirements, however, do *not* apply to certain buildings, including buildings having an *ongoing maintenance program* acceptable to the Building Department for preventive maintenance of the exterior walls and appurtenances thereof.

Other Local Regulations

As indicated earlier, state and local governments may also promulgate numerous laws and regulations, such as:

- Requirement to maintain guest registers

- Restrictions on advertising of rates on outdoor signs

- Requirements relating to adequate lighting

- Specifications as to lifeguards and safety devices at swimming facilities

- Sanitation requirements with respect to bed linens and food preparation

- Restrictions regarding the sale of alcoholic beverages

These examples merely hint at the extent of the operating requirements that state and local governments may impose upon hotel operations.

Taxes

Hotels are subject to and responsible for collecting many kinds of state and local taxes. Such taxes, discussed in more detail in Chapter 35, may include:

- State and local corporation **franchise taxes** or unincorporated business taxes on hotel revenues (applicable to all business entities)

- State sales taxes that the hotel may be responsible for collecting from guests and paying over to the appropriate tax authorities

- State and/or local hotel room occupancy taxes (in addition to and separate from the sales tax)

- Local hotel revenues tax

Important Points for Management

It is impossible to furnish in this book complete information or even a listing of the tens of thousands of laws in all localities in every state. Hotelkeepers must get this information from local authorities or local counsel. The office of the city clerk, town clerk, or village clerk may be one source of information on local laws and regulations. Hotels should also have their local counsel or hotel trade association prepare a list of the local laws and regulations applicable to them, and periodically update it.

Hotelkeepers in each community must also be alert and keep themselves familiar with the activities of local governing bodies through their attorneys, newspapers, trade associations, and so forth. It is only through such watchfulness that hotel personnel can keep informed of proposed local legislation that may adversely affect their interests. It is far better to register opposition in advance to proposed local legislation than to complain about its adverse effect after such legislation has been passed as a local law. (Before taking any such action, consult with local counsel to determine if there are any reporting requirements under state or local lobbying laws.)

Most states and cities require a hotel owner to obtain an operating license. Most states also require licenses to serve alcohol and food. Building codes cover the use of a building, capacity limits, exit requirements, safety features, and standards of design and construction. State laws relating to food cover the topics of sanitation, food storage, cleaning, water supply, sewage, and vermin control. Some state laws require food service operations to post instructions on how to help a choking person.

General health laws cover a multitude of topics such as water supply, sewage, reporting of contagious diseases, and purchase of dairy products only from licensed dealers. These laws vary from state to state. Laws governing swimming pools include not only building codes, but also cover the topics of lifeguards, rescue equipment, warning signs, etc.

References

1. See, for example, *King* v. *City of Tulsa*, 415 P. 2d 606 (Court of Criminal Appeals of Okla. 1966).

2. 217 F. Supp. 661 (E.D. La. 1963).

3. 46 Cal. App. 3d 777, 120 Cal. Rptr. 344 (1975).

4. 46 Cal. App. 3d at 791, 120 Cal. Rptr. at 353 (1975).

Key Terms

appurtenance—An attachment or adjunct to the principal property.

franchise tax—A tax on the franchise of a corporation, that is, on the right and privilege of carrying on business as a corporation.

Review Questions

1. What are three types of licenses that local governments usually require hotels to obtain?

2. Why is it important for a hotel to compile a list of applicable federal, state, and local laws?

3. What are some of the state and local taxes hotels may have to pay or collect?

Internet Sites

For more information, visit the following Internet sites. Remember that Internet addresses can change without notice.

State and Local Tax
http://www.taxsites.com/state.html

Chapter 32 Outline

Competencies

1. Define "telephone resale" as it applies to lodging establishments, and summarize the Telephone Operator Consumer Service Act's posting requirements. (p. 411)

2. Identify circumstances under which surcharges may and may not be imposed on telephone calls. (p. 412)

3. Describe how telephone companies compensate hotels for public coin-operated telephones. (p. 412)

4. Explain how telephone legislation for the hearing-impaired affects hotels. (p. 412–413)

32

Telephone Service and Resale Rights

Resale of Interstate and International Telephone Service

On October 21, 1980, the FCC for the first time permitted hotels and motels to resell *interstate* telephone service. On August 6, 1982, the FCC permitted hotels and motels to resell *international* telephone service. Today, hotels and motels may purchase long distance interstate and international telephone service from AT&T or other common carriers (OCCs) such as MCI or Sprint, and resell such service to their guests.

The FCC allows each hotel and motel to determine its own resale price, without the need for filing **tariffs** with the FCC. Thus, for example, a hotel may purchase long distance telephone service at DDD (direct distance dial) rates, or at bulk rates or WATS (wide area telephone service) rates, or from an OCC, and resell such service to its guests at a rate to be determined by the hotel.

Resale means that hotels may purchase telephone service, including WATS, from common carriers and resell such *interstate* and *international* telephone service directly to their guests. Public service commissions of various states, however, still exercise jurisdiction over *intrastate* telephone calls.

Posting Telephone Notice

The federal Telephone Operator Consumer Service Act of 1990[1] contains the following posting requirements:

> The following notification must be posted at or near each telephone in plain view of the guest.

- Name, address, and toll-free number of the provider of your operator services

- That rates are available on request

- That guests have a right to access the long distance service of their choice

- That guests may not contact their chosen carrier for information on accessing that service from that telephone

- Name and address of the enforcement division of the FCC responsible for enforcing the Act.

In addition, various state laws require the posting of the actual amount of hotel surcharges on telephone calls.[2]

Intrastate Calls

In most states, the hotel's service charge, or surcharge, on local telephone calls and other telephone calls made by hotel guests to another point within the state—intrastate calls—are subject to regulation by the state's Public Service Commission. In many states, Public Service Commissions do not impose any limit upon such intrastate telephone surcharges. However, some states may still preclude hotels from imposing any kind of surcharge on guests' *local and intrastate* telephone calls. Local counsel can advise whether or not a hotel has the right to add any surcharges or charges for the resale of *intrastate* telephone services to guests.

Some states that do not regulate surcharges on guests' telephone calls nevertheless require the hotel to give guests notice of the amount of the surcharge. For example, under the Order of the New York State Public Service Commission "each hotel or motel electing to charge for telephone service shall *affix to each guest telephone notice of the rates and charges that will apply* for the use of the communications system" (emphasis added).

In New York State, hotels are allowed to resell *intrastate* WATS as well as *intrastate foreign exchange* (FX), switched and non-switched private lines, and local exchange services and terminal equipment.

Coin-Operated Telephones

The compensation by telephone companies for public coin-operated and charge-a-call telephones located in hotels is on an entirely different basis. With coin-operated telephones the guest pays for the call, including federal tax, by depositing the money directly in the phone. In charge-a-call telephones the guest uses a telephone company credit card to pay for the call. In either case, the hotel can make no surcharge. However, the telephone company normally pays a commission to the owner of the premises on which pay phone is located, whether hotel or otherwise. Such commissions may be based upon a percentage of either the amount collected by the telephone company from the pay phone, or the total amount of revenues derived from such public telephones. (The telephone company may, in the contract commission schedule, exclude a certain amount of revenues or collections to cover its maintenance costs.) The amount of this commission is fixed by the contract between the telephone company and the owner of the premises who permits the installation of such public telephones.

Some states (such as New York) have now made it possible for hotels, restaurants, bars, and certain other business establishments to purchase and operate coin-operated telephones. This state action followed the Federal Communications Commission (FCC) ruling of June 15, 1984, permitting the private ownership of pay telephones.

Telephone Regulations for the Hearing-Impaired

The FCC has requirements for establishments with 20 or more employees requiring that telephones be text-enabled or hearing aid compatible.[3]

In most cases, it is easy to tell whether a telephone is hearing aid-compatible or not, because it is generally stamped or marked at the base of each telephone set. Most "name brand" telephone systems have been hearing aid-compatible for many years.

The Americans with Disabilities Act (ADA), which is discussed in Chapter 9, has additional requirements with respect to telephones in the guestrooms and public areas of hotels.

Important Points for Management

Telephone calls between states are under the jurisdiction of the Federal Communications Commission (FCC). The FCC has now deregulated hotels and motels to permit the resale of *interstate* and *international* telephone service. Hotels can now resell telephone service and add a surcharge to the cost that the telephone company bills the hotel.

Intrastate means totally within one state. Intrastate telephone service is regulated by the state's public service commission. Some states impose restrictions on the hotel's rights to resell *intrastate* telephone service. What does your state do regarding *intrastate* telephone service? Does it permit hotels to resell telephone service at a profit?

It is recommended that the hotel give the guest notice of the hotel's charges for the resale of any *local, intrastate, interstate,* and *international* telephone service.

References

1. Telephone Operator Consumer Service Act of 1990, 47 U.S.C. § 226.

2. See, for example, N.Y. Gen. Bus. Law § 206-e.

3. See the following FCC regulations on hearing aid-compatible telephones:

   —Title 47, Part 68.4 describes the general requirement for telephones manufactured in the United States or imported for use in the United States after August 16, 1989.

   —Title 47, Part 68.112 describes the scope of telephones to be hearing aid-compatible. This is the section which set the May 1, 1993 and 1994 deadlines for business telephones needing to be upgraded to hearing aid compatibility.

   —Title 47, Part 68.316 is the specific hearing aid compatibility standard referencing the Electronic Industries Association's recommended standard RS-504, "Magnetic Field Intensity Criteria for Telephone Compatibility with Hearing Aids."

Key Terms

tariff—As used in this book, a tariff is a public document filed with the public service commission by a public utility setting forth the services being offered by the carrier, schedule of rates and charges with respect to services, and governing rules, regulations, and practices relating to those services.

Review Questions

1. What regulations govern the hotel's resale of telephone service to guests?

2. What notices should you give your guests as to the telephone company and the charges for telephone service?

3. What telephone equipment and service should you provide a hearing impaired guest in the guestroom? in the lobby?

Internet Sites

For more information, visit the following Internet sites. Remember that Internet addresses can change without notice.

Americans with Disablities Act (ADA)
http://www.usdoj.gov/crt/ada/adahom1.htm

Federal Communications Commission (FCC)
http://www.fcc.gov

Chapter 33 Outline

Competencies

1. Explain the effect of the Copyright Act of 1976. (p. 417)

2. Name the three major copyright associations, and explain when royalties are payable. (pp. 417–418)

3. Describe exemptions allowed under the Copyright Law of 1976. (p. 418)

4. Explain the purpose of the Communications Act of 1934. (pp. 418–419)

5. Explain the implications of the Copyright Act of 1976 as it pertains to cable television broadcasts. (pp. 419–420)

6. Describe the state legislation and common law causes of action regarding unauthorized use of cable television broadcasts. (p. 420)

7. Explain why the Cable Communications Policy Act of 1984 was enacted. (p. 420)

8. Describe concerns regarding videodisc and videocassette movies. (pp. 420–421)

33

Copyright Laws for Music, Television, Video, and Movies

As a general rule, the owner of a copyrighted music composition has the *exclusive* right to print, reprint, publish, copy, and sell the copyrighted work. In addition, the owner of the copyrighted music composition has the right to control the public performance of that work unless the performance falls within certain narrow exceptions specified in the Copyright Act of 1976 as amended.[1]

The effect of the Copyright Act is that no person can give a public performance of copyrighted music unless he/she falls within the limited exemptions provided in the Copyright Act, or has permission from the copyright owner or an organization representing the owner in what is commonly known as a license agreement. Thus, a hotel/motel that plays live music, recorded background music, or rebroadcasts radio music generally has to enter into a license agreement to permit the performance of such music. Otherwise, the hotel/motel may be liable for **copyright infringement**, regardless of the lack of intent or knowledge of the infringement.

Copyright Associations

Associations hold many **copyrights** of music works. The three largest of these associations are the American Society of Composers, Authors & Publishers (ASCAP), Broadcast Music, Inc. (BMI), and the Society of European Stage Authors & Composers (SESAC). These associations ordinarily make license agreements under which hotels, motels, and others can permit copyrighted works to be performed on their premises. All three associations offer standard forms of license agreements to hotels, under which the hotel pays an annual fee based upon the amount of its expenditures for music or entertainment or on the number of rooms in a hotel. Hotels may also make arrangements with associations of copyright owners other than ASCAP or BMI or with individual copyright owners.

When Royalties Are Payable

The net effect of these restrictions is that, if copyrighted music is heard or performed in the public rooms of a hotel or motel, the operator is liable for infringement of the copyright unless he/she has a license agreement covering the copyright owner and pays a **royalty,** or the operator falls within certain exceptions to the rights of the copyright owner. This is the law whether the music is performed by live musicians in the establishment, by wired music, by record player or tape recorder, or by any other mechanical means.

417

The ASCAP and BMI master license agreements for hotels do not authorize music performances as part of a conference, congress, convention, exposition, industrial show, institute, meeting, seminar, teleconference, trade show, or any other business presentation at the premises. Consequently, these events require a separate license from ASCAP and BMI by the parties holding such events.

Exemptions Under Copyright Law of 1976

The Copyright Act provides that the "communication of a transmission embodying a performance or display or a work by the public reception of the transmission *on a single receiving apparatus of a kind commonly used in private homes*" is not an infringement of copyright unless (1) "a direct charge is made to see or hear the transmission"; or (2) "the transmission thus received is further transmitted to the public" (emphasis added).[2] "Transmission program" is defined in § 101 of the Act to be a "body of material, that as an aggregate, has been produced for the sole purpose of transmission to the public in sequence and as a unit." Thus, qualifying small establishments using standard radio and television equipment might be exempt from the requirement to pay copyright royalties.

Unauthorized Interception of Cable Television Broadcasts

Any unauthorized interception and transmission to guestrooms of cable television broadcasts through the use of "satellite signal" receivers may violate the Communications Act of 1934 as well as the laws of various states. Furthermore, any unauthorized interception, decoding, and retransmission of a copyrighted broadcast could constitute an act of copyright infringement under the Copyright Act.

The Communications Act of 1934—47 U.S.C. § 605

All radio and television communications, *except broadcasts intended for the general public*, are protected by the Federal Communications Act of 1934 (47 U.S.C. § 605). In *Chartwell Communications* v. *Westbrook*[3] the U.S. Court of Appeals of the Sixth Circuit held that the scrambled microwave broadcasts of a subscription television (STV) service were not intended to be broadcast to the general public, and, therefore, any unauthorized interception of the STV would violate § 605 of the Communications Act of 1934. Because the microwave transmissions are scrambled and subscribers must use decoding devices to unscramble the broadcasts, the court held that the plaintiff did not intend the general public to use the broadcast without paying the subscription fee.

In the *Chartwell Communications* case, the court cited a decision by a federal district court, *Home Box Office, Inc.* v. *Pay T.V. of Greater New York, Inc.*[4]* The *Pay T.V.* decision had concluded that the unauthorized interception of scrambled

---

* The Sixth Circuit rejected the reasoning in another federal court decision, *Orth-O-Vision, Inc.* v. *Home Box Office, Inc.*, 474 F. Supp. 672 (S.D.N.Y. 1979), which had held that the interception of scrambled broadcasts did not violate § 605.

microwave signals violated § 605 because the scrambling shows the broadcaster's intent not to allow the general public to receive the broadcast.

In light of the *Chartwell Communications* and *Pay T.V.* decisions, a hotel's unauthorized interception of broadcasts could be held in violation of § 605 of the Communications Act of 1934 and might subject the hotel to a private lawsuit for damages.

On May 10, 1996, the Hurley Mountain Inn in New York is alleged to have "unlawfully intercepted, received, and/or descrambled the encrypted satellite signal" of the Evander Holyfield-Bobby Czyz heavyweight boxing match "in order to broadcast the program to its patrons."

Joe Hand Promotions claimed that it had rights to distribute the broadcast, and that the inn had not obtained the right to rebroadcast the fight to its patrons. The promoter sued the inn under the Federal Communications Act and won.[5] For a number of reasons, hotels should be cautious when dealing with such matters as the broadcasting of sports and entertainment events.

The Copyright Act of 1976, as Amended

A hotel that commits an unauthorized interception of STV broadcasts by satellite signal receivers, decodes the scrambled radio waves, and retransmits the broadcast to guestrooms can also violate the Copyright Act of 1976. Section 106(5) of this Act prohibits the public performance of a copyrighted "audiovisual" work without authorization from the holder of the copyright or his/her agent. Section 111(b) provides that a secondary transmission made to the public constitutes infringement if the primary transmission is "not made for reception by the public at large but is controlled and limited to reception by particular members of the public." The legislative history to this provision explicitly states,

> …[T]he secondary transmission to the public of a primary transmission embodying a performance or display is actionable as an act of infringement if the primary transmission is not made for reception by the public at large but is controlled and limited to reception by particular members of the public. Examples of transmissions not intended for the general public are background music services such as MUZAK, closed circuit broadcasts to theatres, *pay television (STV) or pay-cable* [emphasis added].[6]

A secondary transmission of a copyrighted work has been held to constitute a performance of a copyrighted "audiovisual" work for purposes of the federal copyright legislation. Section 111(a)(1) of the Act makes certain exemptions from copyright infringement liability for secondary transmissions "not made by a cable system" that consist "entirely of the relaying, by the management of a hotel, apartment house, or similar establishment…to the private lodgings of guests" provided "no direct charge is made to see or hear the secondary transmission." However, as the legislative history to this exemption makes clear, "The exemption would not apply if the secondary transmission consists of anything other than the mere relay of ordinary broadcasts…. [A]ny other change in the signal relayed would subject the secondary transmitter to full liability."[7]

Also, § 111(a)(1) expressly provides that under the narrow exception for hotels, the secondary transmission cannot be made by a "cable system." Whether a hotel that intercepts cable television broadcasts by microwave receivers and retransmits them to guestrooms would be considered a "cable system" is not clear. Nevertheless, in light of the prohibition against anything more than merely relaying the primary transmitter signal, the narrow exception provided by § 111(a)(1) would not appear to protect hotels that decode scrambled signals without authorization.

Infringement of rights protected by the federal copyright legislation may be subject to an action by the copyright owner for actual damages suffered and any additional profits of the infringer, or, at the option of the copyright owner, the infringer may be liable for damages specified in the statute. The statutory damages are between $750 and $30,000, as the court so decides; damages may be increased to $150,000 if the court finds a willful infringement.

State Statutes and Common Law Causes of Action

Many states have enacted laws imposing additional civil or criminal penalties on persons who use electronic or mechanical means to obtain unauthorized use of cable television broadcasts. For example, § 165.15, subdivision 4 of the New York Penal Law provides that a person is guilty of the crime of "theft of services" when "with intent to avoid payment by himself or another person of the lawful charge for any telecommunications service, including...cable television service" he/she obtains or attempts to obtain by means of "tampering or making connection with the equipment of the supplier, whether by mechanical, electrical, acoustical or other means" or by any other "artifice, trick, deception, code or device."

Other states have similar statutes that may impose additional civil or criminal penalties for the unauthorized interception of cable television broadcasts. If hotels have any questions concerning state or local laws, they should contact local counsel.

California has a statute, § 593d of the California Penal Code, prohibiting a person from "knowingly and willfully" making unauthorized physical or electrical connections to any wire or component of a franchised cable television system for the purpose of intercepting cable television broadcasts. In addition, § 593e prohibits the manufacture, distribution, or selling of any device, plan, or kit for the unauthorized "interception or decoding...of any over-the-air transmission by a subscription television service."

The Cable Communications Policy Act of 1984

The Cable Communications Policy Act of 1984 makes it clear that satellite antennae may not be used for private financial gain. The Act provides substantial penalties for unlicensed commercial use of video entertainment programs obtained from satellites.

Videodisc and Videocassette Movies

The U.S. Court of Appeals (Ninth Circuit) has affirmed the U.S. District Court's (C.D. Calif. - L.A.) decision that a resort hotel's practice of renting videodisc movies to its guests, who then took the videodiscs to their rooms for viewing on VHS players, did not violate the copyright interests of the movie producers.

In this case, *Columbia Pictures Industries, Inc.* v. *Professional Real Estate Investors, Inc.*,[8] eight movie studios brought a copyright infringement action against the resort hotel, arguing that when guests took the videodisc movies to their rooms and played them, this constituted an unauthorized "public performance." Here, the hotel had bought the videodiscs from RCA Corporation. The hotel had installed VHS players in each guestroom, and guests could rent the videodiscs for viewing in their guestrooms. The VHS players were not located in any common areas of the property.

The eight movie producers claimed that the rental of the videodiscs to guests for viewing in their guestrooms constituted public performances of the movies in violation of copyright laws. The U.S. District Court in California disagreed. It noted that hotel rooms traditionally have been considered "private places" under both Fourth Amendment and common law privacy jurisdiction and the occupant is entitled to such privacy. Thus, in this respect, hotel rooms are no different than rooms in private homes, said the court, and the use of the videodiscs was a private, not public, performance. Stated the court, "A hotel room is not a place open to the public under the Copyright Act, and the viewing of movies in such accommodations is not a public performance under the Act."

Caution: It is not currently apparent how other district courts might rule on this question. Because the law is unclear in this area and the monetary damages can be high for violation of the Copyright Act, you should consult with legal counsel in your state before renting video movies to guests to take to their room for viewing.

Many hotel operators have wondered whether they can use a replay unit in the front office, and buy videocassette movies that they would then "rebroadcast" into guestroom television sets (for example, on Channel 8). This particular "rebroadcasting" of videocassette movies into the guestroom can constitute an unauthorized "public performance" and thus a violation of federal copyright laws.

Motion picture distributors have been placing a number of warnings in lodging industry magazines and sending letters to properties warning against such unlawful uses. Lawsuits have also been brought in California and other states.

Important Points for Management

A hotel or motel that plays live music or background music by means of a tape recording or record player or by rebroadcasting radio music generally has to enter into a license agreement with a copyright association (ASCAP, BMI, or SESAC) to permit the performance of such music. Otherwise, the hotel or motel may be liable for copyright infringement.

Using a replay unit in the front office to "rebroadcast" videocassette movies into guestroom television sets can constitute an unauthorized "public performance" and thus a violation of federal copyright laws.

References

1. 17 U.S.C. § 101 *et seq.*
2. 17 U.S.C. § 110(5).
3. 637 F.2d 459 (6th Cir. 1980).
4. 467 F.Supp. 525 (E.D.N.Y. 1979).
5. *Joe Hand Promotions, Inc.* v. *Hurley Mountain Inc.*, 18 F. Supp. 2d 214 (1998 U.S. Lexis 13613, Aug. 28, 1998).
6. H.R. No. 94-1476, p. 92.
7. H.R.94-1476, p. 91.
8. 866 F.2d 278 (9th Cir. 1989) 113 Sup. Ct. Rep. 1920 (1993).

 # Key Terms

copyright—Common law and/or statutory rights to publish and reproduce works of art or literature and the exclusive privilege of printing, or otherwise multiplying, publishing, and vending copies of certain literary or artistic productions. The legal effect of a copyright is to create in the owner an exclusive property right with the incidental power to lease or license the use thereof by others on stipulated terms.

copyright infringement—The unauthorized use or performance of a copyrighted musical composition.

royalty—A payment made by a licensee for the right to perform music.

 # Review Questions

1. Why does the hotel have to pay a royalty fee when it plays music at the hotel?
2. Generally speaking, what are the rights of the owner of copyrighted music?
3. What is a copyright music license agreement?
4. What happens if a hotel uses a satellite receiver to intercept cable television signals, and rebroadcasts the programs to guestrooms?
5. When is a hotel liable under the copyright laws for playing movie videos?

 # Internet Sites

For more information, visit the following Internet sites. Remember that Internet addresses can change without notice.

American Society of Composers, Authors & Publishers (ASCAP)
http://www.ascap.com

Broadcast Music, Inc. (BMI)
http://www.bmi.com

Society of European Stage Authors & Composers (SESAC)
http://www.sesac.com

Chapter 34 Outline

Competencies

1. Describe the Occupational Safety and Health Administration regulations on fire brigades. (pp. 425–426)

2. Identify fire equipment standards promulgated by OSHA. (pp. 426–429)

3. Distinguish between Class A, B, and C fires. (p. 427)

4. Cite some recent examples of state and local fire legislation. (pp. 429–431)

5. Describe pending federal legislation regarding fire safety. Give examples of major hotel fires that occurred in the 1980s. (pp. 431–433)

6. Describe penalties for non-compliance with fire codes. (pp. 433–434)

7. Summarize some private sector sources of fire safety information. (pp. 434–435)

34

Fire Safety Laws

Nothing in recent times has caused more concern to the hotel industry than the several unfortunate hotel fires that occurred in 1981, 1982, and 1986. The publicity given to the fires at the MGM Grand Hotel, Stouffer's Inn of Westchester, the DuPont Plaza in Puerto Rico, and others has had a serious impact on federal, state, and local legislation, liability litigation, and public relations for hotels and motels. As a result, there have been changes in governing concepts of fire safety legislation and practices. This chapter focuses on some of these concerns and also discusses the legal implications of the new developments in hotel fire safety.

Hotels are subject to a multitude of federal, state, and local laws, codes, and regulations relating to fire safety. Fire safety requirements are found in building codes, licensing laws, so-called multiple dwelling laws, public assembly laws, labor laws, occupational safety and health laws (OSHA, for example), sanitation laws, and so-called general business laws of the state.

Hotels should consider having their own attorneys make a list of laws relating to fire safety for the particular property. The local fire chief should also be consulted as to steps that should be taken by a particular property to comply with federal, state, and local fire laws in effect in the local community.

Federal Laws—OSHA

The Occupational Safety & Health Administration (OSHA) of the U.S. Department of Labor has promulgated regulatory standards relating to (1) "fire brigades"* established by employers, and (2) the inspection and maintenance of fire fighting equipment.[1] A brief discussion of these OSHA standards follows.

OSHA Regulations on Fire Brigades

Section 1910.156 of OSHA regulations relates to "the organization, training, and personal protective equipment of fire brigades *whenever they are established by an employer*" (emphasis added).[2] Therefore, this section does not make the establishment mandatory. But if a hotel does have a fire brigade, it is subject to the following OSHA requirements (in addition to any other requirements of state and local laws):

---

* A "fire brigade" is defined as "an organized group of employees who are knowledgeable, trained and skilled in at least basic fire fighting operations."

1. The employer must prepare and maintain a statement or written policy that establishes the brigade, notes the type, amount, and frequency of training for fire brigade members; determines the number of members; and defines the functions of the fire brigade for the property.

2. The employer must obtain from the employee a physician's certificate of fitness for the employee to perform fire brigade duties.

3. The employer is required to provide training and education for all brigade members commensurate with the various duty assignments. Such training must be given before the members perform any emergency fire duties. Training will be provided at least annually and frequently enough to assure that the fire brigade member will perform duties in a safe manner so as to not endanger other brigade members or other employees. Employees specifically assigned to fighting structural fires will be trained on a quarterly basis. The quality of training will be similar to that available in such fire training schools as Maryland Fire and Rescue Institute, Iowa Fire Service Extension, Georgia Fire Academy, New York State Department, etc. (Usually the fire brigade in a lodging establishment will not be involved with interior structural fire fighting but will use the portable fire extinguishers or standpipe systems to control or extinguish fires on a "first aid basis" prior to the arrival of professional fire fighters. Or, as the law states, "fire only in the incipient stage.") NOTE: Any establishments with a fire brigade assigned to duties that make it the equivalent of a professional fire department should contact the OSHA offices in Washington, D.C., for more details on the legal requirements for such a fire unit. Certain requirements relating to protective clothing supplied to such persons fighting "internal structural fires" are contained in § 1910.156(e).

4. The employer is charged with the responsibility of informing the fire brigade members of any special hazards, such as storage of flammable liquids and gases, toxic chemicals, radioactive sources, and water reactive substances to which they may be exposed during fire or other emergencies.

The concept of the brigade as compared with an emergency fire response team on premises is the difference in training and equipment. The brigade will attain the capability of a volunteer fire department and will fight structural as opposed to incipient fires. (An incipient fire is a fire, for example, that is just getting started on an upholstered piece or in a wastebasket.) If your location is in a resort or rural area or you are otherwise remote from a fire service with a resultant significant delay in response time due to distance, you may have to consider the fire brigade option. under those circumstances, you are advised to review 29 Code of Federal Regulations, Ch. XVII (7-1-94 Edition), Section 1910.156. This provides information on the special training schools and locations, and the special personnel proective equipment required for a brigade member as compared with an emergency response team member.

Fire Equipment Standards of OSHA

Extinguishers. Unless the employer has established a detailed emergency action plan for employees (pursuant to 29 C.F.R. § 1910.38), the employer must provide approved* portable fire extinguishers that are mounted, located, and identified so that they are readily accessible without subjecting the employees to possible injury. (Carbon tetrachloride or chlorobromomethane extinguishing agents in fire extinguishers are forbidden.) Also, the employer must permanently remove from service all soldered or riveted shell self-generating foam or gas cartridge water type portable fire extinguishers that are operated by inverting the extinguisher to rupture the cartridge or to initiate an uncontrollable pressure-generating chemical reaction to expel the fire extinguishing agent.

Extinguishers for Class A fires (ordinary combustibles such as wood, paper, or cloth) must be located so that employees need not travel more than 75 feet to any Class A unit. (There is an exemption from Class A extinguishers where a uniformly spaced standpipe system or hose stations connected to a sprinkler system are provided. This system must provide total coverage of the area to be protected and employees must be trained at least annually in its use.)

Extinguishers for Class B fires (flammable liquids, grease, gasoline, paints, oils, etc.) must be located so that the employee need not travel more than 50 feet to access a Class B extinguisher.

Extinguishers for Class C fires (electrical equipment, motors, switches, etc.) must be distributed on the basis of an appropriate pattern for the existing Class A or Class B hazards. The dry chemical in Class C extinguishers is also effective in Class A and B hazards.

The employer is responsible for inspecting, maintaining, and testing the fire extinguishers. Extinguishers or fire hoses must be visually inspected monthly.

Portable fire extinguishers require an annual maintenance check. Stored pressure extinguishers do not require an internal examination. An annual maintenance record is to be maintained for one year after the last entry or the life of the extinguisher shell, whichever is less. Stored pressure dry chemical extinguishers require a 12-year hydrostatic test but must be emptied and subjected to applicable maintenance procedures every six years. Where a non-refillable disposable container is part of the chemical extinguisher, this regulation does not pertain. The hotel must maintain evidence of this testing. This report must show that the testing program has followed proper time intervals, giving the date of test, the test pressure used, and person or agency that performed the test. These records must be maintained until retesting or the extinguisher is removed from service.

The employer must provide alternate equivalent protection when portable fire extinguishers are removed from service for maintenance or recharging.

Standpipe and Hose Systems. The OSHA regulations do not mandate the installation of a standpipe and hose system, but do require proper maintenance and use of such a system if it is installed.** A summary of the regulations follows.

---

* "Approved" generally means that the equipment has been certified to be safe by a nationally recognized testing laboratory such as the Underwriters Laboratories Inc., or the Factory Mutual System.[4]

** Other applicable state and/or local laws, however, may require such systems.

1. Pipes, hose reels, and/or cabinets must be protected against damage; must be conspicuously identified, and restricted to fire emergency use only. Without reference to a specific height, the regulation stipulates that the hose and connections be high enough above the floor to be unobstructed and accessible.

2. Threads on hose outlets and connections must be compatible with fire department equipment.

3. Except in extremely cold climates, the hose will be connected and ready for use. Where weather might damage the hose, it may be stored in a readily accessible location near the connection.

4. Standpipe systems installed after January 1, 1981, for employee use must be equipped with lined hose. Unlined hose may continue in use for existing systems but must be replaced with lined hose when removed from service due to wear or damage.

5. Hose shall be of such length that friction loss from water flowing through the hose will not reduce nozzle pressure below 30 psi (pounds per square inch).

6. The employer shall assure that standpipe hose is equipped with shut-off type nozzles.

7. The minimum water supply to the standpipe and hose system must be capable of delivering 100 gallons per minute for at least 30 minutes.

8. In a technically detailed section, the hydrostatic testing of the piping and hose is presented. It is recommended that hotels review this requirement with a reputable local fire protection service organization. This requirement is directed to systems and hose provided after January 1, 1981.

9. The employer must assure that water tanks are at the proper level, except during repairs; or that the proper pressure is maintained in a pressurized system.

10. The valves in the main piping connections must be fully open at all times, except during repairs.

11. The employer must assure that hose systems are inspected at least annually and that the hose is in place, available for use, and in serviceable condition.

12. When the system or any portion is found to be unserviceable, the employer must immediately provide replacement or repair, and assure equivalent protection through extinguishers or fire watches until replacement or repair is accomplished.

13. Where hemp or linen hoses are provided in existing systems, the hose must be unracked, physically inspected for deterioration, and re-racked using a different folding pattern. This should be done at least once each year.

14. The employer must designate trained persons to conduct all inspections required under this section.

In addition to these specific regulations for established fire brigades and fire fighting equipment, OSHA has also promulgated more general fire safety rules, many of which may also be covered by state or local laws. For example, Subpart E of the OSHA Regulations[5] generally requires employers, including hotels, to maintain a safe means of egress from fire and like emergencies.[6] These requirements include the proper marking of exits by signs, proper lighting, and providing an adequate number and size of exit doors.

Section 1910.36(b)7 prohibits the use of any "lock or fastening to prevent free escape from the *inside*" of a hotel or motel building (emphasis added).

The American Hotel & Lodging Association (AH&LA) has various publications available regarding OSHA regulations.

The National Safety Council and the National Fire Protection Association can also be consulted for suggestions as to the needs of a particular property.

State and Local Fire Legislation

The 1981 MGM Grand Hotel fire in Las Vegas, Nevada, the 1982 Stouffer's Inn fire in White Plains (Westchester County), New York, and the 1986 DuPont Plaza Hotel fire in Puerto Rico were each followed by a flood of proposed state and federal legislation to change the fire codes governing hotels and other commercial properties and to provide stricter standards of fire safety.

Perhaps the strictest fire code ever adopted was that enacted by Clark County, Nevada, where the MGM Grand Hotel is located.[7] This code provides that in all buildings that rise higher than 55 feet above the lowest fire department access, automatic sprinkler systems must be installed in all exit corridors, and each guestroom must be protected by at least one sprinkler head. It also provides for the installation of automatic sprinklers in the building's basement if the entire floor area exceeds 1,500 square feet, or in any portion of the basement which is more than 75 feet from an exit. This code also sets down more stringent standards regarding the air supply to guestrooms. Supplying air to guestrooms from the source of the exit corridors is strictly prohibited, and openings between guestrooms and exit corridors must be sealed unless:

1. approved smoke detectors are installed at specified spacing, fire dampers are installed in the air vents, and the activation of the corridor smoke detectors automatically causes the air supply system for the corridors to stop and the fire dampers to close; or

2. an approved smoke and fire damper is installed in an approved manner in the corridor; or

3. the entire building has an automatic sprinkler system.

In addition, the code states that there must be a voice communication system, at least one way, to the guestrooms, public assembly areas, exit corridors, and stairways. There are also standards on emergency lighting, exit illumination, and fire alarm systems without manual delays, as well as the installation of self-closing devices on doors. The many other provisions in this fire safety code include posting requirements with which the hotels must strictly comply.

Other states have also adopted more stringent fire laws.

In *Louisiana*, a 1981 statute[8] requires hotels and motels to post notices on the back of the main entry door to each room including a map indicating the fire exits.

Louisiana has also officially adopted the 1976 Life Safety Code of the National Fire Protection Association to set standards for new construction of high-rise buildings in the state.

New York State has a posting law[9] that requires hotels and motels with two or more stories to post floor plans by each stairway and elevator indicating the exits on each floor. Following the Stouffer's fire, the New York State Legislature passed a bill that the governor signed into law establishing a State Fire Prevention and Building Code Council. One purpose of the law and the Council is to draft legislation revising the state building code to provide for a statewide uniform fire safety code.[10]

New York City has enacted Local Law No. 41 requiring all new and existing places of assembly in hotels (when required by the building code) to have sprinkler systems, fire alarms, and emergency lighting. This law also requires hotels to maintain exit or directional signs in meeting rooms and other public rooms.

Another New York City law[11] requires hotels to install approved smoke detecting devices in each guestroom. According to this law, a plan for the installation of smoke detectors has to be submitted and approved by the New York City Department of Buildings.

In October 1981, the New York City Building and Fire Commissioners jointly issued regulations that require hotels exceeding 75 feet in height and having more than 30 sleeping rooms to file with the Departments a "Fire Safety and Evacuation Plan." These regulations also require the designation of an employee as fire safety director and a sufficient number of other employees as deputy fire safety directors. These employees are certified "to conduct fire drills, evacuations and related activities such as organizing, training and supervising a fire brigade when required." Also, according to the regulations, hotels must post signs on the back of each guestroom door indicating the location of the fire exits and the number of doorways onto the public corridor that must be passed in order to reach the exit stairways.

Under the New York State Uniform Building and Fire Code, hotels which are more than three stories in height or which have 30 or more guestrooms are required to have portable smoke detectors that are both audible and visual.

Georgia has also adopted stringent regulations requiring hotels and motels to post specific fire instructions on the side of every exit door in every "sleeping room, meeting room or other room open to the public."[12] These instructions include 9 general "Safety Tips," 18 instructions to guests on what to do "in case of fire," and 12 points regarding the operation of fire safety equipment and the hotel's protections. The new regulations also require a conspicuous notice to be fixed above the call buttons for elevators on each floor stating, "In the event of fire, do *not* use this elevator" and showing an "evacuation route" indicating the direction to the nearest fire exit.

Some states have considered enacting tax incentive legislation to promote sprinkler installation in hotels. For example, in 1980, the Alaska legislature enacted a statute allowing an exemption of 2% of assessed value for property taxes. Also, the legislation provided loan funds at discounted interest rates as an incentive to install sprinkler systems.

Failure to comply with applicable fire laws and regulations can result in fines and criminal penalties. As discussed below, noncompliance can also be the basis of liability for damages in a civil lawsuit filed by guests injured in a fire, or by their representatives in the event of death.

Federal Fire Safety Act

The federal Hotel and Motel Fire Safety Act[13] was signed into law September 25, 1990. This Act requires hotels that host federal government employees to have hard-wired smoke detectors in all guestrooms in conformance with National Fire Protection Association (NFPA) Standard 74. In addition, hotels higher than three stories are required to have an automatic fire sprinkler system in compliance with NFPA Standard 13 or 13R.*

Most jurisdictions now require full sprinkler systems in the new construction of any commercial occupancy regardless of the height of the structure. Even in the few jurisdictions that have not addressed the problem, a property that is not required to have smoke detection or sprinklers will find it difficult, if not impossible, to defend against a plaintiff action. The plaintiff's attorney would note that smoke detectors and sprinklers are "state of the art." In other words, while they may not be a standard for a particular community, such protection is so widey used in the industry that a prudent business person would install such protection.[14]

As of October 1, 1994, meetings that are federally funded (in whole or in part) can no longer be held in properties that do not satisfy the Act's fire safety guidelines. The law also requires that 65% of all federal agencies' employee room nights must be spent in properties that meet the fire safety guidelines. The law also stipulates that by October 1, 1995, 75% and by October 1, 1996, 90% of each federal agency's room nights must be spent at hotels in compliance with the law.

The Act required state fire marshals to compile and forward to the Federal Emergency Management Agency (FEMA) a list of complying properties by September 25, 1992. The U.S. Fire Administration (USFA), the federal agency charged with overseeing implementation, then published a National Master List of complying hotels. If a hotel is not on this USFA master list (which is updated periodically), it will not be listed in the *Federal Travel Directory* (FTD).

Because the FTD is published monthly and distributed to federal employees who travel on official business, it serves as their primary lodging information resource. Properties that are on the USFA master list can be included in the FTD, but only if they also participate in the General Services Administration's discount lodging program.

---

* See Raymond C. Ellis, Jr., "A Guide to Occupational Safety and Health Standards Compliance for the Lodging Industry," *Lodging,* American Hotel Foundation (1997) p. 33.

Court Cases

Civil Action

Many lawsuits have been filed in state and federal courts arising out of major hotel fires in 1981, 1982, and 1986. The plaintiffs include guests of the hotel at the time of the fire who were allegedly injured, as well as representatives of deceased victims of the fires.

The MGM Grand Fire. With regard to litigation stemming from the MGM Grand Hotel fire, in which 84 persons died and 679 were injured, about 900 negligence lawsuits seeking over one billion dollars in damages were filed against the hotel.

The complaints in these cases generally allege that the hotel was negligent for not taking specified steps to protect the guests against fire, such as installing sprinklers and smoke detectors and providing adequate instructions for escape. The complaints also cite alleged violations of state and local fire codes. The defendants include the hotel owner and manager, the parent corporations, and even local governmental officials charged with enforcing local fire codes.

In a Los Angeles County Superior Court,[15] 18 guests from Mexico brought a **class action** seeking $175 million in punitive damages from MGM Grand in addition to an unspecified amount of general damages for injuries and property losses for "all Mexican guests" staying at the hotel at the time of the fire (an estimated 375 people). Besides alleging inadequate sprinklers and smoke detectors, this complaint alleges that the hotel solicited these Mexican and foreign-speaking customers, but failed to provide special multilingual fire drills and multilingual safety signs for them.

In an action brought in the Southern District of New York, a husband and wife sued the MGM Grand for alleged injuries caused by smoke inhalation. The complaint sought $40 million in compensatory damages and $100 million in punitive damages.[16]

In another case brought in Federal District Court in Detroit, one couple, allegedly trapped in their room for three hours, sued the MGM Grand for damages arising out of smoke inhalation, minor cuts, and for mental anguish.

Nevada state law allows the plaintiffs who are survivors of victims to be awarded damages for their emotional distress, as well as damages for lost maintenance and support.

Some of the MGM Grand Hotel cases were settled for $75 million in 1983.

The Stouffer's Inn Fire. In the Stouffer's Inn fire in White Plains, New York, in 1982, 26 business executives died in the blaze. One suit was brought by the relatives of four victims for $40 million in damages. One of the deceased was an executive with Nestlés Corporation, the owner of Stouffer's.

Note, however, that in *Arrow Electronics, Inc.* v. *The Stouffer Corporation, et al.,*[17] the plaintiff-corporation, Arrow Electronics, Inc., sued the owners of the hotel for $5 million in compensatory damages and $5 million in punitive damages for the loss of its management, costs of recruiting new employees, loss of books, records, and papers, death benefits to widows and estates of its employees, and lost profits caused by the hotel fire. Arrow had 13 employees who died in the fire.

The complaint alleged that Stouffer had agreed to rent guestrooms and meeting rooms to plaintiff for its senior management-level annual budget meetings, and that the agreement implied that the portions of the hotel furnished to Arrow were suitable and safe for the use contemplated, reasonably free of fire hazards, and reasonably equipped with devices to minimize the danger of fire. The complaint also stated that the defendants had warranted that the hotel was safe when in fact it was not. The complaint alleged causes of action in negligence, for wrongful, wanton, willful and intentional conduct, breach of express and implied warranty, breach of contract, and strict liability.

The trial court held that the Arrow Corporation had no right to recover damages sustained when one of its employees is injured. In other jurisdictions with similar wrongful death statutes, courts have held that the employer has no right of recovery for the death of the employee. The court pointed out that if recovery could be had by all who are "injured in fact, the resources available to compensate an injured person or the survivors of a deceased person would be diluted."

The DuPont Plaza Hotel Fire in Puerto Rico. The DuPont Plaza Hotel fire in San Juan, Puerto Rico, took 97 lives, and at least 140 persons were injured. It is reported that the fire was arson.

Puerto Rico's Occupational Safety and Health Office charged the hotel with a number of violations of safety and health standards. The authorities said an inquiry found 44 violations that investigators considered willful, including two inadequate exits, five locked exits, 15 exits unprotected by self-closing fire doors, and 10 blocked passageways. The hotel was also charged with 15 "serious" violations, including missing exit signs, blocked fire alarms, and stairways without handrails.

A Motel Fire. In *Garrett v. Holiday Inns, Inc.*,[18] the New York Court of Appeals held that a town that issued a certificate of occupancy to a motel despite the existence of blatant fire and safety violations may also be liable for resulting injuries in a subsequent fire. The court stated:

> If, as is alleged in the complaints, known, blatant, and dangerous violations existed on these premises, but the town affirmatively certified the premises as safe, upon which representation the owners and operators justifiably relied in their dealings with the premises, then a proper basis for imposing liability on the town may well have been demonstrated. While such liability would plainly encompass direct injury to the owners and operator, it may also properly include the economic damages they may suffer as a result of judgment against them in favor of the motel guests. Thus, the town may be held proportionately liable for such damages if it is found that such exposure to potential tort liability was a foreseeable harm resulting from the town's alleged breach of duty....
>
> The town had a duty, in the face of the alleged blatant and dangerous code violations, to refuse to issue a certificate of occupancy.

Criminal Actions

In certain jurisdictions there is a possibility of criminal action against individuals for failing to comply with local or state fire codes. In addition, the failure to report a fire or fire alarm may also violate state or local laws. Penalties for noncompliance vary and usually depend on the circumstances of each particular case.

For example, under New York City Local Law No. 62 of 1981, the failure of a hotel to install smoke detectors in guestrooms is considered a "hazardous" violation under the New York City Housing Maintenance Code. Such a violation is a misdemeanor and may result in a criminal penalty of imprisonment of up to one year and/or a fine of between $10 and $1,000 for each violation.[19]

Private Sector Aids

The private sector has strongly responded to public requests for more information on fire safety. One of the more active organizations with respect to promoting fire safety awareness is the National Fire Protection Association (NFPA). The 1981 NFPA publication "Information on Hotel and Motel Fire Safety for Meeting Planners" was distributed to professional meeting planners. It provides general and specific checklists and questions which meeting planners may consider when booking a meeting or convention at a particular property.

The NFPA has also published a voluntary "Life Safety Code." Some jurisdictions may refer to, or adopt, this model NFPA Code in whole or in part when drafting legislation. The Life Safety Code in itself is not binding (unless its provisions have been enacted into law in the local jurisdiction).

The American Automobile Association (AAA) publishes information on the availability of smoke detection and/or sprinkler systems in each hotel or motel property listed in AAA Tourbooks. The AAA also adopted an official resolution (RE-13) urging hotels and motels to install and maintain "approved protection signalling systems...to assure the early detection of smoke, fire or heat." This resolution also states that:

> All establishments should comply with all standards of the Life Safety Code as published by the National Fire Protection Association. NFPA makes available publication No. 101 outlining the specific details of fire protection for various types of public structures. NFPA recommends that all establishments provide a system for life safety from fire incorporating building design and construction, public protection and employee training. In most localities, there are local and state laws and ordinances on fire safety enforced by the building officials and fire department. All establishments should comply with these laws and ordinances.

The fire safety standards mentioned in the AAA resolution are also part of its criteria for listing hotels in AAA Tourbooks.

For the past 40 years AH&LA has sponsored a Safety & Fire Protection Committee which states as its purpose:

> To assist the lodging industry by working with appropriate federal, state and local government agencies on safety and fire protection programs for guests and employees. To provide and disseminate safety and fire protection information.

> To coordinate its activities with the National Safety Council, the National Fire Protection Association and other fire protection and national code organizations.

The committee is actively involved with the National Fire Protection Association, United States Fire Administration, and the Educational Institute of AH&LA in an effort to develop educational programs and materials concerning fire safety.

A monthly bulletin is produced and distributed to member associations under the auspices of the committee.

AH&LA has continuing close working relationships with the NFPA, the National Bureau of Standards, and the U.S. Fire Administration.

AH&LA has worked with the NFPA to make available to members as a matter of information the NFPA instructional materials, including the production of several films on hotel fire safety.

AH&LA and its state association members have also conducted a great number of seminars on fire safety to provide information on applicable laws and regulations and information published by NFPA and other voluntary organizations.

AH&LA has also worked with other interested groups, such as the Council of Insurance Legislators and the Foundation for Fire Safety (Technical Advisory Committee), to seek solutions to the problems of toxicity and smoke generation. AH&LA has also lent its support to efforts to control arson through legislation as conducted by the National Legislative Conference on Arson.

AH&LA and its state member associations are not, however, standard-setting organizations and therefore do not establish, promulgate, or endorse any industry standards for member properties, all of which have different requirements and needs. AH&LA does, however, encourage its affiliated state associations and their 11,000 member properties to be involved in the national, state, and local legislative processes so that the lawmakers formulating new fire safety codes may take into account the myriad different problems the thousands of different large and small hotels face.

Important Points for Management

Hotels are subject to a multitude of federal, state, and local laws, codes, and regulations relating to fire safety. Fire safety requirements are found in building codes, licensing laws, so-called multiple dwelling laws, public assembly laws, labor laws, occupational safety and health laws, sanitation laws, and so-called general business laws of the state.

Hotelkeepers should consider having their own attorneys make a list of laws relating to fire safety for their properties. The local fire chief should also be consulted regarding steps that each property should take to comply with federal, state, and local fire laws in effect in the community.

The Occupational Safety & Health Administration (OSHA) has promulgated regulatory standards relating to (1) "fire brigades" established by employers, and (2) the inspection and maintenance of fire fighting equipment.

Under the federal Hotel and Motel Fire Safety Act, hotels must meet specific National Fire Protection Association (NFPA) fire safety standards in order to be listed in the *Federal Travel Directory* of lodging for federal government employees or to host federally funded meetings. The Act specifies the requirements for smoke detectors and automatic fire sprinklers that such properties must meet.

The American Automobile Association (AAA) publishes information on the availability of smoke detection and/or sprinkler systems in each hotel or motel property listed in AAA Tourbooks.

References

1. Occupational Safety and Health Standards—Fire Protection, 29 C.F.R. § 1910.155 *et seq.* See also Raymond C. Ellis, Jr., and David M. Stipanuk, *Security and Loss Prevention Management*, Second Edition (East Lansing, Mich.: Educational Institute of the American Hotel & Motel Association, 1999).

2. 29 C.F.R. § 1910.156.

3. 29 C.F.R. § 1910.155 (c) (iv) (D) (18).

4. 29 C.F.R. § 1910.155 (c) (iv) (D) (3).

5. 29 C.F.R. § 1910.35-1910.40.

6. 29 C.F.R. § 1910.35.

7. Clark County Nev., Code § 22.10.

8. La. Rev. Stat. Ann. § 40:1580.

9. N.Y. Lab. Law § 473-a.

10. N.Y. Exec. Law § 370 *et seq.*

11. New York, N.Y., Local Law 62 (1981). See also N.Y. Local Law 16 (1984).

12. Ga. Code § 120-3-3:05.

13. 15 U.S.C. § 2201

14. Raymond C. Ellis, Jr., and David M. Stipanuk, *Security and Loss Prevention Management*, Second Edition (East Lansing, Mich.: Educational Institute of the American Hotel & Motel Association, 1999), pp. 135–136.

15. In re: MGM Grand Hotel Fire Disaster, MDL 453.

16. *Vellone* v. *MGM Grand Hotel* consolidated in: MGM Grand Hotel Fire Disaster, MDL 453.

17. 117 Misc. 2d 554, 458 N.Y.S. 2d 461 (Sup. Ct. N.Y. Co., 1982).

18. 58 N.Y. 2d 253 (1983).

19. New York, N.Y., Admin. Code § 27-2118.

 ## Key Terms

class action—A suit in which one or more members of a numerous class, having a common interest, sue on behalf of themselves and all other members of that class.

 ## Review Questions

1. What does OSHA have to do with fire safety?

2. Who determines the laws governing fire safety?

3. What are the state and local laws in your state with respect to hotel fire safety?

4. If a guest is injured in a hotel fire, what rights does he/she have to claim damages, and against whom?

5. What requirements must hotels fulfill in order to comply with the federal Hotel and Motel Fire Safety Act?

6. What actions has the American Automobile Association (AAA) taken with regard to hotels and fire safety?

7. Have you had a hotel fire recently in your state? If so, what caused it?

 ## Internet Sites

For more information, visit the following Internet sites. Remember that Internet addresses can change without notice.

American Automobile Association (AAA)
http://www.aaa.com

American Hotel & Motel Association (AH&MA)
http://www.ahma.com

National Fire Protection Association (NFPA)
http://www.nfpa.org

Occupational Safety & Health Administration (OSHA)
http://www.osha.gov

Chapter 35 Outline

Competencies

1. Define a franchise tax. (p. 439–440)

2. Explain the unincorporated business income tax. (p. 440)

3. Distinguish between a sales and a use tax, and name the basic types of records most businesses must maintain to substantiate the amount of taxable sales. (pp. 441–442)

4. Explain what is meant by a "bed tax." (p. 442)

5. Explain the purpose and jurisdiction of the Bureau of Alcohol, Tobacco and Firearms, and explain federal regulations in regard to liquor taxes, mixing of cocktails, used liquor bottles, and keeping invoices. (pp. 443–444)

6. Describe state liquor taxes and list the criteria considered by some states in determining the amount of state liquor taxes to be charged. (p. 445)

35

Taxes

Hotel and motel operations, like most other businesses, are subject to a variety of state and local tax laws. These tax laws may include corporate franchise taxes, unincorporated business taxes, corporate, state, and local income taxes on gross or net receipts, state and local sales and use taxes, hotel room occupancy taxes (sometimes known as "bed taxes"), and various other miscellaneous state and/or local taxes.* Of course, these taxes vary in form and degree in different jurisdictions.

While some of these taxes are imposed directly upon hotels, others simply impose the duty upon hotels and other retailers to collect the tax from a guest or patron and then turn the tax over to the appropriate authority. For example, in most instances state and local sales taxes (and bed taxes) are added to guests' bills and collected by the hotel for the government. In such situations, hotels have been characterized as "unpaid tax collectors" and are usually subject to assessments, fines, or even criminal penalties for failing to strictly follow their statutory duty of collecting and paying over these consumer taxes.

In other circumstances, the hotel is the actual taxpayer, such as with state and local franchise and business income taxes. Hotels may also be considered consumers when making purchases subject to state and local sales and use taxes (unless the purchase is one characterized as a purchase for resale and there is a specific exemption under the state and/or local sales and use tax law for such purchases).

Hotel and motel owners and operators, and especially hotel comptrollers, must be familiar with all applicable state and local tax laws and how they apply to all facets of hotel operations.

Hotels and hotel chains must also consider the tax consequences of doing business in other states' taxing jurisdictions, thus perhaps subjecting their operations to the additional franchise or business income taxes of other states.

A brief discussion of various types of state and local taxes generally applicable to the operation of hotels and motels follows.

---

* For example, in New York City, there is a Commercial Rent and Occupancy Tax applicable to commercial rentals such as stores and restaurants within the hotel. In *J.C. Penney Co., Inc.* v. *Lewisohn,*[1] the New York Court of Appeals ruled that the New York City Commercial Rent and Occupancy Tax did not apply to a corporation's rental of a hotel suite used only for residential purposes, even though the rent was paid by the corporation and the premises used by its executives and other employees.

Note: There is also a separate New York City Hotel Room Occupancy Tax applicable to the rental of guestrooms, which is discussed later in this chapter.

Franchise Taxes on Corporations

Generally speaking, franchise taxes are imposed by states on corporations authorized to do business within the state. As the name implies, a franchise tax is a corporation's payment to a state government for the privilege of maintaining and operating a business within the state's boundaries. It is also compensation to the state government for services and benefits provided (such as maintenance and use of roads, police, fire departments, and other public services).

Most states base the franchise tax on either the annual earnings or the value of the taxpayer's business. In New York State, for example, Article 9-A of the Tax Law imposes a Franchise Tax on Business Corporations "[f]or the privilege of exercising its corporate franchise, or of doing business, or of employing capital, or of owning or leasing property in this state in a corporate or organized capacity, or of maintaining an office in this state, for all or any part of each of its fiscal or calendar years...."[2] This section further states that the franchise tax is generally based on the corporation's entire net income, unless otherwise provided. The tax for business corporations is computed using the method creating the highest amount, as follows:

1. 9% of the corporation's entire net income base, or the portion thereof allocated within the state as provided by law;

2. one and seventy-eight hundredths mills for each dollar of its total business and investment capital (or for foreign corporations doing business in New York State the portion thereof allocated within the state);

3. 5% of taxpayer's pre-1990 minimum taxable income base (as defined by statute); etc.[4]*

In California, the structure of the corporate franchise tax is much simpler. Generally, corporations doing business in California pay a corporation franchise tax of up to 8.84% of net income.[5] In addition to the state franchise taxes on corporations, there may be separate corporate income taxes.

Unincorporated Business Income Taxes

Some states and local governments also impose income taxes on unincorporated businesses. Income of hotels that are not organized in the form of a corporation may be subject to an unincorporated business income tax, depending on the tax laws of the particular jurisdiction. Generally, this tax is computed as a percentage of net income derived from business carried on within the state or local jurisdiction. For example, in New York City, unincorporated businesses are subject to a tax of 4% on the taxable net income derived from business activity within New York City.[6]

---

* This is an oversimplification of this New York statute; the statute should be reviewed by the hotel's accountant for the actual provisions.

Sales and Use Taxes

State and local "sales and use taxes" are usually "gross receipts" taxes in that the tax is computed as a percentage of the total retail sales receipt for each taxable sales transaction. The use tax (at the same rate as the sales tax) generally complements a state's sales tax by applying to items "used"* within the state but perhaps not subject to the state's sales tax because the sale was actually made outside the state. Every state except Delaware imposes a general sales and use tax. Many county and city jurisdictions impose additional sales and use taxes on the transactions taxable under the state laws.

In general, sales and use taxes are recoverable once for each sales transaction; therefore, in most states it is the retail sale that is taxable. In other words, when an item is purchased for resale in a retail sales transaction, the purchase is often not subject to state or local sales tax.

As stated above, the sales tax is generally imposed on gross receipts. The California Revenue and Taxation Code provides in part:

> § 6051. Levy on retailer's gross receipts; rate
>
> For the privilege of selling tangible personal property at retail a tax is hereby imposed upon all retailers at the rate of . . . 4 $^3/4$ percent of the gross receipts of any retailer from the sale of all tangible personal property sold at retail in this State. . . .

Moreover, California regularly increases the base amount by $1/4\%$ or $1/2\%$ on a temporary basis. Consequently, it is essential that retailers contact the California tax authories to determin current rates.

The law of California, and all other states imposing similar sales taxes, provides many specific exemptions from taxable sales as well as exclusions from what constitutes retail sales receipts subject to the tax. Local counsel can supply details of state and local sales and use tax laws.

As collectors of state and local sales taxes imposed on charges for guest occupancies and related hotel services, hotels have many recordkeeping and reporting duties. In New York State, the Department of Taxation and Finance has issued regulations and a bulletin summarizing the regulations for records that sales tax vendors, including hotels, must keep.[8] The bulletin outlines in detail the four basic types of mandatory records to substantiate the amount of taxable sales and sales taxes collected:

1. sales records—receipts, sales slips, invoices, guest checks, admission ticket stubs, cash register tapes, etc;

---

* For example, in California, the State-Wide Use Tax is "imposed on the storage, use, or other consumption in this State of tangible personal property purchased from any retailer...."[7]

2. purchase records—to substantiate any claimed exemption or to prove taxable status of each purchase and the amount of tax due;

3. miscellaneous records—relating to the sales tax returns such as tax worksheets, general journal ledgers, sales and purchase journals, schedules accounting for the difference between gross sales and services and taxable services and sales; and

4. informational records—that is, the name and address of each occupant of every hotel room, the length of occupancy, and all charges incurred by the occupant.

Many other states have similar requirements and guidelines. Hotels are cautioned to maintain adequate and detailed records to substantiate state and local sales tax payments by proving actual sales and taxes collected, which may be necessary during an audit or whenever a deficiency is alleged by the tax collector.

Hotel Room Occupancy Taxes

Many states (and some local jurisdictions) have enacted hotel room occupancy taxes, often referred to in the industry as "bed taxes." These taxes are often imposed in addition to the sales taxes. States with some form of bed tax or authorizing statute for local bed taxes include Delaware, District of Columbia, Idaho, Illinois, Kansas, Massachusetts, Michigan, Nebraska, New Hampshire, New Jersey, New Mexico, North Dakota, Pennsylvania, Rhode Island, Tennessee, Texas, Utah, Vermont, and West Virginia. Some cities also impose a tax on hotel room occupancies; these include New York City and Salt Lake City. Such bed taxes are often special taxes state and local sales taxes that may be applicable to the rental of transient hotel rooms and facilities. In some instances, the state legislative bodies create a fund from bed tax revenues to be used, in whole or in part, to promote tourism within the taxing jurisdiction. However, this is not always the case. Often revenues derived from the bed taxes go to the states' general funds. Today more and more states and cities are imposing bed taxes as a convenient source of revenues.

Bed taxes are usually either a percentage of the room rate or a lump sum tax collected from the guest according to a tax schedule based on the room charges (as in New York City). Generally, the tax applies only to room rentals on a transient basis. (Statutes will often exempt from the bed tax those occupancies of a specified period of consecutive days.)

Typical of the many bed taxes is The Delaware Lodging Tax.[9] This tax is imposed "at the rate of 8% of the rent upon every occupancy of a room or rooms in a hotel, motel or tourist home within this State."[10] The tax does not apply to "permanent" residents, defined as "any occupant who has occupied or has the right to occupancy of any room or rooms in a hotel, motel or tourist home for at least five consecutive months."[11] The hotel operator must collect the tax from the guest "at the time of the payment of the rent for the occupancy,"[12] and the total amount collected must be reported and paid over to the Delaware Department of Finance by the 15th of each month.[13] Failure to pay the tax as required may result in interest charges of 1% per month.[14]

Federal Liquor Taxes

Certain federal laws apply to the sale of alcoholic beverages. These laws are designed to collect taxes, so they are revenue-producing statutes rather than statutes regulating the manner in which the alcoholic beverages must be sold. There are two basic types of federal liquor tax:

1. A gallonage excise tax on the production of distilled spirits[15]

2. A so-called Special Tax levied upon the occupation of selling alcoholic beverages[16]

Enforcement of Federal Law

Since the federal laws relating to alcoholic beverages are primarily tax laws, responsibility for the enforcement of alcohol taxes and regulations is vested exclusively with the Bureau of Alcohol, Tobacco and Firearms, an independent bureau under the Department of Treasury. The Bureau's officers regularly visit places where liquor is sold. They are concerned with the special tax a hotel pays as a retail dealer in liquor, and also with the law and regulations relating to the proper stamps upon liquor bottles. Officers customarily take samples of liquor and test the proof and color to ascertain whether the contents of the bottles have been tampered with, which would indicate an evasion of the law or regulations relating to the tax stamps. The precautions to avoid such violations are described in more detail below under the particular regulations.

Special Tax on Retail Liquor Dealers

Under the federal law, a hotel that has a bar and sells liquor is classified as a retail dealer in liquors. As such it must pay a special federal tax of $250 per year* which entitles it to sell not only liquors, but also wine and beer.[17] If the hotel sells beer only, it must pay a special federal tax of $250 per year.[18]*

A hotel that sells alcoholic beverages in several areas need only pay the special tax once. Section 194.58 of the regulations states:

> The proprietor of a hotel who conducts the sale of liquors throughout the hotel premises shall pay but one special tax. For example, different areas in a hotel such as banquet rooms, meeting rooms, guest rooms, or other such areas, operated by the proprietor, collectively constitute a single place of business. Where any concessionaire conducts the sale of liquors at two or more areas in a hotel, such areas shall be regarded as a single place of business, and he shall pay but one special tax.[19]

The federal tax ordinarily covers the period commencing on July 1 of the current year and ending on June 30 of the following year. To make a return, the dealer completes Form 11, "Special Tax Return," obtained from the director of the Internal Revenue Service Center or from any district director. The special tax must be paid on

---

* These taxes may increase in future years and are in addition to any state taxes.

or before July 1 of each year operations continue, or, in the case of a new business, before beginning operations.

After paying the tax, the taxpayer will be issued a so-called Special Tax Stamp which must be kept available in the hotel for inspection by any officer of the Bureau of Alcohol, Tobacco and Firearms during business hours.[20]

Mixing of Cocktails

Regulations of the Bureau of Alcohol, Tobacco and Firearms prohibit the mixing of cocktails or the compounding of liquors in advance of sale, "except for the purpose of filling, for immediate consumption on the premises, orders received at the bar or in the expectation of the immediate receipt of orders."[21] Bureau regulations also provide that:

> A retail liquor dealer who mixes cocktails or compounds any alcoholic liquors in advance of sale...may not use liquor bottles in which distilled spirits have been previously packaged for the storage of the mixture pending sale."[22]

Used Liquor Bottles

The regulations of the Bureau of Alcohol, Tobacco and Firearms forbid the reuse of liquor bottles and any alteration of the contents of the bottles. Regulations also prohibit possession of used liquor bottles by anyone other than the person who opened them, with certain exceptions.[23] The hotel may collect the used liquor bottles on the premises:

1. in order to deliver the empty bottles to the bottler or importer upon request of the bottler or importer

2. for purposes of having the bottles destroyed

3. in case of unusual or distinctive bottles, for disposition as collector's items or other similar purposes.

Unusual or distinctive bottles may be sold to collectors, but the sale of used liquor bottles is otherwise prohibited.[24]

Records to Be Kept

The regulations provide that licensees must keep records in book form or keep all invoices or bills for distilled spirits, wine, or beer received showing the quantity thereof, from whom received, and the date of receipt. Any one sale of 20 "wine gallons" (75.7 liters) of spirits, wine, or beer to a single customer must also be recorded. This record must include the sale date, the name and address of the purchaser, the kind and quantity of liquors sold, and the serial numbers of all full cases of distilled spirits sold.

In Conclusion

The federal laws and regulations applying to hotels and motels as retail dealers of liquor, wine, and beer are extensive and technical. Each hotel's own legal counsel can answer specific questions and handle any problems in complying with the federal laws. State laws also apply to the sale of alcoholic beverages by hotels and motels, as discussed next in this chapter.

State Liquor Taxes

States permitting the sale of alcoholic beverages usually impose excise taxes and license fees on the sale of such alcoholic beverages and on the manufacture thereof. We herein briefly describe the general nature of state liquor tax laws as they apply to hotels and restaurants.* States usually impose license fees as well as excise taxes on the hotels and restaurants as retailers of alcoholic beverages.

The term "alcoholic beverages" usually includes three categories: distilled alcohol (liquor), beer, and wine. State alcoholic beverage laws usually distinguish between these categories with respect to tax rates and license fees. For example, in New York State, the annual license fee for hotels and restaurants (in cities with populations of 100,000 or more) for on-premises consumption of is $250; a similar retail license fee for the sale of and beer ranges from $250 (in cities of less than 50,000) to $1,700 in New York County, including the five boroughs of New York City. Therefore, hotels and restaurants even within the same state may be subject to different state taxes depending on such factors as:

1. The type of license—on-premises consumption, off-premises consumption, beer only, liquor (including wine and beer), or wine and beer only

2. The duration of the license, that is, some states provide licenses for part of the year with a proportionately reduced fee

3. The location of the licensed operation within the state

In addition to annual license fees, hotels and restaurants may be subject to licensing and tax requirements for any special events not covered under their existing licenses.

In light of the many factors that affect both the type of license a hotel or motel obtains and the amount of the license tax or fee, each hotel must consult local counsel or state liquor authorities to resolve particular problems or questions.

Important Points for Management

Some state and local taxes that hotels pay include:

- Corporation franchise tax—a state tax for the privilege of doing business as a corporation in that state.

- Corporation income tax—some states also impose an income tax as well as the franchise tax. All businesses are also subject to a federal income tax.

- Unincorporated business income tax—similar to the corporation franchise tax, except that it is imposed on those businesses not organized as corporations.

---

* See Chapter 18 for other state laws relating to alcoholic beverages.

- Sales and use taxes—usually a state tax, although some cities have a similar tax. The sales tax is based on retail sales made in the state. The use tax is based on the retail value of goods used in the state but not sold in the state. The sales and use taxes are the same amount. The hotel is liable for payment of the tax, but can pass it on to its customers.

- Hotel room occupancy tax—often a local tax. Sometimes it is called a bed tax. This tax is in addition to the sales tax. It can be a flat rate or may be based on the room rate paid by transient guests only. Permanent residents do not usually pay it.

Note that not all states and cities have all of the taxes listed.

- Hotels and motels which sell alcohol (beer, wine, or liquor) are subject to a special federal tax as retail liquor dealers. They are also subject to the regulations of the Bureau of Alcohol, Tobacco and Firearms, which collects the tax. Bureau regulations govern such activities as mixing of cocktails, reusing liquor bottles, and keeping records. Most states also impose excise taxes and licensing fees on alcohol retailers, including hotels and motels which serve alcohol.

 ## References

1. 33 N.Y. 2d 528, 347 N.Y.S. 2d 433, 301 N.E. 2d 421 (1973), *aff'g,* 40 A.D. 2d 67, 337 N.Y.S. 2d 472 (1st Dept. 1972).

2. N. Y. Tax Law § 209 (1).

3. N. Y. Tax Law § 210(1)(b).

4. N. Y. Tax Law § 210(1)(a).

5. Cal. Rev. & Tax Code § 23151.

6. N.Y.C. Admin. Code § 11-503 *et seq.*

7. Cal. Rev. & Tax Code § 6201.

8. Technical Services Bureau Bulletin, TSB-M-81(9)S, July 15, 1981.

9. Del. Code Ann., Tit. 30, § 6101, *et seq.*

10. *Id.* § 6102.

11. *Id.* § 6101 (7).

12. *Id.* § 6103.

13. *Id.* § 6104.

14. Del. Code Ann., Tit. 30, § 6104.

15. I. R. C. § 5001.

16. I. R. C. §§ 5091-5142.

17. I. R. C. § 5121(a).

18. I. R. C. § 5121(b).

19. 27 C.F.R. § 194.58.

20. 27 C.F.R. § 194.121, 194.131.

21. 27 C.F.R. § 194.293.
22. 27 C.F.R. § 194.264.
23. 27 C.F.R. § 194.263.
24. 27 C.F.R. § 194.263.

Review Questions

1. What is a bed tax?

2. Why should cities use Occupancy Tax Revenues to build convention facilities?

3. Since the hotel is liable for sales taxes, why does it put these taxes on the guest's bill?

4. What is a corporate franchise tax?

5. What kind of state and local taxes might a hotel have to pay? Which of these may be collected from the guests?

6. What records must a hotel keep because of regulations of the Bureau of Alcohol, Tobacco and Firearms?

7. If an officer of the Bureau visits a hotel, what will he/she be looking for?

Internet Sites

For more information, visit the following Internet sites. Remember that Internet addresses can change without notice.

Federal Tax Law
http://www.taxsites.com/federal.html

State Liquor Excise Tax Rates
http://www.taxadmin.org/fta/rate/liquor.html

Chapter 36 Outline

Competencies

1. Distinguish between express and implied warranties, and summarize Uniform Commercial Code (UCC) express warranty requirements. (pp. 449–451)

2. List the factors considered in an implied warranty of merchantability. (pp. 451–452)

3. Explain implied warranty of fitness for a particular purpose. (pp. 452–454)

4. Describe how warranties can be disclaimed. (pp. 454–456)

5. Summarize UCC rules on warranties of title (pp. 456–457)

6. Describe the function of the Consumer Product Safety Act, and give examples of Consumer Product Safety Commission regulations. (pp. 457–458)

7. Summarize basic standards of responsibility for manufacturers and non-manufacturer product sellers under the proposed Uniform Product Liability Act. (pp. 458–459)

8. Describe state laws on product liability. (pp. 459–461)

36

Warranties and Product Liability

Warranties

This chapter reviews the law of "warranties" and some of the related rights of purchasers and liabilities of sellers of "goods." The discussion is from the viewpoint of a hotel as the purchaser of goods where the seller makes a warranty of some kind.*

As discussed earlier, there are two basic kinds of warranties: express warranties and implied warranties.

Express warranties are oral or written representations made by the seller to the buyer relating to the goods for sale.

Implied warranties are those imposed by law on the sale unless the seller negates or limits them to the extent permitted by the law, that is, by the Uniform Commercial Code (UCC).** Generally speaking, if the seller is a merchant with respect to the kind of goods being sold, a warranty that the goods shall be merchantable is implied in a contract for sale. No particular language or action is necessary to evidence those implied warranties that arise in a sale pursuant to law.

The UCC sets forth in Article 2 the law of warranties as applied to transactions for the sale of "goods."***

Express Warranties

The UCC describes the requirements of express warranties as follows:

§ 2-313. Express Warranties by Affirmation, Promise, Description, Sample

---

   * For a discussion of warranties when the hotel is the seller, that is, the seller of prepared food, see Chapter 16.

  ** The UCC as adopted and modified in each state would govern (except in Louisiana which has not adopted this Code).

 *** The code defines goods as:

> all things (including specially manufactured goods) which are movable at the time of identification to the contract for sale other than the money in which the price is to be paid, investment securities (Article 8) and things in action. "Goods" also includes the unborn young of animals and growing crops and other identified things attached to realty as described in the section on goods to be severed from realty (Section 2-107).

(1)   Express warranties by the seller are created as follows:

(a)   Any affirmation of fact or promise made by the seller to the buyer which relates to the goods and becomes part of the basis of the bargain creates an express warranty that the goods shall conform to the affirmation or promise.

(b)   Any description of the goods which is made part of the basis of the bargain creates an express warranty that the goods shall conform to the description.

(c)   Any sample or model which is made part of the basis of the bargain creates an express warranty that the whole of the goods shall conform to the sample or model.

(2)   It is not necessary to the creation of an express warranty that the seller use formal words such as "warrant" or "guarantee" or that he have a specific intention to make a warranty, but an affirmation merely of the value of the goods or a statement purporting to be merely the seller's opinion or commendation of the goods does not create a warranty.

The whole purpose of the law of warranties is to determine what the seller has in essence agreed to sell. As Official Comment No. 3 to § 2-313 of the UCC states:

No specific intention to make a warranty is necessary if any of these factors is made part of the basis of the bargain. In actual practice affirmations of fact made by the seller about the goods during a bargain are regarded as part of the description of those goods; hence no particular reliance on such statements need be shown in order to weave them into the fabric of the agreement. Rather, any fact which is to take such affirmations, once made, out of the agreement requires clear affirmative proof. The issue normally is one of fact.

As Official Comment No. 4 to § 2-313 of the UCC states:

A clause generally disclaiming "all warranties, express or implied" cannot reduce the seller's obligation with respect to such description and therefore cannot be given literal effect under Section 2-316 [*supra*].

This is not intended to mean that the parties, if they consciously desire, cannot make their own bargain as they wish. But in determining what they have agreed upon good faith is a factor and consideration should be given to the fact that the probability is small that a real price is intended to be exchanged for a pseudo-obligation.

The UCC also makes it clear in Official Comment No. 6 to § 2-313:

6.   The basic situation as to statements affecting the true essence of the bargain is no different when a sample or model is involved in the transaction. This Section includes both a "sample" actually drawn from the bulk of goods which is the subject matter of the sale, and a "model" which is offered for inspection when the subject matter is not at hand and which has not been drawn from the bulk of the goods.

The question to be asked is whether or not the language or samples or models can fairly be regarded as part of the contract.

An express warranty might also be construed from the seller's advertising of the product. For example, see *Drayton* v. *Jiffee Chemical Corp.*,[1] in which the advertisement showed a drain cleaner to be "safe" for contact with the skin.

Implied Warranties

As mentioned earlier, implied warranties are those that are automatically imposed by law on the sale, unless the seller *expressly* negates or limits them to the extent permitted under the UCC, as adopted and perhaps modified by each state (except Louisiana). There are two basic kinds of implied warranties under the UCC: that the goods are merchantable and that they are fit for a particular purpose.

Implied Warranty of Merchantability. Section 2-314 of the UCC states:

§ 2-314. Implied Warranty: Merchantability; Usage of Trade.

(1) Unless excluded or modified (Section 2-316), [the disclaimer provision discussed below] a warranty that the goods shall be merchantable is implied in a contract for their sale if the seller is a merchant with respect to goods of that kind. Under this section the serving for value of food or drink to be consumed either on the premises or elsewhere is a sale.

(2) Goods to be merchantable must be at least such as

   (a) pass without objection in the trade under the contract description; and

   (b) in the case of fungible goods, are of fair average quality within the description; and

   (c) are fit for the ordinary purposes for which such goods are used; and

   (d) run, within the variations permitted by the agreement, of even kind, quality and quantity within each unit and among all units involved; and

   (e) are adequately contained, packaged, and labeled as the agreement may require; and

   (f) conform to the promises or affirmations of fact made on the container or label if any.

(3) Unless excluded or modified (Section 2-316) [below] other implied warranties may arise from course of dealing or usage of trade.

Official Comments No. 3, 4, 5, and 6 to § 2-314 state:

3. A specific designation of goods by the buyer does not exclude the seller's obligation that they be fit for the general purposes appropriate to such goods. A contract for the sale of second-hand goods, however, involves only such obligation as is appropriate to such goods for that is their contract description. A person making an isolated sale of goods is not a "merchant" within the meaning of the full scope of this section and, thus, no warranty of

merchantability would apply. His knowledge of any defects not apparent on inspection would, however, without need for express agreement and in keeping with the underlying reason of the present section and the provisions on good faith, impose an obligation that known material but hidden defects be fully disclosed.

4. Although a seller may not be a "merchant" as to the goods in question, if he states generally that they are "guaranteed" the provisions of this section may furnish a guide to the content of the resulting express warranty. This has particular significance in the case of second-hand sales, and has further significance in limiting the effect of fine-print disclaimer clauses where their effect would be inconsistent with large-print assertions of "guarantee".

5. The second sentence of subsection (1) covers the warranty with respect to food and drink. Serving food or drink for value is a sale, whether to be consumed on the premises or elsewhere. Cases to the contrary are rejected. The principal warranty is that stated in subsections (1) and (2)(c) of this section.

6. Subsection (2) does not purport to exhaust the meaning of "merchantable" nor to negate any of its attributes not specifically mentioned in the text of the statute, but arising by usage of trade or through case law. The language used is "must be at least such as…," and the intention is to leave open other possible attributes of merchantability.

Official Comment No. 13 to § 2-314 states:

> In an action based on breach of warranty, it is of course necessary to show not only the existence of the warranty but the fact that the warranty was broken and that the breach of the warranty was the proximate cause of the loss sustained. In such an action an affirmative showing by the seller that the loss resulted from some action or event following his own delivery of the goods can operate as a defense. Equally, evidence indicating that the seller exercised care in the manufacture, processing or selection of the goods is relevant to the issue of whether the warranty was in fact broken. Action by the buyer following an examination of the goods which ought to have indicated the defect complained of can be shown as matter bearing on whether the breach itself was the cause of the injury.

Implied Warranty of Fitness for a Particular Purpose. Another type of implied warranty that may benefit hotels as purchasers of goods from sellers knowledgeable about the particular uses to which the goods will be put is the implied warranty of fitness for a particular purpose. Section 2-315 states the rule with respect to this implied warranty:

§ 2-315. Implied Warranty: Fitness for Particular Purpose.

Where the seller at the time of contracting has reason to know any particular purpose for which the goods are required and that the buyer is relying on the seller's skill or judgment to select or furnish suitable goods, there is unless excluded or modified under the next section an implied warranty that the goods shall be fit for such purpose.

Section 2-315 with regard to fitness for a particular purpose arises when the goods are intended for a "particular purpose" other than the one for which they are ordinarily used, and the seller understands the specific use a buyer intends for the goods. For example, shoes are generally used for walking on ordinary ground but the seller may know that a particular pair was selected for workers to use on the hotel golf course.

For the implied warranty to apply, the seller

1. must have reason to know of the use to which the buyer will put the purchased goods, and

2. must be aware of the buyer's reliance on the seller's skill or judgment in recommending the purchase of such goods.

A contract may include a warranty of merchantability and one of fitness for particular purposes. Section 2-315 would, of course, require reliance by the buyer upon the seller in any action for breach of the implied warranty of fitness for a particular purpose.

One case that discusses the law of implied warranties is *El Fredo Pizza, Inc.* v. *Roto-Flex Oven Co.*[2] Here the operators of a pizza restaurant sued the manufacturer and seller of the pizza oven on grounds of breach of both the implied warranties of merchantability and fitness for a particular purpose. The plaintiff charged that the oven did not bake pizzas properly because of uneven heating. The plaintiff sued for the costs of the defective oven and its installation as well as lost profits and increased labor costs caused by the defect. The jury at trial found for the plaintiff and awarded damages of $17,500, which included an award for lost profits.

With respect to the breach of implied warranties the court explained,

> Two implied warranties provided for in the Uniform Commercial Code are relevant to this case. Under Section 2-314, U.C.C., a warranty that the goods shall be merchantable is implied in a contract for their sale if the seller is a merchant with respect to goods of that kind. In order for goods to be merchantable under Section 2-314, they must be at least such as are fit for the ordinary purposes for which such goods are used. Under this implied warranty, no reliance upon the seller need be shown. Under Section 2-315, U.C.C., a warranty of fitness for a particular purpose is implied where the seller at the time of contracting has reason to know any particular purpose for which the goods are required and that the buyer in relying on the seller's skill or judgment to select or furnish suitable goods. [citations omitted]

* * *

> Comment 1 to Section 2-315, U.C.C., provides that whether or not the warranty of fitness for a particular purpose arises in any individual case "is basically a question of fact to be determined by the circumstances of the contracting. Under this section the buyer need not bring home to the seller actual knowledge of the particular purpose for which the goods are intended or of his reliance on the seller's skill and judgment, if the circumstances are such that the seller has reason to realize the purpose intended or that the reliance exists. The buyer, of course, must actually be relying on the seller".... The testimony indicated that Roto-Flex ovens

are custom built for Roto-Flex customers, and Roto-Flex was aware of the particular purpose for which the oven was required in this case. Under the circumstances of this case, the evidence was clearly sufficient to raise the factual question of reliance under Section 2-315, U.C.C., and it was proper to submit that question to the jury.

The Supreme Court of Nevada affirmed the lower court's conclusion except that it lowered the jury award to a total of $13,500, finding that the jury award for lost profits was inflated by $4,000.

Seller's Disclaimers of Express and Implied Warranties

In many contracts the seller attempts to disclaim the existence of any express or implied warranties with respect to the goods sold. Section 2-316 of the UCC deals with disclaimers of both kinds of warranties.

§ 2-316. Exclusion or Modification of Warranties.*

(1) Words or conduct relevant to the creation of an express warranty and words or conduct tending to negate or limit warranty shall be construed wherever reasonable as consistent with each other, but subject to the provisions of this Article on parol or extrinsic evidence (Section 2-202)** negation or limitation is inoperative to the extent that such construction is unreasonable.

(2) Subject to subsection (3), to exclude or modify the implied warranty of merchantability or any part of it the language must mention merchantability and in case of a writing must be conspicuous, and to exclude or modify any implied warranty of fitness the exclusion must be by a writing and conspicuous. Language to exclude all implied warranties of fitness is sufficient if it states, for example, that "There are no warranties which extend beyond the description on the face hereof."

(3) Notwithstanding subsection (2)

(a) unless the circumstances indicate otherwise, all implied warranties are excluded by expressions like "as is," "with all faults" or other language

---

* Many states have modified the language of this section of the official text upon enactment into state law. State laws enacting the code should therefore be consulted.

** U.C.C. § 2-202. Final Written Expression: Parol or Extrinsic Evidence

> Terms with respect to which the confirmatory memoranda of the parties agree or which are otherwise set forth in a writing intended by the parties as a final expression of their agreement with respect to such terms as are included therein may not be contradicted by evidence of any prior agreement or of a contemporaneous oral agreement but may be explained or supplemented
>
> (a) by course of dealing or usage of trade (Section 1-205) or by course of performance (Section 2-208); and
>
> (b) by evidence of consistent additional terms unless the court finds the writing to have been intended also as a complete and exclusive statement of the terms of the agreement.

which in common understanding calls the buyer's attention to the exclusion of warranties and makes plain that there is no implied warranty; and

(b) when the buyer before entering into the contract has examined the goods or the sample or model as fully as he desired or has refused to examine the goods there is no implied warranty with regard to defects which an examination ought in the circumstances to have revealed to him; and

(c) an implied warranty can also be excluded or modified by course of dealing or course of performance or usage of trade.

(4) Remedies for breach of warranty can be limited in accordance with the provisions of this Article on liquidation or limitation of damages and on contractual modification of remedy (Sections 2-718 and 2-719).

The general purpose of § 2-316 is explained by Official Comment No. 1 as follows:

1. This section is designed principally to deal with those frequent clauses in sales contracts which seek to exclude "all warranties, express or implied." It seeks to protect a buyer from unexpected and unbargained language of disclaimer by denying effect to such language when inconsistent with language of express warranty and permitting the exclusion of implied warranties only by conspicuous language or other circumstances which protect the buyer from surprise.

2. The seller is protected under this Article against false allegations of oral warranties by its provisions on parol and extrinsic evidence and against unauthorized representations by the customary "lack of authority" clauses.

As § 2-316(2) makes clear, there must be rather specific language to disclaim the *implied* warranties of fitness for a particular purpose and of merchantability. Subsection 3 points out, however, that certain language, such as expressions that the goods are purchased "as is" or "with all faults," will negate any implied warranties. However, one court has held that while an "as is" clause may negate implied warranties, express warranties made by the seller continue to provide a remedy if the sold item or goods did not live up to the express warranty.[3]

As § 2-316 states:

Unlike the implied warranty of merchantability, implied warranties of fitness for a particular purpose may be excluded by general language, but only if it is in writing and conspicuous.

In the Official Comments No. 8 to § 2-316, Paragraph B of Subsection 3 regarding examination reads:

Application of the doctrine of "caveat emptor" in all cases where the buyer examines the goods regardless of statements made by the seller is, however, rejected by this Article. Thus, if the offer of examination is accompanied by words as to their merchantability or specific attributes and the buyer indicates clearly that he is relying on those words rather than on his examination, they give rise to an "express" warranty. In such cases the question is one of fact as to whether a warranty of merchantability has been expressly incorporated in the agreement. Disclaimer of such an express warranty is governed by subsection (1) of the present section.

The particular buyer's skill and the normal method of examining goods in the circumstances determine what defects are excluded by the examination. A failure to notice defects which are obvious cannot excuse the buyer. However, an examination under circumstances which do not permit chemical or other testing of the goods would not exclude defects which could be ascertained only by such testing. Nor can latent defects be excluded by a simple examination. A professional buyer examining a product in his field will be held to have assumed the risk as to all defects which a professional in the field ought to observe, while a nonprofessional buyer will be held to have assumed the risk only for such defects as a layman might be expected to observe.

Sometimes the language of an express warranty might appear to contradict an implied warranty. Section 2-317 of the UCC attempts to resolve this problem:

§ 2-317. Cumulation and Conflict of Warranties Express or Implied

Warranties whether express or implied shall be construed as consistent with each other and as cumulative, but if such construction is unreasonable the intention of the parties shall determine which warranty is dominant. In ascertaining that intention the following rules apply:

(a) Exact or technical specifications displace an inconsistent sample or model or general language of description.

(b) A sample from an existing bulk displaces inconsistent general language of description.

(c) Express warranties displace inconsistent implied warranties other than an implied warranty of fitness for a particular purpose.

This section states that an express warranty does not negate an implied warranty unless they are inconsistent with each other. In addition, to the extent that the seller has led the buyer to believe that all the warranties can be performed, he/she is estopped from setting up any inconsistency as a defense.
Section 2-318 then states:

§ 2-318. Third Party Beneficiaries of Warranties Express or Implied

A seller's warranty whether express or implied extends to any natural person if it is reasonable to expect that such person may use, consume or be affected by the goods and who is injured in person by breach of the warranty. A seller may not exclude or limit the operation of this section.

Warranties of Title

The UCC also provides rules in § 2-312 on warranties of title:

(1) Subject to subsection (2) there is in a contract for sale a warranty by the seller that

    (a) the title conveyed shall be good, and its transfer rightful; and

    (b) the goods shall be delivered free from any security interest or other lien or encumbrance of which the buyer at the time of contracting has no knowledge.

(2) A warranty under subsection (1) will be excluded or modified only by specific language or by circumstances which give the buyer reason to know that the person selling does not claim title in himself or that he is purporting to sell only such right or title as he or a third person may have.

(3) Unless otherwise agreed a seller who is a merchant regularly dealing in goods of the kind sold warrants that the goods shall be delivered free of the rightful claim of any third person by way of infringement or the like but a buyer who furnishes specifications to the seller must hold the seller harmless against any such claim which arises out of compliance with the specifications.

Questions about whether or not a hotel as buyer has a warranty should be referred to a lawyer. Often there are remedies under the law of warranties if the buyer is willing to pursue his/her rights and if the pursuit is worth the projected legal expense.

Federal Laws on Product Liability

Consumer Product Safety Act

The federal Consumer Product Safety Act, 15 U.S.C. 2051-2083, and the regulations of the Consumer Product Safety Commission prohibit the selling, offering for sale, distributing, or importing of any "consumer product" which does not conform to any applicable consumer product safety standard or which has been banned as hazardous by the Consumer Product Safety Commission.[4] The Consumer Product Safety Commission has promulgated regulations under the Act including product safety standards for such products as matchbooks, power lawn mowers, and swimming pool slides.[5] The Commission rules also ban the manufacturing and sale of certain products including unstable refuse bins, extremely flammable contact adhesives, and lead-containing paint. In addition, the rules establish flammability standards for clothing textiles, vinyl plastic film, carpets and rugs, mattresses and mattress pads, and children's sleepwear. The regulations are both specific and technical and provide standards and reporting requirements for manufacturers producing various consumer products, only some of which are mentioned above.

    The Act, in addition to specifying civil and criminal penalties for violations, provides that any person who sustains an injury "by reason of any knowing (including willful) violation of a consumer product safety rule, or any other rule or order issued by the Commission may sue [in federal court] any person who knowingly (including willfully) violated any such rule or order...."[6] The alleged damages in any such action must exceed $10,000. The court, in its discretion, may award to plaintiff the costs of the lawsuit, including reasonable attorney and witness fees. In *Young* v. *Robert-Shaw Controls Company*,[7] a federal district court allowed a private lawsuit to be maintained against the manufacturer of a defective water heater control device which caused an explosion, killing the plaintiff's wife. The defendant-manufacturer's violation of the Act consisted of the manufacturer failing to inform the Consumer Product Safety Commission of other prior incidents involving severe personal injury or death associated with the control devices, as required by the Act and regulations.

Proposed Federal Laws on Product Liability

On July 20, 1978, the administration directed the U.S. Department of Commerce to develop a "model uniform product liability law" for adoption by the states. This legislation preempts, rather than supplements, existing product liability laws based on strict liability, negligence, and warranty *with regard to those claims based on personal injury and damage to property*. However, it leaves actions for other economic losses based on warranties to the UCC (§ 103 of the Model Act) discussed in the first part of this chapter.

While some authorities have criticized the proposed Uniform Product Liability Act as being unnecessary,[8] for purposes of this chapter it is a good introduction to product liability law.

Basic Standards of Responsibility for Manufacturers Under the Act

At the very heart of the proposed Act is § 104, which indicates that a product may be proven to be defective in four basic ways.

1. It was unreasonably unsafe in construction.
2. It was unreasonably unsafe in design.
3. It was unreasonably unsafe because adequate warnings or instructions were not provided.
4. It was unreasonably unsafe because it did not conform to a product seller's express warranty.

With respect to products that were defective in construction or that failed to conform to an express warranty, the Act would apply strict liability. On the other hand, under the Act strict liability cannot be justified for either design defects or defects that are predicated on a failure to warn or instruct.

Design Defects. With products that are allegedly defective in design, the proposed Act adopts a fault standard. The claimant must prove that at the time of manufacture, the likelihood that the product would cause claimant's harm or similar harms and the seriousness of those harms outweighed both the manufacturer's burden of producing a product with an alternative design to prevent those harms, and the adverse effect of that alternative design on the product's usefulness.

Duty to Warn. As to the product seller's failure to provide an adequate warning or instruction with the product, the Act would also adopt a fault standard. The claimant must prove that at the time of manufacture, the likelihood that the product would cause the claimant's harm or similar harms and the seriousness of those harms rendered the manufacturer's instructions or warnings inadequate, and that the manufacturer should and could have provided the instructions or warnings that claimant alleges would have been adequate.

The Act also indicates that the manufacturer must act as a "reasonably prudent product seller" with respect to warning product users about dangers discovered after the product is sold. This is a particularly tough problem in product liability law today, and the Act provides a rule of law to address this problem.

Basic Standards of Responsibility for Non-Manufacturer Product Sellers

The proposed Act also provides liability standards for parties in the distribution chain other than manufacturers; these include, for example, wholesalers, retailers, and distributors. The Act would require product sellers other than manufacturers to exercise reasonable care in handling products. The seller would not be liable for construction and design defects that an ordinary prudent product seller would not discover. The product seller would be responsible for conveying the manufacturer's warnings or instructions intended for the product user. It would also be liable for breach of its own express warranties.

Comparative Responsibility. Perhaps the most important application of these standards of responsibility is with respect to misuse or modification of products. When a product seller proves that product misuse contributed to a claimant's harm, damages could be reduced or apportioned to the extent that the misuse caused the harm. "Misuse" occurs when a product is used in a manner not expected of a reasonably prudent person who is likely to use the product in the same or similar circumstances.

As of this writing, this Act was still only a proposal, and had not been adopted into law.

Other Proposed Federal Actions. Other efforts have been made on the federal level to enact a uniform products liability law applicable to each state. A bill has been introduced in the U.S. Senate to regulate product liability law for products in interstate commerce. The American Bar Association, through a Special Committee, has concluded that such federal legislation is unnecessary and urged defeat of the bill.

State Laws on Product Liability

As the law now stands, the hotel purchaser, in addition to any remedies available under the UCC as enacted in his/her own state, may also have other bases for claims under common law and state product liability laws. The laws of product liability evolved from the common laws on negligence (torts) and warranties (contracts). Today, some states have enacted statutes governing product liability actions and providing for a statutory remedy for strict liability in the case of defective products.

Certain other states have enacted by statute the provisions of the Restatement of Torts 2d relating to the seller's liability for physical harm to the user or consumer of the product.

For example, the South Carolina statute, Chapter 73, Title 15, of the Code of Laws of South Carolina, provides:

Liability of Seller for Defective Product.

(1) One who sells any product in a defective condition unreasonably dangerous to the user or consumer or to his property is subject to liability for physical harm caused to the ultimate user or consumer, or to his property, if

(a) The seller is engaged in the business of selling such a product, and

(b) It is expected to and does reach the user or consumer without substantial change in the condition in which it is sold.

(2) The rule stated in subsection (1) shall apply although

(a) The seller has exercised all possible care in the preparation and sale of his product, and

(b) The user or consumer has not brought the product from or entered into any contractual relation with the seller.

Situation in Which Recovery Shall Be Barred.

If the user or consumer discovers the defect and is aware of the danger, and nevertheless proceeds unreasonably to make use of the product and is injured by it, he is barred from recovery.

In *Kennedy* v. *Custom Ice Equipment Company,*[9] the Supreme Court of South Carolina reviewed some principles of law involved in a product liability suit. In this case the plaintiff, a 15-year-old boy employed by a seller of ice products, was awarded $208,000 for actual damages incurred when he lost his arm in an ice conveyor designed and installed by the defendant-company. The plaintiff sued on both negligence and strict product liability theories. The defendant on appeal argued that the ice manufacturer's installation of a wooden catwalk below the screw conveyor after installation relieved the defendant from liability. In essence, the defendant claimed that "the screw conveyor was not defective when installed because of the insulation provided by height," later reduced by the employer's installation of the catwalk. The court stated,

The test of whether a product is defective when sold is whether the product is unreasonably dangerous to the consumer or user given the conditions and circumstances that will foreseeably attend the use of the product. Under this test, the jury could have determined that the construction of the catwalk by Georgetown [the employer] was a foreseeable circumstance that required the incorporation of protective shields in the design of the conveyor.

Thus, the Supreme Court of South Carolina affirmed the lower court's rulings and the jury award for the injured plaintiff.

In another case in a federal appellate court applying the law of Pennsylvania, a tractor manufacturer was held strictly liable for the death of a purchaser's employee even though it was the purchaser who requested the manufacturer to remove the safety device. In *Hammond* v. *International Harvester Company*[10] the U.S. Court of Appeals for the Third Circuit found that if the safety device had been on the farm machinery, the fatal accident probably would not have occurred. The court said that under the applicable law of Pennsylvania,

> [t]he supplier must at least provide a product which is designed to make it safe for the intended use. Under this standard,…the jury may find a defect where the product left the supplier's control lacking any element necessary to make it safe for its intended use or possessing any feature that renders it unsafe for the intended use.[11]

The court concluded that the tractor sold without the standard safety device was defective under the above standards, and the fact that the purchaser requested the removal of the device did not cure such defect.

In those states that have not adopted product liability statutes, product liability cases are generally governed by the common laws on negligence (torts) and contracts (warranties).

Important Points for Management

- A warranty is a promise by the seller of goods concerning the quality, quantity, or ownership of such goods, etc.

- Warranties may be express or implied. Express warranties can be created by promise, description, sample, or model. Implied warranties are imposed on the sales transaction by operation of law (i.e., Uniform Commercial Code).

- Both express and implied warranties can exist on the same goods.

- Both implied warranties of merchantability and of fitness can exist on the same goods.

- Warranties can be disclaimed by the seller. The implied warranty of merchantability can only be disclaimed by specific language of disclaimer. Other warranties can be disclaimed by general language if it is in writing and conspicuous.

- The Consumer Product Safety Act is a federal law that prohibits selling any consumer product that doesn't conform to a consumer safety standard or has been banned as hazardous.

References

1. 591 F. 2d 352 (6th Cir. 1978).
2. 199 Neb. 697, 261 N.W. 2d 358 (Sup. Ct. Neb. 1978).
3. *Limited Flying Club, Inc.,* v. *Wood,* 632 F. 2d 51 (8th Cir. 1980).

4. 15 U.S.C. § 2068(a)(1) and (2).

5. 16 C.F.R. § 1000 *et seq.*

6. 15 U.S.C. § 2072.

7. 51 U.S.L.W. 2616 (N.D.N.Y. March 7, 1983).

8. Twerski & Weinstein, "A Critique of the Uniform Product Liability Law—a Rush to Judgment," 28 Drake L.R. 221 (1978-1979).

9. 271 S.C. 171, 246 S.E. 2d 176 (Sup. Ct. S.C. 1978).

10. 691 F. 2d 646 (3rd Cir. 1982).

11. 691 F. 2d at 650, *quoting, Azzarello* v. *Black Brothers Co.,* 480 Pa. 547, 559, 391 A. 2d 1020, 1027 (1978).

Review Questions

1. What examples of product warranties can you provide? Examples may include warranties for a TV set, tape deck, curling iron, or new car. Bring examples of warranty labels to class.

2. Why should you check your contracts of purchase to determine the warranties?

3. Why can't you sell consumer products that have been banned by the federal government as being hazardous?

4. How do express and implied warranties differ? What does "implied" mean when we say implied warranty?

5. When do you have an express warranty under the Uniform Commercial Code?

Internet Sites

For more information, visit the following Internet sites. Remember that Internet addresses can change without notice.

Uniform Commercial Code
http://www.law.cornell.edu/ucc/ucc.table.html

U.S. Consumer Product Safety Commission
http://www.cpsc.gov

U.S. Department of Commerce
http://www.doc.gov

Chapter 37 Outline

Competencies

1. State the purposes of the federal antitrust laws. (p. 465)

2. Identify the major statutes comprising the federal antitrust laws. (pp. 465–466)

3. Cite Section 1 of the Sherman Act, define what is meant by a *per se* violation, and describe the "rule of reason" standard used to determine violations of the Sherman Act. (pp. 466–468)

4. Describe how the Clayton Act applies to the hotel and motel industry. Explain how the Federal Trade Commission serves as a consumer advocate in matters related to antitrust. (pp. 468–469)

5. Give some examples of violations of antitrust laws. (pp. 469–470)

6. Describe penalties for violations of antitrust laws. (p. 470–471)

7. Identify some precautions hotel and motel operators and associations should take to avoid antitrust problems. (pp. 471–474)

37

Antitrust Laws and Hotels

N<small>O HOTEL OR MOTEL OPERATOR</small> can afford to be unaware of the federal and state antitrust laws. Their reach is too broad, their enforcement is too strict, and their penalties are too severe to ignore. Moreover, a hotel or motel operator can violate the antitrust laws and be subject to their penalties *without meaning to do so.*

This chapter provides an overview of the basic principles of antitrust laws, and also some practical examples of the application of those laws in the hotel industry. With this knowledge, a hotel operator can be alert to possible violations of antitrust laws and know when to seek legal advice.

It is important that hotel or motel operators provide basic information on antitrust laws to all their managers and employees in decision-making or sales positions. Hotel or motel operators can be held liable for antitrust violations their employees commit even though they neither encourage nor condone their employees' conduct.[1]

The Purposes of Antitrust Laws

The general aim of the antitrust laws is simple: the regulation of business conduct to preserve competition and to prevent economic coercion. Antitrust laws are primarily concerned with limiting collusive conduct between competitors ("horizontal" agreements), and with regulating certain forms of activity between businesses that do not compete but are in a vertical relationship, such as a hotel operator and its customers or suppliers.

The antitrust laws are based upon the simple assumption that vigorous but fair competition results in the most efficient allocation of economic resources and the best terms of sale for consumers.

Major Antitrust Statutes

Three major statutes comprise the bulk of federal antitrust laws: the Sherman Act of 1890,[2] the Clayton Act of 1914 and its amendments,[3] and the Federal Trade Commission Act of 1914.[4] The statutory framework of the antitrust laws is broad; consequently, it is important to analyze the cases interpreting these statutes in

The original co-authors of this chapter were Jack P. Jefferies, Stephen M. Hudspeth, Norman H. Seidler, and Gordon B. Spivack, members of the New York Bar. Mr. Jefferies and Mr. Banks Brown updated this material.

order to understand the application of the statutes in practice.* In addition, many states have enacted their own antitrust laws governing activities conducted exclusively within the state and not in "interstate or foreign commerce."** Some state statutes, in fact, expand the scope of prohibited activity beyond that of the federal antitrust laws on conduct occurring within the state. Furthermore, each state has its own case law interpreting its own antitrust statutes.

The Sherman Act

Section 1 of the Sherman Act is the cornerstone of our antitrust laws. It states in pertinent part:

> Every contract, combination in the form of trust or otherwise, or conspiracy, in restraint of trade or commerce among the several States, or with foreign nations, is declared to be illegal.

According to the U.S. Supreme Court, this broad statutory mandate prohibits every contract, combination, or conspiracy that constitutes an *unreasonable* restraint of trade.[5] The courts have interpreted the word "contract" broadly to mean any form of understanding.*** A duly executed, written agreement is not required. A wink or a nod, or even silence in the face of statements by others, may be enough for a jury to infer that an agreement in violation of antitrust laws has been reached.****

In determining what restraints of trade are unreasonable, the courts apply two general types of standards: the *per se* rule and the rule of reason. Some types of restraints are deemed to be so inherently anticompetitive that they are conclusively

---

   * For example, while § 1 of the Sherman Act forbids all joint conduct which "restrains trade," case law has interpreted the statute to forbid only that joint conduct which is unreasonable. The precise interpretation of what is reasonable and what is unreasonable conduct must be made by reference to the case law. See the discussion of § 1 of the Sherman Act *infra*.

  ** The term "interstate commerce" is a term of art in the law. Loosely speaking, "commerce" means business activity, and "interstate commerce" means business activity which moves between two or more states. However, the meaning of "interstate commerce" has, in fact, become quite broad and encompasses most business activity in the United States today. The federal antitrust laws apply to interstate commerce (and also foreign commerce, that is, commerce that moves between the United States and foreign countries).

 *** This point is discussed in more detail later.

**** In February 2000 the American Society of Travel Agents (ASTA) asked the U.S. Justice Department to investigate possible antitrust violations by the major airlines which are opening a new joint Web site to offer travel services to the public. Twenty-seven U.S. and foreign airlines have said they will open the joint Web site in 2000 to offer many travel services, including air fares, hotels, car rentals, and other products. The travel agents say the joint Web site is "the finishing blow in a campaign calculated to destroy public access to comparative information about air travel services and to end once and for all the hope for a vigorous competitive industry that was the promise of airline deregulation in 1978." (See *Vero Beach Press Journal*, Feb. 18, 2000 at pg. 1, col. 1.)

presumed to be unreasonable. Such restraints are called *per se** violations of the antitrust laws and are absolutely forbidden regardless of the alleged justifications for, or the competitive benefits from, the particular activity.

Among the business practices that the courts have held to be *per se* violations of § 1 of the Sherman Act are:

1. Horizontal or vertical agreements fixing or "tampering with" prices (for example, two or more hotel operators agreeing on the room rates they will charge their customers),[6] or fixing maximum or minimum prices (for example, two or more hotel operators agreeing that they will not charge less than a certain amount for their least expensive rooms),[7] or tampering with prices by adopting common terms and conditions of service and goods (for example, two or more hotel operators agreeing that an advance deposit will be required on room reservations made by guests, individually or as part of a tour group or convention group; agreeing to the establishment of a uniform service charge in the two hotels in lieu of tips; agreeing to charge uniform fees for the tennis courts at the two hotels; or agreeing that the two hotels will impose charges when a scheduled event overruns its allotted time);[8]

2. Horizontal agreements allocating geographic areas,[9] customers,[10] or products or services (for example, two hotel operators agreeing as to which conventions each hotel will bid upon while the other refrains from bidding);[11]

3. Horizontal or vertical agreements boycotting third parties (for example, the members of a hotel association agreeing that they will establish unreasonable terms for any future memberships to block some of their competitors from joining and thereby to prevent them from gaining the competitive benefits of association membership services);[12]

4. In certain circumstances, conditioning the purchase of one product or service on the purchase of another product or service (for example, a hotel operator saying to a customer that the customer cannot rent the grand ballroom unless he/she uses the hotel-owned florist to decorate it).[13]

If a particular activity is not classified as illegal *per se,* then the second standard, the so-called *rule of reason* standard, is applied to determine whether the activity violates § 1 of the Sherman Act. Under this standard, proof that the party engaged in a particular activity is not itself proof of a violation of the antitrust laws. Rather, the court examines the various facts and circumstances surrounding the party's actions and decides whether the party *intended* to restrain trade unreasonably or whether, regardless of intent, its conduct had the *effect* of unreasonably

---

* The term *per se* is derived from the Latin meaning "by itself" and denotes that proof of the alleged conduct alone proves the violation—no defense of the reasonableness or propriety of the conduct under the circumstances will be considered by the courts in determining whether a violation of law has occurred. *Northern Pacific Ry. Co.* v. *United States*, 356 U.S. 1, 5 (1958).

restraining trade. In making that determination, the court analyzes the purpose of the restraint, the length and scope of the particular restraint, and the effect of the restraint on the marketplace, among other relevant factors.[14] An agreement not to compete following the sale of a business is an example of the types of business arrangements commonly judged by the *rule of reason* standard. However, any agreement with a competitor or customer that affects the production, distribution, or sale of a product or service and which is not governed by the *per se* standard is potentially subject to examination under the *rule of reason* standard.

In summary, it can be said as an immutable principle that agreements with competitors to fix or tamper with prices or other terms of sale, or to allocate territories or customers, or to refuse to deal with others are unlawful. Other agreements among two or more hotels that affect the furnishing or sale of a service may be found unlawful under the circumstances. Therefore, before any action is taken to enter into or to implement such an agreement, the plan should first be reviewed by legal counsel.* (See *United States* v. *Hilton Hotels Corporation*, at the end of this chapter, involving questions of violation of § 1 of the Sherman Act.)

The Clayton Act

The present Clayton Act contains the original Act and several amendments, including the Robinson-Patman Act of 1936 and the Celler-Kefauver Amendment of 1950. The Clayton Act describes certain types of prohibited business activity more precisely than does the Sherman Act. However, it is still necessary to examine case law in order to determine whether certain conduct falls within the Clayton Act's statutory proscriptions.

Section 7 of the Clayton Act, as applied to the hotel and motel industry, essentially prohibits a hotel operator from acquiring the stock or assets of another company where that acquisition may "substantially" lessen competition or may "tend to create a monopoly."[15] The standards for proof of a violation of § 7 are beyond the scope of this discussion. There is much case law interpreting § 7, and a proposal for a merger of any magnitude should be submitted for review by legal counsel before consummation of the transaction. In addition, under additional amendments to the Clayton Act, certain mergers cannot be consummated until

1. the companies involved file detailed reports with the two federal agencies responsible for government enforcement of the antitrust laws—the Antitrust Division of the U.S. Department of Justice and the Federal Trade Commission—informing those agencies of the proposed merger, and

2. a statutory waiting period elapses following the companies' filing of those reports.

---

* A discussion of § 2 of the Sherman Act, which prohibits unilateral and joint efforts to monopolize and unilateral attempts to monopolize any part of interstate or foreign commerce, is beyond the scope of this book.

The Federal Trade Commission Act

Section 5 of the Federal Trade Commission Act empowers the Federal Trade Commission (FTC) to enjoin "[u]nfair methods of competition…and unfair or deceptive acts or practices…."[16] Under this statutory mandate, the FTC is empowered to attack anticompetitive practices that violate the Sherman Act and Clayton Act, and to attack practices that, while not Sherman or Clayton Act violations, nonetheless constitute unfair methods of competition.[17] Under § 5, the FTC also has a consumer protection mandate from the U.S. Congress. Under this mandate, the FTC has attacked misrepresentations in advertising and other sales or marketing practices that it judged deceptive to the consumer.

Requirement of an "Agreement"

As this capsule summary suggests, the antitrust laws are primarily aimed at concerted or group action between two or more hotels rather than unilateral conduct. For example, a hotel's unilateral refusal to deal with a potential customer ordinarily does not violate the antitrust laws,* while a contract, combination, or conspiracy between two or more competing hotels to refuse to deal with a certain customer (a "boycott") is ordinarily a *per se* violation of the antitrust laws.

As mentioned earlier, a written agreement is not necessary in order for the courts to find an illegal "conspiracy." Even a casual social conversation with competitors concerning pricing of hotel rooms could lead a jury to infer and conclude that the parties were conspiring to violate the antitrust laws. As the Court of Appeals for the Ninth Circuit explained in *Esco Corp.* v. *United States,*

> Nor are we so naive as to believe that a formal signed-and-sealed contract or written resolution would conceivably be adopted at a meeting of price-fixing conspirators in this day and age. In fact, the typical price-fixing agreement is usually accomplished in a contrary manner.
>
> While particularly true of price-fixing conspiracies, it is well recognized law that any conspiracy can ordinarily only be proved by inferences drawn from relevant and competent circumstantial evidence, including the conduct of the defendants charged…. A knowing wink can mean more than words.[18]

For example, parties have been held guilty of illegal price-fixing when the evidence showed that they had attended meetings with their competitors at which they discussed prices and that thereafter prices and price changes were generally uniform. Similarly, the circulation of a "blacklist" of suppliers by a group of competitors has been held sufficient to establish a group boycott in violation of the antitrust laws.[19]

---

* Of course, if the "unilateral" refusal is in fact part of a conspiracy with others, or is in retaliation for the potential buyer's refusal to continue to adhere to a vertical price-fixing arrangement or is made by one with monopoly power, the refusal could be found to violate the Sherman Act. See *United States* v. *Parke-Davis & Co.,* 362 U.S. 29 (1960). Furthermore, conduct engaged in unilaterally, without any evidence of combination, may be found to be an unfair method of competition in violation of § 5 of the Federal Trade Commission Act. See *FTC* v. *Cement Institute,* 333 U.S. 683 (1948).

Because trade associations provide a forum for meetings of competitors, it is especially important that their programs and operations be closely monitored by legal counsel for compliance with the antitrust laws. For example, the issuance by a trade association of a schedule of suggested prices is forbidden conduct. In *United States* v. *Nationwide Trailer Rental Systems,* the members of a trade association were found guilty of *per se* illegal price-fixing simply upon evidence that they had published a recommended schedule of prices and despite the absence of any evidence that the members actually agreed to adhere to that schedule or that they sought to coerce other members to follow the schedule.[20]

According to the Federal Trade Commision, the South Lake Tahoe Lodging Association (which represents 70 percent of the lodging units on the California side of Lake Tahoe) became concerned about what it viewed to be a "destructive price war" among its members. This battle was being fought with roadside billboards. Consequently, the association adopted a policy prohibiting its members from posting prices on billboards.

In a complaint, the FTC alleged that the association caused a reduction in price competition and kept pricing information out of consumers' hands. The association has entered into a consent order to resolve the complaint, agreeing to refrain from further restrictive activity in the future.[21]

This case is full of warning signs: Competitors, under the umbrella of a trade association, discussing prices and then taking collective action to affect pricing.

What should a hotel representative do if, at an otherwise proper trade association meeting, the discussion turns to an improper subject? For example, suppose a participant suggests that all member hotels would be better off if they raised their room rates for the coming season. Perhaps the participant says, "Wouldn't it be nice if we were able to 'up' our room rates this year?" If some or all of those hotels subsequently raise their rates, a jury can infer from this discussion the existence of an illegal agreement to fix prices among all those hotels represented at the meeting. The best way for a hotel representative to dissociate from the discussion is to stand up and express disapproval of the discussion of this subject immediately and vociferously and then leave the meeting. If minutes of the meeting are being taken, the hotel representative should insist that his/her objection and departure be officially noted in those minutes. The hotel representative should also promptly report the incident to his/her employer and legal counsel should be consulted.

Penalties for Violation of Antitrust Laws

The Antitrust Division of the Department of Justice is empowered to enforce the Sherman and Clayton Acts through criminal and civil actions.

Penalties for a criminal violation of the Sherman or Clayton Acts are quite severe. A criminal violation of § 1 or 2 of the Sherman Act is a felony. An individual violator of those statutory provisions is subject to imprisonment in jail for a maximum period of three years and to a maximum fine of $350,000. Moreover, because a violation of § 1 or 2 is a felony, an individual violator is subject to all of the legal and practical disabilities resulting from a felony conviction, including loss of voting rights and a criminal record. A corporate violator of § 1 or 2 is subject to a maximum fine of $10 million.[22]

A party charged by the federal government with a civil violation of the Sherman or Clayton Acts which is proven is subject to an injunction and other equitable relief. Courts have granted such relief as the divestiture of certain of a company's assets, the cancellation of certain agreements, and the dissolution of a trade association—and have authorized the Justice Department to oversee the party's activities for a significant period of time in order to prevent future violations of the Sherman and Clayton Acts.[23] The United States can also bring a civil suit against any party who violates the Sherman or Clayton Acts to recover any damages resulting to the United States from that party's illegal conduct, plus the costs of the suit.[24]

The federal antitrust laws are also enforced civilly by the FTC. The FTC has concurrent jurisdiction with the Antitrust Division to enforce the Clayton Act, and, as mentioned previously, has sole jurisdiction to enforce § 5 of the Federal Trade Commission Act. The FTC enforces those statutory provisions by orders to cease and desist.[25] In addition, state agencies in a number of states are empowered to bring suit in order to enforce their state's own antitrust laws.

Private corporations and individuals may also act to enforce the antitrust laws by bringing private treble damage actions. A supplier, competitor, or customer who has been directly injured by a violation of the Sherman or Clayton Acts can receive three times the total of damages suffered from a violation, plus costs in bringing the action, including a reasonable attorney's fee.* A supplier, competitor, or customer damaged by a violation of the antitrust laws can also obtain an injunction or other equitable relief.[26]

Application of Antitrust Laws

Relations Between Individual Hotel and Motel Operators

Before discussing or exchanging information with any competitor, a hotel or motel operator should remember two basic principles:

1. Any agreement between competitors jointly to establish rates or any terms or conditions of trade is illegal; and

2. A jury's decision that competitors entered into an unlawful agreement can be, and has been in some cases, premised upon evidence as limited as the mere existence of parallel conduct following an apparently inconclusive and brief discussion with a competitor.

A hotel or motel operator should not enter into an understanding of any sort with any competitor about such sensitive subjects as:

---

* The potential damage liability in private antitrust actions can be enormous. For example, in the corrugated container treble damage actions, certain defendants agreed to pay $300 million in settlement. *In Re Corrugated Container Antitrust Litigation,* M.D.L. 310.

- room rates and conditions and terms of providing rooms (such as deposits, services provided guests, or service charges)
- scope of operations (that is, classes of customers the hotel will serve and its area of operations). For example, a hotel operator should not agree to refer all convention groups to a competing hotel in return for the referral of all high school class touring groups to its hotel.

A hotel or motel operator should not discuss room rates or conditions and terms of providing services with competitors. This proscription includes both written and oral discussions and encompasses *past* room rates, conditions, and terms; *current* room rates, conditions, and terms; the *expected duration* of current room rates, conditions, and terms; and *projected future* room rates, conditions, and terms.

A hotel or motel operator can, of course, lawfully obtain information on its competitors' current room rates, conditions, and terms by asking its customers what others are charging and by consulting publicly published sources.

A hotel or motel operator should not discuss or exchange information with competitors concerning planned conduct with respect to particular customers or suppliers. For example, a hotel or motel operator should not discuss with competitors any planned or actual refusal to deal with a convention bureau or a travel agent.

A hotel or motel operator belonging to a trade association has an individual responsibility to ensure, as best he/she can, that the association's activities do not violate the antitrust laws. Thus, if an improper matter is discussed at a trade association meeting, an individual participant should register objection to the discussion and then leave the meeting.

A proposal by a hotel or motel operator for any sort of joint venture or joint advertising campaign with another hotel or motel should be submitted for review from an antitrust standpoint by legal counsel before any action is taken to enter into or to carry out the proposal.

A hotel or motel of any significant size in its community should not take steps to acquire a competitor without first seeking legal advice on the antitrust implications of the planned acquisition. Legal counsel should not only consider the lawfulness of the acquisition itself under § 7 of the Clayton Act, but should also examine any ancillary conditions to the transaction. For example, this should include any convenants by the seller not to open a new hotel that would compete directly with the hotel being sold, since the geographical scope and the duration of such a covenant must be "reasonable" as determined by the courts or the covenant may be unenforceable.

Relations with Third Parties: Suppliers and Customers

As noted above, hotel and motel operators should not collectively determine whether or not they will deal with certain suppliers or customers. Following are several types of agreements which a hotel or motel operator, even though he/she acts individually and without consulting a competitor, should not enter into with its suppliers or customers. It should be noted at the outset that a hotel or motel operator generally has the right to select the operation's suppliers and customers and to decline to deal with anyone that it does not want as a supplier or customer. However, a hotel or motel operator should never select a supplier or customer, or refuse to deal with a supplier or customer, because the latter will or will not enter into certain arrangements. For example:

- A hotel or motel operator should not restrict a supplier's right to determine individually the prices of its products to others.

- A hotel or motel operator should not require a supplier or customer to deal exclusively with it generally or within a certain geographical area unless the arrangement has been submitted for prior review by legal counsel and has met with counsel's approval after a full analysis of the circumstances.*

Remember that a hotel or motel operator is ordinarily held responsible if its managers or employees engage in conduct violating the antitrust laws even though the operator may not have condoned or encouraged such conduct. Consequently, a hotel or motel should ensure that its managers and its sales and purchasing employees are familiar with the scope and basic principles of the antitrust laws.

Hotel and Motel Trade Associations

Trade associations are perfectly lawful organizations. However, because a trade association is, by definition, an organization of competitors, the members must take special precautions to ensure that their associations do not engage in activities that may violate antitrust laws. If a trade association engages in activities that unreasonably restrain trade, the association and its members are subject to the severe penalties imposed by antitrust laws, regardless of the association's otherwise beneficial objectives.

- Legal counsel should review trade association programs of certification or standardization before they are implemented. Standards that may favor certain competitors and disfavor others are highly suspect, and disciplining members for failure to conform to such standards will in all probability be found to violate antitrust laws.

- Legal counsel should periodically review the association's bylaws and any codes of operating practices for compliance with antitrust laws.

- If possible, the association's membership should be completely open; if not, any restriction on admission to membership must be for a reasonable (that is, non- anticompetitive) purpose and that purpose must be expressly set forth in the association's rules.

---

* Today many sales by suppliers (as well as by hotels) occur over the internet. Such e-commerce is not exempt from the antitrust laws. See Frances H. Casola, "Old Antitrust Doctrine Meets New Economy," *Virginian Lawyer,* Oct. 2000, p. 24 *et seq.*

- Meetings of the association should be conducted in strict accordance with a previously prepared agenda, which legal counsel should examine and approve.

- The chairperson of the meeting should be instructed to silence immediately any remarks on subjects such as room rates, surcharges, conditions, terms and prices of services, allocating or sharing of customers, and refusing to deal with a particular supplier or class of suppliers. The chairperson should silence both serious and flippant comments—a jury may interpret an intended joke as a serious remark.

- The association should not issue any recommendations on any of the above subjects without review by counsel. The association should also refrain from sending members any publications concerning such matters without review by counsel. For example, the association should not recommend for or against rate-cutting, since, because the association is an aggregation of competing members, this could be viewed as participation in a price-fixing conspiracy. Similarly, the association should not advise its members as to whether, for example, to require advance deposits from hotel customers.

- The association should be particularly careful of any role in gathering or dis-seminating information concerning financial results of hotels. It is imperative that any proposed activity of this sort be submitted to legal counsel for review before taking any legal action. If legal counsel determines that such a program may be undertaken, counsel will usually also insist that data be gathered and compiled by an independent organization, such as an accounting firm. Counsel will also require that the independent organization present the data so as not to permit the source of the specific data to be determinable.

- The association should never, under any circumstances, compile or dissemi-nate a list of anticipated future prices for its members' services.

- When an association seeks to obtain group discounts for its members, careful legal analysis of the proposed discount is critical before any action is taken by the association. A group discount on goods or services not directly useful to association members in competition with non-members (for example, a group discount on foreign travel for employees of association members) presents a very different question under the antitrust laws than a group discount obtained on goods or services directly useful in competition (for example, a special hotel and motel association group discount on the purchase of room furnishings). In the latter case, the proof of coercion of the supplier may be found simply from the implicit threat of group action in the event the supplier fails to allow the proposed discount; moreover, in this latter case, non-mem-bers of the association may be found to have been put at a significant competitive disadvantage by their inability to obtain the discount. Thus, any proposal by which an association would seek a group discount for its members should be submitted for review by legal counsel before action is taken by the association.

Important Points for Management

The Sherman Act prohibits a contract, combination, or conspiracy in restraint of trade or commerce.

Certain types of activities are *per se* violations. They are always illegal. Examples of *per se* violations are:

- Horizontal price agreements: two or more competing hotels agreeing on what price to charge for rooms.

- Group boycotts: two or more competing hotels agreeing not to buy supplies from a vendor.

The Clayton Act prohibits specified activities. One example of a prohibited activity is acquiring the stock or assets of a competing company where that acquisition may "substantially lessen competition" or "tend to create a monopoly." The Federal Trade Commission (FTC) may enjoin:

- Unfair methods of competition; and

- Unfair or deceptive acts or practices.

The FTC investigates misrepresentations in advertising, sales, and marketing that are deceptive to consumers.

Agreements among hotels that are antitrust violations of the Sherman Act include:

- Competing hotels agreeing on room rates;

- Agreements between competing hotels about deposits, services, or other charges;

- Competing hotels agreeing not to patronize a particular supplier or customer;

- Competitors dividing a territory to eliminate competition.

Penalties for violating the federal antitrust laws are severe.

It is important to remember that a hotel operator may be held responsible for the conduct of his/her managers or employees which is in violation of antitrust laws, even though the operator has not condoned or encouraged such conduct. Managers who have not had training may not know what activities are antitrust violations. Hotels should see that managers are aware of the antitrust laws and their implications.

References

1. See, for example, *United States* v. *Hilton Hotels Corp.*, 467 F.2d 1000 (9th Cir. 1972), *cert. denied*, 409 U.S. 1125 (1973).

2. 15 U.S.C. § 1-7.

3. 15 U.S.C. § 12-27. The several amendments to the Clayton Act include the Robinson-Patman Act of 1936, 15 U.S.C. §§ 13, 13a, 13b, 21a, the Celler-Kefauver Amendment of 1950 (§ 7 of the Clayton Act), 15 U.S.C. § 18, the Antitrust Procedures and Penalties Act

of 1974, 15 U.S.C. § 16(b)-(h), and the Antitrust Improvements Act of 1976. 15 U.S.C. § 15(c)-(h), 18(a) 66.

4. 15 U.S.C. §§ 41-58.

5. *Standard Oil Co.* v. *United States*, 221 U.S. 1 (1911). The distinction between "reasonable" and "unreasonable" restraints of trade has great practical importance. Otherwise, any business contract by which one party agrees to do something for another could be found to be a "contract in restraint of trade" since it may keep the participants from agreeing to do the same thing or something else with some other party.

6. See, for example, *United States* v. *Socony-Vacuum Oil Co.*, 310 U.S. 150 (1940), *reh'g denied*, 310 U.S. 658 (1940), *Simpson* v. *Union Oil Co.*, 377 U.S. 13 (1964), *reh'g denied*, 377 U.S. 949 (1964), *on remand*, 270 F. Supp. 754 (N.D. Cal., 1967), *aff'd*, 411 F.2d 897 (CA9 Cal. 1969), *rev'd*, 396 U.S. 13 (1969).

7. See, for example, *Goldfarb* v. *Virginia State Bar*, 421 U.S. 773 (1975).

8. See, for example, *United States* v. *Gasoline Retailers Ass'n Inc.*, 285 F.2d 688 (7th Cir. 1961).

9. See, for example, *United States* v. *Topco Associates, Inc.*, 405 U.S. 596 (1972); *United States* v. *Sealy, Inc.*, 388 U.S. 350 (1967); *American Motor Inns, Inc.* v. *Holiday Inns, Inc.*, 521 F.2d 1230 (3d Cir. 1975).

10. See, for example, *United States* v. *Topco Associates, Inc.*, 405 U.S. 596 (1972).

11. See, for example, *Hartford-Empire Co.* v. *United States*, 323 U.S. 386 (1945).

12. See, for example, *United States* v. *General Motors Corp.*, 384 U.S. 127 (1966); *Fashion Originators' Guild of America, Inc.* v. *F.T.C.*, 312 U.S. 457 (1941); *United States* v. *Hilton Hotels Corp.*, 467 F.2d 1000 (9th Cir. 1972), *cert. denied*, 409 U.S. 1125 (1973) (agreement by a number of hotels to refuse to deal with those hotel suppliers that were not members of an association promoting local conventions held *per se* illegal).

13. See, for example, *United States Steel Corp.* v. *Fortner Enterprises, Inc.*, 429 U.S. 610 (1977).

14. See, for example, *Chicago Board of Trade* v. *United States*, 246 U.S. 231, 238 (1918).

15. 15 U.S.C. § 18.

16. 15 U.S.C. § 45 (a).

17. See, for example, *F.T.C.* v. *Brown Shoe Co.*, 384 U.S. 316, 320-22 (1966).

18. *Esco Corp.* v. *United States*, 340 F.2d 1000, 1006-7 (9th Cir. 1965).

19. *Eastern States Retail Lumber Dealers' Ass'n* v. *United States*, 234 U.S. 600 (1914).

20. *United States* v. *Nationwide Trailer Rental Systems, Inc.*, 156 F. Supp. 800, 804-5 (D. Kan.), *aff'd per curiam*, 355 U.S. (1957).

21. See South Lake Tahoe Lodging Association, FTC, File No. 971-0110, 7/28/98.

22. 15 U.S.C. §§ 1, 2.

23. See, for example, *United States* v. *E.I. duPont deNemours & Co.*, 366 U.S. 316 (1961), *motion denied*, 366 U.S. 956 (1961); *United States* v. *Glaxo Group Ltd.*, 410 U.S. 52 (1973); *United States* v. *Manufacturers Aircraft Association, Inc., et al.*, 1976-1 Trade Cases 60.810 (S.D.N.Y. 1975); *United States* v. *Linen Supply Institute of Greater New York, Inc.*, 1958 Trade Cases 69.120 (S.D.N.Y. 1958).

24. 15 U.S.C. § 15a.

25. 15 U.S.C. § 45.

26. 15 U.S.C. § 15.

Review Questions

1. Why do the antitrust laws prohibit agreements between competing hotels on the guestroom prices they will charge the public?

2. When would the hotel owner be responsible for the acts of his/her manager or employees which violate the antitrust laws? even if the owner never encouraged or condoned such conduct?

3. What penalties may a court impose against a hotel operator who violates the antitrust laws?

4. What antitrust lessons are to be learned from the case of *United States* v. *Hilton Hotels Corporation* (illustrative case following this chapter) involving the hotels' boycott of suppliers?

5. Can you name at least three types of agreements between hotels that would violate the federal antitrust laws?

Internet Sites

For more information, visit the following Internet sites. Remember that Internet addresses can change without notice.

Antitrust Division
http://www.usdoj.gov/atr/

FindLaw
http://www.findlaw.com

Federal Trade Commission (FTC)
http://www.ftc.gov

Illustrative Case

United States v. *Hilton Hotels Corporation*

467 F.2d 1000 (9th Cir. 1972),
cert. denied, 409 U.S. 1125 (1973)

BROWNING, Circuit Judge:

This is an appeal from a conviction under an indictment charging a violation of section 1 of the Sherman Act, 15 U.S.C. § 1.

Operators of hotels, restaurants, hotel and restaurant supply companies, and other businesses in Portland, Oregon, organized an association to attract conventions to their city. To finance the association, members were asked to make contributions in predetermined amounts. Companies selling supplies to hotels were asked to contribute an amount equal to one per cent of their sales to hotel members. To aid collections, hotel members, including appellant, agreed to give preferential treatment to suppliers who paid their assessments, and to curtail purchases from those who did not.

I

The jury was instructed that such an agreement by the hotel members, if proven, would be a per se violation of the Sherman Act. Appellant argues that this was error.

We need not explore the outer limits of the doctrine that joint refusals to deal constitute per se violations of the Act, for the conduct involved here was of the kind long held to be forbidden without more. "Throughout the history of the Sherman Act, the courts have had little difficulty in finding unreasonable restraints of trade in agreements among competitors, at any level of distribution, designed to coerce those subject to a boycott to accede to the action or inaction desired by the group or to exclude them from competition." [citation omitted]

Appellant argues that in cases in which the per se rule has been applied to refusals to deal, the defendants intended "to destroy a competitor or a line of competition," while the purpose of the defendants in the present case "was solely to bring convention dollars into Portland." But the necessary and direct consequence of defendant's scheme was to deprive uncooperative suppliers of the opportunity to sell to defendant hotels in free and open competition with other suppliers, and to deprive defendant hotels of the opportunity to buy supplies from such suppliers in accordance with the individual judgment of each hotel, at prices and on terms and conditions of sale determined by free competition. Defendants therefore "intended" to impose these restraints upon competition in the only sense relevant here. [citation omitted] The ultimate objective defendants sought to achieve is immaterial. [citation omitted]

Running through appellant's argument is the theme that the suppliers complied with the urgings of the hotels to contribute because they wished to maintain friendly business relations with these important customers; that this sort of "coercion," and submission to it, is common in American business life, and should not be subject to the Sherman Act unless it is shown that in the particular case it was intended to have, or had, an unreasonable impact upon price, quality, or service.

If the argument is that the evidence did not show an agreement on the part of the hotels to prefer suppliers who paid their contribution over those who did not, we reject it on the ground that the evidence was clearly sufficient to establish such an agreement. If the argument is that such use by the defendant hotels of their combined economic power to coerce suppliers violates the Sherman Act only if price, service, or quality is adversely affected, we reject it on the authority of *Klor's Inc.* v. *Broadway-Hale Stores,* 359 U.S. at 212, 79 S.Ct. 705.

Appellant argues that since the suppliers were also members of the association, the per se rule is inapplicable because "the request for contribution and the alleged coercive action was among members of the same association" and the "implied threat of coercion or preference can be said simply to be an incidental effect of regulations within the group inter se."

The circumstance that both the boycotters and their victims were members of the same trade association would not diminish the impact of the boycott on competition, and appellant does not explain why it should affect the legality of the boycott. This same factual circumstance appears to have been present, for example, in *Fashion Originators' Guild* v. *FTC,* 312 U.S. 457 at 461, 61 S.Ct. 703.

The evidence does not show that the suppliers joined in the agreement that the hotels would cease dealing with those that failed to pay, but the result would not be changed if it had. It is not the primary purpose of the Sherman Act to protect deserving private persons, but to vindicate the public interest in a free market.[1] [citation omitted]

This is not a case in which joint activity having a primary purpose and direct effect of accomplishing a legitimate business objective is also alleged to have had an incidental and indirect adverse effect upon the business of some competitors.[2] [citation omitted] The primary purpose and direct effect of defendants' agreement was to bring the combined economic power of the hotels to bear upon those suppliers who failed to pay. The exclusion of uncooperative suppliers from the portion of the market represented by the supply requirements of the defendant hotels was the object of the agreement, not merely its incidental consequence.

Appellant's president testified that it would be contrary to the policy of the corporation for the manager of one of its hotels to condition purchases upon payment of a contribution to a local association by the supplier. The manager of appellant's Portland hotel and his assistant testified that it was the hotel's policy to purchase supplies solely on the basis of price, quality, and service. They also testified that on two occasions they told the hotel's purchasing agent that he was to take no part in the boycott. The purchasing agent confirmed the receipt of these instructions, but admitted that, despite them, he had threatened a supplier with loss of the hotel's business unless the supplier paid the association assessment. He testified that he violated his instructions because of anger and personal pique toward the individual representing the supplier. *See,* note 1.

Based upon this testimony, appellant requested certain instructions bearing upon the criminal liability of a corporation for the unauthorized acts of its agents. These requests were rejected by the trial court. The court instructed the jury that a corporation is liable for the acts and statements of its agents "within the scope of their employment," defined to mean "in the corporation's behalf in performance of the agent's general line of work," including "not only that which has been authorized by the corporation, but also that which outsiders could reasonably assume the agent would have authority to do." The court added:

> "A corporation is responsible for acts and statements of its agents, done or made within the scope of their employment, even though their conduct may be contrary to their actual instructions or contrary to the corporation's stated policies."

Appellant objects only to the court's concluding statement.

Congress may constitutionally impose criminal liability upon a business entity for acts or omissions of its agents within the scope of their employment. [citation omitted] Such liability may attach without proof that the conduct was within the agent's actual authority, and even though it may have been contrary to express instructions. [citation omitted]

The intention to impose such liability is sometimes express, *New York Central & Hudson R.R. Co. v. United States, supra* 212 U.S. 481, 29 S.Ct. 304, 53 L.Ed. 613, but it may also be implied. The text of the Sherman Act does not expressly resolve the

---

[1] This is also a sufficient answer to appellant's objection to the court's instruction that a boycott would violate the Sherman Act "even if the boycott…resulted from a personal quarrel." *Cf. Klor's Inc.* v. *Braodway-Hale Stores,* 359 U.S. 207, 210, 79 S.Ct. 705, 3 L.Ed. 2d 741 (1959).

[2] Of course, such conduct is not necessarily exonerated: its legality is tested under the "rule of reason." See generally Bird, Sherman Act Limitations on Noncommercial Concerted Refusals to Deal, 1970 Duke L.J. 247, 270-73 (1970).

issue. For the reasons that follow, however, we think the construction of the Act that best achieves its purpose is that a corporation is liable for acts of its agents within the scope of their authority even when done against company orders.

* * *

Despite the fact that "the doctrine of corporate criminal responsibility for the acts of the officers was not well established in 1890," *United States* v. *Wise,* 370 U.S. 405, 408, 82 S.Ct. 1354, 1357, 8 L.Ed.2d 590 (1962), the Act expressly applies to corporate entities. 15 U.S.C. § 7. The preoccupation of Congress with corporate liability was only emphasized by the adoption in 1914 of section 14 of the Clayton Act to reaffirm and emphasize that such liability was not exclusive, and that corporate agents also were subject to punishment if they authorized, ordered, or participated in the acts constituting the violation. *United States* v. *Wise, supra* 370 U.S. at 411-415, 82 S.Ct. 1354.

Criminal liability for the acts of agents is more readily imposed under a statute directed at the prohibited act itself, one that does not make specific intent an element of the offense. *See Standard Oil Co.* v. *United States, supra* 307 F.2d at 125. [citation omitted] The Sherman Act is aimed at consequences. Specific intent is not an element of any offense under the Act except attempt to monopolize under section 2, and conscious wrongdoing is not an element of that offense. The Sherman Act is violated if "a restraint of trade or monopoly results as the consequence of a defendant's conduct or business arrangements." *United States* v. *Griffith, supra,* 334 U.S. 100, 105, 68 S.Ct. 941, 944, 92 L.Ed. 1236 (1948). [citation omitted]

The breadth and critical character of the public interests protected by the Sherman Act, and the gravity of the threat to those interests that led to the enactment of the statute, support a construction holding business organizations accountable, as a general rule, for violations of the Act by their employees in the course of their businesses. In enacting the Sherman Act, "Congress was passing drastic legislation to remedy a threatening danger to the public welfare..." *United Mine Workers* v. *Coronado Coal Co.,* 259 U.S. 344, 392, 42 S.Ct. 570, 576, 66 L.Ed. 975 (1922). The statute "was designed to be a comprehensive charter of economic liberty aimed at preserving free and unfettered competition as the rule of trade. It rests on the premise that the unrestrained interaction of competitive forces will yield the best allocation of our economic resources, the lowest prices, the highest quality and the greatest material progress, while at the same time providing an environment conducive to the preservation of our democratic political and social institutions." *Northern Pacific Ry.* v. *United States, supra,* 356 U.S. at 4, 78 S.Ct. at 517.

With such important public interests at stake, it is reasonable to assume that Congress intended to impose liability upon business entities for the acts of those to whom they choose to delegate the conduct of their affairs, thus stimulating a maximum effort by owners and managers to assure adherence by such agents to the requirements of the Act.

* * *

Because of the nature of Sherman Act offenses and the context in which they normally occur, the factors that militate against allowing a corporation to disown the criminal acts of its agents apply with special force to Sherman Act violations.

Sherman Act violations are commercial offenses. They are usually motivated by a desire to enhance profits.[4] They commonly involve large, complex, and highly decentralized corporate business enterprises, and intricate business processes, practices, and arrangements. More often than not they also involve basic policy decisions, and must be implemented over an extended period of time.

Complex business structures, characterized by decentralization and delegation of authority, commonly adopted by corporations for business purposes, make it difficult to identify the particular corporate agents responsible for Sherman Act violations. At the same time, it is generally true that high management officials, for whose conduct the corporate directors and stockholders are the most clearly responsible, are likely to have participated in the policy decisions underlying Sherman Act violations, or at least to have become aware of them.

Violations of the Sherman Act are a likely consequence of the pressure to maximize profits that is commonly imposed by corporate owners upon managing agents and, in turn, upon lesser employees. In the face of that pressure, generalized directions to obey the Sherman Act, with the probable effect of foregoing profits, are the least likely to be taken seriously. And if a violation of the Sherman Act occurs, the corporation, and not the individual agents, will have realized the profits from the illegal activity.

In sum, identification of the particular agents responsible for a Sherman Act violation is especially difficult, and their conviction and punishment is peculiarly ineffective as a deterrent. At the same time, conviction and punishment of the business entity itself is likely to be both appropriate and effective.

For these reasons we conclude that as a general rule a corporation is liable under the Sherman Act for the acts of its agents in the scope of their employment, even though contrary to general corporate policy and express instructions to the agent.

Thus the general policy statements of appellant's president were no defense. Nor was it enough that appellant's manager told the purchasing agent that he was not to participate in the boycott. The purchasing agent was authorized to buy all of appellant's supplies. Purchases were made on the basis of specifications, but the purchasing agent exercised complete authority as to source. He was in a unique position to add the corporation's buying power to the force of the boycott. Appellant could not gain exculpation by issuing general instructions without undertaking to enforce those instructions by means commensurate with the obvious risks.

[footnote 3 omitted]

[4] A purpose to benefit the corporation is necessary to bring the agent's acts within the scope of his employment. *Standard Oil Co.* v. *United States*, 307 F.2d 120, 128-129 (5th Cir. 1962).

Chapter 38 Outline

Competencies

1. Define the term "franchising." (p. 483)

2. List some of the typical provisions of a franchise contract. (pp. 483–486)

3. State the information the Federal Trade Commission (FTC) requires franchisors to provide franchisees. List acts or practices that violate FTC rules. (pp. 486–488)

4. Describe the purpose of hotel management contracts. (p. 488–489)

38

Understanding Franchising

THE FRANCHISING OF HOTELS and motels has grown by leaps and bounds during the past decade. **Franchise** chains, in both budget and high price ranges, have grown through national and international expansion. It is most important to consider hotel and motel franchise operations and to understand the general nature of the legal agreements governing such operations.

What Is Franchising? *

"Franchising" is simply a method of distribution whereby a franchiser, who has developed a particular pattern or format for doing business, grants to franchisees the right to conduct such a business provided they follow the established pattern. The franchisee receives a proven method of doing business, and the franchisor promises continuing assistance and guidance.

While the franchisor imposes various controls over the franchisee, the franchisee invariably considers himself/herself an independent businessperson. This pride of ownership helps encourage the franchisee to make the business successful. The franchisor's expertise and proven method of doing business also guide the franchisee past the pitfalls that often beset the independent businessperson.

The Franchise Contract

The franchise relationship is based upon the franchise contract. Therefore, before entering into any franchise relationship as a hotel, motel, or restaurant franchisee, a person or corporation should assess the franchisor's business history and reputation, as well as actual operations and the franchise system. Also, the advice and review of an attorney and business consultant should precede any franchise agreement. Of course, the franchisor has similar and corresponding concerns with regard to the prospective franchisee.

The franchise contract for motels or hotels sets forth the contractual arrangements between the franchisor and the franchisee and determines their legal relationships. Its provisions generally cover the following matters, among others:

1. The parties
   .

---

* This particular section is derived, with permission, from Chapter One of the PLI publication, *The Franchise Contract—Reviewing the Franchise Contract*, by George A. Pelletier. Published and copyrighted by the Practicing Law Institute.

2. Definitions

3. Granting of franchise, description of premises, and area of operation. Franchise may include rights to use servicemarks, copyrights, trade secrets and know-how, and patents

4. Franchise fees and service fees

5. Obligations of franchisee, including:

   a. to maintain and operate the franchised property pursuant to some stated high standards (and maintain a high ethical standard)

   b. to comply with the rules and regulations set forth by the franchisor

   c. to comply with all local, state, and federal laws, ordinances, rules, and regulations; to obtain any and all permits or licenses as required by law

   d. to promote use of the franchised property by the traveling public

   e. to permit the franchisor to inspect the property at all reasonable times

   f. to obtain and display on the property one or more (illuminated) signs and logos meeting specifications prescribed by franchisor

   g. to promote and feature the name of the franchisor in all advertising

   h. to participate in the reservation system of the franchisor, and to make reservations and to accept reservations in accordance with the rules, regulations, and procedures of the franchisor

   i. to submit monthly standard operations reports to the franchisor, together with such other reports as the franchisor may require from time to time

   j. to deliver to the franchisor annual statements of operations and balance sheets for the franchisee's property, prepared by certified independent public accountants, showing gross revenues from room rentals, restaurant operations, or from other revenue-producing sales and activities

   k. to permit the franchisor the right to audit the books of the franchisee.

6. Services of the franchisor may include:

   a. providing operations manual(s) and consulting services to franchise personnel

   b. assisting the franchisee in setting up recordkeeping systems, and administering these systems

   c. making available signs, promotional material, and stationery, at costs agreed upon

   d. advertising and promotional campaigns on local, regional, and national levels to encourage traveling public to use franchised properties

    e. sending franchisor's supervisory personnel to visit and inspect franchise property, and observe its operation

    f. providing advance reservations services and systems on agreed-upon terms and conditions and reservation fees, if any

    g. listing franchise property in a directory of the franchised properties, if published by franchisor.

7. Relation of parties—may include a statement to the effect that the franchisor is an independent contractor and the franchise agreement does not create an agency relationship, a partnership, joint venture, or employer-employee relationship between the parties

8. Restaurant facilities

9. Indemnity and insurance provisions

10. Term of agreement, renewal, termination, defaults and transfer (and any rights of franchisor to right of first refusal to acquire the property in the event that the franchisee decides to sell or transfer the property)

11. Rights and duties of the franchisee and franchisor upon termination

12. Warranties and representations of the franchisor

13. Governing law

    Often the franchisor will offer its franchisees highly sophisticated reservations systems, with instantaneous reservations from one franchise property to another. The terminal lease agreement may accompany the franchisor agreement. A reservations terminal will be installed in the property for a fee and costs.

    Appendix B is a hypothetical simplified example of a franchise contract. The terms and conditions of the contract offered by the different hotel and motel franchisors, however, may differ substantially from the terms and conditions contained in this sample.

What to Look for in Reviewing the Franchise Contract

In reviewing the franchise contract, be certain to ask the following questions:

1. Does the territorial grant meet the requirements of federal and state antitrust laws and Federal Trade Commission regulations? Your legal counsel should review any franchising program in order to ensure compliance with the antitrust laws and regulations.

2. Does the franchise grant make the franchisee an agent of the franchisor?

3. Does the franchise contract require the franchisee to include the franchisor as a beneficiary on public liability and other insurance contracts?

4. Under what conditions can the franchisor terminate the contract? In this connection, what performance requirements are placed on the franchisee? Does their breach result in termination of the contract?

Federal Trade Regulations

The Federal Trade Commission (FTC) has issued trade regulations entitled "Disclosure Requirements and Prohibitions Concerning Franchising and Business Opportunity Ventures."[1] The FTC rules require franchisors and franchise brokers to furnish prospective franchisees with information about the franchisor, the franchisor's business, and the terms of the franchise agreement through a "Basic Disclosure Document."

The FTC rules require disclosure of the following information to prospective franchisees:

*   Identifying information as to franchisor

*   Business experience of franchisor's directors and executive officers

*   Business experience of the franchisor

*   Litigation history

*   Bankruptcy history

*   Description of franchise

*   Initial funds required to be paid by a franchisee

*   Recurring funds required to be paid by a franchisee

*   Affiliated persons the franchisee is required or advised to do business with

*   Financial arrangements

*   Restriction of sales

*   Personal participation required of the franchisee in the operation of the franchise

*   Termination, cancellation, and renewal of the franchise

*   Statistical information concerning the number of franchises (and company-owned outlets)

*   Site selection

*   Training programs

*   Public figure involvement in the franchise

*   Financial information concerning the franchisor

Additional information must be furnished in an "Earnings Claim Document" if any claims are made to the franchisee about actual or potential earnings.

This chapter only touches on highlights of the FTC rules on franchises. Prospective franchisees should review the rules in their entirety.

When Disclosures Must Be Made

The Basic Disclosure Documents are to be given to a "prospective franchisee" at the earlier of (i) the first "personal meeting" or (ii) the "time for making of disclosures."*

Other Disclosures

A copy of the franchisor's standard franchise agreement and any related agreements (for example, leases and purchase orders) must also be given to the prospective franchisee when the Basic Disclosure Document is furnished. In addition, the prospective franchisee must receive a copy of the complete franchise agreement and any related agreements that the parties intend to execute at least five business days prior to the day that the agreements are to be executed.

The Basic Disclosure Document must be kept current as of the franchiser's most recent fiscal year. In addition, the document must be updated at least quarterly, or whenever a "material" change occurs in the information contained in the document.

The FTC rules are similar to some state disclosure laws that at least 14 states[2] have adopted, except that the FTC rules require national compliance.

The FTC rules do not prohibit the states to impose different or more stringent requirements upon the franchisors operating in such states.

Uniform Franchise Offering Circular

A number of states use a disclosure format known as the Uniform Franchise Offering Circular (UFOC) to assure compliance with their state registration and disclosure requirements. The FTC may permit the UFOC to be used in lieu of the disclosure requirements set forth in the FTC rules[3] if the UFOC format matches that adopted by the North American Securities Administration Association (NASAA).

On April 25, 1993, new UFOC guidelines were adopted by the NASAA, which go into effect January 1, 1995. These guidelines have been approved by the FTC and most of the states requiring franchise registration.[4]

Acts or Practices Which Violate the FTC Rule and Potential Liabilities

Under § 5 of the Federal Trade Commission Act, it is an unfair or deceptive act or practice for any franchisor or franchise broker to:

---

* The term "time for making of disclosure" is defined in § 436.2(g) as "ten business days prior to the earlier of (i) the execution by a prospective franchisee of any franchise agreement or any other agreement imposing a binding legal obligation on such prospective franchisee, about which the franchisor, franchise broker, or any agent, representative, or employee thereof, knows or should know, in connection with the sale or proposed sale of a franchise or (ii) the payment by a prospective franchisee, about which the franchisor, franchise broker, or any agent, representative or employee thereof knows or should know, of any consideration in connection with the sale or proposed sale of a franchise."

1. fail to furnish prospective franchisees with the Basic Disclosure Document in the manner and within the timetables established in the rules;[5]

2. make any representations about the actual or potential sales, income, or profits of existing or prospective franchises except in the manner and within the timeframes established by the rules, including dissemination of the Earnings Claim Document;[6]

3. make any claim or representation (such as in advertising or oral statements by salespersons) which is inconsistent with the information required to be disclosed by the rules;[7]

4. fail to furnish prospective franchisees, within the timeframes established by the rule, with copies of the franchisor's standard forms of franchise agreements and copies of the final agreements to be signed by the parties;[8] and

5. fail to return to prospective franchisees any funds or deposits (such as down payments) identified as refundable in the Basic Disclosure Document.[9]

A Note on Hotel Management Contracts

Many of the major franchise companies undertake management contracts for hotel properties as an additional or supplemental system to their existing systems of franchise arrangements, direct ownerships, and property leases. At least 10 major chains, including Hyatt, Sheraton, and Hilton, and more than 60 independent companies, now operate more than 700 properties under management contracts.

Pursuant to such management contracts, chain companies furnish management for hotel and motel properties that are owned by other parties throughout the nation. The chain company as manager provides its franchise to the property, and uses its trademarks, logos, and reservations systems in promoting the property.

Many independent companies also provide expertise for operating hotel and motel properties under management contracts. These independent companies may also operate a property using a chain franchise and contract for the use of the chain reservations system.

The use of the management contract has proven very successful to such major chains as Sheraton and Hilton as a means of rapidly expanding their operations with far less investment per property than direct ownership requires. With expertise in franchise operations, financial management, and staffing, marketing, sales, and reservation services, the chain operators would appear to have a definite advantage in many cases over the independent companies in seeking management contracts.

Under the management contract, the manager is responsible for the operation and management of the property. The manager usually pays the operating expenses, and the remaining cash, if any, goes to the owner, who uses this cash to pay debt service, insurance, taxes, etc., after deducting the management fees according to an agreed-upon formula. Some of the management contracts have as much as a 20-year term.

Under the management contract, the owner often retains all or most of the financial, and most of the legal, responsibilities. Often the owners are institutional owners, such as large insurance companies, rather than partnerships or individual businesspersons.

The provisions of the management contract often depend upon the respective bargaining power of the management company and the owner, which, as indicated, may be a large institutional investor.

An excellent description of a management contract's provisions, which are usually quite extensive, is contained in *The Negotiation and Administration of Hotel Management Contracts,* Second Edition, by James Jeffries Eyster, Jr., School of Hotel Administration at Cornell University, 1980.

Important Points for Management

Franchising is a method of distribution whereby a franchisor, who has developed a particular pattern or format for doing business, grants to franchisees the right to conduct such a business provided they follow the established pattern. The franchisee receives a proven method of doing business, and the franchisor promises continuing assistance and guidance.

The franchise relationship is based upon the franchise contract. Therefore, before entering into any franchise contract, you should assess the franchisor's business history and reputation, as well as actual operations and the franchise system. Also, the advice and review of an attorney and business consultant should precede any franchise contract.

The FTC rules require franchisors and franchise brokers to furnish prospective franchisees with information about the franchisor, the franchisor's business, and the terms of the franchise agreement through a "Basic Disclosure Document."

A copy of the franchisor's standard franchise agreement and any related agreements (for example, leases and purchases orders) must also be given to the prospective franchisee when the Basic Disclosure Document is furnished.

The use of the *management contract* has proven very successful to such major chains as Sheraton and Hilton as a means of rapidly expanding their operations with far less investment per property than direct ownership requires.

Under the management contract, the manager is responsible for the operation and management of the property. The manager usually pays the operating expenses and the remaining cash, if any, goes to the owner who uses this cash to pay debt service, insurance, taxes, etc., after deducting the management fees according to an agreed upon formula. Some management contracts have as much as a 20-year term.

References

1. 16 C.F.R. § 436.
2. See *"Franchising Today,"* by Julian E. Jacoby and Lynn McGowan, *L&H Perspective,* Laventhol & Horwath, Spring/Summer 1980, p. 31. (No longer in print.)
3. 16 C.F.R. § 436.1(a)(e).
4. See Mark A. Kirsch, "Franchisors and Franchisees Brace for New Disclosure Regime," *Lodging,* November 1994, pp. 31-38.
5. *Id.* § 436.1(a) 16 C.F.R. § 436.1(a)(e).

6. *Id.* § 436.1(b)(3).
7. *Id.* § 436.1(f).
8. *Id.* § 436.1(g).
9. *Id.* § 436.1(h).

Key Terms

franchise—As used in this book, a franchise is an agreement by which the franchisee undertakes to conduct a business or sell a product or service in accordance with methods and procedures prescribed by the franchisor; the franchiser undertakes to assist the franchisee through advertising, promotion, and other advisory services; the franchise may encompass an exclusive right to sell a product or service or conduct a business in a specified territory.

Review Questions

1. What is franchising?

2. Why would you want to have a franchise when buying or operating a hotel?

3. Why are there federal regulations governing the sale of a franchise? What do these federal regulations require?

4. What does a franchise contract look like? What provisions should you look for in a franchise contract?

Internet Sites

For more information, visit the following Internet sites. Remember that Internet addresses can change without notice.

Federal Trade Commission (FTC)
http://www.ftc.gov

North American Securities Administrators Association
http://www.nasaa.org

Uniform Franchise Offering Circular (UFOC)
http://www.nasaa.org/nasaa/corpfin/UFOC.doc

Chapter 39 Outline

Competencies

1. Describe privacy on the Internet, and explain the Federal Trade Commission's concerns with privacy on the Internet. (pp. 493–494)

2. Identify the antitrust concerns with respect to the Internet. (pp. 494–495)

3. Summarize the Internet's effect on music copyright concerns. (pp. 495–496)

4. Explain how employees use the web, and the importance of an Internet use policy for employees. (p. 496)

39

Legal Issues Involving the Internet

THE INTERNET HAS CREATED a business revolution. Every hotel chain now has a presence on the Internet and virtually every hotel, whether or not part of a chain, can be accessed through the Internet either directly or indirectly through reservation services that are present throughout cyberspace, such as GotRooms, a service of the American Hotel & Lodging Association.

Over the next decade, it can be expected that numerous laws will be passed that will directly control dealings over the Internet. Currently, with one or two exceptions, government authorities, including regulatory agencies and the courts, are applying laws that have been on the books for years to this new market place. Because the Internet provides instant access to the entire world, without regard to state or national boundaries, and because it is exceptionally easy to gather information and to communicate over the Internet, users of the Internet often fall into the trap of thinking that anything goes. This is decidedly not the case.

How the Internet Functions

Today's Internet is a global resource connecting millions of users that began as an experiment over 20 years ago by the U.S. Department of Defense.[1] It began as a collection of computers housed at government institutions and universities that were connected so information could be shared over a network. In the 1980s, when computing power began to decrease in cost, the Internet began to become accessible to more and more people. By the mid-1990s, the Internet had entered the mainstream and was accessible to virtually anyone with a computer and a modem. To gain access to the web, you need an ISP **(server)** and an Internet browser. Some companies—such as MSN and AOL—offer ISP connections and a browser as part of their products and services, thereby making Internet access easy and convenient.

Because the Internet can be easily accessed, and because most businesses, including hotels, provide computer access to their employees, risks of illegality are created daily and in a way that is very difficult for a company to monitor. Some of the most notorious risks are discussed below.

Privacy Concerns

Privacy was the first important legal issue that sparked a debate with respect to the Internet. There is no privacy when you are online. First, whenever you are on the web, your movements are tracked. This is done automatically by use of devices known as **cookies** that create a database of your movements through the web that marketers can then use to try to sell you goods and services. For example, if you log onto a web site about "Dracula," the famous Transylvanian bloodsucker, you may well receive an email advertisement for trips to Transylvania to visit his castle. Second, numerous sites require that you enter information in order to gain access—such as your name and address—and every site that sells something requires you to enter a credit card number in order to complete the sale.

In 1998, the Federal Trade Commission (FTC) issued the first of three reports to Congress concerning privacy on the net. The FTC's concerns were that companies were gathering information on Internet surfers as well as Internet customers, and then using that information for marketing purposes, without giving clear notice. The result of these FTC concerns is that virtually every web site now has a privacy policy that states, in effect, that personal information will not be used, or if it will be used, how it will be used. A good example is the FTC's own privacy policy, found at http://www.ftc.gov/ftc/privacy.htm. If your web site does not have such a policy, you subject yourself to government investigation.[*]

On May 24, 2000, the FTC issued regulations restricting the use of personal information gathered by financial institutions, and requiring clear notice to the consumer of how such information might be used. Included within the scope of the law are certain travel agencies that also offer financial services.[2]

The FTC has also made it clear that it takes an exceedingly dim view toward "profiling" customers by tracking their movements on the web, and then selling such information to marketers. It has moved against web sites that use any element of deception in gathering such information,[3] and has issued a number of reports to Congress on the issue. Given the pressures from the FTC, it is probable that new laws concerning the use of such profiling information will be enacted shortly.

Antitrust Concerns

Use of the Internet also raises antitrust concerns. The first level of risk is created because communication by email is deceptively simple. Specifically, email has become an informal means of instant communication, utilized by virtually every computer user. Users have become accustomed to jotting down random thoughts and emailing them to friends and colleagues. Many believe that once the email is sent, and the copy deleted from the user's system, it disappears for all time. Precisely the opposite is true. Emails are tracked through the systems used to send them. They are stored, whether or not deleted by the user, on hard drives throughout the Internet, and can almost always be recovered. Because of the informality involved, users often write things that they would never put in a business letter or

---

[*] In 1998, Congress enacted the Children's Online Privacy Protections Act, making it illegal to collect information from children (under 13) without parental consent. The act sets specific guidelines to determine whether your web site might be one used by children and sets forth specific procedures to follow if a child attempts to use your web site—the primary one being obtaining parental consent.

would never say person-to-person. The obvious fear of the hotels is that such communications will be used to discuss prices or conditions of service among competitors, thus exposing the hotels involved to antitrust liability. (See Chapter 37 for a discussion of the prohibitions against competitors sharing such information.)

The second level of risk arises out of **business-to-business (B2B)** operations. B2B is used to describe web sites that offer businesses a way to purchase needed products. For example, PurchasePro and Zoho offer marketplaces for hotels, and both are supported by major hotel companies. The concern is that the web site will be used by competitors to share information. This concern arises because the web site becomes a "database" of competitive information since it tracks competitors' purchases. Moreover, competitors often join together to form such web site, or take an ownership interest in them. In such cases, the competitors, at least theoretically, may have access to each others' sensitive competitive information. The FTC is very concerned about such possibilities and continually investigates such services.

Similarly, there is concern when competitors join together to offer services to consumers over the web—a **business-to-consumer (B2C)** web site. The concern is that the competitors might be conspiring to drive out other service providers. As noted in Chapter 37, in February 2000 the American Society of Travel Agents (ASTA) asked the U.S. Justice Department to investigate possible antitrust violations by the major airlines which were opening a new joint web site to offer travel services to the public. Twenty-seven U.S. and foreign airlines said they would establish the joint web site in 2000 to offer many travel services, including airfares, hotels, car rentals, and other products. The travel agents claimed that the joint web site was "the finishing blow in a campaign calculated to destroy public access to comparative information about air travel services and to end once and for all the hope for a vigorous competitive industry that was the promise of airline deregulation in 1978."[4]

Despite these concerns, experts say that B2B and B2C are the most promising business possibilities for the industry.

Music Copyright Concerns

In Chapter 33, the necessity for a hotel to obtain a license to play copyrighted music is discussed. The Internet creates a whole new dimension to that subject matter, because music is readily available on the Internet, can easily be downloaded, and can then be played by the Internet user. Again, like email, this process is deceptively easy and because the Internet is so easy to use, the impression that one has a "right" to such music without compensation is a very common misconception.

In mid-2000 a company known as Napster burst into the newspaper headlines. By accessing Napster, a user could locate and share millions of music files with other users and could download copyrighted music without payment of a fee. Because digital technology was advanced, this meant that those people that downloaded music had no need to purchase CDs or tapes—they could create their own. Representatives of the recording industry sued Napster, asserting that it was engaged in massive violations of the music copyright laws. On July 26, 2000, the United States District Court issued an order, finding that Napster had violated the copyright laws and enjoining it from continuing its operations. Napster appealed and the case was settled by Napster agreeing to charge users a fee. This case followed on the heels of a verdict against another web music provider—MP3.com—for $100 million for copyright infringement (a case that was also settled).

The real target of the lawsuits were music users who accessed and then played copyrighted music without paying a fee. It was rumored at the time that the heavy-metal band Metallica and the rapper Dr. Dre would sue users of the Napster site, along with Napster itself—a ploy mooted by the aforementioned Napster settlement.

Use of music from a web site in a hotel requires a license and the blanket licenses from ASCAP, BMI, and SESAC, discussed in Chapter 33, will cover that use. Do not fall into the trap of thinking that because music is freely available over the web, it can be used in your hotel without appropriate licenses. The cases described above show that the recording industry will act swiftly to shut down illegal use of web-based music.

Employees' Use of the Web

It is widely reported that employees who have access to computers surf the web during their work day—sending personal emails, checking the stock market, shopping, and even visiting pornography sites. Without doubt, most do so under the false belief that their activities are not monitored. However, technology exists which allows an employer to monitor the web surfing of employees, and many employers use this technology.

When businesses provide computers to employees, it is for business reasons; however, it is also with the knowledge that employees, being human, will probably try to use the access for other purposes. It thus becomes imperative for employers to put in writing for the employees the restrictions on computer use, to warn the employee that the computer should not be used for personal reasons, and to make it clear that improper use of the computer can be grounds for sanctions against the employee, including dismissal. Absent such written warnings, a company risks being held liable for activities of the employee on the Internet. Moreover, employees should be warned that their computer activities are being monitored by the employer, in order to avoid employee claims of invasion of privacy. An extensive sample Communication Systems policy appears in the Appendix at the end of this chapter. A more general sample internet policy can be found online at HRZone (http://www.hrzone.com/topics/internet_policy.html).

Important Points for Management

- Make certain your web site has a privacy policy.
- Warn employees concerning the use of email—specifically, that emails are saved and care should be taken in composing them.
- If you use music obtained from the Internet, make certain you have copyright licenses in place.
- Develop an Internet use policy for employees.

References

1. http://www.cis.ohio-state.edu/htbin/rfc/rfc1462.html
   For more information, see Ed Krol, *The Whole Internet User's Guide and Catalog*, (Sebastopol, Calif.: O'Reilly & Associates, Inc., 1992).
2. http://www.ftc.gov/opa/2000/02/glbact.htm
3. http://www.ftc.gov./opa/1998/9808/geocitie.htm
4. http://www.astanet.com/news/releasearchive/05_18_00.html

Key Terms

business-to-business (B2B)—Web sites that market goods or services to businesses.

business-to-consumer (B2C)—Web sites that market goods or services to customers or consumers.

cookies—A small text file that a website can place on your computer's hard drive to collect information about your activities on the site.

server—A computer that "serves" information into the Internet.

Review Questions

1. What is a "privacy policy" as it relates to information gathered by a web site on visitors to the web site?

2. What is a "profiling" of visitors to a web site?

3. To what extent do the anti-trust laws apply to the Internet?

4. To what extent do the music copyright laws apply to the Internet?

5. How should a company restrict employees' use of the Internet?

Internet Sites

For more information, visit the following Internet sites. Remember that Internet addresses can change without notice.

American Hotel & Lodging Association
http://www.ahla.com

American Society of Travel Agents (ASTA)
http://www.astanet.com

Children's Online Privacy Protection Act of 1998
http://www.ftc.gov/ogc/coppa1.htm

Federal Trade Commission (FTC)
http://www.ftc.gov

FTC Privacy Initiatives
http://www.ftc.gov/privacy/index.html

GotRooms
http://www.gotrooms.com

Napster
http://www.napster.com

PurchasePro
http://www.purchasepro.com

U.S. Department of Justice
http://www.usdoj.gov

Zoho
http://www.zoho.com

Appendix
Sample Electronic Communication Systems and Resources Policy

In the course of your job, you may use the Firm's Electronic Communication Systems and Resources to communicate internally with Firm co-workers or externally with clients, consultants, vendors, and other business contacts and to accomplish your job objectives. For purposes of this policy, Electronic Communication Systems and Resources shall be defined as the equipment, systems, and software that is licensed, owned, developed, stored, or provided by the Firm including but not limited to:

- modems
- computer networks
- document scanners
- electronic pagers
- voice-mail systems
- CD-ROM players and disks
- facsimile (fax) machines
- Intranet and Internet access
- telephone lines for modem communication
- office, portable, cellular, and/or digital phones
- desktop and laptop computers and peripheral equipment
- computer software
- electronic files and storage media such as floppy disks, drives, backup tapes, and removable storage media
- Firm and client information created or contained on or accessible through any of the above

(Collectively referred to as "Communication Systems").

The Firm provides some or all of the Communications Systems to you, as an employee of the Firm, to facilitate business communication and to enhance your productivity. As with telephone, there may be occasion to use these Communication Systems for personal communication. Personal use is permitted so long as it does not interfere with your performance of your job, consume significant resources, or interfere with the activities of other personnel. When making use of these Firm-provided Communication Systems for personal use, always remember that you should not assume that these usages or messages are private and confidential. The policy, as set forth below, is intended to assist and protect the Firm and its personnel in the course of conducting work. All personnel are required to comply with this policy. Use of the Communication Systems shall constitute your consent to this policy.

1. All Communication Systems are the property of the Firm and are provided to support the business of the Firm and its customers. All usage of the Communication System must comply with all international, federal, and state laws, or the laws of the United Kingdom, where applicable. Penalties for violations may include discipline, termination, and/or civil or criminal prosecution.

2. Although the Firm respects the personal privacy of our personnel, users of the Communication Systems do not have a right of privacy in messages sent or received or in any files stored on the Communications Systems. Computer files, email messages, voice-mail messages, and other data exchanged or stored on the Communication Systems are Firm property and the Firm retains the right to view any message or information on the Communication Systems without notice to, or permission from, the user and to remove any inappropriate material. Please note, although we use passwords and user IDs to access our computers, voice-mail, and email systems, these access codes are intended to protect the Firm's confidential information from outside third parties and not your personal files and messages. These systems are intended for Firm business use, and all computer information, voice-mail, and email messages are presumptively considered Firm records.

3. The Firm has regular procedures concerning the retention and deletion of email and voice-mail messages.

4. The use of foul, obscene, sexually explicit, or harassing language or images in connection with voice-mail, email, or the Internet (as with other Firm resources) is prohibited. All personnel are expected to act professionally when using the Communication Systems and should not send messages that harass or annoy other personnel or third parties. This includes email or Internet messages meant as a joke but that create either a sexually offensive or otherwise hostile work environment in violation of the Firm's harassment policy. The Firm does not tolerate harassment or discrimination and, accordingly, personnel committing such an offense will be subject to discipline, up to and including immediate termination. Under no circumstances may any posting, voice-mail, or email be in violation of the letter or the spirit of the Firm's Equal Employment Opportunity or Harassment policies.

5. Voice-mail, email, electronic files, and Internet messages should be treated with the same concern for Firm and client security and confidentiality as written documents or oral statements. Accordingly, confidential documents that are to be emailed or sent by fax transmission to clients should be as protected as if receipt by a third party would result in a breach of confidentiality. Similarly, voice-mail messages that contain confidential information should be forwarded only to personnel with a "need to know."

6. Employees are encouraged to discuss with customers their preferred methods of communication via their telecommunications, fax, and computer systems. Some clients provide explicit directions regarding transmittal of information,

especially information that may be confidential or privileged. Some information should not be committed to email, voice-mail, fax, or computer systems if there is risk of the loss of privilege.

7. Users are responsible for any damage caused to the Firm's Communication Systems through willful, reckless, or negligent conduct. A particular concern is when users fail to insure the integrity of electronic data by introducing a virus into the Firm's Communication Systems. All external program and data files received by the Firm, including those received electronically, must be scanned for computer viruses before use on any Firm computer. If found, viruses must be eliminated and reported to the home or local office help desk or the systems administrator in your office.

8. All personnel are prohibited from using any Communication Systems to solicit or conduct non-Firm business or commercial ventures or for political or religious purposes. Personnel should not encourage family members, friends, or non-Firm businesspersons to send non-Firm business messages or information to personnel by means of the Firm's electronic information Communication Systems.

9. The primary use for the Firm's Internet connection is for business purposes. This includes the interaction with other businesses' public areas on the Internet, replies to clients, and using the Internet as a research tool to accomplish your job objectives or other similar business activities. Personnel may not use the Firm's Internet connection or the Communication Systems to obtain pirated software, videos, photographs, or music; to steal passwords for hacking other machines on the Internet; or to participate in the viewing or exchange of pornography or obscene materials, sending discriminatory or harassing email, chain letters, or jokes; or engaging in any other illegal or tortious activities. (For your protection, personnel need to understand that technology permits web page providers to record the email address of any party viewing their web page.) The Firm reserves the right to filter or otherwise block certain sites from being accessed by personnel.

The Firm retains the right to change this policy and its practices with regard to the retention and deleting of email and voice-mail messages at any time with or without notice.

Appendix A
A Glossary of Selected Legal Terms

abandoned property—Property to which the owner has voluntarily relinquished all right, title, claim, and possession with the intention of terminating his/her ownership, but without vesting it in any other person, and with no intention of reclaiming possession or resuming ownership and enjoyment in the future.

"Mislaid property" is that which is intentionally put in a certain place and later forgotten. Under common law, a finder acquired no rights to mislaid property. The general rule now is that the finder is entitled to possession of lost property against everyone except the true owner.

abrogate—To repeal a former law by legislative act, or by usage.

act of God—A casualty, loss, or event caused by direct, immediate, and exclusive operation of the forces of nature, uncontrolled or uninfluenced by the power of human beings.

affirmative duty—The duty or obligation of making proof, in the first instance, of matters alleged or in the pleadings of the court; in other words, the duty to sustain the burden of proof.

a fortiori—(Latin) "With stronger reason." That is, if one fact exists, therefore another fact, which is included therein, must exist.

agency—Presupposes a directing principal and a directed agent under delegation of authority to the agent, either by contract, express or implied, or by operation of law, estoppel, or ratification.

allegation—The assertion or statement of a party to a lawsuit made in a pleading, setting out what the party expects to prove in court.

amicus curiae—(Latin) "A friend of the court." Someone who is not a party to the case but is permitted by the court to furnish information on some matter of the law that may affect the case.

appeal—The removal of a cause from an inferior court to one of superior jurisdiction for the purpose of obtaining a review. The term "appeal" indicates a reexamination by a higher tribunal of issues determined in original trial. The term "appeal" has a double significance and may be used to designate the act of lodging the action in the appellate court and also the action itself, when in the appellate court.

appellate court—A court of review to determine whether the rulings and judgment of the court below on the case were correct. It is not a forum in which to make a new case.

appurtenance—An attachment or adjunct to the principal property.

assault—An attempt to commit violent injury upon the person of another. Physical contact is not necessary. An assault is an act done toward the commission of a battery, and immediately precedes the battery.

bailee—A person with whom personalty (personal property) is entrusted; generally bears a heavy burden of proof to avoid liability.

bailment—The delivery of personalty (personal property) for some particular purpose, or on mere deposit, upon a contract, express or implied, that after purpose has been fulfilled it shall be redelivered to the person who delivered it, or otherwise dealt with according to his/her directions, or kept until he/she reclaims it, as the case may be.

bailor—A person who entrusts his/her property to another.

battery—An actual infliction of a blow without the consent of the person who receives it. While an "assault" is an attempt by violence to hurt another, a "battery" occurs when the violence is accomplished.

binding—Legally enforceable.

bona fide—(Latin) In "good faith"; honestly, openly, and sincerely; without deceit or fraud.

breach of contract—A failure, without legal excuse, to perform any promise that forms the whole or part of a contract.

burden of proof—The burden or duty of satisfying the minds of the jury of the truth of all the material facts alleged by the plaintiff and denied by the defendant.

business invitee—A person who is invited or permitted to enter or to use such part of the premises as the visitor reasonably believes are held open to him/her as a means of access to or egress from the place where that person's business is to be transacted.

cause of action—A matter for which an action may be brought; the ground on which an action may be brought.

caveat—(Latin) "Let him beware."

civil action or civil suit—A proceeding in a court by one party against another for the enforcement or protection of a private right or the redress of a private wrong.

civil rights—Those personal and natural rights of each human being protected by the U.S. Constitution, in particular the Thirteenth and Fourteenth Amendments, and other federal and state laws. Examples of such civil rights include the freedom of speech, press, and religion, the right to be free of discrimination based on race, color, creed, religion, etc.

class action or class suit—A suit in which one or more members of a numerous class, having a common interest, sue on behalf of themselves and all other members of that class.

common law—The general Anglo-American system of legal concepts and the traditional legal technique that forms the basis of the law of the states that have invoked it.

While there have been conflicting theories as to the origin of the common law in the North American Colonies, it is generally settled that the Law of England, as it existed at the time of the colonial settlements, is the basis of the common law in this country (with the exception of Louisiana).

The common law is a system of unwritten law not evidenced by statute, but by traditions and the opinions and judgments of courts of law.

compensatory damages—Awarded to make good or to replace loss caused by a wrong or injury; are confined to compensating for injuries sustained. They do not include punitive damages.

complaint—Gives the adverse party notice of the claims asserted against it. It does not narrow the issues, or give notice of precise factual basis of plaintiff's claim, or provide a means for an early adjudication of a claim.

concession—A privilege or space granted or leased for a particular use within specified premises. An example is a concession for a flower shop on the hotel premises.

constructive bailee—A person who comes into lawful possession of the personal property of another other than by mutual contract of bailment, and may be treated as bailee of such property by operation of law.

constructive possession—The position of exercising dominion or control over a thing.

contempt—A willful disregard of the authority of the court or disobedience of its lawful orders.

contract—A legal agreement creating legally enforceable obligations between two or more parties. To have a contract, there must be an offer, an acceptance, and consideration to support the formation of a legally enforceable agreement.

conviction—The final consummation of prosecution against the accused, including judgment or sentence rendered pursuant to a verdict, confession, or plea of guilty to criminal offense.

copyright—Common law and/or statutory rights to publish and reproduce works of art or literature and the exclusive privilege of printing, or otherwise multiplying, publishing, and vending copies of certain literary or artistic productions. The legal effect of a copyright is to create in the owner an exclusive property right with the incidental power to lease or license the use thereof by others on stipulated terms.

copyright infringement—The unauthorized use or performance of a copyrighted musical composition.

court—A tribunal empowered to hear and determine questions of law and fact, either with or without a jury, upon pleadings either oral or written and upon evidence to be adduced under well-defined and established rules according to settled principles of law.

crime—An act or omission that is prohibited by law as injurious to the public and punished by the state in a proceeding in its own name or in the name of the people.

damages—Pecuniary compensation that may be recovered in court by a person who has suffered a loss or injury to his/her person or property, through an unlawful act, omission, or negligence of another.

derogation—The partial repeal or abolishing of a law.

due process of law—When applied to judicial proceedings, a course of legal proceedings according to those rules and principles that have been established in our systems of jurisprudence for the enforcement and protection of private rights.

essential functions—The fundamental job duties of a particular employment position.

et seq.—(Latin) "And the following."

exculpatory clause—An agreement whereby one party seeks to absolve itself from liability even if negligent.

executor—A person appointed by the testator to carry out the directions and requests in the testator's will, and to dispose of the testator's property according to the will.

ex parte—(Latin) Refers to a judicial proceeding taken or granted at the insistence of and for the benefit of one party only, and without the necessity of the other party's presence.

false imprisonment—The detention of a person without his/her consent and without lawful authority.

family leave—A type of leave that can be taken under the Family and Medical Leave Act for the birth, adoption, or foster-care placement of a child in order to care for that child.

family member—According to the Family and Medical Leave Act (FMLA), one's spouse, child, or parent. The FMLA definition does not include siblings or parents-in-law.

felony—A criminal offense usually punishable by a jail term of over one year (and generally by confinement in the state penitentiary). (See MISDEMEANOR)

fiduciary relationship—A relationship in which one party is under a duty to act for or give advice for benefit of another upon matters within the scope of the trust relation and where a special confidence is reposed in another who in equity and good conscience is bound to act in good faith and with due regard to interests of the person reposing confidence.

foreseeability—In a suit alleging negligence, the plaintiff generally must show in part that the defendant innkeeper had a duty to use reasonable care to protect the plaintiff or victim from foreseeable acts. An injury is foreseeable if a person of ordinary prudence would have foreseen that such an injury might and probably would result from the act of negligence. It does not mean that the negligent party ought reasonably to have foreseen a particular consequence or precise form of injury, or a particular manner of occurrence, or that it would occur to a particular person.

forgery—A crime generally defined as the false making or materially altering, with intent to defraud, of any writing, which, if genuine, might apparently be of legal efficacy, or the foundation of legal liability.

franchise—As used in this book, a franchise is an agreement by which the franchisee undertakes to conduct a business or sell a product or service in accordance with methods and procedures prescribed by the franchisor; the franchiser undertakes to assist the franchisee through advertising, promotion, and other advisory services; the franchise may encompass an exclusive right to sell a product or service or conduct a business in a specified territory.

franchise tax—A tax on the franchise of a corporation, that is, on the right and privilege of carrying on business as a corporation.

fraud—An action calculated to deceive (including acts, omissions, and concealments) involving a breach of a legal or equitable duty, trust, or confidence that results in damage to another.

gratuitous bailee—A person who comes into possession of the personal property of another, receives nothing from the owner of the property, and has no right to recover from the owner for what he/she does in caring for the property. A gratuitous bailee is liable only to the bailor for bad faith or gross negligence.

gratuity—Something given voluntarily or beyond obligation.

gross negligence—Is substantially and appreciably higher in magnitude and more culpable than ordinary negligence. Gross negligence is equivalent to the failure to exercise even a slight degree of care. It is very great negligence, or the absence of slight diligence, or the want of even scant care; and a disregard of consequences that may ensue from the act; and indifference to rights of others. (See ORDINARY NEGLIGENCE)

guest register—A written record of the guest's name, address, date of arrival, and date of departure.

indemnify—To secure against loss or damages.

independent contractor—One who, in exercise of an independent employment, contracts to do a piece of work according to his/her own methods and is subject to his/her employer's control only as to end product or final result of the work.

individual with a disability—Broadly, anyone who has a physical or mental impairment that substantially limits one or more life activities, has a record of such an impairment, or is regarded as having such an impairment.

infra—(Latin) "Below, beneath, hereafter" in the text. The opposite of *supra,* or above.

infra hospitium—(Latin) "Within the inn." Under the doctrine of *infra hospitium,* the innkeeper's liability for loss of a guest's property attaches only where property was within the walls of the inn itself, or, if outside, was in the care and under the charge of the innkeeper.

injunction—A judicial process whereby a party is required by the court to do or refrain from doing a particular thing.

insurer—One who undertakes or is obligated to compensate the other for loss or damage to person or property.

inter alia—(Latin) "Among other things."

jurisdiction—May be defined simply as the court's right or authority to adjudicate concerning subject matter of a particular controversy. The word "jurisdiction" includes jurisdiction over subject matter, over the parties, and power or authority to decide particular matters presented, and lack of any essential is fatal to judgment.

larceny—An unlawful taking and carrying away of personal property without the consent of and against the will of the owner, and with a felonious intent to deprive the person of the property permanently.

liable—Obligated in law or equity to make satisfaction, pay compensation, or make restitution.

lien—A charge upon real or personal property for the payment of a debt or obligation owed. A hold or claim that one person has upon the real or personal property of another as security for some debt or charge.

malicious prosecution—A criminal prosecution instituted upon no, or such slight, grounds of suspicion as to indicate general disregard of the rights of others.

medical leave—A type of leave that can be taken under the Family and Medical Leave Act to care for a spouse, child, or parent with a "serious health condition," or because of a "serious health condition" that makes an employee unable to perform the function of his or her position.

misdemeanor—Generally, a less serious crime that is punishable by fines or jail terms not to exceed one year. (See FELONY)

negligence—In absence of statute, negligence is generally defined as the doing of that thing which a reasonably prudent person would not have done, or the failure to do that thing which a reasonably prudent person would have done, under like or similar facts and circumstances.

ordinary negligence—The failure to exercise care that ordinarily prudent persons would exercise in like or similar circumstances. (See GROSS NEGLIGENCE)

party—A person who is actively included in the prosecution or defense of a legal proceeding.

path of travel—A continuous, unobstructed way of pedestrian passage by which an altered area may be approached, entered, and exited, and which connects the altered area with an exterior approach (including sidewalks, streets, and parking areas), an entrance to the facility, and other parts of the facility. It includes restrooms, telephones, and drinking fountains serving the altered area.

per se—(Latin) In and of itself; taken alone; inherently.

plaintiff—A person who brings a lawsuit against another person.

prima facie **evidence**—That degree of proof that unexplained or uncontradicted by other evidence is sufficient, if credited by a jury, to establish an unlawful intent.

probable cause—Exists when facts and circumstances within one's knowledge, and of which one has reasonably trustworthy information, are sufficient in themselves to warrant a person of reasonable caution to act in the belief that a crime has been or is being committed.

promulgate—To publish; to announce officially.

proximate cause of injury—That primary moving predominating cause from which an injury follows as a natural, direct, and immediate consequence, and without which it would not have occurred.

punitive damages—Damages, other than compensatory or nominal damages, awarded against a person to punish him/her for outrageous conduct. The chief purpose of punitive damages is to inflict punishment as an example and a deterrent to similar conduct.

qualified individual with a disability—A person with a disability who satisfies the requisite skill, experience, education, and other job-related requirements of the employment position that the person holds or desires to hold and who, with or without reasonable accommodation, can perform the position's essential functions.

readily achievable—Easily accomplishable and able to be carried out without much difficulty or expense.

reasonable—Just and proper; ordinary or usual; not excessive.

reasonable accommodations—(1) Modifications or adjustments that are made to a job application process to enable a qualified applicant with a disability to be considered for employment, and (2) modifications or adjustments made to the work environment, or to the manner or circumstances under which a job position is customarily performed, that enable a qualified individual with a disability to perform the essential functions of that position.

rebuttable presumption—Gives particular effect to a certain group of facts in the absence of further evidence, and presumption provides *prima facie* case that shifts to defendant the burden to go forward with evidence to contradict or rebut fact presumed.

remand—To send a case brought into the appellate court back to the lower court it came from so that further proceedings in the case, if any, may be taken there.

royalty—A payment made by a licensee for the right to perform music.

search warrant—An order in writing in the name of the state, signed by a magistrate and directed to a peace officer commanding him/her to search for personal property and bring it before the magistrate.

serious health condition—According to the Family and Medical Leave Act, any illness, injury, impairment, or physical mental condition that involves either

(a) in-patient care in a hospital, hospice, or residential medical care facility; or (b) continuing treatment by a health-care provider.

service of process—Simply defined, a procedure by which the court may obtain jurisdiction over the person of a defendant by service of a writ so that the defendant may be brought into court.

slander—Words falsely spoken that are injurious to the reputation of another. False defamatory words, when written, constitute a libel.

statute—An act of the legislature; a particular law enacted by the legislative branch of the government.

statute of limitations—Any law that fixes the time within which parties may take judicial action to enforce rights or else be thereafter barred from enforcing them.

subpoena—A writ of process in the name of the court authorized by law to issue same. A subpoena is a command to appear at a certain time and place, on a certain date, to give testimony upon a certain matter. Subpoena is the order of an arm of the state compelling the presence of a person under threat of contempt.

A "subpoena duces tecum" is a court process compelling production of certain specified documents and other items, material and relevant to the facts in issue in a pending judicial proceeding, which documents and items are in custody and control of the person or body served with the process.

summary judgment—Loosely defined, a judgment decreed by a court in a case pending before it when, as a matter of law, proceedings show that there is no issue of fact between the parties.

summary proceedings—Any proceedings by which a controversy is settled, case disposed of, or trial conducted in a prompt and simple manner, without the aid of a jury.

summons—A written notice required to bring a defendant into court. A summons is designed to apprise the defendant that the plaintiff in the action seeks judgment against him/her and that at a stated time and place the defendant is to appear and answer the complaint against him/her.

supra—(Latin) "Above." In written text, refers to a previous section.

tort—A civil wrong resulting in damage. The essence of a tort is that it is an unlawful act, done in violation of the legal rights of someone.

Although the same act may constitute both a "crime" and a "tort," the crime is an offense against the public pursued by the government, while the tort is a private injury that is redressed at the suit of the injured party.

tortious—Wrongful.

trespass, common law act of—Every unauthorized entry is a trespass, regardless of the degree of force used.

verdict—A decision made by the jury and reported to the court on matters lawfully submitted to the jury in the course of the trial of a case.

warrantless search—A search of property without a search warrant.

Appendix B
Franchise Contract XYZ Motel Franchise Sysem

Selected Provisions

THIS AGREEMENT OF CONTRACT, entered into at Stardust, Nevada, as of the ____ day of _____, 20____, by and between XYZ MOTEL FRAN-CHISE CORPORATION, a Nevada corporation with principal offices at Stardust Building, Nevada, hereinafter referred to as "Franchisor," and _____ whose address is, _____ hereinafter re-ferred to as "Franchisee";

W I T N E S S E T H:

THAT, WHEREAS, Franchisor has acquired and developed a system (herein-after called the "System") with certain distinctive characteristics for providing the general public a motel and motel service of high quality; and

WHEREAS, Franchisee wishes to acquire and exercise the rights and privi-leges, and have the benefit of the advantages provided to Franchisees arising out of membership in the XYZ Motel System, including the superb reputation for hotel operations which it presently enjoys, and to offer said services to the motoring public; and

WHEREAS, it is recognized by the parties hereto that the continued success of the XYZ Motel System on a nationwide basis depends in large measure upon faith-ful adherence to the principles of the System, including maintenance of the highest standard of quality, efficiency, cleanliness and courtesy at each motel.

NOW, THEREFORE, IN CONSIDERATION OF THE FOREGOING PREM-ISES, the mutual promises of the parties to each other, and other good and valuable consideration, the parties hereto agree as follows:

Granting of Franchise, Description of Licensed Premises and Area of Operation, and Distinguishing Characteristics of System

A. Franchisor hereby grants to Franchisee the non-exclusive right and privilege, subject to the terms and conditions hereinafter set out, to use the System here-inafter described in the operation of a motor hotel to be known and identified as an XYZ Motel and the following location:

A legal description of the premises hereinabove identified is attached to this Contract.

B. Franchisor will grant no similar right or privilege to any other similar motor hotel to operate as an XYZ Motel within _____ miles from the nearest point in the boundary of the premises described in Paragraph A above during the term of this Contract.

C. The XYZ Motel System is identified to members of the public who travel by motor vehicle by:

1. Prominent display of signs, emblems, symbols and logos including the words or terms "XYZ Motel," either alone or in combination with the decor, insignia, color scheme, marks, and/or the distinctive services now or hereinafter prescribed by Franchisor, all as shall be chosen and used in the manner to be determined exclusively by Franchisor, or as used in the System, or as used in connection with the national system of XYZ Motels throughout the United States of America;

2. The System seeks to establish and maintain among all its members uniformly high standards in such features as are most highly regarded by the motoring public, including readily recognizable facilities, lodgings of high cleanliness and staffed by courteous and efficient employees, adequate and safe parking facilities, accessory accommodations and conveniences, scrupulously fair, ethical and honest business practices in its relations with the traveling public, and also with those members of the community wherein the facility is located; and

3. Standardized methods of operation, including reservation service and immediate recognition of reservations made pursuant thereto, courteous management and readily recognizable local and regional advertising based upon use of the distinctive identifying trademarks, service marks, signs, emblems, symbols, slogans and logos, not only in displays available to the motoring public on the road but in its lodgings, advertisements in the media and other facilities of each XYZ Motel occupied or used by the motoring public.

Franchise and Service Fees

In consideration of the promises and assurances of Franchisor, and the services rendered and to be rendered to Franchisee by Franchisor, and other benefits provided by this Contract, Franchisee agrees to make the following payments at the time or times as indicated:

[List]

Obligations and Duties of Franchisee

Franchisee expressly recognizes and acknowledges the property rights and interest of Franchisor in the XYZ Motel System, and all the distinguishing characteristics thereof, including but not limited to the copyrights, trademarks, service marks, trade names, patents, logos, emblems, symbols, and identifying features, and such others as Franchisor may from time to time develop or acquire during the term of this Contract, and expressly recognizes the right of Franchisor to use, and to grant to Franchisee and to others the right to use any or all of said copyright, marks, names and identification devices and others, in connection with said System.

Franchisee agrees to use the rights and privileges granted to it by Franchisor in strict compliance with the provisions of this Contract, and with such reasonable rules and regulations as Franchisor shall adopt, as to which it shall notify Franchisee, and not otherwise, and to conduct its operations as Franchisee at the location(s) herein described. In furtherance thereof Franchisee expressly agrees as follows:

A. To establish and maintain high standards of service and atmosphere at Franchisee's XYZ Motels; to comply with all federal, state and local laws, ordinances, rules and regulations pertaining thereto; to maintain its premises and accommodations in a clean, safe and orderly manner; and to provide high quality, courteous and efficient "XYZ Motel System" service to the public; and to furnish accommodations, services and conveniences of the same quality, type and distinguishing characteristics as are provided in existing XYZ Motels, to the end that the Motel operated by Franchisee under this contract shall help to create good will among the public for the "XYZ Motel System" as a whole, so that Franchisor, Franchisee and each member of said System shall be benefitted and the public assured of uniform high quality, courteous and efficient service on a standardized national basis;

B. To promote and feature in the operation of the Franchisee's Motel covered by this Contract, and in all advertising matter the words "XYZ Motels" together with the distinguishing characteristics of the System;

C. To observe all reasonable rules of operation which Franchisor shall establish or revise or amend from time to time hereafter, the rights of revision and amendment being reserved to the Franchisor, said rules to be promulgated only as necessary for maintenance of uniform quality and standards within the system, and to be communicated with all possible dispatch to Franchisee;

D. The rights and privileges hereby granted to Franchisee are exclusive only as to the specific location described herein. The rights herein granted may be sold, assigned, leased, sublet, pledged or otherwise transferred only in accordance with the provisions for transfer hereinafter set out in this Contract;

E. To permit regular inspection of all accommodations, facilities, premises and procedures by inspectors duly authorized and identified by direction of the Board of Directors of Franchisor;

F. To submit monthly to Franchisor the standard operation report in the form approved by Franchisor and such other reports as may be required by Franchisor from time to time [etc.]; and

G. To cause to be prepared and delivered to Franchisor, no later than ninety (90) days after the close of the fiscal year of Franchisee, whether the same be calendar year or other, a statement of operations and balance sheet for Franchisee's "XYZ Motel" which statement shall bear the certificate of an independent certified public accountant authorized to practice in the State wherein Franchisees XYZ Motel shall be located, which statement shall show gross revenues received from room rentals, from restaurant operations, if any, and from such other sales and activities providing revenue as Franchisee may conduct within said annual period.

Services of Franchisor

In addition to, and implementation of, the grant by Franchisor to Franchisee of the rights and privileges of membership in and identification with XYZ Motel, Franchisor will provide Franchisee certain services as follows:

A. Opportunities for Franchisee's personnel to consult with Franchisors staff upon problems which may be encountered in operating Franchisee's property;

B. To assist Franchisee in installing and carrying out efficient methods of inn operation, as nearly similar to those now practiced in other XYZ Motels operating under the System as Franchisee's circumstances will allow;

C. To assure compliance with Franchisor's standards of cleanliness, efficiency, cour-tesy, and general high quality of accommodations, Franchisor will provide for periodic visits and inspections of Franchisees premises by authorized and qualified inspectors and/or officers of Franchisor;

D. To make available to Franchisee an XYZ Motel sign for rental upon the terms hereinabove described, if Franchisee shall prefer to rent same; also to make available to Franchisee other signs, and all forms, informational bulletins, stationery, and other promotional material which are from time to time made available to other Franchisees;

E. The continued operation, under Franchisor's direction and control, of the System's Advertising Fund, whose principal purpose shall be to encourage the traveling public to use XYZ Motels, on a local, regional and where appropriate national basis, and to take all available opportunities to enhance the image of XYZ Motels as a provider of reliable lodgings for travelers; and

F. Opportunities, upon request of Franchisee, to send Franchisee's supervisory and other responsible personnel to visit other existing XYZ Motels and observe their operations. The expense of any such visits and observations as may be made shall be borne by Franchisee.

Relation of Parties

Franchisee is and shall be an independent contractor and nothing herein contained shall be construed so as to create an agency relationship, a partnership, or joint venture, or employer-employee relationship between the parties. Franchisor shall not regulate the employment or discharge of employees of Franchisee nor shall it supervise their working conditions except to the extent necessary to protect Franchisor's trade names, trademarks, and good will associated therewith.

Franchisor will provide and Franchisee will place in a conspicuous location on Franchisee's premises, a sign which shall state to the public, in effect, that Franchisee's Motel, and each XYZ Motel, is independently owned and operated.

Restaurant Facilities

In the event Franchisee shall operate a restaurant, or lease a portion of the premises to others for such purpose, Franchisee shall be responsible for the maintenance of the restaurant accommodations and will maintain a high quality rating from local health authorities.

Indemnity and Insurance Agreement

Franchisee recognizes that the conduct of its business as a Motel, providing lodging and related services to travelers, and its identification as a member of the XYZ Motel System may result in the misidentification of Franchisee as a subsidiary, partner, joint venturer, agent, or employee of Franchisor, when, in fact, no such relationship exists nor is any intended. Franchisee is an independent contractor. In order to prevent and avoid such misidentification, it is agreed as follows:

A.   Franchisee will not use the name "XYZ Motels" or any combination thereof in any form in the establishment or conduct of its business in operating its motel. Said term shall in no instance be a part of any corporate, partnership, or proprietorship name used in the operation of the Motel. Franchisee further agrees to take all actions and precautions necessary fully to inform trade creditors of Franchisee's sole responsibility for all expenses incurred in the operation of its motel, and to make no purchase in the name of "XYZ Motels." Nor will Franchisee use any of said names or words, nor service marks nor trademarks of the Franchisor in providing products or services, except in providing lodging, accommodations and conveniences for the public of the same nature, type, quality and distinguishing characteristics as may be provided at other existing XYZ Motels. Franchisee agrees to indemnify and hold Franchisor harmless from all losses which may be occasioned by Franchisee's violation or disregard of the foregoing provisions.

B.   Franchisee will obtain and maintain in force at all times during the term of this Contract a policy or policies of general liability insurance, in which Franchisor shall be named as an additional insured, insuring Franchisee and Franchisor against all claims for personal injury, debts, or property damage occurring on or about the premises of Franchisee or adjacent thereto, or arising out of the activities of persons for whose actions Franchisee may be responsible, with policy limits of not less than $_____ for injury to each person, and $_____ for injuries arising out of each accident, $_____ for property damage, and $_____ against liability commonly described as products liability.

Franchisee shall also provide such Workers Compensation, or similar insurance as will comply with the law of the State in which this franchise is to be exercised. Franchisee may, and Franchisor recommends that Franchisee, carry adequate insurance against fire and other hazards called extended coverage, and business interruption insurance and other insurance.

[List]

Notwithstanding the provisions relating to obtaining and maintaining insurance, Franchisee further covenants and agrees that it will indemnify and save harmless Franchisor from any and all claims, liability, responsibility and damage, or any costs or expenses which Franchisor may incur by reason of any loss of life or injury to persons or property that may be sustained in connection with the operation of Franchisee's XYZ Motel or other injury to persons or property occurring on the premises or resulting from the activities of employees of Franchisee for whom it is responsible.

Termination of Agreement. [This section sets forth the reasons for termination, such as the following:]

(1) **Termination for Violation or Breach of Provisions**
(2) **Termination for Bankruptcy**
(3) **Termination Without Fault of Either Party**
(4) **Termination by Franchisee Without Fault**
(5) **Rights and Duties of Franchisee and Franchisor Upon Termination**

Transfer of Franchisee's Rights in the Property Devoted to Use as an XYZ Motel

The Franchisee, upon signing this Contract, grants to the Franchisor the right of first refusal to acquire the property or property interests, whether ownership in fee, leasehold, or other, which Franchisee devotes to use as the premises of the Motel. The rights as a Franchisee acquired pursuant to this Contract shall be included in said right of first refusal, if offered for transfer by Franchisee. Said right of first refusal herein provided shall continue during the term of the Contract and of such extension and renewals thereof as may be entered into between the parties [etc.].

Severability

Any provision of this agreement which is prohibited by law or by court decree, in any locality or state, shall **ipso facto** be inoperative to the extent of such prohibition, without in any way invalidating or affecting the remaining provisions of this agreement, or without invalidating or affecting the provisions of this agreement within states and localities where not prohibited by law or court decree, it being the intention of the parties that the various conditions and provisions herein be severable in nature.

Construction, Integration and Enforcement

A. This instrument constitutes the entire agreement between the parties, and any oral or written representations between the parties which are not set forth herein shall be without force and effect.

B. It is stipulated that this agreement has been negotiated in, and shall be construed and enforced according to the laws of the State of Nevada, without regard to the location in which the signatures of one or more parties may have been affixed.

Notices

A. All notices to Franchisor shall be personally delivered to the President or Secretary of Franchisor or sent by registered or certified mail addressed to Franchisor or such officers at the following address:

XYZ Motel Franchise Corporation
Stardust, Nevada

B. All notices to Franchisee shall be sent by registered or certified U.S. Mail addressed to Franchisee at:

[Address]

Amendments

A. **Amendment to System.** The Franchisor expressly reserves the right reasonably to revise, amend, and change the XYZ Motel System or any part thereof. The System, as so changed, revised or amended from time to time shall be deemed for all purposes to be the System referred to in this agreement. Any such revision, amendment or change shall be promptly communicated to the Franchisee. Any and all improvements in said System developed by the Franchisee, Franchisor or other Franchisees shall be and become the sole and absolute property of Franchisor, and Franchisor may incorporate the same in said System and have the sole and exclusive right to register, copyright, and/or patent such improvements in Franchisor's own name, and Franchisee shall have no right to patent, register, and/or copyright such improvements in Franchisee's name; Franchisee shall have no right to use such improvements except in the manner herein set forth.

B. **Amendments to this Agreement.** The provisions of this agreement shall remain in effect during the term hereof, unless sooner terminated in accordance with the provisions hereof. Provided, nevertheless, any term or provision of this agreement may be amended, revised, or eliminated by mutual agreement in writing signed by duly authorized representatives of the parties hereto.

Waiver

No delay, omission, or forbearance, or failure on the part of Franchisor to exercise any right, option, duty or power arising out of any breach or default by Franchisee, or by any other Franchisee, of any of the terms, provisions or covenants hereof shall constitute a waiver by Franchisor to enforce such right, option or power against Franchisee as to such breach, or as to any subsequent breach or default by Franchisee.

Previous Agreements

The signing of this contract automatically terminates any previous contract or agreement between Franchisor and Franchisee applicable to the premises described herein, and supersedes any previous agreement or contract concerning the XYZ Motel System so applicable.

IN WITNESS WHEREOF, we have fixed our hands hereto this _____ day of _____, 20____.

XYZ MOTEL CORPORATION

By _____

"Franchisor"

_____ [Name of Franchisee] _____

WITNESSED BY:

_____

By _____

Authorized Representative

"Franchisee"

Appendix C

National Labor Relations Act

Codified at 29 U.S.C. ch. 7, subch. II

Selected Provisions Only

§151. Findings and declaration of policy

The denial by some employers of the right of employees to organize and the refusal by some employers to accept the procedure of collective bargaining lead to strikes and other forms of industrial strife or unrest, which have the intent or the necessary effect of burdening or obstructing commerce by (a) impairing the efficiency, safety, or operation of the instrumentalities of commerce; (b) occurring in the current of commerce; (c) materially affecting, restraining, or controlling the flow of raw materials or manufactured or processed goods from or into the channels of commerce, or the prices of such materials or goods in commerce; or (d) causing diminution of employment and wages in such volume as substantially to impair or disrupt the market for goods flowing from or into the channels of commerce.

The inequality of bargaining power between employees who do not possess full freedom of association or actual liberty of contract, and employers who are organized in the corporate or other forms of ownership association substantially burdens and affects the flow of commerce, and tends to aggravate recurrent business depressions, by depressing wage rates and the purchasing power of wage earners in industry and by preventing the stabilization of competitive wage rates and working conditions within and between industries.

Experience has proved that protection by law of the right of employees to organize and bargain collectively safeguards commerce from injury, impairment, or interruption, and promotes the flow of commerce by removing certain recognized sources of industrial strife and unrest, by encouraging practices fundamental to the friendly adjustment of industrial disputes arising out of differences as to wages, hours, or other working conditions, and by restoring equality of bargaining power between employers and employees.

Experience has further demonstrated that certain practices by some labor organizations, their officers, and members have the intent or the necessary effect of burdening or obstructing commerce by preventing the free flow of goods in such commerce through strikes and other forms of industrial unrest or through concerted activities which impair the interest of the public in the free flow of such commerce. The elimination of such practices is a necessary condition to the assurance of the rights herein guaranteed.

Sections 151–169 correspond respectively to sections 1–19 of the National Labor Relations Act as cited in Chapter 23.

It is declared to be the policy of the United States to eliminate the causes of certain substantial obstructions to the free flow of commerce and to mitigate and eliminate these obstructions when they have occurred by encouraging the practice and procedure of collective bargaining and by protecting the exercise by workers of full freedom of association, self- organization, and designation of representatives of their own choosing, for the purpose of negotiating the terms and conditions of their employment or other mutual aid or protection.

§152. Definitions

When used in this subchapter—

(1) The term "person" includes one or more individuals, labor organizations, partnerships, associations, corporations, legal representatives, trustees, trustees in cases under the title II, or receivers.

(2) The term "employer" includes any person acting as an agent of an employer, directly or indirectly, but shall not include the United States or any wholly owned Government corporation, or any Federal Reserve Bank, or any State or political subdivision thereof, or any person subject to the Railway Labor Act [45 U.S.C. 151 et seq.], as amended from time to time, or any labor organization (other than when acting as an employer), or anyone acting in the capacity of officer or agent of such labor organization.

(3) The term "employee" shall include any employee, and shall not be limited to the employees of a particular employer, unless this subchapter explicitly states otherwise, and shall include any individual whose work has ceased as a consequence of, or in connection with, any current labor dispute or because of any unfair labor practice, and who has not obtained any other regular and substantially equivalent employment, but shall not include any individual employed as an agricultural laborer, or in the domestic service of any family or person at his home, or any individual employed by his parent or spouse, or any individual having the status of an independent contractor, or any individual employed as a supervisor, or any individual employed by an employer subject to the Railway Labor Act [45 U.S.C. 151 et seq.], as amended from time to time, or by any other person who is not an employer as herein defined.

(4) The term "representatives" includes any individual or labor organization.

(5) The term "labor organization" means any organization of any kind, or any agency or employee representation committee or plan, in which employees participate and which exists for the purpose, in whole or in part, of dealing with employers concerning grievances, labor disputes, wages, rates of pay, hours of employment, or conditions of work.

(6) The term "commerce" means trade, traffic, commerce, transportation, or communication among the several States, or between the District of Columbia or any Territory of the United States and any State or other Territory, or between any foreign country and any State, Territory, or the District of Columbia, or with the District of Columbia or any Territory or the District of Columbia or any foreign country.

(7) The term "affecting commerce" means in commerce, or burdening or obstructing commerce or the free flow of commerce, or having led or tending to lead to a labor dispute burdening or

obstructing commerce or the free flow of commerce.

(8) The term "unfair labor practice" means any unfair labor practice listed in section 158 of this title.

(9) The term "labor dispute" includes any controversy concerning terms, tenure or conditions of employment, or concerning the association or representation of persons in negotiating, fixing, maintaining, changing, or seeking to arrange terms or conditions of employment regardless of whether the disputants stand in the proximate relation of employer and employee.

(10) The term "National Labor Relations Board" means the National Labor Relations Board provided for in section 153 of this title.

(11) The term "supervisor" means any individual having authority, in the interest of the employer, to hire, transfer, suspend, lay off, recall, promote, discharge, assign, reward, or discipline other employees, or responsibly to direct them, or to adjust their grievances, or effectively to recommend such action, if in connection with the foregoing the exercise of such authority is not of a merely routine or clerical nature, but requires the use of independent judgment.

(12) The term "professional employee" means—

(a) any employee engaged in work (i) predominantly intellectual and varied in character as opposed to routine mental, manual, mechanical, or physical work; (ii) involving the consistent exercise of discretion and judgment in its performance; (iii) of such a character that the output produced or the result accomplished cannot be standardized in relation to a given period of time; (iv) requiring knowledge of an advanced type in a field of science or learning customarily acquired by a prolonged course of specialized intellectual instruction and study in an institution of higher learning or a hospital, as distinguished from a general academic education or from an apprenticeship or from training in the performance of routine mental, manual, or physical processes; or

(b) any employee, who (i) has completed the courses of specialized intellectual instruction and study described in clause (iv) of paragraph (a), and (ii) is performing related work under the supervision of a professional person to qualify himself to become a professional employee as defined in paragraph (a).

(13) In determining whether any person is acting as an "agent" of another person so as to make such other person responsible for his acts, the question of whether the specific acts performed were actually authorized or subsequently ratified shall not be controlling.

(14) The term "health care institution" shall include any hospital, convalescent hospital, health maintenance organization, health clinic, nursing home, extended care facility, or other institution devoted to the care of sick, infirm, or aged persons.

§153. National Labor Relations Board

(a) Creation, composition, appointment, and tenure; Chairman; removal of members

The National Labor Relations Board (hereinafter called the "Board") created by this subchapter prior to its amendment by the Labor Management

Relations Act, 1947 [29 U.S.C. 141 et seq.], is continued as an agency of the United States, except that the Board shall consist of five instead of three members, appointed by the Presi-dent by and with the advice and consent of the Senate. Of the two additional members so provided for, one shall be appointed for a term of five years and the other for a term of two years. Their successors, and the successors of the other members, shall be appointed for terms of five years each, excepting that any individual chosen to fill a vacancy shall be appointed only for the unex-pired term of the member whom he shall succeed. The President shall designate one member to serve as Chairman of the Board. Any member of the Board may be removed by the President, upon notice and hearing, for neglect of duty or malfeasance in office, but for no other cause.

(b) Delegation of powers to members and regional directors; review and stay of actions of regional direc-tors; quorum; seal

The Board is authorized to delegate to any group of three or more members any or all of the powers which it may it-self exercise. The Board is also autho-rized to delegate to its regional directors its powers under section 159 of this title to determine the unit appropriate for the purpose of collective bargaining, to in-vestigate and provide for hearings, and determine whether a question of repre-sentation exists, and to direct an election or take a secret ballot under subsection (c) or (e) of section 159 of this title and certify the results thereof, except that upon the filing of a request therefor with the Board by any interested person, the Board may review any action of a re-gional director delegated to him under this paragraph, but such a review shall not, unless specifically ordered by the Board, operate as a stay of any action taken by the regional director. A vacancy in the Board shall not impair the right of the remaining members to exercise all of the powers of the Board, and three mem-bers of the Board shall, at all times, constitute a quorum of the Board, except that two members shall constitute a quo-rum of any group designated pursuant to the first sentence hereof. The Board shall have an official seal which shall be judicially noticed.

(c) Annual reports to Congress and the President

* * *

(d) General Counsel; appointment and tenure; powers and duties; vacancy

* * *

§154. National Labor Relations Board; eligibility for reap-pointment; officers and em-ployees; payment of expenses

* * *

§155. National Labor Relations Board; principal office, con-ducting inquiries throughout country; participation in deci-sions or inquiries conducted by member

The principal office of the Board shall be in the District of Columbia, but it may meet and exercise any or all of its powers at any other place. The Board may, by one or more of its members or by such agents or agencies as it may designate, prosecute any inquiry neces-sary to its functions in any part of the United States. A member who par-ticipates in such an inquiry shall not be disqualified from subsequently participating in a decision of the Board in the same case.

§156. Rules and regulations

The Board shall have authority from time to time to make, amend, and rescind, in the manner prescribed by subchapter II of chapter 5 of title 5, such rules and regulations as may be necessary to carry out the provisions of this subchapter.

§157. Right of employees as to organization, collective bargaining, etc.

Employees shall have the right to self-organization, to form, join, or assist labor organizations, to bargain collectively through representatives of their own choosing, and to engage in other concerted activities for the purpose of collective bargaining or other mutual aid or protection, and shall also have the right to refrain from any or all of such activities except to the extent that such right may be affected by an agreement requiring membership in a labor organization as a condition of employment as authorized in section 158(a)(3) of this title.

§158. Unfair labor practices

(a) Unfair labor practices by employer

It shall be an unfair labor practice for an employer—

(1) to interfere with, restrain, or coerce employees in the exercise of the rights guaranteed in section 157 of this title;

(2) to dominate or interfere with the formation or administration of any labor organization or contribute financial or other support to it: *Provided,* That subject to rules and regulations made and published by the Board pursuant to section 156 of this title, an employer

shall not be prohibited from permitting employees to confer with him during working hours without loss of time or pay;

(3) by discrimination in regard to hire or tenure of employment or any term or condition of employment to encourage or discourage membership in any labor organization: *Provided,* That nothing in this subchapter, or in any other statute of the United States, shall preclude an employer from making an agreement with a labor organization (not established, maintained, or assisted by any action defined in this subsection as an unfair labor practice) to require as a condition of employment membership therein on or after the thirtieth day following the beginning of such employment or the effective date of such agreement, whichever is the later, (i) if such labor organization is the representative of the employees as provided in section 159(a) of this title, in the appropriate collective-bargaining unit covered by such agreement when made, and (ii) unless following an election held as provided in section 159(e) of this title within one year preceding the effective date of such agreement, the Board shall have certified that at least a majority of the employees eligible to vote in such election have voted to rescind the authority of such labor organization to make such an agreement: *Provided further,* That no employer shall justify any discrimination against an employee for nonmembership in a labor organization (A) if he has reasonable grounds for believing that such membership was not available to the employee on the same terms and conditions generally applicable to other members, or (B) if he has reasonable grounds for believing that membership was denied or terminated for reasons

other than the failure of the employee to tender the periodic dues and the initiation fees uniformly required as a condition of acquiring or retaining membership;

(4) To discharge or otherwise discriminate against an employee because he has filed charges or given testimony under this subchapter;

(5) to refuse to bargain collectively with the representatives of his employees, subject to the provisions of section 159(a) of this title.

(b) Unfair labor practices by labor organization

It shall be an unfair labor practice for a labor organization or its agents—

(1) to restrain or coerce (A) employees in the exercise of the rights guaranteed in section 157 of this title: *Provided,* That this paragraph shall not impair the right of a labor organization to prescribe its own rules with respect to the acquisition or retention of membership therein; or (B) an employer in the selection of his representatives for the purposes of collective bargaining or the adjustment of grievances;

(2) to cause or attempt to cause an employer to discriminate against an employee in violation of subsection (a)(3) of this section or to discriminate against an employee with respect to whom membership in such organization has been denied or terminated on some ground other than his failure to tender the periodic dues and the initiation fees uniformly required as a condition of acquiring or retaining membership;

(3) to refuse to bargain collectively with an employer, provided it is the representative of his employees subject to the provisions of section 159(a) of this title;

(4) (i) to engage in, or to induce or encourage any individual employed by any person engaged in commerce or in an industry affecting commerce to engage in, a strike or a refusal in the course of his employment to use, manufacture, process, transport, or otherwise handle or work on any goods, articles, materials, or commodities or to perform any services; or (ii) to threaten, coerce, or restrain any person engaged in commerce or in an industry affecting commerce, where in either case an object thereof is—

(A) forcing or requiring any employer or self-employed person to join any labor or employer organization or to enter into any agreement which is prohibited by subsection (e) of this section;

(B) forcing or requiring any person to cease using, selling, handling, transporting, or otherwise dealing in the products of any other producer, processor, or manufacturer, or to cease doing business with any other person, or forcing or requiring any other employer to recognize or bargain with a labor organization as the representative of his employees unless such labor organization has been certified as the representative of such employees under the provisions of section 159 of this title: *Provided,* That nothing contained in this clause (B) shall be construed to make unlawful, where not otherwise unlawful, any primary strike or primary picketing;

(C) forcing or requiring any employer to recognize or bargain with a particular labor organization as the representative of his employees if another labor organization has been certified as the representative of such employees under the provisions of section 159 of this title;

(D) forcing or requiring any employer to assign particular work to employees in a particular labor organization or in a particular trade, craft, or class rather than to employees in another labor organization or in another trade, craft, or class, unless such employer is failing to conform to an order or certification of the Board determining the bargaining representative for employees performing such work:

Provided, That nothing contained in this subsection shall be construed to make unlawful a refusal by any person to enter upon the premises of any employer (other than his own employer), if the employees of such employer are engaged in a strike ratified or approved by a representative of such employees whom such employer is required to recognize under this subchap-ter: *Provided further,* That for the purposes of this paragraph (4) only, nothing contained in such paragraph shall be construed to prohibit publicity, other than picketing, for the purpose of truthfully advising the public, including consumers and members of a labor organization, that a product or products are produced by an employer with whom the labor organization has a primary dispute and are distributed by another employer, as long as such publicity does not have an effect of inducing an individual employed by any person other than the primary employer in the course of his employment to refuse to pick up, deliver, or transport any goods, or not to perform any services, at the establishment of the employer engaged in such distribution;

(5) to require of employees covered by an agreement authorized under subsection (a)(3) of this section the payment, as a condition precedent to becoming a member of such organiza-tion, of a fee in an amount which the Board finds excessive or discriminatory under all the circumstances. In making such a finding, the Board shall consider, among other relevant factors, the practices and customs of labor organizations in the particular industry, and the wages currently paid to the employees affected;

(6) to cause or attempt to cause an employer to pay or deliver or agree to pay or deliver any money or other thing of value, in the nature of an exaction, for services which are not performed or not to be performed; and

(7) to picket or cause to be picketed, or threaten to picket or cause to be picketed, any employer where an object thereof is forcing or requiring an employer to recognize or bargain with a labor organization as the representative of his employees, or forcing or requiring the employees of an employer to accept or select such labor organization as their collective bargaining representative, unless such labor organization is currently certified as the representative of such employees:

(A) where the employer has lawfully recognized in accordance with this subchapter any other labor organization and a question concerning representation may not appropriately be raised under section 159(c) of this title,

(B) where within the preceding twelve months a valid election under section 159(c) of this title has been conducted, or

(C) where such picketing has been conducted without a petition under section 159(c) of this title being filed within a reasonable period of time not to exceed thirty days from the commencement of such picketing: *Provided,* That when such a petition has been filed the Board shall forthwith, without regard to the provisions of section 159(c)(1) of this title or the absence of a showing of a substantial interest on the part of the labor organization, direct an election in such unit as the Board finds to be appropriate and shall certify the results thereof: *Provided further,* That nothing in this subparagraph (C) shall be construed to prohibit any picketing or other publicity for the purpose of truthfully advising the public (including consumers) that an employer does not employ members of, or have a contract with, a labor organization, unless an effect of such picketing is to induce any individual employed by any other person in the course of his employment, not to pick up, deliver or transport any goods or not to perform any services.

Nothing in this paragraph (7) shall be construed to permit any act which would otherwise be an unfair labor practice under this subsection.

(c) Expression of views without threat of reprisal or force or promise of benefit

The expressing of any views, argument, or opinion, or the dissemination thereof, whether in written, printed, graphic, or visual form, shall not constitute or be evidence of an unfair labor practice under any of the provisions of this subchapter, if such expression contains no threat of reprisal or force or promise of benefit.

(d) Obligation to bargain collectively

For the purposes of this section, to bargain collectively is the performance of the mutual obligation of the employer and the representative of the employees to meet at reasonable times and confer in good faith with respect to wages, hours, and other terms and conditions of employment, or the negotiation of an agreement, or any question arising thereunder, and the execution of a written contract incorporating any agreement reached if requested by either party, but such obligation does not compel either party to agree to a proposal or require the making of a concession: *Provided,* That where there is in effect a collective-bargaining contract covering employees in an industry affecting commerce, the duty to bargain collectively shall also mean that no party to such contract shall terminate or modify such contract, unless the party desiring such termination or modification—

(1) serves a written notice upon the other party to the contract of the proposed termination or modification sixty days prior to the expiration date thereof, or in the event such contract contains no expiration date, sixty days prior to the time it is proposed to make such termination or modification;

(2) offers to meet and confer with the other party for the purpose of negotiating a new contract or a contract containing the proposed modifications;

(3) notifies the Federal Mediation and Conciliation Service within thirty days after such notice of the existence of a dispute, and simultaneously therewith notifies any State or Territorial agency established to mediate and conciliate disputes within the State or Territory where the dispute occurred, provided no agreement has been reached by that time; and

(4) continues in full force and effect, without resorting to strike or lockout, all the terms and conditions of the existing contract for a period of sixty days after such notice is given or until the expiration date of such contract, whichever occurs later:

The duties imposed upon employers, employees, and labor organizations by paragraphs (2) to (4) of this subsection shall become inapplicable upon an intervening certification of the Board, under which the labor organization or individual, which is a party to the contract, has been superseded as or ceased to be the representative of the employees subject to the provisions of section 159(a) of this title, and the duties so imposed shall not be construed as requiring either party to discuss or agree to any modification of the terms and conditions contained in a contract for a fixed period, if such modification is to become effective before such terms and conditions can be reopened under the provisions of the contract. Any employee who engages in a strike within any notice period specified in this subsection, or who engages in any strike within the appropriate period specified in subsection (g) of this section, shall lose his status as an employee of the employer engaged in the particular labor dispute, for the purposes of sections 158, 159, and 160 of this title, but such loss of status for such employee shall terminate if and when he is reemployed by such employer. Whenever the collective bargaining involves employees of a health care institution, the provisions of this subsection shall be modified as follows:

(A) The notice of paragraph (1) of this subsection shall be ninety days; the notice of paragraph (3) of this subsection shall be sixty days; and the contract period of paragraph (4) of this subsection shall be ninety days.

(B) Where the bargaining is for an initial agreement following certification or recognition, at least thirty days notice of the existence of a dispute shall be given by the labor organization to the agencies set forth in paragraph (3) of this subsection.

(C) After notice is given to the Federal Mediation and Conciliation Service under either clause (A) or (B) of this sentence, the Service shall promptly communicate with the parties and use its best efforts, by mediation and conciliation, to bring them to agreement. The parties shall participate fully and promptly in such meetings as may be undertaken by the Service for the purpose of aiding in a settlement of the dispute.

(e) Enforceability of contract or agreement to boycott any other employer; exception

It shall be an unfair labor practice for any labor organization and any employer to enter into any contract or agreement, express or implied, whereby such employer ceases or refrains or agrees to cease or refrain from handling, using, selling, transporting or otherwise dealing in any of the products of any other employer, or to cease doing business with any other person, and any contract or agreement entered into heretofore or hereafter containing such an agreement shall be to such extent unenforceable and void: *Provided*, that nothing in this subsection shall apply to an agreement between a labor organization and an employer in the construction industry relating to the contracting or subcontracting of work to be done at the site of the construction, alteration, painting, or repair of a building, structure, or other work: *Provided further*, That for the purposes of this subsection and subsection (b)(4)(B) of this section the terms "any employer," "any person engaged in commerce or an industry affecting commerce," and "any person" when used in relation to the terms "any other producer, processor, or manufacturer," "and other employer," or "any other person" shall not include persons in the relation of a jobber, manufacturer, contractor, or subcontractor working on the goods or premises of the jobber or manufacturer or performing parts of an integrated process of production in the apparel and clothing industry: *Provided further*, That nothing in this subchapter shall prohibit the enforcement of any agreement which is within the foregoing exception.

(f)   Agreements covering employees in the building and construction industry

It shall not be an unfair labor practice under subsections (a) and (b) of this section for an employer engaged primarily in the building and construction industry to make an agreement covering employees engaged (or who, upon their employment, will be engaged) in the building and construction industry with a labor organization of which building and construction employees are members (not established, maintained, or assisted by an action defined in subsection (a) of this section as an unfair labor practice) because (1) the majority status of such labor organization has not been established under the provisions of section 159 of this title prior to the making of such agreement, or (2) such agreement requires as a condition of employment, membership in such labor organization after the seventh day following the beginning of such employment or the effective date of the agreement, whichever is later, or (3) such agreement requires the employer to notify such labor organization of opportunities for employment with such employer, or gives such labor organization an opportunity to refer qualified applicants for such employment, or (4) such agreement specifies minimum training or experience qualifications for employment or provides for priority in opportunities for employment based upon length of service with such employer, in the industry or in the particular geographical area: *Provided*, That nothing in this subsection shall set aside the final proviso to subsection (a)(3) of this section: *Provided further*, That any agreement which would be invalid, but for clause (1) of this subsection, shall not be a bar to a petition filed pursuant to section 159(c) or 159(e) of this title.

(g)   Notification of intention to strike or picket at any health care institution

A labor organization before engaging in any strike, picketing, or other concerted refusal to work at any health care institution shall, not less than ten days prior to such action, notify the institution in writing and the Federal Mediation and Conciliation Service of that intention, except that in the case of bargaining for an initial agreement following certification or recognition the notice required by this subsection shall not be given until the expiration of the period specified in clause (B) of the last sentence of subsection (d) of this section. The notice shall state the date and time that such action will commence. The notice, once given, may be extended by the written agreement of both parties.

§158a.   Providing facilities for operations of Federal Credit Unions

Provision by an employer of facilities for the operations of a Federal Credit Union on the premises of such employer shall not be deemed to be intimidation, coercion, interference, restraint or discrimination within the provisions of sections 157 and 158 of this title, or acts amendatory thereof.

§159 Representatives and elections

(a) Exclusive representatives; employees' adjustment of grievances directly with employer

Representatives designated or selected for the purposes of collective bargaining by the majority of the employees in a unit appropriate for such purposes, shall be the exclusive representatives of all the employees in such unit for the purposes of collective bargaining in respect to rates of pay, wages, hours of employment, or other conditions of employment: *Provided,* That any individual employee or a group of employees shall have the right at any time to present grievances to their employer and to have such grievances adjusted, without the intervention of the bargaining representative, as long as the adjustment is not inconsistent with the terms of a collective-bargaining contract or agreement then in effect: *Provided further,* That the bargaining representative has been given opportunity to be present at such adjustment.

(b) Determination of bargaining unit by Board

The Board shall decide in each case whether, in order to assure to employees the fullest freedom in exercising the rights guaranteed by this subchapter, the unit appropriate for the purposes of collective bargaining shall be the employer unit, craft unit, plant unit, or subdivision thereof: *Provided,* That the Board shall not (1) decide that any unit is appropriate for such purposes if such unit includes both pro- fessional employees and employees who are not professional employees unless a majority of such professional employees vote for inclusion in such unit; or (2) decide that any craft unit is inappropriate for such purposes on the ground that a different unit has been established by a prior Board determination, unless a majority of the employees in the proposed craft unit vote against separate representation or (3) decide that any unit is appropriate for such purposes if it includes, together with other employees, any individual employed as a guard to enforce against employees and other persons rules to protect property of the employer or to protect the safety of persons on the employer's premises; but no labor organization shall be certified as the representative of employees in a bargaining unit of guards if such organization admits to membership, or is affiliated directly or indirectly with an organization which admits to membership, employees other than guards.

(c) Hearings on questions affecting commerce; rules and regulations

(1) Whenever a petition shall have been filed, in accordance with such regulations as may be prescribed by the Board—

(A) by an employee or group of employees or any individual or labor organization acting in their behalf alleging that a substantial number of employees (i) wish to be represented for collective bargaining and that their employer declines to recognize their representative as the representative defined in subsection (a) of this section, or (ii) assert that the individual or labor organization, which has been certified or is being currently recognized by their employer as the bargaining representative, is no longer a representative as defined in subsection (a) of this section; or

(B) by an employer, alleging that one or more individuals or labor organizations have presented to him a claim to be recognized as the representative defined in subsection (a) of this section;

the Board shall investigate such petition and if it has reasonable cause to believe that a question of representation affecting commerce exists shall provide for an appropriate hearing upon due notice. Such hearing may be conducted by an officer or employee of the regional office, who shall not make any recommendations with respect thereto. If the Board finds upon the record of such hearing that such a question of representation exists, it shall direct an election by secret ballot and shall certify the results thereof.

(2) In determining whether or not a question of representation affecting commerce exists, the same regulations and rules of decision shall apply irrespective of the identity of the persons filing the petition or the kind of relief sought and in no case shall the Board deny a labor organization a place on the ballot by reason of an order with respect to such labor organization or its predecessor not issued in conformity with section 160(c) of this title.

(3) No election shall be directed in any bargaining unit or any subdivision within which in the preceding twelve-month period, a valid election shall have been held. Employees engaged in an economic strike who are not entitled to reinstatement shall be eligible to vote under such regulations as the Board shall find are consistent with the purposes and provisions of this subchapter in any election conducted within twelve

months after the commencement of the strike. In any election where none of the choices on the ballot receives a majority, a run-off shall be conducted, the ballot providing for a selection between the two choices receiving the largest and second largest number of valid votes cast in the election.

(4) Nothing in this section shall be construed to prohibit the waiving of hearings by stipulation for the purpose of a consent election in conformity with regulations and rules of decision of the Board.

(5) In determining whether a unit is appropriate for the purposes specified in subsection (b) of this section the extent to which the employees have organized shall not be controlling.

(d) Petition for enforcement or review; transcript

Whenever an order of the Board made pursuant to section 160(c) of this title is based in whole or in part upon facts certified following an investigation pursuant to subsection (c) of this section and there is a petition for the enforcement or review of such order, such certification and the record of such investigation shall be included in the transcript of the entire record required to be filed under subsection (e) or (f) of section 160 of this title, and thereupon the decree of the court enforcing, modifying, or setting aside in whole or in part the order of the Board shall be made and entered upon the pleadings, testimony, and proceedings set forth in such transcript.

(e) Secret ballot; limitation of elections

(1) Upon the filing with the Board, by 30 per centum or more of the employees in a bargaining unit covered by

an agreement between their employer and a labor organization made pursuant to section 158(a)(3) of this title, of a petition alleging they desire that such authority be rescinded, the Board shall take a secret ballot of the employees in such unit and certify the results thereof to such labor organization and to the employer.

(2) No election shall be conducted pursuant to this subsection in any bargaining unit or any subdivision within which, in the preceding twelve-month period, a valid election shall have been held.

§160. Prevention of unfair labor practices

(a) Powers of Board generally

The Board is empowered, as hereinafter provided, to prevent any person from engaging in any unfair labor practice (listed in section 158 of this title) affecting commerce. This power shall not be affected by any other means of adjustment or prevention that has been or may be established by agreement, law, or otherwise: *Provided,* That the Board is empowered by agreement with any agency of any State or Territory to cede to such agency jurisdiction over any cases in any industry (other than mining, manufacturing, communications, and transportation except where predominantly local in character) even though such cases may involve labor disputes affecting commerce, unless the provision of the State or Territorial statute applicable to the determination of such cases by such agency is inconsistent with the corresponding provision of this subchapter or has received a construction inconsistent therewith.

(b) Complaint and notice of hearing; answer; court rules of evidence inapplicable

Whenever it is charged that any person has engaged in or is engaging in any such unfair labor practice, the Board, or any agent or agency designated by the Board for such purposes, shall have power to issue and cause to be served upon such person a complaint stating the charges in that respect, and containing a notice of hearing before the Board or a member thereof, or before a designated agent or agency, at a place therein fixed, not less than five days after the serving of said complaint: *Provided,* That no complaint shall issue based upon any unfair labor practice occurring more than six months prior to the filing of the charge with the Board and the service of a copy thereof upon the person against whom such charge is made, unless the person aggrieved thereby was prevented from filing such charge by reason of service in the armed forces, in which event the six-month period shall be computed from the day of his discharge. Any such complaint may be amended by the member, agent, or agency conducting the hearing or the Board in its discretion at any time prior to the issuance of an order based thereon. The person so complained of shall have the right to file an answer to the original or amended complaint and to appear in person or otherwise and give testimony at the place and time fixed in the complaint. In the discretion of the member, agent, or agency conducting the hearing or the Board, any other person may be allowed to intervene in the said proceeding and to present testimony. Any such proceeding shall, so far as practicable, be conducted in accordance with the rules of evidence applicable in the district court of the United States under the rules of civil procedure for the district courts of the United States, adopted by the Supreme Court of the United States pursuant to section 2072 of title 28.

(c) Reduction of testimony to writing; findings and orders of Board

The testimony taken by such member, agent, or agency or the Board shall be reduced to writing and filed with the Board. Thereafter, in its discretion, the Board upon notice may take further testimony or hear argument. If upon the preponderance of the testimony taken the Board shall be of the opinion that any person named in the complaint has engaged in or is engaging in any such unfair labor practice, then the Board shall state its findings of fact and shall issue and cause to be served on such person an order requiring such person to cease and desist from such unfair labor practice, and to take such affirmative action including reinstatement of employees with or without back pay, as will effectuate the policies of this subchapter: *Provided,* That where an order directs reinstatement of an employee, back pay may be required of the employer or labor organization, as the case may be, responsible for the discrimination suffered by him: *And provided further,* That in determining whether a complaint shall issue alleging a violation of subsection (a)(1) or (a)(2) of section 158 of this title, and in deciding such cases, the same regulations and rules of decision shall apply irrespective of whether or not the labor organization affected is affiliated with a labor organization national or international in scope. Such order may further require such person to make reports from time to time showing the extent to which it has complied with the order. If upon the preponderance of the testimony taken the Board shall not be of the opinion that the person named in the complaint has engaged in or is engaging in any such unfair labor practice, then the Board shall state its findings of fact and shall issue an order dismissing the said complaint. No order of the Board shall require the reinstatement of any individual as an employee who has been suspended or discharged, or the payment to him of any back pay, if such individual was suspended or discharged for cause. In case the evidence is presented before a member of the Board, or before an administrative law judge or judges, such member, or such judge or judges as the case may be, shall issue and cause to be served on the parties to the proceeding a proposed report, together with a recommended order, which shall be filed with the Board, and if no exceptions are filed within twenty days after service thereof upon such parties, or within such further period as the Board may authorize, such recommended order shall become the order of the Board and become effective as therein prescribed.

(d) Modification of findings or orders prior to filing record in court.

Until the record in a case shall have been filed in a court, as hereinafter provided, the Board may at any time upon reasonable notice and in such manner as it shall deem proper, modify or set aside, in whole or in part, any finding or order made or issued by it.

(e) Petition to court for enforcement of order; proceedings; review of judgment

The Board shall have power to petition any court of appeals of the United States, or if all the courts of appeals to which application may be made are in vacation, any district court of the United

States, within any circuit or district, respectively, wherein the unfair labor practice in question occurred or wherein such person resides or transacts business, for the enforcement of such order and for appropriate temporary relief or restraining order, and shall file in the court the record in the proceedings, as provided in section 2112 of title 28. Upon the filing of such petition, the court shall cause notice thereof to be served upon such person, and thereupon shall have jurisdiction of the proceeding and of the question determined therein, and shall have power to grant such temporary relief or restraining order as it deems just and proper, and to make and enter a decree enforcing, modifying and enforcing as so modified, or setting aside in whole or in part the order of the Board. No objection that has not been urged before the Board, its member, agent, or agency, shall be considered by the court, unless the failure or neglect to urge such objection shall be excused because of extraordinary circumstances. The findings of the Board with respect to questions of fact if supported by substantial evidence on the record considered as a whole shall be conclusive. If either party shall apply to the court for leave to adduce additional evidence and shall show to the satisfaction of the court that such additional evidence is material and that there were reasonable grounds for the failure to adduce such evidence in the hearing before the Board, its member, agent, or agency, the court may order such addi-tional evidence to be taken before the Board, its member, agent, or agency, and to be made a part of the record. The Board may modify its findings as to the facts, or make new findings by reason of additional evidence so taken and filed, and it shall file such modified or new findings, which findings with re-

spect to questions of fact if supported by substantial evidence on the record considered as a whole shall be conclusive, and shall file its recommendations, if any, for the modification or setting aside of its original order. Upon the filing of the record with it the jurisdiction of the court shall be exclusive and its judgment and decree shall be final, except that the same shall be subject to review by the appropriate United States court of appeals if application was made to the district court as here-inabove provided, and by the Supreme Court of the United States upon writ of certiorari or certification as provided in section 1254 of title 28.

(f)   Review of final order of Board on petition to court

Any person aggrieved by a final order of the Board granting or denying in whole or in part the relief sought may obtain a review of such order in any United States court of appeals in the circuit wherein the unfair labor practice in question was alleged to have been engaged in or wherein such person resides or transacts business, or in the United States Court of Appeals for the District of Columbia, by filing in such a court a written petition praying that the order of the Board be modified or set aside. A copy of such petition shall be forthwith transmitted by the clerk of the court to the Board, and thereupon the aggrieved party shall file in the court the record in the proceeding, certified by the Board, as provided in section 2112 of title 28. Upon the filing of such petition, the court shall proceed in the same manner as in the case of an application by the Board under subsection (e) of this section, and shall have the same jurisdiction to grant to the Board such temporary relief or restraining order as it deems just and proper, and in like manner to make and enter a decree enforcing, modifying, and enforcing as so modified, or setting aside in whole or in part the order of the Board; the findings of the Board with respect to questions of fact if supported by substantial evidence on the record considered as a whole shall in like manner be conclusive.

(g) Institution of court proceedings as stay of Board's order

The commencement of proceedings under subsection (e) or (f) of this section shall not, unless specifically ordered by the court, operate as a stay of the Board's order.

(h) Jurisdiction of courts unaffected by limitations prescribed in chapter 6 of this title

* * *

(j) Injunctions

The Board shall have power, upon issuance of a complaint as provided in subsection (b) of this section charging that any person has engaged in or is engaging in an unfair labor practice, to petition any United States district court, within any district wherein the unfair labor practice in question is alleged to have occurred or wherein such person resides or transacts business, for appropriate temporary relief or restraining order. Upon the filing of any such petition the court shall cause notice thereof to be served upon such person, and thereupon shall have jurisdiction to grant to the Board such temporary relief or restraining order as it deems just and proper.

(k) Hearing on jurisdictional strikes

Whenever it is charged that any person has engaged in an unfair labor practice within the meaning of paragraph (4)(D) of section 158(b) of this title, the Board is empowered and directed to hear and determine the dispute out of which such unfair labor practice shall have arisen, unless, within ten days after notice that such charge has been filed, the parties to such dispute submit to the Board satisfactory evidence that they have adjusted, or agreed upon methods for the voluntary adjustment of, the dispute. Upon compliance by the parties to the dispute with the decision of the Board or upon such voluntary adjustment of the dispute, such charge shall be dismissed.

(l) Boycotts and strikes to force recognition of uncertified labor organizations; injunctions; notice; service of process

Whenever it is charged that any person has engaged in an unfair labor practice within the meaning of paragraph (4)(A), (B), or (C) of section 158(b) of this title, or section 158(e) of this title or section 158(b)(7) of this title, the preliminary investigation of such charge shall be made forthwith and given priority over all other cases except cases of like character in the office where it is filed or to which it is referred. If, after such investigation, the officer or regional attorney to whom the matter may be referred has reasonable cause to believe such charge is true and that a complaint should issue, he shall, on behalf of the Board, petition any United States district court within any district where the unfair labor practice in question has occurred, is alleged to have occurred, or wherein such person resides or transacts business, for appropriate injunctive relief pending the final adjudication of the Board with respect to such matter. Upon the filing of any such petition the district court shall have jurisdiction to grant such injunctive relief or temporary restraining order as it deems just and proper, notwithstanding any other provision of law: *Provided further,* That no temporary restraining order shall be issued without notice unless a petition alleges that substantial and irreparable injury to the charging party will be unavoidable and such temporary restraining order shall be effective for no longer than five days and will become void at the expiration of such period: *Provided further,* That such officer or regional attorney shall not apply for any restraining order under section 158(b)(7) of this title if a charge against the employer under section 158(a)(2) of this title has been filed and after the preliminary investigation, he has reasonable cause to believe that such charge is true and that a complaint should issue. Upon filing of any such petition the courts shall cause notice thereof to be served upon any person involved in the charge and such person, including the charging party, shall be given an opportunity to appear by counsel and present any relevant testimony: *Provided further,* That for the purposes of this subsection district courts shall be deemed to have jurisdiction of a labor organization (1) in the district in which such organization maintains its principal office, or (2) in any district in which its duly authorized officers or agents are engaged in promoting or protecting the interests of employee members. The service of legal process upon such officer or agent shall constitute service upon the labor organization and make such organization a party to the suit. In situations where such relief is appropriate the procedure specified herein shall apply to charges with respect to section 158(b)(4)(D) of this title.

(m) Priority of cases

Whenever it is charged that any person has engaged in an unfair labor practice within the meaning of subsection (a)(3) or (b)(2) of section 158 of this title, such charge shall be given priority over all other cases except cases of like character in the office where it is filed or to which it is referred and cases given priority under subsection (l) of this section.

§161. Investigatory powers of Board

For the purpose of all hearings and investigations, which, in the opinion of the Board, are necessary and proper for the exercise of the powers vested in it by sections 159 and 160 of this title—

(1) Documentary evidence; summoning witnesses and taking testimony

* * *

(2) Court aid in compelling production of evidence and attendance of witnesses

* * *

[paragraph (3) also omitted]

(4) Process, service and return; fees of witness

* * *

(5) Process, where served

* * *

(6) Information and assistance from departments [of the Government]

§162. Offenses and penalties

Any person who shall willfully resist, prevent, impede, or interfere with any member of the Board or any of its agents or agencies in the performance of duties pursuant to this subchapter shall be punished by a fine of not more than $5,000 or by imprisonment for not more than one year, or both.

§163. Right to strike preserved

Nothing in this subchapter, except as specifically provided for herein, shall be construed so as either to interfere with or impede or diminish in any way the right to strike, or to affect the limitations or qualifications on that right.

§164. Construction of provisions

(a) Supervisors as union members

Nothing herein shall prohibit any individual employed as a supervisor from becoming or remaining a member of a labor organization, but no employer subject to this subchapter shall be compelled to deem individuals defined herein as supervisors as employees for the purpose of any law, either national or local, relating to collective bargaining.

(b) Agreements requiring union membership in violation of State law [important]

Nothing in this subchapter shall be construed as authorizing the execution or application of agreements requiring membership in a labor organization as a condition of employment in any State or Territory in which such execution or application is prohibited by State or Territorial law.

(c) Power of Board to decline jurisdiction of labor disputes; assertion of jurisdiction by State and Territorial courts

(1) The Board, in its discretion, may, by rule of decision or by published rules adopted pursuant to subchapter II of chapter 5 of title 5, decline to assert jurisdiction over any labor dispute involving any class or category of employers, where, in the opinion of the Board, the effect of such labor dispute on commerce is not sufficiently substantial to warrant the exercise of its jurisdiction: *Provided,* That the Board shall not decline to assert jurisdiction over any labor dispute over which it would assert jurisdiction under the standards prevailing upon August 1, 1959.

(2) Nothing in this subchapter shall be deemed to prevent or bar any agency or the courts of any State or Territory (including the commonwealth of Puerto Rico, Guam, and the Virgin Islands), from assuming and asserting jurisdiction over labor disputes over which the Board declines, pursuant to paragraph (1) of this subsection, to assert jurisdiction.

§165. Conflict of laws

Wherever the application of the provisions of section 672 of title 11 conflicts with the application of the provisions of this subchapter, this subchapter shall prevail: *Provided,* That in any situation where the provisions of this subchapter cannot be validly enforced, the provisions of such other Acts shall remain in full force and effect.

* * *

[Sections 166, 167, and 168 omitted]

§169. Employees with religious convictions; payment of dues and fees

Any employee who is a member of and adheres to established and traditional tenets or teachings of a bona fide religion, body, or sect which has historically held conscientious objections to joining or financially supporting labor organizations shall not be required to join or financially support any labor organization as a condition of employment; except that such employee may be required in a contract between such employees' employer and a labor organization in lieu of periodic dues and initiation fees, to pay sums equal to such dues and initiation fees to a nonreligious, nonlabor organization charitable fund exempt from taxation under section 501(c)(3) of title 26, chosen by such employee from a list of at least three such funds, designated in such contract or if the contract fails to designate such funds, then to any such fund chosen by the employee. If such employee who holds conscientious objections pursuant to this section requests the labor organization to use the grievance-arbitration procedure on the employee's behalf, the labor organization is authorized to charge the employee for the reasonable cost of using such procedure.

Index